D1503010

CASSELL'S DICTIONARY OF

MODERN GERMAN
HISTORY

CASSELL'S DICTIONARY OF

MODERN GERMAN HISTORY

Tim Kirk

SERIES EDITOR · CHRIS COOK

CASSELL

In memory of my grandmother

This edition first published in the UK in 2002 by

Cassell
Wellington House, 125 Strand, London WC2R 0BB

British Library Cataloguing-in-Publication Data
A catalogue record for this book is available from the British Library

ISBN 0-304-34772-8

Cartography by Technical Art Services

Printed and bound in Great Britain by
Creative Print and Design, Ebbw Vale, South Wales

CONTENTS

INTRODUCTION

For much of its history Germany has been more a state of mind than a state in the political, territorial sense. There have been many German states, certainly, organized for the most part (but not entirely) within the Holy Roman Empire or the German Confederation, but it was not until the establishment of the German Empire by Bismarck in 1871 that any of them claimed to *be* Germany, and even then 'national' identity remained ambiguous for some decades. States such as Bavaria and Saxony retained institutions, traditions and a strong separate sense of identity within a German state that was less 'unified' than it superficially appeared to be. In addition, substantial communities of Germans remained outside the new Reich, above all in Austria, which had been accepted as the dominant political power in modern German history until only a matter of years before. Many Germans in Austria and Bohemia now felt more German than ever, and were unwilling to accept their exclusion from the Reich. For German nationalists *outside* Germany, the German question was by no means resolved and Bismarck's 'little Germany' was one of many possible outcomes.

For these reasons, and also because it reflects my own interests, I have made no distinction between Austria and other German states when selecting items for inclusion in the dictionary from the 18th and much of the 19th century. Similarly I have included some material relating to the Austrian half of the Dual Monarchy, much of it related to culture, but much of it also related to politics. This is not to suggest that 'Cisleithania' constituted another 'German' state (as, for example, the German Democratic Republic did in the second half of the 20th century); after all the rulers of the Austrian half of the Habsburg Empire studiously avoided any attempt to impose a German identity, and even dispensed with the name Austria. Nevertheless, questions of German nationhood and national identity were thrashed out more vehemently in late imperial Austria than in the Reich, and it would be difficult to argue that German-Austrians of this period were without influence on the subsequent course of German history. These questions were far from settled by the outcome of World War I, but the inclusion of items relating to the Austrian Republic are restricted largely to Germany's relations with Austria, the *Anschluss* question, German occupation and so on. The reason for including these entries is that they refer to people, events and institutions that readers will come across in books on the history of Germany.

The criteria for inclusion have been flexible, and this applies as much to the chronological span of the book as to political geography. There are as few natural chronological watersheds for German history as a whole as there are stable physical boundaries. It seemed to me that to start at 1815 was to define 'modern' German history too narrowly, and leave out some of the formative developments in central European politics and culture during the previous half century, not least the attempts made by a succession of reformers, from Frederick the Great and Maria Theresia to Stein, Hardenberg and Metternich, to create modern states. So the approximate starting point is around 1700, but the emphasis is uneven, and much more space is devoted to the early and middle years of the 20th century than to the 18th. Similarly, while the data in the appendices runs up to the turn of the 21st century, there is no attempt to cover contemporary or near-contemporary developments to the same extent as earlier periods. The overriding principle has been to try to cover most comprehensively those parts of German history which attract most interest, and that means disproportionate attention is given to the Weimar Republic, the Nazi dictatorship and the two world wars.

A similar flexibility has been extended to the definition of historical significance. The German states have not been short of kings and queens, emperors and ministers, generals and diplomats – not least because of the sheer number of states, each with its court, government, army, representatives abroad, not to mention the dissidents and revolutionaries planning to replace them. It would be possible to fill the entire dictionary with royal families, governments and public servants alone. But there is much more to history than affairs of state, in fact a work of reference that only dealt with such matters would largely be repeating what is already known or widely available elsewhere. So while it would be absurd to have a *Dictionary of Modern German History* that did not include Hitler, Bismarck or Rosa Luxemburg, the priority was to cover as wide a range of items as concisely as possible. For this reason there are brief entries, for example, on a number of minor parties, ephemeral factions and marginal splinter groups, as well as longer histories of the major political parties; and a number of more obscure cultural figures – self-styled Jacobin poets and *Vormärz* conspirators – appear alongside Mozart and Schiller. (It is, of course, easy to lose a sense of perspective in these matters, and I am grateful to those who occasionally helped me to restore it.) Similarly, there are as few lengthy discursive articles as possible; after all most aspects of German history are covered by very good books, and there is a full discussion of further reading at the end of the dictionary. In some cases, however, the best way to present information relating to an important or controversial issue was to discuss it at some length, and there are longer pieces on subjects such as anti-Semitism and the Weimar Republic.

One of the aims of the dictionary has been to go beyond those areas with which English-speaking readers will already to some extent be familiar, and bring in some of the people, organizations and events which are less well-known outside Germany, such as the *Heimatvertriebene* ('expellees'), those Germans forcibly evicted from eastern Europe after the Second World War. Similarly, a number of German terms, titles and expressions have been included, some of which (*Gastarbeiter, Volk, Weltanschauung*) are more familiar than others (*Bildungsbürgertum, Habilitationsschrift, Vernunftrepublikaner*), while some are increasingly familiar as more German history is taught in schools and universities. The majority of these words and expressions are included because they have appeared in English-language books, and because it was felt that a brief explanation would be a useful or interesting supplement to the translation or definition given in standard German–English dictionaries. All too many words and phrases are simply not translatable, even freely, into an English equivalent without some loss of meaning or cultural significance. Similarly, some entries appear under a number of different headings, both English and German, for example: BRD, *Bundesrepublik Deutschland*, Federal Republic of Germany, FRG, West Germany, so that readers can look up the term under the expression with which they are most familiar. Some geographical names appear in both German and English (Cologne/Köln), with a cross-reference to the main entry.

It is unusual for a reference work such as this to appear under the name of one author, and I should like to thank the many friends and colleagues who contributed their support and expertise: Dermot Cavanagh, Malcolm Gee, Robin Okey, Stephen Salter, and Jill Steward were all immensely helpful. Special thanks are due to Graham Ford and Liz Harvey who read almost the whole typescript at one point or another, and did so with considerable care and attention. Many of my original errors were eliminated thanks to them. Thanks are due too to Richard Milbank and Ian Crofton, who persuaded me to rectify many of the remaining faults, and above all to Rebecca Skipwith whose handling of the 'finished' typescript was meticulous to say the least. Her contribution to the dictionary has been immense. Any flaws that remain in spite of such expert guidance are entirely my own responsibility. Thanks are also due to my friends and family for their support throughout the gestation of the project (and their own contributions, as often as not unwitting): to Chris Cook, who had the idea, was supportive throughout, and is both a colleague and a friend; to Roger, above all, who really has had a great deal to put up with; and to Avram, David, Jeremy, Joan, Hilary, Nonnie and Jill, Patrick, Tony and Willi, and to Matthew, who always asked how things were going, and will no doubt be surprised to be reading this in print.

THE DICTIONARY

A

Aachen, Congress of (1818), also called the Congress of Aix-la-Chapelle, a meeting of the QUADRUPLE ALLIANCE and France. The Quadruple Alliance consisted of the victors in the Napoleonic Wars, namely Great Britain, Russia, Austria and Prussia, who had presided over the Congress of VIENNA of 1815. The Congress of Aachen effectively allowed France to rejoin the 'concert of Europe' and to take part in the maintenance of the new international order on the continent. The Quadruple Alliance agreed to the withdrawal of the occupation army stationed in France since the end of the Napoleonic Wars. It also set out the intentions of the 'concert of Europe' and the CONGRESS SYSTEM in a separate protocol.

Aachen, Peace of (1748), also called the Peace of Aix-la-Chapelle, treaty that brought to an end the War of the AUSTRIAN SUCCESSION. Austria gave up Parma and Piacenza. The rest of the Habsburg empire remained intact except for Silesia, most of which remained with Prussia, and the PRAGMATIC SANCTION was generally recognized.

AB-Aktion (*Ausserordentliche Befriedungsaktion*), 'extraordinary pacification operation', the euphemistic code name for the mass murder of the Polish political and intellectual elites during the German invasion of 1939. The operation was led by Hans FRANK and Arthur SEYSS-INQUART.

Abegg, Philipp Friedrich Wilhelm (1876–1951), civil servant. Abegg was born in Berlin and studied at Berlin and Göttingen before joining the Prussian civil service in 1907. He joined the Prussian interior ministry in 1917, and was head of the police department from 1923 where he reformed the police force in an attempt to make it loyal to the republic. He was appointed state secretary in 1926, but was dismissed following the unconstitutional dismissal of the Prussian government in 1932 (*see PREUSSENSCHLAG*). Abegg left Germany when the Nazis came to power in 1933 and settled in Zurich, where he provided legal advice for refugees.

Abetz, Otto (1903–58), diplomat and Nazi politician. Born in Schwetzingen and educated in Karlsruhe, Abetz was a Nazi supporter from the early 1930s. He joined the diplomatic service in 1935, and specialized in French affairs under RIBBENTROP. Deported from Paris in 1939, he returned after the invasion in 1940 and became ambassador to the VICHY puppet regime. He was sentenced to 20 years' imprisonment by a French military tribunal in 1949, but served only 5 years. He was killed in a motor accident in Germany.

Abgeordnetenhaus ('house of representatives'), term used to refer to the second chamber of the Prussian LANDTAG between 1855 and 1918, and to the lower house of the parliament (the REICHSRAT) in Austria after 1860. It was also used to refer to the legislative assembly in West Berlin from 1950 to 1990, and the legislative assembly for the whole of the city from 1990.

abortion. *See* PARAGRAPH 218.

Abs, Hermann (1901–94), a leading German banker during the Nazi dictatorship. The son of a lawyer, Abs also read law before going into international banking. From 1937 he was a member of the board of the Deutsche Bank, which was involved in the expropriation of Jewish property. In 1940 he became a director of IG FARBEN. Despite the evidence against him he was not tried as a war criminal. After the war he quickly became an important figure in the economic reconstruction of Germany and was a close associate of Konrad ADENAUER.

absolutism, term used to describe the style of government of 18th-century European monarchs under the *ancien régime*. The doctrine implied the centralization of the state under the undisputed authority of the crown. The most obvious examples in Germany are to be found in the so-called 'enlightened absolutism' of MARIA THERESIA and JOSEPH II of Austria, and FRIEDRICH II (Frederick the Great) of Prussia.

Friedrich II, who ruled Prussia from 1740 to 1786, built on the financial and administrative reforms of his father, Friedrich Wilhelm I, and consolidated his absolute rule. Coffee, tobacco and salt became state monopolies, while roads, canals and new villages were built, and agrarian reforms were promoted. Frederick introduced freedom of religion and opinion, and abolished torture. The judicial system was reformed and arbitrary intervention in the legal process by the crown came to an end. Nevertheless, he was conservative in many respects, and left behind a more rigidly stratified society than the one he inherited, where each estate – nobles, burghers and peasants – had its function.

Maria Theresia acceded in the same year as Friedrich, and also introduced important domestic reforms. The Austrian and Bohemian chancelleries were absorbed into a Directory of the Interior (*Directorium in Publicis et Cameralibus*), called the United Bohemian-Austrian Court Chancellery from 1749, and a Staatsrat (Council of State) was established in 1760 to oversee the government of the hereditary lands: effectively the Austrian half of the monarchy became a modern bureaucratic state. A unitary criminal law was introduced in 1768 (the so-called *Nemesis Theresiana*). The education system was reformed: primary schools were established, and the state replaced the clergy as the education authority. (The Jesuit order was dissolved in 1773.)

Despite her notional attachment to the values of the ENLIGHTENMENT, Maria Theresia was cautious and even reactionary in comparison with her son. From 1765 Joseph II was Holy Roman emperor, and ruled along with his mother. In both policy and approach he was more radical, and the pace of reform intensified after her death. The term 'Josephism' (*Josephinismus*) refers to the attempted radical secularization of Austrian society during his reign. His EDICT OF TOLERATION (1781) granted freedom of worship to Lutherans, Calvinists and members of the Orthodox church. Similar freedoms were then also extended to the Jews, who were also freed from a number of impositions (for example, the obligation to wear a yellow star of David), and allowed to take degrees, engage in hitherto prohibited trades and occupations (including agriculture) and to build houses where they wanted. Joseph also took measures to free serfs from their feudal obligations by allowing Bohemian peasants, in a measure of 1781, to leave their villages, take up new occupations, and marry whom they wished. The measures were then extended to Austria and (by 1875) to Hungary.

Abstammungsnachweis, genealogical certificate. The certificate was required as proof of German or German-related ancestry during the Nazi dictatorship. The definition of the term in the 1924 edition of *Meyers Lexikon* explained the term only with reference to a certificate that stated the pedigree of breeds of farm animal, whereas the 1936 edition, reflecting the changed political situation, contained a cross-reference to the NUREMBERG LAWS, in which a person's 'race' was defined by his or her ancestry.

Abwehr, the German military counter-intelligence service from 1929 to 1944. Effectively established under Defence Minister von SCHLEICHER in 1929, it was a military organization in competition with the Nazi Party's internal intelligence, the SD (*Sicherheitsdienst*). It was led by Admiral CANARIS from 1935 until it was dissolved and subsumed into the Race and Settlement Head Office (*Rasse- und Siedlungs-Hauptamt*, or RUSHA) of the SS under Ernst KALTEN-BRUNNER in 1944.

Abwehrpolizei, counter-espionage police. This function was the responsibility of the border police (*Grenzpolizei*), who were subordinate to the GESTAPO.

Ackermann, Anton (1905–73), East German politician, actually called Eugen Hanisch. Born in Thalheim in the Erzgebirge, he was elected to the Politburo of the KPD (German Communist Party) in 1935. He fought in the Spanish Civil War and returned to Germany in 1945 after working for the Comintern. He was a co-founder of the SED (Socialist Unity Party) in 1946, and is best known for his exposition of the specifically 'German road to socialism'. He was expelled from the party for factionalism with ZAISSER and HERRNSTADT, but was rehabilitated in 1956.

actually existing socialism. *See REAL EXIS-TIERENDER SOZIALISMUS.*

ADAV (*Allgemeiner deutscher Arbeiterverein*), the General German Workers' Association. The Association was founded in Leipzig on 23 May 1863 by Ferdinand LASSALLE, who had been invited there by local workers, and twelve delegates from major German cities (Barmen, Dresden, Düsseldorf, Elberfeld, Frankfurt am Main, Hamburg, Harburg, Cologne, Leipzig, Mainz and Solingen). Lassalle was elected the Association's first president. By 1864 it had 4600 members. It never attracted the 100,000 members Lassalle had expected, however, and in 1875 it

was combined with the SDAP (*Sozialdemo-kratische Arbeiterpartei*, Social Democratic Workers' Party) of August BEBEL and Wilhelm LIEBKNECHT to form the SAPD (*Sozia-listische Arbeiterpartei Deutschlands*, Socialist Workers' Party of Germany), which subsequently changed its name to SPD (*Sozial-demokratische Partei Deutschlands*, Social Democratic Party of Germany) in 1890.

Adenauer, Konrad (1876–1967), Christian Democrat politician; the first chancellor of the German Federal Republic (1949–63). Adenauer was born in Cologne, and became deputy mayor of the city in 1909. He was mayor from 1917 to 1933, and president of the Prussian Council of State from 1921 to 1933, when he was removed from office by the Nazis. He was arrested and imprisoned by the Gestapo in 1934. A member of the CENTRE PARTY before the Nazis came to power, he was a co-founder in the British zone of occupation of the Centre Party's postwar successor, the CDU (Christian Democratic Union).

Adenauer was the dominant force in postwar conservative politics in the Federal Republic of Germany. He chaired the PAR-LIAMENTARY COUNCIL (*Parlamentarischer Rat*) in 1948 and 1949, and was elected chancellor of the FEDERAL REPUBLIC OF GERMANY when it was established in 1949. Although he was initially expected to hold office for only a short time, he remained in power for longer than any German chancellor since Bismarck. Adenauer did much to determine the political culture and international orientation of postwar West Germany. Adenauer was an Atlanticist and a European in so far as he was more interested in integrating West Germany into the West, and specifically into a Christian Democratic Western Europe, through the project of European integration, than in pursuing a potentially problematic reunification of Germany as a whole. His government's economic policy, vigorously advocated by his economics minister Ludwig ERHARD, was essentially liberal, and it seemed to be vindicated by Germany's rapid recovery from World War II, the so-called 'economic miracle' of the 1950s.

In many respects, however, the Adenauer period constituted something of a restoration. Responsibility for the Nazi dictatorship and the war was evaded with talk of an 'accident in the works' (*Betriebsunfall*) in the German political system, which depicted Hitler as a maverick leading a band of criminals who had hijacked German history. The government helped to restore attitudes and institutions, which bolstered the middle classes, and left repressive Nazi legislation unrepealed. School and university students remained ignorant of the recent past. The conservative social and political culture of the Federal Republic reflected that of much of the West. Adenauer was compromised by the *SPIEGEL* AFFAIR of 1962, and resigned the following year. He continued to be chairman of the CDU until 1966, when he resigned at the age of 90. Adenauer's legacy was a politically stable, prosperous and democratic Federal Republic. Relations with France had improved remarkably since the end of World War II, and West Germany was fully accepted as a member of the West European state system.

ADGB (*Allgemeiner deutscher Gewerkschaftsbund*, General Association of German Trade Unions), established in 1919, bringing together the FREE TRADE UNIONS (i.e. those close to the SPD) in one organization. Associations for clerical workers (*Allgemeiner freier Angestelltenbund*, or 'Afa-Bund'), and for civil servants (*Allgemeiner Deutscher Beamtenbund*, ADB), founded in 1920 and 1921 respectively, were affiliated to the ADGB. The organization was suppressed by the Nazis in 1933, and replaced by the German Labour Front (*Deutsche Arbeitsfront*, DAF). The German Trade Union Association (*Deutscher Gewerkschaftsbund*, DGB) was established in 1949 as a single trade-union organization.

Adler, Alfred (1870–1937), psychologist. Born in Rudolfsheim near Vienna, Adler qualified as a doctor in several fields, including ophthalmology, before turning to neurology. He opened a clinic in Vienna in 1900 and was a close associate of Sigmund FREUD, but broke with him in 1911. Adler developed the concept of the inferiority complex. He emigrated to America in 1932.

Adler, Friedrich (1879–1960), Austrian socialist, the son of Viktor ADLER. He was party secretary of the SDAP (*Sozialdemokratische Arbeiterpartei*, Social Democratic Workers' Party) from 1911 to 1914. At the beginning of World War I he was one of the leading members of a left oppositional group, along with Max Adler and Robert Danneberg. In October 1916 he assassinated the Austrian minister-president Count STÜRGKH, and used his trial as a platform to speak not only against the government, but against the leadership of the Social Democratic Party (SDAP) as well. He attacked the party executive as an institution for preserving law and order, which, like other such institutions, would have to be swept away if there was to be a revolution in Austria. He was sentenced to 18 years' imprisonment. His action was not only a shot across the bows to a government fully aware of the accelerating crisis in Russia, but a warning too to the SDAP, which did then move to the left and thereby avoided the split that tore apart the SPD in Germany. Adler was granted an amnesty and release from prison after the end of World War I, and was offered the leadership of the newly founded Austrian Communist Party, which he declined. He went on to become secretary of the Socialist International (1923–1940). He emigrated to the United States in 1940 and returned to Europe in 1946.

Adler, Viktor (1852–1918), leading figure in the establishment of the Social Democratic movement in Austria, and the father of Friedrich ADLER. Adler was born into a prosperous Jewish family in Prague, studied medicine in Vienna and was a key figure in the many-faceted Austrian democratic movement of the 1880s. He established and edited the weekly paper *Gleichheit* ('equality') and the *Arbeiterzeitung* ('workers' newspaper'), which became the principal organ of the movement. He was instrumental in bringing unity to the fragmented Austrian workers' movement, and oversaw the founding of the Austrian SDAP (Social Democratic Workers' Party) at the Unity Conference at Hainfeld in Lower Austria (1888–9). He was elected to the Lower Austrian LANDTAG in 1905. Adler died during the collapse of the Austro-Hungarian monarchy, on the eve of the declaration of the First Republic.

Adlertag ('eagle day'), German code name for the beginning of the air war against Britain in 1940.

Adolf Hitler Fund (*Adolf-Hitler-Spende der deutschen Wirtschaft*), fund established in 1933 and made up of donations by German businessmen who profited from their relationship with the regime. It was administered by Martin BORMANN, who used it as a means of exercising power within the party leadership.

Adolf Hitler schools, secondary schools for boys, run and financed by the Nazi Party from 1937 for the training of future political leaders. Prospective pupils were chosen from the DEUTSCHES JUNGVOLK, the junior branch of the HITLER YOUTH, and screened for racial origin, physical appearance and stamina. The schools were run along pseudo-military lines, and physical education and personal hygiene were accorded great importance. Assessment was collective rather than individual, in order to promote teamwork. At the age of 18 successful pupils might go on to one of the ORDENSBURGEN rather than to a conventional university. An alternative route towards a political education was in one of the National Political Educational Institutes (NAPOLAS) founded in 1933 on the model of Prussian cadet schools.

Adorno, Theodor (Wiesengrund) (1903–69), leading member of the FRANKFURT SCHOOL of critical theorists. Adorno was born in Frankfurt am Main and studied at the university there. He completed his HABILITA-TIONSSCHRIFT on Kierkegaard in 1931, a work that was influenced significantly by his friendship with Walter BENJAMIN. In the same year Adorno secured an academic position at Frankfurt University, where he became affiliated to the new interdisciplinary Institute of Social Research. (The Institute had been founded by a millionaire's son, Felix Weil, who wanted its work to contribute to the realization of a Marxist state.) In 1933 Adorno was excluded from the university along with other Jewish academics. The Institute was closed and refounded at Columbia University in New York. Adorno migrated there to rejoin his colleagues in 1938 after a period of study in Oxford, but returned to Frankfurt in 1956. Adorno wrote prolifically on music, literature and the condition of contemporary German society, and his work presented a critical account of 'false consciousness' and a society he considered commodified and conformist. Among his major works are: *Dialectic of Enlightenment* (with HORKHEIMER, 1947), *Minima Moralia* (1951), *Negative Dialectics* (1966) and *Aesthetic Theory* (1970).

AEG (*Allgemeine Elektricitäts-Gesellschaft*, literally 'general electricity company'), major manufacturer of electrical and electronic equipment. AEG was founded in 1887 as the successor to the *Deutsche Edison-Gesellschaft*, established in 1883 by Emil Rathenau. The firm grew rapidly and became one of the most important companies in Germany. It merged with Daimler-Benz in 1985, and was dissolved in 1996.

Aehrenthal, Graf Alois Lexa von (1854–1912), foreign minister of Austria-Hungary (1906–12). The son of a leading Bohemian family, Aerenthal had joined the diplomatic service in 1877, and went to St Petersburg for the first time in 1878. He was Austrian ambassador in St Petersburg from 1899 to 1906. He then succeeded Count Agenor Goluchowski as foreign minister, and his appointment was welcomed by the

Archduke FRANZ FERDINAND, who hoped his Russian experience would help smooth relations between Vienna and St Petersburg. Aehrenthal himself hoped to conduct foreign policy in a more assertive way, and acted decisively on the annexation of BOSNIA AND HERZEGOVINA. The consequences were far-reaching: Serbian hostility towards the Austro-Hungarian monarchy was increased, and Russia and Britain were sufficiently shaken by the action to be drawn together. Relations with Germany were also notably cooler, and there was little real support for the Reich either at the time of the AGADIR crisis or in the matter of the BERLIN–BAGHDAD RAILWAY. In conversation with the French ambassador in 1911 Aehrenthal referred to Austria-Hungary as 'allied to Germany for the moment'. By 1912, however, Aehrenthal was dying. He was succeeded by Count Leopold BERCHTOLD.

Afrikakorps, German army unit that was deployed to assist Italian forces against the British and Commonwealth troops in North Africa between 1941 and 1943. It was commanded by General (later Field Marshal) Erwin ROMMEL. After initial advances towards the Nile Delta and the Suez Canal, the Afrikakorps was forced into retreat by the British and Commonwealth 8th Army under General Montgomery and finally surrendered in May 1943.

Agadir, a small port in Morocco. It became the focus of the second MOROCCAN CRISIS in 1911 when the German gunboat *Panther* was sent there as a protest against perceived infractions of the agreement reached at the ALGECIRAS CONFERENCE. Although Germany tried to insist that the incident was a purely Franco-German matter, David Lloyd George, then chancellor of the exchequer, delivered a warning speech at the Mansion House in London. The Germans eventually recognized French rights in Morocco in return for minor territorial concessions in the French Congo. The Agadir incident was a symptom of the growing tensions between Germany on the

one hand and Britain and France on the other in the years before World War I.

Agrarian League (*Bund der Landwirte*), a pressure group in imperial Germany. Founded in 1893, the Agrarian League represented the interests of large landowners. It was politically close to the German Conservative Party (*DEUTSCHKONSERVATIVE PARTEI*), and the League's protectionist agenda came to dominate the party's political outlook in the last years before World War I. In 1921 it merged with the recently formed *Deutscher Landbund* (1919) to form the *Reichslandbund*. In 1929 the *Reichslandbund* formed an alliance with the Union of German Farmers (*Vereinigung deutscher Bauern*) to form the Green Front (*Grüne Front*), in order to increase the pressure on the government for a more protectionist tariff policy. In 1933 it was absorbed in to the Reich Food Estate (*REICHSNÄHRSTAND*).

Ahnenerbe Forschungs- und Lehrgemeinschaft (literally 'society for the research and teaching of ancestral heritage', and generally abbreviated to *Ahnenerbe*), agency founded in 1935 to promote a racist view of world history through archaeological research and the promotion of mystic theories of the origins of the 'Aryan race'.

Aix-la-Chapelle, French name for Aachen.

Aix-la-Chapelle, Congress of (1818). *See* AACHEN, CONGRESS OF.

Aix-la-Chapelle, Peace of (1748). *See* AACHEN, PEACE OF.

Aktion T4, Nazi euthanasia programme, named after the address of the house, in a fashionable district of Berlin, from which it was run (Tiergartenstrasse 4). The project was part of a broader preoccupation with eugenics, racial fitness and the economic burden of the hereditarily or incurably ill that was restricted neither to the Nazi Party nor to Germany, and opinion polls conducted during the 1920s found some support for such measures. The Nazis passed a 'Law for the Prevention of Progeny with Hereditary Diseases' shortly after they came to power (14 July 1933), and there were plans during the 1930s to initiate a euthanasia programme during the forthcoming war. The programme's immediate origins lay in the formation of the Reich Committee for the Scientific Registration of Serious Hereditarily and Congenitally Based Diseases (18 August 1939) under Karl Brandt and Philipp BOUHLER, the head of the Führer Chancellery, following a father's request to have his deformed child killed. 'Deformed' children were registered, and their cases adjudicated by three paediatricians, before transfer to 'paediatric clinics', where 5200 children were killed either by starvation or lethal injection. The bodies were then passed on to hospitals and university departments for research. An adult euthanasia programme, both illegal and secret like the children's euthanasia programme, was set up during the summer of 1939, initially under the direction of Leonardo CONTI, but ultimately controlled by Bouhler and his deputy Viktor BRACK. Arthur NEBE, chief of the criminal police, was responsible for establishing the most efficient means of killing the victims, and the programme itself involved the widespread complicity of doctors and academics. Refusal to participate was permitted, but overt criticism was prohibited. It was estimated that 70,273 people had been killed by gassing by September 1941, and that over 93,000 had probably been killed altogether. The programme prompted outspoken criticism in a sermon by Clemens von GALEN, bishop of Münster (3 August 1941), although it is likely that by that time it had more or less achieved its objectives. Moreover, although the mass gassings of the mentally and physically handicapped largely came to an end, decentralized euthanasia programmes continued throughout the war. Medication was used on some, and others suffered death through malnutrition and exhaustion. Both the principle and practice of such methods were already familiar, and had to some extent been applied during

World War I. Bouhler committed suicide in 1945; Brandt and Brack were tried and executed at Nuremberg.

Alamein, El, battles of (1942), turning point in the North African campaign during World War II. There were three battles between British and Commonwealth forces on the Allied side, and the combined forces of Germany and Italy, led by ROMMEL on the Axis side. General Sir Claude Auchinleck stopped Rommel's advance towards the Nile in early July, and General Bernard Montgomery prevented Rommel from making another attempt to reach the Suez Canal (August–September). In the third battle (23 October–4 November) the Axis forces were beaten into a 1100-km (700-mile) retreat, leaving behind some 90,000 dead, wounded or prisoners.

Alarich, German code name for the occupation of Italy after the overthrow of Mussolini in 1943. The name was inspired by Alaric, the Visigoth king who sacked Rome in AD 410.

Albers, Hans (1892–1960), film star. Born in Hamburg, Albers worked in the circus and variety theatre before serving in World War I. He then established a successful career in the Berlin theatre, and was one of the first actors to appear in sound films. One of the most popular film actors of the 1930s and 1940s, when he was often cast in the role of heroic patriot, he also appeared in lighter films such as *Die Abenteuer des Barons Münchhausen* ('the adventures of Baron Münchhausen'). Albers' film career continued after World War II.

Albrecht, Heinrich Christoph (1763–1800), radical activist and political publicist. Born in Hamburg and educated at Göttingen, Albrecht was an engaged writer, political journalist and radical Jacobin. He was also a Freemason and a member of the Christian-Jewish lodge *Einigkeit und Toleranz* ('unity and tolerance'). Albrecht was a forceful advocate of republican and democratic ideas, and of the unification of Germany; he published a series of works in the 1790s on Freemasonry,

Rosicrucianism, the rights of man, patriotism and the abuses of the British constitution by William Pitt. He died on his estate at Kielseng near Flensburg in 1800.

Albrecht, Johann Friedrich Ernst (1752–1814), political agitator and writer. Born in Stade and educated at Erfurt, Albrecht became a doctor at Reval in Estonia in 1776 and travelled in Russia. He was also a prolific writer of fiction and an enthusiastic supporter of the French Revolution. He moved to Altona in 1795, where he made contact with local Jacobins, published a radical journal, and founded the Altona National Theatre. Money problems compelled him to take up medicine again in 1806. He contracted the typhus from which he died while working with political refugees.

Algeciras Conference (1906), international conference in the south of Spain, held at the insistence of Germany to settle the disagreements with France that led to the first MOROCCAN CRISIS. It was agreed that France and Spain should police Morocco, overseen by a Swiss inspector general. Germany's intention of creating a rift between Britain and France was thwarted and the Entente Cordiale between them was reinforced.

Alldeutscher Verband. See PAN-GERMAN LEAGUE.

Allgemeiner deutscher Arbeiterverein. See ADAV.

Allgemeiner deutscher Gewerkschaftsbund. See ADGB.

Allgemeiner Kongress der Arbeiter- und Soldatenräte Deutschlands. See CONGRESS OF WORKERS' AND SOLDIERS' COUNCILS.

Allied Control Council, a body set up by the Allies (Britain, France, the Soviet Union and the United States) in accordance with the agreements at YALTA and POTSDAM, to deal with matters affecting Germany as a whole. The council was based in Berlin, and was made up of the supreme commanders of the four occupation powers. The Soviet representative left the control council in 1948, after which it no longer met.

Alltagsgeschichte ('everyday history'), an approach to social history that became popular in Germany during the 1980s. It was criticized by traditionalists, but also by those who felt that 'everyday histories', of the Nazi period in particular, marginalized important political developments. Others have used the techniques of this approach precisely to illuminate mundane complicities with the Nazi regime, or opposition to it.

Alpenfestung, Alpine fortress or redoubt. As the Allies advanced into Germany the notion took hold among leaders of the Reich, and the SS in particular, that a last stand could be made from the Alps. In the event few preparations were made for resistance in the Alps, and little was encountered as the Allies advanced rapidly there in the spring of 1945.

Alpine republic (*Alpenrepublik*), a term frequently used to refer to the Austrian Republic, mainly by Austrian writers.

Alsace-Lorraine (German name: Elsass-Lothringen), French provinces annexed by Germany in 1871. The provinces were part of the Holy Roman Empire during the Middle Ages and remained under German rule until the Thirty Years War. Much of Alsace became French with the treaty of Westphalia (1648), and Lorraine formally became French in 1766. After the FRANCO-PRUSSIAN WAR both provinces were annexed by Germany and administered as an 'imperial territory' (*Reichsland*), a status that was qualified by the granting of some regional autonomy in 1911. Many people emigrated following the German annexation. The population recovered thereafter, and the anticlerical policies of the French state diminished the attraction of emigration. The annexation brought Germany valuable iron-ore deposits and a thriving iron and steel industry, but was resented by the local population. The loss of Alsace-Lorraine remained a grievance in Paris, and both provinces were restored to France by the treaty of VERSAILLES in 1919. Following the fall of France in 1940 Alsace and Lorraine were again incorporated into the Reich. The provinces were restored to France a second time after the end of World War II.

Alte Garde, old guard. Technically the 'old guard' of the Nazi Party consisted of the first 10,000 members.

Alte Kämpfer, literally 'old fighters'. The term was used, generally with positive connotations, to refer to Nazi Party veterans who had been involved in the 'struggle' before the Nazis came to power, as opposed to those who had joined in the spring of 1933 (the so-called '*Märzgefallene*').

Alten, Friedrich Kurt von (1888–1944), public servant. Born in Gross Strehlitz into an educated middle-class family, Alten studied law and pursued a career in the civil service, first in Breslau and Oppeln, and then in Gross Strehlitz. He joined the Nazi Party in 1935 and died in Landsberg prison as a consequence of his connection with the JULY BOMB PLOT of 1944.

Altenberg, Peter (1859–1919), Austrian writer of the *fin de siècle*. Altenberg was born in Vienna, the son of a businessman, and studied both law and medicine without qualifying, and became a bohemian habitué of the Café Griensteidl and friend of Karl KRAUS and Arthur SCHNITZLER. His writing consisted of short prose pieces. He spent much of the last decade of his life in nursing homes.

Altenstein, Karl Siegmund Franz, Freiherr vom Stein (1770–1840), politician. Born in Berlin into an old Franconian noble family, Altenstein studied law, philosophy and science at Erlangen and Göttingen. He joined the public service in Berlin in 1799. He ran the finance ministry from 1808 to 1810, and as head of the culture ministry from 1817 to 1837 he introduced universal primary education and appointed RANKE and HEGEL to positions at Berlin University.

Althaus, Hermann (1899–1966), Nazi functionary. Althaus was born the son of a pastor in Hoyel in the district of Melle, and served on the Western Front during World War I.

In 1919 he started an apprenticeship in agriculture and then went to Leipzig University in 1921 to study economics and agriculture. He abandoned his studies for financial reasons and was a youth worker in Neubrandenburg and Mecklenburg during the late 1920s. He joined the Nazi Party in 1932 and began working for the Nazi welfare organization (NSV) in March 1933. He occupied a number of offices in the NSV, and was a member of the SS. He was captured by the Americans near Innsbruck shortly before the end of the war and was interned until 1948. Althaus was categorized as a lesser implicated member of the regime, and received a great deal of support from the church authorities in his efforts to maintain his relative innocence. In turn he undertook to support others who had worked for the NSV, which he sought to present as a non-political organization. He spent the last years of his life in Kassel, and died there.

Altreich, literally 'old empire', Germany within its 1937 boundaries. The term was used after the ANSCHLUSS to distinguish Germany proper from the 'GREATER GERMANY', which now included Austria (and later the Sudetenland, Carniola, 'South Carinthia', 'Lower Styria' and other directly incorporated territories).

Amann, Max (1891–1957), Nazi politician and press tycoon. Born and educated in Munich, Amann came from a middle-class background, and worked as a legal clerk, served in World War I, and then worked in a bank. He took over the business management of the Nazi Party in 1921, and its publishing house (EHER-VERLAG) in 1922. He was arrested and fined for his part in the 1923 BEER HALL PUTSCH, but was elected to Munich city council in 1924, and to the Reichstag in 1933. He was appointed president of the Reich Press Chamber the same year, and used this position to establish party control of the press. Amann published *Mein Kampf*, oversaw Hitler's personal finances, and ensured that the Führer benefited from the royalties and from his journalism. Amann profited personally from his publishing ventures. He claimed at Nuremberg to be an apolitical businessman, but lost all his property and was sentenced to two and a half years' imprisonment.

Amiens, battle of (8–11 August 1918), last decisive battle of WORLD WAR I. The battle of Amiens brought to an end the Hindenburg offensives of 1918 with a mass Allied attack using 600 British and 90 French tanks with additional armoured vehicles and artillery support. The Allies advanced 10 km (6 miles) deep across a 32-km (20-mile) line on the first day. Although the attack eventually lost momentum, LUDENDORFF and the supreme command of the army were persuaded that the war could no longer be won by military means, and by 29 September it was clear that Germany would have to ask for an armistice.

Amiens, peace of (1802). *See* COALITIONS, WARS OF THE.

Andrássy, Gyula Graf (1823–90) Hungarian revolutionary and first minister-president of Hungary (1867–71). Andrássy left the Habsburg Empire for exile in Britain and France after the REVOLUTIONS OF 1848, and returned ten years later. In 1867 he led the negotiations which brought about the AUSGLEICH and was made minister-president of Hungary. He was Austro-Hungarian foreign minister from 1871 to 1879, agreed the THREE EMPERORS' LEAGUE in 1878, and the alliance with Bismarck of 1879. His ambition was an alliance of Germany and AUSTRIA-HUNGARY with Great Britain against Russia as a means of preserving Austria-Hungary's position in the Balkans.

Anglo-German naval agreement (18 June 1935), treaty recognizing that Germany was effectively no longer bound by the limits on naval capacity imposed by the treaty of VERSAILLES (about 144,000 tons). The idea of such an agreement had been floated shortly after HITLER's appointment, and was proposed again, by Hitler himself, in Novem-

ber 1934. The treaty was negotiated between RIBBENTROP and Sir Samuel Hoare, the British foreign secretary, and allowed the German navy to expand to up to 35% of British naval strength (effectively about 520,000 tons). German submarine strength was to be 45% that of Britain. The agreement was criticized by opponents of APPEASEMENT for condoning the violation of the Versailles treaty. Moreover, as a separate bilateral agreement undertaken without the involvement of France it also undermined collective security within weeks of the formation of the STRESA FRONT (an agreement undertaken at Stresa in Italy by Great Britain, France and Italy to protect the integrity of Austria).

Anhalt, a historical territory in Germany, whose capital was Dessau. Anhalt-Dessau, Anhalt-Bernburg and Anhalt-Köthen were united to form the duchy of Anhalt in 1806–7, during the Napoleonic Wars. In 1945 it was united with SACHSEN-ANHALT, and although it was divided between the districts of Halle and Magdeburg with the reorganization of regional government in the German Democratic Republic (1952), the state of Sachsen-Anhalt was reconstituted with the reunification of Germany in 1990.

Anhaltelager, temporary detention camp.

Anielewicz, Mordecai (1919–43), major leader of the Jewish resistance in the WARSAW GHETTO. He was killed on 8 May 1943.

Anschluss, unification of Germany with Austria, sought by both sides after World War I, but forbidden by the Allies. *Anschluss* was effected with the German invasion and annexation of Austria in 1938.

The German empire created in 1871 effectively amounted to the imposition by BISMARCK'S PRUSSIA of a 'little German' solution to the question of German national unification. It was perceived by many German nationalists both in the Reich and in Austria as an incomplete state. After 1918, with the dismemberment of the Habsburg empire, Austria was reduced to the German-speaking lands previously under the Austrian crown. This 'rump Austria' was considered economically unviable by Austria's major political parties, all of whom supported *Anschluss* with Germany (the GREATER GERMAN PEOPLE'S PARTY most enthusiastically, the CHRISTIAN SOCIAL PARTY most reluctantly). A proposal to establish an Austro-German customs union in 1931 was blocked by the French, who perceived it as a threat to their strategic position and their economic interests in the Danube basin.

Anschluss finally took place in March 1938 after the Austrian dictator, Kurt SCHUSCHNIGG, in response to weeks of German pressure and personal bullying by Hitler, proposed a plebiscite to reaffirm Austrian independence – which never took place. Following the German invasion 99.7% of Austrians voted in favour of the 'reunification of Austria with the German Reich' in a new plebiscite on 10 April. Disillusionment quickly became widespread, however, and Austrians enthusiastically embraced the terms of the Moscow Declaration of 1943, in which the Allies expressed their intention to restore Austria as an independent state with a democratic constitution. Although a persistent minority of Austrians continued to see themselves as German after the war, the possibility of *Anschluss*, and with it the greater German unity to which generations of nationalists aspired, has been a more or less taboo subject in both countries.

Anti-Comintern Pact (25 November 1936), agreement between Germany and Japan, directed against the USSR. (The Comintern was the Soviet-sponsored Third International, an organization of communist parties from around the world.) Italy became a member of the Pact the following year (6 November 1937), and Spain joined in 1939.

Anti-Semitic People's Party (*Antisemitische Volkspartei*), one of a number of marginal anti-Semitic parties in imperial Germany. It was organized by Otto BÖCKEL, a librarian in Hesse.

anti-Semitism, antipathy towards Jews. Anti-Semitism was widespread in Europe from the Middle Ages, and was characterized by social, political and cultural discrimination, pogroms and expulsions. Jews were progressively emancipated in the wake of the ENLIGHTENMENT, but anti-Semitic prejudice re-emerged strongly – in Russia and eastern and central Europe in particular – during the second half of the 19th century.

The modern anti-Semitic movement in Germany was stimulated by the work of radical right-wing publicists at home (such as Wilhelm MARR, founder of the Anti-Semitic League) and abroad (notably Arthur, comte de Gobineau and Houston Stewart CHAMBERLAIN) and found organizational form with the foundation of associations and political parties such as the Anti-Semitic League and the ANTI-SEMITIC PEOPLE'S PARTY. The term itself first appeared in German at the end of the 1870s with the formation of the League, and the publication of Wilhelm Marr's journal *Antisemitische Blätter*: the new term was supposed to lend the movement a scholarly air, thereby giving it more authority than earlier, similar forms of xenophobic bigotry.

Explicitly anti-Semitic parties had little political success in Wilhelmine Germany. Anti-Semitic candidates won 3–4% of the vote in Reichstag elections during the 1890s and 1900s, and 16 members of anti-Semitic parties sat in the parliaments of 1893 and 1907. More importantly, their prejudices gained broader acceptance among conservatives and nationalists. The new 'scientific' anti-Semitism of the *fin de siècle* marked a qualitative shift from the populist bigotry of Christian conservatism, however, in that it exploited the current vogue for biological racism. Jews, it was asserted, were physically different from Germans (or indeed other members of the 'ARYAN' races), and assimilation was neither possible nor desirable, because it would lead to the contamination and dilution of the racial 'stock'. Moreover, many of the Nazi 'solutions' for dealing with the perceived problem of the Jews, including both deportation to a distant island and genocide, were anticipated in pamphlets published before World War I. The anti-Semitism that demonized Jews both as parasitic vermin and powerful adversaries was pervasive in right-wing circles throughout Europe in the early 20th century. Although it was an obsessive preoccupation of the older generation of fascists in Germany and eastern Europe, and of many Nazi Party leaders, it was less central to the concerns of the voters who flocked to the NSDAP during the Depression. Nevertheless, anti-Semitic measures were instituted immediately upon Hitler's appointment as chancellor, and intensified after the establishment of the Nazi dictatorship during the summer of 1933.

The legislative basis for legal and economic discrimination against the Jews – culminating in total expropriation and ghettoization during the 1940s – was laid with the so-called 'NUREMBERG LAWS' of 1935 and the supplementary decrees that followed them. Although arbitrary violence against Jews had long been unpunished in Germany, the pogrom of KRISTALLNACHT ('crystal night', 9 November 1938) marked a turning point. It was followed by the mass internment of Jews in CONCENTRATION CAMPS and the extortion of a 'compensation' fee of 1000 million marks from the Jewish community. This in turn was followed by the wholesale plunder of Jewish property and financial assets by the German state. With the outbreak of war, Jewish emigration was no longer a possible solution to the so-called 'Jewish problem' (which existed only in so far as the German government had entirely created it for itself). Between 1939 and the autumn of 1941 there was widespread and indiscriminate murder of Polish and Soviet Jews by the German armed forces and SS auxiliary units. The massacres perpetrated by special command squads (EIN-SATZGRUPPEN), and the confinement of the

surviving majority of the Jewish population in ghettos anticipated the systematic mass murder of European Jews ordered and carried out by the regime during the early 1940s. Soviet prisoners of war were gassed with Zyklon-B during trials in September 1941, and the construction of EXTERMINA-TION CAMPS in Poland was ordered during the autumn of that year. Following the meeting of ministers participating in the 'final solution' at the WANNSEE CONFERENCE in Berlin (20 January 1942) the evacuation of the Polish ghettos began, and Jews were deported from southern Germany to the camps from March. There were similar deportations from all parts of occupied Europe, carried out with a greater or lesser degree of cooperation from the local political authorities. Some 6 million Jews from all parts of Europe were murdered during the ensuing HOLOCAUST, along with members of other minorities, political prisoners, and prisoners of war.

Public expressions of anti-Semitism in postwar Germany have been restricted to marginal political groups or – in the case of graffiti, and the desecration of Jewish cemeteries – have been undertaken covertly and anonymously.

anti-socialist laws, a series of measures directed against the Social Democratic movement by the BISMARCK regime between 1878 and 1890. In 1876 the Prussian government used the Association Law of 1850 to dissolve the Socialist Workers' Party (SAPD). Two unsuccessful attempts to assassinate the Kaiser in 1878 provided Bismarck with the opportunity to introduce national legislation to suppress the socialist movement.

On 11 May 1878 Max Hödel shot at WILHELM I in Berlin and missed. Hödel, a plumber's apprentice, was described as both mentally and physically ill. He had once briefly belonged to a Social Democratic association, but had been expelled very quickly. He had also belonged to the party led by the radical anti-Semite Adolf STOECKER. Hödel was later executed, but on 17 May, even before the judicial procedures were completed, Bismarck presented a draft anti-socialist law to the Federal Council (Bundesrat). The bill was introduced into the Reichstag on 23 May, but was supported only by the conservatives, and by three academics from the National Liberal Party, one of whom was the right-wing historian Heinrich von TREITSCHKE. As the Social Democrats suspected, the bill was part of a broader strategy that had been in preparation for some time. Bismarck was seeking to introduce legislation that would be repressive enough to alienate the National Liberals, with whom he had difficulties over the introduction of protective economic tariffs. Bismarck calculated that if the National Liberals – who supported free trade – opposed his legislation, they would lose support in the country at the next election, leaving the chancellor free to pursue protectionist policies. Although the bill was defeated by 251 votes to 57, a second assassination attempt provided the government with another opportunity. This time the assassin, Karl Nöbiling, wounded the Kaiser severely, and it was claimed that he expressed sympathy with the socialists before he committed suicide shortly afterwards. The Reichstag was dissolved on 11 June, in the hope that liberal opponents of Bismarck's emergency legislation (and his economic protectionism) would lose seats.

The persecution of the labour movement by the police and the courts had already begun, however, with house searches, arrests and the breaking up of socialist meetings, including the prohibition of the national congress at Gotha. Treitschke called on employers to dismiss socialist workers, and many took measures to do so. In the elections held on 30 July the socialists managed to maintain their share of the vote, losing only 56,000 votes and 3 seats, while the liberals lost 39 seats altogether (28 of them National Liberals). A new draft emergency measures bill was accepted by the Bundesrat

on 13 August, and was passed by the Reichstag by 221 votes to 149 on 19 October. (It was opposed by the socialists themselves, the Centre Party and the Progressive Party).

The measures were renewed four times, and effectively rendered the activities of the socialist labour movement illegal until 30 September 1890. The law gave the police powers to dissolve all public meetings, and to disperse processions and other festive gatherings, to suppress socialist books, pamphlets, newspapers and periodicals and to seize the property of organizations perceived to be a danger to the state (as interpreted by the local authorities). Individuals who broke the new laws could be fined and imprisoned. In addition to party organizations, trade unions and cultural associations with socialist connections were also banned. Socialists were still permitted to compete in elections to the Reichstag and state diets. In comparison with the beatings, torture and murder of socialists during the 1930s, the anti-socialist legislation was relatively mild; but it nevertheless enabled police, employers and officials to practise all kinds of bullying and chicanery with impunity, and deprived many people of their livelihoods. Around 1500 people were sentenced to imprisonment or hard labour, and many others were forced to leave the country.

The effect of the legislation on the labour movement was similar to the impact of the KULTURKAMPF on German Catholics and the CENTRE PARTY. The number of people voting for the socialists rose from 437,158 in 1878 to 1,427,928 in 1890, and the number of seats held by the party in the Reichstag increased by almost fourfold from 9 to 35. It also served to reinforce the independence of the elected deputies from the rank-and-file members of the movement. Socialist deputies in the Reichstag increasingly reflected the more conservative political complexion of their broader electoral constituency than that of the militant illegal activists.

AO (*Auslandsorganisation*, 'foreign organization'), the Nazi organization that dealt with the supervision of Germans abroad. Within the structure of the party the AO was given the status of a separate GAU.

APO (*Ausserparlamentarische Opposition*, 'extra-parliamentary opposition'), political movement formed at the time of the GRAND COALITION (1966–9) when the two government parties, the CDU and the SPD, dwarfed the FDP in parliament. The APO was a protest movement of university students and other young people that adopted the tactics of the American civil-rights movement and anti-Vietnam war protests. The protest movement escalated when Benno Ohnesorg, a student, was shot dead by police at a protest demonstration in Berlin. University classes were disrupted by 'sit-ins' and there were arson attempts on the building of the SPRINGER publishing house and against department stores. A second wave of protests followed an assassination attempt against the student leader Rudi Dutschke on 11 April 1968, which was followed by a demonstration in Bonn in May against emergency laws passed by the government. The movement eventually fragmented into a number of small left-wing splinter groups, many of which survived until the late 1970s. Urban guerrilla groups such as the Red Army Faction recruited from the milieu of the APO. Other supporters went on to join the SPD or other political parties. Many former activists found an ideological home with the GREENS during the 1980s.

appeasement, term used to describe British and French foreign policy towards Nazi Germany in the years immediately before World War II. The policy is particularly associated with the British Conservative prime minister Neville Chamberlain, who sought to avoid war by placating Hitler with concessions, as in the MUNICH AGREEMENT.

Arbeitertum, Nazi publication aimed at industrial workers. It was nominally sold for 10 pfennigs, but in practice often given away free. Its name was the collective term for workers used by the Nazis, which they hoped would replace the word 'proletariat', with its connotations of class conflict.

Arbeiter- und Soldatenräte (Workers' and Soldiers' councils), *see* RAT.

Arbeitsdienst. See RAD.

Arbeitserziehungslager ('labour education camp'), name given to work camps used under the Nazis to punish workers for infringements of labour discipline.

Arbeitsmaid, official designation under the Nazis for a member of the young women's labour service. The word '*Maid*' was obsolete in modern German (*Mädchen* being the modern word for 'girl'), although the Romantics did attempt to revive it, and it was used by Stefan GEORGE. In 1897 a rural school for women was founded where the pupils were referred to as *Maiden*, and here *Maid* was also meant to function as an acronym based on the qualities required of a girl: *Mut, Aufopferung, Idealismus* and *Demut* (spirit or courage, self-sacrifice, idealism and humility).

ARD (*Arbeitsgemeinschaft der öffentlich-rechtlichen Rundfunkanstalten Deutschlands,* Standing Conference of German Public Broadcasting Associations), an organization which brings together the regional public broadcasting stations. Its members were originally radio stations, and now broadcast both radio and television. They transmit a joint evening programme on Germany's first television channel (*Erstes Deutsches Fernsehen,* 'First German television'), and broadcast regional television programmes on a third channel. The first transmissions of German television after WORLD WAR II were broadcast in 1952 by the NWDR (*Nordwestdeutscher Rundfunk;* the station split in 1955 to form the *Norddeutscher Rundfunk* and the *Westdeutscher Rundfunk*). In 2000 the following broadcasting stations were members of the ARD: *Bayerischer Rundfunk* (BR, Bavaria), *Hessischer Rundfunk* (HR, Hesse), *Mitteldeutscher Rundfunk* (MDR, central Germany),

Norddeutscher Rundfunk (NDR, northern Germany), *Ostdeutscher Rundfunk Brandenburg* (ORB, eastern Germany), *Radio Bremen* (RB), *Saarländischer Rundfunk* (SR, Saarland), *Sender Freies Berlin* (SFB), *Südwestrundfunk* (SWR, south-western Germany), *Westdeutscher Rundfunk* (WDR, western Germany).

See also ZDF.

Ardennes offensive (December 1944), German counter-offensive against Allied forces in northwestern Europe towards the end of WORLD WAR II. It is also referred to as the battle of the Bulge. The attack, whose 'unalterable' details were dictated by Hitler, initially took the Americans by surprise, but failed not least because the Germans did not succeed in capturing Allied fuel supplies. The Allies were also helped by the weather, which cleared just before Christmas, enabling the Allies to strike from the air. The success of the campaign depended on the capture of Bastogne, a route centre, and the town was repeatedly but unsuccessfully attacked by the Germans for several days after the battle was clearly lost.

Arierparagraph. See ARYAN CLAUSE.

Army League. See DEFENCE LEAGUE, GERMAN.

Arndt, Ernst Moritz (1769–1860), nationalist writer. Born on the Swedish island of Rügen, the son of a liberated serf, Arndt studied theology at Greifswald and Jena, where he encountered FICHTE. He qualified as a minister, but renounced the ministry in 1798 to travel abroad. When he returned he took up a post as assistant professor of history at Greifswald and published an account of his travels. In 1793 he published *Germanien und Europa* ('Germany and Europe'), a polemic against the French, and established his reputation. In 1806 he published the first of four volumes of *Geist der Zeit* ('spirit of the age'), attacking the French domination of Europe, and was compelled to flee to Sweden when Prussia collapsed. He returned to Berlin, and to Greifswald, but was not permitted to resume teaching, and went to Russia with other German patriots

in 1812. There he became secretary to the German Committee presided over by Freiherr vom STEIN. During the Wars of LIBERATION (1813–15), Arndt was among the most prolific of nationalist writers, and published patriotic songs, political pamphlets and the third volume of his *Geist der Zeit*. His hopes for a liberal, constitutional Germany were dashed by the settlement of 1815, however, and he was arrested for sedition in 1819. He was acquitted, but retired from public life, except for a brief spell in 1848, when he was a liberal member of the FRANKFURT PARLIAMENT.

Art, kind, species. The term was much used by the Nazis, generally as a prefix in a word or phrase expressing relationship to the race, for example *artfremd*, meaning everything opposite to, opposed to or destructive of the race, or *artverwandt* (racially related), to refer to those European 'races' which were considered to be related to the Nordic. It is also found in formulations such as *entartete Kunst* (DEGENERATE ART).

Artaman League, an anti-Semitic, anti-Polish 'blood-and-soil' youth movement of the 1920s. Heinrich HIMMLER, among other Nazis, was a member.

Article 48, provision in the Weimar constitution that granted the directly elected president of the republic the power to rule by decree in an emergency. Although Germany's first president Friedrich EBERT used Article 48 during the early 1920s to defend the republic, it is most closely associated with the economic and political crisis of the Depression. The Reichstag had the right to rescind the president's power at any time, but failed to do so between 1930 and 1933, during which time the authoritarian coalition governments of Heinrich BRÜNING, Franz von PAPEN and Kurt von SCHLEICHER ruled by presidential decree. In March 1933, the necessity for rule through Article 48 came to an end when the Reichstag granted Hitler special powers with the passing of the ENABLING LAW.

Aryan, a term originally used to describe the Indo-European inhabitants of northern India and Iran to distinguish them from the original peoples of the region. It was also used in classical Greek from the time of Herodotus. It was first introduced into the languages of modern Europe by a French translator of Persian scriptures, and was then used of all Indo-European peoples and their languages. The influential racial theorist Arthur, Comte de Gobineau used it in his *Essai sur l'inégalité des races humaines* ('essay on the inequality of the human races', 1853–5) and Wagner used it in 1881, distinguishing 'Aryans' from Jews. It acquired a pseudo-technical meaning in the Nazis' anti-Jewish legislation of the 1930s, and in popular usage came to refer to those north Europeans whose physical features met the criteria of pseudo-scientific racial theorists for the 'Nordic race'.

Aryan clause (*Arierparagraph*), a provision in the Law for the Restoration of a Professional Civil Service of 7 April 1933. Article III stipulated that officials of non-ARYAN descent were to be retired. On 11 April non-Aryan was defined so as to include officials with one non-Aryan grandparent. As a result of the intervention of President HINDENBURG, Jewish veterans of World War I were excluded from the provision. Similar 'Aryan clauses' were inserted in subsequent legislation.

Ascher, Saul (1767–1822), radical thinker. A Jewish writer and ENLIGHTENMENT intellectual, Ascher was born in Landsberg an der Warthe, and married Rahel Spanier in 1789. They had one daughter. He ran a bookshop in Berlin until 1810 when he gained a doctorate at Halle. Ascher was concerned with the question of Jewish emancipation, and his *Bemerkungen über die bürgerliche Verbesserung der Juden* ('observations on the civic improvement of the Jews') (1789) was critical of the EDICT OF TOLERATION of JOSEPH II. He also attacked FICHTE for his anti-Semitism, and the Romantics in general for what he called their 'Germanomania', in a pamphlet that was ceremonially burned by German nationalist students. He was a staunch supporter of Napoleon, and wrote on the theme of 'revolution in historical and philosophical perspective'. Later in life he was preoccupied with the twin themes of a future universal religion and European political unity. He died in Berlin.

asocial, Nazi designation for a category of CONCENTRATION CAMP prisoners deemed 'biologically criminal', including beggars, vagrants and the 'work-shy', as well as 'habitual criminals'. The *Volks-Brockhaus* encyclopaedia of 1939 defined them as 'indifferent to the community'(*'gleichgültig gegenüber der Gemeinschaft'*).

Aspern, battle of (21–22 May 1809), Napoleon's first defeat in battle, during the Wars of the COALITIONS. Archduke Karl and the Austrian army repulsed the French, led by Napoleon, in a two-day battle at Aspern-Essling across the Danube from Vienna. The fighting started on the Sunday of Whitsuntide 1809 and continued sporadically through the night. The French returned to defeat the Austrians at WAGRAM.

Asphalt, a right-wing anti-urban metaphor, frequently used, not least by the Nazis, as a prefix to denote everything that was urban and modern, uprooted from the natural organic society of the countryside. *Asphaltliteraten*, for example, was a damning term for urban intellectuals, and *Asphaltkultur* referred to the supposedly degenerate culture of the WEIMAR REPUBLIC. It was frequently used together with the word 'Jewish' or as a substitute for it, e.g. *'jüdische Asphaltpresse'* ('Jewish asphalt press').

Atlantic, battle of the (1939–43), a prolonged struggle between German submarines and Allied convoys during WORLD WAR II. The British and French navies controlled the Western Approaches in 1939, but the strategic balance was dramatically altered by the fall of France and German control of the French Atlantic coast. Despite losses inflicted by the Allies both on the German surface fleet (including the sinking of the *Bismarck* in May 1941) and on submarines, Admiral DÖNITZ's U-boat fleet had the upper hand until the spring of 1943. During the struggle 2700 Allied ships were sunk and 30,000 sailors killed. The Germans lost some 600 U-boats, 32,000 sailors and several surface ships.

Attila, German code name for the planned occupation (in 1940–1) of the remainder of France (i.e. the southern part, under the VICHY government) in the event of the defection of the French fleet to Britain.

Auersperg, Adolf Carl Daniel, Fürst von (1821–85), minister-president of Austria from 1871 to 1879 and brother of the former minister-president Karl Wilhelm Philipp von AUERSPERG. Auersperg was born in Prague, served as an officer in the imperial cavalry, and was elected to the Bohemian LANDTAG in 1860. He followed Karl von HOHENWART as minister-president of Austria, and presided over a liberal administration that introduced a number of domestic reforms, including a law providing for direct elections to the REICHSRAT (1873), which boosted the electoral strength of the German-speaking middle classes. His ministry, like that of his predecessor, fell on the issue of the nationalities.

Auersperg, Karl Wilhelm Philipp, Fürst von (1814–90), Austrian politician. Born in Prague, Auersperg was a member of the Bohemian LANDTAG before the 1848 revolutions, and a political opponent of Prince METTERNICH. He was president of the Austrian *Herrenhaus* (house of lords) from 1861 to 1867, and minister-president of Austria (1867–8). His brother, Adolf Carl Daniel von AUERSPERG, also became minister-president.

Aufklärung. *See* ENLIGHTENMENT.

Aufnordung, in Nazi racial ideology and rhetoric, the improvement of a people by increasing the proportion of racially Nordic members. There are examples of the use of the term in the work of the Nazi race ideologue Hans GÜNTHER.

Augsburger Hof, a liberal political faction in the FRANKFURT PARLIAMENT of 1848. Like the other groupings within the Parliament, it was named after its meeting place in the town. Almost half of its 42 members were senior civil servants, and many of the remainder were members of the professions.

Aulic Council. *See* REICHSHOFRAT.

Auschwitz (Polish Oświęcim), Nazi CONCENTRATION CAMP and EXTERMINATION CAMP in Poland, 60 km (37 miles) west of Kraków, in the German-annexed territory of eastern Upper Silesia. Established in May 1940 as a concentration camp for Poles, Auschwitz became the largest of the Nazi death camps in German-occupied Poland, and it was systematically planned and built for its role in the HOLOCAUST. Gas chambers were built in June 1941, along with cellars for the storage of bodies and crematoria. Eventually it consisted of three sections: Auschwitz I, the main camp; Auschwitz II (BIRKENAU), which was originally built for Soviet prisoners after the invasion of the USSR, and was subsequently used for Jewish slave labour; and Auschwitz III (Monowitz), the IG FARBEN slave-labour camp, also known as Buna. There were a further 45 smaller slave-labour camps in the surrounding area. Rudolf HOESS, formerly commandant of SACHSENHAUSEN, was placed in command. It is estimated that some 1,600,000 people were murdered at Auschwitz, of which it is believed around 300,000 were non-Jewish victims: Roma and Sinti (Gypsies), homosexuals, Poles and Soviet prisoners of war.

Ausgleich, the 'compromise' reached between Austria and Hungary in 1867 after the defeat of the Austrian empire at the battle of SADOVÁ (Königgrätz) in 1866. From this point Austria became Austria-Hungary and is frequently referred to as the 'Dual Monarchy'. The purpose of the arrangement was to allow Austria to recover from defeat. It was a welcomed by those Hungarian moderates who wanted more independence from Vienna, but did not want to break up the empire entirely. It was the last major constitutional revision in the history of the Habsburg empire, and it marked the end of Austria's role as the leading power within Germany, and the beginning of Vienna's fateful foreign policy reorientation towards the Balkans in the southeast.

The Austrian half of the empire (CISLEITHANIA) consisted of those territories represented in the parliament in Vienna (the REICHSRAT). The Hungarian half of the empire (TRANSLEITHANIA) comprised the lands of the Hungarian crown, whose domestic affairs were now conducted from Budapest. This arrangement was based on provisions governing relations between the two crowns within the PRAGMATIC SANCTION of the 18th century. Each of the two parts of the empire had its own bicameral parliament, its own cabinet for domestic matters and its own prime minister. Only foreign, defence and finance policy were dealt with by 'common ministries' (although the separate parts of the empire dealt with their own domestic financial matters as well). Common 'imperial and royal' ministries were controlled by delegates elected by both parliaments. The *Ausgleich* also marked a turning point for the Austrian half of the monarchy, whose constitution was liberalized considerably.

The *Ausgleich* did not permit the Habsburgs to regain their supremacy in Germany as some had hoped. The Hungarians were against seeking revenge on Prussia, the French were not deemed a suitable ally by public opinion, and Russia was prepared to oppose any Austrian action. Nor did it settle the relationship between Austria and Hungary very effectively. The nationalist Hungarian ruling class pursued a policy of Magyarization and opposed further devolution to the Czechs, Slovaks and South Slavs. Moreover they used the opportunity of the recurrent ten-yearly renegotiations of the terms of the *Ausgleich* to press further demands. Nevertheless, the system survived until 1918, when the state collapsed entirely into its different nationalities at the end of World War I. Its pretensions and deficiencies were affectionately satirized in Robert Musil's description of 'Kakania' in his *The Man without Qualities* – the name of the land he describes is taken from the initials k.k. or k.u.k (*kaiserlich und königlich*, 'imperial and royal'), which were attached to all that was official.

Auslandsorganisation. *See* AO.

Ausserparlamentarische Opposition. *See* APO.

Austerlitz, battle of (2 December 1805), the first decisive battle of the War of the Third Coalition between France and the states allied against Napoleon (Britain, Sweden, Russia, Austria and Naples; *see* COALITIONS, WARS OF THE). Napoleon's victory took place at Austerlitz, now Slavkov u Brna in the Czech Republic. Austria and Russia lost 26,000 men against the loss of 9000 on the French side. Austria was compelled to make peace and Alexander I to return with his army to Russia. The battle is also called the battle of the Three Emperors.

Austria (German name: *Österreich*), now an independent state to the south of the FEDERAL REPUBLIC OF GERMANY. The first mention of the terms '*OSTMARK*' (eastern march) and Österreich are to be found in the late 10th century, and Leopold I of Babenberg, the first ruler of a territory that is recognizably Austria, was margrave from about 976 to 994. Austria was raised from the status of margravate to that of duchy under the Babenbergs (1156), and was acquired by the Habsburgs under Rudolf I (Emperor Rudolf IV) in 1276. Although 'Austria' is used to refer to the Habsburg monarchy throughout the early modern period, political arrangements in central Europe were not so straightforward. The Habsburgs were Holy Roman emperors (*see* HOLY ROMAN EMPIRE) and dukes of Austria until FRANZ II adopted the title of emperor of Austria in 1804 in expectation of the abolition of the Holy Roman Empire. The Habsburg state became Austria-Hungary after the *AUSGLEICH* of 1867.

After the dissolution of the empire in 1918 the remaining German-speaking territories of the First Republic – referred to colloquially as 'rump Austria' and in official proceedings as 'German Austria' – were prohibited from union (ANSCHLUSS) with Germany. When the annexation of Austria by Nazi Germany took place in 1938 and *Anschluss* was achieved, the designation *Ostmark* (eastern march) was revived briefly, but when it was decided to expunge the name of Austria entirely and incorporate its territory directly into the Reich the term *Alpen-und Donaugaue* (literally 'Alpine and Danubian *GAUE*') was used. The Second Republic of Austria was established after World War II, and achieved full independence with the State Treaty of 1955 and the withdrawal of Allied occupation forces.

Austria-Hungary, the HABSBURG 'Dual Monarchy' established in 1867; *see AUSGLEICH*.

Austrian Civil War (February 1934), the brief ill-fated resistance of workers' militias (the Republican Defence League) to fascist HEIMWEHR units and state security forces. The Austrian chancellor Engelbert DOLLFUSS had found it increasingly difficult to rule constitutionally as he saw his party's electoral supporters transfer their allegiance to the Austrian Nazi Party, and in 1933 suspended the NATIONALRAT (parliament) against a background of economic crisis, political polarization and street violence. The government's policy towards the organized working class became increasingly confrontational. In particular the Heimwehr (whose leader, Emil Fey, was also public security minister in the CHRISTIAN SOCIAL administration) provoked a number of conflicts with Social Democrats, including provocative searches of party premises, supposedly in order to find the secret weapons dumps of the Republican Defence League. In February 1934 the Defence League in Linz, Upper Austria, informed the reluctant party leadership that they would respond to the next such provocation with armed resistance. Fighting started on 12 February in Linz and quickly spread to Vienna, where Social Democratic workers demonstrated their support and belatedly called a general strike, but the reserve 'secret weapon' of the labour movement was relatively ineffective in the context of soaring unemployment. In Vienna the government's security forces attacked workers' positions, often with military support, but it was less a civil war than a series of isolated conflicts in the working-class districts on the periphery of the city, where working-class families were bombarded in their council flats by heavy artillery. There was also fighting outside the capital, particularly in the heavy industrial districts of Upper Styria, but order was restored within a few days by the overwhelmingly superior and better-equipped government forces. In some cases workers' militias had themselves been unable to find their weapons caches. The labour movement had effectively been suppressed by armed force. In Vienna alone 131 civilians were killed, including 25 women and children, and 2000 party members were arrested. Summary courts were set up, whose death sentences were carried out almost immediately, and these were followed by lengthy show trials for those who survived. A fascist constitution was promulgated on 1 May 1934.

See also AUSTROFASCISM.

Austrian empire, name given to the empire of the Habsburg monarchy between 1804 and 1867. The emperor FRANZ II adopted the title of emperor of Austria in 1804 during the last days of the HOLY ROMAN EMPIRE in the expectation of the imminent demise of the old Reich. The name 'Austrian empire' is used from that date to the AUSGLEICH, or 'compromise', of 1867, when Hungary gained effective autonomy in internal affairs. After that date the empire is referred to as Austria-Hungary or 'the Dual Monarchy'.

Austrian Netherlands, HABSBURG provinces approximately comprising the territory of modern Belgium and Luxembourg. The territory was inherited by the Spanish Habsburgs from Burgundy, and then by the French when Charles II of Spain died (1700). The Habsburgs, British and Dutch contested the French succession to the Spanish throne in the war of the Spanish succession (1701–14), and the southern Netherlands went to Austria under the terms of the treaties collectively known as the peace of UTRECHT (and in accordance with the Peace of Rastatt, 7 March 1714, which ended hostilities between Austria and France). The end of Austrian rule followed a revolt in the province against the policies of JOSEPH II in 1789, when middle-class conservative leaders took advantage of the French revolution to seize power. Austrian authority was briefly restored by LEOPOLD II in 1790. The French annexed the provinces in 1795. At the Congress of VIENNA Austria gave up the province which then became part of the United Kingdom of the Netherlands.

Austrian Succession, War of the (1740–48), conflict between Austria and Prussia and their respective allies. Following the accession of MARIA THERESIA to the Habsburg throne according to the terms of the PRAGMATIC SANCTION, FRIEDRICH II of Prussia, disputing her right to succeed, invaded Silesia. Saxony, Bavaria and Prussia, allied with France, achieved rapid victories in Silesia, while a Franco-Bavarian army marched on Prague and Linz. Maria Theresa sought help from Hungary, famously appearing before the Hungarian diet at Pressburg (now Bratislava) with the infant Joseph II in her arms. Nevertheless she was forced to cede Silesia at the peace of Breslau (now Wrocław), and Karl Albrecht of Bavaria was elected Holy Roman emperor (KARL VII). These events brought to an end the first phase of the conflict, which has sometimes been called the First Silesian War. Austria now found allies in Savoy, Saxony and Britain, which together formed the so-called 'Pragmatic Army' and defeated France at Dettingen in 1743. A second alliance was then formed between Prussia and France, and the conflict reopened after an interlude; this second phase has been called the Second Silesian War (1744–5), which ended again in victory for Prussia at the peace of DRESDEN. In a separate agreement, however, Bavaria recognized Franz I of Lorraine (Maria Theresia's consort) as Holy Roman emperor. The Anglo-Austrian war against France and Spain continued, however, until the peace of AACHEN in 1748. In this treaty France agreed to return the Austrian Netherlands and British colonial territories.

Austrofascism, term used by contemporaries and historians to describe variously the Austrian HEIMWEHR ('home guard') movement and the DOLLFUSS–SCHUSCHNIGG dictatorship. The validity and usefulness of the term has been disputed since the end of World War II, and has only recently been used extensively in Austria itself. While there has been a measure of general agreement about the fascist nature of the Heimwehr movement, the fascist nature of the 'CORPORATE STATE' (*Ständestaat*) has been disputed and qualified. Contemporaries, however, were less reluctant to use the term, and observers of both left and right, including the then Austrian president, Wilhelm MIKLAS, used it to refer to the dictatorship. Disagreements about the term have been related to the general difficulty in coming to terms with the past in post-fascist Europe.

Although both the Nazi Party and the 'Austrofascists' of the Heimwehr had their origins in the radical right-wing ideology and proto-fascist organizations of imperial Austria, the post-World War I organizational history of Austrofascism begins with the establishment of the avowedly rightwing *Heimwehren*, paramilitary units set up to defend the homeland against frequent foreign incursions, but quickly aligned with the anti-democratic right. Their fascist ideology became clearer after their role in the defeat of the general strike of 1927. It was made explicit in the 'Korneuburg oath', the political and ideological manifesto of the movement, adopted at a rally in Korneuburg, Lower Austria (18 May 1930). This was followed by an attempted coup d'état, the so-called 'march on Vienna' of September 1931. They received sympathy and support from both Italy and Hungary, and stood for parliament as an independent political grouping in 1930. The new government of that year contained Heimwehr ministers, and looked increasingly towards authoritarian solutions to solve its problems. It ruled by emergency decree from 1932 (following the example of Heinrich BRÜNING's administration in Germany), suspended parliamentary government in 1933, and introduced a fascist constitution after the brief AUSTRIAN CIVIL WAR in 1934. All political parties were dissolved and replaced by the VATERLÄNDISCHE FRONT, a patriotic organization founded in the previous year and based on fascist models. It proved to be a failure in terms of mobilizing mass support, however. Parliamentary government was formally replaced with a corporative system but, as in Italy, the corporate state never properly functioned as such, as the system was effectively run by an unaccountable authoritarian clique. Although the federal system was preserved for administrative purposes, authority was centralized, and the autonomy of 'Red Vienna' was brought to an end with the effective imposition of a governor. The FREE TRADE UNIONS were dissolved, and a single government union, the Unity Union (*Einheitsgewerkschaft*), was imposed from above. Heimwehr leaders initially played a leading role in the new regime, but their influence waned under Kurt von SCHUSCHNIGG, who assumed the chancellorship after the assassination of DOLLFUSS in July 1934.

Austro-Hungarian empire, another term for AUSTRIA-HUNGARY; *see AUSGLEICH*.

Austro-Prussian War (1866), conflict in which Prussia rapidly defeated Austria, hence its alternative name of the Seven Weeks War.

The war was precipitated by BISMARCK's German policy of the early 1860s, and also by difficulties arising from the Austrian and Prussian administration of SCHLESWIG-HOLSTEIN, following the acquisition of the duchies in the 1864 war with Denmark. As war became inevitable in 1866, Austria called on the federal diet (BUNDESTAG) of the GERMAN CONFEDERATION to decide the future of Schleswig-Holstein. Bismarck regarded this as a breach of the Gastein agreement of 1865, which had ended a condominium over the duchies and assigned Schleswig to Prussia, and Holstein to Austria. Prussia now occupied Holstein, where the Austrians had recently held a provocative demonstration in Altona, outside Hamburg. Austria asked the diet to mobilize troops against Prussia, and when the proposal was carried, Prussia left the German Confederation, declaring it dissolved. On 16 June 1866 Prussia invaded the north German states of Saxony, Hanover and Hesse-Kassel, which were occupied within a week. The Prussian army then defeated the Austrians decisively at SADOVÁ (Königgrätz) in Bohemia on 3 July, and within seven weeks the war was over. The outcome was the end of Austria's long hegemony in Germany and the granting of effective home rule for Hungary as agreed in the terms of the *AUSGLEICH* or compromise of 1867. Following Italy's military support for Prussia in the war, Austria was also forced to relinquish Venetia to Italy (October 1866). Prussia annexed Frankfurt, Hanover and Hesse-Kassel, thereby uniting the eastern and western parts of the kingdom, and went on to form the NORTH GERMAN CONFEDERATION.

autarky, a term generally taken to refer to the policy of economic self-sufficiency promoted by the Nazis. It had wider currency, however, as part of a broader critique of economic liberalism during the first half of the 20th century. In propaganda terms, the concept reinforced the Nazi ideal of a Germany independent from foreigners, less reliant on the outside world, and as a result more secure. In this context those industrialists who wanted to maintain trade links with the outside world were seen as unreliable and 'cosmopolitan'. Support for autarky in the real world outside Nazi ideology came largely from heavy industry, above all from IG FARBEN, for self-interested reasons, and from the air ministry. It is not clear to what extent the drive for complete self-sufficiency was shared by senior members of the regime, but in so far as it was taken seriously the goal of national economic self-sufficiency was envisaged as achievable only in the longer term, after the acquisition of sufficient LEBENSRAUM to provide Germany with resources such as oil, cotton and the minerals essential for modern industrial production. The conquest of eastern Europe and the western Soviet Union was to provide Germany with raw materials as well as territory for settlement and expansion. Certainly this was the vision of the economic future articulated by Hitler in 1942 during the war against the USSR. Conservatives, including Hjalmar SCHACHT (economics minister and president of the REICHSBANK in the 1930s), were more ambivalent to say the least, on the grounds that it was economic nonsense to pay disproportionately for the domestic manufacture of synthetic *Ersatz* products. In any case, it was acknowledged, isolation from international markets would bring new economic problems once rearmament was completed, especially as the world economy began to recover from the Depression.

autobahns, motorways. Autobahns were first planned by the Weimar Republic during the 1920s. The effects of the Depression persuaded German governments (including the Nazis, who had initially campaigned against the Republic's road-building programme) to invest in public works in general, and the refurbishment of infrastructure in particu-

lar. Labour-intensive projects were prioritized in the emergency programmes of 1932, and over half of expenditure for public works went on transport during the early 1930s. The Nazi programme of road building was begun in 1933–4, and was part of a broader effort to encourage the expansion of motor transport.

Axis, Germany's WORLD WAR II alliance with Italy. The term was apparently first used by Mussolini in 1936 to describe the relationship with Germany established in the agreement of October of that year. Hans FRANK also claimed to be the originator of the term, and to have used it in September in discussions with Count Ciano (the Italian Fascist foreign minister) as part of an extended metaphor in which he compared Europe to a car resting on the Berlin–Rome Axis and driven forward by the twin wheels of Fascism and National Socialism. The Axis was reinforced by the so-called 'Pact of Steel', the military alliance agreed between Germany and Italy in 1939. The term 'Axis powers' came to be applied less rigidly to Germany and her allies in general, including the satellite states in eastern Europe (Hungary, Romania, Bulgaria and the puppet state of Slovakia) and Japan.

See also ANTI-COMINTERN PACT; TRIPARTITE PACT.

Axmann, Artur (1913–96), Nazi youth leader. Born in Hagen, Axmann studied law and founded a Nazi youth group in Westphalia in 1928. He succeeded Baldur von SCHIRACH as Reich youth leader in 1940, and deployed groups of 16- and 17-year-olds in a last desperate attempt to defend Berlin from the Red Army in 1945. He escaped arrest at the end of the war and organized a Nazi underground movement, but was captured by the Americans in December 1945 and sentenced in 1949 to three years' imprisonment.

B

Baader, Andreas (1943–77), one of the leaders of the RED ARMY FACTION (*Rote-Armee-Fraktion*, RAF). Baader was arrested in 1968 but escaped from prison in 1970. He was arrested again in 1976 and was found shot in his prison cell in 1977. His death was recorded as a suicide.

Babi Yar, ravine on the outskirts of the city of Kiev, Ukraine, site of a large-scale Nazi atrocity in which 33,771 Jews were murdered by SS units under the command of Paul Blobel in September 1941. The massacre, which took place in the context of widespread mass murders of Jews by *EINSATZGRUPPEN* in the Soviet Union immediately after the German invasion, was ostensibly a reprisal for a partisan bomb attack on the city's Continental Hotel, where the German 6th Army had its headquarters. On 26 September notices were put up directing Jews to report for resettlement. Over 30,000 turned up, and were then taken to the outskirts of the city to Babi Yar, where a 55-m (60-yard) burial pit had been dug. The victims were taken to the pit in small groups, stripped of their clothes and any valuables, and shot in the back of the neck at the edge of the ravine. Soviet prisoners were also murdered at Babi Yar. Months after the massacre the Germans had to exhume and cremate the decomposing bodies following a number of explosions inside the mass grave. More bodies – mainly Jews but also Communist functionaries and Soviet prisoners of war – were buried at the site during the following two years. In 1943 the site was excavated and the exhumed bodies were burned.

Bach, Alexander, Freiherr von (1813–93), Austrian politician. He was justice minister in 1848, and interior minister from 1849 to 1859. Bach was initially a liberal, but became a clerical-conservative supporter of the policy of NEO-ABSOLUTISM in Austria. As interior minister he undertook the centralization and Germanization of the Austrian dominions. Austria's defeat by France and Italy in 1859 led to his fall from power. He was Austrian minister at the Vatican from 1859 to 1867.

Bach, August (1897–1966), East German publisher and politician. He was a co-founder of the CDU in the German Democratic Republic after World War II, and president of the CDU group in the *VOLKSKAMMER* (people's chamber) up to 1955.

Bach, Carl Philipp Emanuel (1714–88), composer. Born in Weimar, the son of Johann Sebastian BACH, and referred to as 'the Berlin Bach' or 'the Hamburg Bach', he was a student at the Thomasschule in Leipzig, and then later at Frankfurt University. He was harpsichordist at the court of Frederick the Great (Friedrich II), and was director of church music (*Kapellmeister*) in Hamburg from 1767. C.P.E. Bach was associated with the music of the *STURM UND DRANG* period.

Bach, Johann Christian (1735–82), composer. Born in Leipzig, the son of Johann Sebastian BACH, and known as 'the Milan Bach' or 'the

London Bach', he was appointed organist in Milan in 1760 and composer to the London Italian Opera in 1762.

Bach, Johann Christoph Friedrich (1732–95), composer. Born in Leipzig, the son of Johann Sebastian BACH, he studied at the Thomasschule there and then at Leipzig University. He worked as a chamber musician at the court of Graf Wilhelm von Schaumburg-Lippe at Bückeburg, and was appointed Konzertmeister in 1758.

Bach, Johann Sebastian (1685–1750), composer, the best-known of the dynasty of composers and musicians. Bach was born in Eisenach, the son of the musician Johann Ambrosius Bach (1645–95). He attended the Michaelisschule in Lüneburg as a choirboy. From 1703 he was a member of the Weimar court orchestra, and organist first at Arnstadt, and then in Mühlhausen, Thuringia (1707), where he moved shortly after his marriage to his cousin Maria Barbara Bach (October 1707). He moved to the court at Weimar in 1708, and became *Kapellmeister* to the Prince of Anhalt-Köthen in 1717. His wife died in 1720, leaving him a widower with four children. His second wife, Anna Magdalena Wilcken, whom he married in 1721, was to outlive him by ten years. In 1723 he was appointed cantor at the Thomasschule in Leipzig, and he remained there for the rest of his life. During his later life he suffered from an eye disorder that eventually blinded him. Bach was an immensely prolific and innovative composer of choral, chamber, orchestral, keyboard and organ music. Among his best-known works are the *Toccata and Fugue* in D minor for organ, composed during his time in Anhalt-Köthen, the Brandenburg Concertos, which were finished by 1721, and the *St Matthew Passion* (1729).

Bach-Zelewski, Erich von dem (1899–1972), SS general in command of actions against partisans on the Eastern Front during World War II. Born into an aristocratic family in Pomerania, Bach-Zelewski pursued a professional military career. He joined the NSDAP in 1930, and was elected to the Reichstag in 1932. He was the senior SS leader in the Soviet Union in the first months after the invasion of June 1941, and at the end of July took command of 11,000 SS men and 6000 ordinary police officers. In addition 33,000 local auxiliaries had joined the force by the end of the year, bringing the total number under Bach-Zelewski's command to 50,000. The vast majority of the victims of Bach-Zelewski's force were Jews, but his men were also responsible for the murder of Gypsies (Roma and Sinti), and of the mentally and physically disabled. Bach-Zelewski also participated in Nazi war crimes in Estonia and Belarus, and he commanded the units that suppressed the Warsaw Uprising (1944). His testimony against other war criminals at Nuremberg saved him from extradition to the USSR, and he was subsequently sentenced to ten years 'special labour' (in practice house arrest) by a German court in 1951. Although he was never prosecuted for his active role in wartime genocide, he was tried for his part in the Röhm Purge, (*see* NIGHT OF THE LONG KNIVES) and for the murder of six Communists in 1933. He died in a prison hospital.

Backe, Herbert (1896–1947), Nazi minister of food and agriculture. Born and educated in Russia, Backe studied at Göttingen University and went on to teach at the Technical University in Hanover. He joined the Nazi Party after becoming a farmer and was a Nazi member of the Prussian LANDTAG in 1932–3. Appointed Reich food commissioner for the FOUR-YEAR PLAN in 1936, he succeeded DARRÉ as food and agriculture minister and Reich farmers' leader in 1942. He committed suicide in prison at Nuremberg.

Baden, one of the historical states of southwestern Germany. Baden was united in the 18th century, but was forced to cede territory on the left bank of the Rhine to France in the 1790s. Nevertheless it was one of the medium-sized states that benefited from

Napoleon's patronage. It gained territory and its elector was raised to the status of grand duke. It was a free-standing member of the GERMAN CONFEDERATION and of the ZOLLVEREIN. It remained a constituent state of the Reich after 1871, although it ceased to be a grand duchy with the establishment of the WEIMAR REPUBLIC. After World War II the Allied occupation forces of France and the United States divided it between them, along a border formed by the motorway between Stuttgart and Ulm. The division created three new *Länder*: Südbaden and Südwürttemberg-Hohenzollern in the French zone south of the motorway, and Württemberg-Baden in the US zone to the north. The integrity of Baden as a separate state was not subsequently restored and it was eventually subsumed into the state of BADEN-WÜRTTEMBERG in 1952, despite a late appeal to the FEDERAL CONSTITUTIONAL COURT (*Bundesverfassungsgericht*) in October 1951.

Baden, Prince Max von (1867–1929), the last chancellor of imperial Germany. He was appointed (3 October 1918) during the last weeks of WORLD WAR I to appease the Entente powers, and so that Germany's by then quasi-dictatorial military regime might avoid being associated with a humiliating defeat (which the German public was not expecting); the military regime also wanted to avoid responsibility for accepting punitive peace terms.

A moderate conservative, Prince Max introduced constitutional reforms, began negotiations for an armistice, dismissed LUDENDORFF, and in the absence of a definite decision from WILHELM II, announced the emperor's abdication – and his own resignation – to the Reichstag on 9 November. However, these initiatives were insufficient to prevent the outbreak of the NOVEMBER REVOLUTION. He was succeeded by Friedrich EBERT, the leader of the Majority Social Democrats (MSPD).

Badeni, Kasimierz Felix, Graf von (1846–1909), minister-president of Austria (1895–7). Badeni was born in Galicia and studied law at Kraków. He pursued a career as a civil servant, and was appointed governor of Galicia (1888) before becoming minister-president of the Austrian half of the Habsburg monarchy. He is remembered for legislation devised to accommodate the national aspirations of the Slav minorities of CISLEITHANIA (principally in Bohemia and Moravia), including a reform of the franchise that benefited national minority parties, and laws to raise Czech to the status of an official language. This meant that whereas all local officials had had to speak German, they now had to speak and write Czech as well, which would have undermined considerably the position of the German minority in Bohemia and Moravia at a time when there was already anxiety about economic competition from the Czechs. The result of the Badeni laws was intense opposition from the German nationalists and unseemly scenes in the REICHSRAT, which was dissolved. When it reconvened there were further protests, accompanied by public disorder in the streets in Vienna, Graz and Bohemia. Karl Lueger, the mayor of Vienna, whose appointment had been repeatedly blocked by Badeni, now demanded the latter's resignation. Despite the expulsion of some members of the Reichsrat, Badeni was compelled to resign on 28 November 1897. Baron GAUTSCH von Frankenthurn was appointed to succeed him. In 1898 Gautsch issued provisional decrees designed to meet German objections to the Badeni laws, but all the measures were eventually repealed by Prince THUN-HOHENSTEIN in 1899.

Baden-Württemberg, one of the federal states of Germany. It is the only federal state whose (present) borders were fixed by referendum. After World War II both BADEN and WÜRTTEMBERG had been divided between the French and US zones of occupation. To the north of the Stuttgart–Ulm motorway the Americans constructed the state of Württemberg-Baden out of Nordwürttemberg and

Nordbaden in September 1945. To the south, the French occupied territories were designated Südwürttemberg-Hohenzollern and Baden. In November 1946 the constitution of Württemberg-Baden was approved by the electorate in that part of the American zone, and further referenda were held by the French military authorities in Südwürttemberg-Hohenzollern and (French-occupied) Baden on 18 May 1947. The new constitutions of the two territories were approved by 70% and 68% of the electors respectively. At a conference of heads of government in 1950 Gebhard Müller (CDU), state president of Südwürttemberg, proposed that the people of the three states should be consulted about the possibility of constructing a composite '*Südweststaat*' (southwestern state). The results of the 'popular consultation' were deemed unclear, and the matter was referred to the BUNDESTAG, where the law for the redrawing of the state boundaries was eventually passed in March 1951. Baden appealed to the FEDERAL CONSTITUTIONAL COURT, but its appeal was rejected in October 1951, and the state was constituted in its present form in 1952 following approval (94.1%) in a referendum at the end of the previous year (9 December 1951). A provisional government was formed on 25 April by Reinhold Meier.

Baden-Württemberg has been one of the most prosperous states in the history of postwar Germany. The state capital is Stuttgart. It covers 35,752 square km (13,800 square miles) and had a population of just over 10 million by the year 2000, an increase of some 4 million since the establishment of the state in 1952. Of these, 1.3 million were foreigners, 360,000 of them Turks. The CDU has always been the largest single party returned in elections.

Bad Godesberg programme (1959), ideological turning point for the SPD (Social Democrats). It was adopted at an extraordinary party conference in Bad Godesberg in November 1959 to discuss the party programme. Fundamental Marxist positions, no longer much more than rhetoric, and perceived as damaging to the party's electoral chances, were abandoned in favour of a pragmatic repositioning of the party. The new programme, which accepted both NATO and European integration, was adopted virtually unanimously. The SPD's electoral performance improved thereafter.

Baeck, Leo (1873–1956), Jewish leader. Born in Lissa, Prussia, Baeck trained as a rabbi in Berlin and established a reputation as a rabbinical scholar in Oppeln, Düsseldorf and Berlin before World War I. He was elected president of the Union of German Rabbis in 1922 and chairman of the central Jewish Welfare Organization in 1926. He was chairman of the Reich Representation of German Jews, the leading Jewish organization in Nazi Germany, until he was sent to THERESIENSTADT in 1943. Baeck survived to preside over the World Union for Progressive Judaism after the war, and to found the Leo Baeck Institute. He died in London.

Baedeker, Karl (1801–59), publisher. Baedeker was born in Essen, and set up a publishing business in Koblenz, in the Rhineland, in 1827. After publishing a guide to the town, he went on to publish a guide to the Rhineland, and went on to establish the firm's worldwide reputation for authoritative travel guides. Baedeker guides were published in French from 1846 and in English from 1861.

Bahrdt, Karl Friedrich von (1740–92), radical writer. Born at Bischofswerda in Saxony, Bahrdt both studied and taught at Leipzig, where his father had been rector. He then moved on to Erfurt and Giessen and went on to become headmaster of a boarding school, first in Switzerland and then in the Palatinate. Declared a heretic in Vienna, he was forbidden to write or teach theology, and moved to Halle, where he taught classics and gave immensely popular public lectures, but was unpaid. The accession to the Prussian throne of the reactionary FRIEDRICH WILHELM II exacerbated Bahrdt's position, and drove him into a position of outright opposition. He satirized the court, the government and its religiosity, and founded an oppositional secret society, the 'Union of 22', for which he lost his teaching post. The Union expanded rapidly and became a shadow German Freemasonry. (Bahrdt himself was a member of the Grand Lodge of England.) In 1789 Bahrdt was arrested, accused of lese majesty and sentenced to life imprisonment. His Union was persecuted as a subversive organization in several German states. He was released after the French Revolution, for fear that he might become a political martyr, but died after a haemorrhage at the age of 51.

Bamberg Conference (14 February 1926), an important meeting in the early history of the Nazi Party. Leading Nazis met at Bamberg in Bavaria, to resolve differences between ambitious northern members of the party and the Munich leadership. Hitler effectively reimposed his own authority. GOEBBELS was one of the northern rebels, and recorded his feelings about their defeat in his diary. He was subsequently appointed *Gauleiter* of Berlin and became a convert to the Hitler camp.

Barbarossa, code name for the German attack on the Soviet Union on 22 June 1941. Barbarossa (red beard) was the name given to Friedrich I (1123–90), Holy Roman emperor (1152–90), a hero of German medieval history who had been killed during the Third Crusade.

Barlach, Ernst (1870–1938), expressionist artist and writer. The son of a doctor, Barlach studied art in Hamburg, Dresden and Paris (1888–96) Although he had joined up as a convinced patriot, Barlach's artistic response to World War I and the consequences of war was sharply critical, and was attacked by the radical right. Nevertheless, and despite his own self-imposed isolation from the mainstream of artistic life, his work was widely acclaimed and he was awarded the decoration Pour le mérite on the recommendation of Max LIEBERMANN and

Käthe KOLLWITZ in 1933. His work was condemned by the Nazis as degenerate and his sculptures for north German churches were removed and destroyed in 1937. He died in Rostock the following year.

Barth, Emil (1879–1941), trade unionist and Social Democrat politician. Born in Heidelberg, Barth was a plumber by trade, and a member of the SPD. He joined the breakaway USPD during World War I, and was a leader of the Revolutionary Shop Stewards' Movement in Berlin in 1918. He was briefly a member of the COUNCIL OF PEOPLE'S REPRESENTATIVES in the NOVEMBER REVOLUTION of 1918, and was responsible for health and social policy. This was the peak of his political career. He was unseated from his position at the head of the Revolutionary Shop Stewards' Movement in December, and broke with his fellow members of the government shortly afterwards. He subsequently rejoined the SPD and served as an official of the ADGB until 1924.

Barth, Karl (1886–1968), Swiss Protestant pastor and theologian. Born in Basel, he held chairs at Göttingen, Münster and Bonn during the Weimar Republic. In 1933 he took issue with Hitler's Protestant supporters, the GERMAN CHRISTIANS, in his treatise 'Theological Existence Today', which sold 30,000 copies within the year. He strongly influenced the theology of the anti-Nazi BEKENNENDE KIRCHE (the German Confessing Church). Barth was dismissed from his post in 1935 and returned to Switzerland. He became one of the most influential theologians of the 20th century.

Basel, treaty of (1794), treaty between Revolutionary France and Prussia. FRIEDRICH WILHELM II withdrew from the War of the First Coalition (*see* COALITIONS, WARS OF THE) and made a separate, self-interested peace with France at the expense of imperial interests. Prussia effectively agreed to the French annexation of the west bank of the Rhine.

BASF, Badische Anilin- und Sodafabrik, a leading German chemicals company based in

Ludwigshafen on the Rhine. It was founded in 1865, and was part of the IG FARBEN concern from 1925 to 1945. After World War II it was placed under French control (until 1951). It was effectively refounded as a German company in 1952.

Basic Law (*Grundgesetz*), the constitution of the FEDERAL REPUBLIC OF GERMANY. The constitution (literally Basic Law) of the Federal Republic drew heavily on its democratic predecessors, the Reich constitution of 1849 and the Weimar constitution of 1919. It was approved by the PARLIAMENTARY COUNCIL in May 1949 by 53 votes to 12. It was then approved by the military governors of the Western zones of occupation, and was ratified by the *Länder* – except Bavaria, where the LANDTAG rejected the Basic Law on the grounds that it was too centralist. The Basic Law came into force with the establishment of the Federal Republic, subject to 'reserve powers' retained by the Western Allies and pending the adoption of a constitution for the whole of Germany. (It was always referred to as the Basic Law to make the point that it was provisional. The last article stated: 'The Basic Law shall cease to be in force on the day on which a constitution adopted by the free decision of the German people comes into force'.) Article 79 made the constitutional, democratic and federal nature of the constitution amendable, along with the stipulation that the Federal Republic was a 'social welfare state'. The federal states each have their own constitution in accordance with the federal principle, but these must conform to the constitutionalism of the Basic Law.

Basic Treaty (*Grundvertrag*; 1972), treaty between the FEDERAL REPUBLIC OF GERMANY and the GERMAN DEMOCRATIC REPUBLIC, signed on 21 December 1972. The treaty was the culmination of the OSTPOLITIK pursued by the 'social–liberal' (SPD–FDP) administration of Willy BRANDT during the early 1970s. It was opposed by the CDU and especially by the CSU, and the conservative parties threatened not to ratify the treaty if they were returned to power in the election of 1972. (In the event the SPD was not only returned to power, but was the largest party in parliament for the first time since the founding of the Federal Republic.) By the terms of the treaty, the two states recognized each other's boundaries and independence, and each agreed to establish a 'permanent representation' in the capital of the other, but the treaty stopped short of full reciprocal diplomatic recognition. Both states joined the United Nations the following year.

Bauer, Gustav (1870–1944), trade unionist and Social Democratic politician; chancellor (1919–20). Born in Darkehmen, East Prussia, Bauer worked as a clerical assistant in Königsberg, and was an active trade unionist. He was founder and first leader of the office employees' union, and was elected to the Reichstag for the SPD in 1912. Bauer was labour minister in the SCHEIDEMANN administration of 1919. When the Allied peace terms were published on 1 May they were unacceptable to some members of the government, particularly members of the liberal German Democratic Party (*Deutsche Demokratische Partei*, DDP). The government resigned in June and Bauer himself formed a new administration with the support of the CENTRE PARTY. The treaty of VERSAILLES was accepted by a majority of deputies when it came before the Reichstag on 23 June, but the DDP voted against the government. DDP ministers then rejoined the government in October. Bauer's government was forced to flee to Stuttgart during the abortive KAPP PUTSCH the following spring. Although the attempted coup was foiled by a general strike, Bauer himself resigned, and was succeeded by a new coalition under Hermann MÜLLER at the end of March 1920. Bauer himself was appointed transport minister on 1 May 1920 (replacing the Centre Party minister Johannes Bell) and was treasury minister in the two broad coalitions led by Joseph WIRTH (1921–2).

Bauer, Otto (1881–1938), leading Austrian Social Democrat and Marxist thinker. Born in Vienna, Bauer studied law, philosophy and economics there and quickly became a prolific contributor to political debates among the so-called 'Austro-Marxists'. He published his first major work, on social democracy and the Habsburg nationalities, at the age of 26 and became secretary of the Austrian Social Democratic Party (SDAP) in the same year (1907). He was also a co-founder of the party's theoretical journal, *Der Kampf* ('the struggle'). Bauer was an opponent of the Bolshevik revolution, preferring a 'third way' between the policies of the European Communist parties and the compromises of other Social Democratic parties. This was a policy that preserved the unity of the labour movement in Austria, but the party was forced into opposition after a brief period in coalition immediately after World War I, during which time Bauer served as foreign minister. He resigned in July 1919 when his policy of promoting a union (ANSCHLUSS) of Austria with Germany was ruled out by the Allies in the treaty of ST GERMAIN. During the 1920s and 1930s Bauer published a number of theoretical works on contemporary politics, including *Die Österreichische Revolution* ('the Austrian Revolution', 1923), and *Der Faschismus* ('Fascism', 1936). After the AUSTRIAN CIVIL WAR of 1934 Bauer fled to Brno in Czechoslovakia, and then moved to Paris, where he died in 1938.

Bauhaus, avant-garde school of design and architecture in Weimar Germany. It was established in 1919 in Weimar through a merger of the Academy of Fine Arts and the School of Applied Arts, and the first director was Walter GROPIUS. The Bauhaus manifesto claimed that there was no difference between the artist and the craftsman, and among the first members of staff were some of the most prominent painters of the time, including Wassily KANDINSKY, Paul KLEE, Gerhard Marcks and Oskar SCHLEMMER. The Bauhaus moved to Dessau in 1925. Gropius left in 1928 and his successor, Hannes Meyer, prioritized the role of technology and engineering over form. Meyer was succeeded by MIES VAN DER ROHE, who remained director until the school was closed by the Nazis in 1933. Mies van der Rohe then left for the United States, where he became head of architecture at the Illinois Institute of Technology. Other leading members of the Bauhaus staff, including Gropius himself and the Hungarian painter and photographer Laszlo Moholy-Nagy, also went to influential positions in the United States. The Bauhaus has had a dramatic impact both nationally and internationally on modern design and design education. The school's products have been widely copied and their functional, modernist style imitated in the production of domestic articles for mass consumption.

Bäumer, Gertrud (1873–1954), campaigner for women's rights and liberal politician. Bäumer was born in Hohenlimburg, Pomerania, the daughter of a pastor. She trained as a schoolteacher, and was awarded a doctorate in 1904. In 1910 she became president of the League of German Women's Associations (BDF), and was co-editor of its journal, *Die Frau* ('the woman'). Under Bäumer's leadership the BDF moved to the right and sought to encourage women away from confrontation and competition with men. Instead they were to develop their own sphere of activity. Bäumer herself was a supporter of Friedrich NAUMANN, and nationalism and eugenics were increasingly prominent elements in the ideology of the BDF. The organization developed contacts with other organizations on the political right. Bäumer played a prominent role in public life during the Weimar Republic, as a prominent member of the DDP and a Reichstag deputy; as a senior civil servant in the interior ministry; and as a German delegate to the League of Nations. Although she was dismissed from her job by the Nazis in

1933, she cooperated with the regime on a number of minor matters, and continued to publish *Die Frau* until 1944. Bäumer did not resume her political career after the end of World War II, but did continue to publish.

Bavaria (German name: Bayern), after Prussia the largest constituent state in Germany after 1871. The dukes of Bavaria were electors of the HOLY ROMAN EMPIRE, and from 1180 until the end of World War I Bavaria was ruled by the WITTELSBACH dynasty, although the family's entitlement to the crown was unsuccessfully challenged by JOSEPH II in the War of the BAVARIAN SUCCESSION. Bavaria profited from its alliance with Napoleon, promoted by the energetic Count MONTGELAS, gained territory and became a kingdom in 1805. It has existed more or less within its present boundaries since then. Bavaria joined the Reich of 1871, insisting more resolutely than any other state on the rights of the *Länder* (constituent states), and retained an important presence in the federal council (BUNDESRAT), where it commanded 6 of the 14 votes with which it was possible to veto constitutional amendments.

Bavaria continued to assert federal rights after World War I, but events in Bavaria itself and particularly in Munich, the capital, proved a distraction. The Wittelsbach dynasty was deposed during the NOVEMBER REVOLUTION of 1918, and a socialist republic was declared in Munich by the USPD leader Kurt EISNER on 7 November. Following Eisner's assassination in February of the following year, the LANDTAG went into recession and a power vacuum arose during the politically confused interregnum that followed. Three separate factions each claimed political authority, but when news reached Munich of the establishment of a Hungarian councils' republic by Béla Kun, the MSPD fled to Bamberg, and a republic of workers' councils was declared in the capital, with widespread support in the councils movement (*see* RAT), and with the expectation in some quarters that a confederation would be formed comprising Bavaria, Béla Kun's Hungary and revolutionary Austria. In the event the new regime survived only until May, when it was defeated by the army with the assistance of FREIKORPS units. It then became a parliamentary democracy within the WEIMAR REPUBLIC, but was dominated by the right, which tolerated the proliferation of radical right-wing movements, including the Nazi Party (NSDAP). Hitler, who had emigrated to Bavaria before the war, made Munich his base and made his first bid for power there during the abortive BEER HALL PUTSCH of 1923.

Since World War II, Bavarian politics have been dominated by the Christian Social Union (CSU), sister party of the more mainstream CDU, and indirect successor to the prewar Bavarian People's Party (BVP). The party has won over 50% of the vote in all elections to the Landtag since 1970. At the end of the 20th century Bavaria had a population of 11.3 million.

Bavarian People's Party. *See* BVP.

Bavarian Succession, War of the (1778–9), conflict between Prussia and Austria, also called the 'potato war'. The WITTELSBACH dynasty that had ruled Austria since 1180 had two different branches – the Bavarian and Sulzbach lines. The Bavarian line died out in 1777 with the death of the elector Maximilian III, and Bavaria was inherited by the elector palatine, Karl Theodor of the Sulzbach line, who also had no male heirs. JOSEPH II, the Habsburg emperor, was married to the sister of Maximilian, the previous elector of Bavaria, and coveted Bavarian territory. He offered the Austrian Netherlands (modern Belgium) in exchange for territory in Bavaria. The 'war' was an expression of mistrust between FRIEDRICH II of Prussia (Frederick the Great) and Joseph, and ended without their armies having engaged. The issue was settled with the help of French and Russian diplomacy at the peace of Teschen (1779), and Austria gained only the Innviertel district.

Bayerische Volkspartei. See BVP.

Bayern, the German name for BAVARIA.

BdM. *See BUND DEUTSCHER MÄDEL.*

Bebel, August (1840–1913), socialist leader and co-founder of the SPD. Bebel was born in Deutz in the Rhineland, the son of an impoverished officer. He joined the Workers' Educational Association in Leipzig in 1861, by which time he was a master turner. At this time he was an opponent of LASSALLE, of universal suffrage, and of communism. In 1865 he met Wilhelm LIEBKNECHT, and together they founded the Saxon People's Party in 1866 in the wake of the Prussian defeat of Austria. He was elected to the constituent Reichstag of the NORTH GERMAN CONFEDERATION in 1867, the first representative of a workers' party, and was the only person elected in every Reichstag election from 1871 to 1912. In 1867 he was also elected president of the League of German Workers' Educational Associations. In 1869 Bebel and Liebknecht, who had since parted company with their liberal allies, joined a number of dissident Lassalleans to form the Social Democratic Workers' Party (SDAP) at Eisenach. The party's policy differed from that of Lassalle's ADAV in that it reflected Bebel's own opposition to Prussian expansionism. The two parties merged at the 'socialist unity congress' in Gotha in 1875. In 1892 Bebel was elected one of the two presidents of the SPD. He died in Passugg in Switzerland.

Beck, Ludwig (1880–1944), general. Born in Biebrich, Beck served in Alsace-Lorraine before 1914 and in World War I. He was promoted through the ranks of the REICHSWEHR during the Weimar Republic, and was head of general staff of the German army between 1935 and 1938. Beck sought to win a role in political decision-making for military leaders. He resigned in August 1938 in opposition to Hitler's planned invasion of Czechoslovakia, believing Germany to be militarily unprepared for the general war he thought would inevitably follow. He was succeeded

by General HALDER. Beck continued to be associated with oppositional circles in the armed forces, including the JULY BOMB PLOT of 1944, and committed suicide when the assassination attempt failed.

Beck, Max Wladimir, Freiherr von (1854–1943), minister-president of Austria (1906–8). Beck was born in Vienna and pursued a career as a public servant, chiefly in the ministry of agriculture. He succeeded Prince HOHENLOHE as minister-president in 1906, and introduced universal male suffrage in Austria the following year, along with proportional representation in the lower house of the REICHSRAT for the nationalities. The electoral law of 1907 abolished the curiae (separate classes of voter) and gave all Austrian men over the age of 24 an equal vote. The problem of the nationalities was resolved by setting up ethnic registers and constituencies, which meant that members of different ethnic groups did not stand against each other, but against members of the same nationality with different political allegiances. Germans were still over-represented, with 45% of the seats for 35% of the population, while the Czechs had 20% of the seats, yet comprised 23% of the population. The reform had the positive effect of taking some of the racial tension out of elections, and parties based on class interest dominated the new Reichsrat. (The Social Democrats won 85 seats and the Christian Socialists 67.) Beck was also responsible for the difficult ten-yearly renegotiation of the terms of the *AUSGLEICH* with Hungary. He fell as a result of the continuing ethnic tension in Bohemia and the hostility of FRANZ FERDINAND, who resented Beck's opposition to the annexation of BOSNIA AND HERZEGOVINA.

Beckmann, Max (1884–1950), EXPRESSIONIST painter. Born in Leipzig, Beckmann studied in Weimar and was a member of the Berlin and Dresden SECESSIONS. He served as a field hospital orderly in World War I, and the horrors he witnessed are reflected in his subsequent work, much of which depicts appalling violence. He taught at the art school at Frankfurt am Main during the Weimar Republic, and was associated with the NEUE SACHLICHKEIT movement in the 1920s, although his work maintained an expressionist style and greater subjectivity than that of others associated with the movement. His art was condemned as 'degenerate' by the Nazis, and he was dismissed from his teaching post in 1932. He left Germany for Amsterdam in 1937, and died in New York.

Beer Hall putsch (1923), also called the Munich putsch, abortive bid for power by radical right-wing extremists in Munich, led by HITLER with the support of General LUDENDORFF. The political atmosphere was already tense in BAVARIA when passive resistance to the French and Belgian occupiers was ended in the Ruhr on 26 September (*see* REPARATIONS), and the tension was heightened by the appointment of Gustav, Ritter von KAHR as 'state commissioner general'. Poverty was widespread, the police reported political unrest, and there were persistent rumours of a putsch. Both Hitler and the right-wing clique running Bavaria (Kahr, the Reichswehr commander Lossow and Seisser, the chief of police) wanted the WEIMAR REPUBLIC brought down. The latter had their eyes on Berlin, however, and wanted to join forces with others in northern Germany in order to set up a nationalist dictatorship for the country as a whole. The right-wing paramilitary groups, however, wanted to seize power in Munich first, and install Ludendorff and Hitler before taking on the Reich government. In both cases the justification for the march on Berlin would be the necessity of suppressing the left-wing governments in Saxony and Thuringia, but in the event the Reich government did so first, and the army hesitated.

On 6 November Kahr warned Hitler against acting alone, but he had already gone too far to turn back without frustrating the expectations of his supporters and losing face. On 8 November he interrupted a meeting in the beer hall (Bürgerbräukeller) at which August Kahr, Seisser and Lossow were scheduled to speak to the VÖLKISCH faithful on the evils of Bolshevism, theatrically fired a shot and took the speakers into a separate room and attempted – as an armed guard watched over them – to persuade them to join him, assuring them of Ludendorff's support. As soon as they were free the men reneged on their apparent agreement to go along with the putsch, and army reinforcements were ordered to Munich. Hitler and Ludendorff led a procession into the city centre, still hoping that a show of popular support would bring Kahr and his colleagues behind him. Police attempting to control the crowd were spat on and threatened, but the demonstration came to a sudden end when one of the Nazis shot a policeman, the police opened fire, and the demonstrators quickly fled.

Hitler, Ludendorff, and other leaders of the putsch were arrested and tried for high treason. They received exceptional leniency from the courts, but the Nazi Party was banned, and Hitler was compelled to accept that he could not take power without the cooperation of the army, the police and other powerful interests.

Beethoven, Ludwig van (1770–1827), composer. Born in Bonn, Beethoven was the grandson of the *Kapellmeister* to the archbishop-elector of Cologne; his father was also a member of the archbishop's choir. In 1787 Beethoven made a trip to Vienna, where he encountered Mozart, but returned within two months, after receiving news of his mother's death. He moved to Vienna permanently in 1790 after meeting Haydn, and was supported there by Gottfried van Swieten and Prince Karl Lichnowsky, former patrons of Mozart. However, Beethoven – like Mozart before him – rejected the 18th-century system of patronage whereby composers were tied to a particular employer. He supported himself instead by performing, teaching and the publication of his works.

Beethoven's work is usually divided into three periods. The first of these periods corresponded with his first decade in Vienna, when he made his debut as a concert pianist and established his reputation as a composer. The second, or 'heroic', period is generally dated from about the time of his serious depression in 1802, but can also be said to date from the composition of the *Moonlight* Sonata the previous year. It was during this period that the third symphony, the *Eroica*, was composed. (It was originally dedicated to Napoleon, but the dedication was withdrawn when he declared himself emperor.) The third ('silent') period is generally dated from 1813. Beethoven first became aware of hearing difficulties in 1796, and his deafness made it increasingly impossible for him to perform as a pianist in public. His last performance was in 1814, and within another five years he was totally deaf. He became increasingly difficult to live with, and was preoccupied during the last years of his life with attempts to gain custody of his nephew Karl, whose father had died. Beethoven himself died after a long illness in Vienna in 1827.

Quite apart from his innovative contributions to the development of Western music, Beethoven occupies a unique position in the cultural history of Germany and Europe, and has come to personify musical 'genius' – not least because he has avoided being easily categorized, and has instead come to be seen as a pivotal figure between 18th-century classicism and 19th-century Romanticism. Beethoven's music is also seen as representing the humanist spirit, and the dignity and freedom of the individual – reflecting the democratic, liberal ideals of the French Revolution. His choral setting of SCHILLER's 'Ode to Joy' (*An die Freude*) was adopted as the anthem of Europe, and, as 'Ode to Freedom' (*An die Freiheit*), it also became the anthem that accompanied the reunification of Germany in 1990.

Behrens, Peter (1868–1940), industrial architect and designer. Born and educated in Hamburg, Behrens also studied in Karlsruhe, Düsseldorf and Munich. He was one of the founding members of the DEUTSCHER WERKBUND in 1907. As architect to AEG he developed the company's corporate identity, and among his best-known works is the a turbine factory he designed for the company in Berlin (1909). He also designed the IG FARBEN office in Höchst (1920). He subsequently taught at the Vienna Academy (1922–36) and at the Berlin Academy under the Nazis.

Bekennende Kirche, the German Confessing Church, composed of Protestants opposed to the effective Nazification of the German EVANGELICAL CHURCH, and against the GERMAN CHRISTIANS, Hitler's supporters within it. The relationship between the state and the Evangelical Church had always been close, and many senior churchmen were opposed to the Weimar Republic and sympathetic to the Nazis. The German Christian movement, which was popular among the younger clergy, sought to combine evangelical theology with racial nationalism, and hoped thereby to broaden the appeal of the church in the age of the 'masses'. In May 1933 a national constitution was adopted for the church, and on 27 May a Reich bishop elected, Friedrich von Bodelschwingh (1877–1946). He was forced to resign, however, and following new elections to the church synod in July, Ludwig Müller, the candidate of the German Christians and a personal acquaintance of Hitler, was appointed instead. Other Nazi supporters were promoted within the church. The opposition to these developments within the church was organized around the Pastors' Emergency League organized by Martin NIEMÖLLER, and by the 'confessing church', which eventually became a second Evangelical Church (21 October 1934) – albeit one not recognized by the secular authorities, and subject to internal divisions between the Lutheran and Reformed wings.

Its theology was expressed in a declaration at the Synod of Barmen in 1934, which drew heavily on the work of the Swiss theologian Karl BARTH.

Belcredi, Richard, Graf (1823–1902), Austrian politician. Belcredi was minister of state and minister-president from 1865 to 1867. He was born near Svitavy (then Zwittau), the son of a Moravian landowner. He became governor of Silesia in 1860, and succeeded Anton SCHMERLING as prime minister after a brief spell as imperial governor in Prague (1864–5). One of his first acts was to repeal the 'FEBRUARY PATENT', a series of measures by which his predecessor had sought to strengthen the position of the German middle classes. He also permitted the use of Czech as a language of instruction in schools. These moves, effectively concessions to the Slavs of the empire, created tension among the German-speaking population of the linguistically mixed territories of Bohemia and Moravia. Belcredi's ministry was cut short by the double disaster of defeat by Prussia and Italy in 1866. The limitations of his conciliatory approach to the Slavs were reflected in the AUSGLEICH of 1867, which excluded the Czechs from any privileged position similar to that of the Hungarians.

Belsen. *See* BERGEN-BELSEN.

Belzec, Nazi CONCENTRATION CAMP for forced Jewish labour in the Lublin district of Poland. A number of camps existed on this site and in the surrounding area from 1940. Some 11,000 people were accommodated there as forced labourers, many of whom died from exhaustion, malnutrition and the general brutality of their treatment in the camps. The camps were closed down at the end of the year, but during the summer of 1941 work began on the construction of an EXTERMINATION CAMP at Belzec. Jews were deported there first from Poland (mainly from the Kraków and Lvov districts), then from the Reich and occupied Europe. The mass murder of Jewish inmates began in the autumn of 1941, before the introduction of systematic gassing. In October, for example, Jews were taken by members of the transport unit from Lublin barracks to a deserted aerodrome, where they were ordered to dig and get into their own mass graves before being shot or killed by hand grenades. Systematic gassing of the Jewish inmates of Belzec began in the summer of 1942 under the direction of the first commandant of the new camp, Christian WIRTH, first with diesel fumes, and then with Zyklon-B gas. More than 600,000 people were murdered at Belzec before the camp was closed down in 1943.

Benjamin, Walter (1892–1940), cultural theorist and literary critic. The son of an upper-middle-class Jewish family in Berlin, Benjamin was educated at the liberal Kaiser Friedrich School and studied philosophy in Freiburg, Munich and Berlin. He was conscripted for war service in 1914, but was rejected on medical grounds, and spent the later part of the war in Switzerland. On returning to Berlin he became a prolific critic, translator and reviewer, but his academic career came to an end when his *HABILITATIONSSCHRIFT* was rejected by Frankfurt University in 1925. During the early 1920s he made an intellectually important friendship with Theodor ADORNO, and his work was published by Adorno and HORKHEIMER in the *Zeitschrift für Sozialforschung*. He also became close to BRECHT and other left-wing intellectuals, visited Moscow in 1926–7, but did not join the Communist Party. He fled to France in 1933 and resumed his work in Paris. Perhaps his best-known essay is 'The Work of Art in the Age of Mechanical Reproduction', a discussion of the relationship between art, its time and its material and social context. In late September of 1940 Benjamin tried to leave France for the United States, but was prevented from crossing the Spanish border and committed suicide in Port Bou. Many of his essays were collected in 1961 under the title *Illuminations*.

Benn, Gottfried (1886–1956), poet. Born in Mansfeld, Benn studied theology and philosophy at Marburg and then medicine at Berlin. Benn was a military doctor during World War I, and he went on to practise in Berlin in the 1920s. His early work was EXPRESSIONIST and conveyed the sense of a mundane and diseased world dominated by the irrational impulse. In 1932 he published a collection of essays entitled *Nach dem Nihilismus* ('after nihilism'). Initially a supporter of Nazism, he was condemned as degenerate himself in 1933 and expelled from the Nazi writers' organization in 1939. He renounced his sympathy with the Nazis after the war, and received the Georg Büchner prize in 1951. He died in Berlin.

Bennigsen, Rudolf von (1824–1902), liberal politician. Bennigsen was born in Lüneburg, now in Lower Saxony. He became president of the German National Association (*Deutscher NATIONALVEREIN*) in 1859, was elected both to the Reichstag and to the Prussian diet in 1867 and was president of the latter from 1873 to 1879. Bennigsen was a co-founder and leader of the NATIONAL LIBERAL PARTY, and a supporter of Bismarck during the 1870s. In 1883 he resigned from all his public offices, but was elected to the Reichstag again in 1897, and remained a member of parliament until 1898.

Benz, Carl Friedrich (1844–1929), engineer and businessman. Benz was born in Karlsruhe and founded the Benz company in Mannheim in 1883. In 1886 he developed a three-wheeled vehicle powered by a one-cylinder engine. His company merged with DAIMLER in 1926; Benz himself had left the company in 1906.

Berchtesgaden, the small town in Bavaria where Hitler rented the house that later became the Berghof. Above it on the Obersalzberg, linked by a lift cut through the rock, was the so-called 'Eagle's Nest' retreat. Although the Eagle's Nest was private, Hitler used the Berghof for important meetings, such as that with Neville Chamberlain in mid-September 1938, prior to the MUNICH AGREEMENT. The Berghof – which was the home of Hitler's mistress Eva Braun until she joined him in the Berlin bunker in 1945 – was destroyed by Allied bombing in April 1945, and the ruins levelled in 1952 to prevent it from becoming a shrine. However, the Eagle's Nest survives as a tea room.

Berchtold, Leopold, Graf von, (1863–1942), foreign minister of Austria-Hungary (1912–15). Berchtold was a wealthy landowner who had pursued a career in the diplomatic service, and had been Austrian ambassador to St Petersburg from 1906 to 1911, before he was appointed foreign minister on the death of AEHRENTHAL in 1912. His policy, like that of his predecessor, was to attempt to maintain the status quo in the Balkans, a project that was to prove increasingly difficult. He proposed that Turkey adopt an Austrian approach to its subject nationalities in Albania and Macedonia, by granting linguistic freedom in public life and devolving authority to local people, but the suggestion met with little response either from Constantinople of from the international community. When the Balkan League declared war on Turkey he persisted in seeking to maintain the status quo, but also sought to protect the interests of Albania's Catholic subjects, and Austria's own interests on the Adriatic coast. Following Italy's declaration of war on Turkey on 29 September 1911, and the subsequent fall of the anti-Italian Austrian chief of staff CONRAD VON HÖTZENDORF, Berchtold sought a *rapprochement* with Rome, and secured a peace between Turkey and Italy on 18 October. The two powers foresaw the introduction of reforms in Albania under Austrian supervision in the north and Italian in the south. Serbia, meanwhile, was forced to withdraw from Albania and to abandon its hopes of a port on the Adriatic. This not only increased Serbian hostility towards Vienna, but also diverted Serb energies into attempts to create a Yugoslav state. When Archduke FRANZ FERDINAND was assassinated, the hawkish Conrad von Hötzendorf (who had resumed his post as chief of staff in 1912) proposed immediate action against Serbia. Berchtold – who had been a personal friend of the archduke and consulted him in matters of policy – was persuaded by Conrad to issue an ultimatum that Serbia could only reject. When Serbia accepted all but two of the conditions in the ultimatum Conrad persuaded the emperor to declare war. Berchtold resigned shortly after the start of the war (13 January 1915), when Austria faced Italian demands for territory.

Berg, Alban (1885–1935), Austrian composer. Born in Vienna, Berg studied with SCHOENBERG and became one of the leading composers to use twelve-tone music. His opera *Wozzeck*, based on the play *Woyzeck* by the early 19th-century radical Georg BÜCHNER was staged by the Berlin State Opera in 1925. His next opera, *Lulu* (based on a play by Frank WEDEKIND), was unfinished; the unfinished version was first performed in Zurich in 1937, while a version with the final act orchestrated by Friedrich Cerha was first performed in Paris in 1979. Berg also wrote a notable violin concerto. Although he was not himself Jewish, Berg's work was classified as 'degenerate' by the Nazis and he was unable to earn much from his work after 1933. Two years later he died in Vienna of septicaemia following an insect bite.

Bergen-Belsen, Nazi CONCENTRATION CAMP about 16 km (10 miles) to the north of Celle, in what is now Lower Saxony. It was built on the site of a POW camp, and originally intended to accommodate about 10,000 Jewish prisoners. In the event around 60,000 people were forced into the overcrowded camp as Jews were moved from other camps further east during the last months of the war. Some 37,000 people died at Bergen-Belsen, including Anne FRANK, before it was liberated by British forces in April 1945.

Berghof. *See* BERCHTESGADEN.

Berlin, the capital city of Prussia, and then of Germany until 1945. East Berlin was capital of the GERMAN DEMOCRATIC REPUBLIC from 1949 to 1990. When Germany was reunited the capital of the Federal Republic, into which the 'new federal states' were subsumed, remained in Bonn until the summer of 1999, when the BUNDESTAG and ministries moved back to the city. The BUNDESRAT held its last session in Bonn in 2000.

The first mention of Berlin appears in a document of 1244, when it was an insignificant small town. Its significance as a political centre came in 1470 when it was adopted as the seat of the HOHENZOLLERN electors of Brandenburg, later kings of Prussia. It had some 60,000 inhabitants at the beginning of the 18th century, 415,000 at the time of the REVOLUTIONS OF 1848, and 826,341 when it became capital of the German empire in 1871. (It had overtaken Vienna as the largest German city shortly before.) Thereafter it expanded rapidly, and had grown to over 1 million by 1880 and over 2 million by 1905. The brash Berlin of the *GRÜNDERZEIT* was compared with Chicago by contemporaries, and it was during this period that the city established itself as a self-styled '*Weltstadt*', a modern metropolis with an international status and cosmopolitan culture like those of London, Paris or New York. Nevertheless it remained smaller than either London or Paris, and much more of an industrial city than the two western capitals. Its administrative structure remained unreformed on the eve of World War I, when the suburban belt of the emergent 'Greater Berlin' still consisted of a collection of towns and rural districts. It was not until after the war that this structure was rationalized, and these outlying districts incorporated into a city of some 4 million.

Berlin has been an overwhelmingly Protestant city since the Reformation. Three-quarters of its population (3,083,196) were counted Evangelical in 1924, and there were 403,780 Roman Catholics and 172,672 Jews. Over half of its population was employed in industry, and it was a left-wing city: more than 60% of the Berlin electorate voted for the SPD or KPD on the eve of the Depression in 1928 (and almost half of those for the latter), and the city decisively rejected Hitler and the NSDAP in the elections of the early 1930s.

Berlin was one of the German cities worst affected by World War II: 70% of its housing stock was destroyed or severely damaged, and West Berlin lost 94% of what was left of its industrial capacity. The city was divided into four occupation sectors (Soviet, US, British and French) by the Allies (*see* BERLIN, DIVISION OF), and remained under four-power control after the establishment of the two German states in 1949. In the early days of the Cold War, the Soviets blockaded the western sectors in 1948–9, prompting the BERLIN AIRLIFT. Although East Berlin became the capital city of the GDR, the capital of the Federal Republic was to remain in Bonn. West Berlin was not officially part of the Federal Republic, although there were close links. The eastern part of the city was effectively sealed off with the building of the BERLIN WALL in 1961. Unlike the rest of Germany, Berlin remained technically under four-power control until the collapse of the German Democratic Republic in 1989, and the reunification of Germany. The Unification Treaty between the Federal Republic and the GDR of 31 August 1990 stipulated that Berlin would be the capital of Germany and that the seat of parliament and government should be decided after the establishment of German unity. The Bundestag and ministries moved there from Bonn in 1999. At the end of the 20th century Berlin had a population of 3.4 million.

Berlin, Conference of (1884–5), meeting of European powers, mainly to discuss territorial disputes in West Africa and to prevent the scramble for colonies there leading to war. The conference was requested by Portugal, which along with Britain was wary of French, Belgian and German ambitions in the region. The conference met on 15 November 1884 and lasted until 26 February 1885. It was a forum for BISMARCK to preside over the deliberations of the 'Great Powers', and he opened and closed the proceedings with suitably statesmanlike speeches. The decisions of the conference were contained in the Berlin Act of 26 February 1885: the Congo Free State (the personal fief of King Leopold II of Belgium) was recognized, the freedom of navigation on the Congo and Niger rivers was agreed, and slave trading was formally forbidden.

Berlin, Congress of (1878), meeting of European powers, intended to diffuse the international tensions arising out of the 'Eastern Question'. The Congress's deliberations led to the treaty of Berlin, which superseded the treaty of San Stefano. It was called at the request of Austria-Hungary, but was a forum in which BISMARCK was able to dominate the proceedings and to project his desired new image as 'honest broker'. Its main purpose was to achieve political stability in the Balkans and the Near East, and most of its decisions remained in force until after the turn of the century. Territory ceded by the Ottoman empire at San Stefano was returned, the independence of Romania, Serbia and Montenegro was confirmed, and a quasi-autonomous Ottoman province of Eastern Roumelia was created. The treaty satisfied Britain, in so far as it placed checks on Russian expansionism, and also pleased Austria-Hungary, whose right to occupy BOSNIA AND HERZEGOVINA was agreed. The Congress was less sensitive to the aspirations of the Balkan nationalities.

Berlin, division of (1945), the division of BERLIN into four Allied sectors of occupation at the end of World War II. Berlin was attacked by the Red Army in the spring of 1945 and capitulated on 2 May. It was occupied by the Soviets until the arrival of Western Allied forces and the establishment of the Allied City Command on 11 July. When the city was divided, 46% of the surface area and 36.8% of the population remained in the Soviet sector in East Berlin. The remainder (West Berlin) was divided into British, French and American sectors. In August 1947 the Soviet military administration vetoed the ratification of the elected mayor of the city, Ernst REUTER (SPD). Louise Schröder (SPD) took office instead. In 1948 separate city administrations were established in East and West Berlin. The two halves of the city were decisively separated in 1961 by the building of the BERLIN WALL, and reunited in 1989 with the collapse of the GERMAN DEMOCRATIC REPUBLIC.

Berlin airlift (1948–9), the relief of the western (US, British and French) occupation sectors of BERLIN by air, due to the road and rail blockade imposed by the Soviets. With the division of Germany into four zones of occupation, Berlin, which was itself divided into four sectors, was located in the middle of the then Soviet zone of occupation, the future GERMAN DEMOCRATIC REPUBLIC. As relations between the USA and the Soviet Union deteriorated with the onset of the Cold War, the city became increasingly vulnerable, and the Western powers expressed fears that the USSR would attempt to assume control of the entire city. In 1948 the Soviets responded to the currency reform in the west (the US, British and French zones of occupation, comprising what would become the FEDERAL REPUBLIC OF GERMANY) by accusing the Western Allies of breaking postwar agreements on the status of Germany. The Soviet military authorities in the east blocked land access to the western sectors of Berlin through their zone. The Western Allies responded by airlifting supplies of food, fuel and mail to Berlin for almost a year, from June 1948 to May 1949, when the USSR conceded defeat on the issue and relaxed it policy. It was during the airlift that the division of political life in Berlin became more or less complete. The rift between the Soviet and Western authorities in the city became irrevocable, and most of the local authorities

transferred their business to West Berlin in the autumn of 1948 following disruption of their meetings by the Communists.

Berlin–Baghdad railway, a symbol of perceived German ambitions in the Near East between the turn of the century and World War I. BISMARCK had, in 1876, famously told the Reichstag that he could see no German advantage to be gained in the Near East that was worth the bones of a single Pomeranian grenadier, but after 1880 it seemed that this policy had been revised, and that Germany was not so much courting influence in Constantinople as – in the words of a French journalist – taking 'pacific possession'. The proposal to build a railway from Berlin to the Persian Gulf – for which a concession was granted in 1899 – was always more of a matter for such journalistic sabre-rattling than a real diplomatic difficulty. It did, however, remain a potent metaphor for the perceived political and economic penetration of the Balkans by Germany. Russian reservations about the project were settled in an agreement with Germany in 1911, and a similar agreement was reached with Britain and France in 1914. In the event, only a section had been constructed before the outbreak of World War I.

Berlin Wall, barrier that divided the Soviet sector from the western (US, British and French) sectors of BERLIN between 1961 and 1989. When the two German states were established in 1949 Berlin technically remained under the shared jurisdiction of the Allies, and it remained possible to cross from the Soviet sector, now 'East Berlin' and capital of the GERMAN DEMOCRATIC REPUBLIC, to the western sectors and vice versa. The result was a steady stream of emigrants to the west, among them disproportionate numbers of young people and skilled workers. The GDR attempted to stop them by closing border crossings and constructing a wall right across the city. The border was patrolled by armed guards, and many would-be migrants were shot before they reached the west. The wall became a symbol of the division of Germany (and of Europe), and was rapidly dismantled after the collapse of the East German regime in 1989. A small section was preserved as a monument, and much of the rest was sold as souvenirs.

Bernhardi, Friedrich (1849–1930), general. Bernhardi served in the Franco-Prussian War as a young officer. He was head of the military history department of the general staff (1898–1901) and became commanding general of the 7th Army Corps (1909). Bernhardi was a right-wing nationalist, who is best remembered as a military and political commentator, and especially for his book *Germany and the Next War* (1911), which was translated into English in 1914. The book put the case for the right and, indeed, duty to make war, and was the origin of the slogan '*Weltmacht oder Untergang*' ('world power or downfall').

Bernstein, Eduard (1856–1932), influential Social Democrat politician. Born in Berlin, the son of an (assimilated) Jewish railway engineer, Bernstein started work there as a bank clerk with the Rothschilds and joined the SDAP in 1872. He moved to Switzerland, became editor there of the Zurich edition of *Der Sozialdemokrat*, and then moved to London when he was deported in 1888. In 1891 Bernstein drafted the party's ERFURT PROGRAMME with Karl KAUTSKY, adding his own demands for specific immediate reforms to Kautsky's more general and theoretical disquisition on the nature of society and class relations under capitalism. The 'revisionism debate', in which he played a leading part, brought him into conflict with Kautsky. Bernstein advocated a reformist programme, and rejected both the Marxist application of the dialectic to the history of social and economic relations and MARX's labour theory of value.

Bernstein represented the SPD in the Reichstag (1902–6, 1912–18, 1920–8). Although he voted for war credits in 1914, along with virtually all other SPD deputies,

Bernstein very quickly changed his public stance, and together with Hugo HAASE and Kautsky he published a denunciation of the war in 1915. He joined the breakaway USPD in 1917. He was a civil servant in the treasury at the time of the 1918 NOVEMBER REVOLUTION, and supported the introduction of parliamentary government. He returned to the SPD in 1919 and supported the party's cooperation with bourgeois parties within the context of a liberal democratic constitution.

Bernstorff, Christian Günther, Graf von (1769–1835), Danish-born diplomat in the service of Prussia. Bernstorff was born in Copenhagen, the son of Count Peter von Bernstorff, who was Danish foreign minister. The younger von Bernstorff was first ambassador to Sweden (1794–7), and then foreign minister of Denmark from June 1797. In 1812 he was appointed Danish ambassador to Austria, and represented Denmark at the Congress of VIENNA. In 1816 he became Danish ambassador to Berlin, but attended the Congress of AACHEN (1818) as a Prussian diplomat. On his return to Berlin he became Prussian foreign minister, and was a staunch supporter of the METTERNICH system both in Europe and within Germany. Bernstorff was an important figure in the establishment of the German customs union (*ZOLLVEREIN*) of 1834.

Bernstorff, Joachim Heinrich, Graf von (1862–1939), German ambassador in Washington before and during World War I. Bernstorff was a popular party host among the social elite of Washington; his mother was American and he had been born in London. It was Bernstorff's task to protest against American shipments to the Allies, and at the same time to reassure Washington, especially after the sinking of the *Lusitania* and the British steamer *Arabic*, that the Germans were concerned to avoid incidents that led to the deaths of US citizens. When Germany resolved to pursue unrestricted submarine warfare in 1917, Arthur Zimmermann, the

German foreign minister sent a telegram to the German minister in Mexico City, via Bernstorff in Washington, instructing him to approach Mexico with a view to concluding an alliance against the USA, should the latter declare war. Germany proposed to restore to Mexico the states of Texas, New Mexico and Arizona. The telegram containing the instruction was intercepted and deciphered by British naval intelligence, who then sent it on to Washington (*see* ZIMMERMANN TELEGRAM).

Besitzbürgertum, the propertied middle class.

Best, Werner (1903–89), SS officer and Reich commissioner for occupied Denmark during World War II. Born in Darmstadt, Best was brought up and educated in Dortmund and Mainz. He was implicated in plans for a coup following the discovery of the BOXHEIM PAPERS in 1931 and forced to resign from his position in the Hesse justice ministry. Appointed police commissioner in Hesse when the Nazis came to power, he later became governor, and was promoted rapidly during the 1930s. He worked closely with HEYDRICH in building up the GESTAPO and SD in the RSHA in Berlin. He was chief of the civil administration and head of the SD in occupied France until 1942, when he became Reich plenipotentiary for occupied Denmark. He was imprisoned after the war, first in Denmark, where he served a term of five years, and then in Germany.

Bethmann Hollweg, Moritz August von. *See* WOCHENBLATTPARTEI.

Bethmann Hollweg, Theobald von (1856–1921), Reich chancellor (1909–17). Bethmann Hollweg studied law and began his career as a Prussian civil servant in Brandenburg. He became Prussian interior minister in 1905 and chancellor in 1909. A good administrator and moderate reforming conservative, he had little experience of foreign affairs when he took over the Reich chancellorship amid deteriorating international relations. His position in domestic politics was also difficult. Following SPD gains in the 1912 election, he was unable to command a stable parliamentary majority, and his administration depended increasingly on support from the court 'camarilla' and the military. He played an important role in the JULY CRISIS of 1914, and formulated Germany's war aims in the SEPTEMBER PROGRAMME of that year. After the outbreak of war his principal domestic aim was to preserve the fragile wartime political truce (*BURGFRIEDEN*) achieved in 1914, but was increasingly challenged by calls from the left for constitutional reform, which were supported by a radicalized labour movement. Despite the ambitious and expansionist war aims of his government, he also found himself under increasing pressure from the 'annexationist' authoritarian right, and was eventually ousted from the political leadership during the debates on the PEACE RESOLUTION in July 1917. He was succeeded by MICHAELIS, but by this time real power was in the hands of the virtual military dictatorship of LUDENDORFF and HINDENBURG.

Betriebsgemeinschaft, 'factory community', a Nazi term that was intended to characterize industrial relations during the Third Reich. By analogy with the Nazis' 'national community' (*VOLKSGEMEINSCHAFT*) the *Betriebsgemeinschaft* was based on the notion of a coming together of factory leaders on the one hand, and followers or 'retinue' (*Gefolgschaft*) in a community that was supposed to transcend conflict, and that was notionally based on unconditional trust between workers and management.

Beust, Friedrich Ferdinand, Graf von (1809– 86), imperial chancellor and minister-president of Austria (1867–71). Beust was born in Dresden into an aristocratic family and studied law at Göttingen and Leipzig. He pursued a diplomatic career and was posted to Prussia, France, Bavaria and Britain. He was appointed foreign minister in Saxony in 1849 and used Prussian troops to suppress the revolution in Dresden. He was Saxon minister of the interior from 1853.

In the changed political situation of 1866 (*see* AUSTRO-PRUSSIAN WAR) he was forced to relinquish his offices in Saxony and was appointed foreign minister of Austria, ostensibly to seek revenge against Prussia, but in the knowledge that neither the liberals in Vienna nor the Hungarians would countenance another war with Prussia. Beust became foreign minister, minister-president and interior minister in February 1867. He was also given the title chancellor (*Reichskanzler*) at his own request, so that he should be on an equal footing with BISMARCK. He negotiated the *AUSGLEICH* (creating the Dual Monarchy of Austria-Hungary) with Deák and ANDRÁSSY of Hungary. He was dismissed from ministerial office in 1871, and served as Austrian ambassador first to London and then to Paris until his retirement in 1882.

Beuys, Josef (1921–86), artist. Born in Krefeld, Beuys served in the Luftwaffe during World War II before studying art in Düsseldorf. Beuys was a provocative avant-garde artist who often used perishable materials in his work, particularly lard and felt, which he claimed local Tartars used to save his life by keeping him warm when his plane crashed in the Soviet Union during the war.

Biedermeier, an early 19th-century style of design for furniture and other domestic items. The term is sometimes applied more generally to the broader culture of the period between the Congress of VIENNA and the REVOLUTIONS OF 1848, an era dominated by the repressive conservatism of Prince METTERNICH. The term Biedermeier became current only after the period it describes. It derives from the pseudonym used by Adolf Kussmaul and Ludwig Eichrodt for the author of a collection of poetry published by them in a humorous magazine in the 1850s. The real author had been a provincial schoolteacher who had died in 1846, and their aim was to mock the provincialism and domestic preoccupations of the *VORMÄRZ*.

Biegeleben, Ludwig, Freiherr von (1812–92), diplomat and politician. Born in Darmstadt, Biegeleben pursued a career in the Hessian service before joining the Austrian foreign ministry in 1850. As head of the Department of German Affairs there, he was a determined opponent of BISMARCK and his German policies.

Bienerth-Schmerling, Richard, Graf (1863–1918), Austrian politician. He was education minister in 1905, interior minister in 1906 and minister-president from 1908 to 1911. His administration was made up almost entirely of officials and was initially seen as a provisional government, until he brought in some members of parliament. It was dominated by the nationalities problem and was brought down by opposition to his pro-German stance. Bienerth-Schmerling was the governor of Lower Austria from 1911 to 1915.

Bildungsbürgertum, the educated middle class.

Birkenau, German EXTERMINATION CAMP in Poland, also referred to as Auschwitz II. Its name was taken from the village of Birkenau (Brzezinka), where it was situated. Construction of the camp began in October 1941, and was accelerated when the main camp became congested with the arrival of Soviet POWs (for whom the new camp was originally intended). The building work, overseen by Karl Bischoff, resulted in high mortality rates among the Soviet prisoners, and with the faltering of the Russian campaign, the survivors were redeployed in the German arms industries. Instead the camp became an extermination camp for Jews. It comprised 300 prison barracks, four gas chambers along with storage cellars for corpses and crematoria. Its commandant until 1944 was Josef KRAMER.

Bismarck(-Schönhausen), Otto von (1815–98), Prussian minister-president and foreign minister (1862–90), federal chancellor of the NORTH GERMAN CONFEDERATION (1867–71) and Reich chancellor (1871–90). Bismarck was Graf (Count) von Bismarck from 1865, and Prince (Fürst) from 1871. He was also Duke (Herzog) von Lauenburg from 1890.

Bismarck was born in Schönhausen, Brandenburg, the son of a Pomeranian JUNKER of modest means. His mother came from a wealthy bourgeois family. He studied at Göttingen University and first entered public life in 1847 when he attended a meeting of the UNITED DIET in Berlin on behalf of the member for the Altmark, who was ill. He spoke against liberalism and Jewish emancipation, and earned himself a reputation as an extremely conservative countryman. He was elected to the Prussian LANDTAG in 1849, and began a diplomatic career in 1851, first as Prussian representative at the federal diet (BUNDESTAG) in Frankfurt, then as ambassador to St Petersburg from 1858, before moving to Paris in 1862. He was called to resolve the conflict between the king and the Progressives (*DEUTSCHE FORT-SCHRITTSPARTEI*) in the Chamber of Deputies, the lower house of the Landtag, over the question of sovereignty in military matters. The Chamber of Deputies had blocked army reforms by insisting on scrutinizing the budget, and refused to give way.

Bismarck was appointed minister-president on 22 September at the age of 47. He resolved the deadlock by imposing his own interpretation on the constitution and ruling Prussia without the Landtag, claiming that his ministry was responsible only to the king in such a situation. Despite further elections in September the liberals remained in control of the Chamber, and Bismarck continued to govern without it until 1866, during which time he implemented the proposed army reforms anyway. The liberals hoped that the SCHLESWIG-HOLSTEIN crisis might prove to be a way out of the impasse, when Denmark attempted to annex Schleswig in 1863. Bismarck was afraid that if the wave of national feeling in Germany were translated into action against Denmark by the federal diet, the position of the liberals in

Germany would be strengthened, and he tied Prussia's policy to the breaking of Danish promises made specifically to Austria and Prussia, inviting the diet to follow the lead of the two major powers, and thereby underlining the special position of Prussia (and Austria) in internal German politics. Prussia and Austria acted independently and defeated Denmark in the war of 1864. The war ended with a Prussian administration in Schleswig and an Austrian administration in Holstein, but differences soon arose between the two powers, which Bismarck exploited to precipitate the AUSTRO-PRUSSIAN WAR of 1866.

The swift defeat of Austria had a dramatic effect both on political relations within Germany and on the internal politics of both Austria and Prussia. With the effective expulsion of Austria from the new Germany, and the establishment of the NORTH GERMAN CONFEDERATION, 'Germany' (in the broader sense) was divided, and the creation of the German empire in 1871 cemented that division. Austria itself was forced to recognize that Germans were a minority in the AUSTRIAN EMPIRE and to come to terms with Hungary in the *AUSGLEICH* of 1867. In Prussia the victory shattered the liberal opposition to Bismarck: there were important defections from the *Deutscher NATIONAL-VEREIN* (German National Association) and Bismarck gained Liberal support for his indemnity bill, the *post facto* ratification of illegal tax-collecting since 1862. The indemnity bill was also the occasion for a split among the conservatives, with the Free Conservatives (*FREIKONSERVATIVE PARTEI*, later the *Reichspartei*) supporting Bismarck. The south German states – created in their then-present form by Napoleon as an insurance against the hegemonic aspirations of Austria and Prussia – were cowed by threats of French expansionism in the Rhineland, and aligned themselves with Prussia. Bismarck emerged from the conflict immeasurably strengthened.

The opportunity to absorb the south German states arose more quickly than Bismarck had perhaps anticipated, with Prussia's victory in the FRANCO-PRUSSIAN WAR of 1870–1. Bismarck himself had helped to provoke the war by his publication of the EMS TELEGRAM. The south German states were bound by agreements of 1866 to support Prussia, and were drawn both into the war and into the new GERMAN EMPIRE, which was proclaimed on 18 January 1871 at Versailles by the Prussian king, who became Kaiser (emperor) WILHELM I. The establishment of the German empire was bound to change Bismarck's perspectives. His foreign policy now became far more cautious, directed towards the maintenance of the new status quo, and imbued with a consciousness that Prussia-Germany had come well out of the conflicts of the previous decade, but that it had made the other European powers apprehensive. A complicated alliance system was built up with Russia and Austria-Hungary. Bismarck now saw Austria-Hungary as having nothing more to do with Germany, but believed that the Habsburg Empire should be preserved as a bulwark of conservatism. The purpose of the alliance system was to ensure that the French were always so isolated that they could not take revenge for the defeat of 1871 and the loss of ALSACE-LORRAINE. The alliance – the THREE EMPERORS' LEAGUE (*Dreikaiserbund*) – was formalized in 1881 and was renewed in 1884, but thereafter Bismarck made separate arrangements with Russia through the REINSURANCE TREATY.

Bismarck's domestic policy was dominated by conflicts with two important groups: the Roman Catholic population and the Social Democratic Party. Measures were directed against the power of the Roman Catholic Church in 1871 and 1872, when the Jesuit order was banned. In May 1873 the 'May Laws' were passed in an attempt to subordinate the Roman Catholic Church and its religious and secular institutions to the authority of the state. The *KULTURKAMPF* (cultural struggle) that followed served only to reinforce the cohesion of the Catholic community in Germany, and to make its political organization, the CENTRE PARTY, the largest party in the Reichstag. Similarly, the persecution of the socialists in the following decade, inaugurated with the ANTI-SOCIALIST LAWS of 1878, failed to break the Social Democratic labour movement. Moreover, the introduction between 1883 and 1889 of social legislation such as sickness and accident insurance and old-age pensions failed to persuade working-class voters that their best interests would be provided for by the state. Bismarck's domestic policies reinforced confessional and class divisions.

By the time of Wilhelm I's death in 1888 the Germany that Bismarck had brought into being had changed beyond recognition. The prosperity of the founding years of the empire (the *GRÜNDERZEIT*) had given way to different economic circumstances with the crash of 1873, which inaugurated the so-called Great Depression. But more than that, the domestic and international economy had been changed out of all recognition since Bismarck had come to power by industrialization and urbanization. The chancellor's turn to conservative protectionism at the end of the 1870s (the 'pact of iron and rye', which imposed tariffs on imports of industrial and agricultural goods) was a recognition of the changed circumstances. Bismarck was effectively dismissed in 1890 by the young Kaiser WILHELM II, who had acceded to the throne two years earlier. Bismarck retired to his estate, where he wrote the memoirs that constituted an important contribution to the mythologization of his career and the development of a 'Bismarck cult' after his death.

Bismarck(-Schönhausen), Wilhelm von (1852–1901), German politician and son of Otto von BISMARCK. He became *Regierungspräsident* of Hanover in 1889, *Oberpräsident* of East Prussia in 1895, and was a member of the Reichstag for the conservative

REICHSPARTEI from 1878 to 1881 and of the Prussian LANDTAG from 1882 to 1885.

Bitburg, site of a military cemetery with the graves of Waffen-SS men, visited by US President Ronald Reagan in 1985. The visit was seen as a controversial symbolic gesture in the context of the *HISTORIKERSTREIT*, and was seen by the government's critics as a coup for those on the new right who were seeking to relativize the Nazi past.

Bizone, the result of the merger (27 May 1947) of the US and British zones of occupation. Its creation was motivated by a desire to establish an economic bulwark against communism among other things. The administrative centre of the Bizone was in Frankfurt am Main where central offices for post, transport, economy, finance, labour, food, agriculture were situated. It was superseded by the TRIZONE when the French zone was added on 8 April 1949, shortly before the establishment of the FEDERAL REPUBLIC OF GERMANY.

Blank, Theodor (1905–72), Christian Democrat politician. A Christian trade unionist before the Nazis came to power in 1933, Blank was a co-founder of the CDU in Westphalia and of the postwar German Trade Union Federation (DGB). He was elected to the LANDTAG of North Rhine-Westphalia in 1946, and was a member of the BUNDESTAG from 1949 to 1972. In 1951 Blank was charged by Adenauer with responsibility for defence, and the so-called 'Blank office' (*Amt Blank*) was important in preparing the way for West German rearmament. He served as defence minister from 1955 to 1956 and was minister of labour and social order from 1957 to 1965.

blank cheque, the German guarantee of effectively unconditional support for Austria-Hungary against Serbia in 1914.

Blaskowitz, Johannes (1883–1948), army officer. Blaskowitz was promoted to lieutenant in 1900, and to lieutenant general and commander of Defence District II (Stettin) in 1935. He was then appointed field commander of Army Group 3 (Dresden), and took part in the invasions of both Austria and Czechoslovakia. He served in Poland and received the surrender of Warsaw, and was appointed military governor at the head of German occupying forces in Poland in October 1939. He was subsequently dismissed from several army commands for documenting Nazi atrocities. In 1944 he took command of Army Group G, and was then supreme commander in the Netherlands, where he surrendered to the British. He committed suicide in jail while awaiting trial as a war criminal.

Blau, Bruno (1881–1954), director of the Jewish Statistical Office in Berlin and editor of its journal (*Zeitschrift für Demographie und Statistik der Juden*). He was arrested by the Gestapo in 1942, but survived the war and worked at the YIVO Institute for Jewish Research in New York after 1947.

Blaue Reiter (literally 'blue rider'), a group of expressionist artists formed in 1911 in Munich, essentially an exhibiting society. It took its name from a collection of essays in an almanac of the same name (*Der blaue Reiter*, 1912) published by Franz MARC and Wassily KANDINSKY. Other artists associated with the group were August Macke (1887–1914), Paul KLEE, and the Russian artists Alexei Jawlensky (1864–1941) and Marianne von WEREFKIN. The Blue Rider almanac was a major survey of the pre-1914 European avant-garde, inflected by the ideas of Marc and Kandinsky, who favoured the 'spiritual' in art. The group's first exhibition was held in Munich from December 1911 to January 1912, and the almanac was advertised in the catalogue. Its last one was held in Berlin in 1913. The group dispersed with the outbreak of World War I.

Blitz, the (literally 'lightning'), a colloquial term used to describe the sustained aerial bombardment of British cities by the German air force during World War II. The Blitz started in September 1940 during the battle of BRITAIN, and continued until May 1941.

Most damage was done to London, particularly the docks and the working-class areas of the East End, but major commercial and industrial centres in the provinces, such as Sheffield, Liverpool and Manchester, were also severely hit. The raid on Coventry was so severe that the German verb *'coventrisieren'* was coined to describe the complete razing of a city from the air. Raids continued throughout the war. In 1942 towns of cultural and historical interest were targeted in the so-called Baedeker raids, supposedly in revenge for the bombing of the old Hanseatic city of Lübeck; and at the end of the war so-called 'V-weapons' (*Vergeltungswaffen*, 'revenge weapons') were directed at Britain.

Blitzkrieg ('lightning war'), term used to describe the strategy of rapid attacks on limited battle fronts during World War II. It was a method of warfare promoted by a number of writers on military affairs between the wars, but was used most effectively by Germany in Poland (1939) and in Scandinavia, the Low Countries and France (1940). It was then applied in the Balkans in 1941, but was unsuccessful during the German invasion of the Soviet Union. Some historians have argued that *Blitzkrieg* also served domestic purposes, in that it enabled Nazi Germany to pursue a policy of armament in breadth rather than of armament in depth, which would have required total mobilization of the country's resources. This appealed to Hitler, who wanted to win swift victories that would reinforce his authority, without provoking opposition to the war among the German people by expecting sacrifices of them and risking a repetition of the unrest that led to the NOVEMBER REVOLUTION of 1918. Others have argued that this perspective needs to be reassessed, and that the management of the German economy after 1936 suggests large-scale military plans with a view to extensive conquest and annexations: the state investment under the FOUR-YEAR PLAN was intended to provide the raw materials, capital and skilled labour for armament in depth by reorientating the German economy altogether.

Blockwart, the lowest level of Nazi office-holder. The *Blockwart* fulfilled the function of an ideological concierge, representing the Nazi Party in each housing block, and reporting to his superiors any potentially subversive, suspicious or nonconformist behaviour.

Blomberg, Werner von (1878–1946), minister of war (1935–8). Born in Stargard, Pomerania (now Szczecinski in Poland), Blomberg became head of the Reichswehr troop office in 1927 and head of Defence District I (East Prussia) in 1929. He was appointed minister of defence in January 1933 and promoted to infantry general. He became war minister and commander in chief of the Wehrmacht in 1935, and was further promoted to field marshal in 1936. Blomberg was an important member of the conservative faction in Hitler's government until 1938. His downfall was prepared by Himmler and Göring shortly after his marriage to Eva Gruhn, a former prostitute, in January of that year. The Berlin police prepared a dossier on his wife's past, and he was dismissed and ordered to spend a year abroad. His departure, accompanied by those of FRITSCH and NEURATH, constituted something of a purge of leading conservatives in Germany, and amounted to a radicalization of the regime. The war ministry was abolished and replaced by the OKW under KEITEL. Hitler himself became supreme commander of the Wehrmacht.

Blubo, abbreviation of BLUT UND BODEN ('blood and soil'). The term was used to describe Nazi films idealizing rural life, and came from a genre of nationalist literature that idealized the countryside and the idea of HEIMAT.

Blücher, Franz (1896–1959), politician. Blücher was a member of the Frankfurt economic council in 1948, and was vice chancellor and minister for economic cooperation from 1949 to 1957. He was a member of the FDP until 1956, and chairman of the party from 1949 to 1954. In 1956 he left to join the FREIE VOLKSPARTEI (FVP) a right-wing splinter group from the FDP.

Blücher, Gebhard Leberecht von, Fürst von Wahlstatt (1742–1819), Prussian general. Blücher was born in Rostock in Mecklenburg. He joined the Swedish cavalry in 1756 and the Prussian army in 1760. He served in the SEVEN YEARS WAR, and fought against the French during the 1790s and again at the battle of JENA in 1806. He was promoted to lieutenant general in 1801. He retired from active service after the collapse of Prussia and the treaty of TILSIT (1807). He came out of retirement on two occasions, however. In 1813 he defeated the French at Wahlstatt, and was promoted to field marshal for his part in the battle of LEIPZIG. He became prince of Wahlstatt after the first defeat of Napoleon. He returned to the battlefield again in 1815 following Napoleon's return from exile, and although he was defeated at Ligny (16 June 1815) he intervened decisively at the battle of WATERLOO two days later.

Blüm, Norbert (1935–), Christian Democrat politician. Blüm was born in Rüsselsheim, a small town in Hesse. He joined the CDU in 1950, and was elected to the Bundestag in 1972. He was leader of the CDU in parliament in 1980–1, and minister of labour and social order from 1982 to 1998, in which capacity he was responsible for the KOHL administration's reforms of pensions and social security.

Blum, Robert (1807–48), radical politician. Born in Cologne, Blum was a popular speaker and political publicist. He joined the German Catholic movement in 1845, and was leader of the democratic left faction in the FRANKFURT PARLIAMENT in 1848. He was executed in Vienna after the suppression of the uprising there in October of that year.

Blumauer, Aloys (1755–98), Austrian ENLIGHTENMENT intellectual and political radical.

Blumauer was born in Steyr, Upper Austria, and educated at the Jesuit school there. He became a Jesuit novice in Vienna, but following the dissolution of the order he became a magazine editor and at the same time a censor for the state. He was a member of the ILLUMINATI and a supporter of the radical Enlightenment. In his major satirical work he attacked the Vatican's aspirations to temporal power. He was directly involved in politics only on the fringes of Austrian Jacobin circles, and is remembered as a representative of the popular literature of the Josephinian Enlightenment.

Blunck, Hans Friedrich (1888–1961), writer and Nazi functionary. Blunck was born in Altona and studied at Kiel and Heidelberg. He pursued a public-service career, but was also the author of historical novels and mythological stories inspired by his upbringing in northern Germany and by Germanic legends. His work had a distinct VÖLKISCH political orientation, and he has been placed in the blood-and-soil (BLUT UND BODEN) school of literature, along with Hans GRIMM. He was a committed supporter of the Nazis, and was appointed president of the Reich Chamber of Literature in 1934. His memoirs (*Unwegsame Zeiten*, 1952) sought to present Nazi Germany in an unduly positive light.

Blut und Boden ('blood and soil'), Nazi propaganda slogan idealizing and mythologizing the countryside. The earliest known usage is by Oswald Spengler in *The Decline of the West* (1918–22), but it gained currency with its use in the title of a book by Walther DARRÉ, *Neuadel aus Blut und Boden* ('a new aristocracy from blood and soil', 1930). It came to stand for all that was anti-modern and anti-urban in Nazi ideology, and found expression in literature and in the visual imagery of posters and film. Hans Friedrich BLUNCK and Hans GRIMM, among others, are associated with 'blood-and-soil' literature, which built on the HEIMAT genre, depicting the simple and eternal virtues of the *Volk* community, and in particular its relationship with the land and nature. Similarly, 'BLUBO' films frequently used the relationship between community and landscape to illustrate nationalistic or racist themes, to warn against the temptations of the degenerate city and the shallow sophistication of the 'ASPHALT culture' and its promise of emancipation and progress, and to reinforce traditional views of the position of women. In 1933 the Central Office of Agriculture produced a film entitled *Blut und Boden*, which depicted the Nazis' efforts to win the support of the German peasantry with the promise of a brighter future. The appropriateness of the slogan had its limits, however, and party members were advised against emphasizing the indissoluble link between the land and its people when discussing overseas colonies.

Bock, Fedor von (1880–1945), field marshal. Bock commanded an infantry battalion during World War I, and then spent four years at the Reichswehr ministry. In 1921 he escaped trial for anti-Republican collusion with the 'black Reichswehr', military units recruited by the REICHSWEHR in defiance of the condition set by the treaty of VERSAILLES. He preceded BLASKOWITZ as commander of Army Group 3 (Dresden). He led the German troops invading Austria and took part in the invasions of Poland, the Low Countries, France and the Soviet Union. Along with eleven others he was created a Field Marshal of the Reich by Hitler in June 1940. He was dismissed after the failure of the offensive against Moscow, then recalled as commander in chief of Army Group South in 1942. He retired after the battle of STALINGRAD.

Böckel, Otto (1859–1923), right-wing politician and journalist. Böckel was born in Frankurt am Main, and studied law, economics and modern languages at Giessen, Heidelberg and Marburg. From 1883 to 1903 he was a member of the Reichstag. He was an anti-Semitic politician, and founded the ANTI-SEMITIC PEOPLE'S PARTY. He was also editor of the VÖLKISCH journals *Reichsherold*, *Volkskämpfer* and *Volksrecht*.

Boehm, Hermann (1884–1972), admiral. Boehm was commander in chief of the German navy at the beginning of World War II (1938–9), and was supreme commander of naval high command, Norway (1939–40).

Bohemia (Czech name: Čechy; German name: Böhmen), now an area in the western part of the Czech Republic. Bohemia was formerly a province of the Habsburg empire with a substantial German minority. It was made a hereditary kingdom within the Holy Roman Empire from 1198, and was ruled by the Habsburgs from 1526. Czech aspirations to a 'compromise' (AUSGLEICH) similar to that agreed with the Hungarians in 1867 eventually led the Austrian government under BADENI to attempt to introduce equal status for the Czech language. Such attempts were thwarted by the vehement opposition of German nationalists, and the German-speaking minority in the region became increasingly receptive to the VÖLKISCH ideas of the Pan-German movements. Along with Moravia and the formerly Hungarian province of Slovakia it made up the Republic of Czechoslovakia between 1918 and 1939 (and again between 1945 and 1993). During the 1930s the German minority (generally referred to as the Sudeten Germans) agitated for reunion with the Reich, and the SUDETENLAND was annexed by Germany in 1938. The rest of Bohemia and Moravia was annexed and placed under a German 'protectorate' the following year, a measure that effectively incorporated the territories into the Reich. Ethnic Germans were expelled from Czechoslovakia after World War II.

Bohley, Bärbel (1945–), East German artist and dissident. Bohley was born in Berlin two weeks after the end of World War II, and studied art there from 1969 to 1974. She was active in the peace movement in the GERMAN DEMOCRATIC REPUBLIC during the early 1980s, and was imprisoned for six weeks (1983–4), ostensibly on suspicion of passing on intelligence to contacts in Britain and West Germany. Her involvement with the peace movement continued after her release from prison, and she was a co-founder of the *Initiative Frieden und Menschenrechte* (Initiative for Peace and Human Rights) between September 1985 and January 1986. She was arrested again after participating in a demonstration on the occasion of the anniversary of the murder of Karl LIEBKNECHT and Rosa LUXEMBURG. She was a co-founder of the dissidents' movement *NEUES FORUM* in September 1989. She opposed the group's merger with *BÜNDNIS 90*, and stood for the European parliament in 1994. She founded the association *Bürgerbüro e.V.* (Citizens' Bureau) to help those who had suffered at the hands of the East German regime.

Böhmer, Georg Wilhelm (1761–1839), radical intellectual and journalist. Böhmer was born in Göttingen and studied theology at the university there before becoming a teacher in Worms. When Mainz was occupied by French troops in October 1792, he immediately entered the service of the French, became secretary to General Custine and joined the MAINZ JACOBIN CLUB. He occupied a number of important positions and was a deputy in the short-lived Rhineland National Convention. After the Prussian occupation of Mainz in 1793 he was imprisoned until 1795 and then emigrated to France, where he held a number of offices in the service of the Directory and under Napoleon. He was also a co-editor of the Paris-based German-language newspaper *Pariser Zuschauer*. He returned to Germany when the Kingdom of WESTPHALIA was established and was commissioner general of police in the *département* of Harz and Leine. After the end of the Napoleonic Wars he taught at Göttingen University and published a number of works on legal history.

Böll, Heinrich (1917–85), novelist and author of short stories. Böll was born in Cologne into a liberal Roman Catholic family at the end of World War I. He served in France and on the Eastern Front during World War II, and much of his early writing constituted a critique of war. He quickly established himself as a satitrist of postwar society in the Federal Republic, and in particular the materialism and acquisitiveness of the ADENAUER years. He was also critical of the hypocrisies of the Roman Catholic establishment and its values – for example, in *Ansichten eines Clowns* (*The Clown*, 1963). Along with Günter GRASS, Böll was demonized by conservative politicians and the popular press for his criticism of the German government's heavy-handed response to political terrorism during the 1970s. His novel *Die verlorene Ehre der Katharina Blum* (*The Lost Honour of Katharina Blum*, 1974) exposed the chicanery of the right-wing press, and was made into a film by the director Volker Schlöndorff. Böll won the Nobel prize for literature in 1972.

Bonhoeffer, Dietrich (1906–45), anti-Nazi Protestant pastor and theologian. Bonhoeffer was born in Breslau, the son of a doctor and professor of psychiatry, and studied theology at Tübingen and Berlin. He worked as a pastor in Barcelona and London. In 1934 he signed the founding 'Barmen declaration' of the German Confessing Church (BEKENNENDE KIRCHE), a reaction to the Nazification of the Protestant church in Germany. In 1936 he lost his licence to teach at the University of Berlin, and at the beginning of World War II he was banned from preaching. He became involved with conspirators in the military resistance to Hitler, and went to Stockholm in 1942 to attempt to mediate with the Allies on their behalf. He was arrested in 1943 and subsequently imprisoned in Buchenwald concentration camp. He was murdered by the Gestapo in Flossenbürg camp shortly before it was liberated.

Borchardt thesis, argument advanced by the economic historian Knut Borchardt that Chancellor Heinrich BRÜNING could not have saved the Weimar Republic because his political choices were constrained by the state of the economy, and in particular by the burden of the wages of industrial labour. In short his contention, taken up by 'new right' historians, is that social welfare undermined liberal democracy.

Bormann, Martin (1900–45?), Hitler's private secretary and head of the Party Chancellery. Bormann was born in Halberstadt, served in World War I and then joined a FREIKORPS unit and got involved in politics. He was imprisoned for murder for a year in 1924. He joined the Nazi Party in Thuringia on his release in 1925 and became regional press officer there. He was attached to the Supreme Command of the SA between 1928 and 1930. He became chief of staff and secretary to Rudolf HESS in 1933.

Bormann advised Hitler on financial matters during the 1930s and supervised the development of his retreat at BERCHTES-GADEN. His personal power within the Nazi political system increased after the flight of Hess, Hitler's deputy, to Scotland in 1941, when he was appointed head of the Party Chancellery (PARTEIKANZLEI) with ministerial rank. From 1943, when he became Hitler's secretary, he was the pivotal figure in both party and state and used Hitler's increasing isolation to his own political advantage, ultimately undermining the influence of Hitler's closest associates, including Himmler and Göring. An agreement with Hans Heinrich LAMMERS in June 1943 enabled him to extend his power from party to state matters. Bormann was a radical Nazi himself and his increasing influence reflected the accelerating radicalization of the regime. He disappeared in 1945, and reports of his death have never been unequivocally confirmed. He was sentenced to death in his absence at Nuremberg in 1946, and officially pronounced dead by the West German authorities in 1973.

Born, Max (1882–1970), physicist. Born in Breslau, Born was professor of physics at Göttingen from 1921. Dismissed by the Nazis in 1933 on account of his Jewish ancestry, he moved to Cambridge, England, and then in 1936 to a chair at Edinburgh. He continued his work on quantum physics and was awarded the Nobel prize for physics in 1954. He retired to Bad Pyrmont, near Göttingen, where he died.

Borsig, Ernst von (1869–1933), industrialist. During the Weimar Republic, Borsig was an ostensible supporter of the ZAG (*Zentralarbeitsgemeinschaft*), a forum in which labour and capital cooperated, but he was actually a sympathiser of the radical right. He met Hitler twice in 1922, and financed several extremist organizations. An outspoken advocate of private enterprise, he appealed for state help for his business during the Depression, but was unable to prevent its collapse shortly before his death.

Bosch, Carl (1874–1940), chemist and industrialist. Born in Cologne and educated at Leipzig, Bosch joined the chemical company BASF in 1898 and worked on the practical application of Fritz HABER's process for the synthesis of ammonia. An expert witness at the Versailles peace negotiations, he became chairman of the managing board of BASF in 1919, effective head of IG FARBEN (its successor) in 1925, and was chairman of its supervisory board until his death. Bosch was awarded the Nobel prize for chemistry in 1931 (with Friedrich Bergius).

Bosnia and Herzegovina or **Bosnia-Herzegovina,** Balkan provinces annexed by Austria-Hungary in 1908. The Congress of BERLIN in 1878 had conceded to Austria the right to administer the provinces. When it seemed that political developments in Turkey in the wake of the Young Turk movement might lead to a challenge to Austrian control, the provinces were annexed. Emperor FRANZ JOSEPH wrote to the Kaiser on 29 September, and the annexation was formally announced on 6 October. Bosnia became a 'crown land' and was governed jointly by Austria and Hungary under the auspices of the (common) ministry of finance.

Bouhler, Philipp (1899–1945), head of the Nazi euthanasia programme, AKTION T4.

Born in Munich, Bouhler served in World War I before studying philosophy in his native city. He left without completing his studies to work on the *VÖLKISCHER BEOBACHTER*, the Nazi Party newspaper. Bouhler was a centralizing bureaucrat within the party hierarchy, who helped extend the authority of the party leadership over local branches during the 1920s. In 1933 he became a *Reichsleiter*, and took up a Reichstag seat for a constituency in Westphalia. He was also appointed police president of Munich. In 1934 he became head of the Führer Chancellery, which Hitler set up by decree after taking over the office of Reich president, and which organized the euthanasia programme between 1939 and 1941. Bouhler committed suicide in Zell am See in 1945.

Boumann, Johann (1706–76), Dutch-born master builder. Johann Boumann (the elder) was born in Amsterdam. He designed the Dutch quarter of Potsdam following his appointment there in 1732, and in 1748 was appointed senior master builder in Berlin. With Georg Wenzeslaus von KNOBELSDORFF he oversaw the construction of Berlin Cathedral (which was later demolished) between 1747 and 1750, and from 1748 to 1753 the Prince Heinrich Palace, which now houses the Humboldt University.

Boxer rebellion (1900), a Chinese peasant secret society, the Society of Righteous Harmonious Fists, against the dismemberment and piecemeal colonization of the country by Europeans (Germany had acquired KIAOCHOW – now Jiaoxian, in Shangdong province – in 1898). In June 140,000 'Boxers' (as Westerners called the rebels) occupied Beijing, besieged the European compounds and attacked collaborators. The German ambassador, among others, was murdered, and a German expedition was assembled, which, along with other European forces, took severe punitive measures in China. The departing troops were addressed by Kaiser WILHELM II at Wilhelmshaven and at Bremerhaven, where a local journalist noted down and reported bloodthirsty remarks by the emperor that had been deleted from the heavily edited official text. Even in the Europe-wide climate of imperialist chauvinism the Kaiser's remarks stood out as extreme, and the positive comparison he made between Attila's Huns and the German forces provided fuel for Allied propaganda in World War I.

Boxheim papers, plans for a coup in 1931 by a group of Nazis in Hesse under the leadership of Werner BEST. The seizure of the papers embarrassed Hitler and threatened to undermine his attempts to win the support of Rhineland industrialists.

Brack, Viktor (1904–48), SS officer. Brack studied economics at Munich, was appointed to the Health Department in 1936 by Philipp BOUHLER and became the latter's deputy in the Führer Chancellery. Brack's office (AKTION T4) was directly responsible for the euthanasia programme of 1939–41, and Brack himself subsequently assisted in the construction of death camps in Poland. He was tried by an American military court and hanged at Landsberg prison.

Brandenburg, originally a margravate and an electorate of the Holy Roman Empire, now one of the 'new federal states' of eastern Germany. Brandenburg was the territorial power base of the HOHENZOLLERNS and was merged with Prussia in 1701. It was a province of Prussia from 1815 to 1945, lost territory after World War II and was dissolved entirely with the administrative reorganization of the GERMAN DEMOCRATIC REPUBLIC in 1952. It was revived in 1990 when Germany was reunited. Despite its proximity to Berlin, Brandenburg, like the other 'new federal states', has experienced severe economic difficulties since its absorption into the Federal Republic, and support for the PDS (Party of Democratic Socialism), the successor to the East German Socialist Unity Party (SED), increased from 13.4% of the vote in the first elections to the LANDTAG in 1990 to 18.7% in 1994, when its support equalled that of the CDU, and both had the same number of delegates in the house. More strikingly, voter participation in regional elections has declined from 67% to 54%, and the elections of 1999 saw a sharp increase in support for the radical right and the election of five members for the DEUTSCHE VOLKSUNION. At the end of the 20th century Brandenburg had a population of some 2.6 million.

Brandenburg Gate, monument situated at the end of Unter den Linden in Berlin. It was designed and built by Carl Gotthard Langhans between 1788 and 1791. On the top of the gate is Victoria, the goddess of victory, in a chariot. The Brandenburg Gate fell marginally within the Soviet sector, but right on the border, and became a symbol of the division of Berlin during the Cold War and the years of the BERLIN WALL. The gate also symbolized the opening of the border in 1989.

Brandenburg Regiment, a special unit established in 1940 to combat partisan activities in the Soviet Union, Yugoslavia and other occupied territories during World War II. It became a Panzer Grenadier division in 1944. (The original Brandenburg Regiment had first come to notice at VERDUN in 1916.)

Brandt, Willy (1913–92), Social Democratic politician and federal chancellor (1969–74). Brandt was born as Herbert Frahm in Lübeck. He was illegitimate, never knew his father, and grew up in poverty. He was active in Social Democratic politics during the Weimar Republic. He joined the SPD in 1930, but left in 1931 for the Socialist Workers' Party (*Sozialistische Arbeiterpartei*, SAP), a splinter group from the SPD, and was involved in the resistance to the Nazis on the streets before 1933. He left Germany when Hitler came to power, fled to Denmark, and then lived in Norway, where he studied history, and worked as a journalist on the Republican side during the Spanish Civil War. He also returned to Berlin and worked as a member of the Social Democratic underground there before World War II. With the German invasion of Norway in 1940 he managed to escape discovery as a German refugee and fled to Sweden. He continued to work for the anti-Nazi underground during the war, and returned to Germany as a Norwegian citizen.

Frahm had been stripped of his German citizenship by the Nazi regime in 1938, and when it was restored in 1947 he retained his pen name Brandt. He rejoined the SPD in 1947, and was a member of the Bundestag from the establishment of the Federal Republic of Germany in 1949 to 1957, and then again from 1969. He was a member of the Berlin House of Representatives (ABGEORD-NETENHAUS) from 1950, and was a close confidant of the city's Social Democratic mayor, Ernst REUTER. Brandt was president of the Berlin House of Representatives from 1953 to 1957, and as mayor of Berlin from 1957 to 1966 he established an international political reputation. Brandt was one of the key reformers within the SPD, and played an important role in securing the party's acceptance of the BAD GODESBERG PROGRAMME in 1959. He stood unsuccessfully as SPD candidate for the chancellorship in 1961 and 1965, but was vice chancellor and foreign minister during the GRAND COALITION (1966–9).

Brandt became federal chancellor after the election of 1969 and remained at the head of the reforming SPD–FDP coalition until his resignation in the wake of a spy scandal (the GUILLAUME AFFAIR) in 1974. Brandt's social-liberal coalition (with the FDP) pursued progressive welfare policies, developed industrial democracy, and revised or repealed illiberal legislation. Its main achievement, however, was the successful OSTPOLITIK, which permitted the normalization of relations with the German Democratic Republic. His government also introduced so-called radicals' decree (RADIKALENERLASS), which permitted police vetting of public servants (*Berufsverbot*) in response to the rise in political extremism during the early

1970s. After his resignation he remained active in politics, and was president of the Socialist International (1976–92) and of the North–South Commission (from 1977), for whom he compiled the BRANDT REPORT. He received the Nobel Peace Prize in 1971 in recognition of his services to East–West relations.

Brandt report, conclusions of the Independent Commission on International Development Issues. Willy BRANDT, former chancellor (SPD) of the FEDERAL REPUBLIC OF GERMANY was appointed head of the commission (also known as the 'Brandt Commission') in 1977. He spent the following two years compiling his report 'To Ensure Survival – Common Interests of the Industrial and Developing Countries', also known as the 'North–South Report', which he finally delivered in 1980. The report recommended integration of the southern developing world with the industrialized north, involving redistribution of wealth and unilateral disarmament to provide additional financial resources.

Brauchitsch, Walther von (1881–1948), commander in chief of the WEHRMACHT (1938–41). Born into a military family in Berlin, von Brauchitsch was a professional soldier, and was awarded the Iron Cross in World War I. His wife was a staunch supporter of the Nazis, and Brauchitsch himself was loyal to the regime. He played an important part in effecting the expansion of the army after Hitler came to power, and was promoted to general in 1938. He succeeded Werner von FRITSCH as commander in chief of the Wehrmacht, and was promoted to field marshal in 1940 after the successful campaigns in Poland and western Europe. He was retired on health grounds after a heart attack in 1941, and Hitler himself became commander in chief. Von Brauchitsch was compliant in his relations with Hitler, and opposed none of his military plans. He died in Hamburg before he could be tried by a British military court.

Bräuer, Kurt (1889–1969), diplomat. After serving in the German embassy in Paris (1937–9), Bräuer was appointed ambassador to Norway (1939–40) and officiated briefly as German plenipotentiary in Oslo after the German invasion (April–May 1940).

Brauer, Max (1889–1973), Social Democratic politician. Brauer joined the SPD at 16 and pursued his career first in Altona and then as mayor of Hamburg from 1924 to 1933. Brauer was imprisoned by the Nazis, and then left Germany. He spent the following years in China (as a diplomat on behalf of the League of Nations) and in the United States. He was elected mayor of Hamburg again after World War II, and took charge of the material and economic reconstruction of the city, which had been devastated by Allied bombardment. He was elected to the Bundestag in 1961, but retired in 1965.

Braun, (Carl) Otto (1872–1955), Social Democratic politician and long-serving minister-president of Prussia. Born the son of a shoemaker in Königsberg, East Prussia, and a member of the SPD from 1889, Braun was editor of the *Volkstribüne* and a member of the Prussian diet. He was also a leading official in the Agricultural Workers' Union (1909–20). During the NOVEMBER REVOLUTION of 1918 he was a member of the Workers' and Soldiers' Councils (*see RAT*) and subsequently of the National Assembly. He was Prussian agriculture minister (1918–21), and apart from short periods in 1921 and 1925 he served as minister-president of Prussia from 1920 until 1932. He also stood as the SPD candidate in the first round of the presidential elections of 1925, and won almost 8 million votes. Braun's health suffered as the SPD became increasingly beleaguered in Prussia during the Depression, and he was already absent through illness at the time of his government's unconstitutional dismissal by the Reich chancellor Franz von PAPEN (*see PREUSSENSCHLAG*) in 1932. Braun emigrated to Switzerland in 1933 and remained there after the war.

Braun, Eva (1912–45), Hitler's mistress. Braun was born in Munich, met Hitler in 1929, and moved into his flat after the death of his niece. She moved to BERCHTESGADEN in 1936. The exact nature of her relationship with Hitler is unclear, but the two were married on 29 April 1945, the day before they both committed suicide.

Braun, Wernher von (1912–77), rocket engineer. Braun was born in Wirsitz, Prussia, and studied at the Charlottenburg Institute of Technology in Berlin. He was appointed technical director at the rocket research base at Peenemünde in 1937 and worked there on the V1 and V2 rockets (*see* V-WEAPONS). A prototype V1 was first developed in 1938. Braun gave himself up to the Americans in 1945. He continued his research in the USA, where he contributed to the American spaceflight programme.

Braunau am Inn, small town in Upper Austria; the birthplace of Adolf HITLER.

Brauns, Heinrich (1868–1939), Christian trade unionist and Centre Party politician. Brauns was born into a working-class family in Cologne and was an active trade unionist before World War I. He was elected to the 1919 NATIONAL ASSEMBLY for the Centre Party, and was a Reichstag deputy until 1933. Brauns was labour minister in a succession of Weimar coalition governments (1920–8), and was a leader of the German delegations to the International Labour Conferences during the Depression (1929–31). He headed the Brauns Commission on the impact of the Depression at the behest of Heinrich BRÜNING. Brauns retired from public life after the Nazis came to power.

BRD (*Bundesrepublik Deutschland*). *See* FEDERAL REPUBLIC OF GERMANY.

Brecht, Arnold (1884–1977), senior civil servant. Born into a middle-class Protestant family in Lübeck with National Liberal political beliefs, Brecht studied law at Leipzig and served in the Reich Justice Office from 1910. During World War I he called for a peace without annexations, and was appointed secretary to the cabinet of Max von BADEN in 1918. In 1921 he became departmental head of the Reich interior ministry and distinguished himself as a senior public servant of staunchly loyal republican sympathies. He was removed in 1927 on political grounds by the German Nationalist (*DNVP*) Walther von Keudell, interior minister in the fourth centre-right coalition of Wilhelm MARX. He was immediately appointed to a senior position in Prussia by Otto Braun, and became Prussian representative to the REICHSRAT, and at the conferences of the *Länder* dealing with the issue of the reform of the Reich. After the unconstitutional dismissal of Braun's SPD government by Franz von PAPEN in 1932 (*see PREUSSENSCHLAG*), Brecht represented the Prussian government before the Prussian Supreme Court in Leipzig. Brecht was finally dismissed from office by the Nazis in February 1933 and went to New York, where he took up an academic post at the New School for Social Research. After the war he was an adviser in the drawing up of the constitution of the Federal Republic of Germany.

Brecht, Bertolt (1898–1956), Marxist poet, playwright and theatre director. Brecht was born into a middle-class family in Augsburg, studied medicine at Munich, but interrupted his studies to serve as a medical orderly in World War I. Although he went back to medicine at Munich University after the war, he eventually gave up to work in the theatre. His first play, *Baal*, was finished in 1918, and his first stage production was in 1922. He worked at Max Reinhardt's *Deutsches Theater* in Berlin from 1924 and collaborated with Erwin PISCATOR and Kurt WEILL. His first marriage, to Marianne Zoff, ended in divorce, and he married Helene Weigel in 1928 and founded the Berliner Ensemble with her. He fled to Switzerland immediately after the REICHSTAG FIRE in 1933, and then to the United States via Scandinavia and the USSR. Although Brecht had never joined the

KPD he had been a supporter of the Communists during the Weimar Republic and was called before the House Committee on Un-American Activities in 1947. He left the USA shortly afterwards, and returned to Germany (the GDR) in 1949 to refound the Berliner Ensemble in East Berlin.

Brecht's early work reflected the EXPRESSIONIST influences then prevalent in Germany and his engagement with contemporary politics. He later became a committed Marxist and was the chief exponent of 'epic theatre' as opposed to the 'Aristotelian' theatre of illusion. Among his best-known works are *Die Dreigroschenoper* (*The Threepenny Opera*, 1928), *Das Leben des Galilei* (*The Life of Galileo*, 1938–9), *Der gute Mensch von Sezuan* (*The Good Person of Sechuan*, 1942) and *Der kaukasische Kreidekreis* (*The Caucasian Chalk Circle*, 1945). He also published poetry (*Die Hauspostille*, 1927) and essays. His journals have been published in English.

Bredt, Johann Viktor (1879–1940), right-wing politician. Bredt was born in Barmen into a wealthy family of industrialists, and studied law and economics. He was appointed professor of law at Marburg in 1910. He was elected to the Prussian LANDTAG for the Free Conservatives (FREIKONSERVATIVE PARTEI) in 1911, and in 1918 was a co-founder of the German Nationalist DNVP, but left the party after the KAPP PUTSCH. In 1920 he joined the *Wirtschaftspartei* (Business Party), which was renamed *Reichspartei des deutschen Mittelstandes* (Reich Party of the German Middle Estate) in 1925. He was briefly minister of justice in the first BRÜNING administration (March–November 1930). When Hitler came to power he returned to Marburg to resume his career in academic law.

Breitscheid, Rudolf (1874–1944), SPD politician. Born the son of a bookshop assistant in Cologne, Breitscheid joined the SPD in 1912, and the breakaway USPD in 1917. He served as Prussian interior minister (1918–19) and was elected to the Reichstag in 1920.

He rejoined the SPD in 1922, became a leading foreign-policy spokesman for the party, and joined Germany's League of Nations delegation in 1926. He fled to Switzerland in 1933, and later to France, where the Vichy government deported him to Germany. He was murdered in Buchenwald.

Bremen, 'free and Hanseatic city' in northwest Germany. Now Germany's smallest federal state (*Land*), it encompasses the city itself and the port of Bremerhaven (founded in 1827), from which it is geographically separated by part of Lower Saxony. Bremen was a medieval city, the seat of a bishop from 787 and of an archbishop from 845. It joined the Hanseatic League as a secular state in 1358. Its population has been predominantly Protestant since the Reformation. Bremen became an imperial city in 1646 and adopted the epithet 'free and Hanseatic' with the abolition of the Holy Roman Empire in 1806. The city was capital of the French *département* of Wesermündungen between 1810 and 1813 and was an independent member of the GERMAN CONFEDERATION. The city was one of the main centres of revolutionary activity after the First World War, and in January 1919, in the wake of the SPARTACUS UPRISING in Berlin, a Socialist Republic was declared by the local workers' and soldiers' council. Attempts by the Reich government to come to terms with Bremen failed, and the Socialist Republic was eventually defeated and overthrown by military intervention in February.

After World War II Bremen came under the jurisdiction of the United States military authorities (as an American enclave within the British zone). Bremen's current constitution was promulgated on 21 October 1947. The legislature in Bremen is the BÜRGERSCHAFT, an assembly with 100 members elected every four years. The Bürgerschaft in turn elects the senate and appoints the government. The largest party in the Bürgerschaft in every election since World War II has been the SPD. For much of the 1950s and 1960s, and throughout the 1970s and 1980s, the party had an absolute majority of seats. The Greens made their electoral debut in Bremen in 1979, and built up their support from around 5% of the vote in the early 1980s to around 10% in the 1990s (with a peak of 13.1% in 1995). At the end of the 20th century Bremen had a population of 672,000.

Bremer Beiträger (Bremen contributors), north German group of intellectuals. The group contributed to the journal *Neue Beiträge zum Vergnügen des Verstandes und Witzes* ('New contributions to an understanding of reason and wit'), published in Bremen between 1744 and 1748.

Breslau, the German name for Wrocław, a Silesian city now in Poland. A medieval Polish trading and cathedral town, Wrocław attracted German immigration in the 13th century, and passed with Silesia to Bohemia in 1335. It was acquired by Prussia when Frederick the Great (FRIEDRICH II) seized Silesia from the Habsburg empire in 1740–1, during the War of the AUSTRIAN SUCCESSION. For much of the 19th century it was Prussia's second city in terms of population, and doubled in size between the REVOLUTIONS OF 1848 and the founding of the German empire in 1871. The Germanization policies pursued by Bismarck meant that the town's population was largely German by the time of the outbreak of World War I, and it remained in Germany after 1918 along with the rest of Lower Silesia. Many Germans fled westwards during the last months of World War II, and the rest were expelled when Silesia was transferred to Poland after the end of the war.

Breslau, treaty of (11 June 1742), treaty between MARIA THERESIA of Austria and FRIEDRICH II of Prussia (Frederick the Great). The treaty concluded the first Silesian War during the War of the AUSTRIAN SUCCESSION. Austria was forced to cede much of Silesia, which Friedrich II had invaded and annexed, to Prussia. Only the districts of Troppau,

Teschen and Jägerndorf remained Austrian.

Brest-Litovsk, treaty of (3 March 1918), peace agreement in WORLD WAR I between Russia and Ukraine and the Central Powers, following a ceasefire agreed the previous December by the new revolutionary government in Petrograd. Russia relinquished control of substantial territories in the west of the former Russian empire, including Estonia, Latvia, Lithuania and Finland. Independent states were to be created both in Poland and in the Ukraine. In addition the territories of Kars and Batoum were to be ceded to Turkey. War reparations of 3000 million gold roubles were imposed by Germany on Russia, and part of Russia's gold reserves were transferred to Germany in August under a supplementary protocol. The terms of the peace were effectively imposed unilaterally on Russia, which lost about 2.6 million square km (1 million square miles) of territory and some 46 million people. Although the treaty's apologists claimed that it was not annexationist – an important point to argue in the context of the domestic political situation in Germany at the end of World War I – the nominal independence of Ukraine and the Baltic states was little more than a cover for their subordination within a new German-dominated international order in the east. The scope and intentions of the treaty have prompted comparisons with Nazi Germany's war of conquest for LEBENSRAUM in the east during the 1940s, and some historians, most notably Fritz Fischer, have used it to argue for the existence of long-term continuities in German foreign policy (*see* FISCHER CONTROVERSY). The treaty was rendered void by the defeat of Germany in November 1918, and its terms provided Allied politicians with arguments to refute the charge that the treaty of VERSAILLES was unduly harsh.

Brill, Hermann (1895–1959), Social Democratic politician. A teacher by profession, Brill was a member of the Thuringian LANDTAG for the USPD from 1919 to 1922, and for the SPD from 1922 to 1933. He was also elected a member of the Reichstag in 1932. In 1933 he joined the illegal *Volksfrontgruppe Berlin* (Popular People's Front of Berlin) and was arrested and sent to Buchenwald in 1938. After the war he was briefly minister-president and interior minister of Thuringia (1945) before moving to Frankfurt am Main, where he was professor of law. He was a member of the Bundestag from 1949 to 1953.

Britain, battle of (1940), the attempt by Germany to establish air supremacy prior to Operation Sealion, the planned invasion of Britain after the fall of France in 1940. The German air force had about 2800 aircraft and the Royal Air Force 550. The Luftwaffe's first wave of bombers attacked southern England on 15 August. The Germans initially attacked shipping, radar stations and airfields, but despite an enormous onslaught in the middle of August they failed to establish air supremacy and began to bomb London and other British cities, which were subjected to a sustained BLITZ from September. The attack culminated in a massive German air offensive on 15 September, which failed and resulted in the loss of 60 aircraft (as opposed to 26 losses by the RAF). The invasion of Britain was postponed on 17 September and cancelled on 12 October. By the end of September British Fighter Command had lost 678 fighters, while the Germans had lost 1099. The bombing of British cities continued until May 1941.

Brno. *See* BRÜNN.

Brockdorff-Rantzau, Ulrich, Graf von (1869–1928), diplomat and politician. Born into the aristocratic Rantzau family in Schleswig, he studied law, and adopted the name Brockdorff-Rantzau after inheriting an estate from his great-uncle in 1891. He entered the diplomatic service in 1894 and was ambassador to Denmark during World War I. He recognized the importance of the Russian Revolution to the future course of the war, and the necessity of exploiting it to Germany's advantage by encouraging the Bolsheviks. His suggestion that the German empire would avoid the fate of tsarist Russia only by undertaking political reforms was unpopular among conservatives, who nicknamed him 'the Red Count'. His political astuteness impressed the people's deputies of the NOVEMBER REVOLUTION, however, and he was chosen to lead the German delegation at Versailles, where he challenged the charge of German war guilt. He was opposed to the signing of the treaty of VERSAILLES, and withdrew from the delegation in June 1919. He was foreign minister (non-party) from February to June 1919. He went on to become ambassador to the USSR from 1922 to 1928, and died in Berlin.

Brod, Max (1884–1968), Austrian-Jewish writer. Brod was born in Prague, studied law and pursued a career in the Habsburg public service. He then became a theatre and music critic, and was an important figure in Prague cultural circles. He promoted the work of a number of creative artists, but above all Franz KAFKA, whose posthumous reputation rests on Brod's efforts to publish and publicize his major novels. He left Czechoslovakia in 1939 and settled in Palestine. He died in Tel Aviv.

Brownshirts, popular name for the Nazi stormtroopers (SA). SA members wore brown shirts from about 1926. Brown came to be the symbolic colour of the Nazis, and the word was used as a shorthand designation in ways similar to the use of 'red' for socialists and 'black' for supporters of Catholic clerical parties.

Bruck, Karl Ludwig, Freiherr von (1798–1860), Austrian politician. Bruck was a member of the Frankfurt Parliament in 1848, and Austrian trade minister from 1848 to 1851. He was then finance minister (1855–60). His idea for an economic union in central Europe came to nothing. He committed suicide in 1860.

Brücke, Die ('the bridge'), early 20th-century artists' community in Dresden. It was founded in 1905 by a group of artists associated with EXPRESSIONISM, including Ernst Ludwig KIRCHNER, Karl Schmidt-Rottluf and Erich Heckel. Other artists, including Emil NOLDE, joined later. The artists involved developed a style that remained representational but used simplified forms and bold colour. The group dispersed in 1913.

Brüning, Heinrich (1885–1970), conservative politician; chancellor and foreign minister (1930–2). Born the son of a vinegar manufacturer in Münster, Brüning studied philology and economics and graduated from Bonn University in 1915. He worked as a functionary in the Christian trade-union movement from 1920 to 1930, and was elected to the Reichstag for the Centre Party in 1924 and to the Prussian LANDTAG in 1928. He was appointed chancellor in 1930 after the fall of the last grand coalition of the Weimar Republic. The coalition government had fallen on the issue of alterations to the insurance system, which brought the SPD, defending the interests of workers, into conflict with the conservative DVP, which represented the interests of the employers. The crisis led to the effective exclusion of the SPD from government and the formation of a new government by Brüning.

The new chancellor was immediately defeated by his opponents in the Reichstag on 16 July, and used Article 48 of the constitution to pass his government's legislation by means of presidential decree. When an SPD motion to lift the emergency decree was passed two days later the government carried out its threat to dissolve the Reichstag rather than concede to a parliamentary majority. The resort to new elections proved ill-judged, and backfired on Brüning's centre-right government. The Nazis made massive gains, largely at the expense of the DNVP and DVP, two of the parties represented in the government, and smaller, but still significant gains were made by the Communists. The Brüning regime survived only by using

presidential decrees, a measure that was now tolerated by the Social Democrats, who feared that the alternative would be an even greater polarization of political life in Germany if further new elections had to be called. The negotiations and preparations for the installation of an anti-Marxist government that would rule without parliament had begun long before the crisis of March 1930, and Brüning's ultimate objectives included the restoration of the monarchy and the relegation of the Reichstag to an advisory role, aims he shared with many in the conservative establishment of the time. His deflationary economic policies, intended not least to demonstrate Germany's inability to pay REPARATIONS, fuelled the rise in unemployment that did much to undermine popular support for his own government.

Brüning fell not as a consequence of defeat in the Reichstag, but – appropriately enough – because Reich President HINDENBURG refused to give his assent to presidential decrees aimed at breaking up large and uneconomic East Elbian estates for resettlement as small farms. In the elections that his departure precipitated (July 1932) the Nazi vote more than doubled, and the NSDAP became the largest party in the Reichstag. Brüning emigrated to Britain in 1934 and from there he moved to the United States, where he pursued an academic career at Harvard University. He returned to Cologne after the war (1952–5), but died in Vermont, USA.

Brüning's administration was long defended by sympathetic historians as an attempt to overcome the political stalemate generated by the deficiencies of the Weimar political system. However, Brüning's memoirs (published in 1970) revealed the depth of his own antipathy to democracy and his authoritarian ambitions.

Brünn, German name for Brno, the principal town in Moravia, and now the second city of the Czech Republic. Over half the population was German until the end of World

War I and the establishment of an independent Czechoslovak state. It fell to about a quarter in 1919, and the remaining Germans were expelled after World War II.

Brunner, Joseph (1759–1829), priest, Jacobin and radical publicist. Brunner was born in Philippsburg, the son of a schoolmaster, and educated at the cathedral school in Speyer. He studied Roman Catholic theology at Heidelberg, and was ordained as a priest in 1783. He belonged to the ILLUMINATI, and was a supporter of the French Revolution and close to Jacobin circles in Mainz (*see* MAINZ JACOBIN CLUB). His radicalism was largely directed against religious rather than political conservatism, however, and he used his sermons to argue for equality between Christians and Jews. In 1801 he published a popular *Prayer Book for Enlightened Catholics*. Although he was wrongly imprisoned for a scurrilous work he did not write during the 1790s, his later life was rather conventional, and from 1814 to 1826 he was dean at Karlsruhe.

Buch, Walter (1883–1949), president of the Nazi Supreme Court. Born in Bruchsal, Buch was a professional soldier who served in World War I. He was a member of several veterans' organizations before joining the Nazi Party in 1922. In1927 he became chairman of the party tribunal USCHLA (Investigation and Arbitration Board), which carried out surveillance of party personnel and organizations. He was involved in the executions following the NIGHT OF THE LONG KNIVES, and as president of the Party Supreme Court acquitted those involved in the 1938 pogrom (*KRISTALLNACHT*). He committed suicide after his second DENAZIFICATION trial.

Bucharest, treaty of (7 May 1918), agreement between Romania and Germany during WORLD WAR I. Romania had joined the war on the Entente side in 1916, but had to surrender after the collapse of Russia and invasion by German, Austrian and Turkish forces. The Romanian prime minister, Ion Bratianu

(1864–1927), played for time in the hope of an Entente victory, but was eventually compelled to resign. The Germans eventually came to terms with a group of pro-German octogenarian conservatives who had remained in Bucharest, and one of them, Alexandru Marghiloman (1854–1925), eventually became prime minister on 18 March 1918. Marghiloman signed the treaty, which reduced Romania to the status of a satellite within a German *MITTELEUROPA*. The treaty was never ratified by the Romanians, who subsequently claimed to have kept faith with the Entente, and annexed Transylvania from Hungary and Bukovina from Austria after the end of the war.

Buchenwald, one of the first Nazi CONCENTRATION CAMPS. Buchenwald camp was set up in 1937 on the Ettersberg outside Weimar. There were many subsidiary camps in the surrounding region, one of which, at NORDHAUSEN, became a freestanding concentration camp for women (Mittelbau Dora). Although deaths from the mistreatment of prisoners, beatings and torture ran at some 12,000 a month, the main purpose of the camp was the supply of slave labour to local businesses rather than systematic murder. The population of the camp increased massively during World War II, and altogether some 238,000 men and 25,000 women were imprisoned there; 34,000 deaths were registered, and the identity of a further 9000 victims remained unknown. Allied troops reached the camp on 11 April 1945 and found over 21,000 inmates still interned there. The site was used as a prison camp by the Soviet military administration between 1945 and 1950.

Büchner, Georg (1813–37) writer and *VORMÄRZ* radical. Büchner was born the son of a doctor in Goddelau in the grand duchy of Hesse-Darmstadt, and studied in Strasbourg in the early 1830s. He first came to notice as co-author of *Der hessische Landbote*, a revolutionary tract inspired by the events in Paris in 1830. The first draft, written entirely by

Büchner, was toned down by his collaborator, a local pastor called Weidig. The authorities became aware of the pamphlet before the distribution was complete, and despite warnings not to do so, people simply handed it over. Weidig was imprisoned for two years for his part in the project. Büchner himself escaped to France, where he worked on his play *Dantons Tod* (*Danton's Death*, 1835), in which he expressed the pessimism of a frustrated revolutionary. Büchner was something of a radical pioneer not in only in politics, but also in terms of literary form. In *Leonce und Lena* (1836) critics have found a satire on Romanticism, and in *Woyzeck* (1836), his last play, the social criticism and naturalistic form of late 19th-century German literature. Büchner died of typhus at the age of 23. *Woyzeck* was adapted by Alban BERG for his opera *Wozzeck*.

Bulge, battle of the. *See* ARDENNES OFFENSIVE.

Bülow, Bernhard, Fürst von (1849–1929), German chancellor and prime minister of Prussia (1900–9). Bülow was born in Klein-Flottbek, near Hamburg, the son of a senior public servant who served as secretary of state under Bismarck. Bülow himself grew up during the Wars of Unification, which proved to be a formative experience, and he liked to think of himself and his policies in Bismarckian terms. He studied law in Switzerland and embarked on a career in the diplomatic service, including a spell as German ambassador in Rome, before being appointed foreign minister in 1897. German foreign policy under Bülow was characterized by brash diplomacy, assertive sabre-rattling (*see* 'HAMMER AND ANVIL' SPEECH) and, not least, populist presentation (he believed that only a successful foreign policy could 'reconcile, pacify, rally, unite'). Above all, however, his foreign policy lacked focus and clarity of objectives, and it was carelessness and indiscretion – albeit the Kaiser's rather than his own – that brought about his fall in the wake of the DAILY TELEGRAPH AFFAIR of 1908.

In domestic policy Bülow was an arch-conservative and a nationalist. He was intolerant of diversity, and enthusiastically promoted Germanization policies in Poland. He spoke rhetorically of bringing Germany into the modern world, but was a royalist opposed to parliamentary democracy, and at heart committed to conservative Prussian values. He perceived the army and the landowning class as the guarantors of Germany's power. He failed to address Germany's most pressing political and economic problems, such as the urgent need for financial and fiscal reforms, and the necessity of resolving the constitutional relationship between Prussia and the Reich (including the reform of Prussia's three-class voting system). These matters were left unresolved for his successors to deal with. Bülow died in Italy at the age of 80. His memoirs were published after his death.

Bund der Heimatvertriebenen und Entrechteten. *See* EXPELLEES.

Bund der Landwirte. *See* AGRARIAN LEAGUE.

Bund deutscher Mädel (BdM), the League of German Girls. The BdM, part of the broader HITLER YOUTH movement, was a Nazi organization for girls aged between 14 and 18. Younger girls (from the age of 10) were organized in the *Jungmädelbund* (Young Girls' League). The organization sought to inculcate Nazi ideals about appropriate behaviour for German girls, and to prepare them for womanhood according to National Socialist precepts. Member of the BdM had to be German in origin, physically fit, properly dressed and accomplished in domestic skills. Cleanliness, diligence and self-discipline were prized, and girls were expected to be well-acquainted with German culture. The differences between the sexes were made very clear: girls were expected to be docile, passive and sensitive. On the other hand, indolence, frivolity and luxury were frowned upon, and sturdy motherliness was the ideal. The BdM already had 19,244 members at the end of 1932 (and the *Jungmädelbund* had 4600), but the membership had increased more than twelvefold, to 243,750, by the end of the following year. Over 1.5 million girls were members by the time of the outbreak of World War II, and almost 2 million were members of the *Jungmädelbund*.

Bundesakte ('federal acts'), the basic constitutional legislation of the GERMAN CONFEDERATION, agreed at the Congress of VIENNA in 1815. The constitution was finalized with the ratification of the Final Acts of Vienna (*Wiener Schlussakte*) in 1820.

Bundesrat ('federal council'), presently the second, upper, chamber of the German parliament. It is one of the five permanent constitutional bodies of the German political system. The president of the Bundesrat is elected for a year from among the minister-presidents of the *Länder* (federal states), and acts as deputy for the federal president if necessary. Membership of the Bundesrat is confined to the voting members of a state (*Land*) government, generally the minister-president and ministers (in the city-states of Berlin, Hamburg and Bremen the mayor and senators). The Bundesrat has 69 ordinary members and around 130 deputy members. The number of votes depends on the population of the federal state. None has fewer than three votes; those with a population between 2 and 6 million have four votes; those with between 6 and 7 million people have five votes; and those with over 7 million people have six. All the votes for any state are cast together. Laws that affect the interests of the *Länder* need the explicit approval of the Bundesrat. Otherwise objections by the Bundesrat to legislation promulgated in the lower house, the Bundestag, can be overruled by the latter.

The predecessor of the present Bundesrat, the federal council of the NORTH GERMAN CONFEDERATION and then of the empire, was effectively the governing body, and was chaired by the chancellor (BISMARCK, for the first 19 years). It had 43 members in the North German Confederation, and 58 under the empire. In both cases Prussia had 17 of the seats and the rest were divided among the smaller *Länder*.

The second chamber of the Austrian parliament is also called the Bundesrat. It has 64 members, who are elected by the LANDTAG in each of the federal states. The number of members each state elects varies according to the size of the population.

Bundesrepublik Deutschland (BRD). *See* FEDERAL REPUBLIC OF GERMANY.

Bundestag, federal diet or parliament, first of the GERMAN CONFEDERATION, then, since 1949, of the FEDERAL REPUBLIC OF GERMANY, where it is the lower house of parliament and the main legislative assembly. The constituent session of the first postwar German parliament took place in Bonn on 7 September 1949. Eleven parties were represented in the house, and there were 2 independent members; 28 members were women, and 8 members from West Berlin (still technically under Allied jurisdiction) had only limited voting rights. The Bundestag is directly elected for a fixed term every four years on the basis of 'personalized' proportional representation, that is, a mixture of proportional representation by party list and direct election of individual members.

Bundeswehr, the armed forces of the FEDERAL REPUBLIC OF GERMANY, consisting of the army, navy and air force (LUFTWAFFE). The re-establishment of German armed forces was a controversial issue after World War II, both at home and abroad. The Cold War and the Korean War finally prompted Chancellor ADENAUER to respond positively to the suggestion from the United States that the Federal Republic should make a military contribution to the defence of the Western alliance, a response that provoked resistance in West Germany both from pacifists and from nationalists. The Paris treaties that came into force in 1955 made rearmament possible, and West Germany joined NATO the same year. The first volunteers were also recruited in 1955, and the first conscripts were called up in 1957.

All men in the Federal Republic are liable to conscription, and since 1996 the period of compulsory military service has been ten months. According to Article 65 of the constitution (Basic Law), the Supreme command of the armed forces in peace time rests with the minister of defence. If a 'state of defence' is declared, command passes to the chancellor in accordance with Article 115. Following the reunification of Germany in 1990 the Bundeswehr was restructured. In addition to the main defence forces (*Hauptverteidigungsstreitkräfte*) there are crisis response forces that can be deployed for the prevention of conflict or peace-keeping duties, according to the requirements of Germany's alliance commitments. The basic military organization of the Bundeswehr deals with administration, education and liaison with civilians. The strength of the Bundeswehr in peacetime is 338,000, but can be expanded to 370,000 in the event of an emergency.

Bündische Jugend, collective term for youth groups before 1933 that were not associated with a political party or religious organization. Such groups were dissolved by the Nazi regime in 1933.

Bündnis 90 ('Alliance 1990'), an electoral umbrella movement formed by protest groups such as NEUES FORUM ('New Forum') and *Demokratie Jetzt* ('Democracy Now') during the last months of the GERMAN DEMOCRATIC REPUBLIC. It was set up in February 1990 and campaigned in the elections to the VOLKSKAMMER (People's Chamber) held on 18 March that year. It won 12 seats and allied itself with the GREENS and the Independent Women's Movement. It merged with the Greens on a national basis in 1993 to form a new political party, *Bündnis 90–Die Grünen*. The new party won 47 seats in the parliamentary elections of 1998.

Bund Oberland, a radical right-wing paramilitary organization in the Munich of the early 1920s. Its members took part in the BEER HALL PUTSCH.

Bürckel, Josef (1894–1944), Nazi politician and Reich commissioner for the reunification of Austria with the German Reich. Born in Lingfeld, Bürckel was a teacher before he became *Gauleiter* of the Rhineland Palatinate in 1926. He was elected to the Reichstag in 1930. After the 1935 plebiscite in the SAARLAND he was appointed Reich commissioner there, and remained until his appointment as *Gauleiter* of Vienna and Reich commissioner for Austria in 1938. He later returned to the Saarland, and committed suicide in 1944.

Burgenland, Austrian federal state, in the east of the country. Formerly in western Hungary, the territory had been settled by Germans since the Turkish occupation. When the Habsburg empire was divided between Austria and Hungary along the River Leitha with the AUSGLEICH of 1867, the German inhabitants of western Transleithania came under pressure from Hungary's magyarization policies. A movement for secession and union with Austria emerged in the four westernmost *comitats* (counties): Pressburg (Bratislava), Ödenburg (Sopron), Wieselburg and Eisenburg. After 1918 the movement had official backing from Austria, and after lengthy negotiations and much opposition from Budapest the province became a part of Austria in 1922. It was dissolved as a separate state by the Nazis during the German occupation, and restored after 1945.

Bürgerschaft, principal representative body and legislative assembly in the city-states of HAMBURG and BREMEN. It is effectively the city council, and at the same time the provincial diet (LANDTAG).

Bürgertum, 'bourgeoisie' or upper middle class. German usage distinguishes clearly between the lower middle classes (MITTELSTAND) and the upper middle classes. The terms *Besitzbürgertum* (propertied middle class) and *Bildungsbürgertum* (educated middle class) are also widely used to make further distinctions. The term *Bürgertum* is particularly associated with the prosperous upper middle classes of the 19th century. The term *Bürger* was originally used to refer to the inhabitants of towns in the middle ages, but came to be associated with the values and lifestyles of the wealthier citizens and professional groups. The adjective *bürgerlich* (bourgeois) has very clear social, cultural and political connotations of respectability.

Burgfrieden ('fortress peace'), the domestic political truce achieved in Germany at the outbreak of WORLD WAR I. All the Social Democratic members of the Reichstag (except Karl LIEBKNECHT) initially supported the government. The truce had come unstuck by 1917, when the SPD itself split into two over the issue, with the anti-war USPD breaking away from the majority in the party.

Burgtheater, traditionally Vienna's most prestigious theatre. It was founded in 1741 by MARIA THERESIA and declared a national theatre by JOSEPH II. Its name refers to its original location in the Ballhaus at the imperial palace (*Burg*). Since 1888 it has been housed in a purpose-built building on the Vienna Ringstrasse.

Burschenschaften, nationalist student corporations founded at the end of the Napoleonic Wars. The first, which was known as the *Urburschenschaft*, was established at the University of Jena in 1815. Its colours were black, red and gold, those of the patriotic Lützow Freikorps, which had been active during the Wars of LIBERATION. Radical nationalists from the outset, the students burned books of which they disapproved at the WARTBURG RALLY of 1817, along with symbols of absolutism. Another important centre of radical student activity was Giessen. The leader of the 'Giessen Blacks' was Karl Follen, a university teacher, and among his pupils was Karl Ludwig Sand,

who was responsible in the summer of 1819 for the murder of August von KOTZEBUE, a writer of popular melodramas, whom the students accused of being a tsarist agent. The murder provided the political authorities, under the presidency of METTERNICH, with the justification for introducing the authoritarian measures embodied in the KARLSBAD DECREES. Sand was executed. The *Burschenschaften* were prohibited, but persisted and survived.

During the course of the 19th century the *Burschenschaften* became increasingly chauvinist and anti-Semitic, and were associated with the politics of the radical right. Separate Jewish student associations were formed from 1882, and women students' associations from 1906. The Nazis attempted to absorb the *Burschenschaften* into party organizations. Many reformed after World War II in the Federal Republic of Germany. They were banned in the GDR, but some unofficial groups formed and survived into the 1990s. In the later 1990s there were 950 student corporations in Germany with 150,000 members.

BVP (*Bayerische Volkspartei*), the Bavarian People's Party, a regional Roman Catholic party, founded in 1918, when Bavarian Catholics broke away from the CENTRE PARTY. It remained in many respects the Bavarian wing of the Centre Party. The BVP was a particularist rather than a separatist party, and placed great emphasis on Bavaria's autonomy within a national federal framework. Its uncompromising refusal to cooperate with the SPD in Bavaria led it to form alliances with anti-democratic parties and politicians of the right, who thereby gained ministerial posts at the regional level. It voted for the ENABLING LAW along with the Centre Party in March 1933, and dissolved itself shortly afterwards.

C

Caen, battle of (6 June–9 July 1944), engagement in WORLD WAR II during the Allied invasion of northwest Europe. The town was an important communications centre and was Montgomery's first major objective after the D-Day landings. A German Panzer division blocked the first assault, and the fighting then lasted several weeks. The town was eventually captured at the beginning of July.

Café Milani, a conservative faction at the 1848 FRANKFURT PARLIAMENT. Like the other political groups it took its name from its accustomed meeting place. Almost half (18) of the group's 37 members were senior civil servants, and a further 8 were landowners.

Cambrai, battle of (20 November–7 December 1917), engagement on the Western Front during WORLD WAR I, which saw the first large-scale use of British tanks. The initial grenade attack began in the morning and was quickly followed by the deployment of 378 tanks, which drove the Germans to retreat some 10 km (6 miles) and led to the capture of around 10,000 German troops and 123 guns, while there were very few British losses. The British experienced some logistical difficulties, however, and the Germans, who had been ready to withdraw entirely, began to resist and then (on 3 December) to counterattack. The British troops were driven back, the whole of the captured area was won back by the Germans, and advances were made into territory that had been held by the British before the

attack began on 20 November. The battle was important less for the outcome than for the demonstration of what could be achieved by tanks, and the Germans' inability to defend themselves against them.

Cameral Court. *See REICHSKAMMERGERICHT.*

Cameroon (German name: Kamerun), German colony in west Africa acquired in 1884 along with TOGOLAND. It had a population of some 2.5 million, of whom not many more than 1300 were German. It was provisionally divided between Britain and France in 1916, and mandated to the two Allies under the conditions of the treaty of VERSAILLES.

Campe, Joachim Heinrich (1746–1818), philologist and publisher. Campe was born in Deensen, in the rural district of Holzminden, now in Lower Saxony, and taught at the Philanthropinum in Dessau. He was house tutor to Alexander and Wilhelm von HUMBOLDT, and founded educational institutions in Hamburg and Braunschweig. His publishing company became the Hoffmann und Campe Verlag in Hamburg.

Camphausen, Ludolf (1803–90), liberal politician. Camphausen was a leading businessman in Cologne. He was appointed minister-president of Prussia by FRIEDRICH WILHELM IV after the outbreak of the REVOLUTIONS OF 1848 in Berlin. He was caught between the politics of the Prussian diet, which moved to the left, and the king, whose opposition to the revolution became more determined. He resigned in June, but remained a leading figure in the FRANKFURT PARLIAMENT. His younger brother was Otto von CAMPHAUSEN.

Camphausen, Otto von (1812–1896), Prussian politician and younger brother of Ludolf CAMPHAUSEN. Like his brother he was a liberal. He was Prussian finance minister from 1869 to 1878, and vice president of the Prussian state ministry from 1873 to 1878. He was an opponent of Bismarck's protectionism.

Campo Formio, treaty of (1797), treaty between Austria and Revolutionary France during the Wars of the COALITIONS. The treaty ended the War of the First Coalition following Austria's defeat by Napoleon in Italy. The Austrian Netherlands went to France along with parts of Lombardy, in exchange for eastern Venetia (including Venice), Istria and Dalmatia. Austria also agreed to consent to French occupation of the left bank of the Rhine, subject to confirmation by the imperial estates.

Canaris, Wilhelm (1887–1945), German admiral, intelligence chief and anti-Nazi conspirator. Born in Aplerbeck (now part of Dortmund), Canaris joined the imperial navy in 1905, commanded submarines in World War I, and then became involved in counter-revolutionary politics (including the KAPP PUTSCH) during the Weimar Republic. He was appointed head of counter-intelligence (the ABWEHR) in 1935 and remained in that post until 1944, when the Abwehr was taken over by Ernst KALTENBRUNNER. He managed to reconcile his security work with a political sympathy for military and conservative resistance circles, and after his dismissal he became more closely involved with the JULY BOMB PLOT. He was hanged for treason at Flossenbürg concentration camp in April 1945.

Caporetto, battle of (1917). *See* ISONZO VALLEY.

Caprivi, (Georg) Leo, Graf von (1831–99), officer and politician; imperial chancellor (1890–4) and minister-president of Prussia (1890–2). Caprivi was born in Charlottenburg, educated in Berlin, and joined the army in 1849. He took part in the campaign against Austria in 1866, and in the Franco-Prussian War as chief of the general staff of the 10th Army (1870–1). He became chief of the admiralty in 1883, but resigned in protest against the interference of Kaiser WILHELM II in naval matters. Nevertheless in 1890 he was chosen by the Kaiser as Bismarck's successor as Reich chancellor.

Caprivi had a reputation as a moderate, pursued liberal policies and achieved some early successes in trade and colonial policy – including commercial treaties with Russia that led to opposition from the JUNKERS and constituted a catalyst in the establishment of the AGRARIAN LEAGUE (*Bund der Landwirte*). Caprivi initially encountered little opposition from the Kaiser, however, who made him a count. His reform of the army proved difficult but was successfully implemented, but his education bill of 1892 failed amid perceptions that the chancellor was too close to the CENTRE PARTY and ultimately naïve. He attempted to resign in March 1892, but the Kaiser refused to let him go. He then gave up his position as minister-president of Prussia to the conservative Count Botho EULENBURG who, as Bismarck's Prussian interior minister, had drafted the ANTI-SOCIALIST LAWS.

After this the chancellor's authority declined rapidly. Caprivi was unable to exercise any control over the Prussian ministers, which disappointed the expectations of other *Länder*. In 1894 Eulenburg sought to introduce an 'anti-revolution' bill in the Reichstag, with the ulterior motive of provoking a constitutional crisis that would lead to a more authoritarian system of government. Caprivi opposed Eulenburg and threatened to resign unless the Kaiser dismissed him. In the event both were dismissed, and Prince Chlodwig zu HOHEN-LOHE-SCHILLINGSFÜRST became chancellor, Prussian minister-president and Prussian foreign minister. Caprivi retired and took no part in public life during his few remaining years.

Carinthia (German name: Kärnten), constituent federal state of Austria. Carinthia was acquired by Ottakar of Bohemia on his accession to the duchy of Austria in 1253. It was a duchy until 1918, when it was claimed by Yugoslavia on the grounds that it had been predominantly Slovene until the second half of the 19th century. Yugoslav incursions were repulsed by spontaneously formed 'home guards' (*Heimwehren*), which also resisted the demands of the democratic government in Vienna and went on to play a key role in the formation of AUSTRO-FASCISM. Carinthia's boundaries were decided by a plebiscite, in which many Slovenes voted to remain with Austria rather than Yugoslavia. When the Nazis occupied Yugoslavia parts of Slovenia were reintegrated into the Reich as 'South Carinthia'. In the last two decades of the 20th century the Austrian Freedom Party (FPÖ), exploited ethnic tensions in the province, which became a key centre of the party's German nationalist wing. Although nominally liberal, the FPÖ moved more openly towards the radical right under the leadership of Carinthia's governor Jörg Haider.

Carlsbad decrees. *See* KARLSBAD DECREES.

Cassino. *See* GUSTAV LINE.

Cassirer, Paul (1871–1926), art dealer and publisher. Born in Görlitz, Cassirer studied art history and worked on the magazine *Simplicissimus* before settling in Berlin and setting up an art book business (1898) with his cousin Bruno Cassirer (1874–1945). In 1908 he set up a publishing house, and in 1910 he founded the art journal *Pan*. He used his influence and businesses to promote new artists from the Berlin SECESSION. He joined the USPD in 1918, and published socialist pamphlets, including the work of KAUTSKY and BERNSTEIN.

CDU (*Christlich Demokratische Union*), the Christian Democratic Union, the principal conservative party of the German Federal Republic. The party was the effective successor of the CENTRE PARTY of imperial Germany and the Weimar Republic, and retained its moderate conservative ideology while relinquishing the specific defence of Catholic interests in favour of an interdenominational approach. It was established at regional level in the three western zones during the Allied occupation. (A similarly interdenominational Christian Democratic Union was set up in the Soviet zone in June 1945, and continued to exist throughout the history of the GERMAN DEMOCRATIC REPUBLIC, but was never able to operate freely.)

In its Ahlen programme of 1947 the CDU advocated a Christian socialism in opposition to both economic liberalism and social democracy, but moved quickly towards support for free-market policies, not least under the influence of those (largely northern Protestant) members whose pre-war association had been with the DNVP or DVP. These free-market policies were enthusiastically pursued by CDU economics minister Ludwig ERHARD during the 1950s.

In the elections to LANDTAGE during the Allied occupations the CDU won on average over one-third of the vote and emerged as the largest single political party in the western zones. The regional concentration of its support continued to be in Catholic areas, especially Baden and Württemberg-Hohenzollern, where it won over half the vote in Landtag elections of 1947, but also the Rhineland Palatinate and North Rhine-Westphalia, where it was ahead of the SPD. Moreover, both of the party's most successful leaders, Konrad ADENAUER and Helmut KOHL, have been Roman Catholic Rhinelanders. The CDU fared badly initially in the predominantly Protestant *Länder*: many right-wing voters in Lower Saxony and Schleswig-Holstein preferred regional parties. Although the party still does better in the southwest than in the north and east, this increasingly reflects economic conditions rather than confessional allegiance: the CDU represents middle-class interests.

In the first federal elections in 1949 the CDU/CSU group was the largest in the Bundestag (the CSU being the CDU's sister party in Bavaria). The CDU leader Konrad Adenauer became chancellor, a post he retained for the next 14 years. Indeed the CDU/CSU (more often than not in coalition with the FDP) has governed West Germany for much of the postwar period. It was in power continually for the first 20 years of the republic's history (Adenauer being succeeded as chancellor first by Erhard and then by KIESINGER), and then for a further 16 years under Helmut Kohl from 1982. In the election of 1998 it was defeated by the SPD and gained its lowest share of the popular vote (35.1%) since 1949. In 2000 the party elected as its leader Angela Merkel, a Protestant woman from the former East Germany.

The CDU has been the first successful party of pragmatic conservatism in German history. Its domestic priorities have been to restore the social and economic position of the middle class and to defend business interests, while the focus of its foreign policy has been integration into the West through the European communities and NATO.

Central Powers (*Mittelmächte*), a term originally applied to the members of the TRIPLE ALLIANCE (Germany, Austria-Hungary and Italy) but primarily used of Germany and its allies, especially Austria-Hungary. It was extended to include Turkey and Bulgaria during World War I.

Centre Party (*Zentrum*), the principal political party representing the interests of Roman Catholics in Germany between the founding of the Reich and the party's own dissolution in 1933. The party was named after its central physical location among the parties in the Reichstag. The party was established in 1870, and under the leadership of Ludwig Windthorst it became a significant force in defence of Catholic interests during the KULTURKAMPF of the 1870s. In the election to the Reichstag of 1871 it won almost 750,000 votes and was the second largest party in the house. Within ten years its vote had increased to almost 1.2 million. It was the largest single party in the Reichstag during the 1880s and 1890s, and its support became a prerequisite for the passage of legislation.

The party moved to the left during World War I, abandoning its annexationist stance, and advocated a negotiated peace. It was one of the most stable political forces in the WEIMAR REPUBLIC, and although it lost some support to the left in industrial Westphalia and elsewhere, it maintained its share of the vote and participated in almost all the government coalitions. The party shifted to the right again in the late 1920s, and negotiated with HITLER from 1932. It voted for the ENABLING LAW in March 1933 in order to protect Catholic institutions, and the Catholic authorities effectively agreed to abandon their political party when they signed a CONCORDAT with the Nazi regime. This brought about the dissolution of the party later the same year.

The Centre Party was effectively succeeded in the Federal Republic of Germany by the Christian Democratic Union (CDU) and its Bavarian sister party, the Christian Social Union (CSU). A left-orientated Centre Party (*Deutsche Zentrumspartei*) was founded in 1945, but was of political significance only in North Rhine-Westphalia.

Chamberlain, Houston Stewart (1855–1927), British anti-Semite. Chamberlain was born in Portsmouth, the son of a general, and grew up with his grandmother in Versailles. He was educated at a public school, travelled widely and became a great admirer of Richard WAGNER after his first visit to Bayreuth in 1882. In 1889 he moved to Vienna, and ten years later he published his two-volume work *Die Grundlagen des 19. Jahrhunderts* (published in London in 1910 as *The Foundations of the Nineteenth Century*).

The book presented the cultural history of Europe as a racial struggle in which the Germans were depicted as the upholders of European Christian culture against the corrupting influence of the Jews. (He argued that Christ himself was not Jewish at all.) Chamberlain's book was given a rapturous welcome by the VÖLKISCH movement in Germany. The emperor WILHELM II was a particularly influential admirer, whose endorsement reinforced the book's popularity. It was to have an enormous influence on the racial ideologues of the Nazi movement, such as Alfred ROSENBERG and Hans GÜNTHER. In 1909 Chamberlain married Wagner's daughter Eva von Bülow, and moved to Bayreuth. During World War I he published anti-British essays, and in 1916 took German citizenship. In 1923 he met Hitler. His correspondence with the Kaiser was published after his death.

chancellor (German: *Kanzler*), the head of government at federal level in both Germany and Austria. The word originated in the early Middle Ages as a term for a holder of high political office. Its modern usage stems from the early 19th century. The Prussian reformer Karl August von HARDENBERG was designated state chancellor in 1810. In Austria the title 'court and state chancellor' was granted to distinguished statesman such as KAUNITZ, STADION and METTERNICH.

In the GERMAN EMPIRE the Reich chancellor was the 'highest official of the Reich' and was appointed by the Kaiser (emperor). Formally the Reich chancellor was also the only minister of the Reich, and effectively head of a government conducted through 'Reich offices' directed by state secretaries. He also presided over the REICHSRAT. For the most part Reich chancellors were also simultaneously minister-president and foreign minister of Prussia, but Bismarck gave up the post of Prussian minister-president briefly (1872–3). During the chancellorship of his successor CAPRIVI (1890–4), the post of minister-president of Prussia was held by Count Botho EULENBURG from 1892 to 1894.

The post of Prussian foreign minister was, however, retained by Caprivi.

In the WEIMAR REPUBLIC the Reich chancellor and, on his advice, the Reich ministers, were appointed and dismissed by the directly elected Reich president. The Reich chancellor was now responsible to the REICHSTAG, and was bound to resign if he failed to survive a parliamentary vote of no confidence. The Reich chancellor now presided over the cabinet and determined the course of policy.

The constitution of the Federal Republic of Germany defines the chancellorship in essentially similar terms, but has strengthened the office and made the chancellor a stronger political figure.

The term chancellor has also been used since 1918 to describe the head of government in the first and second Austrian Republics.

charismatic leadership, Weberian model applied by historians of Nazi Germany to the type of authority exercised by Hitler. Max WEBER distinguished three categories of leadership: 'traditional', which rested on custom; 'legal' or bureaucratic, which was the outcome of a rational system of politics based on impersonal rules of election; and 'charismatic', a type that is exceptional, unstable and ephemeral, and associated with leadership in crisis rather than with routine government. The charisma in question resides not necessarily in the individual, but in qualities perceived by the followers. Charismatic authority needs to be reinforced by repeated and visible success, and is eroded by failure. Since such a leader must constantly be seen to overcome crises, real or imagined, there can be no stabilization or return to the mundane.

Chełmno, Nazi EXTERMINATION CAMP established in 1941 in a village of that name some 75 km (47 miles) to the west of Łódź in the newly created Reichsgau WARTHELAND (which had been annexed from Poland). Chełmno was the first camp where mass executions were carried out by means of gas, and seems to have been established at the prompting of the *Gauleiter*, Arthur GREISER, after the deportation of 20,000 German Jews and 5000 Sinti and Roma (Gypsies) to the Łódź ghetto. Herbert Lange, an SS officer who had been in charge of euthanasia gas vans, arrived in Chełmno at the end of October 1941 with a special commando unit and took over a local building for the extermination centre. Jews from the surrounding area were brought to Chełmno in December and January, and 55,000 Jews from the Łódź ghetto were murdered there in early 1942, along with 5000 Gypsies. Those who were capable of work remained in the ghetto; those who were not were gassed. The killing was stopped early in 1943 and the centre was blown up. When it was decided in 1944 to kill the remaining Jews in Łódź, however, the commando unit returned and built a new camp. It has been estimated that over 150,000 people were gassed at Chełmno altogether.

chief of civilian administration (*Chef der Zivilverwaltung*, CdZ), Nazi administrative post, usually held by a *Gauleiter*. Territories under a chief of civilian administration belonged to a specific category not directly incorporated into the Reich with immediate effect (like, for example, the Belgian cantons of St Vith, Eupen and Malmédy), but destined for rapid incorporation into the Reich. The territories in question in the west were Alsace and Lorraine (the French *départements* of Haut Rhin, Bas Rhin and Moselle) and Luxembourg. Lorraine was added to Gau Saar-Pfalz, and the Alsatian territories to Gau Baden (under *Gauleiter* Robert WAGNER) to form the new Gau Westmark and Gau Baden-Elsass. Luxembourg was added to Gau Koblenz-Trier to form the new Gau Moselland. Although no specific legal provision was made for the annexation of the territories in the west, Hitler made it clear that he wanted to see them incorporated into the Reich within ten years. Territory that had formerly been part of Yugoslavia (Lower Styria, Upper Carniola, the Miesstal and the commune of Seeland) was incorporated into the *Reichsgaue* Styria and Carinthia. After the invasion of the Soviet Union Bialystok also came under the authority of a chief of civilian administration, Erich KOCH, *Gauleiter* of East Prussia.

Christian Democratic Union. *See* CDU.

Christian People's Party. *See* CHRISTLICHE VOLKSPARTEI.

Christian Social Party (*Christlichsoziale Partei*), German Protestant political party founded in 1878 in Berlin as the Christian Social Workers' Party (*Christlichsoziale Arbeiterpartei*) by Adolf STOECKER, a court preacher. The founding of the party was announced during an SPD meeting by Stoecker himself (the so-called Eiskeller incident). The party's corporatist programme of social reform failed to appeal to the voters of Berlin, particularly the workers, in the general election of 1878. It received only 1422 votes, and it subsequently became simply a vehicle for ANTISEMITISM. Stoecker himself belonged to the extreme anti-liberal KREUZZEITUNG wing of the DEUTSCHKONSERVATIVE PARTEI (German Conservative Party), of which he was a member. In 1881 the Christian Social Party merged with other groups to form the *Antisemitische Deutschsoziale Partei* (Anti-Semitic German Social Party).

Christian Social Party (*Christlichsoziale Partei*), Austrian clerical-conservative party, founded in 1889, whose anti-Semitic platform attracted popular support in Vienna at the turn of the century. In 1895 the Christian Social Party won two-thirds of the seats on the city council, and its leader, Karl Lueger, was elected mayor. However, the emperor refused to confirm his election five times, and it was two years before he could take up the post. The Christian Socials undertook major reforms in the city. The public utilities – gas, water and electricity – were brought into municipal ownership, a modern public transport system was built, and there were new parks, schools and hospitals. Moreover, the party extended its electoral constituency beyond the lower middle classes who were its first supporters to include sections of the educated and propertied bourgeoisie, to some extent uniting the middle classes behind a single conservative party. The success of Karl Lueger impressed the young HITLER, who disliked Lueger's clericalism and the insincerity of his anti-Semitism, but praised his organizational skills and political pragmatism in MEIN KAMPF.

The Christian Social Party survived World War I but lost control of Vienna to the Social Democrats. On the other hand, in the interwar period it became the senior partner in Austria's governing 'Bürgerblock' governments (anti-Socialist coalitions formed with the German Nationalists) and determined the course of Austrian politics throughout the 1920s and 1930s. It provided every chancellor and all the key ministers between 1920 and 1938, but never had a majority in parliament (the Nationalrat). Indeed its numbers of seats fell from 82 in 1923 to 73 in 1927 and 66 in 1930, when the Social Democratic Party became the largest single party.

After the parliamentary election of 1930 the Christian Social Party became increasingly conscious that many of its supporters were switching their allegiance to the Austrian branch of the Nazi Party. In 1932, when half the Austrian electorate voted in regional and local elections, the party's coalition partners were virtually eliminated by the Nazis, and the party's own losses were substantial and significant enough to unnerve the leadership. It also lost control of two symbolically important institutions: the Lower Austrian LANDTAG and the upper house of parliament (the BUNDESRAT). In May 1933 local elections were banned after landslide gains for the Nazis in staunchly Roman Catholic Innsbruck, and in 1932 parliament was suspended on a technicality. From 1934, following the armed suppression of the labour movement in the brief AUSTRIAN CIVIL WAR, the Christian Social chancellor, Engelbert DOLLFUSS, and his successor Kurt von SCHUSCHNIGG, established a fascist dictatorship, the so-called 'CORPORATE STATE', which was swept away in 1938 by the German invasion. The Christian Social Party's successor after World War II was the Austrian People's Party (Österreichische Volkspartei, ÖVP).

Christian Social Union. See CSU.

Christian Social Workers' Party. See CHRISTLICHSOZIALE ARBEITERPARTEI.

Christlich Demokratische Union. See CDU.

Christliche Volkspartei, the Christian People's Party, a political party active in the SAARLAND from the end of World War II. It sought to orientate the Saarland away from Germany and towards France. Its leader, Johannes Hoffmann (1890–1967), was minister-president of the Saarland from 1947 to 1955. The party went into decline when the Saarland was fully reincorporated into Germany, and was eventually absorbed into the CDU (1965).

Christlichsoziale Arbeiterpartei, the Christian Social Workers' Party, founded by Adolf Stoecker in 1878. It became the CHRISTIAN SOCIAL PARTY.

Christlichsoziale Partei. See CHRISTIAN SOCIAL PARTY.

Christlich-Soziale Union. See CSU.

Cisleithania (German name: Zisleithanien), the Habsburg provinces to the west of the River Leitha. The term usually refers to the Austrian half of the empire as opposed to Hungary (TRANSLEITHANIA), after the AUSGLEICH of 1867.

Citadel, codename for the defensive German strategy at the end of World War II (after the failure of Operation BARBAROSSA). It aimed to create a 'Fortress Europe' whose exploitation by Germany would enable a renewed attack on the USSR following a 'breathing space'.

Clam-Martinic, Heinrich, Graf (1863–1932), Austrian officer and politician. He was minister-president from the end of 1916 to June 1917, and then military governor in Montenegro.

Clary-Aldringen, Manfred, Graf von (1862–1928), Austrian politician. He was governor of Styria from 1898 until the end of World War I, and was minister-president of Austria for ten weeks in 1899.

Class, Heinrich (1868–1953), journalist and political agitator. Class became leader of the PAN-GERMAN LEAGUE in 1908, and led it in an authoritarian manner. He was an anti-Semite and proponent of German expansionism in Europe. His best-known work, *Wenn ich der Kaiser wär'* ('If I were the emperor'), was published in 1912 under the pseudonym Daniel Frymann and sold over 20,000 copies before World War I. It argued for a restoration of the ANTI-SOCIALIST LAWS introduced by BISMARCK in 1878, the expulsion of all Social Democratic deputies from the Reichstag and LANDTAGE, and the dismissal of all SPD officials, trade unionists and all editors of left-wing newspapers and journals. There should be 'public' newspapers, and rallies to re-educate the people. In the event of a strike, the affected area should be placed under exceptional rule, and picketing was to be prohibited on pain of arrest and imprisonment. All further Jewish immigration should be stopped, foreign Jews expelled, along with those citizens of ALSACE-LORRAINE who insisted on speaking French, even at home, or reading books published in France. (In fact, he added later, all non-Germans must be expelled from the empire, and German colonists abroad – in Russia, Poland and America – be brought back.) Any resident Jews remaining in Germany should be placed under an aliens law. Decadent art and speculation in the art market were to be banned, and the 'political aspirations of women' were dismissed as neither justifiable nor useful. The book elicited many positive responses, and reflected opinion not only in the *VÖLKISCH* movement, but also among a broader section of German nationalists.

In September 1914 Class published a *Memorandum on German War Aims* setting out an ambitious programme of German annexations in both east and west, which was endorsed by both Gustav KRUPP and STINNES, and during World War I he proved of invaluable support to the annexationist lobby in his ability to mobilize opinion among the educated middle class (which was disproportionately over-represented in the Pan-German League). Class was both an influential and a representative figure among German nationalist circles before World War I.

After World War I Class was proprietor of the *Deutsche Zeitung* newspaper and a significant figure in the right-wing opposition to the WEIMAR REPUBLIC. He supported both the KAPP PUTSCH and Hitler's BEER HALL PUTSCH, and was a vociferous opponent of the YOUNG PLAN in 1929. Although he was a Nazi member of the Reichstag his political influence was insignificant by the time Hitler came to power, and the Pan-German League was prohibited in 1939. After World War II Class settled in Munich. He died in Jena.

Clausewitz, Carl von (1780–1831), Prussian general and military theorist. Born in Burg, near Magdeburg, Clausewitz was an experienced soldier when he became associated with the military reformers around General SCHARNHORST and Graf Gneisenau in the first decade of the 19th century. Although an active professional soldier who was also involved in the diplomacy of the last years of the Napoleonic Wars, he is best known as a military theorist, above all for his incomplete work *Vom Kriege* (*On War*).

Coalitions, Wars of the (1792–1809), series of wars fought against Revolutionary and Napoleonic France by shifting coalitions of other European states; together with the Wars of LIBERATION they constitute what are also known as the Revolutionary and Napoleonic Wars.

The first conflict began in 1792 with the declaration of war by France on Prussia and

Austria. The following year a coalition was formed with Great Britain and was supported by most of the states of western Europe. Prussia made peace in 1795, and Austria in 1797 with the treaty of CAMPO FORMIO.

The second coalition united Austria, Britain, Russia, Turkey, Portugal and Naples against France, but Russia withdrew at the end of the 1799 campaign and the war again ended with the defeat of Austria. With the treaty of Lunéville (1801) Austria recognized French hegemony in the west – Italy, Switzerland and the Austrian Netherlands (modern Belgium) – and confirmed the annexation of the left bank of the Rhine. The war came to an end with the peace of Amiens in 1802.

In 1805 Britain formed a new coalition with Russia, which Austria also joined in August. Within a matter of weeks the Austrian army was encircled at Ulm and suffered a devastating defeat. The French entered Vienna on 13 November and then advanced into Moravia, where the coalition allies were decisively defeated at the battle of AUSTER-LITZ on 2 December. (Britain, however, had established naval supremacy in October with the victory at Trafalgar.) Prussia was awarded Hanover in return for territory in the west (Cleves) and in Bavaria. With the treaty of Pressburg (26 December 1805) Austria lost the Venetian territories it had gained at Campo Formio; it also lost the Tyrol, Vorarlberg and Lindau to Bavaria, and the Breisgau and Konstanz to Baden and Württemberg, which became kingdoms. In return Austria gained Salzburg.

War broke out again in 1806. In the fourth coalition Prussia was allied with Russia and Saxony. Prussia demanded the withdrawal of French troops to the Rhine and the dissolution of the CONFEDERATION OF THE RHINE, which had been created by Napoleon in 1806, the same year as the dissolution of the HOLY ROMAN EMPIRE. Prussia was quickly and decisively defeated at JENA and Auerstedt

(October 1806), and driven back beyond the Elbe. Napoleon's 'continental system' was proclaimed from Berlin (21 November), which was occupied by the French without resistance. Prussia's ally, Saxony, joined the Confederation of the Rhine at the peace of Posen (now Poznań). The court fled to East Prussia, and with it the only remaining army groups that were able to resist Napoleon.

In April 1809 Austria rose against Napoleon, and inflicted a defeat on the French at ASPERN, outside Vienna. This fifth war was also unsuccessful, however. Austria was defeated shortly afterwards at nearby WAGRAM, and lost yet more territory (and access to the sea) with the peace agreed at Schönbrunn in October. Salzburg, the Innviertel and the northern TYROL went to Bavaria, Illyria to France, the SOUTH TYROL to Italy, Galicia to the grand duchy of Warsaw, and extensive territories to Russia. Andreas HOFER, who had led a popular Tyrolean 'resistance', was executed at Mantua in Italy. With the conclusion of the last of the Wars of the Coalitions the whole of Germany had effectively fallen under Napoleonic hegemony. Austria and Prussia were subordinated to French interests, and the rest of Germany was within the Confederation of the Rhine. However, all this was to change after Napoleon's disastrous invasion of Russia in 1812, and the subsequent Wars of LIBERATION.

Cobenzl, Ludwig, Graf von (1753–1809), Austrian diplomat. He was ambassador in Berlin from 1775 to 1778, and in St Petersburg from 1779 to 1801, and played an important role in negotiations over the third partition of Poland in 1795. He negotiated with France at CAMPO FORMIO, Lunéville and RASTATT, and was responsible for Austrian foreign policy as vice chancellor from 1801 to 1805. He was the cousin of Philipp, Graf von COBENZL.

Cobenzl, Philipp, Graf von (1741–1810), Austrian vice chancellor (1779–92) and chancellor (1792–3). In 1779 he negotiated the treaty of Teschen, which brought to an end the War of the BAVARIAN SUCCESSION, and was sent as governor of the Austrian Netherlands in 1787. He replaced Graf von KAUNITZ as chancellor in 1792, and made overtures to Prussia without success. He was removed by the young emperor FRANZ II in 1801, and became Austrian ambassador in Paris (1801–5). He was the cousin of Ludwig, Graf von COBENZL.

Cologne (German name: Köln), one of Germany's oldest and most important cities, situated on the Rhine. It was founded in 38 BC by the Roman commander Agrippa and became a Roman colony (*Colonia Agrippinensis*) in AD 50. It had a bishop from the 4th century and an archbishop from 795. It became an imperial city in 1288. The university was founded in 1388, closed down in 1798 and reopened in 1919. From 1815 Cologne was incorporated into Prussia and in 1946 it fell within the boundaries of the new federal state of North-Rhine Westphalia. Its population increased rapidly during the 19th century, from 50,000 after the Napoleonic Wars to over half a million by the beginning of the 20th century. At the end of the 20th century it had a population of 963,600.

Communist Party. *See* KPD.

Compromise of 1867. *See* AUSGLEICH.

concentration camps (*Konzentrationslager*, KZ), large internment camps erected by the Nazis on coming to power. In the first instance they were used for the mass imprisonment of left-wing political opponents. Unregulated concentration camps were set up by SA stormtroopers during the political terror of 1933, and were used to imprison, beat and torture the party's political opponents on the left. The first 'official' camps were set up near large cities or industrial regions such as Berlin (SACHSENHAUSEN) and Munich (DACHAU). Jews, 'ASOCIALS', ROMA AND SINTI (Gypsies), JEHOVAH'S WITNESSES and HOMOSEXUALS were also interned in them. Some, in Poland, were transformed into EXTERMINATION CAMPS (*Vernichtungslager*) for the the mass murder of Jews and others (*see* HOLOCAUST).

concordat, 20 July 1933, treaty between the papacy and Germany concerning relations between the church and the state. The concordat was effectively a *rapprochement* between the Pope and the new Nazi regime, negotiated by the papal nuncio Eugenio Pacelli. It guaranteed the independence of the church to govern its own affairs within the law in return for giving up the right to its own political representation The CENTRE PARTY was dissolved and in return Articles 23 and 31 of the concordat granted concessions to Catholic schools and organizations respectively. In the case of organizations a distinction was made between purely religious or charitable associations and social or professional associations (including youth groups). The protection of these latter groups was made conditional on their activities being carried out 'outside any political party'. The church understood this to mean the Centre Party, while the Nazis chose to interpret the condition as being any independent demonstrations by Catholic organizations, and the difference in interpretation was the basis for continuing conflict between church and state during the early years of the Third Reich (*see* MIT BRENNENDER SORGE).

Condor Legion (German name: Legion Condor), the air formation that constituted the main contingent of German forces fighting for Franco's rebels during the Spanish Civil War. It was established in 1936 to command German air force units already active in Spain and to provide technical support. It consisted of transport aircraft, fighters, seaplanes, ground support and anti-aircraft artillery. It provided support for infantry and artillery in the most important battles, and was also responsible for attacks on civilians in government-held territory, as at GUERNICA in 1937. Its tactics anticipated tactics used by the German air force in World War II, for which involvement in Spain was an important training exercise.

Confederation of the Rhine (*Rheinbund*), French-dominated German confederation established in 1806 with the dissolution of the HOLY ROMAN EMPIRE. It brought all the German states except Austria, Prussia, Pomerania and Holstein within one political association subordinate to France.

The French advance into Germany during the Wars of the COALITIONS began in the 1790s with the occupation of the left bank of the Rhine and the establishment of a republic at Mainz. When the left bank was formally ceded after the War of the Second Coalition (with the treaty of Lunéville in 1801), the German princes were to be compensated with other territory. Effectively Germany was to be reconstituted under the supervision of princes appointed by the imperial Reichstag, the so-called *Reichsdeputation*. In redistributing territory within Germany, Napoleon hoped not only to secularize the Holy Roman Empire and simplify its structure, but also to reward the larger states, thereby binding them to his international system. Bavaria, Baden and Württemberg all made massive territorial gains, as did Prussia. In addition the rulers of Bavaria and Württemberg became kings, and the elector of Baden a grand duke. The undermining of the Habsburg emperor and the realignment of the new German states with France served to break the constitution of the old empire, and it was effectively dissolved with the final report of the committee of princes (*REICHSDEPUTATIONSHAUPTSCHLUSS*).

The Confederation of the Rhine, which replaced the old empire, was a loose association of French satellites presided over by a princely primate (*Fürstenprimas*), Karl Theodor, Freiherr von Dalberg. It expanded when Saxony joined (as a kingdom), and when it acquired Prussian territories west of the River Elbe. It was dissolved after the failure of Napoleon's Russian campaign in 1812.

Confessing Church. *See BEKENNENDE KIRCHE.*

Congress of Vienna. *See* VIENNA, CONGRESS OF.

Congress of Workers' and Soldiers' Councils (*Allgemeiner Kongress der Arbeiter- und Soldatenräte Deutschlands*), the 'parliament of the revolution', a meeting of delegates from workers' and soldiers' councils (*RÄTE*) throughout Germany between 16 and 20 December 1918 following the NOVEMBER REVOLUTION. The congress was arranged by the executive committee (*VOLLZUGSRAT*) in Berlin, following concerns that no coordinated action was being taken to revolutionize the government and administration of Germany. A meeting was arranged in Berlin for 16 December. Since there was no time to organize elections, local workers' and soldiers' councils were to choose their own delegates. In all, 489 delegates were selected to attend, and the meeting was held in Berlin from 16 to 20 December. At the congress 404 delegates represented workers' councils and 84 represented soldiers' councils. The 288 Majority Social Democrats (MSPD) comprised the largest single group from any party. In addition there were 80 Independent Socialists from the USPD, 25 Democrats, 10 Spartacists (members of the SPARTACUS LEAGUE), 11 United Revolutionaries, 25 delegates attached to a soldiers' delegation and 50 without specific party ties. Although there were calls from the radical left for a transition to a more revolutionary system of government based on the councils, the congress was dominated by Majority Social Democrats, who supported a parliamentary system. Following the withdrawal of the USPD, MSPD delegates controlled all the seats on the central council (*ZENTRALRAT*) elected by the congress to oversee the activities of the provisional Reich government, the COUNCIL OF PEOPLE'S REPRESENTATIVES, and the government of Prussia.

Congress system, a term applied to the international order established at the Congress of VIENNA. The aim of the system was to underpin the essentially conservative order promoted by METTERNICH and Tsar Alexander I (expressed symbolically in the so-called HOLY ALLIANCE). A Quadruple Alliance between Britain, Russia, Austria and Prussia was established on the same day as the second treaty of PARIS (20 November 1815), which concluded the Napoleonic Wars. The alliance was to provide for the diplomatic machinery necessary to enforce the treaty and maintain the peace, principally by means of further regular meetings of the Congress in order to govern the new international order through a 'concert of Europe'. France, which had in the meantime fulfilled the conditions of the second treaty of Paris, was drawn into the system at the Congress of AACHEN in 1818. At the Congress of TROPPAU (1820) the three major powers of the Holy Alliance dominated. Metternich won support for the principle of intervention in the affairs of other states in order to prevent the growth of liberalism and nationalism. Britain distanced itself from the outcome of the Congress of Troppau. Something of a gulf was developing between Britain and continental members of the Congress, particularly the repressive monarchies of eastern Europe (Austria, Russia and Prussia). The Congress of LAIBACH (1821) authorized Austrian intervention against the revolution in Naples, and the Congress of VERONA (1822) authorized military intervention against the liberal revolution in Spain. British ministers were inclined to support liberal movements on the continent, and were increasingly opposed to such action.

Conrad von Hötzendorf, Baron Franz (1853–1925), from 1915 Graf (Count) von Hötzendorf, chief of the Austro-Hungarian general staff (1906–11 and 1912–17). He was suspended from his post in 1911 for advocating a pre-emptive strike against Italy, and the same hawkish attitude characterized his response to the political crisis in the Balkans in 1914. He was dismissed again in 1917, and was an army group commander on the Italian front when the war came to an end.

Consul, a radical right-wing organization during the early years of the Weimar Republic.

Its members Heinrich Schulz and Heinrich Tillessen were responsible for the murder of the Centre Party politician Matthias ERZBERGER in August 1921. The organization was also suspected of responsibility for the assassination of the USPD leader Karl Gareis (1890–1921) in the Black Forest earlier the same year, but no-one was ever charged with the murder. Another member of the organization, the nationalist writer Ernst von SALOMON, was implicated in the murder of the DDP foreign minister Walther RATHENAU in June 1922, shortly after the signing of the treaty of RAPALLO.

Conti, Leonardo (1900–45), Nazi doctor. Born in Lugano, Switzerland, Conti studied medicine and practised in Berlin after World War I. He was an early member of the Nazi Party, and was promoted through the ranks of the SS, eventually to *Brigadeführer*. He founded the *NS-Ärztebund* (the Nazi Doctors' League), was state secretary in the Reich and Prussian health ministry, and also 'Reich health leader' and director of the *Hauptamt für Volksgesundheit* (National Health Head Office) from April 1939 to May 1945. He committed suicide in his cell at Nuremberg on 6 October 1945, and his estate was fined 3000 Marks by a DENAZIFICATION court.

Corinth, Lovis (1858–1925), artist. Corinth was born in Tapiau, East Prussia (now Gvardeisk in Russia). He studied at the art academy in KÖNIGSBERG (now Kaliningrad) and in Munich, Antwerp and Paris. He settled first in Munich in 1891, but after little success there, moved to Berlin in 1901. In Berlin he became friends with Max LIEBERMANN, founder of the Berlin SECESSION, and himself took over the chairmanship of the Secession in 1911 after Liebermann's resignation, later becoming president (1915). Corinth's work, which incorporated a number of styles, was influenced by expressionism in his later years. He died on a trip to Zandvoort in the Netherlands.

Corporate State, the name given to the dictatorship established in Austria in 1934 under Chancellor DOLLFUSS and further developed by his successor Kurt von SCHUSCHNIGG. The establishment of the Corporate State (based on the ideas of CORPORATISM) immediately followed the suppression of the labour movement in the short AUSTRIAN CIVIL WAR of February 1934. The constitution was drafted in May and reflected the influence of the Fascist dictatorship in Italy, and of the anti-democratic doctrines of the Roman Catholic Church (as formulated in the papal encyclical *Quadragesimo Anno* of 1931). Political parties were – theoretically – replaced with corporative institutions based on seven economic sectors, which had a consultative role in the constitution. Parties were replaced by the Fatherland Front, an unsuccessful mass organization with the modish outer trappings of fascism. The Social Democratic and Communist parties were banned, as was the Nazi Party after the assassination of Dollfuss in the attempted Nazi coup of July 1934. The system was never successful. Its conservative economic policies prolonged the Depression and its attempts to mobilize mass support and to foster a separate national identity were largely unsuccessful. It was swept away by the ANSCHLUSS of 1938.

corporatism, a political doctrine (originating in the 19th century but having a wider influence in the 1920s and 1930s) that sought to transcend class conflict in modern industrial societies by means of a system of 'corporations' or 'estates'. Such ideas, originally propagated by the Roman Catholic Church, contributed to fascist social thought, and were more explicit in Italy and Austria (*see* CORPORATE STATE) than in Germany.

Council of Ministers (*Ministerrat*), the government of the GERMAN DEMOCRATIC REPUBLIC. It was formally accountable to the People's Chamber (*VOLKSKAMMER*) but was effectively controlled by the SED.

Council of People's Representatives (*Rat der Volksbeauftragten*), the entirely Social Democratic government of Germany formed during the NOVEMBER REVOLUTION of 1918. Its formation followed negotiations between the Majority and Independent Social Democrats (MSPD and USPD) and representatives of the Revolutionary Shop Stewards. The term 'representative' in the name of the body was proposed by Otto LANDSBERG, as an alternative to the word 'commissar', which was felt to be tainted with Bolshevism. The council had six members with nominally equal rights, but was effectively under the leadership of Friedrich EBERT for the MSPD and Hugo HAASE for the USPD. The government's election was confirmed by a meeting of soldiers' councils in the Reichstag on 9 November, which also elected an executive committee of the Berlin councils movement with a claim of control over the government. The three USPD members left the government on 29 December under pressure from their party, and Gustav NOSKE and Rudolf WISSELL joined it instead. It remained in power until 10 February 1919, when it was superseded by the government formed after elections to the constituent NATIONAL ASSEMBLY.

Creditanstalt, leading Austrian bank whose collapse in 1931 precipitated a financial crisis. The effects of the crash led to a banking crisis in central Europe that deepened the economic depression in Germany.

CSU (*Christlich-Soziale Union*), the Christian Social Union, a German conservative party with Bavarian particularist tendencies. The CSU was founded in Würzburg on 13 October 1945 by former members of the interwar Bavarian People's Party (BVP). It has been consistently to the right of the CDU politically, and – especially under the leadership of Franz-Josef STRAUSS – it adopted a more hawkish attitude towards the Eastern Bloc. Although an independent party it is effectively the Bavarian wing of the CDU in the same way that the BVP was the Bavarian wing of the CENTRE PARTY. The CSU won an absolute majority of votes (52.3%) in the first elections to the Bavarian LANDTAG (1

December 1946). It has formed the government of Bavaria almost continually since the war, albeit at first in coalition with smaller parties, although it has had an absolute majority in the Landtag since 1966, and has won over half the votes in every regional election since 1970 (and 62.1% in 1974).

Cuno, Wilhelm (1876–1933), non-party chancellor (1922–3) during the WEIMAR REPUBLIC. Cuno was born in Suhl, Thuringia, and after graduating in law in 1907 he began a career in the imperial treasury and took over as director general of the Hamburg–America (Hapag) shipping line in 1918. He took part in the armistice and REPARATIONS negotiations, and became chancellor in 1922. Cuno responded to the French and Belgian occupation of the Rhineland in 1923 with an appeal for passive resistance, a policy that crippled the industries of the Ruhr valley and fuelled hyperinflation (*see* INFLATION). He resigned in August after an SPD motion of no confidence in his government, resumed his business career and became chairman of the Hamburg–America Line (1926–30).

Curtius, Julius (1877–1948), conservative politician. The son of an industrialist, Curtius studied law and practised as a lawyer in his native Duisburg until 1910, when he resumed his studies in Heidelberg. He served as an officer in World War I and was a co-founder of the *Deutsche Liberale Volkspartei* (DVP) in Heidelberg in 1919. He was a member of the Reichstag for the DVP from 1920 until his exclusion from the party in 1932 (after which he sat briefly for the *Deutsche Staatspartei*, formally the DDP), and was Reich economics minister under Hans LUTHER, Wilhelm MARX and Hermann MÜLLER from 1926 to 1929. He became foreign minister after the death of STRESEMANN, and worked to ensure that the YOUNG PLAN was accepted. He resigned in 1931 when plans for an Austro-German Customs Union were thwarted. He then practised as a lawyer in Mecklenburg until the expropriation of his estate there by the Soviets in 1945. He then returned to Heidelberg and died there in 1948.

customs union. *See* ZOLLVEREIN.

Czernin von und zu Chudenitz, Count Ottokar von (1872–1932), Austrian diplomat and politician; foreign minister (1916–18). Born in Dymokury, Bohemia, into the Czech aristocracy, Czernin pursued a diplomatic career, and was posted to France and the Netherlands. He was elected to the Bohemian diet in 1903 as a conservative, and defended the interests of the aristocracy against democratization. He was Austro-Hungarian minister in Bucharest from 1913 to 1916, and was appointed foreign minister in 1916 after the death of Franz Joseph and the accession of Karl. He left office in 1918 following the French revelation of earlier secret peace negotiations between Austria and the Entente.

D

Dachau, Bavarian village near Munich, the site of one of the earliest Nazi CONCENTRATION CAMPS. It was established in 1933 under the command of Theodor EICKE and run by SS Death's Head units. It was initially used for the mass imprisonment of the government's political opponents on the left, but the Austrian dictator Kurt von SCHUSCHNIGG and the former French prime minister Léon Blum were also among the inmates. Dachau was famous for the brutal treatment of prisoners, and medical experiments were carried out there on healthy patients during the early 1940s. The camp has been preserved as a museum.

Dada, iconoclastic international art (and anti-art) movement that originated in Zurich, Switzerland, during World War I. It was a nihilistic movement that produced provocative work attacking conventional assumptions of artistic value and bourgeois values generally. It was critical of the war and Germany's conduct of it. The Berlin Dada group, which included John HEARTFIELD, George GROSZ and Hanna Höch, organized an 'International Dada Fair' in the Dada Club in 1920. Dada was introduced into Cologne in 1919 by Max ERNST, and an exhibition there was first closed by the police then allowed to go ahead, prompting the slogan *'Dada siegt'* ('Dada is victorious'). The *Merz* art of Kurt SCHWITTERS in Hanover developed from Dada, which also anticipated the surrealist movement.

DAF (*Deutsche Arbeitsfront*), the German Labour Front, a labour organization set up in 1933 by the Nazis to replace the trade unions. From 2 May 1933 the existing trade unions were dissolved, their offices occupied, their property plundered and their leaders and officials were beaten up or imprisoned (or both) They were replaced by the DAF, led by Robert LEY, and the function of the new organization was to maintain peace within the factory community (*BETRIEBSGEMEINSCHAFT*). It was not permitted to intervene in industrial disputes (which were in any case illegal) or attempt to secure wage increases (although in practice the DAF did sometimes manage to achieve limited concessions for workers at a local level). The regulation of wages and working hours were to be overseen by the Reich trustees of labour appointed in 1933. The role of the DAF was to educate workers into the Nazi system and to mobilize support through propaganda, meetings and parades. It was also responsible for encouraging people to take part in the Nazi leisure organization STRENGTH THROUGH JOY (*Kraft durch Freude*, KdF), but although workers participated in the organization's more modest activities, most of the showpiece trips abroad were reserved for 'bigwigs', which only served to generate scepticism and resentment.

Dagover, Lil (1897–1980), German film star, born in Java. She appeared in *The Cabinet of Doctor Caligari*, and worked in German cinema

89

throughout the Weimar Republic and the Nazi dictatorship. Her career continued until the late 1970s and she died in Munich.

Dahlem, Ernst (1892–1981), Communist politician. Dahlem was born in Rohrbach, Lorraine, into a Catholic working-class family. He joined the SPD in 1913, and then the USPD in 1918 after serving in World War I. He was a member of a Workers' and Soldiers' Council in Allenstein in 1918, and then moved to Cologne, where he became editor of the USPD paper *Sozialistische Republik*. He joined the German Communist Party (KPD) in 1920, and was elected to represent his new party in the Prussian Landtag (1920–4). When the Nazis came to power Dahlem joined the Communist underground resistance, and then went to Paris, where he replaced Walter ULBRICHT as head of the Communist Party's foreign organization there. He was arrested in France in 1941 and imprisoned in Mauthausen concentration camp in Austria until the end of the war. From 1945 to 1953 he was a member of both the Central Committee and the Politburo of the SED (the East German Socialist Unity Party), but was dismissed after further disagreements with Ulbricht. He was gradually rehabilitated between 1956 and 1971.

Dahlmann, Friedrich (Christoph) (1785–1860), liberal politician and historian. Dahlmann was born in Wismar in Mecklenburg, and taught history at Kiel and Göttingen, where he was one of the GÖTTINGEN SEVEN. He then moved to Leipzig, Jena and, eventually, to Bonn. He became one of the most prominent leaders of the liberals at the FRANKFURT PARLIAMENT in 1848. His ideas were written into a draft constitution, which envisaged the creation of a 'small Germany' (*KLEINDEUTSCHLAND*) united under Prussia, and Dahlmann went with the delegation from the parliament to offer the imperial crown of Germany to FRIEDRICH WILHELM IV, who turned it down. A few years after the demise of the parliament Dahlmann retired from public life.

***Daily Telegraph* affair,** the political aftermath of an indiscreet interview given by WILHELM II to the British newspaper in 1908. The Kaiser protested about British suspicions, claiming that he was a true friend of Britain, but that the German authorities were scarcely able to restrain the popular anti-Britishness of the middle and lower classes. The Kaiser had sent a draft of the article to BÜLOW, his chancellor, who said he had not read it. Wilhelm thought that he had done so and approved the text in order to see Bülow humiliated. In any event the chancellor resigned in the wake of the affair.

Daimler, Gottlieb (1834–1900), engineer and businessman. Daimler was born in Schorndorf and studied at the Stuttgart Polytechnical Institute. He was technical director of the engineering firm Deutz AG from 1872 to 1881. In 1882 he opened an experimental workshop in Cannstatt, now part of Stuttgart, with Wilhelm Maybach (1846–1929), and developed engines first for a two-wheeled wooden construction (thought to be the first motorcycle) and then for a boat. In 1889 Daimler and Maybach constructed their first purpose-design four-wheeled automobile. The Daimler Automobile Society (Daimler-Motoren-Gesellschaft) was founded in 1890 and made four-cylinder engines for the first Mercedes cars from 1899. The Daimler company merged with that of Carl Friedrich BENZ in 1926.

D'Alquen, Gunter (1910–), SS officer. Born in Essen, he joined the Hitler Youth in 1925 and the SS in 1931. He was appointed editor of the anti-Semitic SS paper *Das Schwarze Korps* in 1935. After the war he was fined by denazification courts in 1955 and 1958.

Daluege, Kurt (1897–1946), SS officer. Born in Kreuzburg, Upper Silesia, he served in World War I and studied at the Technical High School in Berlin. He joined a FREIKORPS unit, then the Nazi Party (1922), and was leader of the Berlin SA until 1928, before moving to the SS. He was elected to the Prussian LANDTAG in 1932, and later to the

Reichstag. He became director of the Prussian police and head of the ORPO in 1933, and deputy head of the German police in 1936. Daluege was an important figure in the SS, and was appointed deputy protector of Bohemia and Moravia after the death of HEYDRICH. He was executed by the Czechs in 1946.

Danzig, German name for the city of Gdańsk, now in Poland, on the Baltic coast at the mouth of the River Vistula. It was an old Hanseatic port, and in 1919 it was separated from Germany and designated a 'free city' to be administered by the League of Nations. In addition, at VERSAILLES a strip of land was awarded to Poland (the Polish Corridor) to ensure access to the sea. This separated Danzig (and East Prussia) from the main territory of the Reich. German irredentist claims to both territories were the ostensible reason for the invasion of Poland in 1939.

DAP. *See DEUTSCHE ARBEITERPARTEI.*

Darré, Richard Walter (1895–1953), Nazi politician. Born in Buenos Aires, Darré attended school in Germany and England, and served in World War I. After the war he joined first a FREIKORPS unit and then the Nazi Party. He spent time at the German embassy in Riga as a representative of German agricultural interests in 1928 and 1929, and was nominal head of the Nazi Party's agricultural policy section in 1930. He was appointed Reich farmers' leader, Reich minister for food and Prussian minister of agriculture in 1933. He was also a senior SS officer and head of the RUSHA. A proponent of *BLUT UND BODEN* ('blood and soil') ideology, he published a number of racist works on the land and the peasantry, and his ministry introduced the REICH ENTAILED FARM LAW. His inefficiency led to his marginalization, and his corrupt involvement in the black market led to his removal from office in 1942. He was tried and sentenced to five years' imprisonment after the war, and died in Munich after his release.

Däumig, Ernst (1866–1922), socialist politician. Däumig was born in Merseburg into a middle-class family and studied theology. He joined the French foreign legion in 1887, and then pursued a career as an officer in the Prussian army (from 1893). He left the army in 1898 and joined the SPD, working on a number of Social Democratic newspapers before joining the party newspaper *Vorwärts* in 1911. He was on the left of the party, and was a co-founder of the USPD in 1917. He was a leader of the Berlin shop stewards' movement and urged a more radical revolution in government and the economy, particularly at the CONGRESS OF WORKERS' AND SOLDIERS' COUNCILS in Berlin in December 1918. He became president of the USPD in 1919 and was elected to the Reichstag (1920–2). He hesitated to join the KPD (the German Communist Party) but wanted the USPD to join the Communist International. When the USPD split, however, he joined the KPD, but returned to SPD shortly before his death in 1922.

David, Eduard Heinrich (1863–1930), Social Democratic politician. David was born the son of a civil servant in Ediger (Mosel). He began his career as a schoolteacher in Giessen, but was forced out of his job on political grounds. He was editor of a number of Social Democratic newspapers, and after World War I was elected the first president of the Weimar NATIONAL ASSEMBLY (albeit for a matter of days before the presidency passed to the CENTRE PARTY). He was minister without portfolio in the SCHEIDEMANN government, and then interior minister in the administration of Gustav BAUER. He remained a minister (without portfolio) in the next government under Hermann MÜLLER (March–June 1920). From 1921 to 1927 he was the Reich government's representative in Hesse.

DAW (*Deutsche Ausrüstungswerke GmbH*), German Armaments Works, a subsidiary organization of the SS established in 1939.

Dawes Plan, a revised REPARATIONS plan presented to the Allied Reparations Committee in 1924 by Charles G. Dawes (1865–1951), an American banker. Its aim was to devise a more realistic schedule for reparations payments by Germany, which had fallen into default. The state bank was to be reorganized, and loans provided to enable Germany to make its annual payments of 2500 million marks. The loans stabilized the economy, created the illusion of economic (and political) stability in the late 1920s, and enabled Germany to make reparations payments until 1929, when the Dawes Plan was succeeded by the YOUNG PLAN.

DBD (*Demokratische Bauernpartei Deutschlands*), Democratic Farmers' Party of Germany. The party was founded in 1948 in the Soviet zone of occupation. It merged with the CDU of the GERMAN DEMOCRATIC REPUBLIC in 1990.

D-Day (6 June 1944), 'Deliverance Day', code name for the first day of the Allied invasion of German-occupied Europe. Three divisions of British and Canadian troops landed to the west of the River Orne in Normandy on 6 June, along with two divisions from the US army at the mouth of the River Vire. There were 10,000 Allied casualties, but the beachheads were secured.

DDP (*Deutsche Demokratische Partei*), the German Democratic Party, a liberal party of the WEIMAR REPUBLIC. The DDP was founded by a group of intellectuals and businessmen in November 1918, and constituted a merger of the Progressive Party (*DEUTSCHE FORTSCHRITTSPARTEI*) of the imperial period and the left wing of the NATIONAL LIBERAL PARTY. Its members played an important part in drafting the Weimar constitution, and it won 18.5% of the vote in the elections to the constituent NATIONAL ASSEMBLY in 1919. But although it took part in most of the coalitions of the 1920s, its share of the vote declined rapidly after the formation of the DVP. It was renamed the German State Party (*Deutsche Staatspartei*) in 1930, and moved to the right. The party dissolved itself in the spring of 1933.

DDR (*Deutsche Demokratische Republik*). *See* GERMAN DEMOCRATIC REPUBLIC.

Defence League, German (*Deutscher Wehrverein*), one of a number of radical right-wing (*VÖLKISCH*) pressure groups founded in Germany before World War I. It is also referred to in English as the Army League. Founded in 1911 in the wake of the second Morocco (AGADIR) crisis by August Keim, a member of the PAN-GERMAN LEAGUE. Its membership grew rapidly from 33,000 in 1912 to 90,000 in 1914. During World War I it was involved in anti-British agitation in Ireland, the British colonies and the United States, where money was raised for the German war effort. The Defence League was determined to survive defeat and the Weimar Republic, but had only 250 members by 1922. It was dissolved in 1935.

degenerate art (*entartete Kunst*), term applied to modernist and non-representational art deemed by the Nazis to be unsuitable and racially contaminated. The Nazis set up a Combat League for German Culture in 1928, whose purpose was to denigrate modern art as a symptom of social degeneracy. Modern art was disapproved of and suppressed after 1933, and in 1937 two exhibitions were staged at the Haus der deutschen Kunst, a new museum built by the Nazis in Munich. The first was the 'Great Exhibition of Art', which showed work approved of by the Nazis. It was the first of eight annual exhibitions of approved German art between 1937 and 1944. The second exhibition of 1937 was of 'degenerate' art. This exhibition drew on a stock of paintings confiscated by Goebbels, of which many were later sold abroad, and comprised the work of almost every significant artist in Germany.

degenerate music (*entartete Musik*), a term applied to modern music and to some forms of popular music considered by the Nazis to be racially tainted. This included atonal music, which was considered 'abnormal', and works by Jewish composers. Disapproval was expressed, for example, of the work of

Alban BERG, Hanns Eisler (1898–1962) and Ernst Křenek. Composers such as Gustav MAHLER and Arnold SCHOENBERG were rejected by the Nazis because they were Jewish. Richard WAGNER, on the other hand, was celebrated, and Carl ORFF was particularly popular. Other major composers were presented in such a way as to emphasize their ethnic affinity with the German people, among them Bach, Beethoven and Mozart. Modern popular music was seen both as alien and as a product of the decadent West, and jazz especially was considered undesirable on racist grounds. An exhibition entitled 'Degenerate Music' was put on in Düsseldorf in 1938.

Dehler, Thomas (1897–1967), politician. Dehler was a lawyer before World War II, and a member of the liberal DDP. He was imprisoned in a work camp as an opponent of the Nazis. After the war he resumed his political engagement in the FDP and was a member of the PARLIAMENTARY COUNCIL (1948–9). He was justice minister under Adenauer (1949–53) and leader of the FDP parliamentary party (1954–7). He was vice president of the Bundestag from 1960 to 1967.

Delbrück, Adalbert Gottlieb (1822–1890), banker. Born in Magdeburg, Delbrück studied law and practised as a lawyer before founding the banking house Delbrück Leo & Co. in Berlin in 1854. He was a co-founder of the Deutsche Bank in 1870.

denazification, a policy agreed in principle by the Allies at the YALTA CONFERENCE (February 1945), but which was interpreted differently in the different zones of occupied Germany. The Soviets concentrated on eliminating the social and political elites they held responsible for Nazism and the war, while in the western zones, where Nazism was perceived to be a popular phenomenon, mass screening of individuals was foreseen. At the centre of the denazification process were the NUREMBERG TRIALS, but the numbers dealt with there were limited.

The first stage of denazification was a series of mass arrests in all four zones. In the American zone there had been 95,250 such arrests by the end of 1946, and almost half of those detained had been released again. In the Soviet zone 67,179 people had been arrested (of these 8214 were subsequently released); in the British zone 64,500 (of whom more than half had since been freed); and in the French zone 18,963 (8214 of whom had been released).

In the second phase the Allies attempted to categorize Germans according to their degree of culpability and complicity with the regime. The Law for the Liberation from National Socialism of May 1946 divided former Nazis into five such categories, ranging from major offenders to fellow travellers and the exonerated. The process was of such bureaucratic complexity that it quickly ran into the sands. Many of those who found themselves in one of the more serious categories were able to provide evidence of their innocence, often from a clergyman (such documents were called *Persilscheine*, or 'Persil certificates', for their cleansing powers), and the whole procedure was frustrated by a growing reluctance on behalf of the people generally to accept the Allies' charge of collective guilt or to cooperate with the denazification procedures. In addition, a disproportionate number of Nazis had been educated people in administrative, technical or managerial jobs, who were now urgently needed for reconstruction. Moreover, in the context of the Cold War, the Allies realized that such former Nazis were the most reliable anti-communists. Serious offenders were recategorized as fellow travellers on the strength of simple expressions of religious piety, and even Alfred HUGENBERG was eventually classified as a fellow traveller.

The third phase of denazification was left to the FEDERAL REPUBLIC after 1949, and the Bundestag recommended in 1950 that the process be quickly wound up. The last of a number of regional laws bringing the process to a conclusion was passed in Bavaria in 1954. Unsurprisingly, most of those who had been screened by 1949 had been placed in the fourth (1,006,874) or fifth (1,213,873) category, and far fewer in the first three groups. Nevertheless there were striking differences of distribution between the two least culpable groups in the American and British zones. In the US zone over half of those screened were placed in the fourth category (fellow travellers), and only 1.9% were exonerated. In the British zone on the other hand the situation was reversed, and only 10.9% were counted as fellow travellers, while 58.4% were exonerated. The whole procedure generated a degree of scepticism both in Germany itself and among the Allies.

Dertinger, Georg (1902–68), politician. Born in Berlin, Dertinger was a member of the German nationalist DNVP during the Weimar Republic, and editor of the radical right-wing newspaper *Stahlhelm*. He was a co-founder of the CDU in the Soviet zone of occupation in 1945, and secretary general of the party in the Soviet zone from 1946. He was foreign minister of the German Democratic Republic from 1949 to 1953 and in that capacity signed the Görlitz treaty (6 July 1950), which recognized the ODER–NEISSE LINE as a border 'of peace and friendship' between East Germany and Poland. In 1953 he was arrested as a spy, and sentenced to 15 years' imprisonment. He was released in 1964 and died four years later in Leipzig.

Deutsche Arbeiterpartei (DAP), the German Workers' Party, a radical right-wing party founded in Trautenau, Bohemia in 1904. It was an organizational predecessor of the Munich DEUTSCHE ARBEITERPARTEI, which became the Nazi Party. German workers in the towns of Bohemia and Moravia, already resentful of the economic competition from the influx of cheap Czech labour from the countryside, were incensed at the role of Czech strike-breakers in a major local strike

during 1900. Their disaffection was exploited by the breakaway VÖLKISCH unions who formed the DAP. The party has been called 'pre-fascist', and it bore some characteristics that were unwelcome to leading figures on the radical right. Georg von SCHÖNERER considered it too exclusively proletarian, and thought that its racial prejudice arose from a specific local grievance rather than a coherent ideological system. Its anti-Semitism, such as it was, in the early days was directed against the Austrian Social Democratic Workers' Party, which was perceived to be dominated by Jews; and it was resistant to the notion of uncritical obedience to a leader. It renamed itself the *Deutsche Nationalsozialistische Arbeiterpartei* (German National Socialist Workers' Party) in 1918, and split in 1923 into the *Deutschsozialer Verein* (German Social Association) led by Walter Riehl, and the Schulz group. Most members eventually joined the Austrian branch of the German Nazi Party.

Deutsche Arbeiterpartei (DAP), the German Workers' Party, a radical right-wing party that was founded in Munich after World War I by Anton DREXLER and Hermann ESSER. It was one of several similar small groups that emerged from the Fatherland Party (*VATERLANDSPARTEI*). HITLER became member number 7 in September 1919, after being charged by the army with surveillance of the group's activities and making a barnstorming speech at one of the meetings. In April 1920 the party's name was changed to the *Nationalsozialistische Deutsche Arbeiterpartei* (NSDAP) – the Nazi Party.

Deutsche Arbeitsfront. *See* DAF.

Deutsche Aufbaupartei (DAP, German Reconstruction Party), a radical right-wing party founded in West Germany in 1946 by Joachim von Ostau and Reinhold Wulle. It later became the DEUTSCHE RECHTS-PARTEI.

Deutsche Christen. *See* GERMAN CHRISTIANS.

Deutsche Demokratische Partei. *See* DDP.

Deutsche Demokratische Republik (DDR). *See* GERMAN DEMOCRATIC REPUBLIC.

Deutsche Evangelische Kirche. *See* EVANGEL-
ICAL CHURCH; GERMAN CHRISTIANS.

Deutsche Fortschrittspartei, the Progress
Party or the 'Progressives', a political party
founded in June 1861 by a radical group that
broke away from the liberals in the Prussian
LANDTAG. Its leadership was dominated by
landowners and members of the educated
middle classes. In an election of December
of that year they won 110 seats and became
the largest party in the Chamber of Deputies.
It was the Progressives who asserted the
rights of the house against the king, Wilhelm I, precipitating a crisis over the Army
Bill. The king dissolved the house, but the
party then returned after an election in May
1862 with 135 seats and overall control. The
king refused to concede sovereignty on military matters and it was this crisis that BIS-
MARCK was recalled from Paris to resolve.

Deutsche Freisinnige Partei, a liberal party
formed in 1884 from the left wing of the
DEUTSCHE FORTSCHRITTSPARTEI and the *Liberale Vereinigung* (Liberal Union). It was the
only bourgeois party to oppose Bismarck.
'Freisinnig' was a term preferred by north
German left-liberals and carried the sense of
anti-clerical. It has been compared with the
British term 'radical'.

Deutsche Front, a centre-right coalition of
political parties in the SAARLAND in 1933 and
1934. It was dissolved with the reincor-
poration of the Saarland into the Reich
in 1935.

Deutscher Gewerkschaftsbund. *See* DGB.

Deutsche Kommunistische Partei (DKP),
successor party to the KPD, which was declared illegal in the Federal Republic in 1956. The
DKP was founded in 1968, but by then faced
competition from other left-wing groups,
and also carried the stigma of prohibition
and association with the GERMAN DEMOCRAT-
IC REPUBLIC. It failed to attract more than a
tiny following, and its ideological (and material) position was undermined by the collapse of the GDR and the Soviet Union.

Deutsche Konservative Partei (DKP), the
German Conservative Party, a radical right-
wing party formed in 1946 by Hermann
Klingspor and Joachim von Ostau. It won
0.3% of the vote in regional elections in
Hamburg in 1946 and Lower Saxony in April
1947, and 3.1% in Schleswig-Holstein in
September 1947.

Deutsche National-Zeitung. *See* NATIONAL-
ZEITUNG.

Deutsche Partei (DP), the German Party,
founded in 1947. It was a successor party
to the Lower Saxon Regional Party (*Nieder-
sächsische Landespartei*) and to the DEUTSCH-
HANNOVERSCHE PARTEI (German Hanoverian
Party). It was politically conservative and
federalist in orientation in the WELF tradition. It was represented in the centre-right
coalitions of Konrad ADENAUER from 1949
to 1960. It absorbed the short-lived *FREIE
VOLKSPARTEI* in 1957, and was eventually
subsumed into the *Gesamtdeutsche Partei* (All
German Party) in 1961.

Deutsche Rechts-Partei (DRP), a radical right-
wing party established in 1946 by Josef
Bürger, Wilhelm Meinberg, Joachim von
Ostau, Adolf von Thadden, Wolf Graf von
Westarp and others. It was a successor to the
DEUTSCHE AUFBAUPARTEI.

Deutsche Reichspartei, (the German 'Reich
Party') the name of the *FREIKONSERVATIVE
PARTEI* (Free Conservative Party) after the
unification of Germany in 1871. A second,
radical right-wing *Deutsche Reichspartei* was
founded in 1946. It was dissolved in 1964–5,
and most of its members joined the National
Democratic Party (NPD).

Deutscher Flottenverein. *See* NAVY LEAGUE.

Deutscher Hof, the name given to the democratic left faction at the 1848 FRANKFURT
PARLIAMENT. Like other groupings in the parliament, it took its name from the place
where it met in the town. The majority of the
56 members of the group were either senior
civil servants or members of the professions.

Deutscher Kolonialverein, the German
Colonial Association, founded in 1882 by
Baron von Maltzan and Hermann, Fürst zu

HOHENLOHE-LANGENBURG. The association sought to divert German emigration from the English-speaking world to potential settlement colonies under the German flag. It had a membership of 9000 by 1884. In 1887 it joined the Society for German Colonization (*Gesellschaft für deutsche Kolonisation*) to form the German Colonial Society (*Deutsche Kolonialgesellschaft*).

Deutscher Nationalverband (German National League), an umbrella organization for German nationalist deputies to the Austrian REICHSRAT. It was founded in 1907.

Deutscher Ostmarkenverein. *See* OSTMARKEN-VEREIN.

Deutscher Wehrverein. *See* DEFENCE LEAGUE, GERMAN.

Deutscher Werkbund (DWB, 'German association of craftsmen'), an association of artisans, artists, designers and architects founded in Munich in 1907. Among its founding members were the following: Peter BEHRENS, the architect and designer; the architect Theodor Fischer (1862–1938); the Austrian architect Josef HOFFMANN; the architect and art critic Hermann Muthesius (1861–1927); the Bavarian architect and designer Richard Riemerschmid (1868–1957); and the Belgian Art Nouveau architect Henry van de Velde (1863–1957). Similar associations were founded in Austria in 1912 and in Switzerland the following year. The *Deutscher Werkbund* was inspired by the English Arts and Crafts movement, and the people who founded it had been part of an 'applied arts movement' before 1907. It had about 500 members in1908 and almost 2000 in 1914. The importance of individual expression in modern design was important to many of its members, especially Henry van de Velde and his followers. The *Werkbund* also wanted to apply its aesthetic criteria to machine-made goods, and Hermann Muthesius in particular was a proponent of mass production and standard form.

Deutsches Frauenwerk, literally 'German Women's Work', a Nazi organization set up in 1933 as an umbrella for all existing German women's organizations. It was effectively an adjunct of the NS-FRAUENSCHAFT.

Deutsches Jungvolk, Nazi organization for younger boys (aged 10–14), before they moved up to the HITLER YOUTH. It had 28,691 members at the end of 1932, shortly before the appointment of HITLER as chancellor the following January. By the beginning of 1939 it had 2.1 million members.

Deutsche Staatspartei. *See* DDP.

Deutsche Volkspartei. *See* DVP.

Deutsche Volksunion (German People's Union, DVU), a radical right-wing political party founded in 1987. It won its first seat in Bremen in 1987, and was elected to the regional diet in Schleswig-Holstein in 1992. It won almost 13% of the vote and 16 seats in Saxony-Anhalt in 1998, and a further 5 seats in Brandenburg in 1999. From 1987 to 1990 the party formed an electoral alliance with the long-established radical right-wing NPD.

Deutschhannoversche Partei, the German Hanoverian Party, founded in 1866–9 to represent the particularist interests of Hanover in the new Germany. Its mantle was inherited by the *DEUTSCHE PARTEI* after World War II. It was also referred to as the WELF Party.

Deutschkonservative Partei, the German Conservative Party, founded in 1876 from a number of conservative factions. The old Prussian conservatives represented the interests of the JUNKER aristocracy. They dominated the upper chamber of the Prussian diet (*HERRENHAUS*) and were also strongly represented in the lower chamber (*ABGE-ORDNETENHAUS*). They disagreed fundamentally with BISMARCK's policy of German unification, however, and as a result spent much of the 1870s in the political wilderness. They lost 35 of their 57 seats in the Reichstag elections of 1874 and decided to come to terms with the new imperial order, and with Bismarck.

The new German Conservative Party of 1876 was founded with the support of leading representatives of the Prussian landed interest, and with economic issues high on the agenda. Led by Ernst von HEYDEBRAND UND DER LASA, the party recognized the new German constitution, but sought to preserve the old order against further encroachments on the privileges of the monarchy, and against secularization and democracy. The party's regional strength was in northeastern Germany, and its members continued – as they had always done – to defend above all the landed interest. They were opposed to the continuance of free trade, and specifically wanted to reverse the decision of 1873 to remove the iron tariff. Above all, however, they wanted to emphasize the 'agrarian question'. Germany had ceased to be an exporter and become an importer of grain, and the East Elbian landowners were prepared to come to terms both with the Reich and to some extent with industry in order to protect their own interests. In the 1877 elections the German Conservatives increased their vote from almost 359,959 to 526,039, and took 40 seats in the Reichstag. After the next election in 1878 that number increased to 59. Bismarck himself was not averse to a new conservative alliance that would end the hegemony of the NATIONAL LIBERALS, and during the course of the following years the Conservatives helped pass the tariff and tax reforms that broke the National Liberal Party.

When, following the dismissal of Bismarck in 1890, the new chancellor, Leo von CAPRIVI, embarked on a more liberal course, the Conservatives resumed their oppositional stance. Indeed in 1892 they adopted the more radically right-wing Tivoli programme, which not only restated their profound hostility to the Social Democrats (SPD), but also – at the prompting of Adolf STOECKER – expressed antipathy towards the 'destructive influence' of the Jews. The party was somewhat mollified by the protectionist policies of Chancellor von BÜLOW, but remained adamantly opposed to any mea-

sures that might erode the position of the landed aristocracy. Under the influence of pressure groups such as the AGRARIAN LEAGUE the party degenerated into a sectional interest group with a declining electoral constituency. During World War I the party adopted a hawkish stance. It was in favour of a *Siegesfrieden*, a victory peace with annexations. Most of its members and supporters transferred their allegiance to the DNVP after the end of the war.

Deutschlandhalle, a gigantic covered hall built in Berlin in nine months during 1935. The Deutschlandhalle was 140 m (460 ft) long, 120 m (395 ft) wide and 25 m (80 ft) high, and it cost 3.9 million Reichsmarks. Hitler addressed 16,000 people at the opening, but although there had clearly been some consideration given to the possibility of holding rallies there, the Nazis generally preferred the Sportpalast in the Potsdamer Strasse, and the Deutschlandhalle itself was mainly used for sport and entertainment.

Deutschlandlied, poem, also known as *'Deutschland über alles'* ('Germany above everything'), written by Hoffmann von Fallersleben in 1841 and set to Haydn's music of 1797 (which was also used for an Austrian patriotic anthem). It became the German national anthem in 1922. The first verse, which describes the borders of a 'GREATER GERMANY', was abandoned after World War II in favour of the second verse, which begins with the words 'unity and right and freedom'.

Deutschnationale Volkspartei. See DNVP.

Deutschvölkische Freiheitspartei (DVFP, German National Freedom Party or German Racialist Freedom Party). This was the principal party of the radical *völkisch* right outside Bavaria during the early 1920s. It followed the *Deutschvölkische Partei* (German Racialist party) of 1914, which had become the *Deutschvölkischer Bund* (German Racialist League) in 1918. The latter was banned in 1922, and the DVFP was formed in the same year by three dissident members of the nationalist DNVP. Although it was close to the Nazi Party (NSDAP) in many respects, it was perceived as too 'bourgeois' by many Nazis. In the wake of the failed BEER HALL PUTSCH of 1923, however, the disarray on the radical right (and particularly in the Nazi Party itself) was such that the two parties nevertheless combined their resources to fight the election of 4 May 1924 together as the *Völkischsozialer Block.* ('national social' or 'racial social' bloc) and together won 6.55% of the vote. General LUDENDORFF represented the DVFP in the Reichstag from 1924 to 1928.

Deutschvölkischer Schutz- und Trutzbund, radical right-wing anti-Semitic organization formed on the initiative of the PAN-GERMAN LEAGUE. It was founded in 1919 and recruited mainly from the middle classes. It served to channel the support of the Pan-German League in the direction of the Nazi Party.

DGB (*Deutscher Gewerkschaftsbund*, German Trade Union Association), the trade unions' umbrella organization in the Federal Republic of Germany. It was established in 1949 and embraces a number of single trade unions or 'unity' unions (*Einheitsgewerkschaften*) which bring together in a single union all the workers in a particular workplace or industry. The DGB is not explicitly party political and there are supporters of all the main political parties represented in its leadership, but it is dominated by the SPD.

Dickopf, Paul(inus) (1910–73), police officer. A detective from 1939, Dickopf left Germany in 1942, and acted as adviser to the American military administration after the war. From 1952 he was head of the German central office of Interpol, and president of the *Bundeskriminalamt* (federal criminal office) from 1965 to 1971. From 1968 to 1972 he was president of Interpol.

Dieckhoff, Hans Heinrich von (1884–1952), diplomat. Dieckhoff was embassy counsellor in Washington (1922–6) and London

(1926–30), and subsequently (1930–6) head of Section III of the Foreign Office, which dealt with Britain and the United States. He was briefly acting state secretary (1936–7) and then ambassador in Washington (1937–41). He then became ambassador in Madrid (1943–5).

Dieckmann, Friedrich (1893–1969), politician. Dieckmann was born in Fischerhude, now part of Ottersberg near Bremen. He was a member of the conservative German People's Party (DVP) during the Weimar Republic, and worked closely with Gustav STRESEMANN. He was general secretary of the party from 1919 to 1933, when it was dissolved by the Nazis. He was an official in an industrial organization during the Third Reich. He joined the LDPD in the Soviet zone of occupation in 1945, and was deputy president of the party from 1949 to 1969. He was president of the *VOLKSKAMMER* in the German Democratic Republic and deputy chairman of the state council (STAATSRAT).

Diels, Rudolf (1900–57), first head of the GESTAPO. Diels studied law at Marburg after serving in World War I. He became a civil servant in the Prussian interior ministry in 1930 under SEVERING, and was charged with undertaking police measures against political extremists. After the Nazi takeover of power he was appointed head of section Ia of the Prussian state police by GÖRING and was active in the purge of republican public servants. He was unable to negotiate the power struggle between HIMMLER and Göring for control of the police, and was dismissed in 1934. He held other minor posts, and continued a career in local and national administration in the early years of the Federal Republic. He accidentally shot himself in 1957.

Dienstmann, Karl (1885–1962), diplomat. Dienstmann was consul in Leningrad (1922–5), counsellor in the Moscow embassy (1925–6), consul in Odessa (1926–31) and Tbilisi (1931–6). After a spell at the foreign office (1936–40) he returned to Leningrad as consul general (1940–1), and was subsequently consul in Zurich (1943–5).

Diesel, Rudolf (1858–1913), engineer. Diesel was born in Paris and grew up there until his parents were deported in 1870. He worked as an engineer in Munich, Paris and Augsburg, and worked on the development of the diesel engine from 1890. He patented his idea in 1892, and successfully demonstrated it in 1897. His death was mysterious: he disappeared from the deck of the steamer *Dresden* en route to London, where he was to meet representatives of the British Admiralty.

Dietrich, Josef (Sepp) (1892–1966), SS officer. Born in Hawangen, Dietrich joined the Nazi Party early and took part in the MUNICH PUTSCH. He joined the SS full-time in 1928, and became head of the *Leibstandarte Adolf Hitler*. He was elected to the Reichstag in 1930 and promoted to SS general after 1934 for his part in the NIGHT OF THE LONG KNIVES. Dietrich pursued a successful military career on several fronts during World War II and was responsible for atrocities in the Soviet Union. He was tried at Nuremberg for the execution of American prisoners of war and sentenced to life. Released in 1955 he was imprisoned again in 1956 after a trial for the murder of RÖHM and other leading members of the SA during the Night of the Long Knives. He was finally released in 1959.

Dietrich, Marlene (1901–92), film actress. Born Maria Magdalene von Losch in Berlin, Dietrich studied with Max REINHARDT and pursued a career in the German theatre in the 1920s. She established her reputation with Josef von STERNBERG's *The Blue Angel* in 1930. She then moved to America where she made a number of films into the 1960s. During the war she made propaganda films for the Allies in German.

Dietrich, Otto (1897–1952), Nazi press chief. Born in Essen, Dietrich served in World War I, studied politics, and then went into journalism. He was appointed Reich press chief in 1931, organized the propaganda campaigns for the 1932 elections, and mediated between the party and business circles. He was state secretary in the propaganda ministry from 1937 to 1945, and was responsible for the Reich Editors' Law, which made newspaper editors personally responsible for any expression of dissent in their newspapers. In April 1949 he was sentenced to seven years' imprisonment, but was released in 1950.

Dietz, Johann Heinrich Wilhelm (1843–1922), socialist printer, publisher and politician. Dietz was a member of the Reichstag for the SPD from 1881 to 1918. He was the founder of the Dietz publishing house.

Dimitrov, Georgi (1882–1949), Bulgarian Communist. Born in Pernik, he was one of the founder members of the Bulgarian Communist Party in 1919, but fled to the USSR in 1923. He was arrested and tried by the Nazis in 1933 for complicity in the REICHSTAG FIRE, but conducted a defence that put Göring firmly on the defensive and led to his acquittal. He was nevertheless held in custody in the Reich, and only released in 1934 after considerable international pressure. Subsequently Dimitrov was an architect of the Comintern's 'popular front' strategy (1934), and he went on to become the first prime minister of Bulgaria after the war. He died in Moscow.

Dirksen, Herbert von (1882–1955), diplomat. After a spell as chargé d'affaires in Warsaw, Dirksen returned to the foreign office (1921–2) before his appointment as consul general in Danzig (Gdańsk) in 1923. He returned once more to the foreign office in 1925, and then represented Germany in three important embassies: Moscow (1928–33); Tokyo (1933–8), where he officiated at Japan's signing of the ANTI-COMINTERN PACT; and London (1938–9), where he succeeded RIBBENTROP. He retired on his return to Germany after the outbreak of war.

Disarmament Conference (1932–4), a meeting of 60 states under the auspices of the League of Nations in Geneva. Germany withdrew from the conference when it adjourned in July 1932, but reached an agreement with the other major European powers and the United States at the end of the year. The conference resumed in February 1933 but on 14 October GOEBBELS announced that Germany would be withdrawing altogether.

Dittmann, Wilhelm (1874–1954), socialist politician. Dittmann was born into a working-class family in Eutin, Schleswig-Holstein. He was an apprentice joiner after leaving school, and joined the woodworkers' union and the SPD in 1894. He was editor first of the *Norddeutsche Volksstimme*, and then of the *Bergische Arbeiterstimme*, and was elected to the city council in Frankfurt am Main in 1904. Five years later he became the first Social Democrat to preside over it. Dittmann was on the left of the party and was a co-founder of the breakaway USPD in 1917. He was one of the original members of the COUNCIL OF PEOPLE'S REPRESENTATIVES in November and December 1918. He sat in the Reichstag from 1912 to 1918, and again from 1920 to 1933, for the USPD until 1922 and then once more for the SPD. Dittman supported the reunification of the Independent Socialists with the majority party rather than merger with the Communists (KPD). He was also a city councillor in Berlin from 1921 to 1925. He fled to Austria in 1933, and then moved on to Switzerland, where he wrote his memoirs.

Dittmar, Louise (1807–84), early campaigner for women's rights. Born in Darmstadt into a middle-class family with radical connections, Dittmar published anonymously at first, but gained confidence as a member of a group of radicals in Mannheim during the late 1840s. She founded a short-lived journal, *Die Soziale Reform*, and published a collection of essays in 1849, *Das Wesen der Ehe nebst einigen Aufsätzen über die soziale Reform der Frauen* ('the essence of marriage and some essays on the reform of women'). She found it difficult to publish after the suppres-

sion of the REVOLUTIONS OF 1848, and died in relative obscurity.

Dix, Otto (1891–1969), artist. The son of a working-class family, Dix studied art in Dresden (1910–14) and served in World War I, an experience that radically affected his work. He was a co-founder of the SECESSION in Dresden in 1919 and professor at the Academy of Arts there from 1926 to 1933. In the early 1920s he produced works depicting the victims of war and capitalism, including *War Cripples* (etching and painting exhibited at the Berlin Dada fair, 1920) and *Two Victims of Capitalism* (drawing, 1923). He was a leading figure in the NEUE SACHLICHKEIT movement. In 1927 he was appointed professor at the Dresden Academy. He was dismissed by the Nazis in 1933 and expelled from the Prussian Academy of Arts. His work was banned in 1934. He remained in Germany during the Nazi dictatorship and the war, living in obscurity near Lake Constance. After the war he ran an art class at the State Academy of Art in Düsseldorf.

DKP. *See* DEUTSCHE KOMMUNISTISCHE PARTEI; DEUTSCHE KONSERVATIVE PARTEI.

DNVP (*Deutschnationale Volkspartei*), the German Nationalist People's Party, a nationalist party of the WEIMAR REPUBLIC. The DNVP was founded in November 1918 and was heir to the conservative and radical-right traditions of Wilhelmine Germany. It also attracted supporters from the right wing of the former NATIONAL LIBERAL PARTY. Its leaders represented the landed interest, particularly east of the Elbe, and sections of heavy industry. The DNVP was a monarchist party, hostile to the Weimar Republic, opposed to the fulfilment of the treaty of VERSAILLES and committed to revision of its territorial provisions.

The DNVP's support grew from 10% in 1919 to a peak of 20% in 1924, but its uncompromising defence of agrarian interests limited both its social and geographical appeal, and its best electoral performances tended to be in the JUNKER-dominated East Elbian provinces. In 1928 it won only 14% of the vote nationally, but 41.6% in Pomerania and 31.3% in East Prussia. It also attracted some support among the urban lower middle class. Its extremist foreign policy isolated it from the other Weimar parties, and it participated only briefly in government, first in 1925, during the first LUTHER administration, and then again from 1927 to 1928 under Wilhelm MARX.

The policy programme of the DNVP contained explicitly anti-Semitic statements from the outset, and under the leadership of Alfred HUGENBERG it cooperated with the Nazis during the campaign against the YOUNG PLAN. Although much of its support ebbed away to the Nazi Party after 1930, and its share of the vote fell to less than 6% in July 1932, members of the party were appointed to the PAPEN 'cabinet of barons' of that year. The DNVP joined Hitler's government as a junior partner in January 1933, but was dissolved in June.

Döblin, Alfred (1878–1957), modernist writer. A doctor by profession, Döblin was a member of the USPD until 1920, and of the SPD from 1921 until 1930. He emigrated to France in 1933, went on to the USA in 1940, and returned to Germany after the war. His best known work is the novel *Berlin Alexanderplatz* (1929).

Dohnanyi, Hans von (1902–45), civil-service lawyer and opponent of the Nazis. Dohnanyi was a lawyer and senior civil servant in the Reich justice ministry from 1929 until he was dismissed in 1939. He joined the ABWEHR in the same year, and was arrested after Tresckow's attempt to assassinate Hitler in 1943, and again after the JULY BOMB PLOT of 1944. He was missing at the end of the war.

Dolchstosslegende ('stab-in-the-back myth'), the widespread belief on the nationalist right that Germany was not defeated in battle at the end of World War I, but betrayed by socialists and Jews. It was given credence by the testimony of HINDENBURG to a Reichstag committee after the war, and fuelled the ANTI-SEMITISM and hostility to parliamentary democracy that was characteristic of conservative politics during the Weimar Republic. In so far as those on the right who propagated the myth believed it themselves, however, it also – arguably – made the Nazi regime wary of provoking a rebellion among the industrial working class.

Dollfuss, Engelbert (1892–1934), conservative politician; chancellor of Austria (1932–4). Dollfuss came from a farming background. He was born in Texing, near Mank, Lower Austria, the illegitimate son of Josepha Dollfuss, who married his stepfather the following year. Dollfuss attended a seminary, and studied law and theology in Vienna before serving in World War I. His political involvement began in his student days, when he joined one of Vienna's Pan-German student corporations (*BURSCHENSCHAFTEN*). He was director of the Chamber of Agriculture in Lower Austria from 1927. He was appointed Austrian agriculture minister in 1931, and foreign minister and chancellor in 1932.

Dollfuss presided over a regime that increasingly resorted to rule by presidential decree within the terms of the War Economy Enabling Law (promulgated in 1917) and finally provoked a conflict with members of the SDAP (Social Democratic Workers' Party) in 1934, which was the starting point for armed attacks on party and trade-union headquarters and the bombardment of council flats in Vienna by heavy artillery (*see* AUSTRIAN CIVIL WAR). The SDAP was banned and thousands of its members arrested and imprisoned in CONCENTRATION CAMPS after lengthy show trials. Dollfuss was assassinated by Nazis in an attempted coup in July 1934, and was succeeded by Kurt von SCHUSCHNIGG, who completed the transformation of the first Austrian Republic into a fascist 'CORPORATE STATE'.

Dönitz, Karl (1891–1980) German admiral, who was briefly chancellor as Hitler's successor, in May 1945. The son of a civil servant, Dönitz joined the navy in 1910 and served in World War I. He became a submarine commander, and was appointed an adviser to the Navy Inspectorate's submarine section in 1923. He became a rear admiral in 1935 and was given responsibility for the development and deployment of the German submarine fleet. Early in 1943, as Dönitz's submarine force enjoyed its greatest successes in the battle of the ATLANTIC, he succeeded Admiral RAEDER as commander in chief of the German navy, and Hitler switched resources from surface ships to U-boats. Ironically, by May 1943 improved Allied anti-submarine measures forced Dönitz to withdraw his U-boats from the North Atlantic. Finally, he was appointed to succeed Hitler shortly before the end of the war. As German chancellor for one week after Hitler's suicide he surrendered unconditionally to the Allies in May 1945. He was tried at Nuremberg and sentenced to ten years' imprisonment.

Donnersberg, left-wing faction at the 1848 FRANKFURT PARLIAMENT. Of its 47 members 23 were from the free professions.

Dorpmüller, Julius (1869–1945), Nazi transport minister. Born in Elberfeld, Dorpmüller pursued a career in the Prussian railway service and became director general of the German State Railways in 1926. He collaborated closely with the Nazis before his appointment as transport minister in 1937. He died at home in Schleswig-Holstein shortly after the end of the war.

DP. See DEUTSCHE PARTEI.

Drang nach Osten (literally 'push to the east'), a term originally used to describe the colonization of the Baltic by German settlers in the Middle Ages. The term was first widely used in eastern Europe rather than in Germany itself, and was popularized in Russia during the late 19th century, where it was used in popular journalism to criticize the position of the Baltic Germans. It regained currency in the context of aspirations by the Nazis and others of repeating the perceived achievement of bringing German culture to the peoples of eastern Europe, and has been widely used in countries that have been victims of German expansionism, particularly the USSR. The term has rarely been used in Germany itself (except for the Soviet-influenced historiography of the GERMAN DEMOCRATIC REPUBLIC). See also LEBENSRAUM.

Dreikaiserbund. See THREE EMPERORS' LEAGUE.

Dresden, capital city of Saxony, formerly regarded as one of the most beautiful towns in Germany. It was destroyed in an Allied air raid of 13 February 1945 with the aim of disrupting German communications in preparation for a Soviet advance from the east. Over 2500 tons of bombs were dropped on the city by the RAF in one night, and there then followed attacks by hundreds of USAAF planes on the following two days. As a result a firestorm was created, and some 70,000 people were killed.

Dresden, peace of (25 December 1745), treaty that brought to an end the Second Silesian War during the War of the AUSTRIAN SUCCESSION. PRUSSIA gained SILESIA, and Saxony had to pay a considerable indemnity and relinquish all claims to Silesia.

Drexler, Anton (1884–1942), German nationalist politician. Born in Munich, Drexler was one of the founders of the DEUTSCHE ARBEITERPARTEI, forerunner of the Nazi Party. Although he remained a party member until his death, he was rarely involved actively in Nazi politics after 1921, and died in obscurity.

Droste-Hülshoff, Annete, Freiin von (1797–1848), writer. Droste-Hülshoff was born near Münster in Westphalia into a family of Roman Catholic aristocrats and educated at home. She is remembered for her religious poetry and a novella, *Die Judenbuche* (*The Jew's Beech Tree*, 1842). Although she has traditionally been considered a conservative writer, and was for long the only woman included in the canon of 19th-century German literature, her novella and prose sketches have been seen as forerunners of realism.

Droste zu Fischering, Klemens, Graf (1832–1923), Catholic politician. Droste zu Fischering was born into a distinguished family of Roman Catholic aristocrats in Westphalia. He was president of the Association of Catholic Nobleman and a member of the Reichstag from 1879 to 1893. He sat in the Prussian HERRENHAUS (the upper chamber of the parliament) until 1918.

Dual Alliance (7 October 1879), defence treaty concluded in secret between Germany and Austria-Hungary. Each promised to support the other in the event of an attack by Russia, and to observe a benevolent neutrality in the case of attack by any other power. The term of the alliance was agreed for five years in the first instance. In the event its terms remained valid until 1918, and became a TRIPLE ALLIANCE (with Italy) in 1882.

Dual Monarchy. *See AUSGLEICH.*

Duesterberg, Theodor (1875–1950), German nationalist politician. Born in Darmstadt, Duesterberg served in World War I and in the Prussian war ministry before leaving to found (with Franz SELDTE) the STAHLHELM, the largest paramilitary organization in Weimar Germany. An important figure in the agitation against the YOUNG PLAN in 1929, and in the HARZBURG FRONT of 1931, Duesterberg nevertheless turned down an offer of a post in the Hitler cabinet of 1933, and was briefly arrested after the RÖHM purge of the following year (*see* NIGHT OF THE LONG KNIVES). He survived the Nazi dictatorship and attempted, without success, to revive the *Stahlhelm* after the war.

Dühring, Eugen (1832–1921), academic and political theorist. Dühring was a lawyer before obtaining a teaching post at Berlin in 1864. He rejected much of the philosophical canon of his day, including the principal writings of Marx, and although he preached a political economy of self-sufficiency within a controlled economic frame-work, he passed himself off as a socialist, and acquired something of a following among intellectuals in the SPD (including the young BERNSTEIN). This prompted ENGELS' refutation of his views, *Herr Eugen Dührings Umwälzung der Wissenschaft* (*Herr Eugen Dühring's Revolution in Science*), commonly abbreviated to *Anti-Dühring*, which was serialized in *Vorwärts* (the Social Democratic newspaper) and published as a book in 1878. Dühring was also an anti-Semite and an anti-feminist. In 1881 he published his anti-Semitic views in *Die Judenfrage als Racen-, Sitten- und Kulturfrage. Mit einer Weltgeschichtlichenchen Antwort* ('The Jewish Question as a Question of Race, Morals and Culture. A World Historical Response'), in which he argued that feeling, thought and behaviour are racially determined, and that each race must be regarded as natural and immutable. Jews he placed at the bottom of his racial hierarchy as 'one of the least successful of nature's creations'.

Duisberg, Carl (1861–1935), chemist and industrialist. Duisberg was born in Barmen and joined the Bayer chemical company in 1884. He became director general in 1912, and made his political reputation on the right during World War I as an outspoken protagonist of a 'victorious peace' (*Siegfrieden*). He became chairman of the supervisory board of IG FARBEN and president of the Reich Association of German Industry in 1925. Although he was a supporter of the Nazis in 1933, he was subsequently sceptical. He died in Leverkusen.

Dulag (*Durchgangslager*), transit camp, particularly those used during the deportation of European Jews by the Nazi regime, the forced 'resettlement' of non-Germans during WORLD WAR II, and the temporary detention of the opponents of the Nazi political system.

Dunkirk, channel port on the northern coast of France from which British forces were evacuated in 1940. The Germans had broken through in the Ardennes and in the

Netherlands, and were heading for the Channel ports, which would mean that the Allied forces would be cut off from their French coastal bases. Calais and Boulogne were surrounded, but General von KLEIST's forces, which were only a few kilometres from Dunkirk, were held up at the insistence of General von RUNDSTEDT. By that time it became clear that the Luftwaffe was unable to prevent the evacuation of Allied troops. Almost 340,000 were evacuated within a week (between 27 May and 4 June 1940). Dunkirk was the last French town to be liberated (10 May 1945); it had been left encircled as Allied troops moved up the coast to Belgium.

DVP (*Deutsche Volkspartei*), the German People's Party, a middle-class conservative party during the WEIMAR REPUBLIC. Founded in December 1918, and led by Gustav STRESEMANN, the DVP attracted those NATIONAL LIBERALS who felt excluded from the DDP. Although it was an anti-republican party, and committed to revision of the treaty of VERSAILLES, the DVP was consistently represented in Weimar coalition governments, where it defended the interests of businessmen and the upper middle classes. It never commanded a large electoral constituency, and its long-term decline was exacerbated by the onset of the Depression, when its supporters abandoned it, first for splinter parties representing economic interests, and then for the Nazi Party.

DVU. *See DEUTSCHE VOLKSUNION.*

E

Eagle's Nest. *See* BERCHTESGADEN.

Eastern Marches Association. *See* OSTMAR-KENVEREIN.

East Germany. *See* GERMAN DEMOCRATIC REPUBLIC.

Ebert, Friedrich (1871–1925), leading Social Democratic politician; briefly chancellor in November 1918 at the time of the signing of the armistice, and first president (1919–25) of the WEIMAR REPUBLIC.

Ebert was the son of a tailor and pursued a career in left-wing journalism and local politics in Bremen before World War I. He was elected to the Bremen BÜRGERSCHAFT in 1900, and to the Reichstag in 1912. He became president of the SPD in 1913. Ebert was on the right wing of the party, and led the 'Majority Socialists' (MSPD) after the 1917 party split. He became chancellor following the resignation of Prince Max von BADEN on 9 November 1918 and president of the COUNCIL OF PEOPLE'S REPRESENTATIVES during the NOVEMBER REVOLUTION of that year. By agreeing with General GROENER to recognize the independence of the Reichswehr in return for its loyalty to the republic (the 'Ebert–Groener pact') he ensured the survival of parliamentary democracy. The radical left was effectively marginalized as a consequence. Ebert was elected president by the NATIONAL ASSEMBLY in 1919 and was a symbolic guarantor of parliamentary democracy in the Weimar Republic until his death. He was succeeded by Paul von HINDENBURG. His son, also called Friedrich, became a leading politician in East Germany after World War II.

Ebert, Friedrich (1894–1979), East German politician; the son of Friedrich EBERT, the first president of the Weimar Republic. The younger Ebert was a Social Democratic journalist before World War II. He was elected to the Reichstag in 1928, and was briefly interned in a concentration camp by the Nazis. He was chairman of the SPD in Brandenburg after the war, and then from 1946 a member of the executive of the SED (the East German Socialist Unity Party). He joined the party's central secretariat in 1947, and was a member of the Politburo. Ebert was mayor of East Berlin from 1947 to 1960.

Eckart, Dietrich (1868–1923), Bavarian journalist and writer. Eckart was a close companion of Hitler and member of the DEUTSCHE ARBEITERPARTEI (DAP, German Workers' Party). He was also the first editor of the Nazi newspaper, the *Völkischer Beobachter*. He was an alcoholic, and died of a heart attack shortly after his release from imprisonment for participation in the Munich BEER HALL PUTSCH.

Eckart, Felix von (1903–79), journalist and politician. Eckart was press attaché to the German embassy in Brussels until 1932, and then active in the film industry during the Nazi dictatorship (1933–45). He was editor of the *Weser-Kurier* during the early 1950s, head of the federal press office (*Bundespressechef*) and director of the government information office from 1956 to 1962. In

1955 and 1956 he was West Germany's permanent observer at the United Nations, then federal plenipotentiary in Berlin (1962–5). He was a member of the Bundestag for the CDU from 1965 to 1972.

Edelweiss Pirates, a term applied to a number of oppositional youth movements in western Germany during the Nazi dictatorship. Various different groups in the Rhineland and Ruhr valley considered themselves 'Edelweiss Pirates' – so called after the metal edelweiss badge they wore along with other insignia. Although there were clear precursors to such groups, they first appeared at the end of the 1930s and were made up mainly of working-class youths between the ages of 14 and 18 who had rebelled against the authoritarian culture of the HITLER YOUTH and met up with other groups from neighbouring towns on weekend camping trips into the countryside. The Nazi authorities and the police considered them delinquents, and they were responsible for many of the increasing number of violent attacks on Hitler Youth members during the war.

Edict of Toleration, decree enacted by JOSEPH II in 1781, granting freedom of worship to non-Roman Catholics in the Habsburg monarchy. A further measure of the following year ended certain types of discrimination against the Jews.

Eggeling, Joachim Albrecht Leo (1884–1945), Nazi politician. Born in Blankenburg, Harz, Eggeling joined the Nazi Party in 1925 and the SS in 1936. He was deputy *Gauleiter* of Magdeburg-Anhalt from 1935 to 1937, and *Gauleiter* of Halle-Merseburg from 1937 to 1945. Eggeling was a farmer and specialised in agricultural matters. He was appointed Nazi Farmers' Leader (*Bauernführer*) for SAXONY-ANHALT in 1933. He was killed in action in the battle to defend Halle in April 1945.

Eher-Verlag, the central Nazi Party publishing house in Munich. Originally owned by Franz Eher, it was taken over by Max AMANN in 1922.

Ehestandsdarlehen. See MARRIAGE LOANS.

Ehrhardt, Hermann (1881–1971), far-right activist and paramilitary leader. Born in Diersburg, in Baden, into a middle-class family, Ehrhardt joined the imperial navy in 1899, and served as an officer up to and during World War I. After the war he was a radical right-wing agitator and FREIKORPS leader, who organized terrorist attacks on left-wingers, and led the KAPP PUTSCH in Berlin in 1920. Von SEECKT employed him against Communist insurgents in the Ruhr, and he set up the radical right-wing organization CONSUL, which was responsible for the murders of Matthias ERZBERGER and Walther RATHENAU. After the murders he escaped arrest by fleeing to Hungary, and although he was eventually captured in Bavaria, he was only charged with participation in the Kapp putsch. In 1923 he escaped again, this time to Austria. He got to know Hitler in Munich at the end of 1920, and placed his 'brigade' under the command of the SS in 1933. He was also, friendly with Otto STRASSER, however, and fled to Austria after the NIGHT OF THE LONG KNIVES.

Eichmann, Adolf (1906–62), SS officer responsible for the implementation of the 'final solution'. Eichmann was born in Solingen, but grew up in Linz, Austria, and was educated in Thuringia. He joined the Austrian Nazi Party in 1932 and moved to Berlin after its prohibition the following year. In 1934 he joined the SD, the Nazi Party's intelligence service, and in 1935 became head of the Office for Jewish Emigration. Eichmann was closely connected with the origins of the HOLOCAUST. In 1938 he applied Nazi anti-Semitic policies in Vienna, and in 1939 was charged with the deportation of Jews from Austria and Bohemia to German-occupied Poland. In 1940 he was given responsibility for developing plans for the deportation of European Jews to Madagascar after the war. Following the WANNSEE CONFERENCE of 1942, in which he participated, he was placed in charge of the implementation of the 'final solution'. In 1944 he supervised the deportation of Hungarian Jews. He was captured in the American zone at the end of World War II, but escaped and fled to Argentina, where he lived in obscurity until he was discovered in 1960 by Israeli agents. They smuggled him back to Jerusalem to face trial in 1961 for crimes against humanity. He was found guilty and executed in May 1962.

Eicke, Theodor (1892–1943), SS officer. Born in Alsace-Lorraine, Eicke was an anti-republican political activist who was dismissed from a number of positions in the police force. He became a member of the Nazi Party in 1928, and was convicted of bomb attacks in 1932. He was appointed commandant of DACHAU by Himmler in 1933, and in 1934 he became inspector of CONCENTRATION CAMPS and SS Death's Head formations. He shot Ernst RÖHM in 1934 during the NIGHT OF THE LONG KNIVES. From 1939 he led Death's Head formations in Poland, and was promoted to general in the Waffen-SS in 1943. He was killed the same year.

Eigruber, August (1907–46), Austrian Nazi. Eigruber was born in Steyr, Upper Austria, and was a leading Nazi activist there in the 1930s. He was 'Führer' of the city of Steyr from 1931 to 1935, and (illegal) *Gauleiter* of Upper Austria from 1935 to 1938. He then became *Gauleiter* of the new *Reichsgau*, Upper Danube (1938–45), and was also governor (*Reichsstatthalter*) from 1940. He was tried by a US military tribunal in 1946 and hanged at Landsberg prison in Bavaria.

Einem (von Rothmaler), Ernst Günther von (1894–?), radical right-wing politician. Einem was Westphalian leader of FREIKORPS Oberland from 1922 to 1924, and was a member of the DNVP until 1933. He was an officer in World War II, and a founding member of the DEUTSCHE PARTEI (1949–50). He was then a member of the FDP from 1953.

Einem (von Rothmaler), Karl von (1853–1934), army officer. Von Einem was director of the General War Department in the Prussian war ministry from 1900, and Prussian minister of war from 1903 to 1907. Along with other senior officers he opposed expansion of the army on several occasions before the outbreak of World War I. He was supreme commander of the 3rd Army during the war, and commander of Army Group Crown Prince in November 1918.

Einsatzgruppen, special mobile 'task forces' of the security police (*SIPO*) and SS in occupied eastern Europe during World War II. There were four such units, which were subdivided into EINSATZKOMMANDOS. Supported by the order police (*ORPO*) and local recruits, they followed the German armies into Poland and the Soviet Union and carried out mass killings of Jews, Polish national leaders and Soviet political commissars.

Einsatzkommandos, subdivisions of the SS EINSATZGRUPPEN that were deployed on the eastern front during World War II. There were up to six such units in each of the *Einsatzgruppen.*

Einstein, Albert (1879–1955), German physicist. Born in Ulm, Einstein studied in Zurich and became a Swiss citizen in 1901. He worked at the patent office in Bern from 1902 to 1909 and was professor first at the Technical University in Zurich (1912–14) and then in Berlin. He published his special theory of relativity in 1905 and the general theory in 1916, and won the Nobel prize for physics in 1921. Einstein was an active pacifist and protested against German militarism before and after the outbreak of World War I. He was subjected to anti-Semitic attacks by the Nazis, who also refused to accept his work. He left Germany in 1932 and when Hitler came to power he remained in the United States at the Institute for Advanced Studies at Princeton. His property in Berlin was seized and his books burned. In 1939 he wrote to President Roosevelt to warn him about the military possibilities of nuclear fission. He spent much of the last decade of his life campaigning for ways to avoid nuclear war.

Eisenach Congress. *See* SDAP.

Eisler, Hans (1898–1962), composer. Born in Leipzig, the son of a university professor, Eisler studied music with SCHOENBERG and WEBERN in Vienna and then taught music in Berlin. He left Germany in 1933 for the United States, and returned to Vienna in 1948. From 1950 he lived in East Berlin. Eisler's work encompassed orchestral and stage music, work for theatre and film (including *Kuhle Wampe*) and proletarian songs. He also composed the national anthem of the German Democratic Republic.

Eisner, Kurt (1867–1919), journalist and politician. The son of a Moravian immigrant family in Berlin, Eisner joined the *Frankfurter Zeitung* and then the *Hessische Landeszeitung* in Marburg, but was arrested and imprisoned for lese majesty, before joining the Social Democratic *Vorwärts* and going on to edit the party's *Fränkische Tagespost*. He joined the USPD in 1917, and in the wake of the NOVEMBER REVOLUTION in Munich the following year he was elected minister-president of Bavaria by the Workers' and Soldiers' Council (*ARBEITER- UND SOLDATENRAT*). Following the electoral defeat of the USPD in Bavaria in January 1919, and before he was able to announce his resignation, he was assassinated by a radical right-wing aristocrat.

Elsass-Lothringen, the German name for ALSACE-LORRAINE.

Ems telegram, communication sent by the king of Prussia, WILHELM I, to BISMARCK in 1870; an edited version published by Bismarck was a contributory factor in the outbreak of the FRANCO-PRUSSIAN WAR. Following the withdrawal of the candidature for the Spanish throne of Leopold von Hohenzollern-Sigmaringen, a relative of the Prussian king, the French ambassador in Berlin, Comte Benedetti, visited the king at Bad Ems, where he was taking a cure. Benedetti urged the king to reassure Paris not only that the Hohenzollern candidature had been withdrawn, but, on receiving this assurance, that there would be no renewal of the claim. The king refused to see Benedetti again, but telegrammed Bismarck an account of his dealings with Benedetti, adding that the ambassador had requested a second interview, but that he had refused him. Bismarck published an edited version of the telegram, making it appear that Benedetti had sought to humiliate the king – and Prussia – by demanding a second interview, and presenting the king's refusal of his 'demand' as tantamount to a breaking off diplomatic relations with Paris.

Enabling Law (*Ermächtigungsgesetz*, 1933), formally known as the 'Law for the Removal of Distress from People and Reich' (*Gesetz zur Behebung der Not von Volk und Reich*), a law passed by the Reichstag enabling the government to enact legislation, including amendments to the constitution, without recourse to the normal parliamentary procedures. Enabling laws had been passed in order to help resolve crises during the WEIMAR REPUBLIC (for example during the currency crisis of 1923). The purpose of Hitler's 1933 act was to avoid the necessity of ruling by presidential decree as his immediate predecessors had done. The first draft of the law empowered the government to issue emergency decrees, but it was amended to enable laws to be passed without the direct approval of the Reichstag or the Reich president, including constitutional amendments which would normally require a two-thirds majority. In order to get the measure through the Reichstag, however, a two-thirds quorum was essential in the first place. Opposition to the law in the chamber was reduced as a result of the repressive measures taken against the KPD (the German Communist Party) in the aftermath of the REICHSTAG FIRE, and the terrorizing of political opponents during the campaign for the election of 5 March. The Nazis and their conservative allies had managed under these conditions to increase their share of the seats, but still fell far short of the required two-thirds majority. The crucial votes for the

Nazis to win were those of the Catholic CENTRE PARTY, since the Social Democrats (SPD) were determined to block the passage of the law. Hitler won over the waverers with a promise to respect the independence of the church and guarantees about Catholic education. There was also a promise not to interfere with the Reichstag or abolish the *Länder*. The law was passed on 23 March by 441 votes to the 94 of the SPD, following a courageous speech by Otto Wels, the parliamentary leader of the Social Democrats.

The Enabling Law gave the Nazis' subsequent actions a spurious appearance of legality. It authorized the cabinet to enact laws, including laws which deviated from the constitution (provided that they did not affect the position of the Reichstag or the REICHSRAT). The government was also empowered to enter treaties with foreign states without consultation. The Enabling Law was valid for four years, and was renewed in 1937.

Endlösung, 'final solution', the Nazi euphemism for the mass murder of European Jews (*see* HOLOCAUST).

Engels, Friedrich (1820–95), philosopher and Socialist politician. Engels was born into a Protestant liberal middle-class family in Barmen and attended the *Gymnasium* (grammar school) in Elberfeld. He left school before completing his studies and served a business apprenticeship in Bremen. He mixed in left-wing circles in Bremen and Berlin and became a communist during the 1840s. In 1842 he went to England to work with the family firm in Manchester, where he made contact with Chartist activists. Back in Germany he published *Die Lage der arbeitenden Klasse in England* (1845; first published in English as *The Condition of the Working Class in England*, 1887) and then, with Karl MARX, wrote *Die deutsche Ideologie* (*The German Ideology*), which was completed in 1846 but not published for a further 80 years. The two also worked together *on The Communist Manifesto* (*Manifest der Kommunistischen Partei*, 1848) for the Communist Congress.

Engels took an active part in the REVOLUTIONS OF 1848, both in the uprising at Elberfeld (1849) and with the revolutionary forces in BADEN and the PALATINATE. He escaped to Switzerland after the suppression of the revolution, and then returned with Marx to England. Engels worked for the family business in Manchester, supporting both himself and Marx until he sold his share in the firm in 1869 and retired. Engels continued to write during the last 25 years of his life, producing some of most important work. In 1878 he published *Anti-Dühring* (*Herr Eugen Dühring's Revolution in Science*; *see* DÜHRING, EUGEN) and after Marx's death in 1883 he completed volumes 2 and 3 of *Das Kapital* from Marx's notes. One of his last works was *Der Urspung der Familie, des Privateigentums und des Staats* (*The Origin of the Family, Private Property and the State*), published in 1884.

Enigma, a machine used by the Germans to encode messages during World War II. In 1939 the so-called ULTRA project, an intelligence unit for deciphering German signals traffic, was established at Bletchley Park, north of London. German coded messages were intercepted and decrypted by a group of British mathematicians working at Bletchley. The breaking of the Enigma code provided a source of inside information crucial to Allied intelligence.

enlightened absolutism. *See* ABSOLUTISM.

Enlightenment (German: *Aufklärung*), the dominant cultural and intellectual movement in Europe during the 18th century. Its origins were in the humanism of the Renaissance and the scientific revolutions of the 17th century. In its broader European context it is associated with the French thinkers Voltaire and Rousseau and the British thinkers Locke and Hume. The American revolutionaries of the 18th century were influenced by Enlightenment thinking, as were many European monarchs in the age of ABSOLUTISM, including FRIEDRICH II (the Great) of Prussia and JOSEPH II of Austria. In philosophical and political terms the

Enlightenment has generally been seen as a progressive phenomenon, although Enlightened thinkers and writers were frequently dismissive of 'the people' and popular attitudes. The key ingredients were a belief in reason, progress and the perfectibility of humanity. Education and the accumulation of knowledge were seen as good things in themselves, and there was a new emphasis on human happiness. Although most thinkers of the period retained a belief in a God of some kind, the effect of the movement was to contribute to the secularization of European society. Enlightened Christians sought to rid the church of what they perceived to be superstition and irrational dogma.

The dominant cultural style of the Enlightenment was a reaction against the excess and pomposity of the Baroque style, but remained formal and restrained. The movement coincided with the emergence of a national literary culture in Germany, among whose leading figures were Gottfried Ephraim LESSING, Johann Gottfried von HERDER and Moses Mendelssohn (1729–86). During the 1780s the nature of Enlightenment was a question of lively debate among German intellectuals. In December 1783 a Berlin priest, Johann Friedrich Zöllner, published an article against civil marriage in the journal *Berlinische Monatsschrift* ('Berlin monthly') which criticised the 'confusion' generated by the concept of Enlightenment. In response Moses Mendelssohn published the essay 'Über die Frage: was heisst aufklären?' ('Concerning the question: what is Enlightenment?') in the same journal in September 1784. Among those contributing to the debate was the philosopher Immanuel KANT, whose essay 'Beantwortung der Frage: Was ist Aufklärung?' ('An answer to the question: What is Enlightenment?'), also appeared in the *Berlinische Monatsschrift* in December 1784. (Kant was apparently unaware of Mendelssohn's earlier contribution to the debate. Other contributors included the

writer Johann Georg Hamann (1730–88), a critic of the Enlightenment, and the poet and publicist Chistoph Martin Wieland (1733–1813), who argued for Enlightenment values.

The Enlightenment movement failed to survive the revolutionary upheavals of the 1790s. The German STURM UND DRANG movement set itself against the aesthetic values of the Enlightenment, and the cultural and philosophical values of the movement were eventually displaced by Romanticism. It has nevertheless determined philosophical, political and cultural positions since the end of the 18th century, and critiques of the Enlightenment and its legacy have been powerful ingredients in radical right-wing movements.

Entailed Farm Law. *See* REICH ENTAILED FARM LAW.

entartete Kunst. *See* DEGENERATE ART.

entartete Musik. *See* DEGENERATE MUSIC.

Epp, Franz Xaver, Ritter von (1868–1946), right-wing Bavarian general. Born in Munich, the son of a painter, Epp was a professional soldier and served in China and South-West Africa before World War I, during which he was decorated. After the war he returned to Munich to found a FREIKORPS unit, which was responsible for the murder of a number of socialists there in 1919. The Epp unit was also deployed against communists in the Ruhr. He was actively involved in right-wing politics in the early 1920s and a member of the Bavarian People's Party (BVP). He joined the NSDAP in 1928, and was elected to the Reichstag the same year. He was Nazi governor of Bavaria from 1933 to 1945. He died in American detention in 1947.

erbkrank, 'hereditarily sick', a term used for sufferers from mental and physical disabilities deemed by Nazi medicine to be hereditary.

Erfüllungspolitik. *See* FULFILMENT POLICY.

Erfurt programme (1891), revised manifesto of the SPD, written by Karl KAUTSKY and Eduard BERNSTEIN. The party's original

GOTHA PROGRAMME had been drawn up at the founding 'unity conference' of 1875. It had been severely criticized by MARX, whose views, however, had only been published posthumously. The new programme reflected the emergent ideological split in the party between the revisionists, represented by Bernstein, and those who adhered to Marx's analysis of history. After this analysis had been set out by Kautsky in the first part of the programme, Bernstein added the party's more immediate demands in the second section. These included universal suffrage, freedom of assembly, reform of the judicial system, legal equality for women, the secularization of education, welfare measures, a maximum working day of eight hours and legal equality of agricultural workers and domestic servants with industrial workers.

Erfurt Union, a short-lived attempt to unite Germany in 1849. Saxony and Hanover initially agreed to join Prussia, but backed out when other states failed to join. A 'union parliament' was elected, but an agreement signed between Austria and Prussia at Olmütz in 1850 brought the experiment to an end and restored the GERMAN CONFEDERATION.

Erhard, Ludwig (1897–1977), Christian Democrat politician; neo-liberal economics minister 1949–63) and chancellor (1963–6) of the Federal Republic of Germany. Born in Fürth, in Bavaria, Erhard studied economics and became professor of economics at Munich University in 1945. He was appointed head of the Bavarian industrial reconstruction programme and the director of the economic administration of the BIZONE and was responsible for the introduction of the currency reform before joining the administration of Konrad ADENAUER as economics minister in 1949.

A staunch advocate of the 'social market economy', Erhard introduced policies that are widely held to have been decisive in bringing about West Germany's rapid economic recovery in the 1950s (the so-called *Wirtschaftswunder* or economic miracle).

Government regulation of the economy was minimized, restrictions introduced by the Allies abolished, and tax laws were reformed to encourage enterprise. A stringent anti-cartel policy was introduced. The economic recovery was also promoted by the reconstruction programme and assisted by American aid under the MARSHALL PLAN.

Erhard became chancellor after the resignation of Adenauer in 1963. He led the CDU successfully into the 1965 election, but was forced to relinquish his office in 1966 when the FDP refused to agree to tax increases during a brief recession and the governing coalition broke up. He resigned from the leadership of the CDU the following year, and was succeeded by KIESINGER. He died ten years later in Bonn.

Erlach, Johann Fischer von (1656–1723), architect. His buildings in Vienna were constructed in the wake of the Turkish siege of 1683, and defined Vienna as it became the indisputable political, economic and cultural capital of the Habsburg empire. His most famous building is the Karlskirche, but he was also responsible for a number of aristocratic palaces.

Ermächtigungsgesetz. See ENABLING LAW.

Ernst, Max (1891–1976), German artist. Ernst served in World War I and led the Cologne branch of the DADA movement in 1919. He moved to Paris in 1922 where he did most of his best-known work. He joined the Surrealists in 1924 and pioneered frottage, the application of brass-rubbing technique to rough natural surfaces. He was imprisoned by the Nazis after the fall of France, and went to America in 1941. He returned to France in 1949.

Erzberger, Matthias (1875–1921), CENTRE PARTY politician. Born in Buttenhausen, the son of a tailor, and elected to the Reichstag as a Centre Party deputy for the constituency of Biberach in 1903, Erzberger quickly became a leading member of the parliamentary party and an outspoken, if belated opponent of German annexations during

World War I. He was a member of the government of Max von BADEN, and in November 1918 led the German delegation at Compiègne, where he signed the armistice agreement on behalf of Germany. He was Reich finance minister from 1919 to 1921 and instituted major financial reforms. He was subjected to sustained attacks in the conservative press, and was assassinated by right-wing naval officers in 1921.

Escherich, Georg (1870–1941), radical right-wing agitator. A forester by profession, Escherich visited Norway, Bosnia, Ethiopia and the Cameroon before World War I. In 1919 he became head of the right-wing paramilitary 'home guards' (*Einwohnerwehren*) in Bavaria, and in 1920, as leader of the 'Organisation Escherich' (Orgesch), he became head of all such 'self-defence' organizations in Germany and Austria. However, in 1921 the Entente powers insisted that the organization be disarmed and disbanded. In 1928 Escherich founded the Bavarian *HEIMATSCHUTZ*, which was dissolved in 1933 by the Nazis.

Esser, Hermann (1900–81), co-founder of the Nazi Party. Esser co-founded the *DEUTSCHE ARBEITERPARTEI* (DAP) with Drexler in 1919 and became the editor of the Nazi paper, the *Völkischer Beobachter*, in 1920 – the year in which the DAP became the NSDAP. Esser quarrelled with several other leading party members, including the Strasser brothers, Goebbels, Julius Streicher and Adolf Wagner. He was elected to the Reichstag in 1933 and was briefly Bavarian economics minister (1933–5). During the war he held obscure or honorary posts. In 1947 the US authorities released him from detention, but he was imprisoned by a German DENAZIFICATION court in 1950. He was released in 1952.

Eugene of Savoy (full German name: Franz Eugen, Prinz von Savoyen-Carignan) (1663–1736), military leader. The son of the prince of Savoy and a niece of Cardinal Mazarin, he fled from France to Vienna in 1683 and joined the imperial army during the Turkish

siege. He served the Habsburgs in the Turkish wars during the last decade of the 17th century, and was promoted to field marshal in 1693. He led the Austrian troops to victory against the French in Italy and Belgium during the War of the Spanish Succession and conducted peace negotiations on behalf of the emperor. He was governor of the Austrian Netherlands from 1716 to 1724. In Vienna he was keen to establish a reputation as a supporter of scholarship and the arts, and built the Belvedere Palace outside the city walls.

Eulenburg, Botho, Graf zu (1831–1912), Prussian politician; interior minister 1878–81. He drafted BISMARCK'S ANTI-SOCIALIST LAWS. When CAPRIVI succeeded Bismarck in 1890 he took over both the former chancellor's offices, and became chancellor and minister-president of PRUSSIA. In 1892, however, Eulenburg was appointed minister-president and conflict developed between the two. Both men were dismissed in 1894 and Eulenburg joined the Prussian HERRENHAUS in 1899.

Eulenberg und Hertefeld, Philipp, Fürst zu (1847–1921), officer and diplomat. A Prussian officer until 1871, he joined the foreign office in 1877 and was appointed embassy secretary in Paris in 1879. From 1888 to 1891 he was Prussian minister in several German states, and German ambassador in Vienna from 1894 to 1902. He was a member of the HERRENHAUS from 1901, and a member of the Kaiser's circle.

Euro, European unit of currency introduced in Germany and ten other member states of the European Union on 1 January 1999 as part of the third stage of economic and monetary union. Coins and notes were introduced on 1 January 2002, and the German mark was withdrawn on 28 February 2002.

euthanasia. *See* AKTION T4.

Evangelical Church (*Evangelische Kirche in Deutschland*), the overarching organizational framework and legal entity that embodies mainstream Protestantism in the Federal Republic of Germany. It comprises 24

Lutheran, reformed and united churches, along with the *Evangelische Kirche der Union*. The first attempt to unite the regional Protestant churches in Germany took place at Wittenberg in 1848, and although there were regular conferences from 1852, there was no decisive move towards unification, and the independence of the regional churches persisted until the establishment of the Weimar Republic. In 1919 the German Evangelical Conference (*Deutscher Evangelischer Kirchentag*) brought the various churches together. The confederation of churches that emerged from this convergence fell under the influence of the pro-Nazi GERMAN CHRISTIANS (*Deutsche Christen*) in the early 1930s and became the *Deutsche Evangelische Kirche*, notionally the state church of the Third Reich. This body was vehemently opposed by the dissident Confessing Church (BEKENNENDE KIRCHE). The church was re-established as the *Evangelische Kirche in Deutschland* in 1948. At the end of the 20th century it had some 24 million members.

expellees (*Heimatvertriebene*), ethnic Germans expelled from eastern Europe after the end of WORLD WAR II. Germans began to leave the territories invaded and occupied by Germany as the Red Army advanced west towards the end of the war. More Germans had to leave Poland, Czechoslovakia and Hungary after 1945. Altogether some 16 million people were involved, more than 2 million of whom failed to survive the forced exodus. The expellees' association has been a powerful political force in the postwar Federal Republic, and a particular influence on the politics of the CDU. It was founded in 1951 as *Bund der Heimatvertriebenen und Entrechteten* (*see* REFUGEES MOVEMENT). (The name of the association refers both to the expulsion of the Germans from their 'homeland' (*Heimat*) and the concomitant loss of rights.) It was prefixed from 1952 with the further designation *Gesamtdeutscher Block* (*see* GESAMTDEUTSCH). From 1953 to 1955 it was represented in the government led by

Konrad ADENAUER. In 1961 it merged with the DEUTSCHE PARTEI to form the *Gesamtdeutsche Partei*.

expressionism, primarily German cultural movement of the early 20th century, which flourished in a number of important German art centres. The term derives from an exhibition at the Berlin SECESSION in 1911 of primarily French work (including that of Matisse and Picasso), and entitled *Expressionisten*. Expressionist art adopted an exaggerated, often distorted style, sometimes with a deliberately unrealistic use of bright colours, and was perceived by contemporaries as an anti-impressionist movement, which also rejected the spirituality of much 19th-century German art. The focus of the movement in Dresden was *Die* BRÜCKE and in Munich BLAUE REITER ('blue rider', so-called after a picture of the same name by KANDINSKY). Other important individual artists associated with the movement included Oskar KOKOSCHKA in Vienna and Max BECKMANN in Frankurt. In addition Paula Modersohn-Becker and other artists working at WORPSWEDE have been seen as early pioneers of expressionist art. Among the literary expressionists were the poets Franz WERFEL, who published a collection of expressionist poetry in 1912 entitled *Der Weltfreund*; Ernst Stadler (1883–1914), who was killed at YPRES, and whose poetry collection *Der Aufbruch* (1914) was one of the movement's most important and influential; Georg Heym (1887–1912); and Gottfried BENN. Among the best-known works of expressionist drama are Kokoschka's *Mörder, Hoffnung der Frauen* (Murderer, Hope of Women, 1907–10), Kandinsky's *Der gelbe Klang* (The Yellow Sound, 1909–12) and the plays of Georg KAISER and Ernst TOLLER. Carl Sternheim (1878–1942) was known for his grotesque expressionist caricatures of bourgeois society. The journal *Der Sturm* ('the storm') was associated with the movement. Expressionist cinema encompassed some of the best-known German films of the Weimar period. *The Cabinet of Dr Caligari* (Robert Wiene, 1919) employed expressionist devices and motifs in plot and set design, and set the style for a whole genre of horror films, including *Nosferatu* by F.W. Murnau (1922). In 1920 Karl-Heinz Martin filmed Kaiser's *Von Morgens bis Mitternachts* with sets by R. Neppach and Ernst Deutsch. By 1923 there were already ironic references to expressionism (as in *Dr Mabuse the Gambler*, Fritz Lang 1923), but there were echoes of expressionist style throughout Weimar cinema.

extermination camps (*Vernichtungslager*), CONCENTRATION CAMPS used by the Nazis for the mass murder of Jews during WORLD WAR II, and the killing of other unwanted persons , including ROMA AND SINTI (Gypsies), HOMOSEXUALS and JEHOVAH'S WITNE SSES. From 1933 many of the inmates of concentration camps in Nazi Germany were murdered with impunity. Among the first prisoners – usually Communists, Social Democrats, trade unionists or other political opponents – death came as a result of beating and torture as the Nazi stormtroopers took their revenge for the street fights of the Depression era. Many others died during the 1930s as a result of the harsh regime or from overwork.

It was only with the outbreak of the war, and the mass executions of Polish and Soviet prisoners of war and civilians alike – and above all with the beginning of the mass murder of the Jews – that special camps specifically designed for mass extermination were established, most of them in Poland. The first massacres of Jews in Poland and at the beginning of the campaign against the Soviet Union had been by firing squads, but later in 1941 it was decided that a quicker and more anonymous method was needed, and one that was less distressing for those involved in the killing. The first large-scale experiments were with gas vans of a kind that had been used in the euthanasia programme (*see* AKTION T4), but that also proved

crude and inefficient. The first extermination centre was set up in CHEŁMNO, a village near Łódź in Poland.

In early 1941 HIMMLER charged *SS-Brigadeführer* Odilo GLOBOCNIK, the head of the SS and police in Lublin and former *Gauleiter* of Vienna, with the organization of the mass murder of Jews in the *GENERALGOUVERNEMENT* (that part of Poland not incorporated into the Reich). This operation was called 'Aktion Reinhard' to commemorate Reinhard HEYDRICH). The first extermination camp was built at BELZEC in the Lublin district, and when that proved to be not enough a further death camp was built at SOBIBOR. The third camp was built north-east of Warsaw at TREBLINKA. The largest and most important of the death camps was at AUSCHWITZ, which had been a concentration camp since 1940, and where Soviet prisoners were gassed in September 1941.The construction of Auschwitz II at BIRKENAU as a purpose-built death camp began in 1941, and the first transport of Jews arrived at the beginning of 1942. MAJDANEK camp in Lublin had been set up in 1941 as a concentration camp to provide slave labour for the SS, which intended to clear eastern Poland for re-settlement. Although most of the prisoners were Poles and Soviet POWs, there were also large numbers of Jews. Three gas chambers were built in 1942 and it is estimated that a quarter of the people who died at the camp were gassed.

See also HOLOCAUST; ANTI-SEMITISM.

Eyck, Erich (1878–1964), lawyer and historian. Born into a Jewish family in Berlin, Eyck studied law and practised as a lawyer in Berlin from 1906 until 1937. He contributed to the *Vossische Zeitung*, a liberal Berlin newspaper, from 1915 to 1933 and was editor of its legal supplement. He joined the DDP in the 1920s. He emigrated to Britain in 1937. He is known for his history of the Weimar Republic, and for his comparative work on Britain and Germany.

F

factory community. *See* BETRIEBSGEMEIN-
SCHAFT.

Falkenhausen, Alexander, Freiherr von
(1878–1966), military governor of occupied
Belgium and France, 1940–4. A Prussian
career soldier, Falkenhausen was decorated
in World War I and served in World War II
after being recalled from China by Hitler. As
governor of Belgium he had hostages executed and Jews deported. He was imprisoned
on suspicion of complicity in the JULY BOMB
PLOT, and remained in Dachau until the end
of the war. In 1951 he was sentenced to
twelve years' imprisonment by the Belgian
authorities, but was released after three
weeks. He died in Nassau.

Falkenhayn, Erich von (1861–1922), Prussian officer and politician; German army
chief of staff (1914–16). After serving as a
military instructor to the Chinese army early
in his career, Falkenhayn served as a general
staff officer in the BOXER REBELLION, then as
Prussian war minister (1913–15). He replaced
Helmuth von MOLTKE as chief of the general
staff of the German army within weeks of
the outbreak of WORLD WAR I following a
disagreement. He planned the VERDUN
offensive in 1916, but his intentions were
thwarted by the SOMME offensive on the
western front and the Brusilov offensive on
the Eastern Front. In September he took
command of the 9th Army and halted the
advance of Romanian troops at the Vulkan
and Red Tower Passes. He was then sent to

Gaza to command Turkish forces in 1917,
but was unable to prevent their defeat. In
1918 and 1919 he was supreme commander
of the 10th Army.

Falkenhorst, Nikolaus von (1885–1968),
commander of German forces in Norway
during World War II. A career soldier who
served in World War I, and a FREIKORPS
member during the early years of the
Weimar Republic, he was later attached to
the war ministry and the German embassies
in Prague, Belgrade and Bucharest. He took
part in the Polish campaign, and was appointed commander of German troops in
Norway in 1940. He was dismissed after
coming into conflict with the Reich commissioner in Norway, Josef TERBOVEN. Initially sentenced to death after the war by a
British tribunal, he eventually served 6 years
of a 20-year sentence.

Fallada, Hans (pen name of Rudolf Ditzen;
1893–1947), author. Born in Greifswald, the
son of a Prussian judge, Fallada was the
author of the popular novel *Kleiner Mann –
was nun?* (*Little Man, What Now?*, 1933). The
book depicted the life of a sales assistant and
his wife during the Depression, and was
translated into 20 languages. After the Nazis
came to power Fallada wrote children's
books. He served briefly in World War II, and
was appointed a mayor by the Soviets in
1945.

Fassbinder, Rainer Werner (1945–82), writer
and film director. Born in Munich, Fassbinder

was perhaps the most influential director of the 'new German cinema', and directed some forty feature films, as well as writing for the cinema, stage and television. Among his best-known films were *Die bitteren Tränen der Petra von Kant* ('The Bitter Tears of Petra von Kant', 1972), *Effi Briest* (1974), based on the novel by FONTANE, and *Die Ehe der Maria Braun* ('The Marriage of Maria Braun', 1978). He also directed a television adaptation of *Berlin Alexanderplatz* by Alfred DÖBLIN. Fassbinder was a Marxist, who was influenced by the work of Bertolt BRECHT, and much of his work, which was intentionally melodramatic, was politically engaged.

Fatherland Front. *See* VATERLÄNDISCHE FRONT.

Fatherland Party. *See* VATERLANDSPARTEI.

Faulhaber, Michael von (1869–1952), Roman Catholic cardinal and archbishop of Munich. Ordained as a priest in 1892, Faulhaber was appointed professor of theology at Strasbourg (1903), bishop of Speyer (1911) and archbishop of Munich (1917). He was made a cardinal in 1921. Faulhaber was an anti-republican Bavarian legitimist who welcomed the CONCORDAT of 1933, but defended the church against Nazi incursions and preached against ideological 'neo-paganism'. His criticism of the regime was intermittent, partial and mainly limited to the defence of church interests. He was not involved in the 1944 JULY BOMB PLOT, and expressed his opposition to the idea of violent resistance. After 1945 he was also a sharp critic of US DENAZIFICATION policies.

FDGB (*Freier Deutscher Gewerkschaftsbund*), the Association of Free German Trade Unions, the East German trade-union organization. It was founded in 1945 in the Soviet zone of occupation as the coordinating body for 15 separate unions. It deferred to the principle of the leading role of the SED in the German Democratic Republic, and was occupied with the administration of social security, the maintenance of labour discipline, overseeing safety regulations and other similar tasks. There was effectively no right to strike. The FDGB was dissolved in 1990.

FDP (*Freie Demokratische Partei*), the Free Democratic Party, the centrist liberal party of the Federal Republic of Germany. The party was founded in December 1948, bringing together a number of regional liberal parties with different names that had sprung up in the western zones of occupation after World War II. The new party also reunited the two principal strands of German liberalism from the empire and the Weimar Republic. The first had been embodied in the NATIONAL LIBERALS, and later in the DVP (*Deutsche Volkspartei*); the second in the Progressive Party (*DEUTSCHE FORTSCHRITTSPARTEI*) and the DDP. The first president of the FDP was Theodor HEUSS, of the Democratic People's Party (*Demokratische Volkspartei*), which had been founded in Nordbaden-Württemberg in 1946. In so far as the new party had a clearly identifiable constituency, it stood to the right of the CDU. Its regional strength was initially in the traditionally liberal southwest.

The FDP has formed coalitions with both major parties. It was in power with the CDU under ADENAUER from 1949 to 1956, and again from 1961 to 1966. During the 1960s it moved to the left under the leadership of Walter SCHEEL. The party supported the election of Gustav HEINEMANN, the SPD candidate for the presidency, in 1969, and formed the 'social-liberal' coalition with the SPD under Willy BRANDT. Scheel became foreign minister in the Brandt administration, and was then elected president himself in 1974, and Hans-Dietrich GENSCHER became party leader, a post he retained until 1985. In 1982 the FDP switched its support from the SPD to the CDU, Genscher remained foreign minister (until 1992), and the party remained in power until the defeat of the KOHL administration in 1998. Following Genscher's retirement in 1985 the party leadership passed first to Martin Bangemann (until 1988), and then to Klaus Kinkel.

February Patent (1861), revision of the Austrian constitution. Its provisions superseded those of the OCTOBER DIPLOMA of the previous year. The February Patent was introduced by the interior minister Anton Ritter von SCHMERLING, and moved the constitutional emphasis of the empire away from conservative aristocratic federalism towards a more centralized system which favoured the interests of the German-speaking middle classes. It provided for the establishment of a bicameral parliament consisting of a house of lords (*Herrenhaus*) and a lower house (*Abgeordnetenhaus*) of some 300 members elected by the provincial assemblies. Elections to the new REICHSRAT in May 1861 were boycotted by the Hungarians, Croats and Italians, and the other nationalities were also opposed to the new system. The reform raised afresh the problem of Hungary's constitutional status within the empire, and a separate Magyar parliament assembled in Pest in April 1861, voicing demands for the recognition of the Hungarian constitution of 1848. The constitutional arrangements introduced by the February Patent were superseded by those of the 1867 *AUSGLEICH*.

Feder, Gottfried (1883–1941), Nazi politician. Born in Würzburg into a family of Franconian civil servants, Feder studied engineering and was co-proprietor of a Munich building firm from 1908. He was an influential figure in the early Nazi Party. Feder became involved in right-wing Bavarian politics after World War I, propounding anti-capitalist policies that were later rejected by the party leadership in the more pragmatic electioneering of the Depression. Feder was given a minor position in the economics ministry in 1933, but was dismissed in 1934 after provoking powerful opposition to his rural settlements policy and retired from politics.

Federal Constitutional Court (*Bundesverfassungsgericht*), supreme court of the Federal Republic of Germany. It was established in September 1951 to rule in disputes between the federation and the federal states and has the power to declare that the actions of a given party or the contents of a law are unconstitutional. It is independent of all other constitutional bodies and adjudicates between them. Private citizens may also bring cases before the court, if they feel their basic individual rights have been violated by the state and they have not obtained satisfaction in the lower courts. Based at Karlsruhe, the Federal Constitutional Court consists of two senates, each with eight judges, all of whom must be at least 40 years old. They are elected by the BUNDESTAG and the BUNDESRAT and appointed by the federal president for terms of twelve years. The Federal Constitutional Court has come to public attention on a number of occasions, for example in connection with the reform of PARAGRAPH 218, asylum law, conscientious objections to military service and the deployment of German military forces. Most notably it was responsible in 1956 for banning the KPD.

Federal Republic of Germany (FRG; German name: *Bundesrepublik Deutschland*, BRD), state established in 1949 comprising the former US, British and French zones of occupation; in 1990, with the reunification of Germany, it absorbed the GERMAN DEMOCRATIC REPUBLIC.

The impact of the Cold War on occupied Germany during the later 1940s led to the emergence of two separate states based on the Soviet zone of occupation ('East Germany') on the one hand and the western zones of occupation ('West Germany') on the other. The US and British zones merged first, to form the BIZONE (27 May 1947), which was superseded by the TRIZONE when the French zone was added on 8 April 1949. The unification process in the West, which began with the currency reform and the introduction of the Deutsche Mark (the 'Deutschmark'), was accelerated by the Berlin blockade (June 1948–May 1949; *see* BERLIN AIRLIFT). In the spring of 1949 a PARLIAMENTARY COUNCIL (*Parlamentarischer Rat*), representing the political parties of the West and elected by the western *Länder*, concluded its discussions and proposed a 'BASIC LAW' (*Grundgesetz*), which was introduced as a provisional constitution for the western zones pending the acceptance of a permanent constitution for the whole of Germany. The military governors approved the Basic Law on 12 May, and it was ratified by ten of the eleven LANDTAGE in the west a week later. (The exception was Bavaria.) The first parliamentary elections took place in August; the Parliamentary Council had already determined that the seat of government should be in Bonn.

The history of the Federal Republic can be divided into four broad, overlapping periods. The first of these is that dominated by the conservative governments of Konrad ADENAUER, who occupied the chancellorship from 1949 to 1963. It saw the end of Allied occupation in the former western zones, and the integration of the Federal Republic into the Western Bloc. Adenauer made early commitments to cooperate with the Western Allies on the issue of reparations, and the process of integration was accelerated after the outbreak of the Korean War by the expectation that West Germany would make a contribution to the western defence system.

The Bonn treaty of 1952 signed by the Federal Republic, Britain, France and the United States proposed the establishment of a European Defence Community, which would entail the cancellation of the Statute of Occupation, but when the French National Assembly failed to agree to the proposal in 1954, new treaties were agreed in Paris that enabled West Germany to become a member of NATO in 1955. The Federal Republic became a sovereign state the same year, and the SAARLAND was incorporated into the Federal Republic in 1957. The integration of the Federal Republic into Western Europe had been strengthened by West German membership of the European Coal and Steel Community (along with France,

Italy, Belgium, the Netherlands and Luxembourg) since 1951. This relationship was reinforced when the Federal Republic signed the treaty of Rome in 1957 and became a founding member of the European Economic Community (EEC), which came into force the following year.

The domestic political stability of the 1950s was reinforced by economic recovery and prosperity, and in the general election of 1957 the CDU and CSU gained a marginal absolute majority of votes (50.2%). But what looked like stability to some looked like stagnation to others. Moreover the high-handed domination of political life by Chancellor Adenauer attracted increasing criticism. Former Nazis had been promoted to senior positions, while the Communist Party (KPD) had been banned. The turning point came with the *SPIEGEL* AFFAIR of October 1962, and Adenauer announced his resignation the following year. The following six years constituted a transitional period between the Cold War conservatism of the 1950s and the era of the social–liberal coalitions of the 'long' 1970s. Ludwig ERHARD succeeded Adenauer as chancellor, and although it seemed at first that little had changed, the postwar economic boom was already running out of steam, and criticism of the government's economic policy following economic problems (which were felt particularly in the industrial Ruhr valley) led to the formation of the GRAND COALITION (CDU and SPD) in 1966, led by Kurt Georg KIESINGER, a Christian Democrat and former minister-president of Baden-Württemberg. Although the economic reforms undertaken by the new government seemed to have stimulated economic growth, and despite a more flexible approach to foreign policy, the three years of the coalition (1966–9) were dominated by political protest, above all by students and other young people. The coalition itself was riven by internal tensions, and these came to a head with the election of the SPD candidate Gustav HEINEMANN as federal president. Heinemann's election had been made possible by the votes of FDP members of the Bundestag and a new SPD–FDP coalition was widely expected. In the election of 28 September 1969, however, the liberals lost support and it was only with a narrow majority that the new chancellor, Willy BRANDT (SPD), was elected.

Brandt's administration brought fundamental changes, above all to the foreign policy of the Federal Republic. His *OSTPOLITIK* opened up relations with the German Democratic Republic, Eastern Europe and the Soviet Union, and domestic politics saw an extension of the welfare state and a liberalization of society. The popularity of Brandt's policies was confirmed by an increased majority for the social–liberal coalition in the elections of 1972, but Brandt himself was forced to resign following a spy scandal, and was succeeded by Helmut SCHMIDT in 1974. If the early years of the social–liberal coalition had been dominated by a foreign-policy agenda, the Schmidt administration (1974–82) was faced by difficult domestic issues. Not least of these was the problem of political extremism, which peaked in the middle of the 1970s with kidnappings and murders by the Baader–Meinhof group (the RED ARMY FACTION). Schmidt also faced a much more forbidding economic environment than his predecessors. Although the Federal Republic was perhaps less affected by the end of the postwar boom than many other countries, unemployment rose steadily, and economic disagreements prompted the majority of FDP members in the Bundestag to support a no-confidence vote in the government in 1982. This brought down the government and paved the way for a centre–right coalition under Helmut KOHL (CDU), whose position was reinforced by the early general election of 1983 in which the coalition parties won 48.8% of the vote between them.

Kohl remained in office for 16 years, making him the longest-serving chancellor since Bismarck. The first years of the administration coincided with the 'new Cold War' and opposition from the peace movement in Germany to the stationing of new American missiles in the Federal Republic. The commitment of the peace protesters reflected deeper and more long-term changes in the political landscape of the Federal Republic. Those involved in the new social movements of the 1970s – such as the environmentalist movement, the movement for greater equality and emancipation for women and the peace movement itself – were becoming actively involved in electoral politics, above all with the GREENS. The political upheaval that eclipsed all others, however, was the unexpected collapse of the Soviet Bloc, and with it the fall of the East German regime in 1989. During the months preceding the reunification of Germany and the first all-German elections, Kohl stole a march on the East German dissidents organized in BÜNDNIS 90 and his Social Democratic rivals with promises of economic prosperity for the 'new federal states' in a united Germany. The former German Democratic Republic was effectively absorbed by the Federal Republic, and the chancellor succeeded in winning the election of 1990. The Union parties (CDU/CSU) won 43.8% of the vote, and the FDP 11%. While the West German Greens failed to win the 5% of the vote necessary to enter parliament their East German counterparts won 6%. The Party of Democratic Socialism (PDS; the successor to the SED) won 11.1% of the vote in the East and was also represented in Bonn.

With reunification the Federal Republic underwent the most fundamental political changes since its foundation, but despite the continuing economic difficulties of the new federal states, and a resurgence of the extreme right even in some of the most prosperous regions of West Germany, the party-political structure of Germany in the 1990s remained broadly similar to that of the old Federal Republic of the 1980s. The Kohl coalition went on to win the 1994 election, and it was only with its defeat in 1998 and the formation of a coalition at national level by the SPD and the Greens that new political constellations began to take shape.

Fehrenbach, Konstantin (1852–1926), CENTRE PARTY politician; chancellor (1920–1). Born in Wellendingen, the son of a primary school teacher, Fehrenbach was a lawyer by profession and member of the Baden LANDTAG for the Centre Party from 1901 to 1913. He was elected to the Reichstag in 1903 and was both the last president of the imperial Reichstag and the first president of the republican Reichstag. He served as chancellor from June 1920 until May 1921, taking on himself the thankless responsibility of representing Germany at the REPARATIONS conferences at Spa (1920) and in London (1921). His government fell when the DNVP withdrew its support. He died in Freiburg im Breisgau.

Fein, Georg (1803–69), democratic politician and journalist. Fein started his career as editor of the *Deutsche Tribüne* in Munich before emigrating to Paris and Zurich (where he was editor of the *Neue Zürcher Zeitung*). He also spent some time in Britain and the United States. He was a member of YOUNG GERMANY and co-founder of workers' associations. In 1852 he set up a school in Switzerland.

Felix, German code name for the planned occupation of Gibraltar, with Spanish support, in 1940.

Ferdinand I (1793–1875), emperor of Austria (1835–48). He succeeded his father Franz I, but was prevented by his physical and mental disability from taking on any real political role. The government was run by METTERNICH and KOLOWRAT. Ferdinand and his court left Vienna for Innsbruck during the REVOLUTIONS OF 1848, and the emperor abdicated in favour of his nephew FRANZ JOSEPH.

Fichte, Johann Gottlieb (1762–1814), philosopher. Born in Rammenau, near Bischofswerda in Saxony, Fichte studied theology and philosophy at Jena, and was appointed

professor there in 1794. He was subsequently also professor at Erlangen (1805) and the first elected rector of the University of Berlin (1811). Fichte was a follower of KANT, whose philosophy he modified. His *Reden an die deutsche Nation (Addresses to the German Nation*, 1807–8) were powerful appeals to German nationalism in support of the struggle against Napoleon.

Fickert, Auguste (1855–1910), Austrian feminist. Fickert was a primary school teacher and founder (1893) of the General Austrian Women's Association (*Allgemeiner Österreichischer Frauenverein*). She distinguished herself from liberal campaigners for women's rights, and although more sympathetic to the Social Democratic movement and the position of working-class women, she aspired to a moral regeneration of society. Nevertheless she was active in fighting for women's suffrage and educational rights, including admission to universities, and on behalf of poorer women.

final solution (*Endlösung*), Nazi euphemism for the mass murder of European Jews (*see* HOLOCAUST).

Fischer, Joseph ('Joschka') (1948–), GREEN politician; foreign minister (1998–). Joschka Fischer was born in Gerabronn, Schwäbisch Hall, and joined the Greens in 1980. As a leader of the pragmatic wing of the party (the *REALOS*) he helped to bring about the *rapprochement* between the Greens and the SPD, which made possible the formation of 'red–green' coalitions. In the SPD–Green government of the state of Hesse, Fischer himself was a minister for the environment and energy (1985–7) and deputy minister-president, with additional responsibility for the environment and federal issues (1991–4). From 1994 to 1998 he spoke for the Greens in the Bundestag, and became German foreign minister in the red–green coalition that took office at national level in 1998.

Fischer, Ruth (pseudonym of Elfriede Eisler; 1895–1961), Communist politician. Born in Leipzig, Fischer spent her youth in Vienna and was first a member of the Austrian SDAP, and then one of the co-founders of the KPÖ, the Austrian Communist Party. She returned to Germany in 1919 and became leader of the Communist Party (KPD) there in 1924. She was also elected to the Reichstag in 1924, and was a member of the executive and the Presidium of the Comintern from the same year. She was expelled from the party in 1926, and ceased to sit in the Reichstag in 1928. She left Germany for France in 1933, and emigrated to the United States in 1941.

Fischer controversy, debate sparked in the 1960s by Fritz Fischer's *Griff nach der Weltmacht* (1961, published in English as *Germany's Aims in World War I* in 1967), which argued that there were long-term continuities in German foreign policy between and during the two world wars. More seriously, Fischer argued that Germany had deliberately sought war in 1914, and was more responsible for precipitating the conflict than any other power. His thesis, restated more radically in his later book *Krieg der Illusionen* (*War of Illusions*, 1969), challenged the prevalent interpretation among the conservative historical establishment of postwar West Germany that World War I was Germany's fault least of all, and that at most its outbreak was a consequence of the mismanagement of a diplomatic crisis in 1914. It also undermined the argument that World War II was 'Hitler's war'. In such a context Hitler's aggression appeared less anomalous, and World War II less convincingly attributable entirely to Nazism. Fischer was bitterly attacked by other German historians, but the ensuing debate, and the research interest in imperial Germany that it provoked, proved decisively that he was right. Few historians would now dispute Germany's responsibility for the outbreak of World War I.

Fischer Verlag, literary publishing house founded in 1886 by Samuel Fischer (1859–1934).

Flak, abbreviation for *Flugabwehrkanone*, 'anti-aircraft gun'.

Flick, Friedrich (1883–1956), industrialist. A leading Ruhr businessman, and a member of the conservative DVP during the Weimar Republic, Flick made donations to the Nazis (among other political parties) in 1932 and 1933, and to the SS on an annual basis. He joined the Nazi Party in 1937 and profited both from state munitions contracts and the expropriation of Jewish property. During World War II Flick's concerns employed almost 50,000 slave labourers, the overwhelming majority of whom died. Flick was sentenced to seven years' imprisonment in 1947, but released in 1950. Some assets were confiscated, but the Flick business was rebuilt after the war. Flick consistently refused to pay compensation for the exploitation of slave labour on the grounds that he had hired the labour from the SS.

Flick affair, financial scandal of the 1980s. The scandal broke in 1982 following the investigation of Eberhard von Brauchitsch, chief executive of the Flick company, for bribery and corruption. Among the senior politicians implicated were the finance minister Hans Matthöfer (SPD), and the economics minister Graf LAMBSDORFF (FDP), who became the first serving government minister to be indicted while in office when his parliamentary immunity was lifted by the Bundestag in December 1983. Some 700 politicians were investigated for tax evasion by the federal prosecutor, including the agriculture minister, Josef Ertl (FDP). Lambsdorff resigned on 26 June and he was brought to trial less then a week later (2 July 1984), along with Hans Friderichs (FDP), his predecessor as economics minister. The scandal also brought about the resignation of Rainer Barzel (CDU), as president of the Bundestag (25 October 1984).

Florian, Friedrich Karl (1894–1975), Nazi politician and publicist. Florian was born in Essen and served as a volunteer fighter pilot in World War I. He was shot down and captured by the British, returned to Germany in 1919, joined the DEUTSCHVÖLK-ISCHER SCHUTZ- UND TRUTZBUND in 1920, and the Nazi Party in 1925. He was elected to the Reichstag in the Nazi landslide of 1930, and was *Gauleiter* of Düsseldorf from 1930 to 1945, and established a number of local Nazi newspapers in north-west Germany. He was fined and sentenced to six and a half years in prison by a denazification court in 1949, and released in 1951.

Flossenbürg, concentration camp in the Upper Palatinate, Bavaria. The SS built the camp in 1938, and some 30,000 people died there. The victims included many of those involved in the failed JULY BOMB PLOT of 1944.

Fontane, Theodor (1819–98), writer and journalist. Fontane was born in Neuruppin, a small town in Brandenburg, into a Protestant family descended from Huguenots. Like his father he was an apothecary by profession. In 1849 he became a full-time journalist and spent some time in London as a foreign correspondent and travel writer. *Ein Sommer in London* ('A summer in London') was published in 1854, and he also wrote a traveller's account of Scotland. He reported on the GERMAN–DANISH WAR of 1864, the AUSTRO-PRUSSIAN WAR of 1866 and the FRANCO-PRUSSIAN WAR of 1870–1, and was imprisoned (by the Prussians) during the latter conflict on suspicion of spying. He published his first novel, *Vor dem Sturm* ('Before the storm') in 1878. This was followed by *L'adultera* in 1882, *Schach von Wuthenow* in 1883, and *Irrungen, Wirrungen*, the first of his major works, in 1888. *Effi Briest*, perhaps his best-known work in the English-speaking world, was published in 1895. Fontane's work constitutes a chronicle of the social mores of Brandenburg and Berlin society during the rise of Prussia. It is complemented by his journalistic writing on Brandenburg (*Wanderungen durch die Mark Brandenburg*, 'Travels through the Brandenburg March', published in four volumes between 1862 and 1882).

Forster, Albert (1902–54), Nazi politican and regional leader. Born in Fürth, Forster joined the NSDAP in 1923, was elected as a Nazi to the Reichstag for Franconia in 1930 and became *Gauleiter* of Danzig the same year. He was condemned to death by the Poles in 1948 for wartime atrocities, but the sentence was commuted to life imprisonment.

Forster, (Johann) Georg (Adam) (1754–94), writer and revolutionary activist. Born the son of a minister in Nassenhuben, near Danzig (now Gdańsk in Poland), Forster travelled to Russia with his father during his childhood, and then accompanied him on a trip around the world with James Cook. His account of the voyage, which was published in English and German, made him famous. He became a librarian in Mainz in 1788, and his political activity began with the French Revolutionary Wars. When Mainz was occupied by the French general Custine in 1792 Forster joined the pro-Revolutionary/French Society of Friends of Liberty and Equality. He was president of the MAINZ JACOBIN CLUB, and vice president of the Rhineland National Convention. Forster and others demanded the annexation of Mainz by the French, and in 1793 he went to Paris with a delegation to argue the case. In his absence the city was surrounded by counter-revolutionary troops and he died in Paris the following year at the age of 38.

Fortschrittliche Volkspartei (Progressive People's Party, FVP), a liberal party formed in 1910 by members of the FREISINNIGE VOLKSPARTEI, the FREISINNIGE VEREINIGUNG, the *Deutsche Volkspartei* (DVP) and the pre-World War I *Deutsche Volkspartei* (1868–1910, a liberal party whose strength was concentrated in south-west Germany). The core constituency of the *Fortschrittliche Volkspartei* was the educated middle class (*BILDUNGS-BÜRGERTUM*) and the new lower middle class. It was a forerunner of the German Democratic Party (*Deutsche Demokratische Partei*, DDP) of the WEIMAR REPUBLIC.

Fortschrittspartei (Progress Party or 'Progressives'). *See DEUTSCHE FORTSCHRITTSPARTEI.*

Four-Power Agreement on Berlin (3 September 1971), agreement reached by Britain, France, the Soviet Union and the USA. In the context of the OSTPOLITIK of SPD chancellor Willy BRANDT, the ambassadors of the four victorious Allied powers from World War II met in Berlin from 26 March 1970 to discuss the regulation of the status of the city. The Soviet Union eventually agreed to guarantee unimpeded transit to and from west Berlin from West Germany and to recognise the western sectors as effectively part of the west German economy and legal system, but not as a constituent part of the Federal Republic.

Four-Year Plan, a policy devised against the background of the gathering economic (and potentially political) crisis of 1936. Its ostensible aim was to increase Germany's international economic independence, while in practice it brought the regime greater control over the economy as it sought to co-ordinate economic resources in preparation for war. The plan, overseen by GÖRING, was intended to resolve conflicts of interest in the allocation of currency reserves between the demand for raw-material imports for the arms industry and food imports to meet the shortfall that German agriculture was unable to cover. The plan signified a further move away from the collapsing international free-trade system, and more specifically in the direction of policies based on the notion of AUTARKY, or economic self-sufficiency, albeit within the 'greater economic space' (*Grossraum*) that would be created by German territorial expansion. Wages, prices and labour mobility were made subject to stringent controls in an attempt to contain inflationary pressures. The Four-Year Plan had limited success and was superseded from 1938 by the systematic plunder of the economic resources of occupied Europe.

Francis. *See FRANZ.*

Franck, James (1882–1964), physicist. Born in Hamburg, Franck was educated at Heidelberg and Berlin and was decorated with the IRON CROSS in World War I. He was appointed professor of experimental physics at Göttingen in 1921 at the same time as Max BORN, and (with Gustav HERTZ) was awarded the Nobel prize for physics in 1925 for his work on quantum theory. Although his military service entitled him to exemption from Nazi legislation excluding Jews from public service, he resigned in protest in 1933 and moved to America, where he later worked on the development of atomic weapons. In 1945 he warned the Americans against using the atom bomb against living targets.

Franco-Prussian War (1870–1), culminating conflict of the German Wars of UNIFICATION. The changed balance of power in central Europe that arose from the outcome of the AUSTRO-PRUSSIAN WAR and the establishment of the NORTH GERMAN CONFEDERATION was perceived as a threat in France. Napoleon III sought to assert himself with claims to territory on the left bank of the Rhine, and then with an attempt to acquire Luxembourg, which passed without the outbreak of hostilities. (The independence and neutrality of Luxembourg were guaranteed by a conference in London of 7–11 May 1867.)

Tension remained between France and Prussia, however, and was increased by the Spanish succession crisis that followed the revolution there in 1868, and the overthrow of Queen Isabella. The Spanish government offered the throne to Leopold Hohenzollern-Sigmaringen, a Catholic relative of the Prussian ruling family, the Hohenzollerns. In supporting Leopold's claim BISMARCK saw a number of opportunities. The succession of a Hohenzollern would irritate and even humiliate the French, and either weaken Napoleon or lead to a war, either of which would permit the completion of unification without undue interference from France. Under pressure from France, however, the Sigmaringen candidate withdrew his candidature, and it required the crisis prompted by the EMS TELEGRAM to bring France and Prussia into military conflict.

The war started in 15 July 1870. The French forces were 224,000 strong, while the Prussian forces, under General Helmuth Karl von MOLTKE, numbered 475,000, and were generally better organized. Napoleon ordered an advance on Berlin, but the French forces met the Prussians, who were also advancing, at Saarbrücken on 2 August. On 12 August Napoleon handed over command of the Rhine Army to marshals MacMahon and Bazaine, who suffered a defeat at Gravelotte on 18 August. This was followed by the devastating defeat at SEDAN on 1–2 September, where Napoleon was taken prisoner. The Germans marched on Paris as the French declared the Third Republic (19 September) and continued the conflict with partisan warfare. Bazaine surrendered at Metz on 27 October. Peace came with the French surrender in the new year. The German empire was proclaimed at Versailles on 18 January, and the armistice was signed on 28 January, pending the election of a French national assembly. By the treaty of Frankfurt (10 May 1871), Germany annexed Alsace and half of Lorraine, and France had to pay an indemnity of 5 billion francs together with occupation costs until the indemnity was settled. France paid these reparations promptly. Germany was united by war, and the nature of the conflict and the peace terms set a disturbing precedent for the conduct of German foreign policy by Bismarck's 20th-century admirers.

Frank, Anne (1929–45), German-born Dutch Jewish girl, famous for her diary, which was written while she lived in hiding from the Nazis. Anne Frank was born in Frankfurt am Main, but her family moved to Amsterdam in the 1930s to escape from the Nazis and went into hiding there after the occupation of the Netherlands. Anne kept a diary of her time in hiding up to the family's arrest by the Gestapo in 1944. All the members of the family except Anne's father, Otto Frank, died in Nazi extermination camps. Her diary was published after the end of the war.

Frank, Hans (1900–46), Nazi lawyer and governor general of occupied Poland. Born in Karlsruhe, Frank was active in the FREIKORPS and became an early member of the Munich *DEUTSCHE ARBEITERPARTEI* (DAP, the forerunner of the Nazi Party). He practised as a lawyer in Munich from 1926, and became head of the Nazi Party legal office in 1929. In 1933 he became Bavarian minister of justice, and in 1934 Reich minister without portfolio. From 1939 to 1945 he was governor general of the so-called '*GENERAL-GOUVERNEMENT*', the rump of Poland that remained after the German and Soviet annexations. He retained the post until the end of the war despite being stripped of his party and legal positions in 1942, when he made a call for a return to constitutional rule following the execution of a friend. He was tried and hanged as a war criminal at Nuremberg.

Frankfurt, treaty of (10 May 1871), treaty that concluded the FRANCO-PRUSSIAN WAR on the basis of an earlier agreement at Versailles.

Frankfurt am Main, one of the largest cities in Germany, and the country's financial capital. The site of a Roman military encampment, Frankfurt was the seat of Frankish kings in the early Middle Ages. The city was an important commercial city from the 13th century, and a leading publishing centre after the invention of printing. Frankfurt has been closely connected with the constitutional history of Germany. It was an imperial city from 1372 until the abolition of the Holy Roman Empire in 1806. The emperor was crowned in the cathedral in Frankfurt from 1562, and important imperial institutions were located there. The federal diet (Bundestag) of the GERMAN CONFEDERATION met in Frankfurt, the German National Assembly (the FRANKFURT PARLIAMENT) met there during the REVOLUTIONS OF 1848, and the city was considered as a possible capital city for the FEDERAL REPUBLIC OF GERMANY in the wake of the division of Germany after World War II. At the end of the 20th century the city's population was 643,600. It is the seat of the German federal bank (Bundesbank) and of the European Central Bank.

Frankfurter Allgemeine Zeitung, the leading conservative daily newspaper of the Federal Republic of Germany, and the journalistic forum of the establishment. It was established in 1949 and has a circulation approaching half a million. Its pre-war predecessor, the *Frankfurter Zeitung*, was founded in 1856 and was published until 1943.

Frankfurt Parliament (1848), the constituent National Assembly elected at Frankfurt am Main during the REVOLUTIONS OF 1848. A 'PRE-PARLIAMENT' met at the end of March 1848 and called for the election of a constituent assembly. The parliament itself met on 18 May at the Paulskirche in Frankfurt. The election arrangements allowed for 649 members, but a number of districts in Austria had failed to return anybody, and 585 actually met. The delegates formed a number of political factions, ranging from conservatives and liberal constitutionalists to left-wing democrats. Their social background was predominantly in the upper middle and upper classes, and senior civil servants (including university teachers) predominated on the right, while the left-wing factions had more members of the professions. Heinrich von GAGERN was elected president, Archduke Johann was elected Reich 'regent' (*REICHSVERWESER*) and the federal diet (Bundestag) of the GERMAN CONFEDERATION was dissolved. The 'professors' parliament', as it became known, was superseded by events. The revolutions were suppressed in most parts of Germany, and real political power quickly reverted to the princes. The delegates could come to no satisfactory conclusions about where to set the boundaries of Germany, and certainly had no solution that would satisfy both Austria and the rest of Germany. To incorporate German Austria, separating it from the Habsburgs' other, non-German territories, was unacceptable in Vienna (and the idea was also rejected by many Austrian delegates at the parliament); to bring the entire Habsburg empire (which also included Magyars and many Slav peoples) into the new Germany would make nonsense of the delegates' (admittedly confused) cultural, historical and ethnic criteria. The parliament did, however, produce a constitution, which was recognized by 28 separate states. The king of Prussia, FRIEDRICH WILHELM IV, refused to accept the role offered him, however, and famously turned down the imperial crown of Germany. When radicals in the south German states tried to enforce the acceptance of the constitution anyway they were suppressed, with the help of Prussian troops. Following the dispersal of the parliament in Frankfurt, a group of radical democrats set up a 'rump parliament' in Stuttgart, but this too was dissolved, by the Württemberg army.

Frankfurt School, tradition of thinking, also referred to as 'critical theory', associated originally with the Institute of Social Research established at Frankfurt in 1923. It was collectively exiled from Germany after the Nazis came to power and re-established at Columbia University in New York. It moved back to Germany during the 1950s. The 'Frankfurt School' as a reasonably coherent like-minded group of critical intellectuals was much smaller than the whole personnel associated with the Institute, however. They include the Institute's director, Max HORKHEIMER, the cultural theorists Theodor ADORNO, Leo Löwenthal and Walter BENJAMIN, and the philosopher Herbert MARCUSE. Jürgen HABERMAS is also associated with the school. The approach of the school originated in a critical Marxist approach to the relationship between culture, politics and society, and much of the work produced by its leading members was of a pioneering interdisciplinary nature.

Frankfurt trial (December 1963–August 1965), the trial in Frankfurt am Main of the principal SS officers from AUSCHWITZ. Most of the accused were middle-class, well-educated men, and they had a variety of jobs at the camp, ranging from head of the camp pharmacy (Dr Victor Capesius) to guard unit. One of the accused was a prisoner. Most were charged with multiple murders or complicity in multiple murder. Capesius, for example, was accused of complicity in murder on four separate occasions, each time involving some 2000 people. Dr Franz Lucas, the camp medical officer, was accused of complicity in the murder of 1000 people. Dr Willi Frank, chief dentist, was charged with complicity in six multiple murders, each of 1000 people. Most of the defendants denied the charges. Three were acquitted, one case was abandoned on health grounds, and the rest were sentenced to terms ranging from life imprisonment plus 15 years hard labour for Joseph Klehr of the medical section, to 3 years 3 months hard labour (for Lucas).

Franz I (1708–65), Holy Roman emperor (1745–65), the husband of MARIA THERESIA, the archduchess of Austria. Franz was born Francis Stephen in Nancy, and married Maria Theresia in 1736, thereby changing the name of Austria's ruling dynasty to Habsburg-Lothringen. He became Holy Roman emperor in 1745 but played very little part in the affairs of state.

Franz II (1768–1835), Holy Roman emperor (1792–1806) and (as Franz I) emperor of Austria (1804–35). Franz succeeded his father LEOPOLD II, and adopted the title emperor of Austria when the end of the HOLY ROMAN EMPIRE was imminent. He was a conservative who was shocked by the French Revolution and sought to reverse the progressive effects of the reforms of his uncle JOSEPH II in Austria. Prince METTERNICH was chancellor for the latter part of his reign.

Franz Ferdinand (von D'Este) (1863–1914), Austrian archduke and heir to the throne of Austria-Hungary; his assassination in Sarajevo in 1914 was the immediate cause of WORLD WAR I. Born in Graz, Styria, Franz Ferdinand was the eldest son of the emperor FRANZ JOSEPH's younger brother Carl Ludwig, and became heir to the throne after the death of Crown Prince Rudolf in 1889 and of his father in 1896. He married Sophie Chotek von Chotkova in 1900. Franz Ferdinand's private life was happier than his involvement in public affairs. His proposals to reform the monarchy, either by establishing a federation or by establishing the Slavs on an equal footing with the Germans and Hungarians ('trialism'), made him unpopular. He and his wife were shot and killed on a visit to Sarajevo, capital city of BOSNIA-HERZEGOVINA, in 1914, by Gavrilo Princip, a member of the Serbian nationalist group known as the 'Black Hand'. (Austria-Hungary had annexed Bosnia-Herzegovina in 1908, and the Serbs wanted it to be part of a Serb-led Yugoslav state. They were also opposed to Franz Ferdinand's proposed reforms to give Slavs a greater role in the affairs of the empire, seeing it as a strategy to defuse separatist nationalism.) The assassination of the archduke proved to be the starting point of the crisis that led to World War I.

Franz Joseph (1830–1916), emperor of Austria (1848–1916) and king of Hungary (1867–1916). Born in Vienna, Franz Joseph was the eldest son of Archduke Franz Karl, brother of Emperor FERDINAND I. His father renounced his claim to the throne, and Ferdinand abdicated in the wake of the March REVOLUTION OF 1848. Franz Joseph was proclaimed emperor in December. The first part of his reign was characterized by the NEO-ABSOLUTISM of his minister-president, Prince Felix von SCHWARZENBERG, who held office from 1848 until his death in 1852. After the death of Schwarzenberg, Franz Joseph tried to continue ruling as an absolute monarch, but was increasingly forced to make concessions. Yet the multinational Habsburg empire was becoming increasingly anachronistic in the age of industrial nation states, and Italy and Germany were both unified at Austria's expense. After the defeat at SADOVÁ (Königgrätz) during the AUSTRO-PRUSSIAN WAR of 1866 the monarchy was forced to agree to the compromise (*AUS-GLEICH*) that effectively granted Hungary home rule (1867). The emperor attempted to transcend sectional interests and contain the centrifugal pressures undermining the integrity of the empire, and to invest the dynasty with the disinterested authority of the neutral state. He became an important symbol of unity, but ultimately Franz Joseph was admired for his diligent fulfilment of his duties rather than his skills as a statesman.

Frauenschaft, Nazi term (dating from 1931) that referred to the leaders' organization within the *DEUTSCHES FRAUENWERK*, itself an adjunct of the *NS-FRAUENSCHAFT*.

Frauen-Zeitung, weekly women's newspaper, founded in 1849 by Luise OTTO in the wake of the REVOLUTIONS OF 1848. Its concerns were with women's rights, better educational opportunities for women and greater participation by women in public life. The paper continued to publish until 1852, long after the revolution itself had run out of steam. It was revolutionary by virtue of its existence: previous women's papers had conformed to society's expectations of the role and interests of women or had folded quickly. Many of its contributors remained anonymous or adopted pseudonyms, and Otto herself was threatened by the authorities, her house was searched and she was eventually forced to move. But in the context of the emergent women's movement it took a moderate line, distancing itself from the more radical positions of 'emancipated' women. Otto was later a co-founder of the 'General German Women's Association' (*Allgemeiner Deutscher Frauenverein*) (1865) and co-editor of its journal *Neue Bahnen* (New Paths).

Frederick. *See* FRIEDRICH.

Frederick the Great. *See* FRIEDRICH II.

Frederick William. *See* FRIEDRICH WILHELM.

Free Conservative Party. *See* FREIKONSERVA-TIVE PARTEI.

Free Democratic Party. *See* FDP.

Free Trade Unions, those trade unions in both Germany and Austria that were associated with the Social Democratic labour movement rather than sponsored by the Roman Catholic Church or employers in the period between industrialization and the prohibition of independent trade unions by the Nazi dictatorship.

Freie Demokratische Partei. *See* FDP.

Freie Deutsche Jugend, the youth organization of the German Democratic Republic. Initially a nominally non-party organization in the Soviet zone of occupation, its leading positions were quickly filled by members of the Communist Party and subsequently the SED. From 1957 it was defined as the 'socialist youth organization of the GDR' and was the only legally permitted organization for those above the age of 14. (Those younger were members of the Young Pioneers.) It was a proscribed organization in the Federal Republic from 1951.

Freier Deutscher Gewerkschaftsbund. *See* FDGB.

Freie Volkspartei (FVP), the Free People's Party, a short-lived splinter party in the Federal Republic of Germany. It was a right-wing breakaway group from the FDP in 1956, and merged with the *DEUTSCHE PARTEI* (DP) in 1957.

Freiheitssender 904 ('freedom station 904'), an East German radio station that broadcast propaganda to the illegal communist movement in the West after the prohibition of the KPD by the FEDERAL CONSTITUTIONAL COURT. According to West German sources it claimed to transmit from within West Germany, but was actually situated near Magdeburg.

Freiherr, the German equivalent of 'baron'.

Freiin, the German equivalent of 'baroness'.

Freikonservative Partei, the Free Conservative Party, the pro-Bismarckian wing of the German conservatives in the early imperial period. A number of former liberals also joined the party. The party was founded in 1866 and changed its name to *Deutsche Reichspartei* after the founding of the empire. It had no real party organization, and no programme until 1906. The Free Conservatives were more influential than their numbers suggested, and included senior civil servants and big businessmen such as Wilhelm von Kardorff, the founder of the Central Union of German Industrialists. A number of Prussia's ministers during the imperial period were Free Conservatives, as were many of the state secretaries of the Reich. The Free Conservatives were located between the German Conservatives (*DEUTSCH-KONSERVATIVE PARTEI*) and the NATIONAL LIBERAL PARTY. They were in favour of an assertive foreign and colonial policy, and in many respects were close to the PAN-GERMAN LEAGUE. They were conservative in domestic politics, and opposed radical reform, but were more pragmatically open-minded about the cautious modernization of Germany's political and economic systems. The electoral popularity of the Free Conservatives had declined considerably by the time of the last election under the empire (1912), when they won only twelve seats. Most former Free Conservatives were members or supporters of the nationalist DNVP during the Weimar Republic.

Freikorps ('free corps'), a generic term for a range of right-wing paramilitary units active in the early years of the Weimar Republic. (The term had previously been used of German nationalist units that fought the French during the Napoleonic Wars.) The Weimar-era Freikorps were largely manned by ex-officers who had had little or no experience of civilian employment or family life before the war. Although they were involved in campaigns of political terror and assassinations, they were also used by central and local government as auxiliary forces to put down leftist insurrections, including the communist uprising by the SPARTACUS LEAGUE in 1919. Rosa LUXEMBURG and Karl LIEBKNECHT were murdered by Freikorps members. The government proposal to disband the Freikorps – who had developed a taste for looting and vandalism – helped to provoke the KAPP PUTSCH in March 1920. Many Freikorps members went on to join the Nazi Party, and Ernst RÖHM, the head of the SA, was a former Freikorps leader.

Freisinnige Vereinigung, radical liberal party (1893–1910) formed after the break-up of the *DEUTSCHE FREISINNIGE PARTEI.*

Freisinnige Volkspartei, radical liberal party (1893–1910) formed after the break-up of the *DEUTSCHE FREISINNIGE PARTEI.* It placed particular emphasis on economic liberalism.

Freisler, Roland (1893–1945), Nazi lawyer and politician. Freisler joined the Nazi Party in 1925 and was elected to the Reichstag in 1932. He attended the WANNSEE CONFERENCE, and was president of the Berlin *VOLKS-GERICHTSHOF* (the 'people's court') from 1942. Freisler prosecuted the SCHOLLS in 1943 and the conspirators involved in the 1944 JULY BOMB PLOT. He was killed in court during an American air raid in February 1945.

French Revolutionary Wars. *See* COALITIONS, WARS OF THE.

Freud, Sigmund (1856–1939), Austrian psychologist. Born in Moravia, Freud studied medicine at Vienna, where he was appointed professor of neuropathology in 1882. He subsequently practised psychiatry in the Vienna hospital, where he developed his psychoanalytical theories at the turn of the century. He had established an international reputation by 1923, when he was appointed professor of neurology at Vienna, a position he held until the *Anschluss*. He fled to London in 1938. His theories had a profound cultural and social impact during the 20th century.

Freytag, Gustav (1816–95), popular novelist and politician. Freytag taught at Breslau as a young man, but he retired to concentrate on his writing. His most famous novel, *Soll und Haben* (*Debit and Credit*) was published in 1855 and was a best-seller depicting the life of the middle classes. He was a member of the NATIONAL LIBERAL PARTY in the North German Reichstag of 1867–70 and served in the Franco-Prussian War as a staff officer.

FRG. *See* FEDERAL REPUBLIC OF GERMANY.

Frick, Wilhelm (1877–1946), Nazi interior minister (1933–43). Born in Alsenz in the Palatinate into a middle-class family, Frick studied law and worked in the Munich police department from 1904 to 1923, and was designated chief of police by the conspirators in the BEER HALL PUTSCH. He was tried and imprisoned for his part in the putsch, but released in 1924 and elected to the Reichstag, and was leader of the Nazi Party's parliamentary faction from the following year. As interior minister and education minister in Thuringia from 1930 he was the first Nazi to hold ministerial office. He was appointed Reich interior minister in 1933, which enabled him to shape the administrative and civil-service policies of the Nazi regime. In 1943 he was replaced by HIMMLER and appointed protector of Bohemia and Moravia. He was tried as a major war criminal and hanged at Nuremberg.

Friedeburg, Hans Georg von (1895–1945), admiral. A submarine commander during World War I, Friedeburg was promoted to admiral in 1941, and was second admiral of the submarine force from 1943 to 1945. He was appointed supreme commander of the navy in May 1945 (when DÖNITZ took over as Führer), and was responsible for its surrender to the Allies. He committed suicide shortly afterwards.

Friedrich, Caspar David (1774–1840), Romantic painter. Born in Greifswald, Pomerania, Friedrich studied at the Copenhagen academy from 1794 to 1798 before settling in Dresden, where he remained for most of his life. Friedrich is the most widely known of all the German Romantic painters, and his work reflected the current preoccupation

with nature and spirituality. Many of his paintings are of landscapes, both real (the Baltic coast, the Harz mountains, the German forest) and imaginary (the Arctic), into which he introduced religious symbolism. Among his best-known works are *The Cross in the Mountains*, a chapel altar piece, which was exhibited in 1808; *Wanderer above the Sea of Fog* (1818) and *The Shipwreck in the Ice* (1809).

Friedrich I (1657–1713), king of Prussia (1701–13). Born in Königsberg, Friedrich was the son of Friedrich Wilhelm, the 'Great Elector' of Brandenburg. He succeeded to the electorate in 1688 and was crowned king of Prussia in 1701 by an agreement with Austria of the previous year. He was succeeded by his son Friedrich Wilhelm I.

Friedrich II (1712–86), Frederick the Great, king of Prussia (1740–86). Born in Berlin, the son of Friedrich Wilhelm I, Friedrich was mistreated by his father. He married in 1733 and succeeded to the throne in 1740. Known as the 'soldier king', he expanded Prussian territory and power considerably by annexing Silesia from Austria during the War of the AUSTRIAN SUCCESSION, allying himself with Britain on the winning side during the SEVEN YEARS WAR, and making Prussia the most competent military power on the continent. He was an 'absolute' monarch who sought to centralize political authority, and to enforce the subordination of dynastic and individual interests to those of the state. Friedrich liberalized the Prussian legal code and introduced social and economic reforms. He was also an important patron of the arts, played and composed for the flute, and corresponded with Voltaire.

Friedrich III (1831–1888), German emperor and king of Prussia, 1888. Friedrich III succeeded his father, king and emperor WILHELM I, but reigned for only 99 days before his death from throat cancer. As crown prince Friedrich Wilhelm he served in the wars against Denmark, Austria and France between 1864 and 1871.

Friedrich Wilhelm II (1744–97), king of Prussia (1786–97). He succeeded his uncle FRIEDRICH II (the Great). He joined Austria in the War of the First COALITION against revolutionary France from 1792 to 1795, and presided over the expansion of Prussia in the second and third partitions of Poland (1793 and 1795). The Prussian legal code (*Allgemeines Landrecht*) was introduced during his reign. Although cultured, Friedrich Wilhelm was considered a reactionary, whose religious edict (1788) inhibited religious toleration and freedom of expression. He was succeeded by his son FRIEDRICH WILHELM III.

Friedrich Wilhelm III (1770–1840), king of Prussia (1797–1840). He followed a policy of neutrality during the Wars of the Second and Third COALITIONS. After defeat by the French and the collapse of Prussia in 1807 he agreed to constitutional reforms, which were implemented by STEIN and HARDENBERG.

Friedrich Wilhelm IV (1795–1861), king of Prussia (1840–61). The eldest of seven (surviving) children of Friedrich Wilhelm III and Queen Luise, the crown prince was religious and had artistic and literary interests. His experience of growing up during the wars with France made him a romantic nationalist, and he came to believe in the divine nature of royal power and the necessity of an 'organic', corporative, Christian state as an alternative to constitutionalism or democracy. He came to the throne in 1840 and attempted to apply some of his ideas about the relationship between church and state. During the March REVOLUTION OF 1848 he made concessions to the insurgents in Berlin, issued a proclamation leading to the withdrawal of troops, and affected to adopt the cause of German unity. However, he turned down the crown of a united Germany offered to him by the FRANKFURT PARLIAMENT on 3 April 1849. He then retreated to Potsdam, where the clique ('camarilla') that formed around him took action to effect a restoration of the pre-revolutionary order. Berlin was reoccupied by General Friedrich von Wrangel, and the Prussian national assembly was closed down. From 1857 Friedrich Wilhelm suffered from cerebral arteriosclerosis, and his brother Wilhelm (the future WILHELM I) ruled as his regent.

Fritsch, Werner, Freiherr von (1880–1939), head of the army high command (1934–8). Born in Benrath, near Düsseldorf, into a military family, Fritsch served in World War I. He was promoted during the Weimar Republic and reached the rank of lieutenant general and was placed in command of Defence District III (Berlin) in 1932. In 1934 he became commander in chief of the Wehrmacht under the then defence minister General Werner von BLOMBERG. Fritsch was effectively dismissed in 1938 as a result of false accusations of homosexuality. Fritsch, along with Blomberg and von NEURATH, was a critic of Hitler's foreign policy, and all were removed in what became a general purge of potential opponents from the regime's conservative wing. Fritsch returned to his regiment, was found not guilty by a secret military court, and was killed in the Polish campaign in September 1939.

Fritzsche, Hans (1900–53), Nazi head of radio broadcasting. Fritzsche was the son of a civil servant from Bochum. He left university without graduating and joined the nationalist DNVP in 1923. He joined the Nazi Party in 1933 on being appointed head of the news service in the propaganda ministry's press section. He moved to the radio section in 1942 after five years as a political commentator on radio. He was acquitted of war crimes at Nuremberg and released in 1950 after a further trial by a German DENAZIFICATION court.

Führer ('leader'), title adopted by Hitler during the early years of the Nazi Party, presumably on the model of the Italian term *Duce*, the title adopted by Mussolini. It was widely used by the *Völkischer Beobachter*, the Nazi newspaper, in the early 1920s, before the

BEER HALL PUTSCH. After the death of President HINDENBURG in 1934 it became an official designation to denote the fusion of the offices of chancellor and president. In May 1945 Karl DÖNITZ, Hitler's successor, briefly assumed the post of Führer, before surrendering to the Allies.

Führer principle, anti-democratic Nazi slogan. It was used to reinforce the political principles of authority and hierarchy that underpinned Nazi political ideology. In place of the democratic organization of political parties, institutions and the clubs and societies of German associational life there would be leaders and followers.

fulfilment policy (*Erfüllungspolitik*), a term used to describe the foreign policy during the WEIMAR REPUBLIC of German governments who reluctantly agreed to accept the terms of the treaty of VERSAILLES. It was also a rallying point for the nationalist anti-democratic right (most significantly the DNVP), which was against fulfilment of the treaty in principle, but used the treaty's widespread unpopularity as a stick with which to beat the Weimar coalition parties and undermine the authority of successive governments.

functionalists. *See* STRUCTURALISTS.

Fundis, 'fundamentalists' in the GREEN movement. A term used to describe those who opposed the compromises of realists (*REALOS*) on the moderate wing of the movement.

Funk, Walther (1890–1960), Nazi economics minister. Funk was born in East Prussia and studied law at Berlin and Leipzig. In 1916 he became a journalist on the conservative *Börsenzeitung*, which he edited from 1922 to 1932. He joined the Nazi Party in 1931, and mediated between the party leadership and business interests. Appointed government press chief in 1933, he succeeded SCHACHT as economics minister in 1937, a post he held until the end of the war. He was also appointed president of the REICHSBANK in 1939 (again taking over the post from Schacht). He was given a life sentence at Nuremberg, not least for his part in the banking of the valuables of murdered Jews on behalf of the SS. He was released on health grounds in 1957.

Fürst, the German equivalent of 'prince'. The title is derived from an early medieval word meaning 'first'. The feminine (princess) is *Fürstin*.

FVP. *See FORTSCHRITTLICHE VOLKSPARTEI; FREIE VOLKSPARTEI.*

G

Gagern, (Wilhelm) Heinrich (August), Freiherr von (1799–1880), leading liberal politician and president of the FRANKFURT PARLIAMENT of 1848. Born in Bayreuth, Gagern fought at Waterloo, where he was wounded, and was a co-founder of the nationalist student *BURSCHENSCHAFT* movement. He was elected to the Hesse-Darmstadt LANDTAG (1832–6), where he led the liberal group. He was president of the National Assembly (the Frankfurt Parliament) from May to December 1848, and minister-president of the provisional government of Germany from then until the following May. He was later Hessian ambassador to Austria (1864–72).

Galen, Clemens, Graf von (1878–1946), Roman Catholic bishop of Münster (1933), cardinal from 1946. Galen was born in Dinklage, and served as a bishop's chaplain in Münster and as a priest in Berlin before returning to Westphalia as bishop of Münster in 1933. His attitude to the Nazi regime was ambiguous: he swore an oath of allegiance and approved of Hitler's foreign policy from the occupation of the Rhineland to the invasion of the Soviet Union, but opposed anti-Christian elements in Nazi ideology, and took issue with ROSENBERG on the matter in 1934. Above all he defended the interests of the church. His reputation as a leading opponent of Nazism rests on his sermon of 1941 against the euthanasia programme (*see* AKTION T4), which was sus-pended shortly afterwards, arguably as a consequence of his criticism. Galen was arrested after the JULY BOMB PLOT in 1944 and sent to SACHSENHAUSEN until his release shortly before the end of the war. He was created a cardinal in 1946.

Galland, Adolf, (1912–96), air force commander. Galland was one of the first officers to join the German air force that was being secretly rebuilt in the earlier 1930s, served in Spain with the CONDOR LEGION and in France in 1940. He took part in the battle of BRITAIN and was promoted to major-general in 1941 and later to lieutenant general. For much of the latter part of the war he was involved in an intractable struggle for better machines, and in 1945 he was eventually demoted to the command of a squadron following outspoken criticism of resource-allocation priorities.

Gartenlaube, a popular magazine that appealed to the lower middle classes of the German empire. Its title is the German word for a garden arbour or summer house. Its circulation was 382,000 in 1875.

Gärtner, Franz (1881–1941), justice minister (1932–41), who closely collaborated with the Nazis. Born in Regensburg, Gärtner studied law before serving in World War I. A German nationalist, he became Bavarian justice minister in 1922, a position he held until he became Reich justice minister under von PAPEN in 1932. He remained in post until his death in 1941, collaborating with the Nazis in the fusion of state and party organizations, and sometimes protesting at excesses.

Gastarbeiter ('guest workers'), foreign workers employed in the FEDERAL REPUBLIC OF GERMANY since the 1950s, when workers from southern Europe were employed to fill gaps in the labour market brought about by the economic boom (*WIRTSCHAFTSWUNDER*). By 1964 there were a million such 'guest workers' in Germany, and by 1973, at the peak of 'guest worker' employment, the figure had risen to 2.6 million. By 1984 the number had fallen back to 1.6. million. Turkish *Gastarbeiter* are the largest ethnic minority in Germany, and there are lively Turkish communities in many large German cities. In addition there are large contingents of Greek, Spanish, Portuguese and Yugoslav workers in Germany. Guest workers have frequently been the target of xenophobic and racist attacks by radical right-wingers.

Gastein agreement (1865). *See* AUSTRO-PRUSSIAN WAR; SCHLESWIG-HOLSTEIN.

Gau (plural *Gaue*), regional division of the Nazi Party apparatus. The local organization of the party was set up on a hierarchical basis according to the FÜHRER PRINCIPLE, and each level had its own 'leader'. The first territorial division was at the regional level. There were 41 *Gaue* listed in the party's *Organisationsbuch* of 1940, along with the AO (*Auslandsorganisation*). New *Gaue* were added as Austria and other direct annexations of territory were incorporated into the Reich. They varied in size from Saxony, which had a population of over 5 million, to Salzburg, which had fewer than 250,000. Within the Nazi system the GAULEITER was also generally the provincial governor (*REICHSSTATTHALTER*); they were directly responsible to Hitler, and many of them were 'old fighters' with effectively more direct access to him than some politicians and officials in Berlin. The *Gau* was made up of a number of party districts (*Kreise*), and these constituted the next level down in the party hierarchy.

Gauleiter, rank in the geographical hierarchy of Nazi Party office holders. The *Gauleiter* held office at regional GAU level within the party, and reported directly to Hitler. His immediate subordinate was the *Kreisleiter* or district leader. More often than not the party office of *Gauleiter* corresponded with the state office of REICHSSTATTHALTER or provincial governor.

Gauss, (Johann) Carl Friedrich (1777–1855), mathematician, regarded as among the greatest ever. Gauss was born into a poor family in Braunschweig and studied mathematics at Göttingen. He contributed immensely to the development of the discipline, and applied his abilities to astronomical observations and geodetic research. He also contributed to important developments in geometry and physics. He received honorary citizenship of Göttingen, and remained at the university there until his death.

Gautsch, Paul, Freiherr von Frankenthurn (1851–1918), Austrian politician. Gautsch served twice as education minister (1879–81 and 1895–6). He was minister-president in 1897–8, in 1905 and again in 1911. In 1898 Gautsch modified the BADENI language decrees. The principle of official bilingualism was abandoned in an attempt to appease the German population of Bohemia. The Badeni decrees were repealed altogether by Count THUN-HOHENSTEIN in 1899. Gautsch returned to office again in 1905, at the time of a political crisis in Hungary. His refusal to consider reform of the franchise was overturned in the wake of the revolution in Russia and socialist demonstrations in Vienna, and Gautsch legislated in 1906 for the introduction of universal manhood suffrage for elections to the REICHSRAT. His legislation came into effect the following year, along with proportional representation for the nationalities under Minister-president BECK.

GDR. *See* GERMAN DEMOCRATIC REPUBLIC.

GDVP. *See* GREATER GERMAN PEOPLE'S PARTY.

Gefolgschaft ('retinue'), a term used by early 19th-century historians to refer to the ancient Germanic *comitatus*, described by Tacitus, a group of freeborn young men who swore allegiance to their leader and followed him in battle. In return the leader provided accommodation and weapons, and divided the spoils of war with his followers. The term's pseudo-medieval ring appealed to the Nazis, who used it to refer to the followers of a Nazi leader in general, and the workforce in a factory in particular.

Gehlen, Reinhard (1902–79), intelligence officer. Born in Erfurt, Gehlen was an army intelligence chief on the Eastern Front during World War II. From 1942 he ran the 'Foreign Armies East' division of the army general staff. He was employed by the United States after 1945, and built up a covert intelligence service in collaboration with the Americans, the *Nachrichtendienst Gehlen* ('Gehlen intelligence service', popularly referred to as the 'Gehlen Organization'). It was taken over by the West German government in 1955 and in 1956 became the BND (*Bundesnachrichtendienst*), the West German foreign intelligence agency. Gehlen remained as its chief until 1968.

Geiger, Hans (Wilhelm) (1882–1945), German physicist. Educated at Munich and Erlangen, Geiger moved to Manchester University, where he worked with the professor of physics, Arthur Schuster, and his successor, Ernest Rutherford, on the alpha particle and instruments used to detect it, from which Geiger counters were later developed. Geiger moved to Berlin in 1912 and then to chairs at Kiel, Tübingen and the Technical University in Berlin (1936).

Gemeinschaftsfremde ('community aliens'), people deemed outside the 'national racial community' (*VOLKSGEMEINSCHAFT*) of Nazi Germany by virtue of their character, behaviour or other 'defects'. The term embraced 'racial' outsiders such as Jews and Gypsies (ROMA AND SINTI), HOMOSEXUALS, so-called 'ASOCIALS' and recalcitrant political opponents.

General Directory (*Generaldirektorium*), the central administrative body in 18th-century

Prussia. The '*General-Ober-Finanz-Krieges- und Domänen-Direktorium*' was created in 1723 by King Friedrich Wilhelm I by merging the General Finance Directorate and War Commissariat in order to put an end to the rivalry between the two institutions. The heads of the General Directory's four departments had the rank of senior privy councillors, and were effectively ministers. The division of the Directory into four departments was primarily territorial, but each had a number of specific further areas of responsibility. The first department, for example, was responsible for Prussia, Pomerania and Neumark, but also had responsibility for border issues and the provisioning of the army, among other things. Further departments were established throughout the century, each with non-territorial responsibilities. Increasingly the new departments were differentiated by their responsibilities, rather than numbered. The General Directory was superseded by the constitutional reforms of the early 19th century (*see* HARDENBERG and STEIN).

General German Workers' Association. *See* ADAV.

Generalgouvernement ('general government'), that part of Poland not directly incorporated into the Reich during World War II, but governed as a satellite territory by a German civilian administration in Kraków. The governor general was Hans FRANK.

Genscher, Hans-Dietrich (1927–), liberal politician. Genscher was born in Reideburg near Halle, and studied at the university there and in Leipzig after World War II. He migrated from the German Democratic Republic in 1952, became a member of the FDP, and was elected to the Bundestag in 1965. He was appointed interior minister in the BRANDT cabinet (1969–74), and became party chairman and foreign minister in 1974, when his predecessor Walter SCHEEL was elected federal president. When the FDP left to form a new coalition with the Christian Democrats in 1982, Genscher survived a great deal of criticism from within his own party, but continued as foreign minister until 1992. He retired as party chairman in 1985.

George, Heinrich (1893–1946), German film star. George's reputation was established with his parts in *Metropolis* (1926), *Dreyfus* (1929) and *Berlin Alexanderplatz* (1931). He became a Nazi supporter in 1933 and appeared in propaganda films such as *Hitlerjunge Quex* (1933), *Jud Süss* (1940) and *Kolberg* (1945). He was arrested by Soviet troops in East Prussia and died while in detention.

George, Stefan (1868–1933), poet. George was born in Büdesheim, Hesse, near Bingen on the Rhine and studied art history and philosophy in Paris, Munich and Berlin. George was a fin-de-siècle aesthete and built around himself a literary circle (the *George-Kreis*), through which he tried to rejuvenate German literature. He encouraged his radical conservative followers, including the STAUFFENBERG brothers, to believe that Germany could be rescued from materialism and decline by a great leader who would establish a new Reich. He left Germany when the Nazis came to power, despite the new regime's admiration for him, and died in exile in Switzerland.

Gerlach, Manfred (1928–), East German liberal politician. Gerlach joined the LDPD (*Liberal-Demokratische Partei Deutschlands*) in the Soviet zone of occupation in 1945, and was a member of the central council of the FDJ (*FREIE DEUTSCHE JUGEND*, the East German youth movement) at the same time. Gerlach held a number of important posts in the GERMAN DEMOCRATIC REPUBLIC. In 1950 he became a member of the People's Chamber (*VOLKSKAMMER*) and from 1954 to 1967 he was secretary general of the LDPD and deputy president of the STAATSRAT (State Council). From 1967 to 1990 he was president of the LDPD. He was also deputy mayor of Leipzig (1950) and editor in chief of the *Liberal-Demokratische Zeitung* in Halle from 1954. In October 1989 he challenged the monopoly of power of the SED (the East German Communist Party), and then succeeded Egon KRENZ as acting president of the Staatsrat (December 1989–March 1990). Legal action was taken against him after the collapse of the GDR for his alleged involvement in the regime's abuses of power, beginning with the accusation that he had denounced fellow members of the LDPD in Leipzig to the Soviet military authorities. He left the FDP in 1993.

German Christians (*Deutsche Christen*), a pro-Nazi movement within the German EVANGELICAL CHURCH. It emerged in Thuringia in 1927 and was established in Prussia in 1932 with the support of the Prussian NSDAP (Nazi Party). With further assistance from the party the movement won a series of elections in institutions of the church in 1933, and thereby gained control of a number of church offices. The movement was popular with the younger more radical members of the clergy, who hoped, through the Nazification of the church, to adapt Christianity for the age of the 'masses'. It was opposed by the anti-Nazi 'confessing church' (*BEKENNENDE KIRCHE*), and was increasingly eclipsed as the state intruded more and more in the affairs of the official church.

German Confederation, association of German states founded in 1815 on the territory of the former HOLY ROMAN EMPIRE. It had 39 members, including territories whose princes were foreign heads of state (for example, the king of Hanover was also King George III of Great Britain and Ireland). Moreover, much of Prussia and Austria were outside the boundaries of the Confederation. Its only central institution was the federal diet (BUNDESTAG) in Frankfurt; this was effectively a congress of delegates appointed by the governments of the various states and free cities. In practice neither the Bundestag nor the Confederation itself could do anything without the agreement of Austria and Prussia. The Confederation collapsed in 1866 at the time of the dispute between Austria and Prussia over SCHLESWIG-HOLSTEIN, in the lead up to the AUSTRO-PRUSSIAN WAR. Prussia's victory in the war ended Austrian hegemony in Germany, and Prussia went on to establish the NORTH GERMAN CONFEDERATION.

German Conservative Party. *See DEUTSCH-KONSERVATIVE PARTEI.*

German–Danish War (1864), war arising from the conflict of interests between the Germans and Danes over the status of SCHLESWIG-HOLSTEIN. After a short war between Prussia and Denmark in the wake of the REVOLUTIONS OF 1848 (1848–50), the London Protocol (1852) imposed a compromise, which remained in place until the 1860s. When Danish liberals persuaded the king of Denmark to attempt to annex Schleswig in 1863, Austria and Prussia intervened, ostensibly to uphold the principles of the Protocol. The Danes were defeated in two short campaigns and Denmark ceded Schleswig to Prussia and Holstein to Austria.

German Defence League. *See DEFENCE LEAGUE, GERMAN.*

German Democratic Republic (GDR; German name: *Deutsche Demokratische Republik*, DDR), the formal name of the East German state of 1949–90. The German Democratic Republic was formed in 1949 from the Soviet zone of occupation, when the constitution submitted by the People's Council (*Volksrat*) was ratified by the third People's Congress (*Volkskongress*) elected in May. Wilhelm PIECK was elected president (11 October) and Otto GROTEWOHL became minister-president (12 October). The constitution, with its guarantees of civil liberties, resembled that of the FEDERAL REPUBLIC OF GERMANY (West Germany), but in practice the GDR became a 'people's republic' like other states in the Soviet Bloc, and was subject to political direction from Moscow throughout its existence. Diplomatic relations were established with the USSR on 15 October 1949, and with the other Eastern European states and China between 17 October and 2 December. The constitution provided the GDR with a bicameral parliament

consisting of an upper house representing the five *Länder* (the *Länder* were abolished with the reorganisation of regional government in 1952) and a lower house, the People's Chamber (*VOLKSKAMMER*), which ostensibly had greater powers than the West German BUNDESTAG, and in which a range of parties, organized in the National Front, were represented alongside the SED (*Sozialistische Einheitspartei Deutschlands*, the Socialist Unity Party of Germany – effectively the East German Communist Party). Real power, however, lay with the SED itself, at the head of which was the party leader Walter ULBRICHT. The SED was able to determine who was entered on the 'unity lists' of candidates for election, and East German politics effectively became an internal party matter.

Centralized control did not mean that there was no change within the East German system or that there were no real political conflicts. The federal structure was reorganized in 1952 and the five *Länder* replaced with 14 administrative districts. In 1953 the party was faced with an acute political crisis after the death of Stalin when construction workers in the capital, East Berlin, went on strike in protest at government demands for increased productivity (*see* NEW COURSE). Strikes and demonstrations spread to over 270 towns and cities throughout the republic, and although the SED rescinded its decision the strike movement became a popular uprising, with demonstrations in major cities such as East Berlin, Jena, Halle, Leipzig, Dresden and Magdeburg. The revolt was suppressed by Soviet troops. Despite the show of popular disaffection Ulbricht's position was strengthened rather than weakened, and he resisted pressure from within the party and from the East German intelligentsia to introduce genuine de-Stalinization. In 1954 the Council of Ministers was given the power to enact legislation when the People's Chamber was not sitting. With the death of Pieck in 1960 the presidency was abolished and a Council of State established in its place, with Ulbricht at its head, a position he retained until his death in 1973. In 1961 the BERLIN WALL was built to seal the last gap in the borders of the state and so stop the flow of emigrants to the West. (The border between the German Democratic Republic and the Federal Republic had already been closed; the border within Berlin, where people could cross from the eastern to the western sectors, was considered a 'weeping wound'.) In 1963 the distribution of seats in the People's Chamber was fixed, with the SED and affiliated mass organizations controlling 292 of the 500 seats.

Ulbricht retired as first secretary of the SED in 1971 and was succeeded by Erich HONECKER, who remained in power until he was deposed in 1989 during the democratic reform movement that brought about the collapse of the GDR. Honecker's GDR was scarcely less repressive than that of his predecessor, but the economic improvements of the 1970s (albeit exaggerated in official statistics) were sufficient for there to be talk of an East German 'economic miracle'. Despite a degree of cultural liberalization, however, East Germany remained one of the most authoritarian states in the Soviet Bloc until the summer of 1989. When Hungary opened its border with Austria there existed for the first time since 1961 the possibility of escape from the system, and the resulting political pressure, manifested in regular demonstrations, eventually forced the opening of the border between East and West Germany. It was then only a matter of time before the regime was overtaken by a general crisis, and Honecker's successor Egon KRENZ was forced to hand over power to Hans MODROW, a reformist who promised free elections in 1990. The intervention of the West German chancellor, Helmut KOHL, with the promise of rapid unification with the West on the basis of the West German currency, ensured a victory for an alliance of conservative parties. The election spelled the end of the GDR, and the union of the two currencies in July was followed by the incorporation of the East German state into the Federal Republic on 3 October 1990.

German East Africa, former German colony comprising the territory of present-day Tanzania, Rwanda and Burundi. The territory was acquired in 1885, and the first Reich commissioner in the protectorate was Karl PETERS. It had a surface area of almost 1 million square kilometres (386,000 square miles), with a population of 7.5 million, 3500 of whom were Germans. As in the case of other German colonies, expenditure on the colony exceeded income, but a range of raw materials, including rubber, coffee, cotton and other agricultural products were exported to Germany. The British attempted to conquer German East Africa during World War I, but German forces only finally surrendered there after the armistice. Rwanda and Burundi were handed over to Belgium as League of Nations mandates, while the rest (known as Tanganyika) came under British administration.

German empire, proclaimed at Versailles on 18 January 1871 by the king of Prussia, who became Kaiser (emperor) WILHELM I. The empire was short-lived: it came to an end with the abdication of Kaiser WILHELM II and the declaration of the German Republic (commonly known as the WEIMAR REPUBLIC) in 1918, after less than half a century.

The constitution of the empire was based on that of the NORTH GERMAN CONFEDERATION that had preceded it. The king of Prussia became hereditary emperor and BISMARCK, the Prussian minister-president, became Reich chancellor. The federal basis of the empire, with particular provision for the newly absorbed southern states, was embodied in the federal council (BUNDESRAT), which had 58 members nominated by the federal states (*Länder*). Constitutionally this was the executive body of the empire, and was presided over by the chancellor. Prussia had the largest single allocation of seats (17), but by no means a majority. Bavaria had 6 representatives, Saxony and Württemberg 4 each, and Baden and Hesse each had 3. Braunschweig and Mecklenburg-Schwerin accounted for 2 seats each, and the remaining 17 seats were distributed among the other states. Fourteen votes constituted a veto, but the smaller states rarely opposed Prussia in practice. The lower house was the REICHSTAG, elected by universal male suffrage. Ministers were not accountable to the Reichstag, and although it had the right to review expenditure, the right to review the military budget was at first excluded from that provision, and then allowed only every seven years. The Reichstag had 382 seats (increased to 397 in 1873). A total of 7,656,273 electors were eligible to vote in the first Reichstag elections, and the NATIONAL LIBERALS were returned as the largest single party with almost 1.17 million votes and 125 seats. The REICHSPARTEI, conservatives sympathetic to Bismarck's policies, held a further 37. The Reichstag was elected every three years (and from 1888 every five years). The constitution remained in place until October 1918, when the chancellor and ministers were made accountable to parliament.

The German empire began as a very loose federation of states dominated by Prussia, which accounted for some two-thirds of it. Bavaria and Württemberg had separate armies (although they were subject to Prussian leadership in the event of war), and some of the constituent states exchanged diplomatic representatives, as they had done under the GERMAN CONFEDERATION. The Reich controlled the armed forces, trade matters (including customs), transport matters and the post. The states retained control over the administration of justice, cultural matters and education. There was little sense of a common German identity in 1871, and the southern states and their citizens were particularly inclined to insist on their separate rights, traditions and cultures. Most

historians would agree, however, that by 1914 a separate sense of German national consciousness had grown up with the empire, and transcended the particularist identities of locality and region, even if it did not supersede them.

German greeting, 'HEIL HITLER!' accompanied by the raised-arm salute.

German Labour Front. See DAF.

German National Freedom Party. See *DEUTSCHVÖLKISCHE FREIHEITSPARTEI*.

German National People's Party. See DNVP.

German People's Party. See DVP.

German Progressive Party. See DEUTSCHE *FORTSCHRITTSPARTEI*.

German Racialist Freedom Party. See *DEUTSCHVÖLKISCHE FREIHEITSPARTEI*.

German Revolution (1918). See NOVEMBER REVOLUTION.

German Workers' Party. See DEUTSCHE ARBEI-*TERPARTEI*.

Gerstein, Kurt (1905–45), Protestant dissident and member of the SS. Gerstein joined the Christian Association of Young Men, a Protestant youth movement, in 1925 and was a member of the Confessing Church (*BEKENNENDE KIRCHE*). He was head of 'health technology' at the SS head office in Berlin and was sent to introduce Zyklon-B gas into the EXTERMINATION CAMPS in 1942. He tried to pass on his eyewitness knowledge of the HOLOCAUST to the Allies and to the Vatican, to no avail. He left behind a detailed confession when he committed suicide in a French prison in 1945.

gesamtdeutsch, term used to describe a political unification of all Germans both within and beyond the boundaries of the Habsburg and Hohenzollern empires. The prefix *gesamt* ('comprehensive') implied the possibility of a nation that encompassed all Germans anywhere, and a settlement to the question of German national unity that went beyond the GREATER GERMAN (*grossdeutsch*) solution. The term was revived briefly after World War II, in the context of the issue of German refugees from eastern Europe.

Gesamtdeutscher Block/Bund der Heimat-vertriebenen und Entrechteten. *See* EXPELLEES.

Gessler, Otto (1875–1955), liberal politician. Born in Ludwigsburg, Gessler was a lawyer in Straubing and then mayor of Regensburg and Nuremberg before World War I. He was a co-founder of the left-liberal DDP (German Democratic Party) in 1918, but left the party in 1927. He was appointed minister for reconstruction in 1919 and defence minister in 1920. This was a post he held in 13 administrations until 1928, when he was replaced by Wilhelm GROENER. Gessler retired from public life when Hitler came to power, and was imprisoned in Ravensbrück after the 1944 JULY BOMB PLOT. He was briefly president of the German Red Cross after the war (1950–2).

Gestapo, abbreviation of *Geheime Staatspolizei* ('secret state police'). The Gestapo was created by Hermann GÖRING shortly after his appointment as Prussian interior minister in 1933. Each federal state (*Land*) had its own police force before 1933, and the Prussian 'Law for the Establishment of a Secret State Police Office' (*Geheimes Staatspolizeiamt,* or *Gestapa*) of 26 April replaced Police Department Ia of the Prussian interior ministry, which had hitherto dealt with political matters. The new department, under Rudolf DIELS, moved into its notorious headquarters at No. 8 Prinz-Albrecht-Strasse in May. Regional state police offices were then set up throughout Prussia in each government district (*Regierungsbezirk*). A law of 10 November of the same year made the Gestapo an independent branch of the administration, and from 1934 it had effective authority over local state police offices (*Stapostellen*) in Prussia, and since Prussia accounted for roughly two-thirds of Germany, this was the most important such political police force. The development of the political police in Bavaria under Heinrich HIMMLER followed a similar pattern of development, and in November 1933

Himmler became commander in chief of the political police forces of all the *Länder* except Prussia and Schaumburg-Lippe.

Himmler effectively defeated Göring in a struggle for control of the increasingly centralized political police: Göring named him inspector of the Gestapo on 20 April 1934, and two days later Reinhard HEYDRICH was appointed director of the *Gestapa*. Himmler regulated the division of responsibility between the Gestapo and the SD (the Nazi Party's intelligence service) in June 1934. In 1936 Hitler appointed Himmler chief of the German police, and he now used the position to centralize Germany's police force for the first time, and in particular to bring political police and criminal police together in a security police force (*SIPO*) under Heydrich. The Gestapo was involved in the surveillance of political and ideological opponents and the maintenance of industrial discipline. Its numbers were relatively small – by 1944 the force employed about 32,000 people – but it was able to rely on the climate of fear and suspicion generated by its existence, and on denunciation of citizens by each other for real or perceived misdemeanours.

ghetto, originally the separate quarter of a city inhabited by Jews during the Middle Ages. The concept was revived by the Nazis, and parts of certain cities in eastern Europe, notably Łódź Warsaw (*see* WARSAW GHETTO), Minsk, Riga and Vilnius, were effectively transformed into urban prison camps, where Jews were confined and often also worked and starved to death.

Glasenapp, Otto Georg von (1853–1928), vice president of the REICHSBANK (1907–24). A lawyer by training, Glasenapp made his career in the public service at the Reich treasury office (1882–1907), where he dealt with government debt among other things. He was deputy to HAVENSTEIN at the Reichsbank during World War I and the postwar hyperinflation (*see* INFLATION).

Glaube und Schönheit ('faith and beauty'), Nazi youth organization for young women aged between 17 and 21. It was a branch of the BUND DEUTSCHER MÄDEL and was founded in 1938 by Baldur von SCHIRACH. It was intended to prepare young women for marriage with lessons in domestic science and fashion.

Gleichschaltung ('coordination'), the Nazification of German institutions, political organizations and society. The process began immediately in 1933 with the effective centralization of political authority by means of the 'coordination' of the federal states, and the purge of political opponents and Jews from positions in the public service.

Gleiwitz (now Gliwice, in Poland), a town within Germany's pre-war frontier with Poland. Its radio station was attacked on 31 August 1939, ostensibly by Polish soldiers, an incident that provided the justification for the German invasion of Poland and thereby precipitated the outbreak of World War II. The Polish soldiers had in fact been German concentration-camp prisoners in Polish uniforms.

Globke, Hans (1898–1973), civil servant. Born in Aachen, the son of a cloth merchant, Globke studied law and pursued a civil-service career in the Prussian interior ministry, where he was director of the citizenship department in the late 1930s, and although never a party member was responsible for framing much of the Nazis' anti-Semitic legislation. He was state secretary of the Chancellery under ADENAUER from 1953 to 1963.

Globocnik, Odilo (1904–45), Austrian Nazi and SS officer responsible for 'Aktion Reinhard', the organization of the first EXTERMINATION CAMPS. Globocnik was born in Trieste and was an early party member. He was appointed *Gauleiter* of Vienna in 1938 but was dismissed from his office for fraud, and became SS and police leader of Lublin in 1941. Under the patronage of HIMMLER he was given responsibility for the mass murder of European Jews and was responsible for the construction and operation of BELZEC, SOBIBOR and TREBLINKA extermination

camps. He was captured by British troops in Carinthia in 1945, and apparently committed suicide shortly after his arrest.

Goebbels, (Paul) Joseph (1897–1945), Nazi politician; Reich propaganda director of the NSDAP (1929–45) and Reich minister of popular enlightenment and propaganda (1933–45). Goebbels was born in Rheydt, in the Rhineland, studied German literature, history and philosophy at a number of universities, and became involved in radical right-wing politics after graduating from Heidelberg with a doctorate in 1921. He joined the Nazi Party in 1924 and edited the Nazi paper *Völkische Freiheit*. He became a strong supporter of Hitler after the BAMBERG CONFERENCE of 1926 and remained loyal to the end of the war. He was appointed *Gauleiter* of Berlin the same year and Reich propaganda director in 1929. Elected to the Reichstag in 1933, he was appointed Reich minister of popular enlightenment and propaganda. As minister he exercised an unprecedented control over Germany's mass media, cultural life and education system. His power and influence in the Nazi state increased during the war, and his appointment as Reich plenipotentiary for total war in 1944 effectively placed him in overall command of the domestic war effort. Shortly after Hitler's suicide in the bunker, Goebbels killed his wife and family and then committed suicide himself.

Goerdeler, Carl (1884–1945), conspirator in the 1944 JULY BOMB PLOT. Goerdeler was born in Schneidemühl, into a family of Prussian public servants whose political sympathies lay with the Free Conservatives (*FREIKONSERVATIVE PARTEI*). He studied law at Tübingen and Königsberg, embarked on a civil-service career, and distinguished himself as a capable administrator during World War I. He was deputy mayor of Königsberg (1920–30) and mayor of Leipzig (1930–7), making a name for himself in local government during the Weimar Republic. He was frequently suggested as a possible candidate for chancellor during the Depression, and was appointed Reich commissioner of prices by BRÜNING in 1931.

Goerdeler was a conservative nationalist with little time for parliamentary democracy, but his experience of economic management during World War I had made him an economic liberal, and he argued for a grand coalition rather than an authoritarian solution to Germany's political and economic problems. Although never a member of the Nazi Party he remained in office as mayor of Leipzig after Hitler came to power, and was appointed Reich price commissioner again in 1934, but he resigned from both positions in 1937 and became increasingly opposed to Nazi policies. He was the leading civilian in the 1944 July bomb plot, but envisaged a post-Nazi Germany that retained Hitler's territorial gains. He was arrested after the failure of the assassination attempt and executed in 1945.

Goering, Hermann. *See* GÖRING, HERMANN.

Goethe, Johann Wolfgang von (1749–1832), writer. Goethe was born in Frankfurt am Main into an affluent middle-class family and was a student at the University of Leipzig (1765–8), where he started to write poetry in the fashionable Rococo style, and at Strasbourg (1770–1). Goethe met HERDER in Strasbourg, and became an enthusiastic participant in the early Romantic *STURM UND DRANG* movement. Goethe's *Die Leiden des jungen Werthers* (*The Sorrows of Young Werther*, 1774), established his reputation both in Germany and abroad, and his yellow-waist-coated hero became a cult figure among the early European Romantics. Goethe moved to Weimar the following year, where he was endowed with the noble particle (von), and where he entered the government service of Duke Karl August, becoming a privy councillor in 1779. His travels in Italy between 1786 and 1788 are recorded in his travel diary *Die Italienische Reise* (*Italian Journey*, published in 1816–17). Goethe's friendship with SCHILLER during the 1790s was the basis

of a creative collaboration that produced the works associated with Weimar classicism. Goethe's best-known work was *Faust* (Parts I and II, 1808, 1832).

Göring, Hermann (Wilhelm) (1893–1946), leading Nazi, minister of aviation and plenipotentiary for the FOUR-YEAR PLAN. Göring was born in Rosenheim, Bavaria, the son of a colonial official, and was a Prussian officer before serving as a pilot in the RICHTHOFEN Squadron during World War I. After the war he worked as an adviser to the Danish government and as a pilot in Sweden, where he met his first wife, Carin. He joined the NSDAP in 1922, and took charge of the SA the following year. He participated in the abortive BEER HALL PUTSCH in Munich, was wounded and managed to get away to Austria. He remained abroad until the putschists were amnestied, then returned to Germany and rejoined the Nazi Party.

Göring was elected to the Reichstag in 1928, became its president in 1932 and minister-president and interior minister of Prussia in 1933. He was appointed Reich aviation minister after Hitler came to power and undertook the secret reconstruction of the air force (LUFTWAFFE), of which he became commander in chief in 1935. As head of the Prussian secret police, he established the GESTAPO and the first CONCENTRATION CAMPS, but subsequently lost control of the Third Reich's police and security apparatus to HIMMLER. In 1936 he was made responsible for the implementation of the Four-Year Plan, and established a specific organization for that purpose that rapidly eclipsed the agriculture, economics and labour ministries.

Göring was a key figure in the radicalization of the regime during the late 1930s. He assisted in the downfall of leading conservatives (such as FRITSCH, BLOMBERG and von NEURATH) in 1938, and in the arrangements for the expropriation of Jewish property after the November pogrom of that year. His industrial empire expanded in Austria and Czechoslovakia and he made a forthright economic case for their annexation. Although he was promoted to Reich marshal in 1940, his influence declined rapidly after the outbreak of war. The war economy failed to respond to Germany's needs during the crucial period between 1939 and 1941, and the Luftwaffe failed to prevent the evacuation of Allied forces from DUNKIRK, and also failed to win the battle of BRITAIN. Göring, whom Hitler had named as his successor in 1939, withdrew into semi-retirement, and was even expelled from the party in 1945. He was captured, tried and sentenced to death at Nuremberg, but committed suicide in his prison cell.

Gorlice, a small town between Kraków and Lviv (Lvov or Lemberg) that was at the centre of an Austro-German offensive aimed at driving the Russians out of Galicia (and, indeed, out of Austria-Hungary altogether) in 1915. Eight German divisions commanded by MACKENSEN were transferred there and an attack launched on 2 May. The town was taken within a day, and the Russians, who suffered some 2 million casualties, most of whom were taken prisoner, were quickly driven back.

Görres, Josef (1776–1848), Romantic nationalist writer. An early enthusiast for the French Revolution, Görres became active in revolutionary politics during the 1790s. His enthusiasm was somewhat dispelled by the experience of the French occupation of the Rhineland, and his disillusionment was deepened by a visit to Paris in 1799 as part of a delegation to plead the case of local republicans following the dismissal of the German civilian administration of Koblenz by the French military commander. On his return to Germany he abandoned his republican journalism to teach, first in a school and then at Heidelberg University. He became associated with the Romantic German nationalism, and his *Volksbücher* (1807) were an important contribution to the reclamation of German folk culture. In 1814 he founded *Der Rheinische Merkur* newspaper.

He campaigned for a German constitution, became identified with the liberal opposition to the restoration political order, and lived in exile in France and Switzerland from 1816 to 1827, when he returned to Germany to take up a teaching appointment in Munich. An 1837 pamphlet on the conflict between the Roman Catholic Church and the Prussian political authorities in Cologne (*Athanasius*, 1837) made him, at the end of his life, the author of a manifesto for modern political Catholicism.

Gossler, Heinrich von (1841–1927), infantry general and Prussian war minister (1896–1903). Gossler served in the AUSTRO-PRUSSIAN WAR and FRANCO-PRUSSIAN WAR before his appointment to the war department. He was an amateur military historian.

Gotha programme, Social Democratic manifesto agreed at the 'unity conference' of 1875 that merged the ADAV and the SDAP to form the SAPD (the Socialist Workers' Party of Germany), which subsequently became the SPD. The – predominantly Lassallean (*see* LASSALLE, FERDINAND) – programme demanded 'universal, direct, equal suffrage, with secret ballot and obligatory voting for all citizens over twenty years of age in all elections in state and municipality'. It stipulated that the election must take place on a Sunday or public holiday. These demands were written almost verbatim as principles into the 1919 constitution of the WEIMAR REPUBLIC (Article 22).

The programme also proposed a number of reforms to what the delegates saw as the 'foundations of the state'. Some of these were formulated rather vaguely, such as 'legislation by the people', 'decision on war and peace by the people' and administration of justice by the people. Others were more specific, and reflected contemporary conditions, concerns and anxieties. There was a demand for universal military training and a people's militia instead of a standing army. The party also wanted the abolition of all exceptional laws, especially the laws on the press, association and assembly. Both demands were aimed at the removal of means of state coercion.

In the rest of the programme the party set its sights on reforms that would improve the lives of its working-class constituents. It wanted universal and equal public education by the state, universal obligatory school education and free instruction in all educational institutions. The programme also demanded a 'normal' working day and the prohibition of Sunday labour and child labour, along with the banning of all female labour that was 'harmful to health and morals', and protective legislation to safeguard the life and health of workers generally.

The manifesto prompted Karl MARX's famous *Critique of the Gotha Programme*, which was published posthumously when Karl KAUTSKY asked ENGELS to contribute to a debate in the journal *Neue Zeit* in 1891. In 1891 the SPD revised its manifesto in the form of the ERFURT PROGRAMME.

Göttingen Seven, a group of university professors dismissed from their posts for protesting at the suspension of the constitution in 1837 by the king of Hanover. They were the GRIMM BROTHERS, the physicist Wilhelm Weber, the historian Georg Gottfried Gervinus, Wilhelm Eduard Albrecht, Friedrich Christoph DAHLMANN and Georg Heinrich August von Ewald.

Gradnauer, Georg (1866–1946), Social Democratic politician. Gradnauer was born in Magdeburg and studied literature, history and philosophy at Geneva, Berlin, Marburg and Halle and pursued a career in the SPD in Saxony, where he was editor of the *Sächsische Arbeiterzeitung*. He was elected to the Reichstag in 1898, lost his seat in 1907 and was re-elected in 1912. He was a member of the Workers' and Soldiers' Council in Dresden in 1918 and of the revolutionary government in Saxony. He was briefly minister-president of Saxony (1919–20) and Reich interior minister (1921). Gradnauer

was arrested when the Nazis came to power and again in 1944. He survived to the end of the war in Theresienstadt but died shortly afterwards in Berlin.

Graf, the German equivalent of 'count'; a title originally used in the Frankish Empire.

Gräfin, the German equivalent of 'countess'.

Grand Coalition, in general terms a government comprising the major political parties usually opposed to each other. In practice in the Federal Republic this means a government of the CDU and SPD. The only such coalition between World War II and the end of the 20th century was the KIESINGER administration (1966–9), formed following withdrawal of support for the ERHARD government by the FDP. It marked a transition from the ADENAUER era to the social–liberal coalitions of the 1970s. The prospect of a second 'grand coalition' was raised at the end of the KOHL administration in the mid-1990s, when it seemed unlikely that the CDU, CSU and FPD would together win an absolute majority in the next general election.

Grass, Günter (1927–), writer. Born in Danzig (now Gdańsk in Poland), Grass was called up to fight in World War II at the age of 16 and was wounded and taken prisoner by the Americans. After the war he trained as a sculptor and graphic artist in Düsseldorf and Berlin and began to write short stories, poetry and plays. He made his reputation with his first novel, *Die Blechtrommel* (1959, *The Tin Drum*), a novel which provoked much controversy for its close examination of the recent German past, from the rise of the Nazis to the WIRTSCHAFTSWUNDER. The novel was later made into an Oscar-winning film (1979) by the director Volker Schlöndorff. *Die Blechtrommel* formed the central piece of the 'Danzig trilogy' and the other two parts, *Katz und Maus* (*Cat and Mouse*) and *Hundejahre* (*Dog Years*), also dealing with the Nazi regime and its effects upon individuals, were published in 1961 and 1963 respectively.

In the 1960s and early 1970s Grass campaigned for the SPD, and many of his works of this period reflect a politically engaged stance. His play *Die Plebeier proben den Aufstand* (1965, *The Plebeians Rehearse the Uprising*), dealt with the workers' uprising in the German Democratic Republic in 1953, and in 1972 he published an autobiographical novel *Aus dem Tagebuch einer Schnecke* (*From the Diary of a Snail*) in which he constructed a diary of his travels on the election trail for Willy BRANDT and the SPD during the 1969 Bundestag elections. Grass attracted criticism for his radical left-wing views and – along with Heinrich BÖLL – was denounced as an intellectual supporter of terrorism by the SPRINGER press during the 1970s. More recently, Grass has been an outspoken critic of German reunification. His 1992 novel *Unkenrufe* (*The Call of the Toad*) depicted German–Polish relations after reunification and *Ein Weites Feld* (1995, *A Broad Field*), which compared reunification to the ANSCHLUSS of 1938, attracted considerable political hostility. In 1999 Grass was awarded the Nobel prize for literature.

Greater German People's Party (*Grossdeutsche Volkspartei*, GDVP), German nationalist party in interwar Austria. It was formed by the merger of a number of assorted nationalist, liberal and anti-clerical parties. Although by far the smallest of the three ideological groupings in Austrian politics, the GDVP had sufficient electoral support to prevent either of the major parties (SDAP and CHRISTIAN SOCIAL PARTY) from achieving a parliamentary majority. The party supported the clerical-conservative Christian Social Party in the so-called 'bourgeois bloc'. The GDVP participated in administrations throughout the 1920s. The party's electoral support was almost entirely eliminated as its voters switched their allegiance to the Nazis during the Depression. The continuity of the German nationalist tradition was maintained after World War II with the establishment of the League of Independents and the Freedom Party of Austria (*Freiheitliche Partei Österreichs*, FPÖ).

Greater Germany (*Grossdeutschland*), the term used for the expanded Germany created by the annexation (ANSCHLUSS) of Austria in 1938. The term '*grossdeutsch*' was used from the 1840s to describe an outcome to German national unification which would include all Germans.

Greens (*Die Grünen*), a radical environmentalist group that emerged from the West German Ecology Party. The Greens (*Die Sonstige politische Vereinigung – Die Grünen*, 'The other political association – the Greens') first contested a domestic election in 1979 in Bremen, a small city-state in northern Germany with a lively youth culture and a university with a reputation for radicalism. This initial local success was not immediately repeated across the country. They became a political party in January 1980, but in the federal elections of that year received only 1.5% of the vote and failed to enter parliament. They established a presence in the Bundestag in the 1980s with 27 seats in 1983 and 42 in 1987, and (after a setback in the first all-German elections of 1990) became the third largest party, ahead of the FDP. The prospect of a 'red–green' coalition was one that conservatives sought to exploit to keep their own supporters within the fold for fear of unpredictably radical governments, but the Greens successfully formed coalitions with the SPD, first in West Berlin in 1989, then in Hesse in 1991. Following the decisive defeat of Helmut KOHL's conservative–liberal coalition in 1998 the Greens participated in government at national level for the first time, in coalition with the SPD. Joschka FISCHER, as the senior member of the party, became foreign minister. Although the so-called 'realists' (REALOS) within the party eventually triumphed over the more radical fundamentalists (FUNDIS), the party continues to stand to the left of most similar parties in Europe.

Greiser, Arthur (1897–1946), *Gauleiter* of the WARTHELAND. Greiser joined the Nazi Party in 1929 and the SS in 1931. He succeeded RAUSCHNING as president of the DANZIG senate in 1934. He was appointed chief of the civil administration in Posen and *Gauleiter* and Reich governor of the Wartheland in 1939. He was tried in Poland after the war and hanged in 1946.

Grimm, Hans (1875–1959), German nationalist writer. Grimm was born the son of a university professor in Wiesbaden and studied literature. He spent 14 years in South Africa as a young man and wrote a semi-autobiographical novel based on his experiences, *Volk ohne Raum* ('nation without space'), which was both anti-British and imbued with BLUT UND BODEN ('blood and soil') ideology. Published in 1926, it was an enormous success. Grimm never joined the NSDAP but was a staunch supporter of Nazism, and after the war he was unrepentant in his views.

Grimm brothers, Jacob Ludwig Karl (1785–1863) and Wilhelm Karl (1786–1859), philologists and folklorists. They were both born in Hanau and attended secondary school in Kassel. Both became professors at Kassel University (Jacob in 1829 and Wilhelm in 1839) but both lived in Berlin from the 1840s. They were famous for their collections of children's stories, folk tales and heroic national legends. Jacob's pioneering academic research in historical linguistics produced a systematic account of phonetic correspondences between the various branches of the Indo-European languages, which was published in his *Deutsche Grammatik* (German Grammar, 1819–37). The application of 'Grimm's law' to common words in a number of ancient (and modern) languages made it possible to show the ways in which Indo-European languages were related. Although explanations of sound change and the relationships between languages have changed, Grimm's law is still a useful guide to such correspondences.

Groener, Wilhelm (1867–1939), officer and politician. Groener was responsible for war production from 1916, and was second-in-command of the German army at the end of World War I. He cooperated with the moderate Social Democrat, Friedrich EBERT, chancellor during the 1918 NOVEMBER REVOLUTION, and accepted the establishment of the WEIMAR REPUBLIC in return for the suppression of the revolutionary left. He promoted the growth of the FREIKORPS movement, which was used as an instrument of the state in violent political conflicts. He served as transport minister (1920–3) and defence minister (1928–32), and sponsored the rise of General Kurt von SCHLEICHER. The latter subsequently conspired with the Nazis against Groener when, as BRÜNING's interior minister (1931–2), Groener banned the SA (1932). Groener's attempts to defend the republic and keep the army out of politics were unsuccessful, and he resigned in 1932. His resignation contributed to Brüning's downfall and precipitated his own departure from the interior ministry.

Gropius, Walter (1883–1969), architect and founder of the BAUHAUS. Gropius was born in Berlin, and practised as an architect before serving in World War I. He was briefly married (1915–19) to Gustav MAHLER's widow, Alma. In 1918 he was appointed head of the Kunstgewerbeschule in Weimar. The Bauhaus was founded there the following year, and moved to Dessau in 1925. He retired as the school's director in 1928 and emigrated to Britain in 1933 (when the Bauhaus was closed down by the Nazis). He moved to the United States in 1937, where he pursued an academic career at Harvard University.

Groschen, monetary unit worth one-hundredth of the Austrian SCHILLING from the 1920s to 2002. The name originated from the French *gros* (large) and referred to a large silver coin, originally with the same value as a schilling. The Groschen was abolished in Germany in 1873 but the name persisted as a colloquial expression for a ten-pfennig coin.

Grossdeutsche Volkspartei. See GREATER GERMAN PEOPLE'S PARTY.

Grossraumwirtschaft, a term used to refer to an economic policy based on a 'greater economic sphere of interest'. It was specifically used in relation to Nazi foreign and trade policy to refer to the notion of economic integration under German leadership, initially in the Balkans and eastern Europe or *Mitteleuropa,* but more broadly with reference to Europe as a whole under the Nazi new order.

Grosz, George (1893–1959), artist noted for his satirical caricatures. Grosz was born in Berlin and studied art at the Royal Academy in Dresden and the Kunstgewerbeschule in Berlin. After serving in the infantry in World War I he became a leading member of the Berlin DADA movement after the war, and of the *NEUE SACHLICHKEIT* ('new objectivity') school of the mid-1920s. He moved to the United States in 1932, where he remained almost to the end of his life. He died shortly after returning to Berlin in 1959.

Grotewohl, Otto (1894–1964), politician; minister-president of East Germany (1949–64). Born in Braunschweig, the son of a working-class Social Democrat, Grotewohl joined the socialist youth movement in 1910, and became a member of the SPD in 1912. He joined the breakaway USPD in 1918, but rejoined the SPD when the USPD split, and was briefly justice minister in Braunschweig (1923–4) before his election to the Reichstag in 1925. Grotewohl left Braunschweig for Hamburg in 1933, and belonged to an underground socialist resistance group there until his arrest and imprisonment by the Gestapo (1938–9). During the war he was manager of a small business in Berlin, but fled after the failure of the JULY BOMB PLOT in 1944 for fear of being arrested again. He supported the formation of the SED (Socialist Unity Party, effectively the East German Communist Party) as a party activist in Schöneberg after the war, and assumed the leadership, along with Wilhelm PIECK,

in 1946 (until 1954). He was also a member of the Central Secretariat (Politburo) of the new party. He became the first minister-president of the GERMAN DEMOCRATIC REPUBLIC (1949–64).

Gründerzeit (or *'Gründerjahre'*), German term for the 'founding years' of the GERMAN EMPIRE. The early years of the empire were characterized by rapid industrial expansion, economic prosperity and cultural and political confidence. The initial boom that accompanied the establishment of the empire technically came to an end with the *'Gründerkrach'* crash of 1873, but the term is also used more loosely to describe the culture of a rather longer period.

Grünen, die. See GREENS.

Gruppenführer, SS rank equivalent to lieutenant general.

Grynszpan, Herschel (1921–43?), German-Jewish student of Polish extraction living in Paris. In November 1938 he shot and mortally wounded a diplomat from the German embassy after hearing that 17,000 Jews, including his own family, had been deported to Poland and left stranded in the no-man's-land of the border by a Polish government that was unwilling to accept them. His act was then used as an excuse for the organized pogrom that followed, initiating a radicalization of anti-Jewish policy (*see* KRISTALLNACHT). Grynszpan was handed over to the Nazis by the Vichy authorities.

Guderian, Heinz (Wilhelm) (1888–1954), general. A professional soldier, Guderian served in World War I, and between the wars specialized in the development of communications techniques and tank warfare. He was seen as a supporter of the Nazi regime during the BLOMBERG–FRITSCH crisis of 1938, and was appointed chief of motorized troops, which he led during the invasion of Austria that year. He became commander in chief of Panzer troops in 1939 and directed the *BLITZKRIEG* on both the Eastern and Western Fronts in 1939–40. In the summer of 1941 he led the drive towards Moscow and Kiev, but was dismissed in December 1941 after retreating against Hitler's orders. After reverses on the Eastern Front he was recalled as inspector general of armoured forces in 1943. He was promoted to chief of the general staff in the OKW (high command of the armed forces) after the JULY BOMB PLOT of 1944, and purged the army of hundreds of officers. Dismissed again in March 1945 over a further disagreement with Hitler, he was captured by US forces in May. In 1951 Guderian published his memoirs, *Erinnerung eines Soldaten* (published in English as *Panzer Leader*).

Guernica, a small town in the Basque country of northern Spain. In 1937 it was bombed to destruction by German aircraft of the CONDOR LEGION during the Spanish Civil War. Refugees from the town were machine-gunned from the air by the Germans. The bombing of Guernica, commemorated in Picasso's picture of that name, became a Europe-wide symbol of the brutality of fascism, and generated a fear of attack from the air in the anticipated European war.

guilder. *See* GULDEN.

Guillaume affair, a spy scandal that prompted the resignation of Chancellor Willy BRANDT in 1974. Günter Guillaume (1927–95), a member of Brandt's staff in the Federal Chancellor's Office, was exposed in 1974 as an East German spy in the service of the GERMAN DEMOCRATIC REPUBLIC's ministry of state security. The chancellor resigned as a consequence of the political scandal, but there were also rumours of health or personal reasons. Brandt's observations on the affair were published posthumously in 1994.

gulden or guilder, monetary unit. The first guilders (also called florins) were minted in Florence from 1252. The gulden was used in southern Germany from the 14th century and persisted as the name of the Dutch currency until 2002 and (as 'florin') of the

Hungarian currency after the collapse of the Habsburg empire. In Germany it was abolished in 1876.

Günther, Hans (1891–1968), social anthropologist. Günther was appointed to a new chair of ethnology at Jena in 1931, and taught a 'racial science' that saw the Nordic race as an ideal racial type against which other, lesser European races (such as the Slavs) and especially the Jews were to be measured.

Gürtner, Franz (1881–1941), Nazi justice minister (1932–41). Gürtner was born in Regensburg and studied law at Munich. He pursued a career as a lawyer in the Bavarian public service and served in World War I. He joined the nationalist DNVP in 1919 and as Bavarian justice minister was particularly indulgent of right-wing extremists, notably Hitler and the other conspirators in the BEER HALL PUTSCH of 1923. The following year he persuaded the Bavarian authorities to release Hitler from prison and allow him to speak in public. Gürtner was appointed Reich justice minister by von PAPEN in 1932 and remained in post under Hitler until his death in Berlin in 1941. He was responsible for the *GLEICHSCHALTUNG* of the judicial system and for providing legalistic justification for the regime's actions, including the NIGHT OF THE LONG KNIVES of 1934.

Gustav Line, Axis line of defence in Italy during the winter of 1943. The line was established after the Allied landings in Salerno along a chain of mountain fortresses (including Monte Cassino) that stretched across the Italian peninsula north of Naples and south of Rome. Gains by the French expeditionary force in the second week of May 1944 broke the line and forced the Germans to withdraw, only to set up another strong defensive line, the Gothic Line at the northern end of the Apennines.

gymnastics movement. *See TURNBEWEGUNG*.

Gypsies. *See* ROMA AND SINTI.

H

Haase, Hugo (1863–1919), Social Democratic politician. Haase was born the son of a shoemaker in Allenstein and studied law at Königsberg, becoming the first Social Democratic councillor there in 1894. He was elected for the SPD to the Reichstag in 1897, lost his seat in 1907, and was re-elected in 1912. His party career was promoted by senior figures such as August BEBEL and Karl KAUTSKY, and he was seen as somebody who could mediate between left and right. He was an anti-militarist, however, whose support for the party line on war credits in 1914 was reluctant, and he found himself increasingly on the dissident left of the party. He was a co-signatory of the manifesto *Das Gebot der Stunde* ('The Commandment of the Hour') in 1915, and a co-founder of the breakaway USPD in 1917. As leader of the USPD he was a senior member (with Friedrich EBERT) of the COUNCIL OF PEOPLE'S REPRESENTATIVES in 1918 and, effectively, deputy prime minister in the revolutionary government (*see* NOVEMBER REVOLUTION). He was also a member of the NATIONAL ASSEMBLY in 1919, but died that year as a consequence of gun wounds from an assassination attempt.

Haber, Fritz (1868–1934), patriotic chemist. With his brother-in-law Carl BOSCH, he developed the Haber–Bosch process in 1909. This was a method of synthesizing ammonia from hydrogen and atmospheric nitrogen in order to overcome the increasing shortage of natural nitrate deposits (principally Chilean guano). He was appointed director of the Kaiser Wilhelm Institute for Physical Chemistry and Electro-Chemistry in 1911. During World War I Haber worked on making nitric acid for explosives from ammonia, essential now that Germany's supplies of sodium nitrate from Chile were cut off altogether by the British naval blockade. He then worked with other scientists on the military applications of gas and defensive measures against it. He was a German nationalist, who hoped that gas warfare would bring about a breakthrough for Germany on the Western Front, and he was charged with war crimes by the victorious Entente powers after the war (charges which were dropped when he was awarded the Nobel prize in 1918 for his earlier work on the Haber–Bosch process). During the Weimar Republic he promoted the interests of scientific research in Germany, and raised funds from Japan. He also attempted to find a way of extracting gold from sea water, as a way of helping to pay off German REPARATIONS; needless to say, the project proved impractical. Haber's wartime record protected him from the immediate effects of Nazi anti-Semitic measures in 1933, but he resigned in protest at the sacking of Jewish colleagues, and emigrated to Britain. He died of a heart attack while on holiday in Switzerland.

Habermas, Jürgen (1929–), philosopher. Habermas was born in Düsseldorf, and was assistant to ADORNO, before teaching philosophy at Heidelberg (1961–4) and then taking up a chair at Frankfurt. In 1972 he became director of the Max Planck Institute in Starnberg, Bavaria. Habermas built on the theory of the FRANKFURT SCHOOL in order to address problems of contemporary political culture. His work has been involved with the public sphere, critical theory and crises in contemporary capitalism. He was a prominent critic of right-wing revisionist historians during the *HISTORIKERSTREIT* of the 1980s, and proposed a patriotism based on loyalty to the constitution rather than nationalism.

Habilitationsschrift, a post-doctoral thesis submitted as a prerequisite for a senior teaching post in a German university.

Habsburg-Lothringen, Crown Prince Rudolf von. *See* RUDOLF (VON HABSBURG-LOTHRINGEN).

Habsburg, ruling house of Austria from 1276 to 1918, and Europe's longest reigning dynasty. Apart from a brief interregnum (1740–2) and a short period (1742–5), when the office was held by a WITTELSBACH (Charles VII of Bavaria), the Holy Roman emperor was invariably a Habsburg from 1438 onwards, or Habsburg-Lothringen (Habsburg-Lorraine) from the accession of FRANZ I, consort of MARIA THERESIA, in 1745. From 1804 the archdukes of Austria became emperors of Austria with the proclamation of an AUSTRIAN EMPIRE, and in 1806 the HOLY ROMAN EMPIRE was abolished by Napoleon. The Austrian empire became Austria-Hungary with the *AUSGLEICH* of 1867, and the Habsburgs acquired a new kind of constitutional significance in the personal union between the two parts of the monarchy. German AUSTRIA became a republic in 1918, but the Habsburgs technically remained the ruling dynasty of Hungary under the Horthy regency until 1921.

Hácha, Emil (1872–1945), Czech politician. Hácha became president of Czechoslovakia after the German annexation of the SUDE-TENLAND and remained in office as puppet president of the German protectorate of Bohemia and Moravia (1939–45). Jailed by the Soviets, he died in prison in June 1945.

Haecker, Theodor (1879–1945), Roman Catholic publicist. Haecker left school early to start an apprenticeship, but returned to take school-leaving examinations in 1905 and went on to study at Munich University. He started his career with satirical journalism, went on to write a number of books and essays, and translated the work of Kierkegaard and Cardinal Newman. He made his reputation abroad with a number of religious works in the early 1930s, and was forbidden to speak by the Nazis in 1935. From 1938 he was prohibited from publishing any further books.

Haeften, Werner von (1908–44), adjutant to STAUFFENBERG and anti-Nazi conspirator in the 1944 JULY BOMB PLOT. A corporation lawyer in the banking sector by profession, von Haeften served in World War II, but was wounded and transferred to Army High Command in Berlin. He accompanied Stauffenberg to Hitler's HQ with a second bomb in his own briefcase, which was dismantled and disposed of after the first bomb had been planted. Von Haeften was arrested and executed on 20 July.

Hagen, Louis (1855–1932), Cologne banker. Hagen, who later converted to Roman Catholicism, was born into a Jewish banking family that was heir to the banking houses of Levy and Oppenheimer. He was president of the Cologne Chamber of Industry and Commerce from 1915 to his death, and took part in the armistice and peace negotiations in 1918 and 1919 as a representative of the occupied areas. Initially a liberal, he joined the CENTRE PARTY in 1919. Hagen was an influential businessman during the difficult economic circumstances of the early Weimar Republic, and an advocate of a degree of economic autonomy for the beleaguered and occupied RHINELAND, including the establishment of a bank of issue and the creation of a separate Rhenish currency that would be linked to the French franc. Indeed, Hagen and others like him were suspected of separatist political leanings at a time when there was talk of the establishment of a Rhenish Republic.

Hahn, Otto (1879–1968), nuclear scientist. Born in Frankfurt and educated at Marburg, Hahn subsequently worked with Ernest Rutherford in Canada, returning to Germany in 1907. He was appointed professor of chemistry in 1910 and moved to the Kaiser Wilhelm Institute of Chemistry in 1912. With Lise MEITNER he discovered the element protactinium (1917) and carried out research on uranium with Meitner and Fritz Strassmann in the 1930s, contributing to the discovery of nuclear fission. Hahn remained in Germany during the war, and was awarded the Nobel prize for chemistry in 1944. He was shocked by the dropping of the atom bombs on Japan in 1945, and spoke out against nuclear weapons on many occasions in his capacity as president of the Max-Planck-Gesellschaft.

Hainisch, Marianne (1839–1936), Austrian campaigner for women's rights. Born Marianne Perger in Baden, Lower Austria, Hainisch was the wife of a factory owner and a leading member of the League of Austrian Women's Associations (*Bund österreichischer Frauenvereine*). She campaigned for secondary schools for girls and the admission of women to universities during the imperial period, and was active in the peace movement after World War I. She is credited with establishing the celebration of 'Mother's Day' in Austria (from 1924).

Halder, Franz (1884–1972), general. Born in Würzburg into an old Roman Catholic military family, Halder was a career soldier who served in World War I and then joined the Reichswehr ministry (1919). He replaced Ludwig BECK as army chief of staff in 1938 after the latter's resignation. Halder shared his fellow officers' antipathy towards Hitler and the regime, and was opposed to a European war, but after the MUNICH AGREEMENT this opposition waned, and he remained involved in military planning until 1942, when he disagreed with Hitler over the diversion of troops to STALINGRAD and was dismissed. His intermittent dissent seems to have stemmed not from moral or political opposition, but from the view that Hitler was a poor leader who would lead Germany to perdition. He was arrested after the 1944 JULY BOMB PLOT and imprisoned in a concentration camp. He was subsequently director of the Operation History (German) section of the US Historical Division.

Hallstein doctrine, an article of faith in the conservative West German foreign policy of the 1950s and early 1960s, named after an adviser of Chancellor Konrad ADENAUER. The doctrine attempted to subvert the international recognition of the GERMAN DEMOCRATIC REPUBLIC by breaking off diplomatic relations with any state that recognized it. The right of the FEDERAL REPUBLIC OF GERMANY to speak alone for the entire German nation until there should be free all-German elections was written into the country's constitution, the BASIC LAW of 1949. The Bundestag voted to resume diplomatic relations with the USSR in September 1955, but the Hallstein doctrine meant that the Federal Republic effectively had no relations with the rest of the Soviet Bloc until the GRAND COALITION government of 1966–9 established diplomatic links with Yugoslavia and Romania. The doctrine also reinforced East German propaganda, which depicted the Federal Republic as the heir to German fascism, and as a revisionist power with aggressive intentions. The policy was abandoned altogether when Willy BRANDT became chancellor in 1969 and pursued a more flexible and realistic 'eastern policy' (*OSTPOLITIK*).

Hambach festival, a meeting of some 30,000 German liberals and democrats in May 1832. The social basis of the gathering at Schloss Hambach near Neustadt, then in the Bavarian Palatinate, was broader than that of the

WARTBURG RALLY of 1817, and included artisans and workers as well as the intellectuals associated with the liberal movement. The meeting called for German national unity, and civil liberties guaranteed by a constitution, but it had little political resonance, and prompted even more draconian repression than that embodied in the KARLSBAD DECREES.

Hamburg, Germany's second city and one of Germany's constituent federal states (*Länder*). Founded in the 9th century, Hamburg quickly became an important port and major regional city. It was a member of the Hanseatic League and still styles itself 'free and Hanseatic city'. By the end of the 18th century Hamburg had some 70,000 inhabitants, and was one of the largest cities in Germany (after Vienna and Cologne). It became an imperial city in 1770, and joined the GERMAN CONFEDERATION as an autonomous state, a status it retained (along with BREMEN and Lübeck) in the German empire. Hamburg was one of the cities most devastated by Allied bombing during World War II, and much of it was destroyed. After the end of the war it retained its independence as the second smallest of the *Länder*. The state government is the Senate and the parliament is called the Bürgerschaft. The SPD has been the strongest political party in Hamburg since World War II, but the GREENS have also had some of their biggest successes there, and gained 13.9% in the Senate elections of 1997. At the end of the 20th century Hamburg had a population of about 1.7 million.

'hammer and anvil' speech, speech by Bernhard von BÜLOW, German foreign minister, to the Reichstag, 11 December 1899. Bülow argued – to applause from the right and objections from the left – that Germany had the same right to greatness as other great powers, that it was the object of political and economic envy, and that it must have a strong army and strong fleet in order to pursue its legitimate interests. Germans should not tolerate condescension, and must not be the 'slaves of humanity ... In the coming century Germany [would be] a hammer or an anvil'.

Handelskrieg, 'trade warfare'. The term refers to the German naval campaign against Allied merchant shipping in WORLD WAR I, in which U-BOATS played a major role.

Hanfstaengl, Ernst (1887–1975). Head of the Nazi Party Foreign Press Department (a largely nominal position), and an early associate of Hitler. Born in Munich into a wealthy family, Hanfstaengl, whose mother was American, spent ten years in the United States and graduated from Harvard before returning to Bavaria after World War I. Nicknamed 'Putzi', he was close to Hitler during the early 1920s, and provided him with social contacts in Munich high society and financial support, not least to buy the *Völkischer Beobachter* newspaper. Hanfstaengl took part in the BEER HALL PUTSCH and he and his wife hid Hitler in their house afterwards. He was appointed head of the party's Foreign Press Department in 1931, but his influence had diminished with time and he fled abroad in 1937 after rumours of a plot to kill him. He went first to Britain and then to the United States, where he was an adviser to the government during the war, and was interned after it ended. He returned to Germany after his release.

Hanke, Karl (1903–45), Nazi functionary. Born in Lauban, Lower Silesia (now Lubań in Poland), Hanke joined the NSDAP in 1928 and was elected to the Reichstag in 1932 for Berlin East. He was a personal assistant to Goebbels in the propaganda ministry and was *Gauleiter* of Lower Silesia from 1941 to 1945. Hitler appointed him Himmler's successor as *Reichsführer SS* on 29 April 1945 in fury at Himmler's treachery in the last days of the war. He was killed by Czech partisans in August 1945.

Hanover (German name: Hannover), city and state in northern Germany. It originated with the WELF principality of Calenberg, whose capital was in Hanover from 1636.

Duke Ernst August (1676–98) united the territory, and it became an electoral principality in 1692. The elector Georg Ludwig created a personal union with Great Britain when he succeeded to the British throne in 1714, and established the Hanoverian ruling dynasty. The principality became a kingdom in 1814, and was annexed by Prussia after the AUSTRO-PRUSSIAN WAR of 1866. The *DEUTSCHHANNOVERSCHE PARTEI* (German-Hanoverian Party) was formed in opposition to this loss of sovereignty. The present-day city of Hanover, now in the federal state of LOWER SAXONY, has just over half a million inhabitants.

Hansemann, David Justus (1790–1864), reforming liberal politician. Born in Finkenwerder near Hamburg, Hansemann began his career as a businessman in Aachen. He was elected to the Rhineland LANDTAG in 1845 and became Prussian finance minister under CAMPHAUSEN in 1848. Following Camphausen's resignation in June 1848, he formed his own administration but was himself dismissed in September the same year. He was subsequently director of the Prussian Bank from 1848 to 1851.

Harbou, Thea von (1889–1954), writer. Von Harbou wrote the scripts for a number of films made by her husband, the director Fritz LANG, including *Metropolis* (1927) and *Die Frau im Mond* (*The Woman in the Moon*, 1929). She joined the Nazi Party in 1932 and stayed in Germany to work for the Nazis when Lang left for the United States. She was interned briefly after the end of World War II.

Harden, Maximilian (pseudonym of Felix Ernst Witkowski, 1861–1927), journalist. Born in Berlin, the son of a Jewish silk merchant, Harden left school early and spent ten years with an itinerant theatre, where he acquired his pseudonym. From 1888 he earned his living as a journalist, and in 1892 he founded his own journal *Die Zukunft* ('The Future'), which he used to accuse close associates of the emperor, Philipp, Graf zu Eulenberg and Kuno von Moltke, of homosexuality, which was then illegal. (Although Harden was notionally a conservative monarchist, when he had offered to work for the emperor he had been snubbed; he was also a friend of Bismarck.) The accusations precipitated one of the major scandals of imperial Germany: the two men sued for libel, and the government was prompted to legislate for more severe punishments for libels involving accusations of immorality (which almost always meant homosexuality). The scandal ensured that, despite his erratic and contradictory political journalism, Harden was influential. He argued for *Weltpolitik*, the aspiration to make Germany a world power, but against TIRPITZ's navy plans; later, he welcomed the WEIMAR REPUBLIC, but quickly became disillusioned. He retired to Switzerland after he was attacked by right-wing activists.

Hardenberg, Karl August, Fürst von (1750–1822), Prussian minister and reformer. Hardenberg was born in Essenrode bei Gifhorn near Braunschweig into an aristocratic family. He studied at Göttingen and Leipzig, and after a spell at the imperial court in Wetzlar he embarked on a career in the public service in Hanover and Braunschweig. In 1790 he became a Prussian minister in the province of Ansbach-Bayreuth, and became foreign minister of Prussia in 1804. He was dismissed at the insistence of Napoleon in 1807, but returned to public life in 1810 as 'state chancellor', effectively the first prime minister of Prussia. Hardenberg continued the programme of domestic reforms set in train by Freiherr vom STEIN. More flexible (and arguably less principled) than Stein, he was a pragmatist with an objective approach to political reform, as was reflected in the comprehensive statement of his principles embodied in the Riga Memorandum of 1807. He was impatient with custom, tradition and community. Hardenberg sought to promote social and economic freedom within the framework of monarchical government. On his appointment in 1810 he introduced taxes and tariffs to pay off the French indemnity imposed after the collapse of Prussia, and although he never mastered the finances of the state he did, in his attempt to do so, introduce reforms that incidentally had far-reaching political effects. His finance edict (1810) sought to raise revenue by selling off some crown property, secularizing that of the church and reforming the whole revenue system. All businesses were licensed and taxed by the state, which freed them from guild control. Hardenberg also tried to reform the system of local government and rural policing in 1812, but had to surrender to JUNKER resistance. In the same year he also legislated for the emancipation of the Jews. Hardenberg was raised from the status of baron to that of prince in 1814, but his reforms were eclipsed in the conservative political climate of the post-1815 era.

Harlan, Veit (1899–1964), film director. Born in Berlin the son of a novelist and playwright, Harlan was an actor with the Berlin state theatre, and moved into films in 1934. He was a staunch Nazi supporter and directed *Jud Süss* (1940) and *Kolberg* (1945). He continued his film career after the war, claiming that he had been an unwilling Nazi collaborator.

Harnack, Adolf (Karl Gustav) von (1851–1930), theologian and historian of religion. Harnack was born in Dorpat (Tartu), Estonia, in 1851. He was professor of Protestant theology at Leipzig at the age of 25, and founded the *Theologische Literaturzeitung* in 1876. He moved to Giessen in 1879, to Marburg in 1886 and finally to Berlin in 1888, following a conflict between church and state, which was resolved in Harnack's favour following Bismarck's intervention with the Kaiser. He was opposed to annexations during World War I, and an outspoken supporter of the Weimar Republic. In the 1925 presidential election he campaigned for the candidate of the Catholic CENTRE PARTY,

Wilhelm MARX, against HINDENBURG. His liberal positions left him increasingly marginalized among the Protestant establishment, and his influence declined during the 1920s. His son, Ernst von HARNACK, became an anti-Nazi conspirator.

Harnack, Ernst von (1888–1945), anti-Nazi conspirator. Born in Berlin, the son of the theologian Adolf von HARNACK, he studied at Marburg, served in World War I, and pursued a career in the Prussian civil service. A Social Democrat, he was dismissed in 1933 and joined the resistance. He was arrested after the 1944 JULY BOMB PLOT and was executed in March the following year.

Harzburg Front, coalition of right-wing parties opposed to the BRÜNING government. The coalition of the nationalist DNVP, the NSDAP (Nazi Party), the *STAHLHELM* and other radical right-wing movements provisionally formed at Bad Harzburg, Braunschweig, in 1931, was a symbolic milestone in the development of the anti-parliamentary right during the Depression. The initiative came from the newspaper tycoon and DNVP politician Alfred HUGENBERG, and other influential figures included HITLER; the banker Hjalmar SCHACHT, who was later Hitler's economics minister; Franz SELDTE, the head of the *Stahlhelm*; and Fritz THYSSEN, the businessman who introduced Hitler to the Rhineland's industrialists. The meeting at Harzburg was effectively a demonstration of Hitler's importance as a national politician following the previous year's Nazi landslide election victory. Hitler made a point of leaving before the end of the meeting, however, and insisted on maintaining the party's independence of the reactionary right. The leading members of the Harzburg Front were influential in the establishment of the Nazi regime, and many of them held cabinet posts under Hitler.

Hasner von Artha, Leopold (1818–91), Austrian politician. Hasner was born in Prague and was a university teacher in law and economics before taking up the post of Austrian education minister (1867–70). He sought to secularize the education system and set up new, more modern types of state schools. He was briefly and unsuccessfully minister-president of Austria in 1870, after which he confined his political activity to the upper house of parliament.

Hassell, Christian Albrecht Ulrich von (1881–1944), diplomat and anti-Nazi conspirator. Born into an aristocratic family in Pomerania, Hassell studied in England and Switzerland, married the daughter of TIRPITZ and embarked on a career in the diplomatic service, first of all as vice consul in Genoa (1911). He served in the German army during World War I, and then resumed his career. He was ambassador in Copenhagen (1926–30), Belgrade (1930–2), and Rome (1932–8). In Belgrade, Hassell had become friendly with Neville Henderson, who as British ambassador to Berlin (1937–9) was responsible for the implementation of Britain's appeasement policy. Hassell himself was in favour of a *rapprochement* with the West, and found himself increasingly alienated from the foreign policy of the Reich in the late 1930s. He was recalled to Berlin following disagreements with RIBBEN-TROP about the formation of the Axis, and subsequently became involved with the resistance, particularly BECK and GOERDELER, and with them other members of the 1944 JULY BOMB PLOT. He was arrested after the failure of the plot, tried at the *VOLKS-GERICHTSHOF* ('people's court') on 7 September and hanged the following day. His diaries were hidden at his house in Bavaria and have been published in English.

Haugwitz, Christian (Heinrich August Curt), Graf von (1752–1832), Prussian minister in charge of foreign policy (1792–1806). After studying at Halle and Göttingen, Haugwitz pursued a career in the diplomatic service, and was appointed ambassador to Austria in 1791. He was responsible for agreeing the second partition of Poland with Russia in 1793. Most of all he is remembered for the failure during the Wars of the COALITIONS of his foreign policy, which ended with the reduction of Prussia to the status of a French puppet state by 1805.

Hauptmann, Elisabeth (1897–1973), writer. Born the daughter of a country doctor in Westphalia, Hauptmann was a teacher in Pomerania, before moving to Berlin and working with BRECHT. It was Hauptmann who discovered and translated John Gay's *Beggar's Opera*, made famous by Brecht as *The Threepenny Opera*. A Communist, Hauptmann fled to the United States after the Nazis came to power. She returned to Berlin in 1948, and was a member of the Berliner Ensemble.

Hauptmann, Gerhart (1862–1946), playwright and novelist. Born in Obersalzbrunn, Silesia (now Szczawno Zdrój in Poland), into a family of modest means, Hauptmann studied at Breslau and Jena. He made his name as a naturalist writer with *Vor Sonnenaufgang* (*Before Dawn*, 1889) and *Die Weber* (*The Weavers*, based on the Silesian weavers' revolt of 1844), whose premiere in 1892 at the Freie Bühne theatre in Berlin caused a scandal. In 1912 he was awarded the Nobel prize for literature. He was a supporter of the Weimar Republic, but his later writing was less politically engaged. He remained in Germany throughout the Nazi dictatorship.

Haus der jungen Talente (literally 'house of young talents'), the main club house of the Free German Youth (*FREIE DEUTSCHE JUGEND*, FDJ), the youth movement of the German Democratic Republic. It was situated on the Klosterstrasse in East Berlin and dedicated to the youth of the city in 1954, being intended to serve as a model socialist youth centre. It was taken over by the Kulturveranstaltungs-GmbH in 1991.

Haushofer, Albrecht (1903–45), academic and anti-Nazi conspirator. Born in Munich, the son of Karl HAUSHOFER, he became professor of political geography at Berlin University in 1940. Haushofer was a close associate of Rudolf HESS, and although opposed to Nazism, was in favour of the restoration of an authoritarian monarchy. He had contacts with a number of resistance groups, and was arrested after the failure of the 1944 JULY BOMB PLOT. He was shot by the SS when the Soviets captured Berlin, but his poems, written in Moabit prison, were published after his death.

Haushofer, Karl (1869–1946), geographer. Born in Munich, Haushofer travelled extensively in the Far East before 1914. He served as a brigadier general during World War I. He became professor of geography at Munich (1921–39), and taught the young Rudolf HESS. Haushofer is considered the father of geopolitics, and founded the Institute of Geopolitics in Munich. He was the author of *Der Nationalsozialistische Gedanke in der Welt* ('National Socialist Thought in the World', 1934) and *Deutsche Kulturpolitik* ('German Cultural Policy', 1940). His thesis was that geopolitics was a conflict between maritime and continental powers, but that Britain, the dominant maritime empire, was in decline, and that it was now time for a continental power (Germany) to assume leadership. This thesis found a receptive audience not only in the Nazi Party but more broadly among the country's elites. Haushofer believed that Germany needed to expand in eastern Europe, but must remain on good terms with Britain. His ideas reflected the prevalent motifs of German foreign policy from the MITTELEUROPA policies of World War I to the LEBENSRAUM ideology of the Nazis, and made the German invasions of eastern Europe and the Soviet Union a matter of historical necessity. Similarly, his analysis of Britain reflected the ambiguous attitudes of the German ruling class, from WILHELM II to HITLER, to the British empire. Haushofer became embarrassed by his association with the Nazis, and disillusioned with some aspects of the regime's policies. Moreover his son, Albrecht HAUSHOFER, had connections with the resistance and his own wife was half-Jewish. He

committed suicide shortly after his son was murdered by the SS at the end of the war.

Havenstein, Rudolf (1857–1923), president of the REICHSBANK (1908–23). Born in Meseritz, Havenstein trained in law and was a civil servant in the Prussian finance ministry (1890–1900). He was also president of the Prussian State Bank. His presidency of the Reichsbank coincided with the economic preparations for war in 1914, the financing of the war itself, and the INFLATION and hyperinflation of the postwar years. Havenstein died on the day the German currency was stabilized.

Haw Haw, Lord. *See* JOYCE, WILLIAM.

Hayek, Friedrich (August) von (1899–1992), Austrian-born economist. A member of the 'Austrian school', he was also director of the Austrian Institute for Economic Research between 1927 and 1931. He left Vienna for a chair at the London School of Economics in 1931. Hayek's *Road to Serfdom*, first published in 1944, was written under the influence of recent political developments and, anticipating the 'totalitarian' interpretative frameworks of Cold War ideology, conflated Nazism with Soviet Communism. His idiosyncratic intellectual history of Nazism located its 'socialist' roots in the work of 'former Marxists' such as Werner SOMBART and Friedrich NAUMANN. Hayek was especially influential on the political and economic thinking of the new right of the 1970s and 1980s. He shared the 1974 Nobel prize for economics.

Haymerle, Heinrich, Freiherr von (1828–81), Austrian diplomat and politician. Haymerle was Austrian foreign minister in 1879, and was involved in the negotiations for the THREE EMPERORS' LEAGUE.

Heartfield, John (1891–1968), satirical artist. Born in Berlin as Helmut Herzfeld, the son of a socialist writer, Franz Held, he changed his name as an act of political protest against Germany's anti-British propaganda during World War I. He trained as an artist in Wiesbaden and Munich, where he belonged to the artistic circles associated with the journals *Sturm* and *Aktion*, and got to know George GROSZ, with whom he collaborated for many years. After the war he joined the KPD. He collaborated in the establishment of the Malik publishing house (from 1917) and the Berlin DADA group (1919), and was scenic director for Max REINHARDT (1920–3). Among his best-known work is his series of satirical photomontages directed against Hitler and the Nazi movement. In 1933 he left Germany for Prague, where he remained until the end of 1938. He subsequently spent eleven years in England. He returned to (East) Germany in 1950 and worked for the Berliner Ensemble and the Deutsches Theater, but his work was criticized as formalist.

Hebenstreit von Streitenfeld, Franz von (1747–95), Austrian radical activist. Born the son of a university teacher in Prague, Hebenstreit studied at the Charles University there and at Vienna, but did not take a degree. He joined the cavalry in 1768, but was not promoted and deserted in 1773. He was captured and forced to join the Prussian army, but returned to Austria after an amnesty of 1778. He moved to Vienna in the 1780s and met Andreas von RIEDEL there in 1792, with whom he led the Jacobin conspiracy of the mid-1790s. He was arrested for his part in the conspiracy and charged with complicity in subversive attitudes, failure to report those of his friends, planning a military coup, authorship of seditious texts, and the building of a war machine and its delivery to the enemy. (Hebenstreit had constructed a model of a mobile stockade and sent it to Paris with a copy of his *Homo hominibus* and the suggestion that the French might reflect on his work when considering constitutional reform.) The charges were rather exaggerated, given the amateur nature of Hebenstreit's political agitation, but he was sentenced to death and executed for treason in January 1795.

Hecker, Friedrich (1811–81), radical political activist. Born in Eichtersheim, he studied law and history at Heidelberg and was elected to the Baden LANDTAG in 1842. The political opposition in Baden voiced its demands for constitutional reform in February 1848, even before the outbreak of the revolution in France. Hecker and other radicals initially stood alongside the more moderate liberals, but with the escalation of the political situation a rift emerged between the liberal establishment – largely businessmen, civil servants and academics – and the radicals. Along with Gustav von Struve, Hecker became one of the leading spokesmen of the radicals in the Baden Landtag in Karlsruhe and in the Frankfurt PRE-PARLIAMENT, where the 'moderate' majority was alarmed at the radicalism of the left's demands. The political polarization between liberals and radicals was more acute in Baden than in other parts of Germany, and popular rebellion was also more widespread in the south-west than elsewhere. Radicals such as Hecker and Struve saw the appointment of a liberal government in Karlsruhe in March as an unsatisfactory outcome to the revolution and pinned their hopes on a more radical popular uprising, calling for a revolutionary assembly to meet in Konstanz on 14 April 1848. From here a more radical revolution spread through Baden to the rest of Germany. There were few would-be revolutionaries, however, and they were quickly dispersed by deferral troops called out by the Frankfurt authorities. Hecker fled to Switzerland, and briefly edited a radical journal there. He then emigrated to the United States, and returned to Germany only for one brief spell (in May 1849) before the end of the revolution. Although he also visited Germany on subsequent occasions he died in St Louis after participating in the American Civil War.

Heereman von Zuydtwyck, Klemens, Freiherr (1832–1903), politician. A Westphalian landowner with an estate near Münster, Heereman von Zuydtwyck was a member of the Prussian LANDTAG from 1870, and was foremost vice president from 1881 to 1903. He was a co-founder of the CENTRE PARTY and leader of the party faction in the Landtag. He was also a member of the Reichstag (1871–1903), and president of the Westphalian Art Association.

Hegel, Georg Wilhelm Friedrich (1770–1831), philosopher. Born in Stuttgart into a family of public servants and theologians, Hegel was educated in the local German and Latin schools, and the *Gymnasium Illustre*. He studied classics, philosophy and theology at Tübingen, where he became a friend of both HÖLDERLIN and SCHELLING, and he collaborated with the latter on the *Kritisches Journal der Philosophie* ('critical journal of philosophy'). He worked as a private tutor in Bern and Frankfurt and was appointed professor of philosophy at Jena in 1805. In 1807 the war compelled him to leave Jena, and he became editor of the *Bamberger Zeitung*. The following year he became rector of a grammar school in Nuremberg. In 1818 he was appointed to the chair of philosophy in Berlin.

Hegel's first major work was *Phänomenologie des Geistes* (*Phenomenology of Mind*, 1807), and it was followed by *Wissenschaft der Logik* (*Science of Logic*), which was published between 1812 and 1816. His *Encyclopedia of the Philosophical Sciences* was published in 1817. Hegel was influenced by KANT, FICHTE and Schelling, but developed his own philosophy of absolute idealism, in which the world is a reflection of the mind. His dialectical scheme presupposed development of thought through the opposition of a thesis and an antithesis that negates it. This produces a synthesis, which in turn produces its own antithesis, and the whole process starts again.

Hegel's philosophy was declared by those of his disciples on the conservative right to be compatible with and supportive of the political ideology of the post-1815 restoration and the theology of the evangelical church. The YOUNG HEGELIANS on the left used Hegel's philosophy as a vehicle for criticism of the Prussian state. It was through this latter group of radical intellectuals that Karl MARX was introduced to Hegel's philosophy. Marx also interpreted the world in terms of dialectical progression, but from a materialist (rather than idealist) perspective, which he had developed under the influence of Feuerbach.

Heidegger, Martin (1889–1976), philosopher. Heidegger was born in Messkirch into a family of Roman Catholic artisans, and educated at Freiburg University, where he studied first theology and then philosophy. After World War I he was *Assistent* to Edmund HUSSERL. Heidegger moved to Marburg in 1923. His most important work, *Being and Time* (1927), originally planned as a much larger project, made a great impact on the philosophical thinking of the time, but was strongly criticized and even ignored by later philosophers. Heidegger returned to Freiburg in 1929 as professor of philosophy after Husserl's retirement, and was elected rector in April 1933. He joined the NSDAP (Nazi Party), and his inaugural speech (along with other public speeches) was positive about the Nazi regime. In October he was ceremonially inaugurated again, this time as a 'rector-leader'. He resigned as rector in April 1934, and his public enthusiasm for the Nazis diminished rapidly. He was dismissed in 1945 by the Allies and was prohibited from teaching until 1951.

Heiland, Rudolf (1910–65), Social Democratic politician. Heiland worked for the municipal electricity company in Marl. He was imprisoned by the Nazis in 1936. After World War II he was a small shopkeeper in Marl, now in the new federal state of North Rhine-Westphalia, became the town's mayor in 1946, and was a member of the LANDTAG for the SPD (1947–9). He was deputy president of the *Deutscher Gemeindetag* (the German local government conference) in 1949.

Heil Hitler!, Nazi greeting accompanied by a raised-hand salute based on that of the

Italian Fascists. It was introduced as an official greeting among the Nazis in 1925, and became the 'German greeting' after 1933. Its observance was perceived as an index of attitudes towards the regime, both by its opponents and by the police and the authorities.

Heiliger, Max, fictitious holder of an account into which the untaxed funds of SS industrial concerns were deposited, along with valuables looted from the victims of the Nazis.

Heilmann, Ernst (1881–1940), Social Democratic politician. Born in Berlin into a middle-class Jewish family, Heilmann joined the SPD at the age of 17. He studied law, but his political allegiance prevented him from pursuing his chosen career in the public service. Instead he became a journalist, and was editor in chief of the *Chemnitzer Volksstimme* from 1909 to 1914. He volunteered for military service in 1914 and was seriously wounded. He was a member of the Constituent Assembly of the Prussian LANDTAG in 1919, was a member of the Landtag until 1933 and leader of the SPD faction from 1921. He was also a member of the Reichstag from 1928. He was arrested in 1933, spent the next seven years in CONCENTRATION CAMPS, where he was treated with persistent brutality, and was murdered by the SS in Buchenwald.

Heimat, a term that has the approximate meaning of 'home' in the sense of native locality. *Heimatbewegung* generally refers collectively to a range of 19th-century cultural associations (such as Ernst Rudorff's *Bund Heimatschutz*) and the anti-urban and often racist attitudes that underpinned them. It was also used to describe the popular literature of a mythical past (and present) in small rural communities where 'traditional' values are upheld. *Heimat* motifs of this kind quickly found their way into the '*VÖLKISCH*' anti-urban political propaganda of the right.

Heimatschutz, 'home guard', a generic term, applied to home defence militias in Germany,

but also the local name for the HEIMWEHR in Styria. The Styrian *Heimatschutz* was associated with the German-owned heavy industry in the province, and of all the Austrian *Heimwehren* was the most German nationalist and eventually pro-Nazi in its politics.

Heimatvertriebene. *See* EXPELLEES.

Heimwehr, right-wing Austrian paramilitary movement with increasingly fascist tendencies in the late 1920s and 1930s. The *Heimwehren* or 'home guards' were initially set up during the months immediately after World War I, and were deployed against incursions into the territory of the Austrian state, particularly from Yugoslavia. They very rapidly saw themselves as guarantors of 'order' in other ways, and effectively became the military wing of the CHRISTIAN SOCIAL PARTY. The Heimwehr campaigned separately in the 1930 parliamentary elections, and its AUSTROFASCIST ideology was made explicit in the Korneuburg Oath of the same year. In 1931 Heimwehr leaders attempted, unsuccessfully, to march on Vienna, and they played an important part in the establishment of the Austrofascist dictatorship after 1934 (*see* CORPORATE STATE). Prince Starhemberg, one of the most prominent Heimwehr leaders, was head of the *VATERLÄNDISCHE FRONT* (Fatherland Front) until he was dismissed by SCHUSCHNIGG in 1936, after which the Heimwehr movement was effectively marginalized.

Heine, Heinrich (1797–1856), poet. Heine was born in Düsseldorf into a middle-class Jewish family. He studied in Bonn, Berlin and Göttingen, taking a degree in law. He converted to Protestantism so as to be able to enter public service, although he never did so. He was an admirer of the French Revolution and its achievements and a critic of society and politics in restoration Germany. He made his reputation as a poet with the *Buch der Lieder* (*The Book of Songs*, 1827). In 1831 he moved to Paris in the wake of the 1830 revolution, and spent much of the rest of his life there. He published a series of essays on the post-revolutionary political developments (*Französische Zustände*, 'French affairs', 1832), followed by a critique of Romanticism (*Die Romantische Schule*, 'the Romantic school', 1833–5). In the 1840s he collaborated with Marx (whom he met at the end of 1843), and published revolutionary poetry in *Vorwärts*. Nevertheless, he was an unreliable comrade, ungenerous to less gifted political writers, and unsure quite where he himself stood politically. Heine fell ill during the 1848 revolution in Paris, and died there after eight years confined to his sick bed.

Heine, Wolfgang (1861–1944), Social Democratic politician. Born in Posen (now Poznań in Poland), Heine was a member of the Reichstag for the SPD from 1898 to 1918, and was justice minister and then interior minister in Prussia during the revolutionary upheavals after the war. Heine was on the right of the party, and was considered a traitor by the breakaway USPD, but was regarded as one of the few capable Social Democratic leaders by Wilhelm GROENER. Heine was replaced as interior minister of Prussia by Carl SEVERING after the 1920 KAPP PUTSCH. In 1933 he emigrated to Switzerland.

Heinemann, Gustav (1899–1976), politician; federal president (1969–74). Heinemann was CDU interior minister (1949–50) in the first ADENAUER government, but resigned from the cabinet over defence, rearmament and issues in domestic policy in 1950, and from the party in 1951. The following year he was a co-founder of the *Gesamtdeutsche Partei*, which stood for a united and neutral Germany. He was subsequently elected to the Bundestag for the SPD, and was a member of the party executive from 1957. He was justice minister in the GRAND COALITION (1966–9), and federal president from 1969 to 1974.

Heinkel, Ernst (Heinrich) (1888–1958), aircraft engineer. Born in Grunbach, Württemberg, Heinkel studied mechanical engineering at Stuttgart. The Heinkel aircraft works at Warnemünde, established in 1922, developed many designs, including the Heinkel HE-70 and the HE-111 bomber, used by the German air force. Heinkel also developed the first turbojet-powered and the first rocket-powered planes. He was classified as a Nazi fellow-traveller by the Allies.

Heinrici, Gotthard (1886–1971), officer. Heinrici was leader of the XVII and XII Army Corps on the Western Front and commander in chief of the 4th Army in Russia from 1942 to 1944. He was also commander of the First Panzer Army in Hungary (1944–5), and led its retreat into Silesia. In 1945 he replaced HIMMLER as commander of Army Group Vistula, and was made responsible for the defence of Berlin. He was captured by the Russians and released in 1955.

Heisenberg, Werner (1901–76), German physicist. Heisenberg worked with Niels Bohr in Copenhagen before his appointment to the chair of physics at Leipzig in 1926. His work furnished the basis of quantum mechanics, and his uncertainty principle is still accepted by modern physicists. He was awarded the 1932 Nobel prize for physics. Politically Heisenberg was a nationalist, and was appointed director of the German nuclear weapons programme during World War II. It remains unclear whether the programme failed due to the exodus of Germany's Jewish scientists, or due to the reluctance of those remaining to develop such a weapon. He remained a leading West German research scientist after World War II.

Held, Heinrich (1868–1938), politician. Born in Erbach, the son of a Hessian businessman, Held studied law, economics and history at Strasbourg, Heidelberg and Marburg. He was a journalist and became editor of the *Regensburger Morgenblatt* in 1899. He was an important figure in the development of Christian trade unions in the Upper Palatinate and was elected to the Bavarian LANDTAG for the CENTRE PARTY in 1907. Initially on the left of the party, he moved to the right, and was a vocal supporter of an annexationist peace during World War I. Held was a co-founder of the Bavarian People's Party after the war, and was elected minister-president of Bavaria in March 1923, becoming Bavarian foreign minister at the same time. In addition he assumed the trade portfolio in 1927. He remained in office until he was replaced by the Nazis, and then emigrated to Switzerland. He returned to Germany after announcing his resignation.

Helfferich, Karl (1872–1924), director of the Deutsche Bank and finance minister (1915–16). Born the son of a textile manufacturer, Helfferich studied law at Strasbourg. He regulated the currency systems of the German colonies in Africa, and became state secretary at the Treasury in 1915. He also served as state secretary of the interior (1916–17). Helfferich supported the financing of the war through borrowing rather than taxation, and argued that industrialists would be deterred from trying to meet the government's munitions needs if their excessive war profits were cancelled. (The loans would be repaid by REPARATIONS after a victorious peace.) As loans increasingly failed to cover government deficits, more money was printed and inflation set in. In 1918 Helfferich was ambassador in Moscow.

Politically, Helfferich was of the NATIONAL LIBERAL camp, but after the war he moved sharply to the right, joined the DNVP, and was elected to the Reichstag in 1920. He was a vocal opponent of the Weimar Republic's 'FULFILMENT POLICY' and a supporter of the anti-democratic and anti-Semitic 'stab-in-the-back-myth' (*DOLCHSTOSSLEGENDE*), which did much to poison the political atmosphere of Germany during the 1920s. In particular, he was bitterly resentful of Matthias ERZBERGER, the Reich finance minister, whom he regarded as little short of a traitor. (In 1920 Erzberger sued for defamation and Helfferich, who was found guilty, was fined a nominal amount.) The directorate and cen-

tral committee of the REICHSBANK supported his candidature for president of the bank, but he was passed over, and Hjalmar SCHACHT was appointed instead. He was killed in a train crash in Italy.

Heligoland or **Helgoland,** one of the Frisian islands, situated 58 km (36 miles) from Cuxhaven at the mouth of the Elbe. It has some 1600 inhabitants and is technically a part of the local government district of Pinneberg in SCHLESWIG-HOLSTEIN. Its name means 'holy land'.

Heligoland was part of Schleswig from 1402, and was Danish from 1714. It was occupied by British forces in 1807, ceded to Great Britain by Denmark in 1814 and transferred to Germany under the terms of the Anglo-German agreement of 1890 in exchange for Zanzibar. German civil law was introduced in 1900. The island quickly became a popular resort for visitors from the mainland, whose numbers rose from 12,700 in 1890 to 35,000 in 1911. It was an important naval base during both world wars. It was declared a demilitarized area by the treaty of VERSAILLES and its fortifications were demolished after the end of WORLD WAR I. It was refortified from 1935. The settlement on Heligoland was completely destroyed by the RAF in 1945, the military installations were blown up, and the population was expelled. The island was returned to Germany in 1952.

Heligoland Bight, scene of battles between the Royal Navy and the German navy during World War I. The first confrontation came with the sinking of a German ship laying mines in British waters immediately after the outbreak of war in August 1914. There were further skirmishes and losses until the end of the month, when four German light cruisers were effectively ambushed by five British battle cruisers, and a thousand German sailors were lost.

Helldorf, Wolf Heinrich, Graf von (1896–1944), right-wing agitator who eventually became an anti-Nazi conspirator. Born in

Merseburg, Helldorf served in World War I and was awarded the IRON CROSS. After the war he joined the Rossbach FREIKORPS gang and was involved in political violence against the Communists. He also took part in the 1920 KAPP PUTSCH, and fled to Italy when it failed. He was elected to the Prussian LANDTAG when he returned to Germany in 1924, joined the Nazi Party in 1926 and became an SA leader in Berlin in 1931. After Hitler came to power he was made *SA-Gruppenführer* and *SS-Obergruppenführer*, and became a member of the Reichstag in the Nazis' first one-party 'election' in November 1933. He was police president of Potsdam (1933–5) and then of Berlin. He was executed in 1944 after taking part in the JULY BOMB PLOT.

heller, currency unit of the Habsburg empire, a subdivision of the Habsburg crown (*Krone*). The name derives from Schwäbisch Hall, where the coin was minted from around 1200. In Germany it was worth half a PFENNIG until the introduction of the mark.

Hellpach, Willy Hugo (1877–1955), politician. Born in Oels, Silesia, the son of a court official, Hellpach studied medicine at Greifswald and psychology at Leipzig. He became a neurologist in Karlsruhe in 1904. In 1918 he joined the left-liberal DDP, and quickly became a leading member. He was education minister in Baden from 1922 to 1925, and in 1924 he was state president and head of the Baden government. He was the DDP candidate in the Reich presidential election of 1925, and won around 1.5 million votes (5.8%) in the first round. He was elected to the Reichstag in 1928, but resigned in 1930 following sharp differences with the leader of the parliamentary party, Erich Koch-Weser. After his effective retirement from politics he concentrated on his academic work, and died in Heidelberg in 1955.

Henlein, Konrad (1898–1945), leader of the Germans in SUDETENLAND. Born the son of a civil servant in Maffersdorf, Bohemia, Henlein served in World War I on the Italian Front, and then worked in a bank until 1925, when he became a gymnastics teacher for the Sudeten German Gymnastics Association in Asch. He founded the Sudeten German Home Front (*Sudetendeutsche Heimatfront*) in 1933, which subsequently became the Sudeten German Party (from 1935). With financial support from Nazi Germany, Henlein and the Sudeten German Party agitated against the Czechoslovak state. After the occupation of the Sudetenland he was appointed chief of the civil administration and *Gauleiter* (1939). He committed suicide in Pilsen (Plzeň) 1945 after his capture by the Americans.

Heppenheim programme (1847), manifesto drawn up by moderate liberals from southwest Germany, who met at Heppenheim on 10 October 1847 to discuss a common programme. Their meeting took place a month after the OFFENBURG meeting of the region's radicals. The question of German national unity was discussed, along with that of the representation of the people and the issue of civil liberties.

Herder, Johann Gottfried von (1744–1803), writer. Born in Mohrungen, in East Prussia, the son of a schoolteacher, Herder studied theology at Königsberg University from 1762 to 1764, where he encountered KANT. He became a schoolteacher in Riga, and was then appointed to a number of positions in the Lutheran Church. He read seven languages and worked in a number of different fields, ranging from natural history and comparative historical linguistics to theology and philosophy, but his best known works are perhaps in the philosophy of history: *Auch eine Philosophie der Geschichte zur Bildung der Menschheit* (*Another Philosophy of History Concerning the Development of Mankind*, 1774) and *Ideen zur Philosophie der Geschichte der Menschheit* (*Ideas on the Philosophy of the History of Humanity*, 1784–91). He was an associate of GOETHE, many of whose interests he shared. Herder's concern with the *Volk* ('nation' or 'race') as a decisive determinant of human identity, and his work on the relationship between peoples and languages, his research in folklore and his philosophy of history made him an important influence on his contemporaries and on the development of historical thought in Germany during the 19th century.

Hermannsdenkmal ('monument to Hermann'), gigantic monument, 57 m (187 ft) in height, erected near Detmold in 1875 to commemorate the annihilation of three Roman legions in the Teutoburg Forest in AD 9 by the Germanic chieftain Hermann (Latin name: Arminius). In the 19th century Hermann's victory was considered to be a defining moment in the pre-history of Germany, and had already been the subject of three plays before the construction of the monument. The first, in 1769, was by Friedrich Gottlieb Klopstock (1724–1803). Heinrich von KLEIST wrote a political drama on the theme which circulated privately for many years before being published in 1821; and Christian Dietrich Grabbe, who was born in nearby Detmold, published a play about the battle in 1835.

Hermes, Andreas (1878–1964), CENTRE PARTY politician. Hermes was born in Cologne into a lower middle-class family and studied agriculture. He travelled abroad, and worked in the International Institute of Agriculture in Rome before World War I. In 1920 he took over the agricultural department of the Reich economics ministry. He was Reich food minister (the department had been created at his suggestion) from March 1920 to March 1922, and finance minister in the second WIRTH cabinet (1921–2) and then in the CUNO administration (1922–3). He was president of the Union of German Farmers' Associations (1928–33), and was a protagonist of agricultural protectionism and autarkic policies (*see* AUTARKY). He was imprisoned by the Nazis in 1933, worked for the Colombian government after his release, but returned to Germany and became involved with GOERDELER and other members of the

1944 JULY BOMB PLOT. He was arrested after the failure of the assassination attempt and sentenced to death, but was freed by the Allies before the sentence could be carried out. After the war he was a co-founder of the Berlin CDU and deputy mayor of the city, and pursued a career as a political lobbyist.

Herrenhaus ('house of lords'). The term referred to the upper house of the Prussian LANDTAG (from 1855), and to the upper house of the Austrian REICHSRAT from 1861.

Herrnstadt, Rudolf (1903–66), East German politician. Herrnstadt joined the KPD in 1924, emigrated to the Soviet Union in 1933 and returned to Germany in 1945 as editor of the *Berliner Zeitung* newspaper. From 1949 to 1953 he was editor in chief of the SED party organ *Neues Deutschland*. He was a member of the party's Central Committee (ZK) from 1950 to 1953, and a candidate member for the Politburo at the same time. He was expelled from the ZK in 1953 and from the party in 1954 on grounds of 'factionalism'. He subsequently worked in the Merseburg branch of the East German *Deutsches Zentralarchiv* (German Central Archives).

Hertling, Georg (Friedrich), Freiherr (from 1914 Graf) von (1843–1919), CENTRE PARTY politician; Bavarian minister-president and foreign minister (1912–17) and Reich chancellor (1917–18). Hertling was a conservative Roman Catholic academic, who was professor of social policy first at Bonn University and then at Munich. He was a member of the Reichstag for the Centre Party from 1875 to 1890, and then for a second term from 1896 to 1912, when Ludwig III appointed him minister-president of Bavaria. He replaced Georg MICHAELIS as Reich chancellor on 1 November 1917, at a time when power effectively lay in the hands of a virtual military dictatorship headed by generals LUDENDORFF and HINDENBURG. Hertling did not attempt to assert himself against the military during the last year of the war, and eventually resigned (September 1918) rather than lead a government that would be responsible to the Reichstag. He was succeeded by Prince Max von BADEN.

Hertz, Gustav (1887–1975), physicist. Born in Hamburg, the nephew of Heinrich HERTZ, Gustav Hertz also studied physics in Berlin and worked with James FRANCK, demonstrating the quantum theory of Max Planck through experimental work on the impact of electrons on atoms. He and Franck were awarded the Nobel prize in 1925. Despite being Jewish, Hertz was protected against the worst excesses of the Nazis, first by his war record, then by powerful colleagues. After the war he emigrated to the Soviet Union, and was awarded the Stalin Prize in 1951. He returned to Germany and taught at Leipzig University until his retirement. He died in Berlin.

Hertz, Heinrich (Rudolf) (1857–94), physicist. Born in Hamburg, Hertz studied in Berlin and taught in Karlsruhe (1885–9) before moving to Bonn as professor of physics. As part of his experimental investigations of the electromagnetic theory of James Clark Maxwell, Hertz produced electromagnetic waves (specifically radio waves) in the laboratory. This work went on to become the foundation of wireless telegraphy and broadcast radio. The unit of frequency, the hertz, is named after him. He was the uncle of the quantum physicist Gustav HERTZ.

Hertz, Paul (1888–1961), Social Democratic politician. Hertz was born in Worms into a middle-class Jewish family, and joined the SPD in 1905 after a training in business. He graduated in 1914 with a doctorate in government. When the SPD split in 1917 he joined the USPD and was editor of its journal *Die Freiheit* ('freedom'), before returning to the SPD in 1922. He was a city councillor in Berlin from 1919 to 1925, and a member of the Reichstag throughout the Weimar Republic (1920–33). He was elected to the SPD executive in April 1933 and was one of the party's leaders in exile in Prague and then, after 1938, in Paris. In 1939 he

emigrated to the United States, but returned to Germany in 1949 and became a senator in West Berlin. He was senator for the MARSHALL PLAN (1951–3) and then, from 1955 until his death, senator for economics.

Herzfelder, Henriette (1865–1927), Austrian feminist and journalist. Herzfelder was editor of *Der Bund* ('the league'), the journal of the League of Austrian Women's Associations, and then, from 1911 to 1918, edited *Zeitschrift für Frauenstimmrecht*, ('journal for women's suffrage'). She was also active in youth-welfare organizations.

Herzog, Wilhelm (1884–1960), journalist. Herzog was born in Berlin and studied German and art history at the university there. He was a co-founder of the journal *Pan*, and was a friend of Theodor HEUSS. His journal *Forum*, which was sympathetic to the West, was banned in 1915. After World War I Herzog worked on the socialist daily *Republic*, but his Jewish background and political convictions made life in Germany increasingly unsympathetic, and he left to live in France. He was interned when war broke out, but managed to escape in 1941, and spent another four years interned in Trinidad. He lived briefly in New York and California during the 1940s, but returned to Europe, first to Basle in 1947, and then to Munich in 1952.

Hess, (Walther Richard) Rudolf (1894–1987), deputy leader of the NSDAP (the Nazi Party, 1933–41). Hess was born in Alexandria, Egypt, the son of a German businessman. He served in the same regiment as Hitler during World War I, and was wounded at Verdun. In 1919 he joined the radical right-wing THULE SOCIETY, and was a student of the nationalist geographer Karl HAUSHOFER at Munich University. He took part in the BEER HALL PUTSCH, and although he escaped to Austria after it failed, he returned to Germany and was imprisoned with Hitler at Landsberg. In 1925 he became Hitler's secretary, and rose quickly to positions of office within the party. He became deputy party leader on 21 April 1933 and minister without portfolio on 29 June. As 'Führer's deputy for party affairs', Hess (and increasingly his own deputy, BORMANN) played a pivotal role in party–state relations during the 1930s. In 1938 he became one of only six standing members of the Ministerial Council for the Defence of the Reich. On 10 May 1941 he flew alone to Scotland, ostensibly to negotiate peace. He apparently hoped to gain contact with appeasers on the right wing of the British Conservative Party, and to conclude a separate peace with Britain in the context of the planned German invasion of the Soviet Union. Instead he was interned until 1945, and disowned by Hitler. After the war he was tried and sentenced to life imprisonment at Nuremberg, and remained in Spandau prison in Berlin until his death.

Hesse, one of the federal states (*Länder*) of Germany. The present-day *Land* of Hesse was formed in 1945 from the fragmented territories that had carried the name for over 400 years. Its capital is Wiesbaden, but Frankfurt am Main is the largest city. At the end of the 20th century Hesse had a population of over 6 million. For most of the postwar period the largest party in the Hessian Landtag has been the SPD, and most of the state's governing coalitions have been led by the Social Democrats. Joschka FISCHER was appointed environment minister in Hesse by the governing SPD administration in 1985, and the state was governed by a pioneering 'red–green' coalition of GREENS and SPD. Centre–right (CDU–FDP) coalitions have formed governments in Wiesbaden only twice since the end of World War II, from 1987 to 1991, and again from 1999.

Hesse, Hermann (1877–1962), writer. Born in Calw, a small town near Karlsruhe, into a religious family, Hesse pursued a career as a bookseller and began to write poetry. He became famous with his *Bildungsroman, Peter Camenzind* (1904), and then published a series of further novels dealing with youth and education. He moved to Switzerland during World War I as a protest against German militarism, and published a number of essays against the war and critical of the German government and its policy. His best-known books were published during the interwar years and World War II: *Siddharta* (1922), *Der Steppenwolf* (1927), *Narziss und Goldmund* (1930) and *Das Glasperlenspiel* (*The Glass Bead Game*, 1943). He was awarded the Nobel prize for literature in 1946. Although Hesse was a traditionalist in matters of form, his interests in oriental philosophy and psychoanalysis, and the mystical content of his writing, ensured a resurgence of the popularity of his work in the 1960s and 1970s.

Heuss, Theodor (1884–1963), liberal politician and journalist; first president of the Federal Republic of Germany (1949–59). Heuss was born in Brackenheim near Heilbronn, the son of a master builder, and studied economics and history. He wrote for *Die Hilfe*, the organ of the national liberal movement, and became a close colleague of Friedrich NAUMANN. In 1912 he became editor of the liberal *Neckar-Zeitung* in Heilbronn, and after the war he worked on Ernst Jäckh's journal *Deutsche Politik* in Berlin. He wrote extensively on constitutional issues, and in 1923 he became editor in chief of *Die Deutsche Nation*. Heuss was a member of the left-liberal DDP and was twice elected to the Reichstag (in 1930 and then again in the Hitler election of March 1933). Despite reservations he supported the ENABLING LAW. He remained in Germany during the Nazi dictatorship, and wrote biographies of his mentor Friedrich Naumann and others. He resumed his journalistic career after the war, was a liberal (DVP/FDP) member of the LANDTAG of Württemberg-Baden, and became minister of culture in the newly created *Land*. He was president of the FDP, sat on the West German PARLIAMENTARY COUNCIL, and was elected first president of the Federal Republic of Germany, whose constitution he had helped to shape. He retired from the presidency in 1959.

Heydebrand und der Lasa, Ernst von (1851–1924), conservative politician. Heydebrand von der Lasa was born in Silesia and studied law at Heidelberg. He interrupted his studies to serve as a volunteer in the Franco-Prussian War, and then qualified and joined the Prussian public service. In 1888 he was elected to the Prussian *ABGEORDNETENHAUS*, and then in 1893 to the Reichstag, for the German Conservative Party (*DEUTSCHKONSERVATIVE PARTEI*). From 1906 to 1918 he was the leader of the parliamentary party, at a time when it was increasingly seen as a landowners' party, defending agrarian interests in collaboration with the AGRARIAN LEAGUE (*Bund der Landwirte*). In 1911 he became party president. In this post he reflected the attitudes of his party colleagues in his criticism of the shortcomings of the government's foreign policy (which he thought should be more aggressive), his refusal to countenance domestic political or economic reform, and his support for extensive territorial annexations by Germany during World War I. Although no longer active as a political leader after the war, he was a supporter of the German nationalist DNVP.

Heydrich, Reinhard (1904–42), leading SS officer and head of the Reich Security Head Office (*Reichssicherheitshauptamt*, RSHA); Reich Protector of Bohemia and Moravia. Born in Halle into a conservative middle-class family, Heydrich became a naval cadet in 1922 and was promoted to lieutenant in 1928. He was dismissed from the navy for dishonourable conduct in 1931 after an affair, and joined the Nazi Party and the SS. He was promoted very quickly, became head of the SD in 1932, and a lieutenant general in 1934 after the NIGHT OF THE LONG KNIVES. He was HIMMLER's deputy from 1933, and was appointed head of the Reich Central Office for Jewish Emigration in January 1939 and head of the RSHA in September of the same year. He was responsible for the deportation of Jews to the *GENERALGOUVERNEMENT* and the organization of the *EINSATZGRUPPEN* responsible for the mass murder of Jews in eastern Europe. In 1941 he was given overall responsibility for the mass murder of the Jews by GÖRING. He was appointed deputy Reich protector of Bohemia and Moravia in September 1941, to succeed Konstantin von NEURATH, and was assassinated by the Czech resistance in 1942. The village of LIDICE was burned and its inhabitants murdered as a reprisal.

Hilferding, Rudolf (1877–1941), Social Democratic politician; Reich finance minister (1923 and 1928–9). Viennese by birth, Hilferding studied medicine in Vienna and then moved to Berlin before World War I. From 1904 to 1923 he was co-editor with Max Adler of the journal *Marx-Studien*, and in 1907 he became an editor of the SPD newspaper *Vorwärts*. He published his major scholarly work, *Das Finanzkapital*, in 1910. He served as a doctor in the Austrian army during World War I, and joined the USPD following the SPD split of 1917. In 1919 he adopted German citizenship, and in 1922 he returned to the SPD and became one of its most important economic theorists. He was a member of the Reichstag from 1924 to 1933, and was appointed Reich finance minister in STRESEMANN's grand coalition of 1923. It was the first time a socialist had been appointed to such a post, and there was considerable opposition from conservatives, including open incitement to sabotage Hilferding's tax policies by the DNVP. Nevertheless the introduction of the RENTENMARK was resolved during his tenure, and the currency subsequently stabilized. In 1925 Hilferding worked with Karl KAUTSKY on the SPD's Heidelberg programme, and was editor of the theoretical journal *Die Gesellschaft* ('society)' from 1924 to 1933. He was finance minister again during the second MÜLLER administration (June 1928 to December 1929). He fled to Switzerland after the Nazis came to power and settled in France in 1938, but was arrested there by the French police in 1941, and died in Paris in the hands of the Gestapo.

Himmler, Heinrich (1900–45), national leader (*Reichsführer*) of the SS, head of the German police and minister of the interior (1943–5). Himmler was born in Munich, the son of a school teacher who had also been tutor to Prince Heinrich of Bavaria (Himmler's godfather). He received a grammar-school education, and studied agriculture at the Technical University in Munich before becoming involved with the radical right. He took part in the BEER HALL PUTSCH and subsequently became involved with the Nazi movement. Apart from his involvement with the SS, he was also secretary to Gregor STRASSER, deputy *Gauleiter* of Lower Bavaria and Oberpfalz, *Gauleiter* of Upper Bavaria, deputy national director of propaganda, and from 1930 a Reichstag deputy for the district of Weser-Ems.

In 1929 Himmler was appointed head of the SS, then a relatively insignificant organization, and proceeded to make it his own. His appointment to offices within the state security services, first in his native Bavaria, and then throughout the Reich, enabled him to make of the SS police complex an independent focus of power within the polycratic political structure of the Third Reich. In 1933 he became police chief in Munich, and by the end of the year was commander of the political police in all states except Prussia. In 1934 he took over as head of the Prussian police and the GESTAPO. By 1936 he was in control of the entire German police apparatus, a position he used as a power base. In 1939 he was appointed *Reichskommissar für die Festigung deutschen Volkstums* ('Reich commissioner for the consolidation of German nationhood') and was in ultimate command of the Nazi racial extermination campaign, including the mass murder of European Jews. Himmler seemed to take seriously the 'racial' pseudo-science propagated by 'academic' institutes and, although unable to witness violent murder himself (as at Minsk in 1941), he was indifferent to the consequences of his policies.

In 1943 he was appointed Reich interior minister, an indication of the extent to which the power of the SS had expanded within Germany itself. He lost influence towards the end of the war, however, and when he advocated surrender in 1945, Hitler issued an order for his arrest. He fled from Berlin and was captured by British troops, but killed himself before he could be brought to trial.

Hindemith, Paul (1895–1963), composer. Born in Hanau, the son of an unsuccessful businessman, Hindemith was admitted to the Frankfurt Conservatory in 1908 and became leader of the Frankfurt Opera orchestra in 1915. He began to compose after World War I and in 1921 formed the Amar Quartet, which performed mainly contemporary works. Appointed professor of music in Berlin in 1929, he fled Nazi Germany in the 1930s, and settled first in Turkey and then the USA. His music was banned by the Nazis in 1933. He returned to Europe in 1953 and settled in Switzerland.

Hindenburg, Paul (Ludwig Hans Anton) von Beneckendorff und von (1847–1934), army commander in World War I and Reich president (1925–34). After a long military career, which included service in the campaigns against Austria (1866) and France (1870–1), Hindenburg retired as a general in 1911. He came out of retirement in 1914, and with Erich von LUDENDORFF repelled the Russian invasion of 1914 at TANNENBERG and the MASURIAN LAKES. He was promoted to field marshal. His collaboration with Ludendorff continued on the Western Front, and in August 1916 Hindenburg was appointed to replace FALKENHAYN as chief of staff of the German army, with Ludendorff as his chief aide. The partnership became a political one, and the two men more or less turned Germany into a military dictatorship. Hindenburg again returned to private life after the war, until he stood, successfully, as the candidate of the right in the presidential election of 1925. He was re-elected in 1932, when HITLER also stood. His authority guaranteed the governments of BRÜNING, PAPEN and SCHLEICHER, who ruled largely by presidential decree, and his consent was decisive in the appointment of Hitler as chancellor. He remained in office until his death.

Hintze, Paul von (1864–1941), officer and diplomat. Hintze served as naval attaché and military plenipotentiary in St Petersburg (1903–11), and as ambassador to Mexico (1911–14), China (1914–17) and Norway (1917–18). Although he had been considered twice before for the post (in 1914 and 1918), he was only briefly Reich secretary of state for foreign affairs (effectively foreign minister in the Reich government) in 1918 following the fall of Richard von KÜHLMANN in July of that year. A protégé of WILHELM II, his appointment was pushed through against the initial reservations of the chancellor (HERTLING), and without consulting the Reichstag (where the majority opposed him). In general Hintze continued the foreign policy of his predecessor with little modification. He successfully opposed plans to annex the entire Baltic region to the Reich (and Ludendorff's plan to march on Petrograd), but was less successful in containing the military's openly expansionist ambitions in the west, not least because he too believed that there might still be time for a military success which would enhance Germany's negotiating position. In domestic politics Hintze recognised the need for the support of the SPD, and proposed bringing them into government and conceding electoral reform in Prussia, steps that were opposed by Chancellor Hertling. Hintze was replaced by Wilhelm SOLF on 4 October 1918.

Hippel, Theodor Gottlieb von (1741–96), radical writer and early supporter of women's emancipation. Hippel was born in Gerdauen, Prussia, the son of the headmaster of the town school. He studied law and history at Königsberg, and was later mayor of the city. Hippel's writing was intended to popularize ENLIGHTENMENT ideas. His work

on the civic 'improvement' of women (*Über die bürgerliche Verbesserung der Weiber*) appeared in 1792. In it he argued that women should be equal with men, and in particular should have the right to citizenship. He also argued that women should have the right to enter the professions. The work was considered too radical to be taken seriously in the Germany of the 1790s, and was largely ignored.

Hipper, Franz von (1863–1932), admiral. Hipper was a torpedo expert who in WORLD WAR I led a fleet of battle cruisers in the 1914 raids on English North Sea towns that eventually led to the battle of the Dogger Bank in 1915. He also took part in the battle of JUTLAND. As commander in chief of the High Seas Fleet from August 1918, he ordered a final pointless sortie against the Royal Navy, hoping thereby to salvage the honour of the navy and the empire. It was this proposed action that led to the KIEL MUTINY and the outbreak of the NOVEMBER REVOLUTION in 1918.

Hirsch–Duncker unions, liberal labour organizations that emphasized the principle of self-help rather than industrial conflict or political emancipation. They were founded by the liberal politicians Max Hirsch, Franz Duncker and Hermann Schulze-Delitzsch. They formed the *Verband der deutschen Gewerkvereine* (League of German Unions) in 1868, which was subsumed in 1919 into the broader *Gewerkschaftsring deutscher Arbeiter-, Angestellten- und Beamtenverbände* (Circle of Unions of German Workers, Employees and Civil Servants). The Hirsch–Duncker unions had around 100,000 members at the time of the outbreak of World War I.

Hirschfeld, Magnus (1868–1935). Hirschfeld was born in Kolberg. He studied medicine and practised as a doctor before settling in Berlin as a specialist in nervous and psychological disorders, and worked on the nature of human sexuality. He was a campaigner for the decriminalization of male and female HOMOSEXUALITY, and a vocal campaigner against the social prejudices attached to it. To this end he set up the *WIS-SENSCHAFTLICH-HUMANITÄRE KOMITEE* ('scientific humanitarian committee') in 1897. His theory of a 'third sex' between masculine and feminine prompted him to argue against misguided attempts to cure or punish homosexuality. His *Jahrbuch für sexuelle Zwischenstufen* (a yearbook whose theme was 'intermediate sexual stages') and *Zeitschrift für Sexualwissenschaft* ('journal of sexual science') were important in helping to promote academic research on sexuality. Although he had been a loyal monarchist, Hirschfeld welcomed the establishment of the Weimar Republic and the state provision of health services. In 1919 he founded the Institute for Sexual Science (*Institut für Sexualwissenschaft*) in Berlin (later the Magnus Hirschfeld Foundation), and it became an important centre for research, although Hirschfeld's activities were viewed with disapproval by the authorities. When he was so badly beaten up by right-wing thugs after a lecture in Munich in 1920 that the world press reported his death, the Bavarian judicial authorities refused to press charges against his assailants, and instead charged Hirschfeld himself with delivering an immoral lecture and causing a public nuisance. Hirschfeld was elected one of the presidents of the World League for Sexual Reform in 1928. The Institute was ransacked and destroyed by Nazi university students in 1933, and its books were burned. Hirschfeld, who was abroad at the time, did not return to Germany, and resumed his work in Paris instead.

Hirt, August (1898–1945), Nazi doctor. Hirt was born in Mannheim, studied medicine and taught briefly at Heidelberg. He joined the SS in 1939. After killing 20 prisoners while working on an antidote for mustard gas he was appointed head of the Anatomy Institute at Strasbourg. He worked there on the skulls and brains of Jewish and Soviet prisoners until the arrival of Allied troops.

Hirt himself disappeared before the Allies reached Strasbourg and was never found.

Hirtsiefer, Heinrich (1876–1941), trade unionist and politician. Born in Essen into a working-class family, Hirtsiefer took an apprenticeship and worked for Krupp until he became a local official of the Christian-social metal workers' union. He joined the CENTRE PARTY and was elected a city councillor in Essen in 1907. In 1919 he was elected to the Prussian constituent assembly, then in 1921 to the Prussian LANDTAG. In 1921 he replaced Adam STEGERWALD as Prussian welfare minister. Hirtsiefer was on the democratic left of the party and was a staunch supporter of the Weimar Republic's democratic institutions. After the 1930 Reichstag election he urged greater cooperation with the SPD, and was himself a staunch supporter of the SPD-led BRAUN administration in Prussia. He was vocal in his protests against the PAPEN coup of 1932 (*see PREUSSENSCHLAG*). After the Nazis came to power he was arrested – notionally on charges of fraud – and imprisoned in concentration camps. In the event the charges had to be dropped, but Hirtsiefer never recovered from his experience of incarceration.

Hitler, Adolf (1889–1945), leader of the NSDAP (Nazi Party) and chancellor of Germany (1933–45). Adolf Hitler was born in 1889 in Braunau am Inn, Upper Austria, the fourth child of Alois Hitler, a customs official. After a short spell in Passau, Bavaria (1892–5) the family moved back to Austria on the retirement of Hitler's father, who died in 1903. Hitler was educated in Linz and Steyr, but he left school in 1905, having failed to make adequate progress. He moved to Vienna, where he lived as a vagrant. He twice applied for a place to study at the Academy of Arts, and was rejected on both occasions. He finally left Vienna for Bavaria in 1913 in order to avoid Austrian military service, but volunteered for a Bavarian regiment shortly before the outbreak of war in 1914. He spent the war on the Western Front, where he was wounded twice, was temporarily blinded by poison gas and was decorated for bravery. In 1919 Hitler was appointed to a post in the army political department in Munich, where he joined the German Workers' Party (DAP), one of a number of small political groups on the radical right. The party was subsequently refounded as the National Socialist German Workers' Party (*Nationalsozialistische Deutsche Arbeiterpartei*, NSDAP), and Hitler became chairman in July 1921. With Erich von LUDENDORFF he led an unsuccessful rightist putsch (the BEER HALL PUTSCH) in Munich in November 1923, but was treated with exceptional leniency by the court. He served only part of a very brief term of imprisonment at Landsberg in Bavaria, where he dictated *MEIN KAMPF*. After his release in 1924 he relaunched the party, imposed his authority on it (despite serious challenges from party leaders in northern Germany), and eventually transformed it into a mass organization. His experience of the failed Beer Hall putsch made Hitler wary of direct confrontation as a means of winning power, and he set about winning over the middle classes and their leaders, effectively reuniting the German right around himself and the NSDAP.

Despite a massive gain in electoral support in 1930, consolidated and extended in July 1932, the NSDAP consistently failed to win either a majority of seats in the Reichstag or a place in the successive right-wing coalitions of the Depression years. It was only in January 1933, after electoral losses in the general election of the previous November, that Hitler was appointed chancellor at the head of a minority right-wing coalition government, largely made up of the conservatives and nationalists who had served in the previous administration. Moreover, this government, like its predecessors, was dependent on rule by presidential decree until, following the election of 5 March (in which the Nazis won 43.9% of the vote), Hitler acquired unlimited powers for a year

by means of an ENABLING LAW (23 March). He then suppressed all political opposition, and after the death of President HINDENBURG in 1934 styled himself leader (FÜHRER) of the German Reich, and elicited a personal oath of loyalty from the German armed forces. During the 1930s he worked with Germany's traditional ruling elites on a rearmament programme, enforced by an authoritarian dictatorship. From the reoccupation of the demilitarized RHINELAND in defiance of the treaty of VERSAILLES (1936) the Hitler government undertook a programme of military aggression in central Europe. This resulted in the annexation of AUSTRIA (March 1938; *see* ANSCHLUSS), the SUDETENLAND (October 1938), the rest of Bohemia and Moravia (March 1939) and much of Poland (September 1939), which finally plunged Europe into a general war. Much of Europe was occupied or dominated by Nazi Germany between 1940 and 1943, when the tide was turned by the Red Army at STALINGRAD. The domestic policies of the Nazi state also underwent an accelerating radicalization from the mid-1930s. In 1935 the NUREMBERG LAWS initiated a persecution of the Jews that culminated in the HOLOCAUST. Leading conservative politicians, public servants and army officers were purged from high office in 1937 and 1938, when Hitler made a decisive break from his conservative nationalist allies shortly before the start of Germany's aggressive territorial expansion.

The extent to which this radicalization was a consequence of Hitler's own intentions and actions or of the structure and policy-making procedures of the Nazi state has long been a matter of debate among historians, and research has increasingly revealed a rapid collapse of the hitherto efficient German administrative machine into the organizational chaos that stood behind the monolithic facade of the Third Reich. Bureaucratic norms in government and administration were undermined by Hitler's reliance on 'CHARISMATIC' legitimation of political authority; and the situation was exacerbated by his confused and inattentive policy-making in all areas (except, to some extent, foreign policy and the persecution of the Jews). In addition, there was a proliferation of new offices and institutions, which did battle with each other for status, territory and rank within the system in a perpetual 'social Darwinist' struggle. Despite the political disorder at the heart of the Third Reich, the leadership cult established in the party's early days and built up by GOEBBELS' propaganda apparatus, created the myth of the 'man of the people' become heroic leader, and of humble corporal become military genius. When things went wrong, ordinary Germans were willing to blame anybody but the Führer. The myth endured as long as Germany's military success, but was undermined as public morale collapsed in the later war years, and those who had initially collaborated turned against Hitler as defeat seemed increasingly imminent. Hitler survived an assassination attempt by disaffected army officers and leading conservatives from Germany's pre-Nazi elites (the JULY BOMB PLOT) in 1944, only to commit suicide less than a year later with the Allied armies occupying Germany. He left it to his appointed successor, Karl DÖNITZ, to surrender to the Allies. His political testament, written shortly before his death, reaffirmed his radical nationalism and virulent anti-Semitism.

Hitler-Jugend. *See* HITLER YOUTH.

Hitler–Stalin pact. *See* MOLOTOV–RIBBENTROP PACT.

Hitler Youth (*Hitler-Jugend* or HJ), term applied both to the Nazi youth organization as a whole and to the section for teenage boys. It had its origins in an organization called the *Jungsturm*, an offshoot of the SA, and was established as the Hitler Youth in 1926 as a rival to Roman Catholic and left-wing youth movements. It was still insignificant in terms of membership by 1933. It then expanded rapidly, and had almost 4

million members by 1935 – over half of all young Germans. Membership became compulsory in 1939, by which time membership had risen to 7,287,470 out of a total population of 10- to 18-year-olds of 8,870,000. In July 1933 its leader, Baldur von SCHIRACH, was named 'Reich youth leader'.

Within the youth movement there were four separate divisions. The term 'Hitler Youth' applied both to the entire organization, and the sub-organization specifically for boys aged between 14 and 18. Girls aged between 14 and 18 were organized in the *BUND DEUTSCHER MÄDEL* (BdM); young boys between the ages of 10 and 14 belonged to the *Deutsches Jungvolk* and young girls of the same age belonged to *Jungmädelbund* ('young girls' league'). In addition there was a separate organization for young women, *GLAUBE UND SCHÖNHEIT*, which was intended to prepare them for marriage.

As a mass organization the Hitler Youth movement undertook both political indoctrination and, increasingly for male members after 1939, military training. Nevertheless the Hitler Youth failed to create a Nazi generation loyal only to the Führer, despite its image in the popular culture of the postwar West. Its leaders were of poor quality, and its mass membership reflected coercion rather than commitment. Illegal youth gangs (such as the EDELWEISS PIRATES) grew up in industrial areas during the war as the HJ increasingly alienated many young people.

Historikerstreit ('historians' dispute'), a debate among German historians in the 1980s following attempts by conservative historians to reassess the historiography of the HOLOCAUST and relativize it by making comparisons with other massacres in history, and with the Soviet occupation of eastern Germany at the end of World War II.

Hochbaum, Werner (1899–1946), socialist film director. Born in Kiel, Hochbaum worked as an actor and film critic during the 1920s. With the financial support of an SPD councillor in Hamburg he set up a film production business and produced a film about the Hamburg dock strike of 1906. He went on to make films for SPD election campaigns and documented *The Making of the New Altona*. In 1932 he made *Razzia in St Pauli*. Following the international success of his films he was invited to work for the UFA, and made a number of films between 1934 and 1939, when he was expelled from the Reich Chamber of Film.

Hoepner, Erich (1886–1944), Panzer general during World War II. He commanded an armoured division in Thuringia before the outbreak of the war, and served on the Eastern Front. He was dismissed and stripped of his rank after the failure of the Germans to capture Moscow, and became involved in the military resistance. He was intended for high government office if the resistance were to succeed, but was arrested after the failure of the JULY BOMB PLOT of 1944, tried before the People's Court in Berlin and hanged on 8 August.

Hoernle, Edwin (1883–1952), Communist politician. Born in Cannstatt, Württemberg, the son of a pastor, Hoernle studied theology and only became involved in radical politics when he joined the SPD in Berlin after leaving the church and falling out with his family. He became editor of a socialist paper in Stuttgart in 1912 and remained there during World War I and the 1918 NOVEMBER REVOLUTION. He was a co-founder of the SPARTACUS LEAGUE and the KPD (German Communist Party), and was a leading party commentator on agricultural matters and educational theory. He was elected to the Reichstag in 1924, and fled to Switzerland and then the Soviet Union when the Nazis came to power in 1933. In Moscow he was head of the central European section of an international agricultural institute, and belonged (from 1943) to the NATIONAL COMMITTEE FOR A FREE GERMANY. On his return to Germany in 1945 he was a leading figure in the land reforms in the Soviet occupation zone. In 1949 he was effectively retired as professor of agriculture at the German Academy of Administration (*Deutsche Verwaltungsakademie*).

Hoesch, Leopold (1881–1936), diplomat. Born in Dresden into the propertied middle class, Hoesch studied law in Geneva, Heidelberg, Munich and Leipzig, and after a short spell with the Dresdner Bank joined the diplomatic service. He was posted to China, France, Spain and Britain, and served in Bulgaria and then in Constantinople during World War I. He participated in the peace negotiations at BREST-LITOVSK and BUCHAREST, and was also chargé d'affaires in Paris after the recall of the German ambassador during the occupation of the RUHR in 1923, and was subsequently appointed ambassador to France. Hoesch remained in Paris throughout the 1920s, but was transferred to London in 1932, where he died during the crisis following the remilitarization of the Rhineland.

Hoess, Rudolf (1900–47), commandant of AUSCHWITZ. Hoess served on the Turkish front in World War I and received the IRON CROSS, joined a FREIKORPS unit after the war, and was imprisoned for violent murder (1923–8). He joined the SS in 1934 and was posted to DACHAU, SACHSENHAUSEN (1938) and Auschwitz (1940), where he was appointed commandant. Hoess lived at Auschwitz with his wife and family. He prided himself on the efficiency of the extermination camp, and was commended as a model death-camp commandant. He was captured by military police in Germany in 1946, and executed by the Polish authorities at Auschwitz in April 1947 following a trial in Warsaw. Hoess wrote an autobiography, which was published in English as *Commandant at Auschwitz*.

Hoetzsch, Otto (1876–1946), academic and right-wing politician. Born in Leipzig, the son of a craftsman, Hoetzsch studied history and government at Leipzig and Munich. At Leipzig he was a student of the social and

171

cultural historian Karl Lamprecht and later, in Berlin, of the constitutional historian Otto Hintze. He was involved with *VÖLKISCH* student organizations such as the anti-Semitic *Kyffhäuser-Verband der Vereine deutscher Studenten*, and then with the PAN-GERMAN LEAGUE and the NAVY LEAGUE. Hoetzsch specialized in Russian history, and was appointed professor at the Prussian Royal Academy in Posen (1906–13), where he was a proponent of Germanization and chairman of the local branch of the Eastern Marches Association (*OSTMARKENVEREIN*). His view of Russia, as a natural ally of Germany against Britain and a guarantor of the continuing division of Poland, brought him into conflict with Theodor Schiemann, his erstwhile mentor. Hoetzsch replaced Schiemann as foreign-policy commentator on the conservative newspaper *KREUZZEITUNG* (a post he held from 1914 to 1924). Hoetzsch was an annexationist during World War I, arguing for strategic German settlement in Poland along territorial lines not dissimilar to those later espoused by the Nazis. After a long political involvement with the German Conservative Party (*DEUTSCHKONSERVATIVE PARTEI*), Hoetzsch joined the newly-founded DNVP in 1918, was elected to the Reichstag in 1920, and was secretary to the Reichstag Foreign Policy Committee. In 1923 he visited the Soviet Union, and in 1925 he founded the journal *Osteuropa* ('eastern Europe'). He left the DNVP in 1930 and was a co-founder of the Conservative People's Party. He was dismissed from his chair in 1935 for supervising the doctoral thesis of a Polish student who was also Jewish.

Hofer, Andreas (1767–1810), patriotic Tyrolean innkeeper. Hofer was the best-known leader of the popular resistance in the TYROL when it was ceded to Bavaria in 1805 during the Wars of the COALITIONS. When in 1809 the Austrians withdrew from the Tyrol again during the fifth and final war, Hofer and his men fought on and inflicted defeat on the Bavarians at Berg Isel, near Innsbruck.

He was betrayed, however, and executed on Napoleon's orders at Mantua in Italy. His story was the subject of patriotic Romantic poetry in the early 19th century.

Hoff, Hans vom (1899–1969), trade unionist. President of the Lübeck union of white collar employees before World War II, vom Hoff was a member of the trade-union council of the BIZONE (the union of the US and British zones of occupation) in 1947, and of the executive of the German Trade Unions Association (*Deutscher Gewerkschaftsbund*, DGB) in 1949. He was later an adviser to Jean Monnet.

Hoffmann, E(rnst) T(heodor) A(madeus) (1776–1822), writer and composer. Hoffman was born in Königsberg, East Prussia, and was a lawyer in the Prussian public service in Posen (now Poznań in Poland), and later in Warsaw (1804–6). In 1808 he moved to Bamberg, where he worked as a composer and director, and then in 1813 to Saxony, where he was *Kapellmeister* in Dresden and Leipzig. He is famous for his satirical writing and his stories of the supernatural. His best known works are *Lebens-Ansichten des Katers Murr* (*The Life and Opinions of Murr the Cat*, 1819–21) and his short stories.

Hoffmann, Heinrich (1885–1957), Nazi photographer. Born in Fürth, the son of a photographer, Hoffmann served in the Bavarian army, and got to know Hitler in Munich shortly after World War I. Hoffmann introduced Hitler to Munich high society – and to Eva BRAUN. Their relationship was highly profitable: Hoffmann had a monopoly on photographs of Hitler during the early years of the Nazi Party, and published a number of best-selling volumes of these photographs. After the war he was tried as a Nazi profiteer; most of his wealth was confiscated and he was sentenced to ten years in prison. (The sentence was first reduced to three years, and then raised again to five.)

Hoffmann, Josef (1870–1956), Austrian architect. Born in Pirnitz (now Brtnice in the Czech Republic), Hoffmann was one of the most influential figures in Viennese design and architecture at the turn of the century. He was a founding member of the WIENER WERKSTÄTTE and the DEUTSCHER WERKBUND. He designed the famous sanatorium at Purkersdorf, to the south of the city (1903–6), and the well-known Art Nouveau Palais Stoclet in Brussels (1905).

Hofmann, Andreas Joseph (1752–1849), revolutionary activist. Hofmann was born into a middle-class family in Zell, and studied at Mainz and Würzburg. He already had a name as a radical agitator when he joined the MAINZ JACOBIN CLUB in 1792, and was elected president of the Mainz 'National Convention'. He escaped from Mainz with the French army in 1793 and held a number of official positions in the service of the French Republic. After the defeat of Napoleon he retired to his wife's estate.

Hofmannsthal, Hugo von (1874–1929), writer. Born in Vienna, Hofmannsthal was a child prodigy who published poetry under a pseudonym while still at school, and attracted the attention of Vienna's fin-de-siècle intellectual circles. He is best known for his so-called 'Chandos letter' (*Ein Brief*), his short stories and his work as librettist for some of Richard STRAUSS's operas, including *Der Rosenkavalier* and *Ariadne auf Naxos*.

Hohenlohe-Ingelfingen, Friedrich Ludwig, Fürst zu (1746–1818), officer. A Prussian major general (1786), Prince Hohenlohe-Ingelfingen had distinguished himself in the War of the BAVARIAN SUCCESSION. He fought against the French in the 1790s and was promoted to general of infantry in 1798. He commanded one of the two Prussian armies at JENA in 1806, and was decisively defeated there. He was captured by the French, spent two years as a prisoner of war and retired in 1809. Hohenlohe-Ingelfingen was also governor of Breslau in 1791 and Prussian governor of Ansbach-Bayreuth (1804).

Hohenlohe-Langenburg, Ernst, Fürst zu (1794–1860), officer in the service of Hanover and Württemberg. He was also a member of the Württemberg First Chamber, and its president from 1835 to 1845.

Hohenlohe-Langenburg, Ernst, Fürst zu (1863–1950), public servant. Prince Hohenlohe-Langenburg worked in the ministry for Alsace-Lorraine in the 1890s, and was later head of the colonial division of the foreign ministry. He was regent of the duchies of Saxe-Coburg-Gotha from 1900 to 1905 and a member of the Reichstag for the DEUTSCHE REICHSPARTEI from 1907 to 1912.

Hohenlohe-Langenburg, Gottfried, Fürst zu, Austro-Hungarian ambassador in Berlin (1914–18).

Hohenlohe-Langenburg, Hermann, Fürst zu (1832–1913), Prussian cavalry general. Prince Hohenlohe-Langenburg was the founder of the German Colonial Society (*DEUTSCHER KOLONIALVEREIN*) and its president until 1894. He was a member of the Reichstag from 1871 to 1881 and governor of Alsace-Lorraine from 1894 to 1907.

Hohenlohe-Schillingsfürst, Chlodwig Viktor Karl, Fürst zu (1819–1901), Reich chancellor and Prussian minister-president (1894–1900). Born in Rotenburg an der Fulda, Hohenlohe was the sixth Prince (Fürst) zu Hohenlohe-Schillingsfürst, and from 1840 was Prinz von Ratibor and Corvey. He was a *'kleindeutsch'* liberal, and served as Bavarian minister-president from 1866 to 1870. In 1874 he became ambassador in Paris and in 1885 governor of Alsace-Lorraine, a position he held until 1894. He reluctantly accepted his appointment to replace CAPRIVI as chancellor in 1894. His administration was characterized by inertia on his own part and direct confrontation between his ministers and the Kaiser. Hohenlohe was eclipsed in the final years of his administration by the appointment of BÜLOW as foreign minister, and was replaced by him when he resigned.

Hohenlohe-Schillingsfürst, Konrad, Prinz zu (1863–1918), Austrian politician. He was governor of Trieste before becoming minister-president and interior minister of

Austria for a brief spell in 1906. Thereafter he was governor again until 1915, when he was again appointed interior minister. He was also finance minister in 1916.

Hohenwart, Karl, Graf von Gerlachstein (1824–99), Austrian politician. Hohenwart was governor of Upper Austria from 1868 to 1871 and minister-president and interior minister of Austria in 1871. He commanded support from conservative, nationalist and clerical factions, and proposed equality among the nationalities, effectively a federalization of CISLEITHANIA. This approach was rejected by Czechs holding out for a second AUSGLEICH for Bohemia.

Hohenzollern, the ruling dynasty of Prussia and imperial Germany. The family originated in Swabia in the 11th century, and took their name from the location of their fortress there. The Hohenzollerns became electors of Brandenburg in 1415, and Friedrich Wilhelm (the Great Elector, 1640–88) laid the basis for the rise of Brandenburg-Prussia as a great power. The Hohenzollerns became kings of Prussia in 1701 when the elector Friedrich III of Brandenburg became King Friedrich I of Prussia. FRIEDRICH II (Frederick the Great) consolidated the establishment of Prussia as a European power during the War of the AUSTRIAN SUCCESSION and the SEVEN YEARS WAR. From 1871 the Hohenzollern kings of Prussia were also emperors of Germany (*see* GERMAN EMPIRE).

Hölderlin, Johann Christian Friedrich (1770–1843), poet. Hölderlin was born in Lauffen am Neckar and studied in Tübingen, where he got to know HEGEL and SCHELLING. In 1793 he met SCHILLER, who published his poems. Hölderlin's poetry contained elements of both classicism and Romanticism, and combined themes from classical literature and Christianity. Among his best-known works is the novel *Hyperion* (1797–9).

Hollaender, Felix (1867–1931), playwright and journalist. Hollaender worked with Max REINHARDT during the first decade of the 20th century, was manager of the Frankfurt Schaupielhaus from 1913 and director of the Reinhardt-Bühnen in Berlin after World War I (1920–4). He was subsequently theatre critic for a Berlin newspaper.

Holocaust, the term most widely used to describe the mass murder of the Jews of Europe by the Nazis during World War II. Some 6 million Jews were murdered, along with members of other persecuted groups. The word *Shoah*, originally a Biblical term meaning 'widespread disaster', is the modern Hebrew equivalent. The holocaust was the culmination of Nazi ANTI-SEMITISM, the 'final solution' to the 'Jewish problem' that the Nazis had created for themselves. It followed the gradual reversal of Jewish emancipation during the 1930s against a background of incitement to racial hatred by the party and its formations, and by the German states. After the pogrom of 1938 (*KRISTALLNACHT*), the persecution of Jews intensified sharply, but the indifference or hostility of much of the German public towards this persecution, and the horrific nature of the treatment of Jews, prompted an increasing secretiveness on the part of the perpetrators.

The genocide of the early 1940s began with the invasion of Poland in September 1939. Special detachments (*EINSATZGRUPPEN*) followed the German army into Poland, and routinely murdered both Polish Jews and members of the Polish political elites. They were also involved in expropriating property from Jewish individuals and organizations, and there were regular atrocities and some large-scale massacres. But the Jewish population of Poland was perceived by the Nazi authorities to be too large to be dealt with so unsystematically, and orders were issued on 21 September 1939 for the Jews to be moved into the towns. Jews and Gypsies (ROMA AND SINTI) were to be deported from the Reich to Poland, and there were tentative plans for a Jewish 'reservation' in Poland.

The Jews in Poland were subjected to

increasingly repressive measures, including forced labour in CONCENTRATION CAMPS and resettlement in overcrowded and insanitary GHETTOS that were little more than prison compounds within the cities. Throughout 1940 more and more Jews arrived from the Reich and, increasingly, from occupied Europe. A plan to deport all the European Jews to MADAGASCAR, which was worked out in detail by EICHMANN's staff, came to nothing, and the problem of concentrating them in Poland proved increasingly problematic. When the *Einsatzgruppen* followed the German armies into the Soviet Union in the summer of 1941 HEYDRICH issued a directive ordering the 'execution' of all Jews in the service of the Communist Party or the Soviet state, and on 31 July Heydrich was charged by GÖRING with finding a 'final solution' to the 'Jewish problem'. Those who were not murdered in the innumerable massacres that took place throughout the Soviet Union and the Baltic states were transported to the camps in Poland, along with Jews deported from central and western Europe. In September 1941, 900 Soviet prisoners were gassed at AUSCHWITZ in experimental trials of ZYKLON-B, and massive building works were undertaken there and at other concentration camps in Poland.

The systematic mass murder of the Jews had begun with the large-scale killings carried out by the *Einsatzgruppen* in the Soviet Union, but the decision to exterminate the Jews of Europe entirely was taken in stages, and in 1941 it was still unclear how it could be accomplished. The WANNSEE CONFERENCE of January 1942 worked out in detail the course of the evacuation of Jews to the east, but those present spoke only in euphemistic terms of what was to happen once they were there. Only at the end of the conference were the types of 'solution' under consideration discussed, and according to Eichmann's later testimony in Jerusalem 'the talk was of killing, elimination, and annihilation'. Historians disagree about how the

decision to commit genocide was reached. Some have emphasized the apparently unwavering intentions of Hitler and the Nazis ('INTENTIONALISTS'), while others ('functionalists' or 'STRUCTURALISTS') have found the development of the policy confused, incoherent and even improvised. What is clear is that the implementation of mass murder ran parallel with the decision-making process. Gas vans were used in 1941 as a more 'efficient' method of murder than mass shootings, and 55,000 Jews from the Łódź ghetto and 5000 Gypsies were gassed in the winter of 1941–2. Staff were then transferred from the euthanasia programme (AKTION T4) to the Polish camps, where 200,000 Jews were gassed at the EXTERMINATION CAMPS at CHEŁMNO, TREBLINKA and BELZEC in August 1942. By December 500,000 people had been gassed in Belzec alone. Gassings took place between November 1941 and October 1943 in three camps (Belzec, SOBIBOR and Treblinka), which were then dismantled. During the course of the operation Jews were deported from ghettos in Russia and Poland, where organized resistance in the WARSAW GHETTO was put down by STROOP. The most extensive mass murder took place at AUSCHWITZ. Mass deportations to Auschwitz began in the spring of 1942 with transports from France, and were followed by transports of Dutch Jews and a further transport of 'stateless' French Jews in July. The scale of deportations gathered pace from the summer of 1942, with mass deportations from all over occupied Europe, culminating in the deportation and murder of the Hungarian Jews in 1944, when the gas chambers and crematoria were scarcely able to cope. By July 1944 Soviet troops had reached the Majdanek death camp near Lublin, and in November Hitler ordered the cessation of gassing at Auschwitz, which the Red Army reached in January 1945.

Almost 6 million Jews from all parts of occupied Europe had been murdered in the course of the Holocaust. Although the genocide was carried out by the German government, there was extensive local collaboration and collusion, and the nature of what was happening was widely known outside the immediate circles of those directly involved. There was also resistance both from Jews and those who assisted them (as in Denmark, for example). The broader racial project of which the Jewish genocide was part also encompassed other groups. ROMA AND SINTI (Gypsies) were subjected to the same systematic annihilation as Jews; the mentally and physically handicapped were murdered during the euthanasia campaign; and HOMOSEXUALS were imprisoned in concentration camps and indiscriminately murdered. Other interests than racial ideology were also at work. 'Medical' experiments were carried out on camp inmates (for example by Dr MENGELE at Auschwitz), and the Nazis profited enormously from the expropriation of Jewish property. Even personal belongings such as gold tooth fillings and hair were recycled or distributed among the perpetrators. Ultimately, however, the drive to exterminate overcame economic and military considerations as resources were diverted to the Holocaust, and badly needed skilled workers were deported to the camps.

Holstein. *See* SCHLESWIG-HOLSTEIN.

Holtzendorff, Henning von (1853–1919), naval officer. Holtzendorff was chief of the High Seas Fleet (1910–13) , but his opposition to TIRPITZ's expansion plans for the navy led to his resignation. As chief of the Admiralty Staff of the Navy (1915–18) he was an enthusiastic supporter of unrestricted submarine warfare, believing it to be the key to victory. He was forced into retirement in August 1918.

Holy Alliance, agreement between Austria, Prussia and Russia (1815). It was a pious commitment to govern according to Christian ethics at home, and to support each other in international affairs in order to preserve the status quo of the post-Napoleonic restoration across Europe. Effectively, the

most powerful and conservative governments in continental Europe reserved the right to repress progressive or nationalist movements, and to intervene in the affairs of other states where it seemed that a liberal state might be established. The Holy Alliance was the cornerstone of the CONGRESS SYSTEM.

Holy Roman Empire, the term used to describe the loose political association of territories in central Europe that preceded the creation of a modern German nation-state. Although historical tradition dates the founding of the empire to the coronation of Charlemagne in Rome on Christmas day in 800, the term itself was first used only centuries later. 'Holy empire' and 'Roman empire' were both used in the Middle Ages, and the latter term was used to describe the Carolingian empire. The term Holy Roman Empire of the German Nation (*Heiliges Römisches Reich deutscher Nation*) became widespread in the 15th century, and was formally adopted in 1512. What was meant by any of these titles was always rather uncertain, both in so far as the empire's territorial boundaries were never altogether clearly defined, and because it was not always possible to determine where political authority lay. Nevertheless it was the single most important secular institution in western Europe for much of the Middle Ages. By the late 15th century the empire was more or less coterminous with German-speaking central Europe. Its core consisted of what would become the empires of Austria (CISLEITHANIA) and Germany (excluding East and West Prussia and Schleswig) in the late 19th century. In addition the Low Countries were still, in the late 15th century, wholly within the empire, as was Switzerland; so too were Alsace, Lorraine and other territories that later became French; the empire also included a rump of Italian territory (*Reichsitalien*) on the west coast of the peninsula between the Alps and the Papal States. By the time of the peace of Westphalia in 1648, the United Provinces of the Netherlands (the

Dutch Republic) and Switzerland were no longer part of the empire, and the north Italian territories had also gone. There were still 234 distinct territories and 51 imperial cities. The empire remained as a loose constitutional framework for the fragmented political culture of the German states until it was abolished by Napoleon in 1806. AUSTRIA, and increasingly PRUSSIA, dominated, and apart from a brief period in the 18th century the emperor, although nominally elected by a number of German princes, was de facto a hereditary position held by the HABSBURGS.

Holzhausen, Rudolf (1889–1963), public servant. Holzhausen joined the foreign service in 1919. He worked at the Reich archives in Potsdam from 1934 to 1939, then joined the Reich air ministry and was a member of Luftwaffe command. After the war he was employed in the Bavarian civil service, and was then consul general (1950–2) and later ambassador (1952–4) in South Africa.

homosexuals, persecution of. Homosexual acts between men were a criminal offence in Prussia, and after 1871 throughout the German empire. The law was embodied in PARAGRAPH 175 of the Reich legal code. In Austria similar laws applied, and female homosexuality was also illegal. During the imperial period homosexuality prompted ambiguous and inconsistent responses, even from the SPD, the only significant political party to promote liberalization. BEBEL argued in the Reichstag for liberalization in 1898, and Adolf Thiele presented to the Reichstag a petition for the abolition of Paragraph 175 from the *WISSENSCHAFTLICH-HUMANITÄRE KOMITEE* ('scientific humanitarian committee', a body set up by Magnus HIRSCHFELD). The SPD party organ *Vorwärts*, on the other hand, sought to exploit popular homophobia in 1902 by exposing the homosexuality of the industrialist Friedrich Krupp. During the Weimar Republic, attempts by the SPD (supported by the left-liberal DDP and the Communists) to liberalize the law were opposed by the CENTRE PARTY, the conservatives (DVP), the German nationalists (DNVP) and the Nazis, and the right-wing parties sought to make the law more severe.

In February 1933 bars frequented by homosexual men were closed down, and an edict from the Prussian interior ministry (headed by GÖRING) clamped down on erotic literature, but despite these measures anti-Nazis across the political spectrum were keen to use homophobia against the Third Reich. In October 1934 the German police was ordered by HIMMLER to compile lists of homosexuals, which were then to be sent to the Gestapo; in June 1935 Paragraph 175 was extended to cover even the most minor acts that could be interpreted as sexual; and in October 1936 the Reich Central Office for the Combating of Homosexuality and Abortion was established under Josef Meisinger. Prosecutions increased from 766 in 1934 to 2106 in 1935 and 8462 in 1938. In 1939 the number of men charged under Paragraph 175 was 32,360. After 1940 men who had had more than one sexual partner were sent to CONCENTRATION CAMPS, where between 10,000 and 15,000 homosexuals were imprisoned, most of whom died or were murdered, and many of whom were raped, sexually assaulted or subjected to medical experiments. Although proposals to extend the law to women were rejected in 1935, some women were prosecuted for homosexuality, but many more lesbians were persecuted as 'ASOCIALS', and often made to work in concentration-camp brothels.

The Nazi version of Paragraph 175 remained law in West Germany until 1969, when it was repealed by the new SPD-led coalition. Some 50,000 people had been convicted between 1950 and 1965. In the German Democratic Republic the Nazi amendments to the law were withdrawn in 1950, and homosexuality was decriminalized in 1968 for those over the age of 18.

Honecker, Erich (1912–94), Communist politician; leader of the GERMAN DEMOCRATIC

REPUBLIC (1971–89). Honecker was born in the Saarland, the son of a miner, and joined the youth organization of the KPD at the age of 10. He was involved in the Communist underground resistance movement during the Nazi dictatorship and was arrested and imprisoned in 1935. After the war he was involved in rebuilding the Communist youth movement (*FREIE DEUTSCHE JUGEND,* FDJ). He became a candidate member of the Politburo of the SED (*Sozialistische Einheitspartei,* effectively the East German Communist Party) in 1950 and a full member in 1958. He succeeded ULBRICHT as leader of the German Democratic Republic in 1971 by taking over as chairman of the National Defence Council, and was also general secretary of the party and chairman of the Council of State from 1976.

Honecker reversed the trend of Ulbricht's policies by abandoning economic decentralization and bringing party personnel rather than 'experts' back into key positions. Honecker resigned in 1989, ostensibly for health reasons, as the SED lost control of East Germany, and the political system of the German Democratic Republic effectively collapsed around him. After the unification of Germany, Honecker was charged with ordering killings along the border between East and West Germany and at the Berlin Wall. He pleaded ill health, however, and was permitted to emigrate to Chile in 1993.

Höpker-Aschoff, Hermann (1883–1954), politician. Born in Herford, Westphalia, into a family of pharmacists, Höpker-Aschoff studied law and embarked on a career in the Prussian civil service. He was elected to the Prussian LANDTAG for the liberal DDP in 1921, and was Prussian minister of finance under Otto BRAUN. Despite this he was in favour of greater political and economic centralization in Germany and was a leading participant in discussions about the reform of the Reich. He retired in 1931 and spent the Nazi dictatorship in Bielefeld engaged in private pursuits. His financial expertise was called on once more after the war by the British occupation authorities, who made him responsible for finance in the Westphalian provincial government. He became a member of the FDP and was first president of the FEDERAL CONSTITUTIONAL COURT (*Bundesverfassungsgericht*) from 1951 until his death, in Karlsruhe, in 1954.

Horkheimer, Max (1895–1973), philosopher. Horkheimer was born in Stuttgart and studied philosophy. He was appointed professor of social philosophy at Frankfurt in 1930, and took over as director of the Frankfurt Institute of Social Research, a private foundation attached to the university and which was the home of the FRANKFURT SCHOOL of critical theory. In 1932 Horkheimer founded the *Zeitschrift für Sozialforschung* ('journal for social research'), of which he was editor. In 1933 he was dismissed from his professorship as a so-called 'non-Aryan', and the Frankfurt Institute was seized by the regime. Horkheimer re-established the Institute in New York, and the journal was eventually published there too (after a brief spell in Paris). *Dialectic of Enlightenment,* the critique of modernity that Horkheimer wrote with Theodor ADORNO, was published in the United States in 1947. Horkheimer returned to Frankfurt in 1949.

Horn, Hermann (1889–1947), businessman and politician. Horn was an industrialist from Goslar and was president of the chamber of trade there from 1892. He was a member of the Prussian LANDTAG (1892) and of the Reichstag (1898–1907).

Hörsing, Friedrich Otto (1874–1937), Social Democratic politician. Hörsing was born in Gross-Schillingken in East Prussia, where his father was a small farmer, and although he was secretary of the SPD in Oppeln before World War I, his political career was made after the war. During the 1918 NOVEMBER REVOLUTION he was president of the Workers' and Soldiers' Council (*see RAT*) in Upper Silesia, and then state commissar first for Upper Silesia and then for Silesia and Posen.

He maintained law and order in Prussian Saxony as *Oberpräsident* during the turbulent early years of the Weimar Republic, and convened the conference in Magdeburg that led to the formation in 1924 of the REICHS-BANNER SCHWARZ-ROT-GOLD, a union of several pro-republican groups. He was expelled from the SPD in 1932 after wrangles concerning the *Reichsbanner*.

Horst Wessel song, *Die Fahne hoch* ... ('raise the flag'), the Nazi Party's official marching anthem. The words were written by a young Nazi stormtrooper, Horst Wessel (1907–30), who was killed in a fight with Communist Party activists and subsequently represented as a martyr. GOEBBELS arranged for his lyrics to be set to the tune of a music-hall song popular with German soldiers in 1914.

Hossbach, Friedrich (1894–1980), infantry general and author of the HOSSBACH MEMORANDUM. He was Wehrmacht adjutant to Hitler (1934–8) and head of the Central Section of the general staff (1935–8). He took part in the conference of senior officers of 5 November 1937 where Hitler set out his plans for expansion, and his notes became the 'Hossbach memorandum'. Hossbach was dismissed from his post as Hitler's adjutant in 1938, but was recalled to the general staff in 1939 and promoted to infantry general in 1943. He served on the Eastern Front until January 1945.

Hossbach memorandum, controversial minutes of a meeting (5 November 1937) between Hitler, the heads of the armed forces, the war minister and the foreign minister. The meeting was called in response to a request from Admiral RAEDER that Hitler rule on conflicts of interest over the allocation of raw materials and labour. After discussing the state of the economy and the disadvantages of relying on self-sufficiency to be achieved by the policy of AUTARKY, Hitler set out various contingencies for dealing with the situation by force, and his goals were ANSCHLUSS with Austria and the dismemberment of Czechoslovakia. The meet-

ing also marked a turning point in Hitler's foreign-policy thinking, in so far as Britain had become a probable enemy rather than a potential ally. The 'memorandum', based on notes taken by Friedrich HOSSBACH, was used at Nuremberg as evidence of Nazi plans to wage aggressive war.

Hottentot election, the Reichstag election of 1907. It was so-called because the central issue was the determination of the government of Chancellor Bernhard von BÜLOW to have a free hand in the running of Germany's African colonies, particularly SOUTH-WEST AFRICA (now Namibia). The government wanted no interference in colonial matters from the Reichstag. The CENTRE PARTY and the SPD were the two parties most consistently critical of the government's imperial policies, and the Centre Party, on whose cooperation the government relied for the passage of legislation and the routine working of the Reichstag, forced an early general election. A massive smear campaign was mounted against the two parties, whose members and supporters were condemned as unpatriotic. The campaign had little effect on the parties' supporters, and the SPD won an extra 25,000 votes. The vagaries of the electoral system, however, meant that whereas the Centre Party not only maintained but increased its representation in the Reichstag, the SPD actually lost half of its seats, because the liberal Progressive Party (*DEUTSCHE FORTSCHRITTSPARTEI*) voters who normally supported it in second-round run-offs failed to do so.

Huch, Ricarda (1864–1947), writer and literary scholar. Born in Braunschweig into an upper middle-class family, Huch took a degree in history in Switzerland before women were admitted as students in German universities. She is best known for her biographies and for her work on cultural history. Her Christian faith determined her opposition to the Nazis. She received an honorary doctorate from Jena in 1946, and was elected honorary president of the first

German writers' congress the following year.

Hugenberg, Alfred (1865–1951), press baron and nationalist politician. Born in Hanover, Hugenberg was the son of a member of the Prussian LANDTAG, and studied law and economics at Göttingen, Heidelberg, Berlin and Strasbourg. He was a civil servant, banker and company director (of Krupp) before World War I. He was a co-founder with Karl PETERS in 1891 of the General German League (*Allgemeiner Deutscher Verein*), and then in 1894 of the PAN-GERMAN LEAGUE. He was a DNVP deputy to the National Assembly in 1919 and the Reichstag from 1920 to 1933. In 1928 he became president of the DNVP, with quasi-absolute power, and used his position to work towards the dismantling of the Weimar Republic's parliamentary democracy, and towards its replacement with an authoritarian system of government. Hugenberg was a key figure in the 'National Unity Front' of German nationalists and Nazis against the YOUNG PLAN in 1929 and the HARZBURG FRONT of 1931. During the Weimar period he acquired a number of newspapers, periodicals, publishing houses and news agencies, and this press empire was instrumental in Hitler's rise to power. He was minister for economics and food in Hitler's first cabinet, but was forced to resign in June 1933, and the DNVP was dissolved the following day. Although he remained a member of the Reichstag until 1945, he took no further active part in politics, profiting only from the sale of a publishing company to the Nazis in 1943. He retained this property after the war.

Humboldt, (Friedrich Wilhelm Heinrich) Alexander, Freiherr von (1769–1859), scholar and explorer. Born in Berlin, the son of an officer, Humboldt was educated by private tutors along with his brother Wilhelm von HUMBOLDT. He studied at Frankfurt an der Oder, Berlin and Göttingen, and finally went to the mining school in Freiberg in Saxony. He left without completing his studies to work for the Prussian state, organiz-ing the mines of the recently acquired territory of Ansbach-Bayreuth. At the same time he developed his research in the natural sciences around a central discipline that he termed 'physical geography' and which embraced studies in climatology, botanical and zoological geography and the physical properties of the earth. In 1797 he resigned from his post in order to embark on a voyage of exploration to the Spanish colonies in South America, which were then more or less closed to the outside world. After several years exploring the continent and collecting data, Humboldt and his colleague, the French botanist Aimé Bonpland, sailed to Mexico, and then moved on to the United States before returning to France. From 1804 to 1827 Humboldt worked in Paris, writing up and publishing his material. His *Voyage aux regions équinoxiales du Nouveau Continent* appeared in 30 volumes and his *Relation Historique du Voyage aux regions équinoxiales du Nouveau Continent* comprised a further 3. He returned to Berlin when his financial resources were exhausted, and took an active part in life at court, as tutor to the crown prince and as a member of the privy council. He also gave lectures at the university and organized one of the first international scientific conferences. In 1829 he undertook a second, much shorter journey of exploration, this time to the little-known Central Asian regions of the Russian empire. He spent the last 30 years of his life in Berlin, much of it writing the five volumes of his last and most ambitious work, *Kosmos*, a popular and accessible account of the structure of the universe as it was then understood.

Humboldt, (Karl) Wilhelm, Freiherr von (1767–1835), leading ENLIGHTENMENT intellectual and brother of Alexander von HUMBOLDT. Wilhelm von Humboldt visited Paris in 1789 and briefly worked in the Prussian civil service (1790–1) before marrying and moving to his wife's family estate in Thuringia, where he worked closely with

GOETHE and SCHILLER. During the first decade of the 19th century he played a leading role in the reform of the Prussian education system, and was education minister in 1809 and 1810. As ambassador to Vienna (from 1811) he was influential in persuading Austria to rejoin the coalition against Napoleon. At the Congress of VIENNA he was an advocate of a liberal constitution for the GERMAN CONFEDERATION and of civil rights for Jews. He occupied a number of important positions in the service of the state between 1815 and 1819, but was out of place in the conservative new order of restoration Germany and was relieved of all his duties in 1819 after opposing the KARLSBAD DECREES. He spent the rest of his life in retirement at the family estate in Tegel.

Husserl, Edmund (1859–1938), philosopher. Husserl was born in Prossnitz (now Prostejov in the Czech Republic), studied at Leipzig, Berlin and Vienna, where he was influenced by the philosopher Franz Brentano (1838–1917). He then taught at Halle (1887–1901), Göttingen (1901–16) and Freiburg (1916–28), where he was succeeded by his student Martin HEIDEGGER. Husserl is considered the founder of the modern school of phenomenology.

hyperinflation. *See* INFLATION.

I

IG Farben, the most important industrial cartel in interwar Germany. Two groups of companies emerged in the German chemicals industry before World War I: the *Dreibund* (BASF, Bayer and Agfa), and the *Dreiverband* (Hoechst, Cassella and Kalle). World War I increased the need for cooperation between the companies, and a 'community of interest' (*Interessengemeinschaft*, abbreviated to IG) between the two loose associations was established in 1916, which formed the basis for the larger IG of the 1920s. Differences between Carl Duisberg of Bayer and Carl Bosch of BASF held up the final establishment of the cartel until 1925, but it then became the largest single concern in Germany. Although not initially sympathetic to the Nazis, both IG Farben and the regime quickly recognized the advantages of cooperation, particularly after the announcement of the FOUR-YEAR PLAN. Bosch, who had opposed the Nazi persecution of Jewish scientists, was eclipsed, and a new generation of leaders was more sympathetic to Nazi policies. Thus the cartel abandoned its demands for the expansion of export industries in favour of rearmament and self-sufficiency (AUTARKY): Bayer had been an early pioneer of synthetic rubber. Carl Krauch, of the IG Farben executive, was also GÖRING's 'plenipotentiary' for chemicals production. IG Farben was an important supplier for the German state and military during World War II, and benefited from the spoils, in that it was one of the few private companies to acquire foreign concerns as Germany overran central Europe. The company also profited from Germany's impressments of foreign slave labour, and established a plant at AUSCHWITZ in 1943. IG Farben developed Zyklon-B, the gas that was used in the mass murder of the Jews. After the war the cartel was broken up into its constituent companies, and many of the directors were tried by an American tribunal at Nuremberg. Eight were found guilty of plunder in occupied Europe, four were found guilty of using slave labour, and one was found guilty of both charges. Ten others were acquitted. The sentences ranged from 18 months' to 8 years' imprisonment, but all those found guilty had been released by 1951, and most went on to pursue successful business careers in the FEDERAL REPUBLIC OF GERMANY.

Illuminati, radical secret society. The order was founded in Bavaria in 1776 by Adam WEISHAUPT. It was a clandestine organization based on Masonic principles to further the aims of the radical ENLIGHTENMENT. Its internal organization was strictly hierarchical and its outlook elitist, at least in so far as members looked down on the 'masses', who were held to be insufficiently aware of their own best interests. The ideology of the movement was opposed to feudalism, ABSOLUTISM and superstition, which for most members included Christianity. Both GOETHE and HERDER were members of the order. The

Illuminati were originally a local Bavarian organization, but gained significance on a national scale when Adolph von KNIGGE began to organize Illuminati branches in northern Germany. The Illuminati, whose own rhetoric was often extreme, caused something of a hysterical response among German conservatives of the late 18th century, and the organization was persecuted by the state authorities in Bavaria. However, the decline of the movement has been attributed to personal rivalries between Weishaupt and Knigge, the break between the two men and Knigge's departure. The movement was banned in 1786. It was re-established in 1896, and the World League of Illuminati, founded in 1925, is based in Berlin.

Indemnity Law (14 September 1866), statute that settled the constitutional conflict between the Prussian government of Otto von BISMARCK and the Prussian LANDTAG after the battle of SADOVÁ (Königgrätz) and the peace of Prague. The'Law of Indemnity' served to reaffirm the rights of the Landtag while also confirming Bismarck's position. The government was granted an indemnity for the administration conducted unlawfully (i.e. without the Landtag) since the beginning of 1862. The retrospective responsibility of the government was deemed the same as if there had been legally approved estimates for the conduct of government throughout the period.

Independent Social Democrats. *See* USPD.

inflation. Although the hyperinflation of the early 1920s had a number of causes, the inflationary tendency in the German economy began around 1912, and was exacerbated by the German government's approach to financing WORLD WAR I. The government rejected the socially equitable solution of imposing direct income taxes, and instead issued war bonds, to be repaid after the war by imposing enormous reparations on the defeated enemy. In the event the war bonds generated insufficient revenue, and the government resorted to printing money. In addition, the failure to tax meant that purchasing power was not reduced, and despite statutory controls on rents, wages and prices, inflation soared between 1914 and 1918, and was fuelled further as a result of overpricing by industry and the scarcity of food and consumer goods. When the war ended the imperial government bequeathed the problem of financing the war debt – together with that of paying REPARATIONS – to the Weimar Republic. Increasing direct taxation would again have been one possible solution, albeit a politically difficult one. Inflating the Reichsmark, on the other hand, made German goods more competitive on world markets, and also enabled the government to pay off its war debts in an increasingly worthless currency. In practice the policy antagonized the Allies and alienated sections of the middle classes. Allied negotiators came to believe that the Germans were wrecking the currency to avoid payment of reparations, and their frustration culminated in the occupation of the RUHR VALLEY by the French in 1923. The German response, 'passive resistance', brought the German economy grinding to a halt, and the rate of inflation began to increase exponentially, resulting in the issue of notes in meaninglessly enormous denominations, until eventually the resistance was called off. The German government, under the leadership of Gustav STRESEMANN, came to terms with its predicament, negotiated with the Allies, and reformed the currency, introducing the RENTENMARK.

intentionalists, a term used to describe those historians placing greater emphasis on HITLER's personal power and determination to implement a preconceived programme than on 'structures' of power in the Third Reich. Other historians have found their arguments most convincing when applied to those areas of policy-making in which Hitler was personally interested: foreign policy, war, and the persecution of the Jews.

The intentionalist view is opposed by the STRUCTURALISTS.

Iron Cross, a military award for valour, introduced in 1813 by Prussia. There were three categories: second class, first class and Grand Cross. A degree of inflation was introduced during the Nazi dictatorship when higher levels were introduced. The Knight's Cross (*Ritterkreuz*) was the first of these levels, and the higher awards in that category were distinguished by embellishments with oak leaves, oak leaves and sword, oak leaves, swords and diamonds, and golden oak leaves, swords and diamonds.

Iron Curtain, the term used by Churchill in 1946 to describe the closed border between the Communist Bloc and Western Europe. It had already been used by German propaganda during World War II to describe the political barriers created by the Soviet Union. The Iron Curtain ran through the middle of Germany, dividing the GERMAN DEMOCRATIC REPUBLIC (East Germany) from the FEDERAL REPUBLIC OF GERMANY (West Germany). BERLIN, which was in the middle of the East German state, was also divided between the Soviet and Western sectors, and from 1961 the division was reinforced by the BERLIN WALL.

Iron Front (*Eiserne Front*), a movement set up by the SPD in 1932 to defend the WEIMAR REPUBLIC. It involved members of the FREE TRADE UNIONS, the *REICHSBANNER SCHWARZ-ROT-GOLD*, workers' sports associations and the SPD itself. Its aim was to form a political opposition to the radical right-wing HARZBURG FRONT formed the previous year.

Isonzo valley, the scene of several battles between Italy and Austria during World War I. Italy declared war on Austria in May 1915 and mounted a series of offensives along the Isonzo River in northeast Italy from then until September 1917. The casualties were high and little progress was made by either side. The twelfth battle, the battle of Caporetto (October 1917), was a spectacular breakthrough by the Austrians, who were reinforced for the first time in the theatre by German forces. However, they failed to follow up their victory.

Itten, Johannes (1888–1967), Swiss artist. Itten taught at the BAUHAUS from 1919 and then ran his own school from 1926 to 1934. He founded the school for textile design at Krefeld, before returning to Switzerland, where he was director of the Arts and Crafts School and Museum of the Zurich Textile School (1938–54). His most important book, *The Art of Colour*, was published in 1944.

J

Jacobsohn, Siegfried (1881–1926), journalist. Jacobsohn began his career as a theatre critic with the *Welt am Montag* in the early years of the 20th century. In 1905 he founded *Die Schaubühne* ('the stage'), which became one of the most important critical weeklies in Germany during and after World War I and became *Die Weltbühne* in 1918. After Jacobsohn's death, first Kurt TUCHOLSKY and then Carl von OSSIETZKY took over as editor of the journal.

Jagow, Dietrich von (1892–1945), Nazi diplomat. Born in Frankfurt, Jagow was decorated at the end of World War I. He was a Nazi Party member and stormtrooper leader in southwest Germany, and was elected to the Reichstag for the electoral district of Württemberg in 1932. He served in World War II, and was then German minister in Budapest from 1941 to 1945. He committed suicide in Merano, Italy, at the end of the war.

Jahn, Friedrich Ludwig (1778–1852), German nationalist. Jahn was born in Brandenburg and studied at Frankfurt, Göttingen, Greifswald and Halle. In his youth Jahn was a devoted Prussian patriot, and his first book glorified Prussia, but he became an ardent German nationalist, whose ideas about race and nation were set out in a work of 1810 entitled *Deutsches Volkstum* ('German nationhood'). Jahn argued that racial mixing was a danger to the race and had undermined the Roman empire. He hoped to see Germany rise again as the dominant power in Europe (encompassing the Netherlands, Switzerland and Denmark), with a new capital, Teutonia, on the Elbe. The VÖLKISCH national community that would be created in the new Germany, and from which the Jews would be excluded, was contrasted with the liberal individualism of Western Europe. Jahn was a Freikorps fighter against the French during the Napoleonic Wars, and was active in the gymnastics movement (*see* TURNBEWEGUNG) that started up in 1811. (He is known as '*Turnvater*' Jahn, the father of gymnastics in Germany.) In the changed political climate after the end of the Napoleonic Wars, Jahn's energetic promotion of gymnastics and nationalism proved irksome to the authorities, and he was first imprisoned and then forbidden to move to a town with a university or grammar school. He was elected to the FRANKFURT PARLIAMENT in 1848.

Jannings, Emil (1884–1950), actor. Born in Rorschach in Switzerland, Jannings was employed in a number of jobs before he began his stage career in Bohemia in 1910. He made his name on the Berlin stage during World War I. He worked with Max REINHARDT and, after a short spell in Hollywood, returned to Germany and played Professor Unrat in the film *Der blaue Engel* (*The Blue Angel*). He continued to work under the Nazis both in theatre and in film, and died in Strobl, Austria.

Jansenism, a movement within the Roman Catholic Church, named after the Dutch theologian Cornelius Jansen (1585–1638). It was based on the notion that the Counter-Reformation had taken the church too far, and Jansenists were opposed to Baroque expressions of devotion, and in particular to the Jesuits. They were influential in Austria in the middle of the 18th century, and particularly at the court of MARIA THERESIA, whose doctor, Gerhard van Swieten, was a Dutch Jansenist. Other Jansenists were appointed to key positions at court and in public life, and they quickly managed to purge Jesuits from the censorship commission and break their control of higher education. The United Chancellery extended state power over the monasteries (of which 1300 were dissolved), reduced the number of religious festivals and restricted the activities of lay brotherhoods. Direct action against the Jesuits in Austria came only with the suppression of the order by the pope in 1773.

Jarres, Karl (1874–1951), conservative politician. Jarres began his political career as mayor of Remscheid before World War I, and of Duisburg-Hamborn from 1914 to 1933. He was interior minister in the second STRESEMANN administration and then under Wilhelm MARX (November 1923 to January 1925). Jarres stood in the presidential election of 1925 as the 'Reichsblock' candidate, on behalf of the conservative DVP (his own party) and the nationalist DNVP. He polled most votes in the first round (10.4 million), but did not win an absolute majority. When the Weimar coalition parties chose Wilhelm Marx as their candidate in the second round, and it looked as if he might win, the Reichsblock nominated HINDENBURG instead of Jarres, who returned to municipal politics. He was dismissed from his mayoral office by the Nazis in 1933.

Jaspers, Karl (1883–1969), philosopher. Jaspers was born in Oldenburg, studied medicine, and worked in the psychiatric clinic in Heidelberg after graduating from the university there in 1909. Jaspers remained for much of his life in Heidelberg, and was appointed assistant professor first in psychology and then in philosophy. He was one of the earliest proponents of existentialism, and in 1931 he published *Die geistige Situation der Zeit* (translated as *Man in the Modern Age*). The following year came three volumes of *Philosophie*. Jaspers' wife was Jewish and he was excluded from any leading role in the university when the Nazis came to power, and later prohibited from teaching and publishing (1937–8). Heidelberg was occupied by the Allies shortly before Jaspers and his wife were due to be deported, and he survived to take part in the rebuilding of the university. There were too many 'fellow travellers' among the teaching staff, however, to implement his ideal of total DENAZIFICATION. Disappointed that his book, *Die Schuldfrage* (1946, published in English as *The Question of German War Guilt*, 1947), was largely ignored in Germany, he moved to Basle in 1948 and spent the last twenty years of his life in Switzerland. There he worked on his 'world philosophy', emphasizing the necessity of unity and toleration among nations. In 1966 he published *Wohin treibt die Bundesrepublik?* (*The Future of Germany*, 1967), which was received with some hostility in West Germany. As a result, Jaspers gave up his German citizenship.

Jehovah's Witnesses, a Christian sect persecuted by the Nazis for their uncompromising opposition. The Jehovah's Witnesses were founded in the United States in the late 19th century, and had between 25,000 and 30,000 members in Germany at the end of the Weimar Republic. Much of the membership was working-class. Although the Witnesses attempted to avoid conflict with the Nazis, the very character of their organization was anathema to the regime, and their refusal to accept military service was taken as an open provocation. Witnesses were dismissed from their jobs for refusal to confirm with petty requirements such as the Hitler salute (the GERMAN GREETING). Although many were arrested in 1933 and 1934, they were acquitted, but further waves of arrests followed, and the persecution became much more severe after the introduction of general conscription in 1935. Witnesses also incurred the wrath of the state by helping Jews. During the first year of the war over a hundred were executed, and – although a handful recanted – most persisted in their defiance. The total number of such executions has been estimated at 250–300. The society itself estimated that a further 635 died in prison, and some 6000 were imprisoned altogether. A greater proportion of Jehovah's Witnesses were imprisoned and executed than of any other opposition grouping in the Third Reich.

Jena, battle of (1806), major engagement in central Germany during the Wars of the COALITIONS, in which Napoleon decisively defeated Prussia. The defeat at Jena and Auerstedt (which was a few miles to the north) ruined the Prussian army. It also led to the collapse of Prussia and the occupation of Berlin. In the treaty of TILSIT the following year Prussia was forced to give up all territories west of the River Elbe, along with other lands in Poland.

Jodl, Alfred (1890–1946), general. Jodl was a staff officer during and after World War I. He was head of the national defence section of the Supreme Command of the Armed Forces (OKW) from 1935 to 1938, and was head of operations staff, OKW, from 1938 to 1945. Jodl directed all the German campaigns of World War II except the invasion of the Soviet Union, and was promoted to colonel general in 1944. At Reims on 7 May 1945 Jodl signed the surrender of the German armed forces in the west. He was subsequently tried for war crimes, found guilty, and executed at Nuremberg.

Joos, Joseph (1878–1965), journalist and politician. Born in Wintzenheim near Colmar in Alsace, Joos left school and began an apprenticeship. He also worked on the *Ober-Elsässische Zeitung*, and went on to become an editor, then editor in chief of the *Westdeutsche Arbeiter-Zeitung*, a newspaper for Catholic trade unionists. Joos was on the democratic left wing of the CENTRE PARTY. He was elected to the NATIONAL ASSEMBLY in 1919 and was then a member of the Reichstag until his party was dissolved after Hitler came to power. He was an instinctive republican, and favoured cooperation with the SPD. Although he was involved in Centre Party attempts to come to an understanding with the Nazis after the collapse of the BRÜNING government in 1932, he was in the minority within his party that was opposed to the ENABLING LAW. (In the event he voted with his party colleagues.) In 1938 he was stripped of his citizenship, and interned as a foreigner at Dachau after the fall of France. He resumed his career as a political activist after the war, and was chairman of the German Catholic Men's Association.

Jordan, Pascual (1902–80), scientist. Born in Hanover, the son of an artist, Jordan studied physics, mathematics and zoology and graduated with a dissertation on quantum theory from Göttingen in 1924. After working in Göttingen and Hamburg, he was appointed professor at Rostock in 1929. During the war Jordan worked as a Luftwaffe meteorologist, and then in a physics institute with the navy. In 1944 he was appointed to a chair in Berlin, and then in 1947 to another chair in Hamburg. He was a member of the Bundestag for the CDU (1957–61). Jordan wrote popular science books, and was a proponent of the peaceful uses of nuclear power.

Joseph II (1741–90), Holy Roman emperor (1765–90). Joseph became Holy Roman emperor on the death of his father FRANZ I, but ruled the HABSBURG territories jointly with his mother MARIA THERESIA until her death in 1780. Joseph is considered one of the leading practitioners of 'enlightened ABSOLUTISM' and sought to rationalize and centralize the government of the Habsburg empire. His ambitions were restrained somewhat by his mother during her lifetime, and he encountered opposition in Hungary and the AUSTRIAN NETHERLANDS during the final years of his reign. In 1781 personal serfdom and the guilds were abolished. 'Useless' monastic orders were also dissolved, and a degree of toleration extended to Jews, Greek Orthodox subjects and Protestants. State education and civil marriage were also introduced, and a new penal code was promulgated in 1787. Joseph was compelled to rescind some of his reforms, in particular the administrative reorganization of Hungary, but they remained a reference point in Austrian constitutional history.

Joyce, William (1906–46), the real name of Lord Haw Haw, a British traitor who broadcast Nazi propaganda from Germany during World War II. Joyce was born in the United States and grew up in Ireland and Britain. A member of the British Fascist Party from 1933, he left for Germany shortly before the outbreak of war in 1939, and broadcast to Britain throughout the war. He claimed to be German when he was captured after the war, but had kept his British passport, and was hanged for treason.

Juchacz, Marie (1879–1956), Social Democratic politician. Juchacz was born in Landsberg an der Warthe, the daughter of a joiner, and had a number of jobs before she married in 1903. Her marriage was short-lived and she moved to Berlin in 1905, where she joined and then ran a Social Democratic educational association for women and girls. She was SPD women's secretary in Cologne from 1913 to 1917, when she became director of the SPD women's bureau. She was also an editor of the journal *Gleichheit* ('equality'). She was elected to the NATIONAL ASSEMBLY in 1919 and was the first woman to address a German parliament. In 1919 Juchacz was appointed to the chair of the newly established Workers' Welfare Organization (*Arbeiterwohlfahrt*, AWO), a socialist

voluntary organization. The AWO flourished under her leadership and drew many working-class women into public affairs, first through welfare work and then party politics. Juchacz sat in the Reichstag until the SPD was prohibited by the Nazis. In March 1933 she left Germany for the SAARLAND, then under the authority of the League of Nations. She moved on to France after the Saar plebiscite of 1935, and finally to New York State after the fall of France. She returned to Germany in 1949 and became honorary president of the AWO.

judenrein ('cleaned of Jews'), along with *'judenfrei'* ('free of Jews'), a Nazi term used in Germany during World War II to describe a community where the entire Jewish population had been deported or murdered.

Jugendstil, the German term for Art Nouveau. The style was particularly associated with the Vienna SECESSION. Noted practitioners included the painter Gustav KLIMT and the architects Peter BEHRENS and Josef HOFFMANN. The style took its name from the magazine *Jugend: Münchener Illustrierte Wochenschrift für Kunst und Leben* ('Youth: Munich illustrated weekly for art and life') in which the art appeared from 1896.

July bomb plot (1944), an unsuccessful attempt to assassinate Hitler. The conspiracy that led to the July bomb plot was led by Count Claus Schenk von STAUFFENBERG, a conservative intellectual who was chief of staff to the commander of the army reserve. He and many of his fellow conspirators had initially sympathized with the regime, but had subsequently become disillusioned. Many of them – including Stauffenberg himself – did not want to see a return to the parliamentary democracy of the Weimar Republic if their coup d'état were to succeed. Instead they intended to install an authoritarian conservative government under Carl GOERDELER, and favoured a CORPORATIST system where workers and employers shared responsibilities. Although the plotters were increasingly realistic about Germany's international position, they clung to the belief that they could negotiate with the Allies, and if they could not in the end hope to retain the Reich's territorial acquisitions, they nevertheless hoped to avoid unconditional surrender, the division of Germany (or loss of territory) and foreign trials of war criminals. The bomb plot was the most concerted attempt by leaders of Germany's traditional ruling class to get rid of Hitler and the Nazis before it was too late.

Stauffenberg planted a bomb, as planned, at the so-called 'Wolf's Lair', Hitler's headquarters at Rastenburg in East Prussia, on 20 July 1944, and then returned to Berlin without realizing that the Führer had not been killed by the explosion. The conspiracy collapsed and the Nazi leadership responded to the threat with summary justice for those most closely involved, followed by mass arrests, show trials and brutal executions. The regime's retaliation against the JUNKER class in Prussia was so comprehensive as to effect a greater revolution than any that had taken place in 1933. Postwar Germany has remembered the bomb plot as the central event in the history of German resistance to Hitler.

July crisis (1914), the diplomatic crisis immediately preceding the outbreak of World War I in the summer of 1914. The assassination by a Serb nationalist of the heir to the throne of Austria-Hungary, Archduke FRANZ FERDINAND, at Sarajevo on 28 June was followed by a flurry of political and diplomatic activity before the eventual declarations of war.

The protagonists immediately involved were Austria-Hungary and Serbia, but a great deal depended on Germany's response. On 5 July Kaiser WILHELM II promised unconditional support for his ally (the so-called 'blank cheque'), and urged the Austrians to act against Serbia. For much of the following three weeks the crisis had little resonance outside Vienna and Berlin. There was little popular awareness of an impending conflict,

and it was not until the end of the month that events gathered pace. On 23 July Vienna delivered an ultimatum to Serbia, which the Serbs were expected to reject. In fact the Serbs were about to hold a general election and were not sufficiently prepared militarily. On 24 July the regent of Serbia appealed to the tsar for help. The next day the government in Belgrade agreed to almost all Austria's demands, but quibbled with the insistence that Austro-Hungarian officials be involved in the Serbian inquiry into the assassination. Only unconditional acceptance was good enough for Vienna, however, and diplomatic relations were broken off.

The Austrian ambassador, Baron Giesl, left Belgrade for Vienna on 25 July. Russia authorized preparations for partial mobilization the same day. The following day the British foreign secretary, Sir Edward Grey, invited the French, Italian and German governments to join Britain in finding a peaceful resolution, but although Paris and Rome agreed, the Germans rejected Grey's proposal and it failed. On 28 July Austria declared war on Serbia, despite the reservations of General CONRAD, the chief of the general staff in Vienna, who felt that there was little point in a declaration until troops had been mobilized. On the evening of 29 July the German ambassador in St Petersburg warned the Russians of the consequences of mobilization, but the threat backfired and Russia ordered general mobilization. Last-minute efforts were made to avoid war. Grey impressed upon LICHNOWSKY, the German ambassador in London, the consequences of an escalation for Anglo-German relations, and it seemed that both the Kaiser and Chancellor BETHMANN HOLLWEG had reservations. Bethmann Hollweg attempted to keep Britain out of the war by promising to forgo any annexations of French territory should Britain remain neutral. At the same time, however, General von MOLTKE, chief of the German general staff, was urging Conrad to proceed with mobilization, while resisting a proposal from General FALKENHAYN that Germany should also move towards mobilization.

By the time the Prussian cabinet met on 30 July it was clear that no government was in control of the rapidly developing situation. Austria authorized general mobilization the following day, an acceptance that the conflict could no longer be localized on the Serbian front. Germany authorized mobilization the same day, after waiting for news that Russia was mobilizing. This would enable the German government to present Russia as an aggressor, in the hope of securing the support of the SPD. Germany declared war on Russia on 1 August, (while Austria-Hungary delayed until 6 August). On 2 August Germany demanded that Brussels permit German troops to cross Belgian territory as required in order to implement the SCHLIEFFEN Plan. The British fleet was mobilized the same day, and on the following day (3 August) Germany declared war on France. Britain and Belgium declared war on Germany on 4 August.

These bilateral declarations effectively brought about a state of war between the Triple Entente (France, Russia and Britain) on the one hand, and the so-called CENTRAL POWERS (Germany and Austria-Hungary) on the other. Italy was also allied with Germany and Austria-Hungary, but stayed out of the war on the grounds that Austria (and not France) was the aggressor, so that the conflict was outside the terms of the TRIPLE ALLIANCE.

Jung, Carl Gustav (1875–1961), Swiss psychologist. Jung was born in Kesswil, the son of a pastor, studied science and medicine at Basle and Zurich, and completed his education as assistant to Eugen Beuler in Zurich before setting up in private practice as a psychotherapist in Küsnacht. From 1907 to 1913 he worked closely with Sigmund FREUD, and from 1911 to 1914 he was the first president of the International Psycho-analytic Society. Jung questioned, extended and developed many of Freud's ideas, and their collaboration was relatively short-lived. He developed his own 'analytical psychology', identified 'psychological types' (*Psychologische Typen*, 1921) and developed the controversial notion of a 'collective unconscious'. He also proposed the existence of universal 'archetypes' to be found in dreams, mythology and religion. The nature of his work led him to collaborate with orientalists, and to work with the indigenous peoples of North America and North Africa. The implications of his work on dreams and mythology had an important influence on contemporary culture. The work of Jung and his collaborators was published in *Psychologische Abhandlungen* ('psychological treatises') which appeared from 1913 to 1957. From 1933 to 1941 Jung was professor of psychology at Zurich, and, from 1944 until his death, professor of medicine at Basle.

Jung, Edgar (1894–1934), conservative journalist. Born in Ludwigshafen, Jung studied law and worked in the office of a conservative politician in Saarbrücken. He became involved in radical right-wing political violence after World War I. In 1924 he organized an attempt to assassinate the separatist leader Heinz-Orbis, in which five people were killed. He then moved to Munich and practised there as a lawyer, failed to be selected as a parliamentary candidate for the DVP, and began to make his career as a conservative journalist. During the Depression he argued in the pages of the *Deutsche Rundschau* for a conservative revolution, and duly welcomed the appointment of Franz von PAPEN as chancellor. It was in his capacity as speech-writer for Papen that Jung incurred the wrath of the Nazi regime. He was arrested on 23 June 1934, shortly after Papen's famous MARBURG SPEECH against Nazi excesses, and was shot a few days later.

junge Deutschland, Das. See YOUNG GERMANY.

Jünger, Ernst (1895–1998), writer. Jünger was born in Heidelberg, the son of a pharmacist. He ran away and joined the Foreign Legion as an adolescent and then volunteered for military service in 1914. He was posted to the Western Front as an infantry officer, and received the order *pour le mérite*. He remained an officer until 1923 and was active in the radical right-wing paramilitary group STAHLHELM. Jünger was a staunch supporter of the Nazis but was suspicious of Hitler's tactic of a legalistic takeover of power, and he remained outside the movement. He wrote about his wartime experience in a number of books: *In Stahlgewittern* ('the storm of steel', 1920), *Der Kampf als inneres Erlebnis* ('Struggle as inner experience', 1922), *Das Wäldchen 125* ('Copse 125', 1925) and *Feuer und Blut* ('fire and blood', 1925). He was also a proto-fascist publicist, and his ideas for a totalitarian society are contained in *Die Totale Mobilmachung* ('total mobilization') and *Der Arbeiter* ('the worker'), which were published in 1931 and 1932 respectively, at the height of Germany's political and economic crisis. In his later allegorical work he withdrew somewhat from his earlier political enthusiasms. *Auf Marmorklippen* (1939, published in English as *On Marble Cliffs*) has been described by those sympathetic to Jünger as an anti-Nazi parable; others have been more sceptical. The book was banned only after a year. During World War II he served on the staff of the German military commander in Paris until 1944. He turned against the Nazis and was dismissed after the JULY BOMB PLOT. His son was killed in action in Italy at the end of the war and, although Jünger refused to appear before a DENAZIFICATION tribunal, he condemned militarism after the war. He continued to write, but withdrew from public life. Jünger lived to be 102.

Jungmädelbund ('young girls' league'), division of the HITLER YOUTH for girls between the ages of 10 and 14.

Junker, a term used to describe Prussian aristocrats. Originally *junger Herr* or *Jungherr*, a young nobleman, the term came to be applied specifically to the class of large Prussian landowners east of the Elbe. They dominated the institutions of Prussia, and less directly of the Reich, particularly the bureaucracy and the army, and were satirized for their stiff military bearing and clipped speech. In the late 19th century the Junkers were represented by the German Conservatives (*DEUTSCHKONSERVATIVE PARTEI*) in the Reichstag, and organized in the *Bund der Landwirte* (AGRARIAN LEAGUE). Their political vehicle during the Weimar Republic was the DNVP. The Junkers formed the core of the traditional ruling class of Prussia and Germany, but their power was broken after the 1944 JULY BOMB PLOT and the occupation of eastern Germany by the Soviet Union.

Junkers, Hugo (1859–1935), aircraft designer and industrialist. Junkers was born in Rheydt am Rhein, and studied at the Technical University in Aachen. He moved to Dessau in 1888 and set up his first business there five years later. His company worked on technical developments in a number of fields (including domestic heating appliances) and registered some 300 patents. Junkers was eventually the largest employer in the town and was awarded honorary citizenship. In 1919 he set up an aircraft factory and pioneered the use of metal in aircraft rather than the wood and fabric that had hitherto been used. He developed the first successful all-metal aeroplane and his company built one of the first turbojet engines. Various Junkers designs played important roles during World War II, including the Junkers Ju-52 troop transport, the Ju-87 'Stuka' dive-bomber and the Ju-88 medium bomber.

Jutland, battle of (31 May–1 June 1916), the only significant naval battle of World War I. The superiority of the Royal Navy and the failure of submarine warfare had compelled the German navy to attempt to lift the Allied blockade by means of a war of attrition.

In February 1916, however, Vice Admiral Reinhard Scheer, the new German naval commander in chief, began to plan attempts to engage the British Grand Fleet off the Danish coast. The engagement between the two fleets eventually took place on 31 May and 1 June. The outcome was indecisive. The Germans claimed a victory over Britain in terms of the ratio of ships lost – the British lost 14 battle cruisers, cruisers and destroyers compared with the German Fleet's 9 – but failed to break out of the blockade either then or later. (Further unsuccessful attempts were made in August and November 1916, and then in April 1918.)

Jüttner, Hans (1894–1965), SS officer. Jüttner was chief of staff of the WAFFEN-SS from 1940, and head of the Operational Department of the SS (which controlled the Waffen-SS) from 1942.

K

Kafka, Franz (1883–1924), writer. Kafka was born into a German-speaking Jewish business family in Prague, and studied law at the Charles University. It was here that he met Max BROD, who was chiefly responsible for preparing Kafka's work for publication after his death, and thereby ensured his literary reputation. Kafka started to write while he was still a student. He was then employed by insurance companies, and remained at the Workers' Accident Insurance Institute for the Kingdom of Bohemia until he was compelled by poor health to take more and more time off. He was diagnosed with tuberculosis in 1917 and retired in 1922. He went to Berlin to write the following year, but died in a clinic at Kierling near Vienna in 1924. In 1912, while working in Vienna, he began his first novel, published in 1927 as *Amerika* and later as *Der Verschollene* ('missing person'). Little of his work was published in his lifetime, although he had prepared some short stories for publication, and his major novels were published by Brod after his death: *Der Prozess* (*The Trial*) in 1925, *Das Schloss* (*The Castle*) in 1926 and *Amerika* in 1927. Kafka himself had wanted his work destroyed; instead he became one of the most influential writers in 20th-century central European literature.

Kahr, Gustav, Ritter von (1862–1934), conservative nationalist politician. Kahr was born in Weissenburg into a leading Bavarian family, and studied law at Munich before pursuing a career as a public servant. Kahr was not so much a professional party politician as a successful and powerful public servant with strong conservative, nationalist views, who had the support of the local right-wing paramilitary groups (*Einwohnerwehren* or 'home guards'). He became minister-president of Bavaria during the political crisis that followed World War I (1920–1). He was determined to impose order on Germany's most politically turbulent constituent state and immediately forced the Workers' and Soldiers' Councils (*RÄTE*) to disband. Although he resigned his political position in September 1921 after conflicts with both the Reich government and the Allies, he occupied an equally powerful position as *Regierungspräsident* (a local government administrator). In 1923 he was appointed 'state commissioner general' of Bavaria by the government in Munich, which granted him wide-reaching, quasi-dictatorial powers. He hoped to win the support of the early Nazi movement for his plans to secede from the Reich and restore the Bavarian monarchy, but although he was sympathetic to Hitler and was caught up in the BEER HALL PUTSCH of November 1923, he was an unwilling participant, and managed to break away from Hitler and the others as the police and Reichswehr suppressed the putsch. He spent the rest of his career as president of the Bavarian administrative court (*Verwaltungsgerichtshof*), a position that had been occupied by his father before him, and was murdered in 1934 in Dachau during the NIGHT OF THE LONG KNIVES.

Kaiser, emperor (from Latin *Caesar*). Sometimes the term 'the Kaiser' is used in English specifically of WILHELM II.

Kaiser, Georg (1878–1945), EXPRESSIONIST writer. Kaiser was born in Magdeburg and lived in Argentina for three years as a young man before returning to Germany and publishing his first work, *Rektor Kleist* (1903). He wrote some sixty plays, including *Von Morgens bis Mitternachts* (*From Morning until Midnight*, 1916), and a trilogy on capitalism: *Die Koralle* (1917), *Gas I* (1918) and *Gas II* (1920). His work was banned in 1933 and he emigrated to Switzerland.

Kaiser, Jakob (1888–1961), politician. Kaiser was active in the Christian trade unions from 1912, and became deputy president of the Rhenish CENTRE PARTY in 1919. He was elected to the Reichstag in 1933. After the war he was effectively the first president of the CDU in the Soviet zone of occupation, but he was removed from his offices by the military authorities in the Soviet Zone in 1947. From 1949 he was a member of the Berlin parliament and a representative of (West) Berlin on the PARLIAMENTARY COUNCIL in West Germany. From 1949 he was also a member of the Bundestag, and federal minister for relations between East and West Germany (1949–57). From 1956 to 1958 he was deputy president of the CDU.

Kaiser-Wilhelms-Land, a former German colony in the northeastern part of New Guinea, forming the major part of German New Guinea. It became an Australian mandate after World War I.

Kaltenbrunner, Ernst (1903–46), Austrian Nazi. Kaltenbrunner was born the son of a lawyer in Ried im Innkreis in Upper Austria and was educated in Linz, where he became a friend of EICHMANN. He studied law at Graz, and subsequently practised law in Linz. He joined the NSDAP in 1932. He was imprisoned briefly in 1934 and 1935, when the Nazi Party was illegal in Austria, but was appointed Austrian minister of state security by SEYSS-INQUART in 1938. He took charge of the SS in Vienna when the Germans invaded, and succeeded HEYDRICH as head of the RSHA in January 1943. In 1944 he took over the ABWEHR and subordinated it to the RSHA. He was captured in Austria after the war, tried at Nuremberg, and hanged in 1946.

Kamerun. *See* CAMEROON.

Kandinsky, Wassily (1866–1944), Russian-born painter, based in Munich from 1897. Kandinsky was born in Moscow, where he had a musical education and studied law from 1886 to 1892. He emigrated to Munich at the age of 30 to study art, and became a friend of Paul KLEE. A pioneer of abstract painting, he published his treatise *On the Spiritual in Art* in 1912 and was a founding member of the *BLAUE REITER* group of artists in Munich, which became the centre of German EXPRESSIONIST art. In 1914 he returned to Russia, where he worked with the Bolsheviks after the October Revolution, returning to Germany to teach at the BAUHAUS in 1926. He left for Paris in 1933, and was denounced by the Germans as a degenerate artist. He became a French citizen in 1939, and died at Neuilly-sur-Seine.

Kant, Immanuel (1724–1804), philosopher. Kant was born in Königsberg and lived all his life there, both studying and teaching at the university. In 1770 he was appointed to a chair. Kant's work is the most important starting point for modern German philosophy, although for much of his early career he was a minor, if fairly typical, Enlightenment thinker and writer. He was prompted by David Hume's scepticism to question the philosophical basis of Enlightenment thinking, but was afraid that too sceptical a philosophy might prove self-destructive. His 'three critiques' were part of an attempt to suggest a middle way, and to set orientation points and boundaries for philosophy. His first major work, *The Critique of Pure Reason*, was published in 1781, and set him apart from his contemporaries. In response to criticism he published *Prolegomena to any Future Metaphysics* in 1783. A series of further works followed: *Foundations of the Metaphysics of Morals* (1785), *The Critique of Practical Reason* (1788) and *The Critique of Judgement* (1790). Within a decade Kant had become one of the most influential thinkers in Germany, and one of the most productive in modern philosophy. Moreover, many of the most influential philosophers of the following two centuries – not least HEGEL and MARX – have felt compelled to define themselves to some extent in relation to Kant's work.

Kantorowicz, Hermann (1877–1940), academic lawyer. Kantorowicz taught criminal law and the history and philosophy of law at Freiburg from 1908. He volunteered for military service in 1914, but returned from the war a republican pacifist and joined the liberal DDP. His subsequent career demonstrates the difficulties faced by a liberal academic during the 1920s. His academic position was damaged when he was vituperatively attacked by a conservative historian for criticizing BISMARCK's policies. He then worked on the Reichstag committee on the origins of World War I, and demonstrated that Germany was co-responsible for the outbreak of hostilities in 1914, a conclusion that precipitated further hostile criticism from historians. His work on the causes of the war was not published until 1967. His promotion to a chair at Kiel was delayed by misgivings in the foreign ministry, and finally he was dismissed and emigrated first to New York (1933–4), and then to Cambridge, England.

Kanzler, the German word for CHANCELLOR.

Kapp, Wolfgang (1858–1922), right-wing nationalist politician. Kapp was born in New York in 1858, where his father lived as an exile after taking part in the Revolutions of 1848. His father returned to Germany in 1870 and was elected to the Reichstag as a liberal. The younger Kapp studied law, became involved in right-wing politics and was a co-founder of the Fatherland Party (*VATERLANDSPARTEI*) in 1917. After the war he was a representative of East Prussia within the leadership of the nationalist DNVP, and was elected to the Reichstag. In 1920 he became leader of the putsch attempt that bears his name. He died in Leipzig two years after the failure of the putsch.

Kapp putsch (1920), sometimes referred to as the 'Kapp–Lüttwitz putsch', the attempt by officers and right-wing paramilitary groups to establish a conservative dictatorship in Germany during the early days of the Weimar Republic.

The attempt was prompted by the government's decision to disband the Baltic volunteer corps, the EHRHARDT Brigade and other FREIKORPS formations in accordance with the wishes of the victorious Entente powers. On 13 March 1920 Ehrhardt marched his men through the Brandenburg Gate in Berlin. The army refused to suppress the rebellion – notably failing to defend the Republic against the right as it had against the left with the suppression of the SPARTACUS uprising – and the government fled to Dresden. Wolfgang KAPP was declared chancellor by the rebels in Berlin. General von Lüttwitz, chief of Reichswehr Command Area 1 in Berlin, was appointed commander in chief of the army by the rebel government. In parts of northern Germany government officials were forced to resign, and there was support for the coup in the navy. In the event, however, it was defeated by a swift and effective general strike supported by all the political organizations of the left from the USPD to the DDP. The REICHSBANK refused to issue the new 'government' money without proper authorization, and the civil servants in Berlin refused to carry out its orders. In addition, the rebel government failed to attract support either among the middle classes or among senior army officers. It was only four days until it was recognized by the rebels that the coup had failed, and the legitimate government (now in Stuttgart) was approached with a view to coming to terms. Kapp handed over leadership of the new 'government' to Lüttwitz and fled. The failed coup strengthened the conservatives in the military. Walther Reinhardt, the only general who had been prepared to defend the republic by armed force, felt compelled to resign, and his rival, Hans von SEECKT, who had been more ambivalent in his attitude towards the rebels, was appointed chief of the army command. Seeckt's insistence on a politically 'neutral' army made the Reichswehr something of a 'state within the state', a quasi-independent institution whose leaders, despite their oaths of loyalty, had already revealed a marked reluctance to defend the legitimate elected government. The abortive Kapp putsch also failed to produce a reaction against the right in the country: the first general election to the Reichstag, held in June 1920, proved to be a defeat for the moderate 'Weimar parties' and a clear victory for the right.

Karajan, Herbert von (1908–89), Austrian conductor. Karajan studied music at the Mozarteum in Salzburg and made his debut in the town in 1929 before being appointed a conductor in Ulm. He joined the Nazi Party in 1933 and became general musical director at Aachen the following year. He continued to work in Germany throughout most of the Third Reich, and fled to Italy in 1944. His association with the Nazis prevented his resuming work after the war until he was appointed conductor of the Vienna Symphony Orchestra in 1947. He then became principal conductor at the Vienna State Opera, and was director from 1956 to 1964. Much of his later life was spent with the Berlin Philharmonic.

Karl I (1887–1922), the last HABSBURG emperor (1916–18). He succeeded to the throne on the death of his great uncle, the emperor FRANZ JOSEPH, in the middle of WORLD WAR I. His attempts to negotiate an end to the war

through contacts in France were unsuccessful, and his hope of preserving the empire as a federation of nationalities was thwarted by the plans of the Allies and the outbreak of revolution in Austria and Hungary. He left Vienna for Switzerland in November 1918, then went to Hungary where he tried to intervene in Hungarian politics and was exiled to the Portuguese island of Madeira. His wife Zita lived until 1989.

Karl VI (1685–1740), Holy Roman emperor and ruler of the HABSBURG hereditary lands in central Europe (1711–40). The AUSTRIAN NETHERLANDS were acquired during his reign (1714), along with Lombardy, Naples and Sicily. He also acquired territory in the Balkans from the Ottoman empire (1716–18). He issued the PRAGMATIC SANCTION in 1713 in order to secure the accession of his daughter MARIA THERESIA and the indivisibility of the Habsburg empire as a territorial state.

Karl VII (1697–1745), WITTELSBACH elector of Bavaria (1726–45) and Holy Roman emperor (1742–45). Karl was the son-in-law of emperor Joseph I and, as an ally of FRIEDRICH II of Prussia in the War of the AUSTRIAN SUCCESSION, challenged the succession of MARIA THERESIA to the HABSBURG lands. In 1742 he was elected emperor in opposition to Maria Theresia's consort, the future FRANZ I, who succeeded him in 1745.

Karl-Marx-Stadt, the name for Chemnitz under the German Democratic Republic.

Karlsbad decrees (August 1819), a series of repressive measures agreed by the political leaders of the GERMAN CONFEDERATION under the chairmanship of METTERNICH at Karlsbad (now Karlovy Vary in the Czech Republic). The measures were enacted in response to the nationalistic agitation of student corporations (BURSCHENSCHAFTEN), and in particular to the murder of the writer KOTZEBUE. The measures included prohibition of the *Burschenschaften*, censorship of the press, surveillance of the universities and a general prohibition of political meetings. The introduction of these measures reflected both the domination of Austria in Germany – in so far as the decrees were effectively imposed on the Confederation by Metternich – and the authoritarian nature of the post-Napoleonic restoration over which Metternich presided.

Kärnten. *See* CARINTHIA.

Kasche, Siegfried (1903–47), Nazi diplomat. Kasche was born in Strasbourg, then under German rule, joined the NSDAP in 1926 and was a member of the Reichstag for Frankfurt an der Oder from 1930. A former stormtrooper, he was appointed ambassador to the fascist puppet state set up by the Germans in Croatia (1941–4). He was hanged in Yugoslavia after the war.

Kasino, the name given to the grouping of centre-right liberals at the 1848 FRANKFURT PARLIAMENT. The faction was led by Heinrich von GAGERN, and was also associated with DAHLMANN and Droysen. Two-thirds of its members were senior civil servants. It supported the transformation of Germany into a constitutional federation. As with other factions in the parliament, its name was taken from its meeting place.

Katyn, the site in Russia of the massacre of Polish officers in World War II. When the area was captured by the Germans in 1943 they announced that they had discovered the mass graves of 4443 Polish officers, who had been in Soviet custody. The Russians in turn claimed that they had been killed by the Germans when they had captured territory around Smolensk in 1941. The Polish government-in-exile in London demanded an international investigation by the Red Cross, who said there was nothing they could do without an invitation from the USSR. Moscow refused to issue such an invitation on the grounds that the murders had been committed by the Germans. Instead the Germans conducted their own inquiry, which established that the Poles had been killed while the area was controlled by the Soviets. When the territory was recaptured by the Red Army, the Soviets in turn con-

ducted an inquiry that established that the Germans were guilty. Postwar Polish governments officially accepted the Soviet explanation until a non-Communist government was elected. In 1992 the Russians released material showing that the massacre and the cover-up had been the work of the NKVD, the Soviet secret police.

Kaufmann, Karl (1900–69), *Gauleiter* of Hamburg. Born in Krefeld, Kaufmann was a co-founder of the NSDAP in the Ruhr (1921) and was *Gauleiter* of the Rhineland in 1928, when he was sacked for corruption. He was rehabilitated in 1933 and appointed Reich governor of Hamburg, a position he retained until 1945. He was temporarily detained several times after the war before his final release in 1953.

Kaunitz, Wenzel Anton, Graf von (1711–94), Austrian minister. Kaunitz was born in Vienna, studied law and entered the diplomatic service in 1740, the year of MARIA THERESIA's accession to the throne. He served as a diplomat in Italy, and as effective governor of the Austrian Netherlands, before returning to Vienna as head of the Austrian State Chancellery in 1753. He was responsible for the 'diplomatic revolution' in Europe that reversed the accustomed order of power constellations on the continent and realigned France with Austria and Russia, thereby isolating Prussia on the eve of the SEVEN YEARS WAR. After the war he was created Fürst von (prince) Kaunitz-Rietberg, and presided over the State Council (STAATS-RAT) created by Maria Theresia in 1760. Kaunitz's influence declined under JOSEPH II, and he resigned in 1792. One of his granddaughters married Prince METTERNICH.

Kautsky, Karl (1854–1938), Marxist theoretician. Kautsky was born in Prague and grew up in Vienna. He joined the Austrian Social Democrats when he was a student, and was subsequently employed by Karl Höchberg, the patron of the journal *Die Zukunft*, who also employed Eduard BERNSTEIN. In 1880 Kautsky moved to Zurich, and three years later he founded the journal *Die Neue Zeit*, which he edited until 1917. He spent three years in London (1885–8), where he got to know ENGELS and published *The Economic Doctrines of Karl Marx* (1887), which established his reputation. He wrote the opening theoretical passages of the SPD's ERFURT PROGRAMME of 1891, on which he collaborated with Bernstein. He was then commissioned by the party to write a book explaining it, *Das Erfurter Programm* (1892). At the turn of the century Kautsky challenged Bernstein's critique of Marxism, categorizing his revisionism as bourgeois radicalism. In *The Road to Power* (1909), which earned him the wrath of the trade unions, Kautsky restated the necessity of organizing the working class for political agitation and eventually for revolutionary action against the state and the ruling class. Kautsky left the party to join the breakaway, anti-war USPD in 1917. He became a deputy foreign office minister (1918–20). He then moved to Austria and lived in Vienna in the 1920s and 1930s, and fled to the Netherlands in 1938.

KdF (*Kraft durch Freude*). *See* STRENGTH THROUGH JOY.

KdF-Wagen. *See* VOLKSWAGEN.

Keil, Wilhelm (1870–1968), Social Democratic politician. Keil was a turner who joined the SPD and became editor of the *Schwäbische Tagwacht*, the party's local paper, in 1896, and was editor in chief until it was banned by the Nazis in 1933. He was a member of the Reichstag from 1910 to 1932. He was president of the Württemberg constituent assembly in 1919, and pressed for a coalition of the SPD with the middle-class parties. From 1921 to 1923 he was Württemberg's minister for work and food.

Keitel, Wilhelm (Bodewin Johann) (1882–1946), field marshal and chief of staff, OKW, the High Command of the Armed Forces (1938–45). Keitel was born in Helmscherode in the Harz mountains, served in World War I, and then pursued a career in administration in the war ministry, where he was appointed chief of staff to war minister Werner von BLOMBERG in 1935. Keitel was head of the OKW from its inception in 1938. Promoted to field marshal in 1940 he was loyal to Hitler throughout the war and retained his post until 1945. He was tried at Nuremberg, found guilty of war crimes and hanged.

Kelly, Petra (1947–92), environmentalist politician. Born in Günzburg an der Donau, Petra Kelly moved to the United States with her parents in 1959, and studied political science at the American University, Washington. From 1971 she worked for the European Commission in Brussels and became involved in the movement against nuclear power in the 1970s. In 1979 she was a candidate for the GREENS in the European elections, and was a leading figure in the German Green movement from its inception. She stood as a candidate in the Bundestag elections of 1980, and was elected in 1983. In 1992 she was shot dead by her partner Gert Bastian, who then shot himself. The motives for their deaths have never become clear.

Keppler, Wilhelm (1882–1960), industrialist and Nazi politician. An early Nazi Party member, Keppler was an important mediator between the party and big business during the Depression. He was elected to the Reichstag in 1933, and was appointed Reich commissioner for economic affairs in the same year. He was adviser to GÖRING at the FOUR-YEAR PLAN office in 1936, briefly Reich commissioner for Austria in 1938 and administered property expropriated by the SS in Poland and the USSR. He was sentenced to ten years' imprisonment in 1949, but was released in 1951.

Kerrl, Hans (1887–1941), Nazi minister for the churches. Kerrl became a Reich commissioner in the Prussian justice ministry in 1933, minister without portfolio in 1934, and minister for ecclesiastical affairs in 1935. He died in office.

Kesselring, Albert (1885–1960), field marshal. Kesselring served in World War I and was admired for his dynamism and powers of organization. After the end of the war he was a member of the *TRUPPENAMT* and played an important part in reorganizing the REICHS-WEHR. He moved from the army to the new Nazi air ministry in 1933. He helped lay the foundations of the LUFTWAFFE and was its chief of administration until 1936. He commanded the air force in Poland, the battle of Britain and the Soviet Union before his promotion to commander in chief of land and air forces in the south in 1941. He was responsible for supplies to the African campaign, for military-diplomatic relations between Germany and Italy, and eventually for the withdrawal from both Africa and Italy. He was sentenced to death for war crimes by a British military court in Venice in 1947, but his sentence was commuted to life imprisonment. He was released in 1952 and was later president of the re-founded *STAHLHELM*.

Kharkov, battles of (1941 and 1943), key engagements during the Russian campaign of World War II. Kharkov was capital of the independent Ukraine created by the Germans in 1917, and remained its capital within the Soviet Union until 1934. It was also one of the largest industrial cities in the USSR. In 1941 it was captured and occupied by the Germans, who resisted Soviet efforts to retake it in 1942. The city was eventually recaptured during the Soviet counter-offensive of 1943 in a battle that lasted from 11 to 23 August.

Kiaochow (German name: Kiautschou), the main German concession in China (now Jiaoxian in Shandong province). It was acquired in 1898 on a 99-year lease and became the site of a German naval base. In 1914 it was captured by the Japanese and in 1922 it was returned to China.

Kiderlen-Wächter, Alfred von (1852–1912), diplomat and politician; Reich foreign minister (1910–12). Kiderlen was born in Stuttgart and studied law before entering the Prussian diplomatic service. He was German

minister in Bucharest (1899–1910) and a supporter of the BERLIN–BAGHDAD RAILWAY. He was then Reich foreign minister (1910–12). He was a hawkish politician and diplomat in the Wilhelmine style, and precipitated the AGADIR crisis of 1911 by sending a gunboat to Morocco to reinforce his diplomatic insistence on compensation for Germany for the French occupation of Rabat and Fes. His demand for the whole of the French Congo in return for French supremacy in Morocco was rejected, and the eventual outcome – a French protectorate in Morocco for minor territorial concessions in the Congo – was seen as a failure by Kiderlen's critics on the right. His policies did much to aggravate international tensions on the eve of World War I.

Kiel Canal, waterway linking the Baltic and North Seas. The port of Kiel became Prussian with the acquisition of the Danish duchies of Slesvig (Schleswig) and Holstein in the 1860s (*see* SCHLESWIG-HOLSTEIN). The canal was built between 1887 and 1895, and subsequently enlarged and reopened in 1914. The total cost was estimated by the British Foreign Office at £19,068,000, but the original cost per kilometre was reckoned to be cheaper than other similar constructions (such as the Suez Canal and the Manchester Ship Canal). The time saved for shipping by the canal varied: vessels of 1000 tons saved 24 hours between Newcastle and Bornholm, while ships of 400 tons saved 5 hours over the same distance.

Kielmannsegg, Erich, Graf (1847–1923), Austrian politician. Kielmannsegg was the son of the Hanover minister of state (effectively the prime minister). He was governor of Lower Austria from 1899 to 1911, and briefly Austrian minister-president and interior minister in 1895.

Kiel mutiny, sailors' mutiny of November 1918 which precipitated the NOVEMBER REVOLUTION. Its immediate cause was an order to engage the Royal Navy in a last attempt to salvage the honour of the German navy, although the war was already lost. The sailors, however, were unwilling to engage in what seemed a suicidal sortie and mutinied. Around 1000 fleet mutineers were arrested and on 3 November seven people were shot by military police during a demonstration for the release of the prisoners. The mutiny fast escalated to armed rebellion, and by the evening of 4 November the rebels held Kiel and presented demands for press freedom and the moderation of military discipline. The rebellion spread to army units, and by 6 November workers', soldiers' and sailors' councils (*see* RAT) had been set up in all major cities and ports.

Kiesinger, Kurt Georg (1904–88), conservative politician; federal chancellor (1966–9). Kiesinger was born in Ebingen and studied at Tübingen and Berlin. He was a member of the Nazi Party and was interned by the Allies after the war. He joined the CDU and was elected to the Bundestag in 1949. Kiesinger was minister-president of Baden-Württemberg from 1958 to 1966, and president of the Bundesrat from 1962 to 1963. He was chancellor during the GRAND COALITION of 1966–9, and was known for the informality of his meetings with his coalition allies. His administration saw some easing of tension in relations with the GERMAN DEMOCRATIC REPUBLIC, a development that anticipated the *OSTPOLITIK* of his successor, Willy BRANDT.

Kiev, battles of (1941 and 1943), key engagements during the Russian campaign of World War II. Kiev is the capital city of Ukraine, and was considered a vital strategic city both by the Germans during the advance of 1941 and by the Soviets as they drove the Germans west in 1943. It was taken by Field Marshal von RUNDSTEDT's Army Group South and General GUDERIAN's Panzer Group in September 1941, and was recaptured by the Soviets in November 1943.

Killinger, Manfred, Freiherr von (1886–1944), Nazi administrator and diplomat. Born in Lindigt, Killinger served as a naval officer in World War I, and was then a member of the EHRHARDT brigade, a FREIKORPS group. He joined the Nazi Party in 1927, was Nazi Reich commissioner for Saxony from March 1933, and minister-president of Saxony from 1933 to 1935. He was a member of the *Volksgericht* (People's Court) from 1935, and German consul general in San Francisco from 1936 to 1938. He then worked in the foreign office in Berlin until 1941, when he was sent as German minister to Romania. He committed suicide in the German embassy in Bucharest in order to avoid being captured by Soviet troops.

Kinder, Kirche, Küche ('children, church and kitchen'), a slogan used to summarize the role and place of German women as perceived by conservatives and anti-feminists.

Kinkel, Johanna (née Mockel; 1810–58), composer, writer and political agitator. After an unhappy first marriage Mockel settled in Berlin in the 1830s, and then returned to her native Bonn, where she founded the *Maikäfer Bund*, a literary society. She married Gottfried Kinkel, a pastor, in 1843. She aligned herself with the democrats during the REVOLUTIONS OF 1848, and became editor of the *Neue Bonner Zeitung* in 1849. Her husband was arrested and imprisoned in July of that year, but escaped with her help, and the couple fled to London.

Kirchner, Ernst Ludwig (1880–1938). German EXPRESSIONIST artist. An important member of the expressionist group *Die BRÜCKE*, Kirchner suffered a nervous breakdown shortly after his mobilization in 1914. He spent the rest of his life in Switzerland and committed suicide after his work was condemned by the Nazis.

Kirdorf, Emil (1847–1938), industrialist. Kirdorf was director of the *Gelsenkirchener Bergwerksgesellschaft*, an important Ruhr mining company, and a promoter of the Rhineland-Westphalian Coal Syndicate. Kirdorf was a convinced annexationist during World War I, and an energetic promoter of the myth that Germany had not so much been defeated as betrayed at home by Jews and

Bolsheviks (the *DOLCHSTOSSLEGENDE*). He had been a long-serving member of the PAN-GERMAN LEAGUE, and joined the nationalist DNVP in 1919. After retiring from business he was an important mediator between the industrialists of western Germany and the Nazi movement, and he got to know Hitler personally in the late 1920s. He joined the NSDAP briefly, but left again, alienated by its anti-capitalist posturing. He remained on good terms with Hitler, however, and rejoined the party in 1934. He was decorated personally by Hitler on his 90th birthday, and died the following year.

Kladderadatsch, satirical magazine. It was founded in May 1848 as a revolutionary weekly and continued publication until 1944. Its politics were generally anti-establishment, but its anti-clericalism led it to support the *KULTURKAMPF* of the 1870s, and by the imperial period it was considered relatively harmless.

Klee, Paul (1879–1940), Swiss-born artist classified as degenerate by the Nazis. Klee was born the son of a music teacher in München-buchsee near Bern, and studied art in Munich, where he was a student of Franz von Stuck. He returned to Switzerland in 1902 and settled in Bern, but went back to Munich in 1906 and became a member of the *BLAUE REITER* group. After the war Klee taught at the BAUHAUS in Weimar and Dessau (1921–31), and then at the Düsseldorf Academy. Klee's abstract and semi-abstract art, which he described as 'taking a line for a walk', offended the Nazis, and he was dismissed from his teaching position in 1933 when they came to power, and over a hundred of his works were confiscated from art galleries. His position was exacerbated by his leftist political sympathies. He returned to Switzerland, but was prevented from working by illness for much of the rest of his life.

Kleindeutschland, a term used – particularly at the FRANKFURT PARLIAMENT – to describe a possible outcome to the question of German unification which would exclude Austria. In effect the solution imposed by Bismarck in 1871 constructed just such a *Kleindeutschland.*

See also GREATER GERMANY.

Kleist, (Bernd) Heinrich (Wilhelm) von (1777–1811), writer. Kleist was born in Frankfurt an der Oder into a military family, and spent several years in the army before leaving with the rank of lieutenant in 1799. He broke off his engagement to Wilhelmine von Zenge and retreated to a Swiss farmhouse to concentrate on his work. Here he wrote his first tragic drama, *Die Familie Schroffenstein*. At this time he also began *Robert Guiskard*, an unfinished play that has been seen by some as his greatest work. In 1803 he completed the comedy *Der zerbrochene Krug* (*The Broken Jug*).

Following a complete breakdown, ostensibly prompted by his own inability to live up to the aesthetic ideals he had set himself, Kleist joined the Prussian state service in 1805 in Königsberg, and wrote a number of novellas, including *Michael Kohlhaas, Die Marquise von O*, and *Das Erdbeben in Chile* (*The Earthquake in Chile*). In 1807 he left his post and moved to Berlin, where he was arrested by the French on suspicion of spying. The following year in Dresden, with the political philosopher Adam Müller, he founded the short-lived journal *Phöbus*, in which his novellas were published.

After the collapse of Prussia during the Napoleonic Wars Kleist's writing became increasingly political. His patriotic tragedy *Die Hermannsschlacht* ('Hermann's Battle'; *see HERMANNSDENKMAL*) circulated in manuscript form from 1808 (though not published until 1821), and the following year he attempted to found a nationalist journal, *Germania*. The last two issues of *Phöbus* appeared in 1809 and Kleist then left Dresden for a trip to Austria with the historian Friedrich Christoph DAHLMANN. His play *Das Käthchen von Heilbronn* ('Katy of Heilbronn') had its premiere in Vienna at the Theater an der Wien in March 1810.

Kleist and Dahlmann had returned from Prague to Dresden in October 1810, and Kleist settled in Berlin as editor of the *Berliner Abendblätter*, which was censored by the authorities for its conservative criticism of the reforms instituted by STEIN and HARDENBERG. When it folded he had no financial means of support. He became involved with Henriette Vogel, a woman who was ill with a terminal cancer. The couple made a suicide pact, and after spending the night at an inn by the Wannsee, Kleist shot first Henriette and then himself on the shore of the lake the following afternoon (21 November 1811). The premiere of his last play, *Prinz Friedrich von Homburg*, took place at the Vienna Burgtheater in 1821.

Kleist-Schmenzin, Paul Ludwig (Ewald) von (1881–1954), field marshal. Appointed commander of Breslau (Wrocław, now in Poland), he was promoted to cavalry general in 1936. In World War II he commanded the 22nd Army Corps during the Polish campaign, served in France, and commanded the troops that took Belgrade in 1941. He was also commander in chief of the First Panzer Army, which captured KIEV in 1941–2, and was promoted to field marshal in 1943. He was relieved of his post by Hitler in 1944 following reversals in the Ukraine. He was captured by British troops, and handed over first to Yugoslavia and then to the Soviets. He died in a Soviet prison.

Klimt, Gustav (1862–1918) Austrian artist and foremost painter of fin-de-siècle Vienna; co-founder and director (1897–1905) of the Vienna SECESSION. Born the son of a gold engraver from a peasant family in Baumgarten, now a suburban district of Vienna, Klimt studied at the School of Applied Arts in Vienna and, with his brother Ernst, won a number of important commissions during the 1880s, culminating in work on the prestigious new buildings on the Ringstrasse: the imperial court theatre (*Burgtheater*) in 1887–8, and the Art History Museum (*Kunsthistorisches Museum*) in 1890. In 1894 the education ministry commissioned him to decorate the great hall of the university with allegorical paintings (which proved to be unpopular). Klimt was also a society artist, renowned for his portraits of women. Among his best known works are the medicine frieze and the Beethoven frieze for the university, *Judith I* (1901), *The Three Ages of Woman* (1905) *The Kiss* (1907–8) and *Judith II* (*Salome*, 1909).

Knigge, Adolph, Freiherr von (1752–96), ENLIGHTENMENT intellectual. Knigge was born into a noble family and brought up on his father's estate near Hanover. He studied law in Göttingen, was appointed to an official position at court in Kassel in 1771, and married in 1773. He became involved with the ILLUMINATI in Frankfurt in the early 1780s, before moving on first to Heidelberg, then to Hanover and finally to Bremen, where he was appointed a chief magistrate in 1791. He was already ill when he arrived in Bremen and died there five years later. Knigge was mainly a writer of fiction, but also wrote a number of essays. He opposed the political order of the old regime and his sympathy with the French Revolution is clear from his later satirical novels.

Knobelsdorff, Georg Wenzeslaus von (1699–1753), architect and master builder. Knobelsdorff was born near Crossen (now Krosno Odrzańskie in Poland). He embarked on a career as an officer but gave it up to study painting and architecture. He travelled to Italy and France in the course of his studies, and in 1740 was appointed director of the royal palaces and gardens by Frederick the Great (FRIEDRICH II), who had just succeeded to the Prussian throne. From 1740 he oversaw the conversion and extension of Charlottenburg Palace, and from 1741 the construction of the Berlin Opera House. In 1745 he began the construction of SANSSOUCI Palace in accordance with Friedrich's ideas. He was also involved in the design of the park at Sanssouci and the Tiergarten in Berlin.

Koch, Erich (1896–1986), Nazi politician. Koch joined the NSDAP in 1922, became *Gauleiter* of East Prussia in 1928, and was elected to the Reichstag in 1930. He was appointed chief of the civil administration in Bialystok in 1941, and Reich commissioner of the Ukraine the same year. A committed advocate of Nazi racial policies in the East, he was captured after the war and tried by the Poles in 1958. His death sentence was commuted to life imprisonment for health reasons.

Kohl, Helmut (1930–), conservative politician; federal chancellor (1982–98). Born in Ludwigshafen in the Rhineland, Kohl studied political science at Heidelberg, where he graduated with a doctorate in 1958. Kohl was active in the CDU from the age of 17, was elected to the LANDTAG of Rhineland Palatinate in 1959, and became regional party chairman in 1969 and minister-president in 1969. He became federal chairman of the CDU in 1973 and was the party's chancellor candidate in the Bundestag election of 1976. He was passed over for the candidature in 1980 in favour of the CSU leader Franz-Josef STRAUSS, but was then instrumental in persuading the FDP to abandon the 'social–liberal' coalition of Helmut SCHMIDT and to help form a centre–right coalition under Kohl's own leadership. Although not at first taken seriously by the opposition, and not expected to remain in office for long, Kohl remained chancellor from 1982 to 1998. With the endorsement of increased support in the 1983 general election Kohl embarked on a neo-liberal programme of redistributing wealth by reducing taxation and cutting public expenditure at the cost of higher unemployment. His administration survived an electoral setback in 1987 to take advantage of the subsequent economic recovery, but Kohl profited above all from the collapse of the GERMAN DEMOCRATIC REPUBLIC and the opening of the Berlin Wall in 1989. He supervised the reunification of Germany in 1990, and campaigned actively in the East during the elections of that year, which proved to be a resounding victory for the CDU. Kohl was defeated in the 1998 election and suffered the indignity of revelations of financial impropriety in CDU party funding during his leadership.

Kokoschka, Oskar (1886–1980), Austrian EXPRESSIONIST painter. Kokoschka moved to Berlin in 1910, served in World War I, and was wounded in battle. He moved to Dresden after the war and then spent several years travelling. He fled to London in 1938 after the condemnation of his work as degenerate (remarked on by the artist in his *Self-Portrait of a Degenerate Artist*, 1937) by the Nazis, and finally settled in Switzerland in 1953.

Kollwitz, Käthe (1867–1945), artist. Kollwitz was born in Königsberg, and settled in Berlin after her marriage to a doctor in 1891. She was a committed socialist and pacifist whose subjects were poverty and the horror of war. Her son was killed in World War I and her grandson in World War II. She was professor at the Berlin Academy from 1919 to 1933, when she was removed from her post by the Nazis. She remained in Germany but was prohibited from exhibiting her work.

Köln. *See* COLOGNE.

Kolonialverein. See DEUTSCHER KOLONIAL-VEREIN.

Kolowrat(-Liebsteinsky), (Franz) Anton, Graf von (1778–1861), Austrian politician. Kolowrat was a Bohemian aristocrat who was mayor of Prague, governor of Bohemia and then a minister in the Austrian government in the later 1820s. Kolowrat's was the dominant voice in domestic affairs, and as something of a liberal he was an opponent of METTERNICH. He briefly became chief minister during the REVOLUTIONS OF 1848, but was forced to retire on health grounds.

Königgrätz, battle of. *See* SADOVÁ, BATTLE OF.

Königsberg, German name for Kaliningrad, a city of the USSR from 1945 to 1991 and of the Russian Republic since then. Königsberg was an old Hanseatic city, which had originally been established around a German fortress in the 13th century. It was the site of a university, the home of KANT, and became an important naval base. In 1945 it was almost totally destroyed by the Red Army, and rebuilt as a Soviet city when the northern part of East Prussia was transferred to the USSR after the end of World War II.

Konzentrationslager. *See* CONCENTRATION CAMPS.

Körner, Theodor (1873–1957), Austrian officer and politician. Körner served as an officer in World War I and was then director of the Army Office during the First Republic. He joined the Austrian Social Democratic Party (SDAP) in 1924, and was arrested and imprisoned without trial for eleven months during 1934. He was subsequently mayor of Vienna (1949–51) and federal president (1951–7).

Kotzebue, August von (1761–1819), writer. Kotzebue was born in Weimar and studied law at Jena. He travelled to Russia during the 1780s, and became a Russian government official in Estonia. He established a reputation as a popular playwright and travelled abroad on behalf of Russia and was assassinated as a 'Russian spy' in 1819 by a German radical, Karl Sand. His assassination prompted the repressive KARLSBAD DECREES introduced by the German princes under the leadership of Prince METTERNICH.

KPD (*Kommunistische Partei Deutschlands*), the German Communist Party. Founded between 30 December 1918 and 1 January 1919 on the basis of a merger between the Bremen radical left and the SPARTACUS LEAGUE, a group of radical socialists led by Karl LIEBKNECHT and Rosa LUXEMBURG. The formation of the party had important consequences for the German labour movement, which was split for the duration of the Weimar Republic. The party did not make an electoral impact initially. After the suppression of the Spartacus rising in Berlin in January 1919, and the murder of both

Liebknecht and Luxemburg by FREIKORPS members, the KPD boycotted elections to the constituent NATIONAL ASSEMBLY, and gained only 2.1% of the vote in the first Reichstag elections in June 1920. The party attracted new supporters with the collapse of the USPD in October of that year, however, and was involved in insurrections in 1921 and 1923. Its electoral success remained limited during the 1920s, but it attracted disillusioned Social Democrats during the Depression and won 16.9% of the vote in the November elections of 1932, by which time it had almost a third of a million members. Its principal constituency was among the unskilled working class and the unemployed. The party was affiliated to the Comintern, and accepted the 'social fascism' thesis, which identified the Social Democratic Party (SPD) as the principal impediment to a communist revolution in Germany. This policy exacerbated the division within the labour movement, and weakened the effectiveness of working-class resistance to the rise of the Nazis.

The KPD was the Nazis' first target after the appointment of Hitler as chancellor in January 1933, and the REICHSTAG FIRE was used as an excuse not only to smash the party, arrest and imprison its leaders and officials and close down its presses and other activities, but to suspend civil liberties in Germany as well. Communists accounted for a large proportion of the inmates of the first CONCENTRATION CAMPS. In the two years that followed, the party's underground organization was detected and destroyed by the Gestapo. While the party had expected prohibition it had not expected persecution and arrests on the scale that took place between 1933 and 1935, and its strategy for underground activity, based on hierarchical cells and easily detectable propaganda activity, was inadequate for survival. Disproportionate numbers of members suffered arrest, imprisonment, beatings, torture and murder as a result. Despite adopting a more flexible strategy, the party was unable to rebuild its resistance network, and its activities were compromised in any case by the Nazi–Soviet pact (the MOLOTOV–RIBBENTROP PACT) of 1939. Resistance activities were resumed with more success after the invasion of the Soviet Union, and regional networks were built up in large cities and conurbations where the party had formerly enjoyed strong support, such as Hamburg, Berlin and Munich, and the industrial regions of Saxony, Thuringia, the Rhineland and the Ruhr.

The KPD fared badly in West Germany after the end of World War II, not least as a consequence of the continuing presence of the Soviets in East Germany. In the East the party was merged in 1946 with the SPD to form the SED, the Socialist Unity Party of Germany – in effect a new East German Communist Party. In the West the KPD won 1.3 million votes (5.7%) in the election of 1949, and 15 seats in the Bundestag. In 1953, however, it won only 608,000, and with only 2.2% of the vote failed to enter parliament. The party was banned in West Germany during the Cold War by a decision of the FEDERAL CONSTITUTIONAL COURT (17 August 1956). A new communist party, the DKP (*DEUTSCHE KOMMUNISTISCHE PARTEI*), was established in the Federal Republic in 1968.

KPÖ (*Kommunistische Partei Österreichs*), the Austrian Communist Party. Founded in 1918 during the revolutionary upheavals that followed World War I, the KPÖ failed to win significant support either during the First Republic or after World War II. The relative radicalism of the Austrian Social Democratic Workers' Party (*Sozialdemokratische Arbeiterpartei*, SDAP) prevented the KPÖ from gaining a foothold in the 1920s, and it was only with the collapse of the parliamentary system and the establishment of the AUSTRO-FASCIST dictatorship under DOLLFUSS in 1933–4 that it attracted more followers. Communists were disproportionately overrepresented both in the resistance to Dollfuss and his successor SCHUSCHNIGG, and to

Nazism. After World War II the party participated in the provisional government of 1945. Its popularity declined rapidly, however, during the ten-year occupation of eastern Austria by the USSR, and it was last represented in the NATIONALRAT in 1959.

Krafft-Ebing, Richard, Freiherr von (1840–1902), psychiatrist. Krafft-Ebing was born in Mannheim and appointed professor of psychiatry at Strasbourg University at the age of 32. His interests were wide-ranging, but he is remembered above all for his work on sexual psychopathology. His best-known work, *Psychopathia sexualis*, was published in 1886.

Kraft durch Freude (Kdf). *See* STRENGTH THROUGH JOY

Kramer, Josef (1907–45), commandant of BIRKENAU and BERGEN-BELSEN concentration camps. Before this, Kramer served in a number of camps (Auschwitz, Dachau, Esterwagen, Sachsenhausen, Mauthausen and Natzweiler). He was condemned to death by a British military court in 1945.

Kraus, Karl (1874–1936), Austrian satirist and editor of the journal *Die Fackel* ('the torch'), which he wrote almost single-handedly from 1911. He was a scathing critic of Austrian politics and society, and was particularly sharp in his observation of the misuse of language by politicians, the state bureaucracy and the press. His best-known work is *Die letzten Tage der Menschheit* ('the last days of mankind'), an apocalyptic play written in 1918 and directed against World War I.

Kreipe, Werner (1904–67), air force officer. Kreipe began his career as a military cadet in an artillery regiment and moved to the air force in 1937. He served as chief of general staff of the 1st Flying Corps (1941–2) and chief of general staff of Air Fleet Command Don (1942–3). He was commander of the Air Force Academy at the end of the war, and subsequently head of the aviation division of the transport ministry (1961–7).

Kreisau circle, an anti-Nazi resistance group during the Third Reich. It took its name from the estate of Helmuth James, Graf von MOLTKE, one of the leaders of the group. The group first met in 1940, and consisted mainly of aristocrats, officers and civil servants, for the most part in their thirties and forties. They established contacts with the Social Democratic resistance and Roman Catholics. The members held discussions in 1942 and 1943, deliberating on the future of Europe after the collapse of the Third Reich, an eventuality for which they planned in some detail. The group was less conservative politically than the group around STAUFFENBERG, but many of them supported the 1944 JULY BOMB PLOT (although as a group they opposed a coup d'état in principle).

Krenz, Egon (1937–), East German politician. Krenz was born in Kolberg, Pomerania, and trained to be a teacher in Putbus on Rügen during the 1950s. He joined the *FREIE DEUTSCHE JUGEND* (FDJ) in 1953, became a member of the SED in 1955, and volunteered for service in the *NATIONALE VOLKSARMEE* in 1957. From 1967 to 1983 he was secretary of the central council of the FDJ, and became a close associate of Erich HONECKER. In 1983 he became a member of the Politburo, and the following year he effectively became Honecker's deputy when he was appointed deputy president of the STAATSRAT (State Council). He succeeded Honecker as party leader on 18 October 1989, and as head of government on 24 October, in the middle of the political collapse of the GERMAN DEMOCRATIC REPUBLIC. On 3 December he resigned along with the rest of the party leadership, and on 6 December he gave up the presidency of the Staatsrat. He was subsequently brought to trial for his responsibility for deaths on the border between East and West Germany, and sentenced to a term of imprisonment.

Kreuzberg, a district of Berlin. The area took its name from the cross carried by a statue of Victory erected on a hill there after the Wars of LIBERATION (1813–15). It became known during the cold-war division of Berlin for its political dissent and youth counter-culture.

Kreuzer (or **kreutzer**), old German silver coin widespread in the south from the 13th century, and generally worth about four PFENNIGS. Its name derives from the double cross on one side. It was abolished in 1873 (1892 in Austria).

Kreuzzeitung, name given to the *Neue Preussische Zeitung*, a conservative newspaper founded in 1848, on account of the iron cross emblem it carried on its title page. The name *Kreuzzeitungspartei* was applied to an extreme right-wing group within the *DEUTSCHKONSERVATIVE PARTEI*. The newspaper had a circulation of 8–10,000 in the three decades before World War I.

Kripo, short for *Kriminalpolizei*, criminal police. Under the Nazis the *Kripo* was a branch of the centralized police network run from Berlin by the Reich Security Head Office (*Reichssicherheitshauptamt*, RSHA) In the FEDERAL REPUBLIC OF GERMANY the criminal police has been organised on a federal basis, with a regional criminal police office (*Landeskriminalamt*) in each state. This office liaises with the federal criminal office (*Bundeskriminalamt*).

Kristallnacht (9–10 November 1938), 'crystal night' or 'night of broken glass', the pogrom organized by the Nazis after the assassination of Ernst vom Rath, a German diplomat in Paris by a Polish-Jewish student, Herschel GRYNSZPAN. On a single night, synagogues and other Jewish institutions were burned down, Jewish businesses and homes were looted and destroyed, and individual Jews were attacked, beaten and murdered. Jewish men were arrested and interned on a large scale immediately afterwards. The pogrom marked a sharp radicalization in the German government's ANTI-SEMITIC policies.

Krogmann, Karl Vincent (1889–1978), Nazi mayor of Hamburg. Krogmann was a wealthy shipping merchant who was elected president of the Hamburg senate and *Bürgermeister* in March 1933 during the Nazi takeover or 'coordination' (*Gleichschaltung*) of the federal states (*Länder*).

Krüger, Friedrich Wilhelm (1894–1945), SS *Obergruppenführer* and police chief in the GENERALGOUVERNEMENT (occupied Poland) during World War II. Krüger was born in Strasbourg, then under German rule, joined the NSDAP (Nazi Party) in November 1929 and was elected to the Reichstag for Frankfurt an der Oder in 1932. He joined the SS in April 1931 at the rank of *Sturmführer*. He was promoted to *Obergruppenführer* in 1935, police general in 1941, and Waffen-SS general in 1944. It is thought that he committed suicide in Austria in May 1945.

Krupp, Alfred (1812–87), industrialist. Born in Essen the son of Friedrich Krupp, whose ailing workshop he ran from the age of 14 following his father's death in 1826. He introduced technical innovations, and made the business a success, particularly with the advent of the railways. He bought out his mother for 40,000 TALER in 1848, at which point the firm employed 70 workers. In 1852 he developed a seamless railway tyre, and in 1862 was the first to use the Bessemer process (imported from Britain), which made possible the mass production of steel. In 1869 he was also the first manufacturer in Germany to use the Siemens–Martin process, which superseded it.

Krupp began to produce arms around 1847 and exhibited a cannon at the Great Exhibition in London in 1851. He was initially unable to sell arms in Prussia, however, and exported to Egypt and Russia. After the FRANCO-PRUSSIAN WAR the Krupp concern become synonymous with the German arms industry. The firm was inherited by his son Friedrich Alfred Krupp.

Krupp (von Bohlen und Halbach), Alfried (1907–67), German arms manufacturer. The son of Gustav KRUPP, Alfried studied engineering at Aachen Technical Institute before joining the family business. He joined the NSDAP (Nazi Party) in 1936 and took over the Krupp empire in 1943. Under his direction the company plundered the industrial plant of occupied Europe and exploited concentration-camp labour and foreign slave workers. He was tried at Nuremberg as a war criminal and sentenced to twelve years' imprisonment, but was released in 1951 following American intervention, and his estate was restored to him.

Krupp (von Bohlen und Halbach), Gustav (1870–1950), German arms manufacturer. He was 'Leader of the Reich Estate of German Industry' during the Third Reich. Born in Den Haag, Netherlands, Gustav von Bohlen und Halbach studied law at Strasbourg, Lausanne and Heidelberg after completing his military service in the Second Baden Dragoons. He then joined the diplomatic service and served in Washington, Beijing and the Vatican before marrying the sole heiress of the Krupp fortune, Bertha Krupp, in 1906. He changed his name at the time of his marriage (by special dispensation from the emperor) and, now Gustav Krupp von Bohlen und Halbach, he took over his wife's family company, maintaining its independence despite financial difficulties. Although his own politics were nationalist and he was hostile to the left and unsympathetic to parliamentary democracy, he was not actively involved in party politics during the Weimar Republic. His sympathies were a mixture of inherited Pan-Germanism and economic liberalism – he was opposed to state intervention and autarkic economic policies (*see* AUTARKY). As president of the German employers' organization, the Reich Association of German Industry (*Reichsverband der deutschen Industrie*, RDI) from 1931 he maintained a policy of political neutrality. After HITLER came to power he became director of the *Adolf-Hitler-Spende der deutschen Wirtschaft* (ADOLF HITLER FUND), a means of combining industry donations to the Nazis in a single payment.

Although the Krupp concern was perceived by the Nazis as indispensable to the rearmament process, the firm remained committed to the production of a range of goods. Like the German economy as a whole, however, it came under increasing pressure from the state to concentrate on arms and arms-related production. In the event Krupp proved a loyal servant of the regime and complied with its demands. He was named 'leader of the defence economy' in 1937 and awarded a Nazi party medal. During the war the Krupp concern employed some 100,000 slave workers, around 80% of whom died while working for the firm.

Krupp's own health deteriorated during the war. He suffered from progressive arteriosclerosis from 1939 and had a stroke in 1942. He retired to his estate in Austria in 1944 after persuading Hitler to pass a law (the so-called Lex Krupp of 1943, which made his son Alfried KRUPP von Bohlen und Halbach the sole heir) converting the firm back to the status of a family business, thereby avoiding tax on his inheritance. He was injured in a car accident in December 1944, and suffered a further stroke at the beginning of 1945, which resulted in loss of speech and severe brain damage, leaving him semi-paralysed and incontinent. This infirmity prevented him from being tried at Nuremberg despite being indicted as a major war criminal.

Kühlmann, Richard von (1873–1948), Reich secretary of state for foreign affairs (foreign minister), 1917–18). Following diplomatic postings in London (1908–14) and Constantinople (1914–15), Kühlmann was ambassador to the Netherlands (1915–16) and Constantinople (1916–17). As secretary of state for foreign affairs from August 1917 to June 1918, he negotiated the treaties of BREST-LITOVSK and BUCHAREST. He was dismissed after telling the Reichstag that the war was not winnable solely by military means.

Kulturkampf, the 'cultural struggle' or 'conflict' during the 1870s between BISMARCK and the liberals on one hand and the Roman Catholic community in Germany on the other. The *Kulturkampf* was also located, however, in a broader, long-term conflict between the Vatican and the forces of 'modernity', especially liberalism and the nation-state. Pope Pius IX condemned civil marriage and civil education in his *Syllabus errorum* of 1864, thereby marking out the territory on which the struggle between church and state would take place for over a century. In 1870 the Vatican adopted the doctrine of papal infallibility. The more specific conflict between German Catholics and the Bismarckian empire in the NATIONAL LIBERAL era immediately followed the unification of Germany. Although there had already been anti-Catholic legislation in 1871 and 1872, including interference in Catholic education and the prohibition of the Jesuit order, the *Kulturkampf* is generally dated from the promulgation of the so-called 'May Laws' of 1873. Civil marriage was introduced in 1875 and monastic orders other than those that cared for the sick were closed down. The Catholic community was strengthened rather than weakened by the laws, however, and the Catholic CENTRE PARTY more than doubled its electoral support in 1874. With the death of the pope in 1878 Bismarck took the opportunity of opening negotiations, and most of the anticlerical measures were repealed. Such a conflict between church and state was not unusual in Europe during the second half of the century, particularly where liberals were in power, and the new pope, Leo XIII, pursued a more pragmatic policy in an effort to come to terms with modern social and political developments.

Külz, Wilhelm (1875–1948), liberal politician. Born in Leipzig into a conservative family of Protestant pastors, Külz studied law and in 1904 became mayor of Bückeburg in Schaumburg-Lippe (now in Lower Saxony). He was also president of the LANDTAG in Schaumburg-Lippe. He was Reich commissioner in German SOUTH-WEST AFRICA (1907–8), and returned to Germany to become mayor of Zittau in Saxony in 1912. Külz joined the liberal DDP in 1919, and was elected first to the NATIONAL ASSEMBLY and then to the Reichstag, where he sat first for the DDP and then (from 1930) for its successor, the *Deutsche Staatspartei* (until 1932). He was interior minister in the second LUTHER administration and in the third MARX government (May–December 1926).

Kursk, battles of (1943), key engagement during the Soviet campaign of World War II. Kursk had fallen to the Germans with little resistance, and was retaken by the Soviets in February 1943 after the German debacle at STALINGRAD. At Kursk the Soviets had established a salient that projected westwards into German-held territory. In Operation Citadel of spring 1943, Hitler made it a priority to 'pinch out' the Kursk salient in a manageable operation that would set the Soviets back, and give the impression of an offensive to the home public, despite the fact that Germany's overall strategy was now effectively determined by defensive considerations. The transformation of a limited operation into a major offensive with potential political repercussions caused sufficient delay to allow the Soviets to assemble an army of 1.3 million men. The battle began in early July and the Soviets wiped out the northern pincer of the attack almost immediately. The southern pincer was then also repulsed in a decisive conflict on 11–12 July, the biggest tank battle of the war, and the German offensive was held, undermining the rationale of the larger operation. The Germans never recovered from their losses at Kursk, and it became the last significant German offensive of the war on the Eastern Front.

KZ (*Konzentrationslager*). *See* CONCENTRATION CAMP.

L

Labour Front. *See* DAF.

Labour Service. *See* RAD.

Labour Service Law (26 June 1935), Nazi law making labour service obligatory for all men between the ages of 18 and 25 for a period of six months. Labour service for women was voluntary until 1939. Part of the intention of the Reich Labour Service (the RAD), enshrined in the wording of the law, was to educate people into the dignity of labour, and especially manual labour. In the event, however, it served to alienate more than educate.

Lagarde, Paul Anton de (1827–91), writer. Born Paul Bötticher in Berlin, Lagarde was a biblical scholar, professor of oriental languages at Göttingen University, and a radical right-wing polemicist. His academic work included several translations of the Old Testament and gospels into oriental and ancient languages as well as writings on theology and the church. He decried the effects on German society of liberalism, materialism and secularism, and published extensively on current affairs in the second half of the 19th century. Lagarde was a xenophobic anti-semite, whose work was particularly influential in the *völkisch* movements, and an intellectual hero of the Nazi party.

Laibach, Congress of (1821), a meeting of the European powers in order to resume the business of the Congress of TROPPAU (1820). The king of the Two Sicilies was also present. Austrian troops were charged with the busi-ness of restoring order in Italy following the outbreak of revolution in Naples and Pied-mont, and they quickly suppressed the insurgents in both states. In a circular sent to all their ambassadors at foreign courts, the members of the HOLY ALLIANCE (Russia, Austria and Prussia) jointly reaffirmed their reasons for intervening in the affairs of another state where the monarchy there was threatened.

See also CONGRESS SYSTEM.

Lambsdorff, Otto, Graf (1926–), liberal politician. Lambsdorff was born in Aachen and came to prominence as a politician in the FDP during the 1960s. He was party trea-surer from 1968 to 1978, and was elected to the Bundestag in 1972. From 1978 to 1982 he was economics minister in Helmut SCHMIDT's 'social–liberal' coalition, and was party chairman of the FDP from 1988 to 1993. Lambsdorff was implicated in a scan-dal surrounding the financing of political parties during the 1980s (*see* FLICK AFFAIR).

Lammasch, Heinrich (1853–1920), Austrian politician; minister-president (27 October– 10 November 1918). An academic lawyer by profession, Lammasch was professor at Inns-bruck in the 1880s and Vienna from 1899. Lammasch was an associate of Archduke FRANZ FERDINAND, whom he advised on reform of the Austrian criminal law, and at the end of World War I served briefly as the last Austrian minister-president of the empire. After the war he was a member of the Austrian delegation negotiating the treaty of ST GERMAIN.

Lammers, Hans Heinrich (1879–1962), head of the REICH CHANCELLERY (1933–45). Born in Upper Silesia, Lammers studied law at Breslau and Heidelberg and entered the Prussian civil service before serving in World War I. After the war he was a ministerial counsellor in the interior ministry (from 1922). He got to know Hitler in the same year, but did not join the Nazi Party until 1932. He was state secretary and head of the Reich Chancellery from 30 January 1933, when Hitler became chancellor. He remained head of the Reich Chancellery until 1945, with the rank of minister without portfolio from 1937, and was appointed a member of the Ministerial Council for the Defence of the Reich in 1939. An honorary SS general from 1940, Lammers (along with BORMANN) controlled access to Hitler, and chaired the cabinet in his absence. He lost favour in 1945 by supporting GÖRING in a bid to assume the leadership. After the war he was tried for war crimes at Nuremberg (1949) and sentenced to 20 years' imprisonment, but the sentence was reduced (twice) and he was released in 1954.

Land (plural: *Länder*), a province, or (federal) state, for example, Bavaria.

Landsberg, centre-right faction in the 1848 FRANKFURT PARLIAMENT. Almost two-thirds of its members were senior civil servants.

Landsberg, Otto (1869–1957), Social Democratic politician. Landsberg was born into a middle-class Jewish family in Rybnik, Upper Silesia. His father was a country doctor. He studied law at Berlin, joined the SPD in 1890, and was elected to the Reichstag for Magdeburg in 1912. Landsberg was on the right of the party, and a staunch ally of Friedrich EBERT. As one of the three original MSPD (Majority SPD) members of the COUNCIL OF PEOPLE'S REPRESENTATIVES during the NOVEMBER REVOLUTION of 1918, he had responsibility for justice and finance. He was also a member of the German peace delega-

tion to Versailles. He was justice minister in the SCHEIDEMANN administration, but resigned in protest at the treaty of VERSAILLES in June 1919, and went as German ambassador to Brussels in 1920. He returned to Germany in 1923, and practised as a lawyer. He was elected to the Reichstag again for the SPD in 1924, and remained a deputy until the Nazis came to power in 1933, when he fled to the Netherlands. He stayed in the Netherlands during and after the war, surviving the German occupation. He died in Baarn near Utrecht. Landsberg was a founding member of the Association for Defence against Anti-Semitism (*Verein zur Abwehr des Antisemitismus*) in 1890.

Landsberg am Lech, small town in Bavaria where Hitler was briefly imprisoned after the failed BEER HALL PUTSCH of 1923. He composed *MEIN KAMPF* while incarcerated there.

Landtag, provincial or federal state diet, the parliament of a *LAND*.

Lang, Fritz (1890–1976), Austrian film director. Lang, the son of an architect, was born in Vienna and studied architecture at the Technische Hochschule there. He left Vienna when he was 20 to travel abroad in Africa, Turkey, Russia and the Far East. He settled in Paris in 1913, and returned to Vienna the following year, serving in the Austrian army during World War I. He was wounded several times and was discharged in 1916. He began writing screenplays while recovering in hospital. After the war he moved to Berlin to work for the Decla Bioscop Company, and in 1920 he married the writer Thea von HARBOU. He directed a number of important silent films between the end of the war and the release of his best-known film, *Metropolis* (1927), a dystopian expressionist drama that depicted a futuristic slave society. His other well-known film, *M* (1931), the story of a child killer, was the first German sound film. In *Das Testament des Dr. Mabuse* (*The Testament of Dr Mabuse*, 1932) he showed a madman spouting Nazi ideology, and was invited by GOEBBELS to take over as director of the Nazis' film production. He left Germany for Paris, however, and was divorced by his wife, who stayed behind to work for the Nazis. *M* was denounced as degenerate. He settled in America in 1935 and directed a further 23 mainly undistinguished Hollywood films over a period of some twenty years. He returned to Germany in 1960 to make *The Thousand Eyes of Dr Mabuse*.

Langemarck Schools, Nazi institutions for children in their mid-teens. Their objective was to provide 18 months' training for university entry for the benefit of pupils from disadvantaged backgrounds.

Langhans, Carl Gotthard (1732–1808), architect and director of the Court Planning and Building Department (*Oberhofbauamt*) in Berlin. Langhans was born in Landeshut, Silesia, and studied law in Halle. He worked as an architect in Silesia until 1788, when he was called to Berlin by Friedrich Wilhelm II and appointed director of the *Oberhofbauamt*. In this capacity he was responsible for overseeing the construction of the BRANDENBURG GATE (1788–91). He was a member of the Prussian Academy of Arts from 1786, and was also responsible for the construction of a number of theatres in Berlin, Potsdam and Charlottenburg.

Lasch, Agathe (1879–1942?), philologist. Lasch was the first female professor of linguistics. She worked initially on the history of the written language in Berlin up to 1600, and then on language and languages in cities. She published a history of Berlin dialect, *Berlinisch: Eine berlinische Sprachgeschichte* ('Berlinisch' a history of the language of Berlin') in 1928. Lasch was Jewish, and was deported to the Łódź ghetto in 1942, where she died.

Lassalle, Ferdinand (1825–64), socialist politician. Lassalle was born in Breslau into a well-to-do Jewish family and studied philosophy at Berlin. In 1863 he organized the General German Workers' Association (ADAV), effectively Germany's first labour party. Lassalle had got to know Karl MARX in the Rhineland

during the REVOLUTIONS OF 1848, but there was some rivalry between them, and Marx and ENGELS thought Lassalle's knowledge of economics superficial and his political tactics questionable: in 1863, for example, Lassalle began to meet Bismarck in the hope of achieving universal suffrage and welfare measures within the political framework of the existing state. Marx also objected strongly, and in some detail, to the Lassallean GOTHA PROGRAMME adopted at the 1875 'unity conference' where the ADAV merged with the Social Democratic Workers' Party (SDAP) to form the SPD. Lassalle led a flamboyant life and was killed in a duel.

LDPD (*Liberal-Demokratische Partei Deutschlands*), the Liberal Democratic Party of Germany, an East German political party. The LDPD was founded on 5 July 1945 as a fourth political grouping in the Soviet zone of occupation. The party was forced into the so-called 'National Front' during the late 1940s, and was from then on effectively subordinate to the ruling SED (the Communist-dominated Socialist Unity Party). The LDPD's president from 1962 to 1990 was Manfred GERLACH. As the political system of the German Democratic Republic began to collapse the party sought to take advantage of events to relaunch itself as a genuinely liberal democratic party, and to assume a new political role. An extraordinary conference was held in 1990, where the party was renamed simply Liberal Democratic Party (*Liberal-Demokratische Partei*, LDP). The LDP was subsumed into the FDP.

League of Nations, an international organization established in 1920 (under the terms of the treaty of VERSAILLES) to preserve the peace and mediate in international disputes. Although it was supported by President Wilson, the USA never joined. Its initial membership consisted of 32 states hostile to Germany and 13 neutrals. The CENTRAL POWERS were initially excluded. Germany joined on 8 September 1926 following negotiations at LOCARNO, and was admitted as a permanent member of the League Council. The admission of Germany marked a milestone in STRESEMANN'S policy of *rapprochement* with France. Germany left the League again, in October 1933, within months of the establishment of the Nazi dictatorship.

League of Outlaws, revolutionary sect of the 1830s. In 1834 it issued a declaration of human and citizens' rights containing a mixture of political and economic demands. It wanted reform of the judicial system, and an end to the arbitrary powers of the state and to oppression or disproportionate punishment. It also asserted that society should aim to ensure the well-being of all its members by guaranteeing people the means of earning a living that would afford them the possibility of a dignified life, and not merely one that would ensure them the barest minimum for existence.

Lebensborn ('fountain of life'), SS society founded in 1935. According to HIMMLER it was started on the premise that there was a need to provide both antenatal and postnatal treatment and accommodation for 'racially satisfactory' women bearing illegitimate children. It was an initiative that formed part of a broader 'racial' challenge to conventional morality. If the parents and child were racially acceptable, then procreation was to be encouraged, and the stigma of illegitimacy should not be allowed to stand in the way. Women were accommodated in maternity homes, nominal legitimation of the children was arranged, as was adoption if it was necessary. It was not a charitable organization, however: the racial credentials of the parents and their families were to be thoroughly checked by the SS Race and Settlement Office (RUSHA). The history of the *Lebensborn* homes has been obscured by their depiction as SS brothels or 'stud farms' in postwar popular culture and journalism.

Lebensraum ('living space'), term used to describe territory to be gained for German settlement in eastern Europe and Russia.

Premised on the notion that Germany was overcrowded and had no overseas outlet for its dynamic energies, the concept of *Lebensraum* in the east was an important element in the rhetoric of Nazi foreign policy. It was an idea that grew out of the experience of blockade during World War I, when Germany had also been briefly successful in subordinating eastern Europe and the Ukraine to German domination, following the 1918 treaty of BREST-LITOVSK with Russia. The conquest of the territory for settlement and exploitation by Germany seemed not only achievable to the Nazis, but also compatible with *VÖLKISCH* (Nazi and German nationalist) notions of racial superiority over the Slavs. The territory that was conquered in eastern Europe and Russia during World War II was subjected to brutal plunder. Local elites were massacred, Jews deported to death camps and murdered, and thousands of slave workers (*Ostarbeiter*) transported to the Reich to work.

Leber, Julius (1891–1945), Social Democratic politician and journalist. A Reichstag deputy, he was imprisoned in concentration camps between 1933 and 1937 and became involved with resistance circles after his release. He was close to the KREISAU CIRCLE and Claus von STAUFFENBERG, but was arrested before the assassination attempt of 1944 (*see* JULY BOMB PLOT) and executed in October of that year.

Leers, Johann von (1902–65), anti-Semitic writer. A member of the NSDAP from 1929, Leers was employed by the Nazi regime to write crude anti-Semitic propaganda for popular consumption. He was also appointed professor at Jena. After the war he fled to Italy and Argentina, was employed by General Nasser in Egypt, and died in Cairo.

Legion Condor. *See* CONDOR LEGION.

Leichter, Käthe (1895–1942), Austrian socialist. Leichter was an active trade unionist and director of the women's section of the Vienna Chamber of Labour. After the suppression of the Social Democratic Workers'

Party (*Sozialdemokratische Arbeiterpartei*, SDAP) in 1934 she was involved in the underground resistance activity of its radical wing, the Revolutionary Socialists. She was arrested in May 1938 and imprisoned at Ravensbrück concentration camp, where she died.

Leipzig, battle of (16–19 October 1813), also called the 'battle of the nations', engagement during the Wars of LIBERATION in which Napoleon was decisively defeated by Austrian, Prussian, Russian and Swedish armies numbering 205,000 men against his 190,000. Following the retreat from Moscow of 1812 it marked the end of Napoleon's ambitions in the east.

Lenya, Lotte (1898–1981), Austrian actress and singer. Lenya studied ballet and drama in Zurich (1914–20), and established a reputation in the German theatre during the Weimar Republic. She was most closely associated with the works of BRECHT and WEILL (to whom she was married). In 1933 she moved to Paris and then to the United States.

Leopold II (1747–92), Holy Roman emperor (1790–2), and king of Hungary and (from 1791) Bohemia. Leopold was the son of MARIA THERESIA and the emperor FRANZ I and was Archduke of Tuscany (1765–90) before succeeding his brother JOSEPH II. His short reign came at the turbulent end of a long period of reforms, some of which he repealed. He took Austria into the War of the First COALITION with Prussia shortly before his death in 1792.

Lessing, Gotthold Ephraim (1729–81), ENLIGHTENMENT writer and critic. Lessing, the son of a pastor, was born in Kamenz, Saxony, and was a student at Leipzig University. He moved to Berlin in 1748 and published the pioneering journal *Briefe, die neueste Literatur betreffend* ('letters on the most recent literature') between 1759 and 1765. Lessing moved to Breslau (now Wrocław in Poland) in 1760, where he remained until 1765. He lived in Hamburg (1767–9), and then moved on to Wolfen-

büttel, where he was librarian to the duke of Braunschweig. Lessing was one of the most important figures of the 18th century in establishing an indigenous German literature and cultural life. His own best-known works are the plays *Miss Sara Sampson* (1755), *Minna von Barnhelm* (1767), *Emilia Galotti* (1772) and *Nathan der Weise* (1779).

Leuschner, Wilhelm (1890–1944), trade unionist and Social Democratic politician. Leuschner was Hessian interior minister for the SPD from 1929, but was arrested by the Nazis in May 1933 and sent to a concentration camp. After his release he became involved with resistance circles around BECK and STAUFFENBERG. He was arrested after the failure of the JULY BOMB PLOT and hanged in September 1944.

Ley, Robert (1890–1945), leader of the German Labour Front (DAF). A chemistry graduate and World War I pilot, Ley worked for IG FARBEN after the war and joined the NSDAP (Nazi Party) in 1924. He was elected to the Prussian LANDTAG in 1928 and the Reichstag in 1930. He became Reich organization leader in 1932 and leader of the German Labour Front, created to replace the FREE TRADE UNIONS, in 1933. He committed suicide in 1945.

Liberal-Demokratische Partei Deutschlands (Liberal Democratic Party of Germany). See LDPD.

Liberation, Wars of (1813–15), European conflict following the retreat of Napoleon from Russia; together with the earlier Wars of the COALITIONS they constitute what are also known as the Revolutionary and Napoleonic Wars. The Wars of Liberation were an important factor in the gestation of a modern German national consciousness.

The wars had their origins in the convention of Tauroggen, which permitted Russian troops to enter East Prussia and provided for a levee en masse there against Napoleon (the so-called *Landwehr*). Prussia then declared war on France in March 1813. METTERNICH, on behalf of Austria, negotiated with both sides and effected a temporary truce (the armistice of Pleiswitz, June 1813). Austria declared war in August, however, and Napoleon was defeated at the battle of LEIPZIG in October 1813. Napoleon's hegemony in Europe came to an end and the French-dominated CONFEDERATION OF THE RHINE was dissolved. While the Duke of Wellington led a British army into France from Spain, BLÜCHER and SCHWARZENBERG pursued Napoleon to Paris, where France accepted defeat in 1814. By the first treaty of PARIS France was reduced to its 1792 boundaries and the monarchy restored. The peace was disturbed again, however, when Napoleon returned from exile in Elba, landed in Cannes in March 1815, raised an army and engaged the coalition forces at WATERLOO. After his defeat there he was exiled to St Helena. There followed the second treaty of PARIS.

Count STADION, the Austrian foreign minister, had appealed to German patriots (and patriots of the other HABSBURG nationalities) during the War of the Fifth Coalition (1809), and the first significant generation of German nationalists had felt humiliated by the course and consequences of the Wars of the COALITIONS. The Wars of Liberation – which began with the raising of popular armies against the French, the organization of independent units (*Freikorps*) and Freiherr vom STEIN's call for a national German constitution – proved to be a formative experience in the development of German nationalism. However, German nationalist hopes were for the moment dashed by the restoration of the prewar status quo by the Congress of VIENNA, and by the establishment of the Austrian-dominated GERMAN CONFEDERATION.

Lichnowsky, Karl Max, Fürst (1860–1928), diplomat. Following minor diplomatic appointments in London, Stockholm, Constantinople, Dresden and Bucharest, Lichnowsky was ambassador to Austria, Britain, Russia and Italy in turn. In 1912 he was recalled from retirement by the Kaiser and sent back to London, where he was German ambassador during the two years leading up to the outbreak of World War I in 1914. There he played a key role in the so-called JULY CRISIS of 1914, attempting to defuse the crisis, and arguing against unconditional German support for Austria-Hungary. Following discussions with the British foreign secretary, Sir Edward Grey, Lichnowsky made it clear to Berlin on 27 July 1914 that the British government was convinced the key to resolving the diplomatic crisis lay in Berlin. Two days later he passed on a warning from Grey that Britain would not stay neutral if Germany attacked France. Ultimately, however, Lichnowsky's own interpretation of the developing situation led him to suggest – misguidedly – that Britain might remain neutral even if France were attacked; and even after the outbreak of war, he suggested that Britain was bound to break off the war quickly, not least for economic reasons.

Lidice, a small village in central Bohemia. It was the site of a massacre on 10 June 1942, ordered by Hitler as a reprisal for the assassination of deputy Reich protector of Bohemia and Moravia, Reinhard HEYDRICH. Along with another village (Lezaky), Lidice was razed to the ground. 189 men were shot, 184 women were sent to Ravensbrück and eleven others to prison. The children were placed with German families under the LEBENSBORN programme.

Liebermann, Max (1847–1935), German artist. Born in Berlin, Liebermann spent several years in Paris in his youth and returned to Germany in 1878 to establish a reputation as a leading German impressionist. A co-founder of the Berlin SECESSION, he was president of the Academy of Arts from 1920 to 1930. He was forced to resign in 1933 and died two years later in Berlin. His work was categorized 'degenerate' by the Nazis (*see* DEGENERATE ART).

Liebknecht, Karl (1871–1919), revolutionary socialist. Liebknecht was born in Leipzig, the son of the Social Democrat politician and journalist Wilhelm LIEBKNECHT and his wife Nathalie. He studied law and economics at Leipzig and Berlin, and took a doctorate in Würzburg in 1897. He joined the SPD in 1900, and was elected to the Berlin city council the following year. In 1900 Liebknecht married Julia Paradies. They had two children, but his wife died in 1911. He was president of the Socialist Youth International from 1907 to 1910, but in 1907 was sentenced to one and a half years in prison for high treason following the publication of his pamphlet *Militarismus und Antimiltarismus* (1907). He was elected to the Prussian LANDTAG in 1908, during his term of imprisonment. He was elected to the Reichstag for the SPD in 1912, and belonged to the extreme left of the Social Democratic parliamentary party. In the same year he married his second wife, the art historian Sophie Ryss.

Liebknecht was the only member of the Reichstag to break the domestic truce (*BURGFRIEDEN*) between the government and the political opposition at the beginning of World War I. Although he adhered to SPD party discipline and voted for war credits at the outbreak of war in August 1914, he refused to vote for further war credits on 2 December, the only member of the Reichstag to do so. Along with Rosa LUXEMBURG he was the leader of a dissident group of Social Democrats, the so-called *Gruppe Internationale*, which was founded on 1 January 1916, and was also known by the name of its journal, *Spartakus*. He was expelled from the parliamentary party. On 1 May 1916 he helped to organize a peace demonstration on the Postdamer Platz in Berlin and was arrested and sentenced to four years for high treason. He was released with the general amnesty of October 1918, and, with Rosa Luxemburg, assumed the leadership of the SPARTACUS LEAGUE. He was a co-founder of the German Communist Party (KPD) at a meeting of 30 December 1918–1 January

1919, and helped to organize the Spartacus uprising in Berlin two weeks later. Along with Rosa Luxemburg he was abducted, brutally interrogated and then murdered by members of a right-wing paramilitary FREIKORPS unit deployed by the government to suppress the uprising.

Liebknecht, Wilhelm (1826–1900), socialist activist and politician. Born in Giessen, the son of a Hessian civil servant, Liebknecht was orphaned in 1832 and brought up by relatives. He was educated at the *Gymnasium* (grammar school) in Giessen, and studied philology, theology and philosophy at Giessen, Marburg and Berlin. He took part in the Paris REVOLUTION OF 1848, and was imprisoned briefly. After his release he fled to Switzerland, where he was also arrested and deported for his activities in Swiss-German labour politics. He then travelled to London, where he joined the Communist League and got to know Karl MARX and Friedrich ENGELS. In 1862 he returned to Germany following a general amnesty for participants in the 1848 revolutions, and the following year he joined LASSALLE's *Allgemeiner Deutscher Arbeiterverein* (General German Workers' Association, the ADAV). Liebknecht was expelled from the party following differences with Jean-Bapiste von Schweitzer, the editor of the journal *Der Social-Demokrat*, to which he had contributed. He was also expelled from Berlin, and settled in Leipzig, where he got to know August BEBEL. With Bebel he founded the Saxon People's Party (*Sächsische Volkspartei*), and both men were elected to the diet of the NORTH GERMAN CONFEDERATION. Liebknecht subsequently became a leader of the Social Democratic Workers' Party (*Sozialdemokratische Arbeiterpartei*, SDAP). In 1871 Liebknecht voted against further war credits for the Franco-Prussian War. After a further spell in prison he was elected to the Reichstag in 1874, and was closely involved in the merger of the ADAV and the SDAP to form the Socialist Workers' Party (*Sozialistische Arbeiterpartei*, SAPD, later the

SPD) in Gotha in 1875. During the years of anti-socialist repression in the 1880s (*see* ANTI-SOCIALIST LAWS) Liebknecht used his Reichstag seat as a platform to criticize the government, and also travelled widely abroad. He became editor of the party journal (*Vorwärts*) in 1891, and was closely involved in the reshaping of the SPD as a Marxist party at Erfurt (*see* ERFURT PROGRAMME). In 1896, at the age of 70, he was arrested and imprisoned on a charge of lese majesty. His son was the revolutionary socialist Karl LIEBKNECHT.

Lippe, a principality in northern Germany until the end of WORLD WAR II. It was integrated into NORTH RHINE-WESTPHALIA in 1947.

List, Friedrich (1789–1846), economist. Born in Reutlingen, the son of an artisan, List was appointed to a chair in government at Tübingen in 1817 and was elected to the Württemberg LANDTAG in 1820. He made his reputation as a liberal opponent of tariffs on behalf of the south German industrialists. As a result he lost his teaching post in 1820 and his seat in the Landtag in 1821. He was imprisoned for his political views, and released only when he undertook to emigrate to the United States. On his return to Germany he argued for the construction of a German national railway network and campaigned on behalf of a customs union. He also now argued for protectionist measures to assist German industry through its early stages. He proposed a semi-protectionist 'national system' in Germany, and envisaged its expansion into southeast central Europe: Austria should be in the German customs union (*ZOLLVEREIN*), he wrote in 1843; its railway connection to Trieste would bring that port a 'German national' significance. He also proposed subsidies to divert German emigrants from North America to southeastern central Europe. Impoverished and disappointed at the lack of response to his ideas, List committed suicide in Kufstein, Austria, in 1846.

List, Johann Georg (1753–1806), revolutionary activist. Born in Karlsruhe, the son of a privy councillor and surgeon to the marquis of Baden, List studied medicine and in 1789 became manager of the Battier company in Basle. There he organized a revolutionary society, and was forced to move to Strasbourg after undertaking espionage expeditions against the Austrian army. He became one of the leaders of the revolutionary movement in southern Germany, and eventually moved to Mainz, where he worked in the French service as a hospital inspector.

Little Entente, an originally pejorative term for alliances between Czechoslovakia, Yugoslavia and Romania in 1920 and 1921 against the possibility of Austrian or Hungarian revisionism.

Litzmannstadt, German name invented during the Third Reich for the Polish town of Łódź.

Löbe, Paul (1875–1967), Social Democratic journalist and politician. Born in Liegnitz, the son of a joiner, Löbe was editor of *Die Volkswacht* in Breslau from 1899. He was elected to Weimar's constituent NATIONAL ASSEMBLY (1919) and was a member of the Reichstag (1920–33) for the SPD. Imprisoned by the Nazis briefly in 1933 and in a concentration camp from 1944, he resumed his political career after the war. He was a member of the PARLIAMENTARY COUNCIL in the western zones of occupation (1948–9) and served in the Bundestag from 1949 to 1953.

Locarno treaties (16 October 1925), the outcome of a multilateral conference called to regulate Germany's relations with the other major powers in western Europe. The conference built on German proposals and produced a series of treaties that were informally agreed at the conference, and then formally signed in London on 1 December 1925. The principal outcome was the treaty of Mutual Guarantee, in which Germany, Belgium, France, Italy and the United Kingdom recognized the Reich's western borders and the status of the demilitarized zone. Britain and Italy were guarantors of the agreement. In addition bilateral arbitration conventions were agreed between Germany and Belgium, and Germany and France. There was no similar general agreement to recognize Germany's eastern frontiers. Instead, separate arbitration treaties were agreed between Germany and Poland, and Germany and Czechoslovakia. These were guaranteed in turn by separate treaties between France and Poland, and France and Czechoslovakia respectively. The Locarno treaties generated resentment on the revisionist, anti-VER-SAILLES right of German politics, despite the fact that they were at best an ambivalent recognition of the new international order – conciliatory towards the more powerful West, but less so to the weaker successor states in eastern central Europe. Nevertheless, the treaties were an enormous success for the German foreign minister, Gustav STRESEMANN, a revisionist VERNUNFTREPUB-LIKANER himself. By recognizing Germany's western borders he hoped to prevent a further French incursion into German territory like the occupation of the RUHR VALLEY in 1923, and thereby to reassure foreign investors, principally in the United States, that German industry was a secure investment. Stresemann also negotiated the dissolution of the Inter-Allied Military Control Commission. In the longer term Germany joined the League of Nations with a permanent seat on the council, and Allied troops withdrew from the west bank of the Rhine in 1930, five years ahead of schedule. In 1926 Stresemann and the French foreign minister, Aristide Briand, shared the Nobel Peace Prize for their work on the Locarno treaties.

Lohse, Heinrich (1896–1964), Nazi administrator. Lohse was *Gauleiter* of Schleswig-Holstein from 1925 until the end of the war and Reich commissioner for the 'Ostland' (the Baltic and Belorussia) from 1941 to 1944. He was arrested and tried by a de-nazifica-tion court in Bielefeld, but although sentenced to ten years' imprisonment in 1948, he was released in 1951. He died in his native Mühlenbarbek, Schleswig-Holstein.

London, treaty of (5 September 1914), agreement signed immediately after the outbreak of WORLD WAR I by France, Russia and Britain, by which the three powers of the Triple Entente undertook not to conclude a separate peace with the CENTRAL POWERS.

London Protocol (1852). *See* SCHLESWIG-HOLSTEIN.

Lothringen, the German name for Lorraine (*see* ALSACE-LORRAINE).

Lower Saxony, the second largest of the constituent federal states (*Länder*) of modern Germany. Its state capital is Hanover. At the end of the 20th century Lower Saxony had a population of 7.4 million. The SPD has been the largest party in the LANDTAG for much of the postwar period. It was overtaken by the CDU in 1974, and did not regain its leading position until 1990. The FDP won no seats in the elections of 1970, 1978, 1994 and 1998, but the GREENS have been represented consistently since 1982. Radical right-wing parties won seats for the first twenty years after the war, culminating in ten seats for the neo-Nazi NPD in 1967. The Communists (KPD) won a diminishing share of the vote and a handful of seats before the party was banned in 1956.

Lubbe, Marinus van der (1909–34), Dutch Communist. Lubbe was found in the burning Reichstag building in 1933. He was charged with starting the REICHSTAG FIRE, found guilty of high treason in an unconvincing show trial and executed.

Ludendorff, Erich (1865–1937), military leader during WORLD WAR I and supporter of the radical right during the WEIMAR REPUBLIC. Ludendorff was born, the son of a landowner, in Kruszwenia in the Prussian province of Posen (Polish: Poznań). He was educated at the cadet school in Gross-Lichterfelde, Berlin, and pursued a military career before the outbreak of World War I.

He led the assault and capture of Liège in 1914, and was then moved to the Eastern Front, where his expertise was invaluable to HINDENBURG in the German victories of TANNENBERG and the MASURIAN LAKES. In 1916 Ludendorff contributed to the downfall of army chief of staff, General FALKENHAYN. Falkenhayn was succeeded by Hindenburg, and Ludendorff became the latter's second in command as quartermaster of the German army. Along with Hindenburg he began to extend his power into the political sphere, and was instrumental in the overthrow of the chancellor, BETHMANN HOLLWEG (July 1917), after which the two men established a virtual military dictatorship in which Ludendorff played the key role. At the end of the war Ludendorff suffered a nervous breakdown and resigned. He subsequently took part in the BEER HALL PUTSCH of 1923 with Hitler, sat as a Reichstag deputy for the *DEUTSCHVÖLKISCHE FREIHEITSPARTEI* (German National Freedom Party) from 1924 to 1928 and stood against Hindenburg in the 1925 presidential election. The same year he founded an ostensibly religious 'Germanic' society, the TANNENBERG LEAGUE, from rightwing youth groups and veterans associations. He broke with the Nazis in 1928 and founded another religious society called the *Deutschvolk* in 1930. His politics became increasingly eccentric and he was estranged from most of his former colleagues before his death. In 1933 both the Tannenberg League and the *Deutschvolk* were banned by the Nazis, and although Ludendorff gained permission from Hitler in 1937 to set up a new religious community, he died in December of the same year.

Ludin, Hanns Elard (1905–47), Nazi diplomat. Ludin was born in Freiburg, and was a Reichswehr officer in the 1920s. He was detained for political activities on behalf of the Nazi Party during the Depression (1930–1), and served briefly during World War II (1939–40) before going to Bratislava as German minister to the Nazi puppet state

of Slovakia. He was hanged in Czechoslovakia after the war.

Ludwig II (1845–86), 'Ludwig the mad', king of Bavaria (1864–86). Ludwig acceded to the throne in 1864 on the death of his father Maximilian II. Ludwig was a political conservative, and something of a German patriot. In 1870 he joined Prussia in preference to an alliance with France, and in return for privileged status for Bavaria within the new Reich, he appealed for the support of all the German princes in the establishment of a new GERMAN EMPIRE. He very quickly became disillusioned with the new Germany, however, and was particularly disappointed with Bavaria's subordinate role and his failure to gain territorial acquisitions for his kingdom within the new order. He retired increasingly from public life, and is perhaps better known for his patronage of the arts than his interventions in affairs of state. In particular he was a patron of the composer Richard WAGNER, and responsible for the construction of the fairy-tale castle at Neuschwanstein, among other extravagant building projects. He became increasingly reclusive during the 1880s, and was declared insane in 1886. He drowned the same year in a lake (the Starnberger See) near his retreat at Schloss Berg.

Luftwaffe, German air force. During WORLD WAR I the German air force had been part of the army, and was prohibited by the treaty of VERSAILLES. It was re-established by the Nazi regime, with GÖRING at its head.

Lunéville, treaty of (1801). *See* COALITIONS, WARS OF THE.

Lusitania, a British passenger ship sunk by German torpedoes off the coast of Ireland in 1915. The deaths of a number of American passengers prompted tension between Germany and the then neutral United States, and led to a temporary relaxation of submarine warfare.

Luther, Hans (1879–1962), non-party politician during the Weimar Republic; chancellor (1925–6). After a career in municipal politics and ministerial appointments under CUNO, STRESEMANN and Wilhelm MARX, Luther served as chancellor from January 1925 to May 1926. He was president of the REICHS-BANK (1930–3) and ambassador to the United States under the Nazis (1933–7). After the war he was involved in the reconstruction of the financial and banking sector in the western zones of occupation, and was subsequently an honorary professor of political science at Munich. He published his memoirs in 1960 under the title *Politiker ohne Partei* ('politician without party').

Luxemburg, Rosa (1870–1919), revolutionary socialist and theoretician. Luxemburg was born at Zamosc in Russian Poland, and studied law and political economy at Zurich University, where she gained a doctorate in 1898. In the same year she acquired German citizenship through marriage, and moved to Berlin. A co-founder of the Polish Social Democratic Party (in Switzerland) and a participant in the Russian Revolution of 1905, she spent World War I in prison in Germany. As a member of the SPARTACUS LEAGUE (which she founded with Karl LIEBKNECHT), and of the KPD (the German Communist Party), she was a participant in the January 1919 uprising in Berlin. She was murdered, along with Liebknecht, by radical right-wing FREIKORPS members employed by the government to suppress the rebellion.

M

Machtergreifung, 'seizure of power' (by the Nazis). The term 'seizure' implies a revolutionary takeover of power from outside the existing political system, and many historians avoid using it on the grounds that this distorts our understanding of the processes by which the Nazis came to power, and plays down the political continuities between the last years of the WEIMAR REPUBLIC and the dictatorship itself. It also understates the role of the established elites – both within and outside the political parties in HITLER's coalition cabinet of 1933 – in assisting the political transition.

Mackensen, August von (1849–1945), field marshal during WORLD WAR I. Mackensen was born in Saxony, and began his military career in 1869. He took command of the 9th Army for the Polish campaign in the autumn of 1914, and then commanded the combined Austro-German 11th Army in 1915 for the successful GORLICE offensive in Galicia. As field marshal and commander of Army Group Mackensen he led the campaign against Romania from August 1916. This led to the fall of Bucharest in December, and Mackensen then remained as supreme commander of the German occupying forces in Romania. An admirer of Hitler, Mackensen became a Prussian state councillor in 1933. One of his sons, Eberhard von Mackensen (1889–1969), served in World War II as general-commander of the 11th Army Group in Italy, and was a

writer on military matters. Another son, Hans Georg von MACKENSEN, was a diplomat.

Mackensen, Hans Georg von (1883–1947), diplomat, the son of Field Marshal August von MACKENSEN. After taking up minor posts in Copenhagen, Rome, Brussels and Tirana between 1919 and 1929, Mackensen was appointed German minister in Budapest, where he served from 1933 to 1937. He was then ambassador to Rome (1938–43). Mackensen married the daughter of the Nazi foreign minister, von NEURATH.

Madagascar plan, Nazi plan to deport all European Jews to Madagascar and to create a Jewish colony there under an SS governor. In the conference at the aviation ministry that followed the KRISTALLNACHT pogrom of November 1938, HEYDRICH made clear his preference for large-scale emigration as a solution to the 'Jewish problem', and he suggested that otherwise there might be difficulties in getting more than 10,000 of the increasingly impoverished Jews out of the country each year. In the event the possibility of emigration was all but closed off with the outbreak of war. After the fall of France in 1940, however, a plan was proposed by Franz Rademacher, legation counsellor in the foreign ministry, to deport all European Jews, possibly to Madagascar. He also suggested, as alternatives, holding some Jews hostage in Poland, and creating a Jewish state in Palestine – which the Nazis feared would make Jerusalem a second

Vatican. The number of Jews in territory occupied by Germany was now over 3 million, and the 'problem' could not be solved by emigration. France, it was anticipated, would be compelled to cede Madagascar in the peace treaty. Its French inhabitants would then be resettled elsewhere, and a German military base established on the island. The rest would be given over to a Jewish 'reservation'. The idea appealed to the Reich Security Head Office (RSHA), and EICHMANN's department worked out the details. The plan was approved by HIMMLER and put before RIBBENTROP. It was in accord with Hitler's wish to see all the Jews deported from Europe, and it was also welcomed by Hans FRANK, the governor general of occupied Poland. In practical terms, however, it could not be implemented until a peace was agreed with France, and that in turn seemed dependent on a victory over Britain, which appeared increasingly unlikely after the battle of BRITAIN. Jews continued to be deported from the Reich, but only as far as Poland (or in some cases VICHY FRANCE).

Mahler, Gustav (1860–1911), late-Romantic Austrian composer. Born in Kalischt, Bohemia (now Kaliště in the Czech Republic), the son of a brewer, Mahler studied at the Vienna Conservatory (1875–8) and was appointed artistic director of the Vienna Court Opera in 1897, despite the obstacle of his Jewish origins. He resigned his post in 1907, and went to New York, where he was appointed conductor at the Metropolitan Opera. Among his best-known works is *Das Lied von der Erde*. He also wrote ten symphonies, the last of which was unfinished, and a number of other musical works.

Mainz Jacobin Club, the 'Society of Friends of Liberty and Equality', founded in 1792 by local supporters of the French Revolution, among them Matthias METTERNICH. It was the chief forum for political radicals in the Rhineland. After the surrender of Mainz to the French (21 October 1792) the club organized elections to a Rhineland German Convention which declared a Mainz Republic the following year (17 March 1793). The Republic attempted to secede to France, but was reconquered by Austrian and Prussian troops while negotiations were taking place.

maize programme, agricultural plan adopted in the German Democratic Republic in the 1950s in imitation of Khrushchev's ill-fated enthusiasm for planting maize in the Soviet Union. The area devoted to maize production was increased from 10,000 hectares (25,000 acres) in 1955 to over 4,238,000 (10,472,000 acres) in 1960.

Majdanek, Nazi concentration camp and extermination camp in Poland. The camp was initially set up as forced-labour camp for the SS in Lublin, where the organization established a base from which to implement plans for the 'racial' resettlement of eastern Poland by Germans in a manner similar to the attempted racial reordering in the WARTHELAND. Its inmates were mostly Poles or Soviet POWs who worked for the SS in the area, but some Jews were also sent there, and three gas chambers were built for the purpose of mass murder in September and October 1942. It is estimated that 60,000 Jews died at Majdanek, and some 200,000 people altogether, most of them from fatigue, malnutrition and disease. In 1943 there were mass shootings of Jews in Polish labour camps, and all of those remaining at Majdanek were shot in early November.

Malicious Attacks on the State and Party, Law against (20 December 1934), the so-called malice law (*Heimtückegesetz*), which made criticism of Hitler, the Nazi Party and its subsidiary organizations an arrestable offence. It criminalized dissent and political humour, and since many of the people charged were denounced to the Gestapo by their fellow citizens, it provided people with a means of redressing grievances quite unconnected with political opposition to the regime.

Mann, Heinrich (1871–1950), liberal writer, the brother of Thomas MANN, with whom he quarrelled on political grounds. During World War I Mann was very much the spokesman of German liberalism. His best known novels are *Professor Unrat* (1905), on which the film *The Blue Angel* was based, *Der Untertan* (1918), translated into English as *Man of Straw*, and *König Henri Quatre* (1935–8). He fled first to Czechoslovakia in 1933, and then via France to the United States. He died in California after the war.

Mann, Thomas (1875–1955), writer, the younger brother of Heinrich MANN. Politically conservative before and during World War I, Mann wrote an essay on Frederick the Great (FRIEDRICH II) that served as an apologia for the violation of Belgian neutrality, and developed his observations on the cultural conflict between Germany and the West in *Betrachtungen eines Unpolitischen* (*Reflections of an Unpolitical Man*, 1918). Mann was a postwar convert to republicanism of a pragmatic, faint-hearted kind: he became a 'pragmatic republican' (*VERNUNFT-REPUBLIKANER*). He won the Nobel prize for literature in 1929. Among his best-known novels are *Buddenbrooks* (1901), *Der Tod in Venedig* (*Death in Venice*, 1912), *Der Zauberberg* (*The Magic Mountain*, 1924), *Josef und seine Brüder* (*Joseph and his Brothers*, 1933–43) and *Doktor Faustus* (1947). Mann fled to Switzerland in 1933 and subsequently to the United States. He returned to Europe after the war and settled in Switzerland in 1952.

Mannheim school, a group of composers at the court of the Elector Palatine in Mannheim during the 18th century, led by Johann Stamitz (1717–57). The group helped to establish the symphony as a musical form.

Manstein, Erich von (1887–1973), field marshal during World War II. Manstein served on both the Eastern and Western Fronts in World War I, and was an experienced infantry commander by the time he took part in the Polish campaign in 1939. He also commanded the infantry during the invasion of France, having managed to persuade

Hitler to adopt his plan to invade through the Ardennes, and was promoted to field marshal in June 1940. He then went to Russia, first as commander of a Panzer corps during the German advance on Leningrad. He moved south to the Crimea, and north again to Leningrad, before taking part in the attempt to relieve STALINGRAD and in the defence of KHARKOV, where his tactics lured weakened Soviet troops into a trap. His strategy at KURSK was less successful, and his disagreements with Hitler increasingly frequent. He was dismissed in 1944. He was captured by the British, tried for war crimes and acquitted, but remained in prison until 1953. He was subsequently an adviser to the West German army.

Manteuffel, Edwin (Hans Karl), Freiherr von (1809–85), soldier and diplomat. Born in Dresden, Manteuffel, a cavalry officer, was appointed adjutant to FRIEDRICH WILHELM IV of Prussia during the REVOLUTIONS OF 1848, and was advised on the historical context and implications of the crisis by his friend Leopold von RANKE. Manteuffel was present at other critical moments over the following quarter of a century. He persuaded Russia and Austria to withdraw from the brink of war during the Crimean War (1853–6). From 1857 he was head of the Prussian military cabinet, and in 1862 he urged the king to defy the LANDTAG. He served in the GERMAN–DANISH WAR of 1864, and then led Prussian troops from Schleswig into Holstein in the AUSTRO-PRUSSIAN WAR of 1866. He served in the FRANCO-PRUSSIAN WAR, commanded the German occupation forces in France, and was later (from 1879) governor of the *Reichsland* of ALSACE-LORRAINE.

Manteuffel, Hasso, Freiherr von (1897–1978), army officer and liberal politician. Manteuffel was the grand-nephew of Edwin von MANTEUFFEL. He served in World War II in the North African campaign, and on both the Eastern and Western Fronts. He was a member of the Bundestag for the FDP from 1953 to 1957. In 1959 he was tried and briefly imprisoned for shooting an adolescent deserter in 1944. He died in the Tyrol.

Manteuffel, Otto, Freiherr von (1844–1913), conservative politician, the son of Otto Theodor von MANTEUFFEL. Manteuffel was a member of the Reichstag for the German Conservative Party (*DEUTSCHKONSERVATIVE PARTEI*) from 1877 to 1898, and was then *Landesdirektor* of Brandenburg (1896–1911). He sat in the HERRENHAUS from 1883, and was a member of its presidium from 1896 to 1911.

Manteuffel, Otto (Theodor), Freiherr von (1805–82), politician. Manteuffel became minister-president of Prussia in 1850, and negotiated the agreement (*Punktation*) at OLMÜTZ with Austria, which brought an end to the plans for a German union. A constitutional conservative who embodied the post-1850 political climate, he nevertheless recognized the spirit of the times, dismissing his colleagues' fantasies about a 'corporate state'. His son, also Otto von MANTEUFFEL, was also a politician.

Maquis, collective name for anti-Nazi partisans in occupied France, many of whom initially fled to the hills in order to avoid conscription as forced labour to the Reich. It is estimated that there were 40,000 such resisters by 1944. Some were armed and trained by the British SPECIAL OPERATIONS EXECUTIVE, and many were able to enlist in the First French Army before the battle for Germany. The word *maquis* is a Corsican term for the brushwood used as cover by the partisans in the south of France, but became a shorthand term for the French resistance generally.

Marburg speech (17 June 1934), speech delivered by Franz von PAPEN at Marburg University. Ex-Chancellor von Papen was Hitler's vice chancellor, and the chief spokesman of the conservatives within the Hitler cabinet and the regime. His speech, largely written by Edgar JUNG, a protagonist of the 'conservative revolution' during the later 1920s, was an attack on the excesses of the Nazis during the 'NATIONAL REVOLUTION' of 1933–4,

and culminated in references to the 'selfishness, lack of principle, insincerity, unchivalrous behaviour, the arrogance' of the Nazis. Von Papen was concerned that the Nazis represented a permanent uprising from below. The speech came at a critical time for Hitler, when many members of the SA were disillusioned about what they perceived to be a lack of radicalism. Reporting of the speech was banned, and von Papen was sent as German ambassador to Vienna. Jung was murdered in the wave of summary executions that followed the NIGHT OF THE LONG KNIVES.

Marc, Franz (1880–1916), EXPRESSIONIST artist. Marc was born in Munich, where he studied modern languages at the university before attending the art academy. He visited Paris in 1903 and 1907, and he held his first exhibition in Munich in 1910. He was a member of the *Neue Künstlervereinigung* ('new artists' association') in 1911, and was a close associate of the artist August Macke (1887–1914). He was also a friend of KANDINSKY and a founding member of the group BLAUE REITER (1911–13). He was co-editor, with Kandinsky, of the *Blaue Reiter* almanac. Marc's work was a formative contribution to the development of German modernism. Under the influence of cubism and futurism he sought to express himself through the independent power of colour and form. He studied anatomy in order to pursue his objective of the 'animalization' of art, and paintings of animals are among his best-known works: *The Red Horses* (1911), *Blue Horse I* (1911) and *The Tiger* (1912). He was killed at Verdun in 1916. The Nazis considered his work degenerate and removed it from museums.

March Revolutions. *See* REVOLUTIONS OF 1848.

Marcuse, Herbert (1898–1979), philosopher and political activist. Marcuse was a Marxist theorist and a member of the FRANKFURT SCHOOL who also made use of the theories of FREUD. He published *Der eindimensionale Mensch* (*One Dimensional Man*), a critique of contemporary society, in 1964. Marcuse was a hero of the radical left in Germany in the late 1960s, not least on account of his call to oppose the economic order of 'late capitalism'.

Maria Theresia (1717–80), archduchess of Austria and queen of Hungary and Bohemia (1740–80). The accession of Maria Theresia to the HABSBURG territories was secured through the strenuous efforts of her father, the emperor KARL VI, with the PRAGMATIC SANCTION of 1724, but when she ascended the throne at the age of 23 nothing in her education (by the Jesuits) had prepared her for government. She faced the immediate crisis of the War of the AUSTRIAN SUCCESSION, with the Prussian invasion of Silesia and a Bavarian claim to the Habsburg hereditary lands (*Erblande*).

After the war Maria Theresia was persuaded by the young Privy Conference (cabinet) secretary, Johann Christoph, Freiherr von Bartenstein (1689–1767), to reform the administration of the empire. Her measures reflected the principles of 'enlightened ABSOLUTISM'. A new foreign ministry, the Chancellery of State (*Staatskanzlei*), was established in 1742, and a centralized war ministry was established in 1744. An interior ministry for the monarchy was also effectively established from 1749 under Graf Friedrich Wilhelm von Haugwitz. If these measures, arguably, reflected the centralizing tendencies of absolutism, others reflected the influence of the ENLIGHTENMENT: education was promoted with the introduction of the *Volksschule*, the church was increasingly subordinated to the state (despite Maria Theresia's own piety), and torture was abolished. After the death in 1765 of her husband Franz I (who had become Holy Roman emperor in 1745), she remained in mourning for the rest of her life. Her son, the emperor JOSEPH II, was made co-regent.

Marita, code name in use between 1940 and 1941 for the German offensive against Greece (1941).

mark, unit of currency. Originally, in the Middle Ages, the mark was a unit of weight. With the *Reichsmünzordnung* (imperial coin decree) of 1524 the Kölner (Cologne) mark of *c*.234 grams became the basic unit of weight for the Holy Roman Empire. From the 16th century the mark was also the name of the currency of north German cities such as Hamburg and Lübeck, and in 1861 Saxony suggested the name 'mark' for a single currency to supersede the GULDEN of the south and the TALER of the north German states. The Coin Act (*Münzgesetz*) of 9 July 1873 made the gold mark the currency of the German empire. In 1923 the RENTENMARK was introduced to reform and stabilize the currency in the wake of the hyperinflation of that year (*see* INFLATION), and became the Reichsmark in 1924. The Deutsche Mark (or 'Deutschmark') was introduced into the western occupied zones of Germany in 1948. Its East German equivalent was the *Mark der Deutschen Notenbank* (1964–7) and then the *Mark der DDR* (1968–90). The mark was superseded by the EURO in 2002.

Marne, battles of the (1914 and 1918), key engagements in the valley of the River Marne in France during WORLD WAR I.

In accordance with the SCHLIEFFEN Plan, the first battle of the war was to be fought during the German advance to the west. When MOLTKE transferred troops from the German right wing to Russia, however, the plan was weakened. The French were expecting a direct attack on Paris, but the German 1st Army advanced southeast of the city rather than to the west, and the French and British attacked its flank at the Marne (6–9 September 1914), checking the German advance and forcing a retreat to the River Aisne. The Schlieffen Plan had failed, and about 1 million men had been lost in the three weeks since the beginning of the war.

The second battle was fought in July 1918. It witnessed the final collapse of the German spring offensives of that year on the

Western Front, and was followed by a series of Allied counter-offensives that by November had helped to bring the war to an end.

Marr, Wilhelm (1819–1904), radical right-wing journalist who popularized the term 'anti-Semitic'. Marr was born in Magdeburg the only son of the actor Heinrich Marr. He went with his father to Vienna in 1839 after completing his apprenticeship, and became involved in republican politics there. He then moved to Switzerland (1841), where he was also involved in radical politics. In 1845 he was expelled from Lausanne, and eventually settled in Hamburg (1846).

In 1848 Marr launched his first attack on the Jews, whom he accused of manipulating the revolution of that year for their own ends (*see* REVOLUTIONS OF 1848). From 1852 to 1859 he lived in Costa Rica, but then returned to Hamburg, where he was elected to the BÜRGERSCHAFT. He also became president of the Democratic Association. In 1862, however, he lost his seat, and was removed from the presidency of the Association after he launched an anti-Semitic attack on the Jewish leader of the Bürgerschaft, Gabriel Riesser (1806–63). He then worked as a journalist, and after separating from his first wife in 1873 married a Jewish woman in 1874, Sophia Behrend, who died the same year. His third marriage (1874–7), was also to a woman with one Jewish parent, and ended in divorce. In 1879 he published an anti-Semitic pamphlet that blamed the crash of 1873 on the Jews, and argued that they were coming to Germany to found a new Palestine. Marr's *Der Sieg des Judentums über das Germanentum vom nichtkonfessionellen Standpunkt aus betrachtet* ('Jewry's victory over Germandom from the non-confessional point of view'), which was published in 1873 in Switzerland by Rudolf Costenoble, ran to twelve impressions. In the same year Marr founded the *Antisemitische Hefte* ('anti-Semitic journal') and the Anti-Semitic League.

See also ANTI-SEMITISM.

marriage loans, financial provision introduced in the Law for the Reduction of Unemployment (1 June 1933). Loans of up to 1000 marks were available for couples of German nationality, provided that the wife had spent six months in employment in Germany between June 1931 and May 1933, and was now giving up her job. The wife also had to undertake not to work as long as her husband earned more than 125 marks per month. The loans were interest-free, and paid in vouchers that were redeemable for furniture and other household goods. The original purpose of the loan was to reduce male unemployment by encouraging young wives to stay at home. Very quickly, however, it was used to try to reverse the decline in the birth rate (which had been more dramatic in Germany than elsewhere in Europe). A supplementary decree was issued on 20 June, which provided for the cancellation of a quarter of the debt with the birth of each child, and a moratorium on remaining repayments between birth and the child's first birthday. The number of marriages increased during the mid-1930s (not least as a consequence of the recovery of the economy) and one-third of marriages (700,000 up to January 1937) were assisted with marriage loans. When wives were allowed to claim marriage loans and also work (from 1937), the proportion of marriages so assisted rose to 42%. Although the measure was intended to help the poorest marry and have children, the political conditions attached to it excluded some of the most needy. If either partner had any connection with the Communist Party (KPD) or its affiliations they were denied a loan. Similarly, marriage loans were also denied to various 'ASOCIAL' categories: the 'work-shy', vagrants and alcoholics.

Marshall Plan, popular name of the European Recovery Programme announced by the US secretary of state General George Marshall at Harvard University on 5 June 1947. The plan was devised to prevent postwar reconstruction in Europe from grinding to a halt, and with it the attendant economic recovery in both Europe and the United States. Exports of European goods were low, and the repayment of war debts by the European Allies to the United States, combined with the reliance of Europe on American imports, created a dollar shortage. Moreover, inflation in the United States (which made European goods dearer) and the failure of the 1947 harvest in Europe (which increased the need for agricultural imports) made the currency shortage so severe that European countries had to cut their imports of American industrial and manufactured goods so dramatically as to threaten the American adjustment from war production to a peace-time economy premised on free world trade. Under the terms of the European Recovery Programme of 1948–52, aid was offered to the whole of Europe, including the Soviet Bloc, and one of the aims of the plan was to undermine the influence of communism in Europe during the early days of the Cold War. In 1948 Moscow turned down such assistance for the Soviet Union and its East European puppet states, but the remaining 17 states received some 15 billion dollars of loans and grants from the United States. The plan was a success in that West European production had reached pre-war levels again by 1950, and the depression that had followed the end of World War I was avoided.

Marx, Karl (1818–83), philosopher, economist and political activist. Marx was born into a Protestant family of Jewish origin in Trier and studied politics, philosophy and history at Bonn and Berlin (where he became an adherent of the YOUNG HEGELIANS between 1835 and 1841. He became editor of the *Rheinische Zeitung* newspaper in Cologne in 1842, married Jenny von Westphalen in 1843 and moved to France as co-editor with Arnold Ruge of the *Deutsch-Französische Jahrbücher* ('German–French yearbooks', later *Deutsche Jahrbücher*). It was in France that he began to work with Friedrich ENGELS. Together they published *Die heilige Familie* (*The Holy Family*) in 1845, the year that Marx composed *Die deutsche Ideologie* (*The German Ideology*, first published in 1926). Marx was expelled from France and moved to Brussels, where he published *Misère de la Philosophie* (*The Poverty of Philosophy*,1847) and founded the German Workers' Educational Association (*Deutscher Arbeiter-Bildungsverein*) and the *Association Démocratique*. The *Communist Manifesto* was published the following year, when Marx was expelled from Brussels and returned to Cologne as editor of the *Neue Rheinische Zeitung*. Following the suppression of the newspaper he moved on to London.

In London Marx rejoined the Communist League, and was actively involved with the First International (the International Working Men's Association), of which he became the leader; but he spent most of his time in the British Library. Two extended pamphlets on the political upheavals in France were published shortly after he arrived in England: *The Class Struggles in France* (1850) and *The Eighteenth Brumaire of Louis Bonaparte* (1852). During the 1850s he was preoccupied with the draft of a work on capital, land, wage labour and trade, which was published only in 1941 and has come to be known as the *Grundrisse* ('outlines'). *The Critique of Political Economy* appeared in1859, and the first volume of *Das Kapital* (*Capital*) in 1867. Volumes 2 and 3 were edited by Engels after his death.

Marx had an immeasurable influence on the international labour movement, but his involvement with workers' parties in Germany was less direct. The first German labour party, LASSALLE's General German Workers' Association (ADAV), was outside Marx's influence, as was the Social Democratic Workers' Party (SDAP), with which the ADAV eventually merged in 1875 to form the SAPD (the Socialist Workers' Party of Germany). Marx criticized the SAPD's founding

GOTHA PROGRAMME (although the critique was published only much later and posthumously). The party that eventually developed from the merger, the SPD (the German Social Democratic Party), was influenced by Marxism much more directly, but by the time it had become established and was free to operate openly in Germany, there was already emerging a pragmatic revisionist critique of Marx's and Engels' analysis of political change. The SPD abandoned Marxism with its BAD GODESBERG PROGRAMME of 1959.

Marx, Wilhelm (1863–1946), Catholic politician; leader of the CENTRE PARTY (1921–8) and chancellor (1923–4 and 1926–8). Marx was born in Cologne, the son of a Catholic primary-school headmaster, and became active in the Centre Party in the 1890s. He was a member of the Prussian LANDTAG from 1899 to 1921, and of the Reichstag from 1910 to 1918, and again from 1920 to 1933. He was also a member of the constituent NATIONAL ASSEMBLY of 1919.

Marx's first administration was formed in November 1923 after the fall of the STRESEMANN government, in the aftermath of the postwar crisis, the Franco-Belgian occupation of the RUHR VALLEY and the hyperinflation (see INFLATION). Marx's government's business was conducted under an emergency law, and when the Reichstag refused to renew it in March 1924 the government collapsed. Marx formed a second government, but that too fell in December 1924, largely over the issue of the DAWES PLAN.

In 1925 Marx was briefly minister-president of Prussia (February–April), then stood as presidential candidate with the endorsement of the Centre Party. In the first round he won 3.9 million votes, sufficient to win him the support of the three republican or 'Weimar' parties in the second round, but not the Bavarian Catholic Party, the BVP, whose right-wing instincts overcame its confessional loyalty and prompted it to support the (Protestant) candidate of the right, Paul von HINDENBURG. The outcome was close:

Marx won 13.7 million votes and Hindenburg 14.6 million.

Marx went on to serve as justice minister in Hans LUTHER's second administration (January–May 1926), and then formed a government himself. Apart from the new chancellor, the cabinet itself remained virtually unchanged. It was a minority government based on a narrow coalition of mainly small parties (the liberal DDP, the Centre Party, the conservative DVP, and the BVP), and was dependent on SPD toleration for survival. The DVP maintained contacts with the German Nationalists (DNVP), with a view to forming a broad conservative coalition in the future. The working agreement between the Social Democrats and the government broke down in December, and Marx formed his fourth government in January 1927. Ministers from the DNVP, which had supported the SPD's no-confidence motion now joined the cabinet. The new administration was now very firmly on the right, but at the same time it was a government in which a range of very divergent interests and aspirations were subsumed. In the event it was not the anticipated intransigence of the German Nationalists on foreign-policy matters that led to the government's collapse, but disagreement between the Centre Party and the DVP (heirs to imperial Germany's NATIONAL LIBERALS) over education. The Centre Party sought to introduce Catholic schools into states where the education system had hitherto been non-denominational, a policy that the DVP successfully opposed. The Centre Party then served notice on the coalition, and new elections were called that resulted in a clear victory for the left (20 May 1928). Marx resigned his leadership of the party, but remained active in politics until 1933.

Märzgefallene, 'those fallen in March', a sarcastic term for the perceived opportunists who only joined the Nazi Party in the spring of 1933, following the Nazi electoral success in the election of 5 March. The term was originally used to describe those who fell during the March REVOLUTIONS OF 1848.

Masuria (German name: Masurenland), a region now in northern Poland but formerly part of East Prussia. Its population was largely Germanized by the beginning of the 20th century. The battles of the MASURIAN LAKES were important victories over the Russians at the beginning of World War I. The German population was expelled from the area after it became Polish in 1945.

Masurian Lakes, battles of (September 1914 and February 1915), two German victories over the Russians on the eastern frontier of East Prussia. The first battle took place shortly after the battle of TANNENBERG, and forced the Russians out of East Prussia. The second victory came with the 'winter battle of Masuria', and forestalled a Russian invasion of East Prussia.

Mauthausen, CONCENTRATION CAMP near Linz in Upper Austria. It was opened in summer 1938, within weeks of the ANSCHLUSS, and was closed only in May 1945, days before the end of the war. It was notorious for its particularly brutal conditions.

Max von Baden, Prince. See BADEN, PRINCE MAX VON.

May, Ernst (1886–1970), architect and town planner. May studied at London, Darmstadt and Munich, and was a member of the British Fabian Society. He established himself as an architect in Frankfurt in 1913, served in World War I, and then worked on a number of housing estates in Silesia during the early 1920s. His greatest influence was in Frankfurt, however, where he was responsible for planning. By 1930 there were 20,000 new dwellings in the city, mostly in terraces on peripheral estates. The new housing was fitted with standardized equipment for kitchens and bathrooms, and with gardens, central washrooms and other communal facilities. It was conceived as a new type of accommodation for a 'reformed' style of living, and was publicized in *Das neue Frankfurt*, a journal edited by May. May went to work in the Soviet Union in 1934, and

returned to West Germany in 1953 after spending some time in Africa.

May, Karl (1842–1912), popular writer. May was one of the bestselling authors of the 19th century. He wrote mainly genre fiction (Westerns and children's books), and remained popular well into the 20th century.

Mayerling. See RUDOLF, CROWN PRINCE.

Mayreder, Rosa (1858–1938), Austrian writer, 'utopian' feminist and pacifist. Mayreder was born and lived in Vienna, where she was a co-founder of the General Austrian Women's Association (*Allgemeiner Österreichischer Frauenverein*) in 1893. She was president of the Women's League for Peace and Freedom. She was sceptical about cooperation with the Social Democrats, suspecting that men on the left were only interested in women's emancipation for as long as they themselves were excluded from power. Mayreder wrote novels and poetry and published a number of essays and discursive works. An edition of her diaries was published in 1988.

Mecklenburg, a historic region on the Baltic coast of northern Germany. It was divided in 1701 into Mecklenburg-Schwerin and Mecklenburg-Strelitz. The two states, both overwhelmingly Lutheran by confession, were members of the GERMAN CONFEDERATION, then joined the NORTH GERMAN CONFEDERATION and the GERMAN EMPIRE as separate *Länder*. Mecklenburg-Schwerin had a population of 625,000 at the turn of the 20th century, and Mecklenburg-Strelitz 103,000. The two territories were united by the Nazis in 1934 into a single state of Mecklenburg, which – with some acquisitions from western Pomerania – survived as one of the *Länder* of the GERMAN DEMOCRATIC REPUBLIC until 1952. It was then split up into three districts during the East German local-government reforms, but reconstituted as Mecklenburg-Vorpommern ('hither' or western Pomerania) in 1990. The local economy has remained dominated by agriculture, and the population was 1.9 million by the later

1990s. In the first regional elections in 1990 there was no overall majority in the LANDTAG, but the CDU was the largest party, with 29 of the 66 seats and 38.3% of the vote. During the 1990s both the SPD (which became the largest party in 1998) and the PDS (the Party of Democratic Socialism, formerly the ruling East German Socialist Unity Party, the SED) increased their share of the vote at the expense of the CDU and the FDP, which failed to win seats in 1994 and 1998. The position of the smaller progressive groups has declined steadily, while that of the radical right increased slightly during the later 1990s. None of the smaller parties of right or left has been represented in the Landtag.

Mefo bills, bills of exchange used by Hjalmar SCHACHT, economics minister and head of the REICHSBANK, to boost the German economy during the early 1930s. Mefo bills took their name from the bogus Metall-Forschungsgesellschaft AG, formed by four munitions firms in 1933 on the understanding that its debts would be covered by the government. As a result the Reichsbank was able to discount the Mefo bills, which were accepted by government contractors and banks. In practice Mefo bills were a form of short-term credit that enabled the government to finance rearmament. By the time the bills were reaching their redemption date, taxation and loans had replaced Mefo bills as a means of financing rearmament, but Schacht was rapidly losing influence and the Reichsbank was forced, reluctantly, to give the government further credit. Between 1934 and 1936 half of German arms expenditure was accounted for by Mefo bills.

Meinecke, Friedrich (1862–1954), German historian. Meinecke was born in Salzwedel, the son of a Prussian civil servant. He was editor of the prestigious historical journal *Historische Zeitschrift* from 1893 to 1933, professor of history at Strasbourg (1901–6), Freiburg (1906–14) and Berlin (1914–28). A conservative nationalist, he was an 'intel-lectual republican' during the Weimar Republic and was dismissed from the *Historische Zeitschrift* by the Nazis. He was appointed the first rector of the Free University of Berlin in 1948 and published a critical book on the Nazi dictatorship, *Die deutsche Katastrophe*, in 1946.

Mein Kampf ('my struggle'), Hitler's political *magnum opus*, originally written as two separate books while Hitler was in Landsberg prison after the failed BEER HALL PUTSCH of 1923. It was published (by Max AMANN) in two volumes: *Eine Abrechnung* ('a reckoning', 1925) and *Die Nationalsozialistische Bewegung* ('the National Socialist movement', 1926). About half a million copies had been sold by the time of Hitler's appointment as chancellor. Sales were then boosted by the semi-official status of the book, and bulk purchases by government departments and institutions. Total sales are estimated at some 8 or 9 million by the time of Hitler's death. *Mein Kampf* has been reprinted in English since the war, but is banned in both Germany and Austria. Hitler dictated a second book to Amann, which was published only posthumously in 1961 as *Hitlers Zweites Buch* (published in English as *Hitler's Secret Book*).

Meitner, Lise (1878–1968), Austrian physicist. Meitner was appointed to a chair in Berlin in 1922, but along with other Jewish scientists, had to give up her position in 1933, when the Nazis came to power. She emigrated to Denmark in 1938 and subsequently moved to Stockholm. She worked with Otto HAHN and discovered a number of radioactive isotopes. She contributed to the theoretical work explaining nuclear fission, publishing results that Hahn had been reluctant to. Niels Bohr then took the information to the United States.

Memel, former German seaport on the Baltic. It is now in Lithuania, and is called Klaipeda. The treaty of VERSAILLES removed Memel from East Prussia and transferred it to Lithuania. It became an objective of German revisionism, and was ceded to Germany by

Lithuania under pressure in March 1939. It remained part of Germany under the terms of the MOLOTOV–RIBBENTROP PACT, but was absorbed into the Soviet Union in 1945.

Mengele, Josef (1911–79), EXTERMINATION CAMP doctor. After a career at the Institute of Hereditary Biology and Racial Hygiene in Berlin, in 1943 Mengele was appointed chief doctor at AUSCHWITZ, where he conducted medical experiments on the Nazis' victims. He fled to South America after the war and in 1959 became a citizen of Paraguay, whose government refused to agree to his extradition. His body was found in Brazil in 1985.

Messerschmitt, Willy (Emil) (1898–1978), aircraft engineer. Messerschmitt was a friend of Rudolf HESS. His design for a new fighter aircraft, the Me109, was accepted by the Luftwaffe in 1935. The Me109 was first deployed in the Spanish Civil War and remained in use throughout World War II. The Me110 was a long-range fighter, and one was used by Hess to fly to Scotland in 1941. The Me262 was the world's first operational jet fighter, but was developed too late to make a significant contribution during World War II.

Metternich, Klemens Wenzel, Fürst von (1773–1859), chancellor of Austria and dominant political figure in post-Napoleonic restoration Germany and Europe. Metternich was born into an imperial aristocratic family in Koblenz. He was shocked by the popular disorder during the early days of the French Revolution in Paris. During the Revolutionary Wars the family estates of the Metternichs were occupied and their property confiscated. Their privileges and social position were dependent on the survival of the old regime, and with the disappearance of the minor provincial courts of western Germany, their stage and status were both gone. Metternich remained a committed conservative all his life.

Following Metternich's marriage to the granddaughter of Prince KAUNITZ, he enjoyed the patronage of the HABSBURGS and went as ambassador first to Dresden in 1801, then to Berlin, and finally to Paris, where the French refused to accredit him as imperial ambassador rather than Austrian minister. He was recalled to Vienna as foreign minister in 1809, and although he personally found the rise of Napoleon and his German allies distasteful, he pursued a pragmatic policy of Austrian *rapprochement* with the French within the continental system. Even after Napoleon's retreat from Russia, Metternich hesitated before committing Austria to the Wars of LIBERATION, not least because he was suspicious of the appeal to popular resistance and national consciousness. During the first onslaught against Napoleon in 1813, Metternich acted as mediator, leaving the fighting to Prussia and Russia, backed by Britain. Only when he had a sense that the tide had turned against France, and it was clear that his attempts to negotiate with Napoleon against Russia had come to nothing, did Austria declare war.

Metternich presided over and dominated the Congress of VIENNA. Subsequently he dominated Austrian politics until the REVOLUTIONS OF 1848, and presided over the policing of domestic order in the GERMAN CONFEDERATION and of international order in restoration Europe, by means of the CONGRESS SYSTEM. Metternich was alarmed by any sign of opposition, or even, it seemed, of political activity – from the establishment of parliaments (albeit with very limited powers) in the liberal southwestern states of Germany to the nationalist agitation among university students that ultimately led to the KARLSBAD DECREES of 1819. The murder of KOTZEBUE came in time for Metternich to persuade the king of Prussia to abandon plans for a constitution, and he thereby prevented what he regarded as the dangerous spread of constitutionalism throughout Germany. Metternich's politically repressive regime remained in force until he was overthrown during the March Revolution of 1848 in Vienna, when he was forced to flee to England. He returned to Vienna, but never regained his position in public life.

Metternich, Matthias (1741–1825), revolutionary activist. Born at Steingrenz, near Limburg, Metternich studied mathematics at Mainz, and was appointed to a chair at the university there in 1785. He was an active participant in the revolutionary movement of the 1790s, and was a founding member of the MAINZ JACOBIN CLUB. During the Mainz Republic he was a prolific publicist on behalf of French ideas and the new revolutionary order. He was both a competent administrator and reliable collaborator, who argued for Rhinelanders to have the same rights as the French. Sceptical of the possibility of an independent republic surviving in the Rhineland, he hoped for the spread of the revolution to the rest of Germany.

Michaelis, Georg (1857–1936), public servant and politician; imperial chancellor (July–October 1917). Michaelis was undersecretary in the Prussian ministry of finance (1900–17), then food minister (1917), before succeeding BETHMANN HOLLWEG as imperial chancellor. As Michaelis had no political support of his own in the Reichstag, real power during his chancellorship lay in the hands of the virtual military dictatorship of LUDENDORFF and HINDENBURG. After the end of World War I Michaelis was ministerpresident of Pomerania (1918–19).

Mielke, Erich (1907–2000), East German politician. Born in the Berlin suburb of Wedding into a working-class family, Mielke joined the Communist youth movement in 1921. When two policemen were shot at a demonstration in 1931, Mielke, as leader of the Communist paramilitary group that was present, was charged with their murder and sentenced to death in his absence after he had fled, first to Belgium and then to the Soviet Union. He was a member of the International Brigades during the Spanish Civil War, and returned to Germany in 1945. In February 1947 a warrant was issued by the West Berlin police for his arrest for the murders of 1931, and in August he took over the DENAZIFICATION procedures of the Soviet zone. From 1950 to 1989 he was a member of the Central Committee (ZK) of the SED, and he was minister of state security in the GERMAN DEMOCRATIC REPUBLIC from 1957 to 1989. He became a member of the Politburo in 1976. After the collapse of the East German state he was repeatedly arrested and tried on a number of charges, including damage to the economy and attempted murder by means of supporting the RED ARMY FACTION. In the end he was sentenced to six years for the murder of the two policemen in 1931, but released early on health grounds.

Mies van der Rohe, Ludwig (1886–1969), influential modernist architect. With GROPIUS, Mies was an assistant of BEHRENS before World War I, and became an original and acclaimed architect in his own right during the Weimar Republic. He succeeded Gropius as director of the BAUHAUS in 1930 and remained there until the institution was closed by the Nazis in 1933. He emigrated to the USA in 1937, and continued to pursue a successful architectural career.

Miklas, Wilhelm (1872–1956), conservative politician; president of Austria (1928–38). Miklas was born in Krems, and was a schoolteacher by profession. He was a member of the REICHSRAT for the CHRISTIAN SOCIAL PARTY from 1907 to 1918, and then a member of the NATIONALRAT from 1920 to 1928. He also sat in the LANDTAG of Lower Austria from 1908 to 1918. He was elected federal president in 1928, and again for a second term in 1931. As president he failed to resist the unconstitutional activities of the chancellor and Christian Social leader Engelbert DOLLFUSS. When Dollfuss was unable to rely on a parliamentary majority, Miklas permitted him to rule by presidential decree, a strategy that was notionally legitimized by a 'war economy enabling decree' of 1917. Miklas effectively presided over the transformation of republican Austria from parliamentary democracy to fascist dictatorship. He resigned with the German invasion of 1938, and did not return to public life after World War II.

Milch, Erhard (1892–1972), field marshal. Milch was a member of the executive of the airline Deutsche Lufthansa (1926–33), then state secretary for aviation under the Nazis (1933–45). He was also inspector general of the LUFTWAFFE.

Milice française, a right-wing paramilitary force formed in VICHY FRANCE in 1943 to assist the Germans in the suppression of the French Resistance.

Miquel, Johannes von (1828–1901), liberal politician. Miquel was born in Neuenhaus, and was a lawyer by profession. He was a founding member of the German National Association (*Deutscher NATIONALVEREIN*) in 1859, and of the NATIONAL LIBERAL PARTY in 1866. He was also Prussian finance minister from 1890 to 1901.

Mischling, a term used by the Nazis to describe those with a mixture of Jewish and non-Jewish ancestry. The Law for the Protection of German Blood and Honour, one of the NUREMBERG LAWS of 1935, set out the distinction between a *Mischling* of the first degree (with two Jewish grandparents) and a *Mischling* of the second degree (with one).

Mit brennender Sorge ('with ardent concern'), an encyclical of Pope Pius XI on the Roman Catholic Church and the German Reich, issued on 14 March 1937. It expressed the disappointment of the church with the Nazis' failure to keep the terms of the CONCORDAT of 1933, particularly in educational matters: 'If the State organizes a national youth, and makes this organization obligatory to all,' the encyclical asserted, 'then, without prejudice to rights of religious associations, it is the absolute right of youths as well as of parents to see to it that this organization is purged of all manifestations hostile to the Church and Christianity.' The church had no fundamental objection to

the VOLKSGEMEINSCHAFT (the Nazi concept of a harmonious society) – indeed, the CORPORATIST rhetoric that accompanied the encyclical was reminiscent of the social teaching embodied in earlier papal encyclicals: 'No one would think of preventing young Germans establishing a true ethnic community in a noble love of freedom and loyalty to their country. What We object to is the voluntary and systematic antagonism raised between national education and religious duty'.

Mitteldeutschland ('central Germany'), a term used by right-wing West German propagandists after World War II to describe the territory of the GERMAN DEMOCRATIC REPUBLIC in preference to the prevalent 'East Germany', in order to reinforce the point that Silesia and East Prussia were merely 'under Polish/Soviet administration'. The term was revived by radical right-wing activists after 1990 to describe the NEW FEDERAL STATES.

Mitteleuropa ('central Europe'), a shorthand slogan for the expansionist plans espoused by the annexationist camp on the right of the German political spectrum during World War I. The term was used during the 19th century, but was popularized during the imperial period, particularly through the book entitled *Mitteleuropa* (1915) by the liberal journalist Friedrich NAUMANN. The term was used across the political spectrum with a variety of different meanings, both politically and geographically. However, by the end of World War I it had become associated with Prussian militarism and Pan-Germanism, and fell from use in Germany, only to be revived with the doctrines of geopolitics under the Nazis.

With the emergence in the 1980s of a consciousness in Budapest and Prague that an orientation towards central Europe was more promising than association with the Eastern Bloc, the term *Zentraleuropa* was invented to replace the older, discredited term, and was widely used by Czechs, Austrians and Hungarians at the end of the Cold War.

Mittelmächte. *See* CENTRAL POWERS.

Mittelstand (literally 'middle estate'), the lower middle class. German distinguishes clearly between the lower and upper middle classes, *Mittelstand* and *BÜRGERTUM*. The origin of the term *Mittelstand* is to be found in pre-modern social ideology based on the concept of estates, but after the industrialization of Germany the term came to be used increasingly as a self-designation by those whose social anxieties were expressed in terms of fear of proletarianization and nostalgia for a mythical age of economic prosperity and political stability. It was a subjective term used to articulate pleas for economic assistance: the *Mittelstand* should be supported, its advocates argued, because a healthy 'middling estate' was essential to the well-being of the nation. During the second half of the 19th century the term came to be accepted more broadly as a social category that included master artisans, independent retailers and small farmers or independent peasants. Distinctions have been made between this 'old' *Mittelstand* and the 'new' urban *Mittelstand* of white-collar workers in both the public and private sectors. Members of the *Mittelstand* were over-represented in the membership and electoral constituencies of radical right-wing parties in both Germany and Austria. The issue of whether the NSDAP – the Nazi Party – was a *Mittelstandspartei* or a *Volkspartei* (a popular party appealing to the whole people and transcending sectional interests) is at the centre of the debate about the social base of Nazism.

Möbius, August Ferdinand (1790–1868), astronomer and mathematician. Born in Schulpforta, Saxony, Möbius was professor at Leipzig from 1815, and was director of the observatory there. Apart from astronomy his chief concerns were with geometry and topology (the study of properties retained by an object that is deformed). He is remembered for the Möbius strip (a continuous one-sided surface, formed by half twisting a rectangular length of material and then joining the two ends), and the Möbius net, which was important in the development of projective geometry.

modernization theory, a general explanatory model of the transformation of 'traditional' societies into 'modern' ones. It has been applied by some non-Marxist historians to Nazi Germany, to the extent that the effects of Nazi policies had, arguably, a modernizing effect on German society and politics while the regime was trying to achieve anti-modern ends. In fact the most dramatic modernization came with the destruction of the last years of World War II, and changes brought about during the Allied occupation. Moreover, the relationship between Nazism and modernity is now recognized to be a more complex one, and historians are less willing to take Nazi propaganda at its word, whether the tone is modern or anti-modern.

Modrow, Hans (1928–), last leader of the GERMAN DEMOCRATIC REPUBLIC. Modrow was born in Jasenitz into a working-class family. At the end of World War II he was drafted into the *VOLKSSTURM*, and taken prisoner by the Soviets. In 1949 he returned to Germany and joined the ruling SED, the East German youth movement (*FREIE DEUTSCHE JUGEND*, FDJ) and the FDGB (the East German trade-union organization). From 1967 to 1989 he was a member of the Central Committee (ZK) of the SED, and from 1973 first secretary of the party in Dresden. In 1989 he became a member of the Politburo, and opened a dialogue with opposition parties. As president of the GDR council of ministers he attempted to manage the political changes taking place with the aim of preserving the East German state as an independent political entity, and pursued the possibility of a confederation with the FEDERAL REPUBLIC. In 1994, after reunification (1990), his parliamentary immunity was lifted by the BUNDESTAG, and he was accused of abuse of office in the former GDR. He was found guilty of falsifying local election results and given a suspended prison sentence. In 1999 he was elected as one of six PDS members of the European Parliament.

Moldenhauer, Paul (1876–1947), conservative politician and academic. Moldenhauer was born in Cologne into the middle-class business establishment of the Rhineland, and studied at the Cologne *Handelshochschule* (commercial university). He was a member of the German People's Party (DVP) and was elected to the Prussian constituent assembly in 1919 and to the Reichstag the following year. He was first economics minister, then minister of finance (1929–30). He remained in the BRÜNING cabinet briefly after the collapse of the MÜLLER coalition in 1930, and his own political views were not dissimilar to those of the new chancellor. Later, he had a certain amount of sympathy for the Nazi regime's policies, approving of the dissolution of political parties in 1933, and of Germany's break with the LEAGUE OF NATIONS. From 1931 to 1943 he was honorary professor at the *Technische Hochschule* in Charlottenburg, and at the University of Berlin, and in 1933 he took part in the Geneva DISARMAMENT CONFERENCE. After World War II he worked on the regulation of pension funds.

Molotov–Ribbentrop pact (23 August 1939), also called the Nazi–Soviet pact or the Hitler–Stalin pact, a non-aggression pact between Germany and the USSR signed in Moscow by RIBBENTROP, the German foreign minister, and his Soviet counterpart, V.M. Molotov. The agreement contained an additional secret protocol providing for the division of Poland between Germany and the Soviet Union. Germany also acknowledged Soviet interest in the Baltic states and Bessarabia. As a result Poland was partitioned after the brief campaign of September 1939. Western Poland (Katowice, Pomorze and Poznań) was annexed directly by Germany and these provinces, along with Danzig, went to make up the new *GAUE* of Danzig-West Prussia and the WARTHELAND. (Some territory from these districts was added to East Prussia and Silesia, and Tešín became part of the latter); central Poland became a German protectorate (the *GENERALGOU-VERNEMENT*), and the rest of Poland was occupied by the Soviet Union. The treaty was revised on 28 September 1939, when the USSR ceded Lublin district and part of Warsaw district to Germany in return for unchallenged control of Lithuania. Shortly afterwards the Baltic republics, Estonia, Latvia and Lithuania were absorbed into the Soviet Union (15–17 June 1940), and Bessarabia and the northern part of Bukovina were annexed by the USSR later the same year. Local communist parties were ordered by Moscow to cease their anti-fascist activities. The pact came to an end with the German invasion of the Soviet Union in June 1941.

Moltke, Helmuth (James), Graf von (1907–45), great-grand nephew of Field Marshal Helmuth von MOLTKE and a legal adviser to the German high command (OKW). Moltke was an opponent of the Nazi regime, and a co-founder and leading member of the KREISAU CIRCLE, which met at the family estate in Kreisau, Silesia. He was arrested after the failed JULY BOMB PLOT of 1944, and tried for treason on the grounds that he had not reported the activities of the conspirators to the authorities. He was executed at Plötzensee prison on 23 January 1945.

Moltke, Helmuth (Johannes Ludwig), Graf von (1848–1916), chief of the general staff of the army (1906–14). Moltke was the nephew of the elder Helmuth von MOLTKE, and was his adjutant from 1882. He succeeded Alfred von SCHLIEFFEN as chief of the general staff, and inherited his predecessor's plan for the invasion of France, which he attempted, unsuccessfully, to implement in 1914. He failed, it has been argued, to retain control of the developing military situation, and as a consequence the German advance was checked at the battle of the MARNE. The swift victory over France that the Germans had hoped for eluded them, and Moltke was effectively dismissed on September 14. He was succeeded by FALKENHAYN.

Moltke, Helmuth (Karl Bernhard), Graf von (1800–91), field marshal. Moltke was born into the Prussian aristocracy in Parchim, Mecklenburg. His father emigrated to Denmark when he was a small boy and he was educated with the Royal Cadet Corps in Copenhagen. He gained a commission in the Prussian army in 1822. His career was interrupted by poor health, and he studied modern languages and turned to writing fiction and translating before returning to the military as an officer in the general staff in 1832. He then spent four years in Turkey, advising on the modernization of the army. In 1855 he was appointed personal aide-de-camp to the future FRIEDRICH III and he was appointed chief of the Prussian general staff on the eve of the wars of UNIFICATION in 1858. He reorganized the Prussian army, which had been thoroughly rearmed with modern weaponry throughout the previous two decades, and he was quick to recognize the importance that railways would make to troop movements and provisioning. His strategic planning was central to the defeat of Denmark (1864; see GERMAN–DANISH WAR), Austria (1866; see AUSTRO-PRUSSIAN WAR) and France (1870–1; see FRANCO-PRUSSIAN WAR). Moltke's rewards came in cash, rank and social status. He received enough money after his victory over Austria at SADOVÁ (Königgrätz) to buy an estate at Kreisau, near Breslau (now Wrocław in Poland), and after defeating the French at SEDAN was created a count (*Graf*) and promoted to field marshal. He remained chief of staff until 1888, when he retired to Kreisau. He died during a visit to Berlin three years later. He was succeeded as chief of general staff by Alfred von Waldersee. His nephew, also Helmuth von MOLTKE, also became chief of the general staff of the army.

Mommsen, Theodor (1817–1903), historian. Born in Garding, Schleswig, the son of a Protestant minister, Mommsen studied law at Kiel, and then spent three years in Italy, where he worked on Latin inscriptions. When he returned he was appointed to a chair of civil law at Leipzig in 1848, but lost his post after taking part in revolutionary activities in Saxony. He was subsequently professor at Zurich and at Breslau (now Wrocław in Poland). A liberal nationalist, Mommsen was a member of the Prussian LANDTAG from 1873 to 1879, and of the Reichstag from 1881 to 1884. The first three volumes of his great historical work on Roman history, *Römische Geschichte*, were published between 1854 and 1856, and a fifth volume was published in 1885, but it was never completed. (The fourth volume, was to have been on the emperors, but Mommsen abandoned it.) His work on Roman constitutional law was published as *Römisches Staatsrecht* between 1871 and 1888. He also remained engaged in contemporary political issues, as in 1880 when he challenged Heinrich von TREITSCHKE's attribution of the negative effects of modernization to the influence of Jews.

Monowitz, also called AUSCHWITZ III or 'the Buna camp', it was the largest of the Auschwitz satellite camps, and supplied slave labour to IG FARBEN and other German firms.

Mons, battle of (August 1914), the first engagement between German forces and the British Expeditionary Force during World War I. Despite superior firepower the British were defeated, and the 'retreat from Mons' came to represent the failure of the Allies to prevent the German invasion of France.

Montgelas de Garnerin, Maximilian Joseph, Graf von (1759–1838), minister-president of Bavaria during the Napoleonic Wars (the Wars of the COALITIONS). Born in Munich, the son of an aristocrat from Savoy, Montgelas became first minister of Bavaria in 1799, and introduced reforms to modernize the political system. He was also finance minister (from 1803) and interior minister (from 1807). In 1808 he produced a written constitution that abolished serfdom and established modern legislative and judicial institutions. His aim was to establish an independent Bavaria, but this aspiration was thwarted. Bavaria remained subordinate to France, and then, after the Napoleonic Wars, joined the GERMAN CONFEDERATION. Montgelas was dismissed in 1817.

Monumenta Germaniae Historica, a collection of documents pertaining to the history of medieval Germany. They were collected and published, originally at the behest of Freiherr vom STEIN.

Morgenthau Plan, plan for the treatment of defeated Germany, proposed at the Quebec Conference of 1944 by Henry Morgenthau, secretary of the US Treasury, who was dismayed by what he saw as plans to assist German recovery without sufficient consideration of how to prevent further aggression in the future. He urged the de-industrialization of the defeated Nazi Germany after the end of the war. The plan was briefly given approval by Roosevelt and, reluctantly, by Churchill. In the end, however, it was considered unrealistic by both Britain and the USA, but was used in Nazi propaganda.

Moroccan crisis of 1905, international crisis provoked by an agreement between France and Spain, supported by Britain, to partition Morocco. Chancellor von BÜLOW attempted to use the situation to isolate France and weaken the Entente, and Kaiser WILHELM II duly paid a visit to Tangier, where he made a speech in support of the Moroccans. Counsellor von Schoen, an envoy in the imperial suite, reported that there were no unfortunate events, a good impression was made on the Moroccans, and that the Kaiser was very satisfied with the visit, and especially with the sultan's reassurance that he would consult Germany before instituting any reforms. The confrontation was defused, however, by the close cooperation of Britain and France at the ALGECIRAS CONFERENCE. A second Morocco crisis (the AGADIR crisis) was prompted by the sending of a German gunboat, the *Panther,* to Agadir in 1911, ostensibly to protect German interests.

Möser, Justus (1720–94), public servant and influential conservative political theorist. Möser was born in Osnabrück into a leading local family, and studied law at Halle and Göttingen. He then returned to Osnabrück (1744), and apart from a trip to England in 1764, he spent the rest of his life there. He was appointed secretary to the *Ritterschaft,* which represented local aristocratic interests, while still a student, and settled down to a distinguished career as a lawyer and leading public servant in his tiny and institutionally conservative native state. He was appointed *advocatus patriae,* a judicial post overseeing the financial interests of the state and the local aristocracy, and in 1762 he was appointed to a judicial position by the cathedral chapter. In addition to fulfilling his complicated administrative duties Möser was a prolific writer. His three-volume *Osnabrückische Geschichte* (1768–1824) had a significance and resonance far beyond Osnabrück and HERDER reprinted part of it in his collection *Von teutscher Art und Kunst.* Möser was a political conservative whose ideas ran counter to the prevalent ideology of the ENLIGHTENMENT. He articulated a local patriotism, arguing that the 'organic' peasant community was the ideal form of society, along with the 'home town' that housed its local institutions. In 1766 he founded the *Wöchentliche Osnabrückische Zeitung,* which served not only as the official bulletin of the government, but also as the repository of Möser's own thoughts on life and politics. His articles were reprinted as *Patriotische Phantasien* (1774–86). Möser's influence as a thinker on political and constitutional issues was widespread, and although he can be seen as a founder of modern German conservatism, he influenced not only other conservatives such as Freiherr vom STEIN, but liberal reformers such as HARDENBERG, literary figures such as Herder, and Enlightenment intellectuals such as his biographer Friedrich Nicolai (1733–1811).

Mozart, Wolfgang Amadeus (1756–91), composer. Mozart was born in Salzburg, which was not yet then a part of Austria. His father, Leopold Mozart, was court composer to the archbishop, and taught him piano, violin and composition from an early age. Mozart toured the capitals of Europe as a child performer, along with his father and sister, Maria Anna (Nannerl). He began to compose his first symphonies in London in 1764. He spent a short time in Vienna in 1767 where he composed an opera for the emperor, but returned to Salzburg and became *Konzertmeister* to the archbishop, an honorary (that is, unpaid) position. He composed *La finta giardiniera* and *Il rè pastore* after extended visits to Italy in the early 1770s, and visited Augsburg, Mannheim and Paris between 1777 and 1779.

After eventually gaining employment as organist at the archbishop's court in Salzburg and working on *Idomeneo* (1781), a commission from Munich, Mozart left again for Vienna in 1781 for the coronation of Joseph II. The following year he married Constanze Weber and wrote *Die Entführung aus dem Serail* (*The Abduction from the Seraglio*), a *Singspiel* (opera with spoken dialogue) for the *Nationalsingspiel*, which was promoted by Joseph II. Between 1784 – the year he became a Freemason – and 1786 he produced twelve piano concertos, and *Le Nozze di Figaro* (*The Marriage of Figaro*, 1786), based on the revolutionary play by Beaumarchais. In 1787, the year of the first performance of *Don Giovanni* in Prague, he was appointed to a position at the imperial court that carried a salary of 800 gulden in return for the composition of dance music for court balls. In 1789 Mozart travelled to Berlin, stopping at Prague, Dresden and Leipzig en route. The following year he composed *Così fan tutte* and travelled to Frankfurt for the coronation of the new emperor LEOPOLD II. In 1791 he composed *Die Zauberflöte* (*The Magic Flute*), a subversive Masonic *Singspiel* based on a collection of fairy tales, which was performed in a small suburban theatre. In the same year he wrote *La clemenza di Tito*. He also began work on an anonymous commission for a requiem mass, but died before completing it, in Vienna in December 1795.

Mozart's stature as, arguably, the greatest composer in the European musical tradition, has generated a great deal of distorted mythology about his life – not least about his prodigious musical genius (at the expense of his conscientiousness and painstaking attention to his work), and the melodramatic circumstances surrounding his death suggested by 20th-century popular theatre and cinema. Like other major figures in the cultural canons his reputation in many ways transcends his musical achievements, and his name has been put to both political and commercial uses, not least by the tourist industries of Vienna and Salzburg. He has been celebrated as an outstanding (and above all positive) figure in the German cultural tradition, and as a reference point in the politics of Austrian national identity.

MSPD (*Mehrheits-Sozialdemokratische Partei Deutschlands*, Majority Social Democratic Party of Germany), a term used to describe the rump of the SPD following the departure of left-wing members to form the Independent Social Democratic Party of Germany (*Unabhängige Sozialdemokratische Partei Deutschlands*, USPD) in 1917. When the USPD split in 1922 some members joined the Communist Party (KPD), and others returned to the SPD.

Mülhausen, battle of (19 August 1914), early engagement in World War I. The French occupied Mülhausen (Mulhouse) during their advance into Alsace-Lorraine in early August 1914. The Germans mounted a counter attack, but the French managed to occupy the town again on 19 August.

Müller, Friedrich (1823–1900), philologist. Müller, the son of the poet Wilhelm Müller, pursued a career in comparative linguistics at Oxford University (1849–75). Müller was an orientalist, who used the term 'Aryan' to describe the Indo-European family of languages.

Müller, Georg von (1854–1940), admiral. Von Müller was head of the imperial naval cabinet from 1906 to 1918. His diaries and memoirs were published in English in 1961.

Müller, Heinrich (1901–?), head of the GESTAPO. Born in Munich, Müller served on the Eastern Front during World War I and then pursued a career in the Bavarian police. He was head of the Gestapo from 1935 until the end of World War II, and was closely involved in the routine administration for the implementation of the 'final solution' (*see* HOLOCAUST). He disappeared at the end of the war and was never found.

Müller, Hermann (1876–1931), Social Democratic politician; chancellor (1920 and 1928–30). Born in Mannheim, the son of a factory manager, Müller joined the SPD in 1893. He was editor of the *Görlitzer Volkszeitung* newspaper from 1899, but subsequently became a full-time paid official of the party. He was elected to the party leadership in 1906 and to the Reichstag in 1916. Müller was on the right of the party, and was ready for the SPD to cooperate with the government during World War I. He remained with the Majority Social Democrats (MSPD) when the party split in 1917, but played an important part in the Workers' and Soldiers' Councils movement (*see* RÄTE) in 1918. He was appointed foreign minister in the BAUER government (1919), in which office he was one of the principal German cosignatories of the treaty of VERSAILLES.

Müller was chancellor twice (from March to June 1920 and from 1928 to 1930). His first administration was a 'Weimar coalition' (MSPD, liberal DDP and Catholic CENTRE PARTY) formed after the fall of the Bauer government, without fresh elections, and on the basis of representation in the NATIONAL ASSEMBLY. The coalition was beleaguered by extremist agitation on the part of right-wing paramilitary groups, and by the Communists. It failed to survive the polarization of political attitudes revealed by the first Reichstag elections, and was replaced by a centre–right coalition led by Konstantin FEHRENBACH of the Centre Party in June 1920. Müller remained chairman of the SPD (1919–27).

Müller's second administration took office following a shift to the left in the elections of 1928, which made a government without the SPD impossible. This was a problem in a political climate where both the conservative DVP and the Centre Party were inclined to exclude the Social Democrats from office and influence if at all possible. In this context the death in 1929 of Gustav STRESEMANN (Müller's DVP foreign minister) was a blow to the coherence of the government. The administration was bedevilled not only by differences between the coalition parties – which represented divergent sectional interests in a deteriorating economic climate – but also by differences between ministers attempting to compromise and their own backbenchers. The government fell against the background of the slump, and in the face of a frontal assault by business and industrialists (represented primarily by the DVP) on the basic welfare provisions of the Weimar system. The changes to the unemployment benefit system that prompted the collapse of the government merely provided the focus for a far broader conflict of interests between capital and labour: negotiations on the right for the installation of an anti-Marxist government that would rule without parliament had begun long before the crisis of March 1930. The fall of the government marked the effective end of parliamentary government in Weimar Germany, as Müller's successor, Heinrich BRÜNING, failed to secure a parliamentary majority, and ruled by presidential decree.

Munich agreement (30 September 1938), pact between Britain, Germany, France and Italy to partition Czechoslovakia by forcing the cession of the SUDETENLAND to Germany, as Hitler had demanded. The Sudeten Germans, the German-speaking inhabitants of Bohemia and Moravia (formerly Austrian territories of the HABSBURGS, and part of the new republic of Czechoslovakia since 1918), were the focus of German foreign policy after the ANSCHLUSS of Austria in March 1938. Nazi Germany created an atmosphere of international crisis in response to alleged mistreatment by Prague of the German minority. Various attempts were made by the Western democracies to mediate between the two countries, and in the end a four-power conference was held at Munich, where the United Kingdom, France and Italy agreed to Germany's demands for the cession of the territories. The agreement deprived Czechoslovakia of important border defences, alienated the Soviet Union and generated a disillusionment with the democracies among oppositional circles within Germany itself. The agreement was the culmination of British Prime Minister Neville Chamberlain's appeasement policy.

Munich putsch. *See* BEER HALL PUTSCH.

Murr, Wilhelm (1888–1945), *Gauleiter* of Württemberg-Hohenzollern. He became state *REICHSSTATTHALTER*, interior minister and economics minister in Württemberg in March 1933 during the Nazi takeover or 'coordination' (*GLEICHSCHALTUNG*) of the federal states (*Länder*).

Mussert, Anton (1894–1946), Dutch Nazi leader. Mussert was the founder of the Dutch Nazi movement (*Nationaal-Socialistische Beweging*). The movement, one of many marginal fascist groups, was always unpopular in the Netherlands, but by 1941 it had absorbed its rivals and was the only party permitted by the Nazis. Mussert was named 'leader' of the Dutch people in 1942, and formed a consultative cabinet the following year. Leading members of the movement were assassinated, and Mussert himself was hanged for treason in 1946.

N

Nacht-und-Nebel-Erlass. *See* NIGHT AND FOG DECREE.

Nadolny, Rudolf (1873–1953), diplomat. Nadolny was German minister in Sweden from 1921 to 1925, and then ambassador first to Turkey (1925–32) and then to the Soviet Union (1933–4). He was also the head of the German delegation to the Geneva DIS-ARMAMENT CONFERENCE in 1932.

Nahrungsfreiheit ('nutritional freedom'), a term used to denote the self-sufficiency in food supplies to which the Nazis notionally aspired.

> *See also* AUTARKY.

Napolas (*Nationalpolitische Erziehungsanstalten*, 'national political educational institutes'), elite schools for 10- to 18-year-olds, founded in 1933 by the Nazis. They were formally under the jurisdiction of the education ministry, but effectively run by the SS and SA. In all, 23 such schools were set up, and their purpose was to train a future generation of politicians and bureaucrats. The overwhelming majority of the schools were for boys; only two 'Napolas' for girls were ever in operation.

Napoleonic Wars. *See* COALITIONS, WARS OF THE; LIBERATION, WARS OF.

National Assembly (1848). *See* FRANKFURT PARLIAMENT.

National Assembly (1919), the constituent assembly of the WEIMAR REPUBLIC. It was the aim of the Social Democrats to convene a national assembly as soon as possible after the NOVEMBER REVOLUTION of 1918, but the decision on a date for the elections was to be made by the First National CONGRESS OF WORKERS' AND SOLDIERS' COUNCILS, which met in Berlin in December. Elections were held within a few weeks, on 19 January 1919, and the Majority Social Democrats (MSPD) emerged as the largest single party with 38% percent of the vote and 165 of the 423 seats. The breakaway, more radical USPD, which had left the COUNCIL OF PEOPLE'S REP-RESENTATIVES on 29 December and the Prus-sian government on 3 January, received only 7.6% of the vote and 22 seats. This meant that the majority was with the middle-class parties, the largest of which were neverthe-less the two most moderate, the Catholic CENTRE PARTY and the liberal DDP, with 91 and 75 seats respectively.

Hugo PREUSS, a democratic liberal and state secretary in the interior ministry since November, was charged with drafting a con-stitution that reflected the dominant polit-ical coalition of moderate Social Democrats and middle-class liberals. In addition, a com-mittee of the German federal states was established on 25 January, which was effec-tively a precursor of the Weimar upper house, the REICHSRAT. The assembly itself met in Weimar on 6 February, away from the polit-ical upheavals of Berlin (*see* SPARTACUS UPRISING), and elected Friedrich EBERT as president (11 February) with the power to appoint a provisional cabinet responsible to the assembly. The assembly thereby became a provisional parliamentary legislature, and the cabinet a new provisional government, replacing the Council of People's Representatives. The Weimar constitution was adopted by the assembly on 31 July, and signed by Ebert on 11 August.

National Committee for a Free Germany (*Nationalkomitee Freies Deutschland*), central committee of the Soviet-inspired anti-Nazi movement *'Freies Deutschland'*. The committee was founded in 1943 by German émigrés and prisoners of war in Krasnogorsk, near Moscow. One of its members was the KPD leader Wilhelm PIECK. Many of its members were appointed to key positions in the Soviet zone of occupation after 1945.

National Democratic Party (*Nationaldemokratische Partei Deutschlands*). *See* NPD.

Nationale Volksarmee (NVA), the National People's Army, armed forces of the GERMAN DEMOCRATIC REPUBLIC. It was formed in 1956 from the armed police units of the barracks police (*kasernierte Volkspolizei*) and the limited air and naval forces that had been discreetly built up by East Germany.

Nationalkomitee Freies Deutschland. *See* NATIONAL COMMITTEE FOR A FREE GERMANY.

National Liberal Party (*Nationalliberale Partei*), political party founded on 17 November 1866. The party was formed by members of the Progressive Party (*DEUTSCHE FORTSCHRITTSPARTEI*) in the Prussian diet, who left to support BISMARCK. Its heyday was the *GRÜNDERZEIT*, under the leadership of Rudolf von BENNIGSEN and Johannes von MIQUEL. The party was the largest in the 1871 Reichstag with 125 seats, and it increased its lead over the conservative parties in the 1874 election by gaining a further 30 seats while the Conservatives lost 25. It supported Bismarck throughout the 1870s, but its hopes for a ministry accountable to the Reichstag and parliamentary control over finance were frustrated, and its relationship with the chancellor became cooler. It lost seats in the elections of 1877

(falling back to 128) and 1879 (99) and the party split in 1880.

The rump of the party was reorganized by Miquel and came to terms with Bismarck, while the left wing and the unwavering supporters of free trade formed or joined other parties. The reorganized National Liberals represented the interests of big business. Neither Bennigsen nor Miquel were industrialists, and nor was Ernst Bassermann (1854–1917), who led the party from 1898, but the influence of industry was particularly strong in the Prussian LANDTAG, where the interests of the Rhine and Ruhr industrialists were represented. These industrialists therefore benefited from Bismarck's pro-tariff and ANTI-SOCIALIST policies during the 1880s. Conservatives and Liberals cooperated formally in the *Sammlung* ('politics of concentration' or nationalist 'rallying together') of the late 1890s. Most of the party's remaining members joined the DVP after World War I.

Nationalrat ('national council'), the lower house of the Austrian parliament since 1918.

National Revolution, a term used by the Nazis to describe the reign of terror by Nazi stormtroopers after the appointment of Hitler as chancellor, and more specifically after the March 1933 election and the passing of the ENABLING LAW. It began with the brutal suppression of the Communist Party (KPD) after the REICHSTAG FIRE, and of the SPD and trade unions in May, and involved the dissolution of the other parties and the establishment of a one-party state during the summer of 1933. The federal states were also brought into line or 'coordinated' during 1933, and the civil service was purged of Jews and Social Democrats. Hitler called an end to the 'National Revolution' at a conference of REICHSSTATTHALTER (Reich governors) on 6 July, but arbitrary interference in routine matters of administration by all sections of the Nazi Party – but most particularly and most violently by members of the SA – continued into 1934. This caused disquiet among the middle-class supporters of the Nazis' conservative allies, and prompted von Papen's MARBURG SPEECH deploring the continuing political disorder. A definitive end to this phase in the Nazi consolidation of power was reached with the NIGHT OF THE LONG KNIVES on 30 June 1934.

National Socialist German Workers' Party. *See* NSDAP.

Nationalverein, Deutscher (German National Association), a liberal political organization founded in 1859 in Frankfurt am Main. It had some 30,000 members, and embraced both 'national liberals' and radical liberals, and under the leadership of Rudolf von BENNIGSEN it campaigned for the unification of Germany under Prussian leadership. It was dissolved in 1867, and most of its members went on to support the NATIONAL LIBERAL PARTY.

National-Zeitung, originally the *Deutsche Soldaten-Zeitung*, a newspaper founded in 1950 by Helmut Damerau, a former Nazi Party functionary, and Paul Steiner, a former SS officer, among others. The paper was subsidized by the Americans and by the federal press office, but its circulation sank from 30,000 to 9000 before it was taken over by Gerhard Frey, who founded the DSZ-Druckschriften- und Zeitungsverlag publishing company in 1958. Since 1963 the paper has been called the *Deutsche National-Zeitung*, and is aimed at the radical right. For as long as it was legal the *National-Zeitung* sought to question, obscure and deny the historical existence of the HOLOCAUST. German intellectuals petitioned the government to take action against the newspaper in the 1960s, but when the centre–left coalition of the early 1970s attempted to act against Frey, its case was dismissed by the FEDERAL CONSTITUTIONAL COURT.

Nations, battle of the. *See* LEIPZIG, BATTLE OF.

Natzweiler, a Nazi CONCENTRATION CAMP in Alsace.

Naumann, Friedrich (1860–1919), liberal politician. Naumann was born, the son of a pastor, in Störmthal near Leipzig. He

studied theology at Leipzig University and was a co-founder of the nationalist German Students' Association (*Verein Deutscher Studenten*) in 1881. He became the pastor of Langenberg in the Erzgebirge in 1883, and married Maria Magdalena Zimmermann three years later. In the Evangelical Social Congress he led a group of liberals opposed to the conservative and anti-Semitic politics of Adolf STOECKER. In 1896 he founded the *Nationalsozialer Verein* (National Social Association), whose liberal-democratic domestic agenda was influenced by Max WEBER. The association was dissolved in 1903, and Naumann joined the small liberal *Freissinnige Partei*.

Navajos, an oppositional working-class youth gang from Cologne during the early 1940s. They were one of a number of such groups from the Rhineland and Ruhr.

See also EDELWEISS PIRATES.

Navy League (*Deutscher Flottenverein*), one of a number of radical right-wing (*VÖLKISCH*) pressure groups that flourished in Germany before World War I. It was founded in 1898, following the campaign for the First Navy Law. It started with just over 14,000 members, a figure that had risen to over 330,000 by 1914 (over a million with corporate affiliations). Ostensibly representative of a wider coalition of interests, the Navy League's executive was initially controlled by a clique of businessmen and conservative politicians representing the 'alliance of iron and rye'. Its grass-roots membership was more typically drawn from lower middle-class nationalist circles, over which the political elites within and outside the organization were unable to establish control.

Nazarenes (*Nazarener*), a group of artists of the early 19th century who sought to regenerate religious art in Germany. The group's founder and leader, Johann Friedrich Overbeck (1789–1869), emigrated to Italy along with several like-minded friends and worked in a deserted monastery in Rome, painting in the style of the 14th century. The group was an influence on the English Pre-Raphaelites.

Nazi Party. *See* NSDAP.

Nazi–Soviet Pact. *See* MOLOTOV–RIBBENTROP PACT.

Nebe, Arthur (1894–1945), head of the criminal police (*Kripo*) from 1933 to 1945. The son of a school teacher, Nebe served in World War I, and then joined the criminal police. He joined the NSDAP (Nazi Party) and the SS in 1931, and was responsible for reorganizing the criminal police during the 1930s. In 1939 he was appointed head of Amt (department) V of the RSHA (Reich Security Head Office). During World War II Nebe was commander of EINSATZGRUPPE B, an SS murder squad operating from Minsk in 1941, and responsible for 46,000 'executions'. Although he was not a suspect in the JULY BOMB PLOT, Nebe went underground in 1944, and was executed the following March.

negative integration, an analytical concept borrowed from the social sciences and used by historians of the German empire – such as Hans-Ulrich Wehler – to describe the political strategy of the BISMARCK regime, which, they argue, sought to distract attention from the ill effects of social change by diverting popular attention towards a common enemy.

neo-absolutism, a term used to refer to the system of rule in Austria after the suppression of the REVOLUTIONS OF 1848, under interior minister Alexander, Freiherr von BACH. The end of the regime, and the introduction of constitutional government, came with Austria's defeat by France in Italy in 1859.

neo-Nazis, a generic term used to describe a range of radical right-wing groups in Germany and Austria since the end of World War II. Despite the prohibition of Nazi movements and the notion of a 'zero hour' (*Stunde Null*) in 1945, implying an abrupt discontinuity between the Third Reich and its successor states, a substantial number of former Nazis remained politically active in right-wing organizations during the early

days of the Federal Republic. During the late 1940s and early 1950s there was a plethora of such groups, foremost among them the *SOZIALISTISCHE REICHSPARTEI* and the *DEUTSCHE REICHSPARTEI*, precursors of the marginally more successful NPD (National Democratic Party). In addition, the *DEUTSCHE VOLKSUNION* was founded in 1971, 'on the eve of the centenary of the founding of the Second Reich', as a supra-party movement of the radical right. The REPUBLICANS, founded in 1983, had a brief spell of electoral success in West Germany during the late 1980s. In the German Democratic Republic, meanwhile, the NDPD (*National-demokratische Partei Deutschlands*, National Democratic Party of Germany) was formed specifically as an organization designed to draw former Nazis away from the ranks of the ruling SED, and more importantly, to prevent them emigrating to the West. In Austria more than 500,000 people were affected by the laws dissolving Nazi organizations after World War II. The League of Independents (*Verein der Unabhängigen*, VdU), precursor of the FPÖ (the present *Freiheitliche Partei Österreichs*, Austrian Freedom Party), was formed in 1949 as an alternative to the two major parties, and became a potential political home for those isolated by the anti-Nazi legislation.

Neu Beginnen, a Social Democratic resistance group during the Nazi dictatorship. The group was made up of radical members of the *Sozialistische Arbeiterjugend* ('Young Socialist Workers', the youth branch of the SPD) and former Communists, who had got together as early as 1931 to prepare to oppose a Nazi seizure of power. The group was linked to the SPD after 1934, and received financial help from the party's exiled leaders. In 1935 its leader, Walter Löwenheim, attempted to dissolve the group in the belief that resistance to the new regime was futile, but was opposed and replaced by the radical majority of the membership in Berlin. Shortly afterwards most of the Berlin organization was suppressed by the Gestapo, but other groups survived in the south.

Neuengamme, a CONCENTRATION CAMP near Hamburg, set up in 1940. Its main function was to supply labour for the munitions industry.

Neue Rheinische Zeitung, a left-wing newspaper published in Cologne during the REVOLUTIONS OF 1848, and associated with Karl MARX (who was editor), Friedrich ENGELS, and other members of the Communist League. By the time of its demise in 1849 it had a circulation of some 6000.

Neue Sachlichkeit ('new objectivity'), cultural movement that emerged in the 1920s as a reaction to EXPRESSIONISM and DADA. The *Neue Sachlichkeit* movement has been perceived as a short-lived but optimistic coming to terms with mass culture. The term embraces the art of Otto DIX and George GROSZ, and the literary genre of urban 'reportage' that had been popular since the turn of the century.

Neues Deutschland, the official party paper of the SED, and then of its successor party, the PDS.

Neues Forum, East German 'citizens' movement' (*Bürgerbewegung*). The movement was founded on 9 September 1989 by dissident intellectuals and political activists in the GERMAN DEMOCRATIC REPUBLIC, including Bärbel BOHLEY and Jens REICH. The group merged with other GDR opposition groups to form BÜNDNIS 90 ('Alliance 1990') in February 1990.

Neumann, Heinz (1902–37), Communist politician. Born into a middle-class family in Berlin, Neumann joined the KPD in its very early days in 1920. He abandoned his university studies and became a full-time party functionary and editor of the *Rote Fahne* ('red flag') newspaper. He visited the Soviet Union in 1922 and met leading members of the Soviet Communist Party (CPSU). He was KPD representative on the Comintern in Moscow during the mid-1920s, and promoted the Kremlin's line when he re-turned to Germany in 1928, encouraging not only a radical anti-fascist line, but also an intensified opposition to the 'social fascists' (i.e. the German SPD). He was a member of the Reichstag from 1930 to 1932. He was ousted from the party leadership and abandoned by Stalin in 1932, but after Hitler came to power he emigrated to the Soviet Union. He was arrested there in 1937, and is presumed to have been executed or murdered.

Neurath, Konstantin, Freiherr von (1873–1956), German foreign minister (1932–8). Von Neurath was born in Klein-Glattbach into an old Württemberg aristocratic family. He studied law and began his career in the foreign office in 1901. After World War I he was posted to Copenhagen (1919–21), and then was ambassador in Rome (1921–30), and London (1930–2). He was appointed foreign minister in 1932 and remained in office until Hitler's purge of the conservatives in 1938, when he was replaced by RIBBENTROP. He subsequently became Reich protector of Bohemia and Moravia (1939–43; on leave after 1941). He was tried at Nuremberg and sentenced to 15 years, but released in 1954 on health grounds.

New Course, reforms imposed on the Soviet Bloc from Moscow after the death of Stalin in 1953. In the GERMAN DEMOCRATIC REPUBLIC, the Politburo of the SED officially adopted the New Course on 9 June, and the Council of Ministers explained it two days later (11 June) with reference to the 'serious mistakes' that had been made and the damage that had been caused to the interests of small farmers, small tradespeople, artisans and the intelligentsia. Repressive measures and price increases would be rescinded, and the regime undertook to increase the production of consumer goods. It did not repeal its call of 28 May for a 10% increase in work norms, a policy that was defended in the trade-union newspaper *Die Tribüne*. This led to a construction workers' strike on the STALINALLEE, which spread to other parts of East Germany and involved demonstrations in over 270 towns and some 300,000 workers, people almost exclusively employed in heavy industry, mining and construction. The crisis escalated with the declaration of a state of emergency by the Soviet army, and the articulation of political as well as economic demands by the strikers. The SED announced that the New Course would continue, but also announced wage increases.

New Era. *See* WILHELM I.

new federal states (*neue Bundesländer*), five new federal states created out of the territory of the former German Democratic Republic when East Germany was reunited with the Federal Republic. The states are BRANDENBURG, MECKLENBURG-Vorpommern, SAXONY, SAXONY-ANHALT and THURINGIA. Berlin was also reunited and became a separate federal state. (However, since the term was most widely used during the 1990s as a euphemism for the former GDR, Berlin was not generally counted as a 'new' *Land*. West Berlin had de facto been a *Land* of the Federal Republic.) In the regional elections of October 1990 the CDU was the strongest party in all but one of the new federal states (Brandenburg), and won an absolute majority in Saxony.

new order, the proposed economic and political integration of Europe under German domination planned by the Nazis. The phrase has been widely used both before and after the early 1940s, by both left and right, and has referred to both domestic and international 'new orders'. The term was also used in discussions within Germany of plans to reorganize Europe after a successful war. However, the first detailed discussion of the specifically Nazi 'new order' came with the fall of France and an address to journalists by Walther FUNK, the Nazi economics minister, in July 1940. During the two years or so that followed, when German victory in the war seemed a distinct possibility, the term was widely used in the German media to discuss the European initiatives to be undertaken by the Reich. At the same time it

was taken seriously in London, where John Maynard Keynes was asked to devise a rebuttal and alternative to the Nazis' plans for a post-liberal political and economic order in mainland Europe. Hitler and many others in the Nazi leadership were more sceptical about Germany's European mission (at least until the end of the war, when German propaganda made the Soviet threat to the Nazis a Bolshevik threat to European civilization). Although many German businessmen and bureaucrats saw opportunities in a German-dominated postwar Europe, the regime's policy was the rather more short-term one of plundering the continent of human and capital resources to fuel the war effort while avoiding the total mobilization ostensibly demanded by Nazi rhetoric. The only aspect of the 'new order' pursued with single-mindedness was the racial reordering of the continent, and in particular the genocide of Europe's Jewish population in the HOLOCAUST.

new plan, policy adopted by economics minister Hjalmar SCHACHT in 1934 in order to deal with Germany's urgent foreign exchange crisis. It involved halting the repayment of foreign debts and regulating imports with permits so that hard currency would only be used for the purchase of vital food and raw materials imports. The prior notice required from importers wishing to be allocated foreign exchange gave the government greater control over the regulation of imports. The 'new plan' was a first step towards the AUTARKY (self-sufficiency) for which some economists had long argued, and it went some way in helping the regime to subordinate the economy to the needs of rearmament. It failed to solve the main balance-of-payments problem in the long term, however, and further measures had to be taken in 1936, when the FOUR-YEAR PLAN was introduced.

Niederdonau ('lower Danube'), Nazi name for *Niederösterreich* (Lower Austria). The new *Reichsgau* (*see* GAU) also absorbed the northern part of the BURGENLAND, and former Czech territory from the SUDETENLAND.

Niemöller, Martin (1892–1984), anti-Nazi Protestant pastor. Niemöller was awarded the *Pour le Mérite* for his service as a U-boat commander in World War I. He studied theology after the war and was a pastor in Berlin when the Nazis came to power. An antirepublican nationalist, he was initially approved of by the Nazis, but was a cofounder of the *Pfarrernotbund* (Pastors' Emergency League) and leader of the Confessing Church (the BEKENNENDE KIRCHE). He spent seven years in Sachsenhausen and Dachau for outspoken criticism of the Nazis. After the war he was elected president of the Protestant church in Hesse and Nassau, and was active in the peace movement and the World Council of Churches.

Nietzsche, Friedrich (1844–1900), philosopher. Nietzsche was born in Röcken, Saxony, the son of a Lutheran pastor. He studied theology and classics at Bonn, then at Leipzig (where he met WAGNER), and was appointed to a chair in classical philology at Basle in 1869. His first major work, *Die Geburt der Tragödie aus dem Geiste der Musik* (*The Birth of Tragedy from the Spirit of Music*), was published in 1872. In 1876 he took sick leave from his academic post, and he retired in 1879. His work was greeted with indifference by contemporaries, and the fourth part of *Also sprach Zarathustra* (*Thus Spake Zarathustra*, 1883–5) was published privately. His ideas were to be taken up by the radical right, however, who saw in his concept of the 'will to power' a justification for the rejection of conventional morality by the 'superman'. Despite Nietzsche's disparagement of German nationalism and anti-Semitism, he was to be associated – thanks not least to the efforts of his sister Elisabeth – with the Nazis. Nietzsche collapsed in Turin in 1889, and was mentally ill for much of the rest of his life.

Night and Fog Decree (*Nacht-und-Nebel-Erlass*), secret order of 7 December 1941. It followed a number of attacks on German personnel in occupied western Europe. In order to prevent martyrs being created during trials of resistance activists, Hitler ordered that they should be arrested 'in night and fog', deported to Germany and detained there in isolation. The decree was issued as an OKW (Armed Forces High Command) order, and was signed by Field Marshal KEITEL. A few of the prisoners were tried by military courts. The rest came before the 'People's Court' (*VOLKSGERICHTSHOF*) or the 'special courts' (*Sondergerichte*), a procedure that was formalized by an OKW order of 26 June 1942, stipulating that those acquitted in the military courts should be handed over to the GESTAPO. Many were then sent to CONCENTRATION CAMPS (mainly Gross-Rosen and Natzweiler). There were about 7000 such prisoners, the majority of whom came from France.

Night of the Long Knives (30 June 1934), the popular name given to Hitler's purge of the SA leadership; also called the Röhm purge. The purge followed unease on the part of the Nazis' conservative allies about aggressive behaviour on the part of rank-and-file members during the so-called NATIONAL REVOLUTION of 1933. The army was also concerned about the ambitions of the SA (the Nazi stormtrooper organization), and the party leadership, including Hitler, was apprehensive about the increasingly strident demands from radicals for a 'second revolution'. The SS was used to raid a hotel in Bavaria where SA leaders were staying. A number of prominent stormtroopers (including the SA leader, Ernst RÖHM) were killed immediately, and other murders followed in the wake of the raid. Hitler used the occasion to settle old scores (with SCHLEICHER, Gregor STRASSER and Gustav von KAHR, all of whom were murdered), and to silence von PAPEN, who had been the spokesman for his conservative critics. Edgar JUNG, the author of von Papen's MARBURG SPEECH, was also killed.

Noebel, Willy (1887–1965), public servant and diplomat. Noebel was a Polish expert in the foreign office (1927–33), and then German ambassador, first in Tokyo (1933–8) and then Peru (1938–42).

Nolde, Emil (1867–1956), EXPRESSIONIST artist. Born near Nolde, in Schleswig-Holstein, as Emil Hansen, he studied at Munich, Paris and Copenhagen. Before World War I he was associated with *Die BRÜCKE*, a group of avant-garde artists based in Dresden, and became one of the leading exponents of expressionist painting in Weimar Germany. A number of his paintings were seized as 'degenerate' by the Nazis in 1937, and in 1941 he was forbidden to paint.

Nordhausen, Nazi CONCENTRATION CAMP. Nordhausen was a subsidiary of BUCHEN-WALD, and employed forced labour on the production of V-WEAPONS. Around 20,000 people, about one-third of the total work force, died at the camp.

Northern Light (*Nordlicht*), code name for the anticipated capture of Leningrad, which from 1941 to 1944 was subjected to a siege of 900 days by German forces.

North German Confederation, confederation of German states created by BISMARCK in 1867 after the defeat of Austria in the AUSTRO-PRUSSIAN WAR of 1866. Prussia annexed territories between the eastern and western parts of the kingdom, uniting the two for the first time. Saxony remained independent at the insistence of France and Austria. The confederation encompassed all states north of the River Main. The king of Prussia became hereditary president, and the minister-president of Prussia (Bismarck) became chancellor. The constitution provided for a federal council appointed by the constituent states. Prussia occupied 17 seats out of a total of 43. In addition a Reichstag was established, which was elected by direct universal and equal manhood suffrage. Although in the event the North German Confederation was a provisional arrangement, these constitutional arrangements

served as a model for the GERMAN EMPIRE of 1871. The constitution was accepted on 17 April 1867, and came into force on 1 July.

North Rhine-Westphalia (*Nordrhein-Westfalen*), the most populous of modern Germany's constituent federal states (*Länder*), with a population of around 17 million at the end of the 20th century. Some of Germany's largest and most important cities are there, including Cologne (Köln), Düsseldorf, Bonn, Essen and Dortmund, and the RUHR VALLEY industrial conurbation is wholly within it. The LANDTAG was elected every four years until 1970, and subsequently every five years. Until 1980 the largest single party represented in the Landtag was generally the CDU, which consistently won over 40% of the vote in all regional elections up to that time. Its support declined during the 1980s, as did support for the party's national coalition partner, the FDP (which twice failed to get over the 5% hurdle). Support for the SPD increased to 52.1% in 1985 and was 50% in 1990, and only fell back in the 1990s as the GREENS increased their electoral base. The KPD (Communist Party) won 14% of the vote and 28 seats in 1947, but their electoral support had already declined quite sharply before the party was banned in 1956.

Noske, Gustav (1868–1946), Social Democratic politician. Noske was born into a working-class family in Brandenburg an der Havel and was active in the trade-union movement during the 1880s while Bismarck's ANTI-SOCIALIST LAWS were still in force. He became editor of the *Chemnitzer Volksstimme* newspaper in 1902 and was a member of the Reichstag for the SPD from 1906 to 1920. He was the party's spokesman on military and colonial affairs, and spoke in favour of Germany's right to a colonial empire. Noske was on the right of the party and after World War I helped to contain the radicalism of the NOVEMBER REVOLUTION. He was appointed to fill one of the seats on the COUNCIL OF PEOPLE'S REPRESENTATIVES left vacant by the USPD members who left in December 1918. He negotiated a peaceful end to the KIEL MUTINY, and was elected chairman of the Sailors' Council there and governor of Kiel. As Reich defence minister from 1919 to 1920, he was responsible for the suppression of the SPARTACUS UPRISING and of the Bremen Councils Republic. Further unrest in Berlin was brutally suppressed during the spring of the same year. Noske won support on the right both at home and abroad, but was loathed by the radical left, and unpopular within the SPD and among its working-class constituency. He relied on army officers to support his strategy, but they betrayed him during the KAPP PUTSCH, and the trade unions whose general strike defeated the attempted coup demanded his resignation. With his career in national politics at an end he was appointed governor (*Oberpräsident*) of Hanover (1920–33). He was arrested after the 1944 JULY BOMB PLOT, but survived the end of the Nazi dictatorship.

November criminals, a term used by the Nazis to describe those who were perceived to be responsible for the supposed 'stab in the back' that had led to Germany's humiliation in 1918 (*see DOLCHSTOSSLEGENDE*). It referred more or less to anybody who supported the WEIMAR REPUBLIC, but especially Jews and socialists.

November Revolution (1918), political upheaval in Germany at the end of WORLD WAR I. German politics and society were polarized and radicalized by the experience of the war, and the unequal burden of deprivation that fell on the poorest sections of society. In April 1917 a new party of independent, anti-war Social Democrats (USPD) broke away from the majority party (now referred to as the 'majority Social Democrats' or MSPD), which continued to support the war, while the CENTRE PARTY moved to the left. At the same time, the formation of the *VATER-LANDSPARTEI* (Fatherland Party) in 1917 reflected the drift to the right among sections of the conservative middle classes.

From 1916 there were serious strikes throughout German industry, and new forms of political organization grew up both within and outside the trade-union movement. In April 1917 workers' councils were formed for the first time, and in January 1918 the strike movement peaked in massive stoppages, not only in Germany, but also in Vienna, Budapest and other industrialized regions of Austria and Hungary. The outcome of the January strike movement in the short term was little more than an increased political polarization both within the labour movement (between the MSPD and the USPD), and outside it. Revolution came only in November, at the very end of the war.

Constitutional changes preceded the first insurrections in the autumn by a matter of weeks. Having lost the war, Germany's military leaders (HINDENBURG and LUDENDORFF) and Paul von HINTZE, the state secretary in the foreign ministry, hoped to evade responsibility for it by ceding authority to a new government under Prince Max von BADEN (3 October 1918), and ensuring that constitutional changes were introduced. The new government was responsible for the first time to parliament. The military leadership hoped that the Allies would deal more leniently with a parliamentary government, and in addition the ignominy of the humiliating peace treaty that they anticipated would be associated with the democratic parties that had the majority in parliament. In October the new chancellor introduced the constitutional changes, which removed the monarchy's privileged relationship with the army and navy, made ministers accountable to parliament, and embarked on a reform of the Prussian three-class franchise.

These constitutional reforms from above were outpaced, however, by the revolution from below that they were designed to prevent. Dismayed at the navy's lack of action during the war, and determined to save Germany's honour, Admiral von HIPPER ordered a final sortie against the Royal Navy, which provoked a sailors' mutiny in the Baltic port of Kiel, which then spread to Wilhelmshaven (*see* KIEL MUTINY). The rebellion spread to army units, and by 6 November workers', soldiers' and sailors' councils (*see* RAT) had been set up in all major cities and ports. There was no resistance from the old order and scarcely any bloodshed. Ludendorff's successor, General GROENER, attempted to persuade the MSPD to collaborate with the army in maintaining order, but the concessions demanded at that point by EBERT, the party leader, seemed at the time to be too extreme. Among other things the Social Democrats wanted the abdication of the Kaiser in favour of a regent, and Groener was not prepared to go that far. In the event the problem was superseded by events, and within days a republic had been declared. On 7 November revolution broke out in BAVARIA, the WITTELSBACH dynasty was overthrown and a Bavarian republic declared (8 November). The next day, 9 November, Max von Baden resigned from the Reich chancellorship, which passed to Ebert, and the Kaiser abdicated. A republic was hurriedly declared by Philipp SCHEIDEMANN in order, as he thought, to prevent Karl LIEBKNECHT of the SPARTACUS LEAGUE declaring a councils' or soviet republic first.

Ebert's chancellorship had the legitimacy of continuity, but without the support of the councils movement – which was the real focus of political power in November 1918 – it had no real political authority to begin with. Despite fears of a Bolshevik revolution, however, it rapidly became clear that most members of the councils were Social Democrats of one kind or another (Independents in the larger cities, and MSPD in the smaller towns) and were more inclined towards a Western-style parliamentary democracy than a soviet system. Their chief concern was the maintenance of civil order in their own localities, and they were for the most part content to leave the business of national government to the COUNCIL OF PEOPLE'S REPRESENTATIVES, a core government consisting of three USPD and three MSPD members, pending elections to a constituent NATIONAL ASSEMBLY. The moderation of the councils was reflected in their decision to call elections for such an assembly as soon as possible, rejecting the possibility of making themselves the supreme legislative body and executive authority.

Already, however, there was an incipient, if ill-fated, realignment of political forces. In December the USPD withdrew from the Council of People's Representatives, leaving the running of the country in the hands of the Majority Social Democrat ministers, the conservative imperial bureaucracy and the army, with which Ebert had concluded a secret agreement of mutual support. This agreement was put to the test in January 1919 when the government, army and paramilitary FREIKORPS formations cooperated to suppress the SPARTACUS UPRISING in Berlin. Further revolts, and attempts by the newly formed KPD (Communist Party) to seize power were similarly put down – although the army proved far less willing to act against coup attempts from the right, most notably in the case of the 1920 KAPP PUTSCH.

With elections to the constituent National Assembly in January 1919, the radical phase of the German revolution was over. The elections themselves reflected the support of the vast majority of German electors for democratic parties, and the SPD was the largest single party by far. The WEIMAR constitution established not only a parliamentary democracy, but also the most progressive welfare state of its time. It failed, however, to alter social and economic relations in Germany sufficiently. It left land, industry and public services unreformed in private hands, and important institutions (the civil service, armed forces and universities) largely in the hands of the conservative upper and upper middle classes, many of whom were embittered anti-republicans from the outset.

NPD (*Nationaldemokratische Partei Deutschlands*), the National Democratic Party, a West German party of the extreme right founded in 1964. Despite the presence of twelve former active members of the NSDAP on its executive, the party sought to avoid being identified as a group of former Nazis and cultivated a conservative image. The party won only 2% of the vote in the Bundestag election of 1965, but in subsequent regional elections during the brief economic depression of the mid-1960s it managed to enter regional parliaments. It won 7.9% and eight seats in Hesse in November 1966, and in the next year and a half won over 5% of the vote (the minimum necessary to enter the LAND-TAG) in Bavaria, the Rhineland-Palatinate, Schleswig-Holstein, Lower Saxony, Bremen and Baden-Württemberg, where it gained 9.8%. It was much less successful in Hamburg, and virtually non-existent in North Rhine-Westphalia. In the national parliamentary elections of 1969, however, it just failed to enter the Bundestag, and its support declined during the 1970s. Nevertheless the NPD has provided continuity between the radical right of the 1940s and a younger generation, and its fortunes have been revived by poverty and political disaffection in the NEW FEDERAL STATES (the former East Germany) since 1990.

NSBO (*Nationalsozialistische Betriebszellenorganisation*), the National Socialist Factory Cell Organization. Cells of Nazi factory workers were first established in 1927 and legitimized by the party leadership the following year. Their purpose was to convert industrial workers to Nazism, and Reinhold Muchow was appointed leader (*Organisationsleiter*) of the NSBO. The organisation's journal, *ARBEITERTUM*, was published from 1931, initially with a circulation of 13,000, which (according to its own figures) had increased to 176,000 by April 1933. Membership of the NSBO itself, which stood at 4000 at the beginning of 1931, reached 100,000 by the middle of 1932, and 260,000

by January 1933. This was still a negligible proportion of the workforce, and even after Hitler's appointment the NSBO were unable to win significant support in elections to works councils, despite the purging of Social Democrats and Communists (they only achieved 25% in March 1933). Even the NSBO was too assertive for employers, however, and the power to regulate wages was transferred to the newly created Reich Trustees of Labour on 19 May 1933. The NSBO was in turn purged of its more radical members and subordinated to LEY's German Labour Front (DAF).

NSD (*Nationalsozialistischer Dozentenbund*), the National Socialist University Teachers' Association. Membership was obligatory, and lecturers were required to take a six-week training course with the association before taking up an academic post. This involved political education and physical training. The national director of Nazi academics (*Hauptamtsleiter*) was Walter Schultze.

NSDÄB (*Nationalsozialistische Deutscher Ärztebund*), the Nazi Doctors' League, established in August 1929. The Reich doctors' leader in 1936 was Gerhard Wagner (1888–1939).

NSDAP (*Nationalsozialistische Deutsche Arbeiterpartei*), the National Socialist German Workers' Party (or Nazi Party), an extreme right-wing party that grew out of the DEUTSCHE ARBEITERPARTEI (DAP, German Workers' Party) founded in Munich in 1919. Its broader precursors are to be found in the VÖLKISCH movements of both Germany and Austria at the end of the 19th and beginning of the 20th century. The NSDAP itself was founded on 1 April 1920, and HITLER became leader, with dictatorial powers, in 1921. It was still one of a number of small regional groups on the radical right during the early 1920s, but based as it was in Munich it benefited from the Bavarian authorities' indulgence towards the extreme right. It was only after the abortive BEER HALL PUTSCH of November 1923, and

Hitler's imprisonment in Landsberg prison, that the party built up a national infrastructure and a mass membership, which enabled it to compete with other parties in the Weimar political system in order to win power 'legally'. The party had disintegrated during Hitler's absence, and it was only with some difficulty that he re-established his own authority, first on the Bavarian wing of the movement, and then, at the BAMBERG CONFERENCE (14 February 1926) on the North German section of the party. The Nazis had little electoral success before the Depression. Then there were gains in local elections during 1929, and the party won power at regional level for the first time as coalition partner in an 'anti-Marxist' bloc with the nationalist DNVP and the conservative DVP in Thuringia.

The NSDAP's propaganda effort was directed increasingly (and successfully) at the middle classes and peasants – when the electoral breakthrough at national level came in 1930, it came predominantly in the countryside, in small towns and in well-to-do suburban districts. The party was stronger too in the Protestant north and east than in the Roman Catholic south and west. More straightforwardly, in party-political terms, the party's fortunes rose as those of the middle-class Protestant parties declined, while overall support for the Catholic CENTRE PARTY and the combined support for the two left-wing parties (the SPD and KPD) remained more or less stable. Despite its breakthrough during the Depression, however, the Nazi Party was no more successful than any other party in winning the votes of a majority of German electors: the most it managed in a free election was 37.3% in July 1932. By 1933, however, parliamentary majorities had long ceased to be the most important requirement for government. The crucial factor was the confidence of President HINDENBURG and the small clique of JUNKERS, officers and industrialists at the centre of power, and in January 1933

Hindenburg was persuaded to appoint Hitler chancellor in a government that was still overwhelmingly conservative in terms of its members.

Certain social groups were disproportionately over-represented in the membership of the Nazi Party, above all the self-employed, civil servants (including teachers in schools and universities) and white-collar workers. Other groups were under-represented among the party's rank-and-file membership: industrial workers, peasants and the unemployed. The majority of leaders and senior office holders at local and national level were from middle-class backgrounds.

With the accession of the party to political power in Germany the NSDAP was transformed. The party had about 3000 registered members in 1921, and almost 130,000 by 1930. Membership increased rapidly during the Depression, and had reached almost 850,000 by the time of Hitler's appointment. Thereafter – and particularly following the Nazis' success in the election of March 1933 – the ranks were swollen by opportunists and careerists (referred to as '*Märzgefallene*', 'those fallen in March'). The party had 2.5 million members by May 1933, and a temporary membership freeze was imposed. Party membership in the one-party state was clearly not so much a matter of political commitment as a functional decision, permitting access to certain careers or privileges, and by the middle of World War II there were some 7 million members.

The function of the party itself was also different following the establishment of a one-party state. It had been formed and built up in order to win political power. Once that had been achieved it had served its purpose, and new tasks had to be found for it. After 1933 it increasingly became an organization – or an agglomeration of organizations – involved in various kinds of propaganda and charity work, whose members were often local bigwigs of one kind or another and who were perceived as pedantic busybodies. With the capitulation of Germany in May 1945 the party became defunct, and was declared an illegal organization both by the Allies and the provisional political authorities in Germany and Austria.

See also DENAZIFICATION; NEO-NAZIS.

NSDStB (*Nationalsozialistischer Deutscher Studentenbund*), the National Socialist German Students' Association, a body recognized by the Nazi Party leadership in February 1926. The 'Reich student leader' was Gustav Adolf Scheel.

NS-Frauenschaft, Nazi women's organization, intended to recruit an elite cadre of Nazi women. It was founded in 1931 by Elsbeth Zander, and then reorganized after 1933 by Gertrud BÄUMER. From 1934 its leader was Gertrud SCHOLTZ-KLINK. It had over 3 million members in 1939, and 6.2 million in 1942 – roughly 20% of German women. From 1933 its members were no longer required to be members of the NSDAP as well. 'The Reich women's leadership' (*Reichsfrauenführung*) was subordinate to the Reich leadership (*Reichsleitung*) and oversaw the Reich Committee of Nurses and Carers, the German Red Cross and the women's section of the labour front (DAF). All other activities within the scope of the *NS-Frauenschaft* were organized in theory within the DEUTSCHES FRAUENWERK. This model was repeated at all the hierarchical levels of the party: the *Gau-Frauenschaftsleiterin* was subordinate to the *Gauleiter,* but otherwise responsible for the work of the *Deutsches Frauenwerk* within the GAU. The *Kreis-Frauenschaftsleiterin* occupied a similar position at district level, and so on. This meant that despite the profound anti-feminism of the Nazis, there were structures in place from Reich level down to the locality and the party cell for women to occupy formal positions in the life of the party that reflected exactly the hierarchical structures of men's party careers.

The work of the women's organization remained on traditional territory, however.

Women were prepared for war, and educated in efficient home economics, including nutrition and the preserving of fresh food. The organization ran courses in other household skills (such as sewing), provided carers to supplement the work of medical professionals and social workers, and organized charity collections through the Winter Aid organization (*WINTERHILFSWERK*).

NSKK (*Nationalsozialistisches Kraftfahrerkorps*), the Nazi Motor Corps, one of the Nazi Party's paramilitary organizations. The NSKK was responsible for the pre-military training of recruits for the army's motorized units. The leader of the NSKK in 1936 was Adolf Hühnlein (1881–1942).

NSLB (*Nationalsozialistischer Lehrerbund*), the League of National Socialist Teachers, established in August 1929. The head of the association was Fritz Waechtler.

NSRB (*Nationalsozialistischer Rechtswahrerbund*), the Nazi Lawyers' League, so called from 1936. It was originally the *Bund Nationalsozialistischer Juristen*, and was recognized by the party leadership in September 1928. Hans FRANK was the leader of the organization.

NSSB (*Nationalsozialistischer Schülerbund*), the Nazi School Students' League, established in 1929, and incorporated into the Hitler Youth in June 1932.

NSV (*Nationalsozialistische Volkswohlfahrt*), the Nazi welfare organization. It sought to expand its control of welfare services by taking over welfare activities hitherto provided by the public authorities and the welfare associations affiliated with the churches. It also created facilities of its own, for example, *Mutter und Kind* ('mother and child'), and was responsible for the Winter Aid organization (*WINTERHILFSWERK*), which was announced in September 1933.

Nuremberg Laws (1935), the Reich Citizenship Law (*Reichsbürgergesetz*) and the Law for the Protection of German Blood and Honour (*Gesetz zum Schutze des deutschen Blutes und der deutschen Ehre*), announced at the

Nuremberg party conference on 15 September 1935.

The Reich Citizenship Law deprived German Jews of their citizenship and redefined them as subjects. A citizen of the Reich was in a slightly narrower category, and was defined as a subject 'who is of German or related blood', and only a citizen enjoyed 'full political rights in accordance with the provision of the laws'. The first order under the Reich Citizenship Law (1 November 1935) also revoked the section in the Law for the Restoration of a Professional Civil Service (1933) that had exempted Jewish veterans of the armed forces from dismissal. The Law for the Protection of German Blood and Honour outlawed marriages between Jews and non-Jews, and prohibited Jews from employing German women of childbearing age, or from displaying the German flag.

Many additional regulations were attached to the two main statutes, and these provided the basis for removing Jews from all spheres of German political, social and economic life. This process was slow at first, largely because the Nazis wanted to ensure that the Olympic Games were held in Berlin in 1936, but senior Jewish doctors were required to resign from hospitals by the second order under the Reich Citizenship Law (21 December 1935), and there then followed a stream of supplementary orders affecting pharmacists, publicans and restaurateurs, private tutors, dieticians, legal consultants and inspectors of abattoirs. In addition, civil servants introduced new measures, for example, stopping the payment of family allowances to large Jewish families, ending the right of Jews to apply for a hunting licence, and suspending the award of doctoral degrees.

Although the Nuremberg Laws also carefully established pedantic definitions of Jewishness based on 'bloodlines', the process of deciding who was legally Jewish was very arbitrary. Many Germans of mixed ancestry, the so-called 'MISCHLINGE', faced ANTI-SEMITIC discrimination if they had one or more Jewish grandparents, but there were no consistent criteria spelled out for determining whether the grandparents themselves were Jewish.

Nuremberg rallies, the party conferences of the NSDAP (Nazi Party), held every year in September. Party rallies were held in Nuremberg from 1923, but the theatrical set pieces that were to become familiar during the Third Reich began with the rally of 1929. Rallies were held annually from 1933 to 1938, and Nuremberg was awarded the privilege of calling itself 'City of the Party Congresses' (*Stadt der Reichsparteitage*). Each such congress carried a sloganistic name, for example the 'Congress of Victory' in 1933. The following year the rally was filmed by Leni RIEFENSTAHL as the *The Triumph of the Will*. The rally at which the anti-Semitic NUREMBERG LAWS were announced was the 'Congress of Freedom', and the rally of 1937 was the 'Congress of Labour'. The theme of the final rally, in 1938, was 'GREATER GERMANY'.

Nuremberg trials (1945–6), war crimes trials of 22 of the leaders of Nazi Germany (including Martin BORMANN, who was tried *in absentia*), conducted by the Allies after World War II. The trials were a joint four-power initiative undertaken by the Allies for didactic as well as retributive reasons. HITLER, HIMMLER and GOEBBELS had already committed suicide, LEY committed suicide in prison, and Gustav KRUPP was considered too ill to be tried. The trials were held before an international military tribunal presided over by Lord Justice Geoffrey Lawrence and were conducted in four languages. The tribunal sat from 20 November 1945 to 1 October 1946. All but three of the accused were found guilty: SCHACHT, PAPEN and FRITZSCHE – the conservatives who had assisted the Nazis in the establishment of the dictatorship – were acquitted, despite strong objections from the Soviet Union. HESS, FUNK and RAEDER were sentenced to life imprisonment (the latter two were released in 1957 and

1955 respectively). Von SCHIRACH and SPEER were each sentenced to 20 years, and von NEURATH and DÖNITZ to 15 and 10 years respectively. Von Neurath was released in 1954 on health grounds. The rest – GÖRING, FRANK, FRICK, STREICHER, SAUCKEL, JODL, Bormann, RIBBENTROP, KEITEL, KALTENBRUNNER, ROSENBERG and SEYSS-INQUART – were sentenced to death.

In addition to the trials of the major war criminals, the tribunal was also responsible for determining whether certain institutions were criminal: the cabinet, the Nazi Party (NSDAP) leadership, the SS and SD, the GESTAPO, the SA and the general staff and the OKW (High Command of the Armed Forces). If these organizations were proved to be criminal, individuals belonging to them could be brought to trial for having been members. The SS, the SD, the Gestapo and the party leadership were found to be criminal organizations, but the indictments against the SA, the cabinet, the general staff and the OKW were dropped.

O

Oberdonau ('Upper Danube'), Nazi name for *Oberösterreich* (Upper Austria). The new *Reichsgau* also absorbed Czech territory from the Sudetenland.

Oberkommando der Wehrmacht. *See* OKW.

October diploma, (1860), constitutional reform for the HABSBURG empire, largely the work of Agenor Goluchowski (1812–75), minister of the interior (1759–60). The diploma granted assemblies to its constituent *Länder*, effectively making the empire a federal state, and conceded to the recently expanded, but effectively impotent REICHSRAT participation in legislation on economic matters. The constitutional arrangements introduced by the diploma were short-lived and were superseded with the promulgation of the FEBRUARY PATENT of 1861.

Odal, an old Norse word for a family farm taken in 1934 by Walter DARRÉ as the new name for his journal *Deutsche Agrarpolitik*, founded two years earlier. In 1936 the journal became *Odal. Monatschrift für Blut und Boden* ('blood and soil monthly').

Oder–Neisse line, the frontier between Germany and Poland provisionally agreed by the Allies at Tehran (1943) and at the POTS-DAM CONFERENCE (July–August 1945), and established at the end of World War II by the United Kingdom, United States and the Soviet Union. The GERMAN DEMOCRATIC REPUBLIC accepted the frontier in 1950, and the permanence of the border was reiterated by East Germany and Poland in 1955. The Federal Republic of Germany refused to accept the frontier until 1970, when, as part of his OSTPOLITIK, the Social Democratic chancellor Willy BRANDT signed an agreement with Poland acknowledging the status of the frontier as 'inviolable'. Final acceptance and recognition of the boundary came only in 1990, however, in the course of Germany's own reunification.

Odessa (*Organisation der ehemaligen SS-Angehörigen*), 'Organization of Former SS Members', an underground network established at the end of World War II. Its purpose was to help SS officers and Nazi functionaries escape justice after the defeat of Germany.

Oeser, Rudolf (1858–1926), liberal politician. Born in Coswig, Anhalt, Oeser studied philosophy and economics in Berlin before becoming a journalist on the *Frankfurter Zeitung*, and then editor of the *Ostsee-Zeitung* in Stettin. He was a member of the Reichstag from 1907 to 1912, and of the Prussian LANDTAG from 1920 to 1924 for the DDP. After World War I he was Prussian minister of public works (1919–21), and then interior minister in the CUNO cabinet (1922–3) and transport minister under STRESEMANN (1923). From 1924 he was head of the state railways (REICHSBAHN).

Offenburg manifesto (12 September 1847), political programme published by the Baden democrats at a meeting on the eve of the REVOLUTIONS OF 1848. The Baden liberals replied with a similar declaration at HEP-PENHEIM on 10 October. These divisions in the Baden LANDTAG foreshadowed the political alignments, and with them the difficulties for the liberals, in the FRANKFURT PARLIAMENT.

Ohlendorf, Otto (1908–51), SS officer. An economist by profession, Ohlendorf was head of Amt (Department) III in the Reich Security Head Office (RSHA) from 1936. During World War II he commanded EINSATZ-GRUPPE D in the Ukraine, and between June 1941 and July 1942 he was responsible for the murder of some 90,000 Jews. He then returned to a desk job in Berlin. He was brought to trial at Nuremberg along with other members of the *Einsatzgruppen*, found guilty of complicity in mass murder and executed in 1951.

Ohnesorge, Wilhelm (1872–1962), Nazi politician; Reich post minister (1937–45). Ohnesorge was born in Gräfenhainichen. He was a civil servant in the post office, joined the NSDAP in 1920 and founded the first Nazi Party branch outside Bavaria, in Dortmund (1920). He became state secretary in the ministry of posts in 1933 when the Nazis came to power, and was appointed Reich post minister in 1937. He was tried as a major offender after the war, but was given a lenient sentence on health grounds.

OKW (*Oberkommando der Wehrmacht*), High Command of the Armed Forces. The *Oberkommando der* WEHRMACHT was established in February 1938 as a headquarters from which Hitler could operate as supreme commander in chief of the armed forces. The independence of all branches of the armed forces was diminished, and they were all rendered equally subordinate to Hitler. The army lost the privileged status it had previously held in Prussia and Germany. Field Marshal KEITEL was head of the OKW.

Olmütz, treaty of (1850), also called the *Punktation*, an agreement that brought an end to Prussian plans – following the REVOLUTIONS OF 1848 and the FRANKFURT PARLIAMENT – for

a union to replace the GERMAN CONFEDERA-TION, to be led jointly by Prussia and Austria. Austria resisted the idea of equality with Prussia and proclaimed the restoration of the Confederation. Prussia was also compelled to replace Josef Maria von RADOWITZ with the more accommodating Otto von MANTEUFFEL. The Olmütz agreement constituted a severe diplomatic defeat for Prussia and fuelled a bitter rivalry between the two states, culminating in the AUSTRO-PRUSSIAN WAR of 1866.

Oma-Bewegung ('grandma movement'), an initiative organized by local committees of the East German Democratic Women's League (*Demokratischer Frauenbund Deutschlands*, DFD) to arrange for female pensioners to take on housework and childminding for unrelated young families. The women thus released from domestic work would be able to take up paid employment.

Oradour-sur-Glane, scene of a Nazi atrocity in France, in which 600 villagers were murdered by an SS Panzer division on 10 June 1944.

Ordensburgen, Nazi schools for selected graduates of ADOLF HITLER SCHOOLS. The curriculum was politics, ideology and physical culture.

Orff, Carl (1895–1982), composer. Orff was born in Munich and worked in musical education after World War I, co-founding the Günther School for gymnastics, dance and music in Munich in 1924. His most famous work is *Carmina Burana* (1937), based on medieval poetry found in a Bavarian monastery. Orff's music was popular with the Nazis, and he is reputed to have been one of Hitler's favourite composers.

Orgesch. *See* ESCHERICH, GEORG.

Orpo (*Ordnungspolizei*), the regular uniformed police force in Nazi Germany.

Ossietzky, Carl von (1889–1938), left-wing journalist. A member of the German peace movement, Ossietzky was a co-founder in 1924 of the unsuccessful Republican Party with Fritz von UNRUH. He was an editor with a number of publications in the 1920s, including the *Berliner Volkszeitung* and *Das Tagebuch*, and from 1927 was editor in chief of *Die WELTBÜHNE*. Jailed in 1931 and released the following year, he was re-imprisoned under the Nazis and died as a consequence of his treatment in prison. He was awarded the Nobel Peace Prize in 1935.

Ostarbeiter, ('eastern workers'), forced labourers drafted from the Soviet Union to work in Germany during World War II.

Österreich, the German name for AUSTRIA.

Osthilfe ('eastern aid'), economic assistance for the depressed agricultural sector east of the Elbe during the WEIMAR REPUBLIC. JUNKER interests dominated the formation of agricultural policy during the last years of the republic, and they ensured that they received financial assistance from the state at the expense of industry, the peasants and urban consumers in order to preserve the uneconomic East Elbian estates. In the words of the industrialist Paul Silverberg, 'long-term political purposes would be served by the maintenance on their soil of families who through tradition and character are closely connected to the state'. As a consequence, during the political and economic crisis of the early 1930s billions of Reichsmarks went to the landowners of the east, where the money was used mainly to pay off debts. President HINDENBURG himself received as a gift the return of the family estate at Neudeck in East Prussia, which had been lost as a result of indebtedness. The purchase of the estate was organized by a committee after Hindenburg was elected president, and was funded by donations, but its return to viability was ensured by *Osthilfe* money. In 1933 SPD and Centre Party members of the Reichstag budget committee found serious irregularities in the use of *Osthilfe* funds by landowners, and serious charges were made: the money, it was alleged, had been used to pay gambling debts, keep mistresses, buy racehorses and travel to the Riviera.

Ostmark ('eastern march'), the name used for Austria in VÖLKISCH, and, later, in Nazi circles. When Austria was annexed in 1938, however, the designation was quickly dispensed with on the grounds that other border territories were also effectively eastern marches, but also to avoid attributing a collective identity to Austria (*see* ANSCHLUSS). Instead the names of the individual GAUE were to be used, and even here the word Austria was replaced with *Donau* (Danube) in the *Reichsgaue* formed from the Austrian federal states of Upper and Lower Austria.

Ostmarkenverein (Eastern Marches Association), right-wing pressure group in imperial Germany. It was founded on 3 November 1894 as *Verein zur Förderung des Deutschthums in den Ostmarken* (Association for the Promotion of Germandom in the Eastern Marches). Its remit referred to the Germanization policies then taking place in the Prussian province of Posen (now Poznań in Poland). The association changed its name to simply *Deutscher Ostmarkenverein* in 1900 and was also commonly known as the *Hakatistenverein*. It was a private association supported by membership subscriptions but also received donations from industrialists such as the KRUPP family. The association supported government legislation promoting German settlement at the expense of the indigenous Polish population. It had ceased to have any significance by 1914 and was eventually dissolved by the Nazis in 1934.

Ostpolitik ('eastern policy'), a collective term for the various policies and agreements with which the social–liberal coalition led by Willy BRANDT in the early 1970s effected a *rapprochement* with the Soviet Bloc, and in particular with the GERMAN DEMOCRATIC REPUBLIC. The SPD leadership abandoned the HALLSTEIN DOCTRINE when it came to power in 1969 as the dominant partner in a coalition with the Free Democrats (FDP). Brandt visited the Soviet Union in 1970, and agreed to recognize the existing frontiers between the two German states; and on a visit to Warsaw in December of that year he also agreed to recognize (as 'inviolable') the border between East Germany and Poland (the ODER–NEISSE LINE). The policy caused bitter controversy in the Federal Republic, where the CDU/CSU was still bitterly opposed not only to recognizing the 'pariah' East German state, but also to accepting the loss of German territory to Poland and the Soviet Union. (Such territories had hitherto officially been described as 'under Polish (or Soviet) administration' and marked as such in atlases.) After the election of 1972, when the coalition was returned with a larger majority and the SPD became the largest party in the Bundestag for the first time, the policy was reinforced with a BASIC TREATY (*Grundvertrag*) between the two German states, whereby each recognized the other's independence and frontiers. In 1973 *Ostpolitik* was extended to Czechoslovakia with the signing of a similar treaty.

Otte, Bernhard (1883–1933), Christian trade unionist. Otte was president of the Association of Christian Trade Unions (*Gesamtverband der christlichen Gewerkschaften Deutsch-lands*) and of the International League of Christian Trade Unions.

Otto, code name for the invasion of Austria in the event of an attempted restoration of the Habsburgs.

Otto, Luise (also Luise Otto-Peters or 'Otto Stern'; 1819–95), writer and journalist. Luise Otto was born in Meissen and was an activist in the early days of the German women's movement. She founded the FRAUEN-ZEITUNG, a women's journal, in 1849 and was a co-founder, in 1865, of the General German Women's Association (*Allgemeiner Deutscher Frauenverein*), which campaigned for women's education, emancipation and equal rights. She was married to the writer August Peters.

P

Pact of Steel (1939), a term used for the military alliance between Germany and Italy signed on 22 May 1939. The agreement reinforced the Rome–Berlin AXIS.

palatine, a title originally given to officials of the late Roman court, and to civil servants of the early HOLY ROMAN EMPIRE. It came to mean a plenipotentiary of the sovereign, and by extension the territory where he exercised power. In the 10th century there were counts palatine in Lorraine, the Rhineland, Swabia, Bavaria and Saxony. The office became hereditary and remained until the dissolution of the empire in 1806. The term 'palatinate' (*Pfalz*, from the Latin *palatium*) came to describe the territory of the count palatine, and originally referred to a complex of palace buildings for the accommodation of the king and his retinue. It was used as a seat for the court, and later as an administrative centre. There were a number of such seats from Carolingian times, including Worms, Frankfurt am Main and especially Aachen, in the palatinate of Lorraine (Lotharingia), where Charlemagne's royal palace was established in the 790s. As other palatinates were absorbed by local aristocrats only the county palatine of the Rhine remained. It was acquired by the WITTELS-BACH rulers of Bavaria in 1214. In 1329 the Rhine palatinate was separated from Bavaria, along with the Upper Palatinate (*Oberpfalz*) under a separate branch of the Wittelsbach family. The name Pfalz now refers specifi-cally to the central and southern part of the government district (*Regierungsbezirk*) Rhein-land-Pfalz (RHINELAND-PALATINATE), one of the states of the German Federal Republic. *Oberpfalz* remains the name of a district in Bavaria.

Pan-German League (*Alldeutscher Verband*), one of the most vocal and influential pressure groups in imperial Germany. It was originally the General German League (*Allgemeiner Deutscher Verband*), which was established in 1891 by Alfred HUGENBERG and Karl PETERS. Its leader, from 1893, was Ernst Hasse, and it became the Pan-German League in 1894. In the spring of 1896 the League had 8601 members, but by 1900 it had over 20,000. Its membership peaked at the turn of the century, and it never attracted the numbers that joined the NAVY LEAGUE or the DEFENCE LEAGUE. Academics constituted the largest single group among the members of the League, followed by businessmen and the professions, and its leaders were well placed in the universities, civil service, politics and journalism to influence both public opinion and policy-making. Hasse himself was a professor of politics and economics and a member of the Reichstag. Among its other most active members were Count Stolberg-Wernigerode (president of East Prussia and president of the Reichstag), Alfred HUGENBERG, Ernst Bassermann (leader of the NATIONAL LIBERALS in the Reichstag), Dietrich Hahn (member of the

Reichstag and leader of the AGRARIAN LEAGUE) and Heinrich CLASS (a lawyer from Mainz, and the future leader of the League).

The formally expressed aims of the Pan-German League were vague: 'to work for a united, fundamentally patriotic view of life' and 'to bring together the nationally minded citizens without consideration of party'. Its immediate rationale was opposition to the CAPRIVI administration and its policies, but it developed into a self-appointed watchdog, critic and adviser to successive governments. It was a radical nationalist organization that supported the *Weltpolitik* but became increasingly disillusioned with the government. Heinrich Class became leader of the League in 1908, and in 1912 published a programmatic pamphlet, *Wenn ich der Kaiser wär'* ('If I were the Kaiser'), a radical right-wing, anti-Semitic manifesto calling for authoritarian measures at home and recommending the annexation of territory abroad if Germany should be forced into a war. When war did break out in 1914, the executive committee of the League set out its programme of pan-German war aims, pressing for extensive German annexations in both eastern and western Europe. The First World War and the November revolution of 1918 altered the political climate in Germany and the Pan-German League was superseded by new radical right-wing parties which proved to be more successful in building up a popular base, above all the Fatherland Party (*VATER-LANDSPARTEI*) and the Nazis (*Nationalsozialistische deutsche Arbeiterpartei*, NSDAP).

Papen, Franz von (1879–1969), conservative politician; chancellor (1932) and Hitler's deputy chancellor (1933–4). Papen was born into an old Catholic aristocratic family in Werl, Westphalia. He began his military and diplomatic career before and during World War I, starting with a commission as lieutenant in a cavalry regiment. He was posted to the general staff in Berlin in 1913, and then took up a diplomatic position as military attaché in Washington (1914–15). He

was effectively expelled from the United States, and returned to Germany to serve on the Western Front and in the Middle East. After the end of the war he went into politics, and was elected to the Prussian LANDTAG for the Catholic CENTRE PARTY in 1920. He was on the far right of the party, and his career was undistinguished until he was appointed chancellor in June 1932 at the head of the so-called 'cabinet of barons'. During his short term in office he sought to undermine the power of the labour movement, not least through his illegal removal of the elected SPD-led government of Prussia in July 1932 (*see* PREUSSENSCHLAG). He also repealed the previous government's ban on the Nazi stormtroopers. Papen's cabinet was massively defeated in a no-confidence vote in the Reichstag on 12 September, when the Nazis aligned themselves with the Centre Party for the purpose of forcing new elections. Although the Nazis lost votes in the elections there was no resolution to the political impasse, as any of the major parties was able to block the government's business if it chose to do so. Plans for an authoritarian coup d'état were blocked by SCHLEICHER, and Papen was dismissed (December 1932).

In January 1933, after Schleicher's own short-lived and unsuccessful administration, Papen returned as deputy chancellor in Hitler's first cabinet. However, following his assertive criticism of the new regime in the MARBURG SPEECH of June 1934, and the subsequent NIGHT OF THE LONG KNIVES, he was sent as minister to Vienna (1934–8). After the *ANSCHLUSS* he was appointed ambassador to Turkey (1938–44). He was acquitted at Nuremberg, but sentenced to eight years' imprisonment in a labour camp and confiscation of his property by a German DENAZIFICATION court in 1947. He was released on appeal in 1949.

Papen coup. *See* PREUSSENSCHLAG.

Paragraph 175, section of Reich legal code making homosexual acts between men illegal. Paragraph 143 of the Prussian statute of 1851was taken over as Paragraph 175 by all German states with the founding of the German empire in 1871. Paragraph 175 made 'unnatural intercourse' between two men equivalent to intercourse between men and animals and punishable by imprisonment. (Homosexuality had been decriminalized in most of Germany by the French with the introduction of the Napoleonic Code.)

Attempts were made to amend the paragraph during the early years of the Weimar Republic. In the draft revision of the statute law proposed by SPD justice minister Gustav RADBRUCH in 1922 there was no provision for judicial punishment of 'simple homosexuality'. However, provisions were then introduced by the next government, a centre–right coalition, to make the law more severe. Although the Criminal Law Committee (*Strafrechtsausschuss*) of the Reichstag decided narrowly in favour of the more liberal law (when Wilhelm Kahl of the DVP cast his vote with the SPD, KPD and DDP members), the draft never came before the Reichstag and the law was never liberalized. It was used by the Nazis for persecution of HOMOSEXUALS, reinforced by the more draconian Paragraph 175a in 1935.

Paragraph 218, part of the Reich penal code that made abortion a criminal offence. In 1926 it replaced paragraphs 218–220, in a reform that reduced penalties for the aborting woman, but increased them for paid abortionists to a maximum of 15 years penal servitude. In the Federal Republic of Germany abortion was legalized for the first three weeks of pregnancy by the SPD–FDP coalition in 1974, but the reform was overturned by the FEDERAL CONSTITUTIONAL COURT following an appeal by the Roman Catholic *Länder* and members of parliament from the CDU and CSU. As a result women were able to get abortions if doctors agreed that the mother's health would be harmed by pregnancy, which meant that it effectively remained illegal in the Catholic south.

A further attempt was made to liberalize the law after reunification, since abortion had been legal and free on demand in the German Democratic Republic, and remained so in the NEW FEDERAL STATES. Despite backing from a majority in parliament, however, reform was blocked when Bavaria appealed again to the constitutional court with the support of the CDU and CSU in the Bundestag. This left abortion legal in the east, semi-legal in the north, and effectively illegal in the south.

Paris, first treaty of (30 May 1814), peace agreement concluded between the victorious powers in the Napoleonic Wars (Great Britain, Russia, Austria and Prussia) and France. France lost all its conquests from the Wars of the COALITIONS of the previous 22 years, and the French frontiers were restored to the position of 1 January 1792. It was also stipulated that the navigation of the Rhine be free. It was superseded by the second treaty of PARIS, which was concluded after the final defeat of Napoleon at WATERLOO.

Paris, second treaty of (20 November 1815), peace agreement imposed on France by the victorious powers (Great Britain, Russia, Austria and Prussia) following the final defeat of Napoleon at WATERLOO. The treaty restored the French frontiers of 1790, reasserted the losses of territory outlined in the first treaty of PARIS (1814), imposed an indemnity of 700,000,000 francs, and provided for the occupation of strategic points along the border by an allied army of occupation.

Paris Peace Conference (1919–20), the peace conference following WORLD WAR I at which the treaties of VERSAILLES and ST GERMAIN (among others) were negotiated and signed.

Parliamentary Council (German: *Parlamentarischer Rat*), institution established in 1948 to draw up the basic constitutional law for the Federal Republic of Germany. The council's members were delegates from the *Länder* parliaments. It convened on 1 September 1948 and elected Konrad ADENAUER as its president. It wrote the BASIC LAW, which was then passed on to the assemblies of the participating *Länder* for approval. Despite objections from Bavaria, the Basic Law was accepted by the *Länder* and effectively became the consitution of West Germany.

Partei des Demokratischen Sozialismus. *See* PDS.

Parteigenosse or ***Pg.*** ('party comrade'), the official Nazi designation for party members. The term 'comrade' was taken from the labour movement to add radical edge and to reinforce the importance of the collective as opposed to the individual. The duties of a 'party comrade' were summarized in the 'commandments of the National Socialist', the first of which was 'the Führer is always right'.

Parteikanzlei, the Party Chancellery, the name given to the staff of the Führer's deputy in May 1941 after the flight of HESS to Scotland. Its head was Martin BORMANN, who became a member of the Reich government and of the Ministerial Council for the Defence of the Reich, and therefore had ministerial authority in his dealings with other leading figures and institutions in the regime. The Party Chancellery became Bormann's power base and he sought to use it to extend the power of the party in relation to the state, and at the same time to increase his own power and influence.

partisans, term used above all in the USSR and Yugoslavia to describe Communist guerrillas operating behind enemy lines.

Paulskirche, meeting place of the first German National Assembly (the FRANKFURT PARLIAMENT) in March 1848.

Paulus, Friedrich (1890–1957), field marshal. Paulus was born in Breitenau, joined the army as a cadet in 1910 and served in World War I. In 1939 and 1940 he served in the Polish, Belgian and French campaigns, and was appointed deputy chief of staff in 1940. In 1942 he was promoted to general and appointed commander in chief of the 6th Army, which was defeated at STALINGRAD.

Against Hitler's wishes, Paulus surrendered his army to the Soviets in 1943. He remained in prison in the USSR until 1953, and settled in East Germany after his release.

Payer, Friedrich von (1847–1931), liberal politician. Payer was a member of the Reichstag from 1877 to 1920, first for the DEUTSCHE FORTSCHRITTSPARTEI (the Progressives), then for the DDP. He was deputy chancellor at the end of World War I (1917–18) at a time when real power lay in the hands of the virtual military dictatorship of LUDENDORFF and HINDENBURG.

PDS (*Partei des Demokratischen Sozialismus*), the Party of Democratic Socialism, successor party to the SED. From December 1989 its first president was Gregor Gysi (1948–). He was succeeded in 1993 by Lothar Bisky (1941–). The party has largely failed to make an impact outside the former GDR, but has managed to hold its own in elections in the new federal states. The party participated in government for the first time at regional level in Mecklenburg-Vorpommern in 1998.

peace resolution (19 July 1917), parliamentary motion that marked the intervention of the Reichstag in the discussion of war aims. The domestic truce (*BURGFRIEDEN*) that had been achieved at the beginning of WORLD WAR I had given way to political polarization, and a coalition of SPD, CENTRE PARTY and the 'Progressives' of the DEUTSCHE FORTSCHRITTSPARTEI now formed a majority in the Reichstag that was opposed to an annexationist peace. Led by Matthias ERZBERGER of the Centre Party, this coalition was critical of the government's conduct of the war, and in particular the resumption of unrestricted submarine warfare. The peace resolution proposed an end to the war without annexations and was opposed by the right, which now found organizational expression in the Fatherland Party (*VATERLANDSPARTEI*) under the leadership of TIRPITZ and KAPP. The peace resolution could not alter government policy, but brought together the opposition parties which later formed the basis of the so-called 'Weimar coalition'.

permanent representations (*ständige Vertretungen*), diplomatic missions opened in place of embassies by the German Democratic Republic in Bonn and the Federal Republic in East Berlin in 1974.

Pester Lloyd, the newspaper of the German-speaking minority in Hungary, founded in 1854. The paper was taken over as an instrument of the Nazis during World War II and was forced to close in 1945. The paper was reopened in 1993 as *Der neue Pester Lloyd*.

Pétain, Philippe (1856–1951), French collaborator. A national military hero for his service during World War I, Pétain retired from the army in 1931 and entered politics. He was appointed war minister in 1934 and prime minister in 1940, a short time before the defeat. He immediately negotiated peace with the Germans and established an authoritarian puppet regime in unoccupied France, whose government was based at Vichy (*see* VICHY FRANCE). Civil rights were removed, trade unions abolished and political opposition prohibited. Pétain's regime also passed anti-Semitic legislation and its leaders assisted in the deportation of French Jews. Vichy France was directly occupied by Germany in 1942 and Pétain himself was taken to Germany in 1944. He was tried as a traitor in 1945, but his death sentence was commuted to life imprisonment.

Peters, Carl (1856–1918), founder of the Society for German Colonization (*Gesellschaft für deutsche Kolonisation*, 1884). Peters then went to Tanganyika, where he secured land rights from local chiefs, and established the Peters German East Africa Company, which received an imperial charter in 1885 (*see* GERMAN EAST AFRICA). He became Reich commissioner of the German protectorate in East Africa, but was dismissed in 1897 for abusing his power and mistreating local people. Peters was also a co-founder, with Alfred HUGENBERG, of the General German League

(*Allgemeiner Deutscher Verein*), the precursor of the PAN-GERMAN LEAGUE.

Pfalz. *See* PALATINE.

pfennig ('penny'), unit of currency. The pfennig originated with Charlemagne's currency reform of 794, which instituted the division of a pound into 20 shillings and 240 pence. The use of both names persisted until the introduction of the EURO: the pfennig as a subdivision of deutschmark; and the schilling as the principal currency unit in Austria from the 1920s until 2002.

Pieck, Wilhelm (1876–1960), first president of the GERMAN DEMOCRATIC REPUBLIC (1949–60). Pieck was born into a working-class family in Guben, Niederlausitz, and was apprenticed as a joiner from 1890 to 1896. He joined the SPD in 1895, and was a member of the Bremen Bürgerschaft from 1905 to 1910. He opposed the *BURGFRIEDEN* (political truce) during World War I, and was called before a military court in 1917 for spreading antiwar propaganda, but escaped to Berlin and lived there illegally until the end of the war. He was active in the SPARTACUS LEAGUE, and took part in the founding conference of the KPD (German Communist Party). He was a member of the Prussian LANDTAG from 1921 to 1928, when he was elected to the Reichstag, and deputized for THÄLMANN as KPD president after the latter's arrest in 1933. In 1935 Pieck was elected president of the Central Committee (ZK) of the KPD for the duration of Thälmann's imprisonment and moved to Moscow in the same year. In 1943 he was a co-founder of the NATIONAL COMMITTEE FOR A FREE GERMANY. He returned to Germany from exile in Moscow in 1945, and the following year he became one of the two presidents of the SED (*Sozialistische Einheitspartei*, Socialist Unity Party). His co-president was Otto GROTEWOHL. In 1949 he was elected president of the German Democratic Republic by the provisional People's Chamber, and was confirmed in that office for a second term in 1953. He died in Berlin in 1960.

Piscator, Erwin (1893–1966), theatre director. Piscator became a socialist after serving in World War I. He was involved with the Berlin DADA movement and the Proletarian Theatre, and was director of the Berlin *Volksbühne* theatre (1924–7) before forming his own company. He developed the 'epic theatre' approach later taken up by BRECHT, and is noted for his striking EXPRESSIONIST style of staging. He went to the USSR in 1931 and Paris in 1938, before emigrating to America. In 1939 he set up the Dramatic Workshop at the New School for Social Research. He returned to West Berlin in 1951, where he continued to produce political works. From 1962 until his death he ran the *Freie Volksbühne* theatre.

Planck, Max (1858–1947), physicist who developed the quantum theory. Educated at Munich and Berlin universities, Planck was appointed professor of physics at Berlin in 1892, a post he held until 1926. He was awarded the Nobel prize for physics in 1918, and in 1930 he became president of the Kaiser Wilhelm Institute. Planck opposed Nazi racial policies, protesting directly to Hitler, and defended EINSTEIN, but failed to slow the process of dismissal of Jewish scientists. Planck resigned in 1937 in protest, and in 1945 his son Erwin was killed by the Gestapo for his part in the 1944 JULY BOMB PLOT. After the war Planck was reappointed president of the Institute, which in 1945 changed its name to the Max Planck Institute.

Plate, battle of the River (1939), a naval skirmish off the coast of South America at the beginning of World War II. The German armoured cruiser *Graf Spee* had been preying on Allied shipping, and was attacked by three Royal Navy cruisers on 13 December 1939. The German ship was forced to shelter at Montevideo in Uruguay, and was scuttled there by its captain, who believed that a stronger British force was lying in wait beyond the mouth of the river.

pogrom, an organized attack on Jews (originally in tsarist Russia), such as occurred on *'KRISTALLNACHT'* in November 1938.

Polish Corridor, land transferred from Germany to Poland after WORLD WAR I to give the Poles access to the sea. The cession of this territory by the treaty of VERSAILLES separated East Prussia from the rest of Germany, and it was an object of revisionist foreign policy during the Weimar Republic and the Nazi dictatorship to reclaim it.

Polykratie, variously translated as 'polycracy' or 'polyocracy', a term used to refer to the nature of government in Nazi Germany by historians who emphasize the importance of institutional rivalry rather than the role of HITLER.

Pomerania, historical German territory along the Baltic coast. Hinterpommern (Eastern Pomerania) became part of Poland in 1945. Vorpommern became part of the German Democratic Republic and now constitutes a part of the *Land* MECKLENBURG-Vorpommern.

Popitz, Johannes (1884–1945), civil servant. Popitz was born in Leipzig and studied law, economics and politics. He became a privy councillor in 1919, and was appointed to a chair at Berlin University in 1923. He became state secretary in the finance ministry in 1925, and had an enormous influence on German financial policy during the 1920s. He resigned in 1929 after criticism from Hjalmar SCHACHT, who was then president of the REICHSBANK. He took charge of the Prussian ministry of finance after the PAPEN coup of 1932, and was minister without portfolio and Reich commissioner at the Prussian finance ministry under the Nazis (1933–44). Originally a political conservative, he was sympathetic to the Nazis, but then became involved with conservative resistance circles. He was arrested after the failed JULY BOMB PLOT of 1944 and hanged in Plötzensee prison, Berlin.

Popp, Adelheid (née Dworak; 1869–1939), Austrian Social Democrat. Popp was born in Vienna and worked in a factory there from the age of 8. She joined the Vienna Association for the Education of Working Women in 1889, and became a leading figure in the Austrian women's movement. She was chief editor of the *Arbeiterinnenzeitung*, a newspaper for women workers, and a leading member of the Social Democratic Party, on whose executive committee she served for 30 years. She was a member of the city council (1919–23) in the early days of RED VIENNA, and a member of the Nationalrat (the lower house of the Austrian parliament) until it was shut down by the AUSTROFASCIST coup of 1933–4. She published *Die Jugendgeschichte einer Arbeiterin* ('the story of a working woman's youth') in 1909.

Porsche, Ferdinand (1875–1951), Austrian engineer and designer. Porsche was born in Maffersdorf, now in the Czech Republic, and worked at the Lohner-Werke in Floridsdorf, Vienna (1898–1905). From 1906 to 1923 he was technical director of the Austro-Daimler Motor Works in Wiener Neustadt, built aeroplane motors from 1908, and the Sascha sports car in 1921. From 1929 to 1931 he worked at the Steyr-Werke in Upper Austria, where he constructed the Steyr 30 and the Steyr 100. From 1931 he had his own business in Stuttgart, and began work on a cheap 'people's car' for mass consumption. The Nazis took up the idea and he was employed by the German Labour Front (DAF) as technical director at the VOLKSWAGEN factory in Wolfsburg from 1937. The design for the first VW car was produced by his son Ferdinand ('Ferry', 1909–98). During the war, Porsche (and his son) designed military vehicles, and then returned to Austria, where he worked on the Porsche sports car, which was launched in 1950. He was briefly imprisoned by the French after the war.

Potocki, Alfred, Graf (1822–89), Austrian landowner, diplomat and politician; minister-president (1870–1). Potocki's early career was in the diplomatic service. He became a member of the HERRENHAUS in 1861, and minister of agriculture in 1867. He became minister-president in 1871, continued as agriculture minister, and also became minister of defence at the same time. He was in favour of neutrality during the FRANCO-PRUSSIAN WAR, and repudiated the concordat with the church (agreed in 1855 under Freiherr von BACH). He was unable, however, to get the nationalities to work together in the Reichstag, despite the conciliatory nature of his nationalities policy: the Slavs criticized the centralizing elements of his policy, and the Germans were opposed to the federal elements. Emperor FRANZ JOSEPH, alarmed at the growth of German nationalism in Austria, replaced him in 1871 with HOHENWART, a pro-clerical nationalist conservative. Potocki was later governor of Galicia.

Potsdam Conference (17 July–2 August 1945), the last of the major Allied wartime conferences, involving Britain, the United States and the Soviet Union. The USSR was represented by Stalin, the United States by Truman, while Churchill was replaced by Attlee after his defeat in the British general election. The central item on the agenda was the future of Germany, and the three powers agreed on the 'complete disarmament and demilitarization of Germany and the elimination or control of all German industry that could be used for military production.' Moreover all German land, naval and air forces, and the SS, SA, SD and Gestapo, 'with all their organizations, staffs and institutions, including the general staff, the officers' corps, reserve corps, military schools, war veterans' organizations and all other military and semi-military organizations, together with all clubs and associations which served to keep alive the military tradition in Germany' were to be completely abolished. All arms and ammunition were also to be destroyed, and arms production facilities were to be destroyed or held by the Allies.

The Allies also agreed on DENAZIFICATION and democratization, which included ensuring the destruction of the Nazi Party, the repeal of its repressive legislation and the reform of education and the judicial system. It was agreed that local government would be restored, but that there should be no central government for the time being. Similarly the economy should be decentralized, and economic reconstruction should concentrate on agriculture and 'peaceful domestic industries'. The issue of reparations was also agreed at Potsdam. They would be in kind rather than in monetary form, and each occupying power was authorized to seize capital goods from its own zone. The Soviet Union would export food from the eastern zone, in return for industrial plant from the western zones. It was agreed that the USSR, which had suffered disproportionately at the hands of the Germans, would also receive a further allocation of goods from the western zones with no exchange. Germany was to be administered in the meantime by the ALLIED CONTROL COUNCIL, but real executive authority lay with each of the occupying powers within its own zone. These were arrangements that were meant to be temporary, pending the convening of a peace conference, but no such conference took place, and the Allies were unable to agree on terms for peace with a united Germany until after the collapse of East Germany (the GERMAN DEMOCRATIC REPUBLIC) in 1990.

Pragmatic Sanction, a measure, first published in 1712–13, intended to ensure that the HABSBURG lands remained undivided despite the fact that Emperor Karl VI had no sons. The emperor succeeded in persuading the Austrian estates to recognize his daughter MARIA THERESIA as his heir, and the Pragmatic Sanction became law in 1724. Its first article affirmed that Austria was an indivisible unit, thereby establishing the Habsburg monarchy as a territorial state. In the long term this was a more important stipulation than the immediate right of Maria Theresia to succeed, and the Pragmatic Sanction can be seen as something of a fundamental

constitutional measure. The other European powers were not so easily persuaded of its validity, however, and although all the major states of Europe recognized the Pragmatic Sanction while the emperor was alive, Bavaria and Prussia contested it after his death, and the invasion of Silesia by FRIEDRICH II (Frederick the Great) in 1740 led to the War of the AUSTRIAN SUCCESSION.

Prague, peace of (23 August 1866). *See* SADOVÁ, BATTLE OF.

Prandstetter, Martin Joseph (1760–98), Austrian radical. Born in Vienna into an upper middle-class background, Prandstetter attended the Jesuit school, and studied philosophy and law. He was a Freemason, and member of the same lodge as Aloys BLUMAUER. Prandstetter grew up in the reforming era of JOSEPH II, and the accession of the reactionary FRANZ II in 1792 was a shock to him as to much of educated Vienna, where there was probably more sympathy for the aims of the French Revolution than in any other German city other than Mainz. Prandstetter, like other Josephinian bureaucrats, was drawn into the ineffectual Jacobin conspiracy. He was arrested in 1794 and charged with aiding and abetting a conspiracy, and with the publication of subversive texts. He received a prison sentence of 30 years, but had served only 3 when he died in jail.

Pre-Parliament (*Vorparlament*) (1848), a meeting of German legislators and other leading public figures in Frankfurt in the wake of the REVOLUTIONS OF 1848. It was convened by a committee of the federal diet (Bundestag) of the GERMAN CONFEDERATION. The Pre-Parliament met from 31 March to 3 April 1848, and consisted of 574 members, mainly parliamentarians from the diets of the individual states or city councillors. The Pre-Parliament had limited power and a limited task. Its main business was to prepare the way for elections to a constituent National Assembly (the FRANKFURT PARLIAMENT), which met in Frankfurt on 18 May.

Pressburg, the German name for Bratislava, now the capital of Slovakia. As Pozsony, Pressburg was the capital of Hungary from 1526 until 1784, and the seat of the Hungarian parliament until 1848.

Pressburg, treaty of (1805). *See* COALITIONS, WARS OF THE.

Preuss, Hugo (1860–1925), liberal constitutional lawyer and politician. Preuss was born into a middle-class Jewish family in Berlin, and completed his *Habilitation* (*see* HABILITATIONSSCHRIFT) at the University of Berlin before he was 30. But because he was an active member of the liberal Progressive People's Party (*FORTSCHRITTLICHE VOLKSPARTEI*), and Jewish, he was not appointed to a chair. However, he was appointed professor at the new Commercial University (*Handelshochschule*) in 1906. Preuss was a co-founder of the liberal DDP in 1918, and as Reich interior minister (1918–19) he was commissioned by EBERT to work on the new constitution. His original radical draft, which recommended a strong centralized state, was altered under pressure from sectional and regional particularist interests. He resigned from the cabinet in February 1919, along with other DDP ministers, in protest at the government's acceptance of the terms of the treaty of VERSAILLES.

Preussen, the German name for PRUSSIA.

Preussenschlag, term used to refer to the constitutional coup whereby the federal chancellor, von PAPEN, deposed the elected SPD-led government of Prussia in 1932. The move followed the lifting of the ban on the SA during the summer of 1932, and the condemnation of the Prussian government, by Reich interior minister Wilhelm von Gayl, for continuing to restrict the SA. Preparations were made to depose the Prussian government and install a Reich commissioner instead. President HINDENBURG signed a decree on 'the Re-establishment of Order in the Territories of the State of Prussia' on the strength of information from a police department informer in Berlin that the KPD (the German Communist Party) had been encouraged to join forces with the SPD in resisting the Nazis. The decree was enforced after the street fighting of 'bloody Sunday' (17 July 1932) in Altona. The decree was unconstitutional, a point conceded by the Prussian supreme court at Leipzig, which did not, however, rule that the measure be reversed. The illegal dismissal of the Prussian government was followed by a wholesale purge of Social Democratic and liberal state employees and their replacement by conservative civil servants. The so-called 'Papen coup' probably did more than any other single act before January 1933 to ease the way for the establishment of the Nazi dictatorship.

Progress Party or **Progressives.** *See* DEUTSCHE FORTSCHRITTSPARTEI.

propaganda ministry (*Reichsministerium für Volksaufklärung und Propaganda,* 'Reich ministry for popular enlightenment and propaganda'), ministry established by law on 13 March 1933. It was headed by GOEBBELS from its establishment until 1945.

Protection of People and State, Decree of the Reich President for the (28 February 1933), decree that followed the REICHSTAG FIRE. It was suggested by Ludwig Grauert of the interior ministry in order to legalize the arrests of Communists, but redrafted by Wilhelm FRICK, the interior minister, with the aim of extending his authority over the still autonomous federal states in the event of a threat to public order, a provision that laid the basis for the GLEICHSCHALTUNG ('coordination' or Nazi takeover) of the states in March. The decree suspended several sections of the constitution, thereby permitting restrictions on civil liberties and the freedom of expression and assembly. It also enabled the government and security forces to intercept mail, telegraphic communications and telephone calls, and allowed for the confiscation of property.

protective custody. *See* SCHUTZHAFT.

Protectorate of Bohemia and Moravia, protectorate established following the German occupation of the remainder of Czechoslovakia in March 1939, and the creation of an 'independent' puppet state in Slovakia.

Prussia (German name: Preussen), the dominant constituent state of the GERMAN EMPIRE and the WEIMAR REPUBLIC. The original Prussia was located on the southern coast of the Baltic Sea, and inhabited by people speaking a Baltic language. It was settled by Germans in the Middle Ages and was ruled by the knights of the Teutonic Order. It became a duchy in 1525, and a kingdom in 1701 under FRIEDRICH I, son of the 'Great Elector' of Brandenburg. Prussia expanded during the 18th century at the expense of Austria, notably under FRIEDRICH II (Frederick the Great), who annexed Silesia and turned Prussia into one of the leading military powers of Europe. Later in the century Prussia benefited territorially from the partitions of Poland. The kingdom acquired more territory in the west after the Napoleonic Wars (*see* COALITIONS, WARS OF THE), and seemed to many German nationalists during the REVOLUTIONS OF 1848 to be the natural leader of the emergent German nation. However, FRIEDRICH WILHELM IV declined to accept the crown of Germany from the commoners of the FRANKFURT PARLIAMENT, and Prussia's belated bid for equality with Austria within a new constitutional arrangement was thwarted by the treaty of OLMÜTZ. During the 1860s, however, under ministerpresident Otto von BISMARCK, Prussia manoeuvred Austria into a military confrontation (the AUSTRO-PRUSSIAN WAR), which led to the latter's defeat and effective expulsion from Germany.

In 1871, following the FRANCO-PRUSSIAN WAR, Germany was united under Prussian leadership, with the king of Prussia becoming Kaiser (emperor) WILHELM I. Prussia accounted for the overwhelming majority of the population and surface area of the new GERMAN EMPIRE, and much of Germany's economic power was also concentrated on Prussian territory, above all in the RUHR VALLEY and the Rhineland. Throughout the imperial period the king of Prussia was also German emperor, and the minister-president of Prussia was Reich chancellor. Prussia continued to dominate Germany during the WEIMAR REPUBLIC, but whereas Prussian governments were led by the SPD throughout the 1920s, the Social Democrats were often excluded from the Reich government. The traditional Prussian ruling class, the JUNKER aristocracy, also continued to exert political influence in Weimar Germany, although through different channels: they dominated the army, the bureaucracy and – eventually – the political leadership. The power of the Junkers was decisively broken during and after World War II: first by the Nazis after the failed JULY BOMB PLOT of 1944, which had involved a good number of Prussian aristocrats; and then by the loss of East and West Prussia, Silesia and other territory to Poland. The confiscation of large estates during the postwar land reforms in the GERMAN DEMOCRATIC REPUBLIC, and the establishment of the East German state itself, brought the power of the aristocracy to an end.

public holidays (GDR). A number of new public holidays were introduced in the German Democratic Republic in addition to May Day (*Internationaler Kampf- und Feiertag*), which was also a public holiday in West Germany, as in most of mainland Europe, where it is celebrated, appropriately, on 1 May. A law of 21 April 1950 established the following as public holidays: Liberation Day (*Tag der Befreiung*) on 8 May; and Republic Day on 7 October. In 1961 the 'Day of the National People's Army' (*Tag der Nationalen Volksarmee*) was established on 1 March; and *Vereinigungstag* (Unification Day) on 21 April. The unification in question was that of the SPD and KPD, which established the SED, East Germany's governing party. In addition, 21 April became the 'International Day of Youth against Colonialism and for Peaceful

Existence', and 10 November 'World Youth Day'. The work of various occupations was also celebrated: railway workers on 11 June, teachers on 12 June, and miners on 2 July. Victims of fascism were remembered on 10 September.

Pünder, Hermann (1888–1976), public servant and politician. Pünder was a civil servant in the Reich finance ministry (1921–5), and then state secretary in the Reich Chancellery (1926–32). He was *Regierungspräsident* in Münster (1932–3), and served in the army from 1935 to 1943. After the war he was mayor of Cologne and a member of the Bundestag for the CDU (1949–57). From 1948 until the end of 1949 Pünder was president of the council (*Verwaltungsrat*) of the united economic area (*Vereinigtes Wirtschaftsgebiet*) in the western zones of occupation.

putsch, a sudden, violent political uprising, such as the KAPP PUTSCH (1920) and the BEER HALL PUTSCH (1923).

Q

Quaatz, Reinhold Georg (1876–1953), conservative politician. Quaatz was a member of the Reichstag for the nationalist DNVP from 1920 to 1933, and co-founder of the CDU in Berlin after the end of World War II.

Quadruple Alliance (20 November 1815), agreement signed by Russia, Austria, Prussia and Great Britain. The aim of the alliance, established at the Congress of VIENNA, was to ensure the enforcement of the provisions of the second treaty of PARIS (concluded the same day) and to uphold the peace in mainland Europe by means of the 'CONGRESS SYSTEM'. The alliance also provided for regular further meetings of the Congress.

Quidde, Ludwig (1858–1941), politician, historian and pacifist. Quidde was a member of the South German Democratic People's Party (*Süddeutsche demokratische Volkspartei*) and of the liberal DDP. He was a member of the NATIONAL ASSEMBLY in 1919, and president, from 1914 to 1929, of the *Deutsche Friedensgesellschaft* (German Society for Peace), and of the *Deutsches Friedenskartell* (German Cartel for Peace) from 1920 to 1929. After the Nazis came to power he went into exile in Switzerland.

Quisling, Vidkun (1887–1945) Norwegian collaborator. As leader of the Norwegian fascist movement, *Nasjonal Samling*, Quisling assisted the German invasion of Norway and was appointed head of the puppet government installed there by the Nazis (1940–5). He was executed for treason after the war. His name became a general term for collaborators throughout Europe.

R

Raab, Julius (1891–1964), conservative Austrian politician. Raab was born in St Pölten and was a civil engineer by profession. He was a member of the NATIONALRAT for the CHRISTIAN SOCIAL PARTY (1927–34) during the First Austrian Republic. He was also a HEIMWEHR leader, and was briefly trade minister under the SCHUSCHNIGG dictatorship in 1938. After World War II he was a co-founder of the conservative Austrian People's Party (ÖVP), and chancellor from 1953 to 1961.

Rabinowitsch-Kempner, Lydia (1871–1935), scientist. Born in Kovno, Lithuania, into a Jewish family, Rabinowitsch-Kempner studied in Switzerland and in 1903 was appointed assistant professor at the Berlin Institute for Infectious Diseases, where she worked on the transmission of tuberculosis through cow's milk. She was the first woman in Berlin to be appointed professor (1912) and to edit an academic journal. She was director of the bacteriological institute in the Moabit municipal hospital from 1920, but was dismissed by the Nazis in 1934.

RAD (*Reichsarbeitsdienst*), the Reich Labour Service, a Nazi organization for the conscription of labour. Unemployed workers were 'voluntarily' drafted into service on public-works projects after the Nazis came to power, and a compulsory six-month labour service was introduced for all young men with the Reich LABOUR SERVICE LAW of 26 June 1935. Labour service remained voluntary for young women until 15 February 1938, when all single women under the age of 25 were required to undertake a 'duty year' of labour service.

Radbruch, Gustav (1878–1949), Social Democratic politician (MSPD). Born in Lübeck, Radbruch was a member of the Reichstag for the SPD from 1920 to 1924, and was Reich justice minister under Joseph WIRTH (October 1921–November 1922) and Gustav STRESEMANN (August–October 1923). Radbruch was a pioneer in the humanitarian reform of German criminal law. He was also professor at Königsberg, Kiel and Heidelberg.

Radetzky, Josef, Graf (1766–1858), Austrian field marshal. Radetzky fought in the Turkish war of 1788–9, and in the Napoleonic Wars (the Wars of the COALITIONS), when he took part in the battle of WAGRAM, and planned the 'battle of the nations' at LEIPZIG in 1813. He was chief of the Austrian general staff from 1809 to 1829, and was an adviser to the Archduke Karl in Hungary from 1818 to 1828. He was promoted to field marshal in 1836. From 1831 he was general commander of the Austrian army in Lombardy and Venetia, and although he was forced to abandon Milan during the REVOLUTIONS OF 1848, and Austria was also forced to withdraw from Venice, Radetzky's victories at Santa Lucia, near Verona (6 May), Vicenza (10 May), and Custozza (25 July), and at Mortara and Novara (21 and 23 March 1849) restored Austrian authority. He then starved

Venetia into surrender. Radetzky was Austrian governor of Lombardy and Venetia until his retirement in 1857. The *Radetzky March*, by Johann STRAUSS the elder, is named after him.

Radikalenerlass, the 'decree concerning radicals' of 1972. This measure, introduced by the social–liberal (SPD–FDP) coalition, was intended to standardize existing practice in relation to the proscription of extreme political organizations, which varied between the different states. However, it was used mainly to intensify discrimination against the left, and to prevent those with links to arbitrarily defined suspect organizations from taking up jobs in the public sector; this practice became known as *Berufsverbot* ('job ban').

Radowitz, Joseph Maria von (1797–1853), diplomat and politician. Radowitz was a member of the Gerlach circle of conservatives in the 1830s and was an advocate of Prussian leadership in the reform of the GERMAN CONFEDERATION. He was a delegate to the 1848 FRANKFURT PARLIAMENT, and leader of the right there. In 1850 he was briefly the first minister of Prussia and proposed a new 'German union' in which Prussia and Austria would be equal leaders. The plan was thwarted by the OLMÜTZ agreement, and Radowitz was replaced by Otto von MANTEUFFEL. He retired from public life in 1851.

Radowitz, Joseph Maria von (1839–1912), diplomat. Radowitz was German ambassador in Athens (1874–82), Constantinople (1882–92) and Madrid (1892–1908).

Raeder, Erich (1876–1960), admiral and commander in chief of the German navy (1928–43). Raeder served in World War I, and took part in the battle of JUTLAND (1916). He was promoted to rear admiral in 1922, and commander in chief of the navy in 1928. He was promoted to grand admiral in 1939 and led the naval offensive against Britain from the north European coast. He resigned in 1943 and was replaced by DÖNITZ. He was sentenced to life imprisonment at Nuremberg, but was released in 1955.

RAF. *See* RED ARMY FACTION.

Rahn, Rudolf (1900–75), diplomat. Following minor postings in Ankara, Lisbon and Paris, during which time he was also employed at the Foreign Office, Rahn was appointed ambassador to the German-occupied northern rump of Fascist Italy (1943–5).

railways. Railways were constructed throughout Germany from 1835, when the first line was built between the towns of Fürth and Nuremberg in Franconia. Railway technology was originally imported from Britain, and was supported by enthusiasts such as the economist Friedrich LIST, who was influential in bringing about the construction of the first long-distance railway (between Dresden and Leipzig) in 1837. The first train was pulled by a British locomotive and had a British driver, but in 1841 the German firm August Borsig began making locomotives. Finance was raised by joint-stock companies, and these were encouraged by the state. Prussia guaranteed a 3.5% rate of interest for such companies, ensuring that anybody who invested would make a profit. By 1840 there were already 549 km (340 miles) of track, and within ten years there were over 1000 km (620 miles). By 1870 the railway network had expanded to 25,000 km (15,500 miles), and by the 1920s there were over 50,000 km (31,000 miles). The railways were effectively nationalized after World War I, and between 1920 and 1945 most were run by the Deutsche Reichsbahn. (There were also private companies, which accounted for 6–7% of the total amount of track.) After World War II separate railway authorities were established in each of the four zones of occupation. A central authority was created for the western zones in 1946, and the Deutsche Bundesbahn (DB) was created in 1949 (known as Deutsche Bahn since 1994). The German Democratic Republic retained the name Deutsche Reichsbahn for its railways, which merged with the Deutsche Bundesbahn in 1990.

Ramek, Rudolf (1881–1941), Austrian politician; chancellor (1924–6). Born in Teschen (now Cieszyn in Poland), Ramek made his career as a lawyer, and was a member of the NATIONALRAT for the CHRISTIAN SOCIAL PARTY from 1920 to 1934. He was state secretary for justice under RENNER (1919–20) and minister of the interior and education in 1921. In 1924 he succeeded SEIPEL as federal chancellor. He was forced to resign in 1926 following a financial scandal involving his minister of justice. After this, Seipel returned to office.

Ranke, Leopold von (1795–1886), historian. Ranke was born in Thuringia into a family of Protestant clergymen, and studied theology and classics at Leipzig. He was a school teacher (1818–25) and then taught at Berlin University, where he was appointed to a chair in 1834. Ranke helped establish history as a separate scholarly discipline based on the aspiration to objectivity expressed in the phrase *'wie es eigentlich gewesen'* ('how it actually was'). Ranke insisted that historians should ascertain the reliability of their sources, and where possible use primary sources, such as contemporary documents and eyewitness reports. His approach was influential both within and beyond the Germany of his day, and constitutes in essence the core practice of modern historical research.

Rapallo, treaty of (1922), treaty between Germany and the Soviet Union. By the terms of the treaty Germany became the first state to recognize the USSR, and both countries renounced claims to debts and REPARATIONS and agreed to cooperate in economic matters. In accordance with secret agreements negotiated in connection with the treaty, the Soviet authorities went on to allow German troops to train in the USSR, in violation of the treaty of VERSAILLES, and assisted Germany in developing prohibited weaponry. The agreement was reinforced by the treaty of Berlin (1926), but lapsed when the Nazis came to power in 1933. (An earlier Rapallo treaty, of 1920, had regulated the border between Italy and Yugoslavia.)

Rasse- und Siedlungs-Hauptamt. *See* RUSHA.

Rastatt, Congress of, conference convened in 1797 during the Wars of the COALITIONS to decide the future of the HOLY ROMAN EMPIRE. The Congress was effectively a series of negotiations between the princely representatives of the empire and those of Revolutionary France, who insisted on recognition of their gains from the War of the First Coalition. Indirectly, the Congress inaugurated the winding up of the Holy Roman Empire after a thousand years of existence. It was still in session at the beginning of the War of the Second Coalition.

Rastenburg, location of the 'Wolf's Lair', Hitler's headquarters in East Prussia. It was here that STAUFFENBERG attempted to assassinate Hitler on 20 July 1944 (*see* JULY BOMB PLOT).

Rat (plural ***Räte***), council. The word is used as part of the name of various legislative bodies, such as the NATIONALRAT ('national council'), the lower house of the Austrian parliament) and BUNDESRAT ('federal council'), the upper house of the German parliament. The term is also used extensively in connection with the councils movement (*Rätebewegung*) which grew up at the end of WORLD WAR I. Councils were formed by German workers from April 1917, as an alternative to the existing institutions of the labour movement. The SPD and FREE TRADE UNIONS were cooperating with the government and the military at a time of unequal material sacrifice by their constituencies in the industrial working class. The political crises of 1917 saw the tabling of the PEACE RESOLUTION in the Reichstag, the end of the *BURGFRIEDEN* (domestic political truce), the fall of Chancellor BETHMANN HOLLWEG and the secession of the left wing of the SPD to form the USPD. At this critical time, councils were formed spontaneously 'from below' as democratic organizations representing industrial workers. These councils then reappeared in the January strikes of 1918, and most of all during the 1918 NOVEMBER REVOLUTION, when sailors' and soldiers' councils were set up throughout Germany as well. The leadership of the labour movement found the councils a disturbing phenomenon, outside the control of the bureaucratized party and union structure, while the middle classes saw in them the threat of Bolshevism. In the event, most council members supported either the SPD or USPD, and were in favour of parliamentary democracy. In the autumn of 1918 the councils' movement proved to be far more level-headed and even-handed in their response to the collapse of the empire than the dispossessed elites of imperial Germany. The national CONGRESS OF WORKERS' AND SOLDIERS' COUNCILS met in Berlin on 16 December 1918. A clear majority of delegates were supporters of the MSPD (Majority Social Democrats), and the issue of holding elections for a national assembly was never in doubt. On 4 February 1919 the central council transferred all power granted to it by the national Congress of Workers' and Soldiers' Councils to the constituent NATIONAL ASSEMBLY in Weimar, which drew up the constitution of the WEIMAR REPUBLIC.

In Austria the soldiers' and workers' councils movement was weaker and its organization less coordinated. It did not exercise any influence on the formation of a central government, and the Austrian Social Democratic Workers' Party (SDAP) had not experienced a split between moderates and radicals, and so was in any case already in a stronger position than its German counterpart. When an all-Austrian conference of councils met in March 1919 it was called by the SDAP, and membership of the party and of a trade union was a precondition of election.

Rat der Volksbeauftragten. *See* COUNCIL OF PEOPLE'S REPRESENTATIVES.

Räte. *See* RAT.

Rath, Ernst vom (1907–38), German diplomat in Paris, whose assassination by a Jewish youth, Herschel GRYNSZPAN, on 7 November 1938 was used as an excuse for the anti-Jewish pogrom of 9–10 November (*KRISTALLNACHT*).

Rathenau, Walther (1867–1922), industrialist and liberal politician; foreign minister (1922). A physicist and chemist by training, Rathenau was president of AEG, and in 1914 was appointed director of the raw materials department in the Prussian war ministry. In 1919 he joined the liberal DDP, and became minister for reconstruction in 1921 and foreign minister in 1922. Rathenau was conciliatory in his dealings with the West, and recommended fulfilment of the treaty of VERSAILLES. He was also responsible for concluding of the treaty of RAPALLO with the USSR. He was assassinated in Berlin by right-wing extremists in 1922. Among those implicated in the murder was the writer Ernst von SALOMON.

Rau, Heinrich (1899–1961), politician. Rau was born in Feuerbach near Stuttgart and was a metal worker after leaving school. He joined the socialist youth movement in 1913, left the SPD for the breakaway USPD in 1917 and was a founding member of the KPD (the German Communist Party). From 1928 to 1933 he was a member of the Prussian LANDTAG. He was imprisoned for two years under the Nazi regime (1933–5), and then emigrated, first to Czechoslovakia and then to the Soviet Union. He served in Spain with the International Brigades, and fled to France in 1939, where he was interned and, in 1942, handed over to the Nazis. He spent the rest of the war in MAUTHAUSEN concentration camp. In 1945 he rejoined the KPD and became economics minister of the GERMAN DEMOCRATIC REPUBLIC in 1949. In 1950 he became deputy minister-president, and president of the State Planning Commission. In 1953 he was minister for the machine industry, and in 1955 trade minister. Rau was a member of the presidium of the COUNCIL OF MINISTERS.

Rauscher, Joseph Othmar von (1797–1875), Austrian theologian. Rauscher was philosophy teacher to Emperor FRANZ JOSEPH, professor of ecclesiastical history at Salzburg and an adviser to the METTERNICH government. He was elected archbishop of Vienna in 1853 and from 1855 he was also a cardinal. Rauscher was the author of the Austrian concordat with the Vatican of 1855, and went on to become a member of the upper house of parliament (the *HERRENHAUS*) in the 1860s.

Rauschning, Hermann (1887–1982), Nazi politician. Born in West Prussia, Rauschning served in World War I and moved to DANZIG in 1926. He was appointed president of the Danzig Senate in 1933 after the Nazi election victory. He fled to Switzerland in 1935, renounced his previous political convictions and published books seeking to warn the outside world against the dangers of Nazism (*Revolution of Nihilism* and *Hitler Speaks*).

Ravensbrück, a CONCENTRATION CAMP (largely for women) in Mecklenburg, northern Germany. Opened in 1936, it was built to accommodate 6000 prisoners, but as in the case of other concentration camps, Ravensbrück was overcrowded, and in 1944 there were twice as many prisoners as its nominal capacity, and up to six times as many in 1945. Prisoners were subjected to medical experiments, and some 50,000 died at the camp.

real existierender Sozialismus ('real existing socialism' or 'actually existing socialism'), a term applied to the stabilized 'Marxist-Leninist' system in the GERMAN DEMOCRATIC REPUBLIC of the HONECKER period (1971–89). It was a term frequently used ironically by East German citizens, and by right and left alike in the west.

Realos, 'realists' in the GREEN movement. It was a term used to describe the moderate wing of the GREENS during internal debates with their opponents, the uncompromising '*FUNDIS*' (fundamentalists).

Realpolitik, 'realistic' or 'pragmatic' politics – in effect power politics. It was a term that was applied to BISMARCK's politics, although it had been coined some years earlier.

Rebmann, Andreas Georg Friedrich (1768–1824), political journalist and revolutionary activist. Rebmann studied at Erlangen and Jena, and graduated in 1789. He became increasingly radical after the Jacobins came to power in France, and published the revolutionary journal *Das neueste graue Ungheuer* ('the newest grey monster') in Erfurt. He was persecuted by the authorities, and fled to Altona and then to Denmark. There he was a co-founder of the radical publishing house Verlagsgesellschaft von Altona. Rebmann was appointed a judge in Mainz after the French occupation of the Rhineland. He continued to serve in the judiciary after 1815, in the Bavarian Palatinate.

Rechberg, Johann Bernhard, Graf von (1806–99), Austrian diplomat and politician. Born in Regensburg, Rechberg entered the Austrian diplomatic service and was posted to Sweden and Brazil. He was appointed minister-president and foreign minister in 1859. He held the former post until 1861, but continued as foreign minister until 1864. However, he was unable to assert himself on Austria's behalf against BISMARCK in the matter of the SCHLESWIG-HOLSTEIN question.

Rechtsstaat, a constitutional state that is based on the rule of law, and forgoes the possibility of arbitrary intervention of monarch, executive or dictator in legislative or judicial processes. The term first became current during the reform era of STEIN and HARDENBERG in Prussia. Although the establishment of the principles of the *Rechtsstaat* are often seen as part of the progressive development of modern parliamentary democracy, such a state need not in principle be either a democratic state or a liberal one.

Recke, Wilhelm, Freiherr von der (1819–1910), Prussian politician. Von der Recke was a member of the Prussian LANDTAG for the German Conservative Party (*DEUTSCH-KONSERVATIVE PARTEI*).

Red Army Faction (*Rote-Armee-Fraktion*, RAF), a left-wing terrorist organization in West Germany during the 1970s, also known as the 'Baader–Meinhof gang'. The authorities held the RAF responsible for a number of bombings, bank robberies and kidnappings, along with some 50 attempted murders, between 1968 and 1972. One of the leaders, Andreas BAADER, was arrested in 1968 but escaped from prison in 1970. He was re-arrested along with other members, including Ulrike Meinhof, in 1976. Meinhof was found dead in her cell in suspicious circumstances in 1976, and Baader apparently committed suicide in prison in 1977. The remaining members of the group continued to stage attacks during the 1980s.

The RAF's activities were directed against the 'military–industrial complex' and they claimed to be seeking to provoke the West German state into revealing its latent authoritarianism. Although there was criticism of some of the measures taken to defend the state against terrorism – such as the 'radicals decree' (*RADIKALENERLASS*) of 1972 – there was very little sympathy for the RAF in German society, and the populist right-wing press helped to direct popular anxiety against political radicalism and youthful non-conformity in general.

Red Baron. *See* RICHTHOFEN, MANFRED, FREIHERR VON.

Red Vienna, a term used to describe the Austrian capital during the 1920s. Vienna had become an autonomous federal state after World War I, and unwaveringly returned large Social Democratic majorities until its administration was unconstitutionally dismissed in 1934 by the AUSTROFASCIST regime of Engelbert DOLLFUSS. Before this the city's autonomous status had enabled the council to pursue progressive economic and social policies, particularly in the fields of housing and social policy. Although these successful policies were based on sound capitalist economics and constitutional methods, the city was a political thorn in the side of Austria's right-wing 'bourgeois-bloc' governments during the 1920s.

Refugees Movement (*Bund der Heimatvertriebenen und Entrechteten*), association formed in West Germany after the parliamentary elections of 1949 to represent the interests of Germans expelled from the SUDETENLAND, Poland and East PRUSSIA following the redrawing of frontiers at the end of World War II. In 1953 the Refugees Movement won 27 seats in the Bundestag, and joined the ruling right-of-centre ADENAUER coalition. Although the association ceased to stand for election, its members and their demands remained an important influence on the CDU.

See also EXPELLEES.

Reich, empire or state. The term was used to refer to the state in successive German constitutional arrangements, including the Holy Roman Empire, the German empire of 1871 (the 'Second Reich') and in certain contexts the Weimar Republic, as well as the Nazis' 'Third Reich'.

Reich, Jens (1939–), East German civil rights activist. Reich was born in Göttingen into a middle-class family, and studied medicine and molecular biology at the Humboldt University in East Berlin, and biochemistry at Jena. He became an academic scientist, and from the late 1970s a dissident known to the STASI. In 1984 he was demoted as a result of his political activities and contacts in West Germany. Reich was one of the leading dissidents associated with the NEUES FORUM group at the time of the collapse of the GERMAN DEMOCRATIC REPUBLIC in 1989.

Reich Chamber of Culture, state cultural organization under the Nazis. It was established by law on 22 September 1933, under the presidency of GOEBBELS and with FUNK as vice president. It encompassed the Reich Chamber of Literature (whose president was Hans Friedrich BLUNCK), the Reich Press Chamber (under Max AMANN), the Reich

Chamber of Broadcasting (under Horst Dressler-Andress), the Reich Theatre Chamber (under Otto Laubinger), the Reich Chamber of Music (under Richard STRAUSS), the Reich Chamber of Fine Arts (under Eugen Hönig), and the Reich Film Chamber (already established on 14 July under Fritz Scheuermann). Membership of the appropriate sub-organization was obligatory for practising artists, who were subject to ideological surveillance and exclusion on racial or political grounds.

Reich Chancellery (*Reichskanzlei*), office established in May 1878 to deal with the Reich chancellor's cabinet business and relations with the federal states. During the Weimar Republic the Reich Chancellery remained the chancellor's office, but was also responsible for coordinating government business. With the marginalization of the legislature under the Nazis it gained in importance, and from 1939 was also responsible for the business of the Ministerial Council for the Defence of the Reich (*Ministerrat für die Reichsverteidigung*). It also faced increasing competition from the office of the Führer's deputy and the Party Chancellery (*see PARTEIKANZLEI*).

Reichenau, Walter von (1884–1942), German officer. Reichenau was born in Karlsruhe, joined the army in 1903 and served in World War I. He was a supporter of Nazism and was appointed chief of staff in 1933. He was commander of the 10th Army during the invasion of Poland in 1939, and of the 6th Army for the 1940 offensive in western Europe. He was made a field marshal, and in the Soviet Union took over Army Group South from RUNDSTEDT. He endorsed both Hitler's war plans and the racial atrocities in the east. He died of a stroke.

Reich Entailed Farm Law (*Reichserbhofgesetz*) (29 September 1933), measure that aimed to ensure the survival of small peasant farmers. It defined all farms or forests of between 7.5 and 125 hectares (18.5 and 310 acres) as 'entailed' property, which belonged by definition to a 'peasant', and could only be inherited undivided by his heir. A 'peasant' in this definition could only be a German citizen 'of German blood'. The law failed in its main purpose in that its criteria covered relatively few farms. Moreover, many peasants whose farms were defined as 'entailed' felt dispossessed, and those of their children who had been expecting cash or a dowry (in lieu of inheritance in return for long years of employment for very low wages) felt cheated by the provisions of the law.

Reich governor. *See REICHSSTATTHALTER.*

Reichsarbeitsdienst. *See RAD.*

Reichsbahn, German state RAILWAYS. The name was retained in East Germany. The West German railway became the Deutsche Bundesbahn. The two were merged in 1990 and renamed Deutsche Bahn AG in 1994.

Reichsbank (*Deutsche Reichsbank*), Germany's central bank from 1875 to 1945. The Reich was excluded from the management of the bank in 1922, and it became an institution independent of the state in 1924, in accordance with the DAWES PLAN. State control was reasserted by the Nazis in 1937, and the bank was placed under the direct authority of HITLER in 1939. The Reichsbank survived the end of World War II and was dissolved in 1961, but its functions were taken over by central banks of the German states, and eventually (in the west) by the *Bank deutscher Länder* (1948). This in turn was superseded by the *Deutsche Bundesbank* in 1957. The equivalent central bank in the German Democratic Republic was the *Deutsche Notenbank*, and from 1968 the *Staatsbank der DDR*.

Reichsbanner Schwarz-Rot-Gold (literally 'Reich flag black-red-gold'), an unarmed patriotic formation during the Weimar Republic. It was founded in 1924 by the Social Democrat Friedrich Otto HÖRSING for defence against attacks on the republic or constitution by 'political enemies'. Although the *Reichsbanner* was intended to be non-partisan, in so far as it was open to all pro-republican parties, it was run and financed by the SPD and the FREE TRADE UNIONS.

Reichsdeputationshauptschluss ('final report of the imperial deputation') (1803), the document that dissolved the HOLY ROMAN EMPIRE after a thousand years, and effectively also the peace settlement that followed the War of the Second COALITION. Written at Regensburg and enacted in Vienna (6 August 1806), the report recognized France's victory and territorial claims. At the same time it dramatically simplified the territorial boundaries and political structure of Germany. It abolished all but six of the imperial free cities, secularized virtually all the ecclesiastical territories (which were absorbed by their larger neighbours) and created the medium-sized German states that played such an important role in the internal politics of Germany during the 19th century.

Reichshofrat, the Imperial Aulic Council, which, along with the REICHSKAMMER-GERICHT, was one of the two supreme courts of the Holy Roman Empire. Of the two, the *Reichshofrat*, which was established in Vienna in 1498, was more directly under the emperor's own control.

Reichskammergericht, the Imperial Cameral Court (or Tribunal), which, along with the REICHSHOFRAT, was one of the two supreme courts of the Holy Roman Empire. It was established in 1495.

Reichskanzlei. *See* REICH CHANCELLERY.

Reichskristallnacht. *See* KRISTALLNACHT.

Reichsnährstand, the Reich Food Estate, a corporate organization for German agriculture established by the Nazis in 1933 under the leadership of Reich farmers' leader, Walter DARRÉ, who was also Reich agriculture minister (from June 1933, when he replaced HUGENBERG). The *Reichsnährstand* was the largest of the regime's occupational organizations and was set up in response to the demands of agricultural associations themselves. Its organization conformed to the hierarchical pattern of the Nazi Party itself (*see* NSDAP), and beneath Darré there were tiers of regional, district and local farmers' leaders, whose job it was to oversee the implementation of the organization's attempts to regulate the production, distribution and pricing of agricultural produce. Measures were also introduced to regulate the import of foreign agricultural produce.

Reichspartei, the name for the FREIKONSER-VATIVE PARTEI (Free Conservative Party) in parliament after 1871. The party consisted of those conservatives who approved of BISMARCK's policies and supported the government in the Reichstag. They were involved, with the NATIONAL LIBERALS, in the drafting of the imperial constitution, although there was no explicit provision for such a role, and the party organization of both groups was rudimentary. Wilhelm von Kardorff and Baron Stumm-Halberg were among the most active of the party's members in parliament. The party was superseded by the German Nationalist People's Party (DNVP) in 1918.

Reichsrat (Austria), the parliament of CISLEITHANIA. The Reichsrat was initially an advisory council comprising six Austrian and two Hungarian members, established by the emperor FRANZ JOSEPH in 1851. In 1860 the emperor announced plans for it to be enlarged by bringing in archdukes, senior office holders and high-ranking members of the church, all of whom were to be appointed for life. A second group within the expanded parliament would consist of 38 representatives of the *Länder*, who would be appointed by the emperor from lists of candidates submitted by the estates. These would be appointed for terms of six years and were to include representatives from Hungary and the South Slav lands. The new body marked the end of NEO-ABSOLUTISM in Austria, but was a typical creation of 'sham constitutionalism', in that it had no real authority in the state and was convened only on the whim of the emperor and his closest advisers. Moreover, it overwhelmingly represented the landed interest. The new body met from May to September 1860, and served only to frustrate liberal expectations of a greater degree of constitutional government and to reveal redundancy of the old regime. The constitution was reformed again in October 1860, this time in the interests of conservative federalism, with the OCTOBER DIPLOMA, which conceded to the Reichsrat the power of participation in legislation, although the body itself was left unreformed. The FEBRUARY PATENT of 1861 reformed the basic constitutional arrangements in Austria by establishing a bicameral parliament with a house of lords (including hereditary and life peers) and a house of representatives of about 300, elected by the provincial estates. Elections were held in May 1861, but were boycotted by the Hungarians, Croats and Italians. The other nationalities were also opposed to the new constitution on account of its centralizing tendencies, which reflected the interests of the German-speaking liberals. A separate Hungarian parliament convened in Pest in 1861.

The Austrian constitution of 1867 made the Reichsrat 'the common representative body of the kingdoms of Bohemia, Dalmatia, Galicia and Lodomeria with the grand duchy of Krakow, of the archduchies of Lower and Upper Austria, of the duchies of Salzburg, Styria, Carinthia, Carniola, and Bukovina, of the margravate of Moravia, of the duchy of Upper and Lower Silesia, of the princely county of Tyrol and the territory of Vorarlberg, of the margravate of Istria, of the princely county of Gorz and Gradizia, and of the city of Trieste with its territory'. The Reichsrat was composed of a house of lords (*Herrenhaus*) and a house of representatives (*Abgeordnetenhaus*). It was abolished with the dissolution of the HABSBURG empire in 1918.

Reichsrat (Germany), the upper house of parliament during the WEIMAR REPUBLIC. The Reichsrat was established by Articles 60 to 63 of the constitution. Its purpose was to give the federal states a say in legislation,

and every state had at least one vote. It was indirectly elected by the states, which were represented by members of their own governments. Larger states had a vote for every 1 million inhabitants (reduced to one vote per 700,000 inhabitants in 1921), with the proviso that no one state should command more than 40% of the total votes. The Reichsrat was empowered to protest against legislation passed by the REICHSTAG, but the lower house was able to override such objections with a two-thirds majority.

Reichsstatthalter ('Reich governor'), head of a provincial or state government. Ten Reich governors were appointed in May and June 1933 following the 'coordination' (*GLEICHSCHALTUNG*) of the *Länder*. They were representatives of the central government, and their principal function was to ensure that the *Länder* complied with government policy as decided by Hitler. They were also to ensure that there were no attempts within the Nazi Party to form local power bases. The Reich governor was normally a local *GAULEITER* (regional party leader), but for a number of reasons there were more *GAUE* (the regional administrative divisions of the party) than Reich governorships: Hitler himself was Reich governnor of Prussia, and there were no Reich governors for the Prussian provinces (the equivalent position was *Oberpräsident*); Bavaria had six *Gauleiter* but only one Reich governor, von EPP; and, finally, some of the smaller *Länder* were combined under one Reich governorship.

Reichstag, originally the imperial diet of the HOLY ROMAN EMPIRE; the term was revived to refer to the parliament of the NORTH GERMAN CONFEDERATION from 1867, and then the parliament of unified Germany from 1871 to 1945.

A 'permanent imperial diet' met between 1663 and the end of the empire in 1806, comprising representatives of the princes, dignitaries, electors and imperial cities. The diet was nominally presided over by the emperor, and he was notionally bound by its decisions. In effect, however, any decision-making was difficult, and internal German relations during the last decades of the Holy Roman Empire were increasingly dependent on the realpolitik of relations between the major powers, especially Austria and Prussia. The Reichstag disappeared with the end of the Holy Roman Empire, and was replaced by the BUNDESTAG of the GERMAN CONFEDERATION.

A Reichstag was elected for the North German Confederation in 1867, and after the proclamation of the GERMAN EMPIRE in 1871 the Reichstag became the principal parliamentary body. Unlike the Prussian LANDTAG or the diets of the constituent states it was directly elected on the basis of an equal franchise for all males over the age of 25. This meant that despite the other constitutional shortcomings of imperial Germany, the Reichstag could fulfil important political functions on the basis of a popular legitimacy, which was reinforced by the relative lack of interference in elections. However, the Reichstag became increasingly unrepresentative, as there was no redistribution of seats to take account of changing demographic patterns. Although the chancellor was technically accountable to the Reichstag it had only nominal power over the government until the constitutional reforms of the last weeks of WORLD WAR I.

The relative importance of the Reichstag was dramatically increased during the WEIMAR REPUBLIC, Germany's first parliamentary democracy. Electoral procedures were reformed by the constituent NATIONAL ASSEMBLY of 1919. Article 22 of the new constitution extended the franchise to women on an equal basis with men, and reduced the age of voting to 20. Proportional representation was introduced at the insistence of the SPD, but it was also supported by the middle-class parties, who were aware that a majority system rewarded larger parties disproportionately, and that the main immediate beneficiaries of retaining it would be the SPD and the CENTRE PARTY. The role of the Reichstag was undermined from 1930 by the 'presidential cabinets' of Heinrich BRÜNING and his successors, who by-passed parliament by using presidential decrees. However, the situation was tolerated by the Reichstag, which had the right to block such measures.

The Reichstag continued to exist during the Nazi dictatorship, and one-party plebiscitary elections were held, but it had no real political function. The Reichstag ceased to exist with the capitulation of Germany in 1945, but its building has been used by the BUNDESTAG, which moved from Bonn to Berlin in 1999.

Reichstag (Austria), parliament convened after the REVOLUTIONS OF 1848. It was opened on 22 July 1848, and moved to Kremsier (now Kroeměříž in the Czech Republic) on 22 October. It was dissolved on 7 March 1849. There were 383 members from the German and Slav territories.

Reichstag fire (27 February 1933), the event that provided the Nazi regime with a justification for its first repressive measures. The Reichstag fire took place within four weeks of Hitler's appointment as chancellor, and in the middle of the Reichstag election campaign. The Decree of the Reich President for the PROTECTION OF PEOPLE AND STATE, which was issued the following day, permitted the more-or-less wholesale suspension of civil liberties in Germany, and allowed the Nazis to terrorize the KPD (the Communist Party) – a Dutch Communist, Marinus van der LUBBE, had been found in the burning parliament building and arrested. Despite the open terror, and the thousands of arrests, the Nazis failed to win a majority in the election of 5 March. Van der Lubbe was brought before a show trial by the Nazis in September. This proved to be a public-relations disaster for the regime, when van der Lubbe's co-accused, the Bulgarian Communist Georgi DIMITROV, put GÖRING on the defensive. The inconclusive debate about who really started the fire has tended on the whole to attract more attention than the consequences for the individual victims of the terror that followed.

Reichstreuhänder der Arbeit ('Reich trustees of labour'), twelve regionally based state officials responsible for the regulation of industrial relations. Established by the Law on Trustees of Labour (1933), they were accountable directly to the ministry of labour.

Reichsverweser ('imperial regent'), the office held from 29 June 1848 by Archduke Johann following his election by the FRANKFURT PARLIAMENT. Archduke Johann moved to Frankfurt in July and appointed a provisional German government under Prince Karl zu Leiningen, which was effectively paralysed by the assembly's failure to agree. The provisional Reich government was replaced by a federal commission approved by Austria and Prussia, and the imperial regent resigned in December 1849.

Reichswehr, German army created after World War I. It was limited to 100,000 men by the terms of the treaty of VERSAILLES. The Reichswehr became the WEHRMACHT in 1935.

Reinhard, Aktion ('Operation Reinhard'). *See* EXTERMINATION CAMPS.

Reinhard, Karl Friedrich (1761–1837), revolutionary republican and foreign minister of France. Born in Schorndorf, Württemberg, the son of a Lutheran pastor, Reinhard studied at Tübingen University, and after holding a number of minor posts in the church travelled to Switzerland (1787) and France at the time of the French Revolution. He welcomed the Revolution enthusiastically, and in 1791 he moved to Bordeaux, where he became involved with the Girondin party. Reinhard joined the French diplomatic service, and was posted to several European capitals, despite the suspicions of the Jacobins. After the fall of Tuscany in March 1799 he was head of the French occupation government. He was called back to Paris and served briefly as French foreign minister, the only foreigner ever to occupy the post, until the 18 Bru-

maire (9 November 1799), when he was replaced by Talleyrand. He remained in the French diplomatic service, and became ambassador to the German Confederation after the restoration. He retired from the post in 1829.

Reinhardt, Max (1873–1943), Austrian actor and director. Born in Baden, near Vienna, Reinhardt began his career as an actor in Salzburg. From the 1890s Reinhardt lived and worked in Berlin, where he was director of the Deutsches Theater from 1894. He worked with Richard STRAUSS and Hugo von HOFMANNSTHAL on the idea for the Salzburg Festival, and then moved to Vienna and took over the directorship of the newly restored Theater in der Josefstadt in 1924. Reinhardt went back to Berlin in 1929, but left Germany for Vienna again in 1933 to escape Nazi anti-Semitism. He emigrated to the USA in 1938.

Reinsurance Treaty (18 June 1887), treaty between Germany and Russia. It was effectively a separate renewal by Russia and Germany of the terms of the THREE EMPERORS' LEAGUE, without Austria-Hungary. The two powers agreed to support each other in the event of a war unless it arose from an attack by either party on Austria-Hungary or France. Germany recognized the rights historically acquired by Russia in the Balkan peninsula, and particularly the legitimacy of its influence in Bulgaria. The two powers agreed to preserve the status quo in the Balkans. In a separate protocol Germany agreed to accord Russia benevolent neutrality should the tsar have to defend the entrance to the Black Sea. The treaty remained valid only until 1890.

Remagen, a small town on the Rhine. The capture of the bridge there on 7 March 1945 enabled the Allies to cross the river into Germany.

Remarque, Erich Maria (1898–1970), novelist. Born in Osnabrück, Remarque served in World War I and was wounded twice. His novel *Im Westen nichts Neues* (*All Quiet on the Western Front*), a realistic depiction of the experience of war published in 1927, sold millions of copies, and was burnt by the Nazis in 1933. His other works were banned and he left Germany for the USA in 1939, returning to Switzerland after the war.

Renner, Karl (1870–1950), Austrian Social Democratic politician; chancellor (1918–20). Born in Unter-Tannowitz, Moravia, Renner studied law at Vienna University, and made a significant contribution to Marxist legal theory. His other main intellectual interest was the nationalities problem in the HABS-BURG empire. Renner was the leader of the right wing of the Austrian Social Democratic Workers' Party (SDAP). In 1918 he became the first chancellor of the First Austrian Republic. He also took over the foreign ministry from Otto BAUER in June 1919, and remained in both posts until the SDAP left office in 1920. Renner was the first president of the Second Austrian Republic, from 1945 to 1950, and – briefly – foreign minister for a second time, from April to December 1945. He died in office on New Year's Eve 1950.

Rentelen, Theodor Adrian von (1897–1946), commissioner general of Lithuania during World War II. Born in Russia and educated at Berlin and Rostock, von Renteln joined the Nazi Party in 1928 and was appointed Reich youth leader and students' leader in 1931. He was appointed commissioner general of Lithuania in 1941, and was hanged by the Russians in 1946.

Rentenmark, the new currency introduced in 1923 that ended the German INFLATION of the early 1920s. The Reich government settled on a scheme by which the currency would be based on the value of land and industrial capital. The Rentenbank, an institution constituted for the purpose, issued a loan to the REICHSBANK, which was backed by a mortgage on land and industrial property. The Reichsbank was thereby empowered to issue Rentenmarks, each of which had a value of one gold mark. Since the loan was limited there could be no backsliding into inflation, and the government was

compelled to attempt to balance its books. As a result the new currency held its value. The Rentenmark became the Reichsmark in 1924.

Renthe-Fink, Cecil von (1885–1964), diplomat. Renthe-Fink was secretary general of the Elbe Commission (1923), a member of the political section of the League of Nations secretariat (1926–33), German minister in Copenhagen (1936–40), and then plenipotentiary in Denmark (1940–2). He was also plenipotentiary in VICHY FRANCE (1943).

reparations, payments in cash and kind demanded by the victorious power at the end of a war. Although the term is usually associated with the reparations imposed on Germany by the Allies after the end of WORLD WAR I, indemnities of one kind or another had long been demanded by the victor in wars. In recent history, the Germans themselves had imposed an indemnity on France after the FRANCO-PRUSSIAN WAR of 1870–1; this had been repaid in full, and had helped to fuel the boom of the GRÜNDERZEIT.

During World War I each side intended, if victorious, to make the other pay for the war and, more than any of the other belligerents, Germany had relied on borrowing to finance it. The Reich government had repeatedly expressed its intention of reclaiming the whole cost of the conflict from its defeated enemies, and set out to do so when Russia collapsed. Although the question of indemnities was specifically excluded from the BREST-LITOVSK negotiations, 6 billion marks were demanded in reparations when supplementary treaties were negotiated with Soviet Russia in August 1918, and the REICHS-BANK demanded part payment of the indemnity in gold as a means of supplementing reserves.

There were differences among the Western Allies about the nature and extent of compensation to be demanded from the defeated CENTRAL POWERS, and the peace treaties failed to stipulate either the total amount or the proportions to be paid by each of the defeated states. In 1921 a reparations commission was set up to determine the scale of damage done by the Central Powers, and an initial payment of 20 billion gold marks was demanded. By the time the commission came to its decision in May 1921 the Allies estimated that they had received 2.6 billion gold marks worth of goods (including almost the entire German merchant fleet, 5000 railway locomotives and over 100,000 each of railway wagons, horses, cattle and agricultural machines). In addition, the value of the SAARLAND coal mines (which had been awarded to France) was reckoned at a further 2.5 billion marks. The Germans, on the other hand, claimed to have made payments up to the value of 37 billion marks. In the event the total reparations bill was determined to be 132 billion marks, a sum that was decided with scarcely any consideration of Germany's ability to pay.

Germany defaulted repeatedly on its reparations payments, and in 1923 French and Belgian troops occupied the RUHR VALLEY with a team of engineers in order to attempt to force the Germans to comply with their demands. The Ruhr occupation, and the passive resistance with which it was met, only made Germany's economic situation worse, and turned the INFLATION present in the economy since the beginning of the war into hyperinflation. In 1924 the Germans agreed to a revised reparations schedule (the DAWES PLAN). With the help of American loans, Germany was able to make the repayments throughout the 1920s, but by 1928 there was dissatisfaction with the system. The Germans resented the continuing occupation of the RHINELAND, and the authority of the Reparations Agency to scrutinize the Reich budget – the agent general for reparations, S. Parker Gilbert, was concerned that the payments were being funded by loans. A new committee was set up in Paris in 1929 under the chairmanship of Owen D. Young

to prepare evidence for a definitive settlement of the issue. The YOUNG PLAN reduced the total amount to be paid by about three-quarters, and brought to an end the surveillance of Germany's budget and the occupation of the Rhineland. The annual payments required by the plan were suspended in 1931 by the Hoover moratorium, and all but wiped out at the Lausanne Conference of 1932.

Reparations again proved to be a divisive issue among the Allies at the end of WORLD WAR II. The Western powers rejected most of the demands made by the Soviet Union. Reparations were to be an internal zonal matter, with each occupying power taking its reparations from its own zone of occupation. In addition the Soviet Union, whose territory had been devastated by the Germans, was to receive an extra 10% from the west. In its own zone the USSR dismantled 1900 industrial plants, halving East German industrial capacity in comparison with 1939.

Republikaner ('Republicans'), a radical right-wing movement that emerged in West Germany during the 1980s. The success of the Republicans before the fall of the Berlin Wall was an indication of a resurgence of NEO-NAZISM before the attention of the media switched to the particular problems of right-wing extremism in the NEW FEDERAL STATES. The Republicans' first major success was in West Berlin, where they entered the city parliament in 1989 after winning 7.5% of the vote. (They lost all 11 of their seats in new elections for the whole of the reunited city the following year.) They also won 6 seats in the European Parliament in 1989, and went on to win 15 seats in Baden-Württemberg in 1992, all but one of which they retained in 1996. The Republicans' long-term electoral strength has therefore been in one of the most affluent regions of Germany, and the one with the longest and most consistent liberal traditions. The Republicans are extreme nationalists, and advocate the reunification of Germany within its 1937 borders and a halt to the employment of foreign labour in Germany. They have also included appeals to environmentalism in their propaganda.

Residenzstadt, 'residential city', generally built around a princely palace, such as Karlsruhe and Potsdam. The term is also used to refer to such capital cities as Vienna ('*Haupt- und Residenzstadt*', capital of the Habsburg monarchy and seat of the emperor), Munich and Dresden. The permanent courts established in such towns from the late 17th century generated a particular kind of society. The aristocracy was also attracted to the city by the presence of the court, and built palaces there, displacing the old urban elites; and the political importance of *Residenzstädte* generated the growth of a centralized bureaucracy of senior civil servants, an officer class, journalists and a whole range of service personnel, along with purveyors and manufacturers of luxury goods. Culture was dominated by the prince's court, and by the aristocratic salons that imitated it.

resistance, the general term for opposition to the Nazis in occupied Europe during World War II. There was some resistance in France from 1940, but it became more widespread after the invasion of the Soviet Union with the large-scale involvement of underground Communist groups (partisans). In many parts of eastern Europe such Communist movements vied with rival nationalist groups for control, and in some countries the war ended amid civil war between the two factions, as in Greece, or with nationalist 'resisters' collaborating with Axis forces against the Communists, as in Albania. These divisions were reflected in the competing Cold War narratives of resistance. The politics of post-Nazi Europe made any objective assessment of the extent and nature of resistance to Nazism virtually impossible, and whereas the central role of the Communist resistance was asserted by the USSR and the Soviet Bloc, their role was mini-

mized in the West or dismissed altogether. In Germany itself the failed JULY BOMB PLOT to assassinate Hitler has largely eclipsed the much longer conflict between the Nazis and their left-wing political opponents during the early 1930s, first on the streets, and then underground. In Austria, the Allies' guarantee of postwar independence was made conditional on the country contributing to its own liberation, and such opposition to Hitler as there had been between 1938 and 1945 was thoroughly documented after the end of the war.

Restoration of a Professional Civil Service, Law for the (7 April 1933), a measure that effectively purged the German bureaucracy of Jews and political opponents. Officials of 'non-Aryan' descent were to be retired, but an exception was made, following the intervention of President HINDENBURG, for those who were on active service on 1 August 1914, or who fought for Germany during World War I.

reunification. *See* FEDERAL REPUBLIC OF GERMANY; GERMAN DEMOCRATIC REPUBLIC.

Reuss, Heinrich VII, Fürst von (1825–1906), diplomat. Reuss was German ambassador to St Petersburg, Constantinople and Vienna. He was also adjutant general to Kaiser WILHELM I.

Reuter, Ernst (1889–1953), left-wing politician. Reuter was born in Apenrade, northern Schleswig and joined the SPD (1912) before serving in World War I. He was a prisoner of war in Russia, and returned to Berlin, where he joined the Communist Party (KPD). He was general secretary of the party (from 1921) before his expulsion (1922). He rejoined the SPD and was mayor of Magdeburg (1931–3) and a member of the Reichstag (1932–3) until the Nazis came to power. Like many other Social Democratic politicians he was imprisoned in a concentration camp (twice between 1933 and 1935) and then emigrated to Turkey, where he remained until 1946. In 1947 he was elected mayor of Berlin, but as a consequence of

Soviet objections he took office only in 1948. He was mayor of the city during the Berlin blockade (1948–9; *see* BERLIN AIRLIFT). He died in Berlin in 1953.

Revolutionary and Napoleonic Wars. *See* COALITIONS, WARS OF THE; LIBERATION, WARS OF.

Revolutions of 1848, political upheavals that swept across much of mainland Europe following a revolution in Paris in February. The 1848 'March Revolution' was preceded by two decades of political agitation in central Europe, during the period known in German history as the *VORMÄRZ* ('pre-March'). More immediately, there had been several years of bad harvests and food shortages, and then in 1847 there was an economic depression of a new kind, which affected manufacturing and created unemployment.

The first uprising in Germany took place in Baden, where a mass meeting in Mannheim on 27 February made a series of political demands, including the convening of a German parliament. The revolution then spread to Austria and Hungary, where there were demonstrations in Vienna, Prague and Budapest. On 13 March the Lower Austrian estates met in Vienna, and revolutionaries took to the streets of the city with their political demands. Chancellor METTERNICH was deposed and fled to England, and the emperor promised a constitution. In Berlin concessions were made immediately: FRIEDRICH WILHELM IV, the king of Prussia, promised a constitution and support for German unity. Other, smaller states in the 'THIRD GERMANY', followed suit, and Prussia undertook to lead the reform of the GERMAN CONFEDERATION. When a crowd gathered in Berlin to cheer the king, however, shots were fired by nervous and inexperienced troops, and street fighting broke out. The troops were withdrawn from Berlin, a liberal ministry was established under Ludolf CAMPHAUSEN and a national assembly promised. In Bavaria Ludwig I abdicated in favour of his son Maximilian II. In late March and April the HABSBURG empire seemed to disintegrate:

Austrian troops were on the retreat in Italy, a Venetian republic was declared, and Piedmont declared war on Austria. In April further disturbances followed in Bohemia (which was promised a constitution), Moravia, Galicia, Transylvania and Italy.

With liberal administrations now in power in many states, the federal diet of the German Confederation also moved to the left, and set up a committee under DAHLMANN to draft a constitution, and the FRANKFURT PARLIAMENT met in May to set in place the constitutional structures for a new order in Germany. The triumph of the revolutions was short-lived, however, for a number of reasons. The parliament itself was divided between radical democrats and liberals, and also between those who preferred a 'greater German' solution to the question of German unification (a *Grossdeutschland* that would include the German-speaking parts of the Austrian empire), and those who preferred a smaller Germany led by Prussia (a *Kleindeutschland*).

Outside the parliament the forces of revolution were weaker than they had at first appeared, and they were disproportionately concentrated in the capital cities and other important towns, where they temporarily forced concessions from the authorities. Moreover, the disparate coalitions that constituted the 'revolutions' had diverse aspirations. In particular, middle-class liberals took fright at the more radical demands of the democrats, and were quickly inclined to compromise. The old rulers were stronger than they appeared at the height of the civil disturbances in March, and quickly regained their self-assurance. In June, Prague was bombarded by the forces of Prince WINDISCHGRÄTZ; the Czech revolution was suppressed, and Bohemia placed under martial law. By the end of the summer the parliament in Frankfurt and the liberal ministries in the various states had been overtaken by events, and the provisional executive was compelled to put down disorder, further fuelling polarization and division in the revolutionary movement.

Counter-revolution was far from straightforward, however. The authorities delayed elections and fudged reforms, but when a restricted franchise was announced for parliamentary elections in Austria, a second uprising broke out in Vienna in May, and the court was forced to flee to Innsbruck. A REICHSTAG was convened for Austria, and this ordered the emancipation of the serfs. There were further disturbances in Baden and Frankfurt in September, and in Vienna again in October. But Windischgrätz now besieged and captured Vienna, and the old regime was restored under the NEO-ABSO-LUTIST regime of Prince SCHWARZENBERG, albeit with a new emperor after the abdication of FERDINAND I in favour of FRANZ JOSEPH. Hungary's autonomy was withdrawn, and the republic that was then proclaimed in Budapest was defeated with the support of Prussia and Russia. In Berlin the national assembly was forced to move to Brandenburg, and was then dissolved by General Wrangel. In April 1849 Friedrich Wilhelm refused the German crown offered to him by the Frankfurt Parliament. Although there were further uprisings in the spring of 1849 in Baden and Saxony, the revolution was effectively over, and the Frankfurt Parliament disbanded.

The Revolutions of 1848 have been interpreted by many historians as 'failed revolutions', in which the German middle classes missed the opportunity to take real political power. As a result Germany was, arguably, propelled on a 'peculiar path' (SONDERWEG) to modernity, with the reactionary, premodern political forces that triumphed over the revolutionaries still the dominant force, impeding political development along Western lines. But although the revolutions were suppressed, they were not a complete failure. Politically, there was no unqualified restoration of the old order, and many German states retained some form of constitu-

tional government after 1850. In addition, important economic reforms remained in place, and one of the consequences was that the social and cultural position of the bourgeoisie was strengthened, and despite the limitations of Germany's political institutions, middle-class men of property and education were able to exercise much more political influence than previously. Finally, the national consciousness that was so much a part of the revolutions, both among Germans and among the non-German nationalities of the Habsburg empire, was scarcely suppressed at all, and within two decades the German unity that had been thwarted at Frankfurt had been achieved (albeit by bloodier means and in alliance with the old order), and Hungary had regained its autonomy from Vienna.

RFSS, abbreviation of *Reichsführer SS (und Chef der deutschen Polizei)* ('Reich leader SS and head of the German police'), HIMMLER's official title.

Rheinhaben, Werner, Freiherr von (1878–1975), politician. Rheinhaben was a member of the Reichstag for the conservative DVP from 1920 to 1930, and was state secretary in the Reich Chancellery in 1923.

Rhine, Confederation of the. *See* CONFEDERATION OF THE RHINE.

Rhineland, demilitarization of the, a condition of the treaty of VERSAILLES. German territory on the left (west) bank of the Rhine, along with the Bavarian PALATINATE and Cologne, Kehl, Koblenz and Mainz, were placed under Allied occupation for 15 years. The Rhineland and adjacent RUHR VALLEY were centres of acute political tension during the early years of the WEIMAR REPUBLIC. The French encouraged separatist tendencies, and a series of separatist putsches took place in towns up and down the Rhineland in 1923, while Social Democrats in the Bavarian Palatinate wanted independence from the right-wing regime in Bavaria (and possibly from the Reich as well). The peculiar status of the Rhineland led to fears that the reformed currency (the RENTENMARK) might not be introduced there, and there were important advocates in the region – not least in the Catholic CENTRE PARTY – for a reassessment of the Rhineland's relationship with Prussia (of which the Rhineland formed a part) and the Reich. For example, Konrad ADENAUER suggested separating the region from Prussia, and contemplated the possibility of a political arrangement that would also separate the Rhineland from the Reich, if that meant an end to the occupation and some relief for the rest of Germany. In the event the Rhineland remained fully a part of Germany, and the region was more settled after the 1923 currency reform.

The last Allied occupation troops left in 1930, and in 1936 HITLER ordered the remilitarization of the Rhineland, in violation of the treaties of Versailles and LOCARNO. It was one of the first steps towards Germany's renewed self-assertion in the international arena. In many respects the move was a bluff on Hitler's part, since the German troops had orders to retreat if they encountered opposition, and the German air force of which GÖRING boasted scarcely existed. The passive response of the Western Allies was an important signal to Hitler, however, and central to German diplomatic assumptions in the events of the following four years.

Rhineland-Palatinate (German name: Rheinland-Pfalz), one of modern Germany's constituent federal states, created on 8 August 1946. Its state capital is Mainz, and at the end of the 20th century it had a population of around 3.7 million. The state was created by the French occupation forces out of the former Bavarian PALATINATE, parts of the Prussian Rhine province, Rhinehessen and Hesse-Nassau. The strongest political party in the province until the 1990s was the CDU, and chancellor Helmut Kohl made his early career there. In LANDTAG elections from 1971 until 1983 the party won over 50% of the vote and governed alone. The election of 1991 saw a reversal of fortunes and the SPD

became the largest party and formed a coalition with the FDP under the leadership of Rudolf Scharping. He was succeeded as minister-president in 1994 by Kurt Beck. The FDP have won seats in every election except 1983, and the GREENS have been represented in the Landtag since 1987. The minority parties of the extreme right have performed less well and less consistently. The *DEUTSCHE REICHSPARTEI* was active up to the election of 1963, but was superseded by the NPD, which won four seats in the election of 1967. The *REPUBLIKANER* have campaigned since 1987, with very little success, and the presence of the Communists (KPD up to the election of 1955 and DKP from that of 1971) has been negligible.

Rhine–Main–Danube canal system, a network of waterways linking the Atlantic seaboard to the Black Sea. Over 3500 km (2100 miles) in length, the system was completed in 1992.

Ribbentrop, Joachim von (1893–1946). Nazi foreign minister (1938–1945). Born in Wesel, a small town on the lower Rhine, the son of a middle-class army officer, Ribbentrop was educated in Germany, Switzerland, France and England, and went to Canada in 1910. He returned to Germany in 1914 and served in a cavalry regiment during World War I. Ribbentrop was a wine salesman after the war, and something of a social climber who married a rich woman and was adopted by a titled relative. He joined the NSDAP in 1932 and became Hitler's foreign-affairs adviser in 1933. He was appointed Reich commissioner for disarmament at Geneva in 1934, and ambassador to Britain in 1936, after negotiating the ANTI-COMINTERN PACT with Japan. He was appointed foreign minister in 1938 in place of von NEURATH. In May 1939 he signed the PACT OF STEEL with Italy, and in August negotiated the German–Soviet non-aggression treaty (the MOLOTOV–RIBBENTROP PACT) that opened the way for the German invasion of Poland. He was less influential during the later war years, and was tried and hanged at Nuremberg.

Richter, Willi (1894–1972), trade unionist and politician. Richter was a member of the Bundestag for the SPD from 1949 to 1957, and from 1956 to 1962 he was also president of the German trade-union association.

Richthofen, Ferdinand Paul, Freiherr von (1833–1905), geographer and geologist. Richthofen was born in Carlsruhe, Upper Silesia (now Polzój in Poland), and began his geological explorations in the Dolomites. In the 1860s he undertook a lengthy trip to the Far East and California, and published a number of works on contemporary geography, and the findings of his own explorations. He did much to help establish the modern discipline of geography, particularly geomorphology.

Richthofen, Hartmann, Freiherr von (1878–1953), diplomat and liberal politician. Richthofen was a member of the Reichstag from 1912 to 1928, first for the NATIONAL LIBERAL PARTY and then for the DDP.

Richthofen, Manfred, Freiherr von (1892–1918), cavalry officer and World War I pilot, nicknamed the 'Red Baron'. Richthofen was born in Breslau (now Wrocław in Poland) into a well-to-do military family. He was an officer in a Prussian cavalry regiment from 1912 and served on the Eastern Front at the beginning of World War I. He then moved to the Western Front and joined the infantry, but transferred to the German imperial air service in 1915, and flew reconnaissance aircraft. In September 1916 he started flying fighters, and immediately established his reputation by shooting down a number of enemy aircraft. He was commander of a fighter group (nicknamed the 'Flying Circus' by the Allies) from June 1917, and was shot down and killed by ground fire in an air battle near Amiens on 21 April 1918. His final tally of 80 planes shot down made him the leading German air ace of the war.

Richthofen, Oswald, Freiherr von (1847–1906), public servant. Richthofen was director of the colonial department (1896–7), and

then state secretary in the foreign office. He was foreign minister from 1900 to 1906.

Riedel, Andreas, Freiherr von (1748–1837), Austrian Jacobin. Riedel was born in Vienna, and attended the prestigious *Theresianische Militärakademie* in Wiener Neustadt. In 1779 he became tutor to the future FRANZ II, and advised LEOPOLD II on constitutional reform, with plans to turn Austria into a constitutional monarchy. After the accession of Franz II, whose policies were markedly more reactionary, Riedel became the leader of a group of disaffected officers, and worked on an appeal to all Germans to join an 'anti-aristocratic league of equality' with the aim of leading an uprising on 1 November 1792. Some copies were distributed, but Riedel's Vienna Jacobins were denounced to the authorities, and over 30 people were arrested on charges of treason. Riedel was sentenced to 60 years' imprisonment, and served his sentence in harsh and degrading conditions until he escaped in 1809. He lived in poverty, mainly in Paris, until his death.

Riefenstahl, Leni (1902–), Nazi film director. Riefenstahl was born in Berlin, and began her career as a dancer and actress there. She opened her own film production company in 1931, and was chosen personally by Hitler to make propaganda films for the Nazi regime, including *Reichsparteitag* (1935), *The Triumph of the Will* (1935; a celebration of the previous year's NUREMBERG RALLY) and *Olympia* (1938; a documentary on the 1936 Berlin Olympics). She was blacklisted until 1952, but then resumed her career.

Riezler, Kurt (1882–1955), speech writer to Kaiser WILHELM II and private secretary of Chancellor BETHMANN HOLLWEG. He was later a member of the liberal DDP and a supporter of the Weimar Republic. After Hitler came to power he left Germany with his Jewish wife. Riezler's diary from World War I became an important source for historians of German foreign policy, but its reliability was questioned when it was shown by Bernd

Sösemann that his entries for the JULY CRISIS of 1914 were written on different paper to the rest of the journal, and attached as a loose-leaf collection. This suggested that the original diary notes were revised after the end of World War I. The original editor of the diaries, Karl Dietrich Erdmann, responded to Sösemann's points in an exchange in the *Historische Zeitschrift*, but was unable to dispel doubts about the reliability of these sections of the diary as an uncorroborated source.

Riga, battle of (1917), engagement in Latvia during WORLD WAR I. Riga was then the Russian empire's third industrial city, and was attacked by the German 8th Army on 1 September 1917. The city was taken by surprise, and those Russians who were unable to escape were compelled to surrender. The city was also the scene of fighting in 1944, as the Germans retreated.

Rintelen, Anton (1876–1946), Austrian lawyer and politician. Before World War I Rintelen was professor of law at the German university of Prague (1903–11) and then professor at Graz. A member of the CHRISTIAN SOCIAL PARTY, he was *Landeshauptmann* (head of the provincial government) of Styria from 1919 to 1926 and again from 1928 to 1933. He was federal education minister (1932–3) under DOLLFUSS. He was appointed Austrian ambassador in Rome (1933) and was proclaimed chancellor by Nazi putschists after the assassination of Dollfuss in 1934. After the failure of the putsch he unsuccessfully tried to commit suicide. He was tried and sentenced to life imprisonment, but was amnestied in 1938.

Rintelen, Enno von (1891–1971), infantry general. Von Rintelen served in World War I and was awarded the Iron Cross in 1914. He was German military attaché in Rome from 1936 to 1943. He was promoted to infantry general in 1942 and retired at the end of 1944.

Ritter, the German equivalent of 'knight' or 'baronet'.

RKFDV (*Reichskommissariat für die Festigung des deutschen Volkstums*), Reich Commission for the Strengthening of German Nationhood. HIMMLER was appointed to head the RKFDV on 7 October 1939, with responsibility for the 'repatriation' of Germans abroad, the elimination of those who were perceived to constitute a danger to the Reich, and the settlement of new territory by Germans. The RKFDV resettled over 1 million Germans during World War II.

rococo, 18th-century style of interior decoration, which also gave its name to the wider culture of the early and mid-18th century. The word is originally from the French *rocaille* (rock-work), and the style is characterized by the use of scrolls and curves. The style is found in a whole range of artefacts, such as porcelain, gold and silverware, cabinet work and marquetry panels. It is also reflected in the sculpture and painting of the time, and was popular in the churches of the Catholic south of Germany, particularly Austria and Bavaria.

Röhm, Ernst (1887–1934), leader of the SA (*Sturmabteilung*), the Nazi stormtroopers. Born in Munich, the son of a senior railway official, Röhm was educated in a *Gymnasium* (grammar school), and became an officer cadet in 1906 and an officer in 1908. He served in World War I and received the IRON CROSS (First Class). After the war he served as an officer with the FREIKORPS von Epp, where he was involved in a secret gun-running operation for the radical right, and was himself a founding member of a right-wing paramilitary group, the *Eiserne Faust* ('iron fist'). He met HITLER in 1919 and was persuaded to join the DAP (*DEUTSCHE ARBEITERPARTEI* – which became the Nazi Party). Röhm joined the SA, became its effective leader, and resigned from the army in order to participate in the abortive BEER HALL PUTSCH of 1923. After the failure of the putsch he was imprisoned briefly, and released in April 1924. He became a member of the Reichstag and set up the *Front-*

bann, a cover organization for the SA, which had been dissolved after Hitler's release. When it became clear that the new SA would be subordinate to Hitler, Röhm resigned in May 1925. In 1930, however, he was recalled and appointed head of the SA, whose street violence and intimidation was central to the terminal political crisis of the Weimar Republic and the rise of the Nazi Party to power. After 1933 the stormtroopers were not only regarded as dispensable by Hitler, but also, in so far as their persistent violence alienated conservative support, as a threat to the consolidation of Nazi power. Röhm was murdered in 1934 in the purge known as the NIGHT OF THE LONG KNIVES.

Röhm purge. *See* NIGHT OF THE LONG KNIVES.

Roma and Sinti, ethnic minorities known as *Zigeuner* (Gypsies) in German. Originally from India, they first came to Germany in the 15th century, where – as elsewhere in Europe – they were generally outcasts from society. They were discriminated against before the Nazis came to power, but after 1933 the system of persecution was centralized and measures taken against Roma and Sinti were increasingly radical. Their origins in India made them Aryans in the logic of the racial theory of the day, but Robert Ritter, an academic psychologist from Tübingen University employed by the ministry of health, claimed that most had interbred and were impure, so that while those who were purely Aryan might be allowed to survive on supervised reservations, the others should be resettled and sterilized. The NUREMBERG LAWS were applied to Roma and Sinti in order to establish their racial background, and they were then to be rounded up and sent to Poland. Many were arrested in any case as 'ASOCIALS'.

At the beginning of the war EICHMANN suggested that the 'Gypsy question' be resolved along with the 'Jewish question', and many were in fact deported from western Germany and from the BURGENLAND, and either worked to death or murdered at

CHEŁMNO. Priority was given to the deportation of Jews, however, and many others remained in temporary camps, where they succumbed to disease or the regime of hard labour. After the invasion of the Soviet Union, the SS, army and police started systematically shooting Sinti and Roma in eastern Europe and Russia. On 16 December 1942 Hitler signed an order providing for the deportation of 'Gypsies' to Auschwitz, and almost all those who arrived at the camp were murdered. Postwar recognition of these crimes was slow, partial and – at first – limited to the last two years of the war. It was only in 1982 that the full enormity of the genocide of the 1940s was recognized officially (by the SCHMIDT administration).

Rommel, Erwin (1891–1944), field marshal. Born in Heidenheim an der Brentz, Württemberg, into a middle-class family, Rommel joined the 124th Württemberg infantry regiment as an officer cadet in 1910. He was commissioned as a lieutenant in 1912, served in France, Romania and Italy during World War I, and was decorated for valour. In 1937 he published a military textbook, *Infanterie greift an* ('infantry attacks'). After the ANSCHLUSS of Austria in 1938 he was posted to the officers' school in Wiener Neustadt.

In World War II Rommel took part in the invasion of France before his transfer to North Africa, where, as commander of the Afrikakorps (1941–3), he initially reversed the disastrous military position of the Axis following the collapse of the Italians. However, deprived of reinforcements as resources were diverted to the Eastern Front, from late 1942 he was forced into retreat by massive Allied superiority on two fronts. After the German withdrawal from Africa he commanded the Army Group in France (1943–4). Rommel was implicated in the 1944 JULY BOMB PLOT to assassinate Hitler, but his prestige in Germany prevented the Nazis from publicly humiliating him with a trial and execution. He was forced to poison himself, and was then buried with full military honours.

Roon, Albrecht, Graf von (1803–79), field marshal. As a young officer von Roon served at the Berlin War Academy, and later assisted in the suppression of the REVOLUTIONS OF 1848 in Baden. He became Prussian war minister in 1859 and navy minister in 1861. His conflict with the Prussian LANDTAG over the financing and reform of the army led to the appointment of BISMARCK as minister-president in 1862. Von Roon's military reforms were vindicated by the swift victories in the AUSTRO-PRUSSIAN WAR of 1866 and the FRANCO-PRUSSIAN WAR of 1870–1. He retired in 1872.

Rosen, Friedrich (1856–1935), diplomat and politician. Rosen was ambassador to Romania, Portugal and the Netherlands. He also served briefly as foreign minister during the first WIRTH administration (1921).

Rosenberg, Alfred (1893–1946), Nazi ideologue. Born in Reval, Estonia, Rosenberg witnessed the Russian Revolution in Moscow, when his school was moved there during World War I. After returning to Reval in 1918 he fled to Bavaria, where he met Adolf Hitler and joined the NSDAP in 1920. He took part in the BEER HALL PUTSCH in Munich, and temporarily took over the Nazi Party leadership during Hitler's imprisonment. His racist ideology was formulated in *Der Mythus des 20. Jahrhunderts* (*The Myth of the Twentieth Century*, 1930) which was enormously influential on the German right. He was in charge of ideological training within the party from 1934 and was appointed minister for occupied eastern territories in 1941. He was tried and hanged at Nuremberg.

Rosenberg, Frederic Hans von (1874–1937), diplomat and politician. Rosenberg was ambassador to Vienna (1920–2), then Copenhagen (1922), Stockholm (1924–33) and Ankara (1933–5). He was briefly foreign minister in the CUNO administration (1922–3), and also head of the German delegation to the League of Nations Assembly in 1932.

Rote-Armee-Fraktion. *See* RED ARMY FACTION.

RSHA (*Reichssicherheitshauptamt*), the Reich Security Head Office, formed in 1939 with the merger of the head office of the SD and the head offices of the security police (*SIPO*) and criminal police (*KRIPO*). Reinhard HEYDRICH was head of the RSHA until his death in 1942. Ernst KALTENBRUNNER was head from 1943 to 1945. From 1941 the RSHA was divided into seven offices.

Rudolf (von Habsburg-Lothringen), Crown Prince (1858–89), archduke of Austria and heir to Emperor FRANZ JOSEPH. He was married in 1881 to Stephanie, daughter of Leopold II of Belgium. Rudolf was opposed to much of his father's domestic and foreign policy, and had sympathies with the liberals. Among his friends were radical journalists, and this enabled him to publish critical articles anonymously. Rudolf killed himself in the hunting lodge at Mayerling in a suicide pact with a 17-year old girl with whom he had been having an affair.

Ruhr Statute, agreement that established an international control authority for the RUHR VALLEY in 1949. It was signed by the Federal Republic of Germany, the Netherlands, Belgium, Luxembourg, France, Italy, Britain and the United States. The first six signatories later signed the founding treaty of the European Coal and Steel Community, a forerunner of the European Union.

Ruhr valley, Germany's most important industrial region. The '*Ruhrgebiet*' (Ruhr area) extends along the Ruhr valley east of Duisburg and encompasses a number of major German cities, including Essen, Bochum, Gelsenkirchen, Wuppertal and Dortmund. Urbanization was rapid during the Industrial Revolution, and the region (together with the adjacent cities of the northern Rhineland, above all Düsseldorf and Cologne) is one of the largest and most densely populated conurbations in the world. Its economy was built on coal mining and steel production, but engineering, chemicals and other manufacturing industries have also been important. In 1923 the Ruhr was occupied by French and Belgian troops attempting to force Germany to deliver its REPARATIONS payments.

Rundstedt, Gerd von (1875–1953), field marshal. Rundstedt served in World War I, and in World War II successfully commanded Army Group A in the German attack on Poland in 1939. He was also a key figure in the German invasion of France the following year, but was dismissed by Hitler for defeatism during the Soviet campaign in December 1941. Although he was reinstated as commander in chief of German forces in the west in 1942, he was again dismissed, and again for ostensible defeatism, when he suggested coming to terms with the Allies in 1944. He was reinstated again, however, and served a final stint in command of the ARDENNES OFFENSIVE (the battle of the Bulge).

RUSHA (*Rasse- und Siedlungs-Hauptamt*), the Race and Settlement Head Office. The RUSHA was responsible for establishing the racial purity of members of the SS.

Rust, Bernhard (1883–1945), Nazi education minister. Rust was born in Hanover and studied German and classics before serving in World War I. After the war he worked as a schoolmaster until he was sacked in 1930 for molesting a pupil. He joined the NSDAP in 1922, was *Gauleiter* of Hanover and Braunschweig from 1925, and was elected to the Reichstag in 1930. In 1933 he was appointed Prussian minister of science, and in 1934 Reich minister of education. He committed suicide in 1945.

Rwanda and Burundi, parts of GERMAN EAST AFRICA that were mandated to Belgium after World War I.

S

SA (*Sturmabteilung*), 'storm division', the Nazi stormtroopers' organization. The NSDAP's paramilitary force was founded in August 1921. It quickly became a uniformed guard, always present at party meetings, and by 1923 had a membership of 55,000, many of them ex-combatants who had also been involved with various FREIKORPS organizations. By 1933 membership was approaching half a million. From about 1926 SA members adopted the brown-shirt uniform, which gave them their popular name.

The principal function of the SA was violent political intimidation of a kind that reassured the Nazis' more genteel electoral constituency of the party's opposition to the left. During the Depression the SA engaged repeatedly in street-fighting with Communists and other political opponents, and in the spring and summer of 1933 they were responsible for the brutal suppression of the labour movement and its organizations, the ransacking of the buildings and property of left-wing parties and trade unions, and the beatings and arbitrary imprisonment endured by individuals. Although the SA was briefly a proscribed organization in 1932, stormtroopers were treated with considerable leniency by the judicial system and political authorities.

With the consolidation of the Nazi dictatorship the SA had more or less outlived its usefulness. The party's middle-class supporters found the continuing disorder unnecessary and distasteful, and the regime's allies in the bureaucracy, the armed forces and among Germany's political and economic elites found the SA's ambitions disturbing. Following outspoken criticism of its activities the SA was effectively neutralized in 1934 by the NIGHT OF THE LONG KNIVES, during which its leader, Ernst RÖHM, and a number of other leading stormtroopers, were murdered. It was deployed once more, however, during the KRISTALLNACHT pogrom of 1938.

Saarland, a small federal state in southwestern Germany with a population of around 1 million. It was occupied by France between 1792 and 1815, and then integrated into Prussia as part of the Rhine Province. Its economy flourished during the imperial period, but its coal mines were awarded to France after World War I, and it became a political unit separate from Germany in 1920. It was placed under the administration of the League of Nations for 15 years, and returned to Germany after a plebiscite held on 13 January 1935. The territory was occupied by France after World War II, and the first state parliament proposed the establishment of an autonomous Saar state in an economic union with France. In 1954 Paris and Bonn agreed on a plan that would place an independent Saarland under the authority of a European commissioner. The Saar electorate rejected the proposal, however, and the territory became part of the FEDERAL

REPUBLIC. Its capital city is Saarbrücken and it has engineering, chemicals, glass and ceramics industries, as well as coal mining. Until 1985 the largest party in the LANDTAG was the CDU; from then until 1999 the SPD had a majority of seats. In the regional elections of 1999 the CDU had a majority of one.

Sachsen, the German name for SAXONY.

Sachsen-Anhalt. *See* SAXONY-ANHALT.

Sachsenhausen (also called Sachsenhausen-Oranienburg), Nazi concentration camp outside Berlin. Half of its 200,000 prisoners died or were killed at the camp. Sachsenhausen was liberated by the Soviet army on 27 April 1945.

Sadová, battle of (also called the battle of Königgrätz; 3 July 1866), decisive defeat of Austria by Prussian forces at the end of the AUSTRO-PRUSSIAN WAR. The Prussians attacked from two directions and had the decisive advantage of the new breech-loading needle gun, which was superior to the Austrian rifles. This enabled them to achieve a swift victory bringing the short (seven weeks) war to an end. The Peace of Prague was concluded between Austria and Prussia on 23 August the same year.

Sahm, Heinrich (1877–1939), politician and diplomat. Sahm was president of the DANZIG senate (1920–9), and then mayor of Berlin (1931–5). He was ambassador in Oslo from 1936 to 1939.

St Germain, treaty of (1919), peace treaty concluded with AUSTRIA at the end of WORLD WAR I. Austria and Hungary were separated, and the HABSBURG empire's Slav-speaking territories were integrated into a number of newly independent successor states (Poland, Czechoslovakia and Yugoslavia). In addition, the SOUTH TYROL, Trentino and Istria were ceded to Italy, and the southern border of CARINTHIA (where the Yugoslavs asserted irredentist claims) was to be decided by plebiscite. The Austrian armed forces were not to exceed 30,000 men, and the fleet was surrendered to Yugoslavia, and then divided among the victorious powers. Austria, like Germany, was blamed with 'war guilt', but the country was so destitute that very little was paid in reparation. The principle of self-determination that underpinned these territorial adjustments was denied the German-speaking former subjects of the empire, however. The Austrian Republic was forbidden to become a part of Germany on the grounds that the defeated aggressor could not be allowed to acquire territory. Germans in Bohemia and Moravia and in the South Tyrol were perceived to have been 'handed over' to Czechoslovakia and Italy respectively without the plebiscites conducted in some of the other reassigned territories, creating ethnic tensions and political problems for the future.

Salieri, Antonio (1750–1825), composer who was long believed to have poisoned MOZART. Salieri was born in Venice and moved to Vienna in 1766. He was court composer to JOSEPH II from 1774, and court music director from 1788. He retired after the death of the emperor, but returned to organize the music for the Congress of VIENNA.

Salomon, Erich (1886–1944), photojournalist. Born in Berlin, the son of a banker who was subsequently ruined by the 1923 INFLATION, Salomon studied law and worked in the publishing department of the publishing house ULLSTEIN. He became a freelance photojournalist in 1928, working in Berlin. In 1931 he published his collection *Berühmte Zeitgenossen in unbewachten Augenblicken* ('famous people in unguarded moments'). Salomon fled to the Netherlands in 1933, but following the German occupation was sent to Auschwitz with his family in 1943 and murdered in 1944.

Salomon, Ernst von (1902–72), German nationalist writer. Sentenced to five years for his part in the murder of Walther RATHENAU, he was released in 1928 and became a popular writer of *VÖLKISCH* fiction. During the Nazi dictatorship he wrote mainly films scripts and apolitical fiction, but published a popular right-wing critique of DENAZIFICATION after the war.

Sammlung, a term for the 'politics of concentration' or nationalist 'rallying together' of the late 1890s.

Sanssouci, ROCOCO palace built for FRIEDRICH II (Frederick the Great) near Potsdam. The palace was designed by KNOBELSDORFF, and built during the 1740s. The new palace (*Neues Palais*) was built in the 1760s.

SAPD (*Sozialistische Arbeiterpartei Deutschlands*), the Socialist Workers' Party of Germany, the forerunner of the SPD. It was formed at the 'socialist unity conference' in Gotha in 1875 by the merger of the ADAV of Ferdinand LASSALLE and the SDAP of August BEBEL and Wilhelm LIEBKNECHT. Its manifesto was the GOTHA PROGRAMME. It subsequently (1890) became the SPD (*Sozialdemokratische Partei Deutschlands*).

Sauckel, Fritz (1894–1946), Nazi *Gauleiter* of Thuringia and plenipotentiary general for labour mobilization. Sauckel was a merchant sailor before World War I and was imprisoned in France during the war. He joined the DEUTSCHVÖLKISCHER SCHUTZ- UND TRUTZBUND in 1919 and the Nazi Party in 1922, and gave up his study of engineering to become a local party official in Thuringia. He founded one of the first Nazi newspapers, and after the refounding of the party became regional party manager (*Gaugeschäftsführer*) in Weimar (1925). In 1927 he was elected to the Thuringian LANDTAG and appointed *Gauleiter*. In 1932 he became minister-president and interior minister of Thuringia, and was appointed Reich governor of the province in 1933. During World War II Sauckel was responsible for the mobilization of foreign slave labour for the war effort, and for the murder of Jews in Poland. He was tried and hanged at Nuremberg.

Savigny, Karl Friedrich von (1814–75), diplomat and politician. Born in Berlin, Savigny was the son of an academic lawyer. He studied law in Berlin and Paris, and then pursued a diplomatic career. He was the last Prussian representative at the BUNDESTAG (federal diet) of the GERMAN CONFEDERATION in Frankfurt am Main (1864–6) and was a close political colleague of Bismarck. He was a member of the Reichstag from 1867 to 1875, and leader of the CENTRE PARTY there from 1870.

Saxony (German name: Sachsen), one of the NEW FEDERAL STATES. Present-day Saxony was reconstructed in 1990 on the basis of the East German Saxony of the first three years of the GERMAN DEMOCRATIC REPUBLIC (GDR). Historically, however, the name has been applied to a number of territories. In the early Middle Ages it referred to territory to the west of the River Elbe in the region of the present-day LOWER SAXONY, SAXONY-ANHALT and parts of WESTPHALIA and THURINGIA. In the later Middle Ages the name was applied to territories both east and west of the river. From the 15th century, however, Saxony was the name of one of the more substantial German states. Napoleon made Saxony a kingdom in 1806, but some territories were ceded to Prussia at the Congress of VIENNA, and a separate Prussian province of Saxony was created alongside the remaining kingdom of Saxony. The kingdom of Saxony joined the GERMAN CONFEDERATION as an independent state, and remained a separate federal state, and a kingdom, within the GERMAN EMPIRE. Saxony ceased to exist as a *Land* in 1952, when the GDR divided it into the administrative districts of Chemnitz, Dresden and Leipzig.

During the imperial period industrial Saxony was an important centre of support for the Social Democrats, who won 55% of the vote there in the last elections to the imperial Reichstag (1912). During the Weimar Republic support for the left in Saxony was split between the SPD and the KPD (German Communist Party), and some of the Communists' best electoral performances outside Berlin and Hamburg were in the electoral districts of Saxony, particularly Chemnitz –

which also recorded one of the highest votes for the Nazis. Since 1992 support for the left has been similarly split between SPD and the PDS, and in the LANDTAG elections of 1999 the Social Democrats were overtaken by the former Communists and won only 10% of the vote. At the end of the 20th century Saxony had a population of about 5 million, and was the most populous of the new federal states.

Saxony-Anhalt, a state created in the Soviet zone of occupation, and since 1990 one of the NEW FEDERAL STATES. Saxony-Anhalt was formed between 1945 and 1947 from the Prussian provinces of Halle-Merseburg and Magdeburg (part of Prussian Saxony until 1944), the state of Anhalt and territory from Braunschweig and Thuringia. The capital city was Halle. In 1952 the state was divided into the administrative districts of Magdeburg and Halle. It was restored in 1990 from Magdeburg, most of Halle and part of Cottbus district. The largest party in the first LANDTAG after German reunification was the CDU, with 48 out of 106 seats, but the election results of 1994 led to the so-called 'Magdeburg model', a red–green coalition of the SPD and the GREENS, tolerated by the PDS. The capital is now Magdeburg, and at the end of the 20th century the state had a population of 2.8 million.

SBZ (*Sowjetische Besatzungszone*), the SOVIET ZONE OF OCCUPATION.

Schacht, Hjalmar (1877–1970), banker and politician. Schacht was brought up in America, but returned to Germany to study economics and take up a career in banking. From 1916 he was director of the Nationalbank (later the Darmstädter Nationalbank). In 1923 he was appointed Reich currency commissioner, and his introduction of the RENTENMARK halted the hyperinflation crisis (*see* INFLATION). Later in the same year he was appointed head of the REICHSBANK. Subsequently, Schacht was an important participant in the DAWES PLAN and YOUNG PLAN negotiations.

Initially a liberal, and a co-founder of the DDP (which he left in 1926), Schacht joined the nationalist HARZBURG FRONT in 1931, and supported Hitler's claim to the chancellorship the following year. The Nazis reappointed him head of the Reichsbank in 1933 and economics minister in 1934. He went on to devise the economic strategies that financed Germany's rearmament (including the MEFO BILLS). His NEW PLAN of 1934 attempted to regulate imports into Germany by means of government supervision of the allocation of foreign exchange. He was appointed plenipotentiary general for the war economy in 1935, but the economic crisis of 1936, the increasing influence of the AUTARKY lobby, and the establishment of the FOUR-YEAR PLAN under GÖRING contributed to his eclipse. He was removed from the economics ministry in 1937 (where he was succeeded by Walther FUNK) and from the presidency of the Reichsbank in 1939, but remained a minister without portfolio until 1943. He was imprisoned following the 1944 JULY BOMB PLOT, and was subsequently captured by the Allies. He was cleared at Nuremberg and resumed his banking career after the war.

Schäffer, Fritz (1888–1967), conservative Bavarian politician. Schäffer was born in Munich the son of a minor civil servant and studied law at Munich University. He served in World War I, and then joined the Bavarian public service in the interior ministry. A staunch conservative and royalist, he was elected to the Bavarian LANDTAG for the BVP (Bavarian People's Party) in 1920, and was its president from 1929 until it was disbanded in 1933. He was a strong supporter of the BRÜNING government, and his attitudes towards the Nazis seem to have been ambivalent. According to PAPEN, he offered to serve in a Reich government led by Hitler, but he supported the restoration of the WITTELSBACH dynasty in Bavaria in February 1933. He retired from public life when the BVP was dissolved, and was arrested by the authorities at the time of the abortive JULY BOMB PLOT of 1944 and imprisoned at Dachau. Following the liberation of Dachau by the Allies he was appointed minister-president of Bavaria by the military authorities, but was dismissed on account of his leniency towards former Nazis. He was a member of the Bundestag for the CSU (1949–61), and was federal finance minister from 1949 to 1957, then minister of justice (1957–61).

Schäffer, Hans (1886–1967), civil servant. The son of a Jewish industrialist, Schäffer pursued a public-service career in the economics ministry during the 1920s, and was appointed state secretary in 1929. His political sympathies were with the SPD, but he was a supporter of free-market economics and contributed to the legislation regulating cartels. He was an important participant in the REPARATIONS conferences, and helped to secure foreign loans for Germany. Schäffer was the architect of BRÜNING's deflationary economic policies, but resigned in 1932 over differences with the chancellor. He emigrated to Sweden in 1933, and remained there after the war.

Scharnhorst, Gerhard Johann David von (1755–1813), officer in the service of Hanover (1793–5) and Prussia (from 1801). He was a leading figure in Prussia's military reforms, and director of the newly created war ministry (1807–10). He was severely wounded at the battle of Lützen, and died in Prague from his wounds.

Schattendorf, scene of a Social Democrat demonstration in the Burgenland, Austria, on 30 January 1927. Attacks on local Social Democratic functionaries by members of the radical right were frequent in the district, and the *Frontkämpfer*, a right-wing paramilitary organization, attempted to stop the demonstration. When they were unable to do so, they opened fire on the demonstrators from behind as they passed through the main street of the village. As a consequence an 8-year-old child and a disabled war veteran were killed. The murders led to large-scale demonstrations by the labour movement in the Burgenland, Lower Austria and Vienna, but the Social Democratic leader Otto BAUER insisted on awaiting the outcome of a trial. When the murderers were acquitted in Vienna in July there was a spontaneous demonstration during which the Palace of Justice was burned down.

The Schattendorf incident was seen as a turning point in the history of the First Austrian Republic, and the beginning of a political crisis that ended with the imposition of the AUSTROFASCIST dictatorship. It was interpreted on the left as a double attack on the labour movement by means of violent intimidation on the streets and unapologetically partial justice in the courts.

Scheel, Walter (1919–), liberal politician. Scheel was born in Solingen, and served in World War II. He was a member of the Bundestag from 1953 until 1974, vice president of the Bundestag from 1967 to 1969, and leader of the FDP from 1968 to 1974. Scheel was federal minister for economic cooperation from 1961 to 1966, and then foreign minister and vice chancellor in Willy BRANDT's social–liberal coalition (1969–74). He then became federal president (1974–9). Scheel was a leading figure in the development and implementation of the coalition's *OSTPOLITIK*.

Scheidemann, Philipp (1865–1939), leading Social Democratic politician. Born in Kassel into a working-class family, Scheidemann was a printer by trade, and joined the SPD in 1883. He pursued a career in journalism, and was appointed editor in chief of the *Kasseler Volksblatt* in 1905. He stood for election to the Reichstag in 1898, but was not successful until 1903. After the death of BEBEL in 1913 he became one of the party's three presidents. Scheidemann was on the moderate right of the party, and supported the government during World War I. In 1918 he joined the short-lived coalition government formed by Prince Max von BADEN, and opposed the radicalism of the left during the

NOVEMBER REVOLUTION. It was Scheidemann who declared Germany a republic on 9 November 1918, albeit to forestall and counter the proclamation of a 'Socialist Republic' elsewhere in Berlin by Karl LIEB- KNECHT and the SPARTACUS LEAGUE. Scheidemann was a member of the COUNCIL OF PEOPLE'S REPRESENTATIVES, and as minister-president of the provisional government that emerged from the 1919 NATIONAL ASSEMBLY he was effectively the first Weimar chancellor. He was subsequently mayor of Kassel from the end of 1919 until 1925, and survived an assassination attempt in 1922. Scheidemann fled when the Nazis came to power and died in exile in Copenhagen.

Schellenberg, Walter (1910–52), head of the Nazi intelligence service. Born in Saarbrücken, Schellenberg studied law at Bonn and joined the Nazi Party and SS in 1933, and the Gestapo in 1934. He organised SS 'special units' for the occupation of Czechoslovakia, and was later responsible for establishing the autonomy of the same units in their actions in the occupied eastern territories. He was promoted rapidly within the SS and RSHA, and was appointed supreme head of military and SS intelligence in 1944. He was acquitted of complicity in genocide, but sentenced to six years for the murder of Soviet prisoners of war. He was released after serving only half his sentence.

Schelling, Friedrich Wilhelm Joseph von (1775–1854), philosopher. Schelling was born in Leonberg in Württemberg and studied in Tübingen where he met HEGEL and HÖLDERLIN. He was appointed to a chair at Jena in 1798, where he became involved with Romantic writers. He moved to another chair in Würzburg in 1803 and then to a chair in Munich in 1827 and in Berlin in 1841. He published a number of philosophical works based on a very consistent Romantic interpretation of the world at the centre of which was the Absolute (sometimes referred to as God). He saw history as man's journey within the mind of God starting at the centre and moving away only subsequently to return.

Schiele, Egon (1890–1918), Austrian painter. Schiele was a student at the Vienna Academy of Art from 1906 to 1909. He was initially influenced by the *Jugendstil* (Art Nouveau) of the Vienna SECESSION, and went on to become one of the greatest of the Austrian EXPRESSIONISTS. In 1911 he was imprisoned briefly as a consequence of complaints from his neighbours to the police, who confiscated a hundred or so erotic paintings as pornography. He was also accused of seducing a girl below the age of consent, and although the charges were dropped, the judge burned one of his paintings in the courtroom. Schiele was conscripted four days after his wedding to Edith Harns in 1915. He died of Spanish influenza in 1918.

Schiele, Martin (1870–1939), conservative politician and agrarian leader. Schiele was born in Gross-Schwarzlosen and studied estate management. He was a member of the German Conservative Party (*DEUTSCH-KONSERVATIVE PARTEI*) from before the turn of the century, and was elected to the Reichstag in 1914. After World War I he was a co-founder of the nationalist DNVP, and joined the first administration of Hans LUTHER as interior minister in January 1925, bringing the DNVP into government for the first time. The experience was short-lived: the DNVP ministers came under internal party pressure to vote against the LOCARNO TREATIES, which were seen on the right as the result of a supine 'FULFILMENT POLICY' (*Erfüllungspolitik*), and Schiele himself was a particularly vehement critic of STRESE-MANN's foreign policy. The DNVP ministers resigned on 25 October before the Reichstag vote on the issue, which took place on 27 November. The government survived only a matter of days after the vote, and there ensued a political crisis that lasted several weeks until a minority government was formed by Luther (without the DNVP). The DNVP rejoined the government in Wilhelm

MARX's fourth administration (1927–8), and Schiele was appointed agriculture minister. This position enabled him to help his agrarian constituency by introducing emergency aid for farmers and calling for import tariffs on agricultural produce – while the rest of the government was trying to get tariffs reduced. Schiele was subsequently appointed executive president of the National Agrarian League (*Reichslandbund*). In 1929 he left the DNVP and joined a small splinter party, the Christian National Peasants' and Agrarian People's Party (*Christlich-Nationale Bauern- und Landvolkpartei*, or more briefly *Christliches Landvolk*), an agrarian interest group organized to oppose both the DNVP and the Nazis in the countryside. He resigned his DNVP seat in the Reichstag, and joined BRÜNING's government as minister for food (1930–2). Schiele was single-minded in his defence of the landed interest, and determined in his demands for protectionism and financial support for agriculture. With the support of President HINDENBURG he pressed the government into delivering the programme of measures known as OSTHILFE ('eastern aid'), designed to benefit the inefficient agricultural sector east of the Elbe. In doing so, however, Schiele alienated his colleagues, and was also criticized for not doing enough by the AGRARIAN LEAGUE, which was becoming increasingly radical. The *Osthilfe* scheme became embroiled in financial scandals (in which Hindenburg himself was implicated), and when Schiele left office with the fall of the Brüning administration he retired from public life.

Schiess, Franz, Freiherr von Perstorff (1844–1932), Austrian diplomat. Schiess was a diplomatic attaché at the Austrian embassy in St Petersburg (1870), and the legation secretary in Tehran (1872), St Petersburg (1874), Athens (1875), Constantinople (1878), Belgrade (1882), Constantinople again (1887) and Berlin (1891). He was then ambassador in Tehran (1894) and Belgrade (1895).

Schiffer, Eugen (1860–1954), liberal politician. Schiffer was born into a middle-class Jewish family in Breslau (now Wrocław in Poland) and studied law before entering the Prussian public service. He was a member of the Reichstag for the NATIONAL LIBERAL PARTY from 1912 to 1917, and a prominent supporter of the peace resolution of that year. He joined the liberal DDP in 1918 and represented the party in parliament from 1919 to 1924. He was finance minister in 1919 under Philipp SCHEIDEMANN, and then justice minister (1919–20 and 1921). He was German plenipotentiary in Upper Silesia from October 1921 until May 1922, responsible for regulating the partition of the territory, and then represented Germany at the International Court in the Hague. He retired from the Reichstag in 1924, but remained active in politics for the rest of his life. His central political project was the attempt to construct a coherent, united centrist liberal grouping in German politics. Although Schiffer was Jewish, he remained in Berlin during the Nazi dictatorship and organized a discussion group of prominent liberals and conservatives from the 1920s. He survived the dictatorship and the war to become the leader of the Liberal Party (LDPD) and head of the central judicial administration in the Soviet zone of occupation. He was also general director of the zone's central judicial administration.

Schifferer, Anton (1871–1943), conservative politician. Schifferer was a member of the Reichstag for the DVP from 1930 to 1932.

Schiller, Friedrich von (1759–1805), writer and critic. Schiller, the son of an army officer, was born at Marbach in Württemberg, and was a student of medicine at the military academy in Stuttgart. He fled from Württemberg when the duke took exception to his writing and had him arrested. He settled in Mannheim, where his first play, *Die Räuber* (*The Robbers*), had been performed (1782). A political drama, it bore the inscription *in tyrannos* ('against tyrants') on the title page. It was followed by *Die Verschwörung des Fiesco zu Genua (Fiesco's Conspiracy at Genoa*, 1783) and *Kabale und Liebe (Intrigue and Love*, 1784), both of which had their first performance in Mannheim. In 1785 he founded a theatrical journal, *Rheinische Thalia*, and moved to Leipzig, where he composed the poem *An die Freude (Ode To Joy)*, which was set to music by BEETHOVEN. (The poem was later adopted as the anthem of a united Europe, and was also sung as *An die Freiheit* – 'to freedom' – when the postwar division of Germany came to an end in 1989).

In Dresden (1786) Schiller began work on the play *Don Carlos* (1787), and then moved to Weimar, where he met HERDER and GOETHE. His historical research on the struggle of the Netherlands for independence from Spain (published in 1788) helped him to a chair at the University of Jena. He published a history of the Thirty Years War in three volumes between 1790 and 1792, but was forced to give up his university position on health grounds in 1791.

He went on to study the philosophy of KANT and published a number of essays on aesthetics, including *Über die ästhetische Erziehung des Menschen* ('On the Aesthetic Education of Humanity', 1793) and *Über naive und sentimentale Dichtung* ('On Naïve and Sentimental Poetry', 1795). He formed a close working friendship with Goethe, and returned to writing poetry and drama. It was in the years immediately before his death that he wrote his most famous plays: *Wallenstein* (1797–8), a play that reflected his interest in the Thirty Years War, *Maria Stuart* (1800), *Die Jungfrau von Orléans (The Maid of Orleans*, 1802) and *Wilhelm Tell* (1804). He also translated the work of foreign writers (such as Shakespeare and Racine) for the Weimar National Theatre.

schilling (shilling), unit of currency. The schilling originated with Charlemagne's currency reforms of 794, which divided the pound into 20 shillings and 240 pence. It was a common unit of currency in many parts of Germany and remained in use in some areas until the establishment of the empire in 1871. It became the principal unit of currency in the Austrian Republic during the 1920s, and again after 1945.

Schindler, Franz Martin (1847–1922), Austrian politician. Born in Motzdorf (now Mackov), Schindler was professor of theology at Vienna University for 30 years (1887–1917). He was an early member of the CHRISTIAN SOCIAL PARTY, and exercised considerable influence on its ideology. He was a member of the upper house of the Austrian parliament from 1907 to 1918.

Schirach, Baldur von (1907–74), Nazi Reich youth leader and governor of Vienna. Schirach was born in Berlin into a prosperous and well-connected family. His father had been a Prussian officer and then a theatre director, and his mother was an American from a distinguished family. He studied the history of art at Munich and joined the Nazi Party in 1924 while he was a student there. He was head of the National Socialist German Students' League from 1929, Nazi youth leader from 1931 and Reich youth leader from 1933 to 1940. After a brief spell of military service, Schirach was appointed *Gauleiter* and governor of Vienna in 1940. He was sentenced to 20 years' imprisonment at Nuremberg for his part in the deportation of Jews, and was released in 1966.

Schlange-Schöningen, Hans (1886–1960), conservative politician. Schlange-Schöningen was born into a landed family in Pomerania and pursued a military career as an officer cadet with a Prussian regiment before serving in World War I. He was a conservative nationalist, and joined the DNVP after the war. He sat in the Prussian LANDTAG for the DNVP from 1920 to 1928, and in the Reichstag from 1924 to 1932 for the DNVP, the *Volkskonservative Vereiningung* (the Popular Conservative Union of Gottfried TREVIRANUS) and the *Christliches Landvolk* (an agrarian interest group organized to oppose both the DNVP and the Nazis in the countryside). In 1931–2 he was Reich minister and Reich commissioner for OSTHILFE ('eastern aid') in the second BRÜNING administration. The East Elbian landowners reacted against some of Schlange-Schöningen's plans to break up unproductive and inefficient estates, and to resettle unemployed workers in the east. The JUNKERS had a powerful ally in President HINDENBURG, and the *Osthilfe* debacle was an important factor in the fall of the Brüning government. Although Schlange-Schöningen was associated with people in the conservative opposition to Hitler, he was not sufficiently involved to be arrested after the failure of the JULY BOMB PLOT in 1944. After World War II he was elected to parliament again for the CDU (1949–50), and then took up a diplomatic posting in London (1950–5).

Schlegel, August Wilhelm von (1767–1845), critic and translator. Born in Hanover, the son of a pastor who was also a writer, Schlegel – along with his brother, the critic and philosopher Friedrich von Schlegel (1772–1829) – was one of the leading literary figures of German Romanticism. He studied at Göttingen, and was appointed to a chair at Jena in 1798. Schlegel is perhaps best remembered for his translation of many of the plays of Shakespeare into German. He also translated Spanish, Italian and Portuguese writers.

Schleicher, Kurt von (1882–1934), general and politician; the last chancellor (1932–3) of the WEIMAR REPUBLIC. Schleicher was born into a minor aristocratic family in Brandenburg and began his military career as a subaltern in 1900. He served in World War I and won the Iron Cross, and then held various posts at Supreme Headquarters before being appointed adjutant to General GROENER in 1918. He was then head of the *TRUPPENAMT* in the defence ministry from 1920 to 1926, when he was promoted to colonel and moved to the leadership of the Wehrmacht department.

By the end of the 1920s Schleicher had a network of excellent political contacts, and in 1932 he was appointed minister of defence in PAPEN's government, having helped to engineer the downfall of Chancellor BRÜNING. When Papen fell in December 1932 Schleicher was appointed chancellor after considerable intrigue on his part against his predecessor. During his very brief period of office Schleicher attempted to build a 'national' coalition by attempting to win over the working class with job-creation measures, and by seeking support from the STRASSER faction within the NSDAP (Nazi Party). After only a few weeks in office he was replaced by Hitler (January 1933), with whom Papen had conspired. Schleicher was murdered by the Nazis during the NIGHT OF THE LONG KNIVES (30 June 1934).

Schleiermacher, Friedrich (1768–1834), philosopher and evangelical theologian. Schleiermacher was born in Breslau (now Wrocław in Poland) and studied at Halle. He was appointed to a chair at the University of Halle in 1804, but left after the French invasion and moved to Berlin. There he assisted in the founding of the new university, and was appointed to a chair in the year of its opening. He was considered the major Protestant theologian of his time, and his most important work, *Der christliche Glaube* (*The Christian Faith*, 1821–2, revised 1831), was immensely influential.

Schlemmer, Oskar (1888–1943), painter, sculptor and stage designer. Schlemmer studied at the Art Academy in Stuttgart from 1909 to 1914, and then served at the front in World War I until 1916, when he was wounded. He worked at the BAUHAUS from 1920 to 1929, and ran the stage-design workshop there. In 1929 he moved to the Breslau Academy and from 1932 worked in schools in Berlin. He was dismissed in 1933.

Schlesien, the German name for SILESIA.

Schlesinger, Therese (1863–1940), Austrian feminist. Born Therese Eckstein in Vienna, Schlesinger was a leading figure in the

Austrian women's movement before World War I. She was elected to the board of the *Frauenverein* (Women's Association) in 1894, and joined the Austrian Social Democratic Party (SDAP) in 1897. She was a founding member of the *Verein sozialdemokratischer Frauen und Mädchen* (the Association of Social Democratic Women and Girls), and was elected to parliament after World War I. She fled to France in 1939 and died there the following year.

Schleswig-Holstein, a federal state in northern Germany. The 'Schleswig-Holstein question' was the first testing ground of the foreign policy pursued by BISMARCK in the 1860s. The king of Denmark was duke of Schleswig and Holstein, which had been united since the Middle Ages. The population of Holstein, which had joined the GERMAN CONFEDERATION in 1815, was largely German, however, and there was also a substantial German minority in Schleswig. After the Napoleonic Wars the rise of nationalism in both Germany and Denmark led to increased tension over the duchies. The Danish nationalists wanted Schleswig incorporated into Denmark, while the German minority there – with backing from German nationalists generally – wanted it to remain with Holstein and thereby become part of Germany. A revolt of the Germans in both provinces against Denmark in 1848 was supported militarily by Prussia and led to war between the two countries. The fighting came to an end in 1850, and in the London Protocol of 1852 the major European powers expressed their interest in seeing Denmark preserved intact. Austrian troops entered Holstein under the terms of the OLMÜTZ agreement and returned the duchy to Denmark. In 1851 Denmark promised not to annex Schleswig, and to respect the rights of the Germans. In practice there were difficulties throughout the 1850s, and anti-Danish German nationalism was revived in Holstein.

In 1863 Denmark attempted to bring Schleswig under Danish law and exclude Holstein. Austria and Prussia protested, but Denmark pressed ahead and published a new constitution uniting Schleswig and Denmark. It was signed by the new king, Christian IX, who had acceded to the throne on the death of his father in November. The duke of Augustenburg, whose late father had renounced his title to the duchies after the London Protocol, now proclaimed himself duke of Schleswig-Holstein. The crisis precipitated the GERMAN–DANISH WAR of 1864, which ended with the peace of Vienna and the cession by Denmark of Schleswig and Holstein to Prussia and Austria. The treaty of Gastein (1865) regulated the occupation of Holstein by Austria and Schleswig by Prussia. After the 1866 AUSTRO-PRUSSIAN WAR both provinces became part of Prussia, but North Schleswig voted to become part of Denmark in a plebiscite after World War I.

Schleswig-Holstein remained a Prussian province during the Weimar Republic. It became one of the constituent *Länder* of the FEDERAL REPUBLIC OF GERMANY in 1949. The provincial capital is Kiel. The CDU has been the leading government party for much of the postwar period, but the SPD has been the biggest party in the LANDTAG since 1987. At the end of 20th century Schleswig-Holstein had a population of about 2.6 million.

Schlieffen, Alfred, Graf von (1833–1913), general; chief of the general staff (1891–1905). Schlieffen was born in to a family of Prussian aristocrats, joined the army in 1854 and fought in the German wars of unification against Austria (1866) and France (1870–1). The so-called 'Schlieffen Plan', an operational plan for the invasion of France, was delivered on his retirement as chief of the general staff, and more or less put into practice in the first days of WORLD WAR I, shortly after his death.

Schlieffen's objective was to knock out France with a rapid strike, leaving the German army free to concentrate on the war with Russia. The quickest advances against France were to be made through the Low Countries rather than the wooded, hilly terrain to the south. The plan was devised only to deal with the Western Front – Schlieffen thought Germany should adopt a defensive strategy against Russia, which at the time of the first draft was weakened by its war against Japan in the Far East, and would in any case be slow to mobilize.

In the event Schlieffen's plan was modified by the younger Helmuth von MOLTKE, his successor. Moltke made the defensive left wing in the south stronger at the expense of the critical right wing in the north. This modification of what was considered a masterly strategy was long held to have been the reason for the Germans' failure to capture Paris. In fact, when the plan was published after World War II it was established that Moltke's deviations differed less from the original than had been thought, and modern historians are more inclined to locate Germany's weakness in a general unpreparedness for effective resistance from all quarters.

Schmerling, Anton, Ritter von (1805–93), Austrian diplomat and liberal politician. A lawyer by profession from a family with a tradition of public service, Schmerling was a member of the 1848 FRANKFURT PARLIAMENT. He served in Frankfurt first as interior minister in the Leiningen administration, and then as minister-president himself. He resigned in 1848 when his 'greater-German-Austrian' programme collapsed, not least as a result of the intervention of Prince SCHWARZENBERG, the newly appointed Austrian minister-president. From 1849 he was justice minister in the Schwarzenberg cabinet in Vienna, but resigned in 1851 in protest against the NEO-ABSOLUTIST policies of the government. In 1860 he succeeded Goluchowski as interior minister (1860–5) and effectively reformed the Austrian constitution, replacing the essentially federalist 'OCTOBER DIPLOMA' with a series of

measures referred to collectively as the 'FEBRUARY PATENT', which strengthened the position of the German-speaking middle classes. He was forced to resign in 1865 after the emperor appointed a new minister for Hungarian affairs, an act that undermined the basis of his policy.

Schmidt, Auguste (1833–1902), political activist. Schmidt was born in Breslau (now Wrocław in Poland). She was a co-founder of the General German Women's Association (*Allgemeiner Deutscher Frauenverein*) in 1865, of the General German Association of Women Teachers (*Allgemeiner Deutscher Lehrerinnenverein*) in 1890), and of the League of German Women's Associations (*Bund deutscher Frauenvereine*) in 1894. She died in Leipzig in 1902.

Schmidt, Helmut (1918–), Social Democratic politician; federal chancellor (1974–82). Born the son of a schoolteacher in Hamburg, Schmidt served in World War II and studied government and economics at Hamburg University. He joined the SPD in 1946, and was federal president of its student association (the *Sozialistischer Deutscher Studentenbund*) in 1947 and 1948. He began his political career at regional level in Hamburg, and made his name as the city's senator for internal affairs during the early 1960s. He was elected to the Bundestag in 1953. He was defence minister (1969–72) and then finance minister (1972–4) in the social–liberal coalition of Willy BRANDT, before becoming chancellor himself after Brandt's resignation in 1974. The coalition was re-elected in 1976 and 1980, but was broken up in 1982 when the FDP left the coalition and formed a centre–right alliance with the CDU/CSU under Helmut KOHL. Schmidt quickly developed a high profile as a statesman of international standing, and his chancellorship saw further improvements in Germany's relationship with France and Germany's NATO allies. Although he retired from politics in 1987, Schmidt continued to contribute to political debate through his writing and his co-editorship of the prestigious liberal weekly newspaper *Die Zeit*.

Schmidt, Robert (1864–1943), trade unionist and Social Democratic politician. Born into a working-class family in Berlin, Schmidt had an apprenticeship as a piano-maker. He worked on the SPD newspaper *Vorwärts*, and was elected to the Reichstag in 1893. He was on the right of the parliamentary party, remaining with the MSPD (Majority Social Democrats) following the 1917 split, and was appointed to a minor post in the government of Prince Max von BADEN in 1918. Schmidt pursued a successful career as a minister in several governments during the 1920s. He was minister for food in the SCHEIDEMANN and BAUER cabinets (1919–20) and economics minister under MÜLLER (March–June 1920), and again under WIRTH (1921–2). Under STRESEMANN he was vice chancellor and minister for reconstruction (1923). The SPD resigned from coalition in protest at heavy-handed government intervention against disturbances in Saxony and Thuringia, and Schmidt returned to government only once more, in December 1929, when he replaced Paul MOLDENHAUER as economics minister. He served for only three months before the government fell, and he retired from politics.

Schmitt, Carl (1888–1985), conservative German jurist and constitutional theorist. Born in Plettenberg, Westphalia, Schmitt studied law in Berlin, Munich and Strasbourg, and pursued a career as an academic lawyer. He was professor of law at Greifswald, Bonn, Cologne and Berlin, where he held the chair from 1933 to 1945. Schmitt was an anti-republican figure opposed to political pluralism, parliamentary politics and conventional notions of the rule of law. His controversial essay *'Der Begriff des Politischen'* ('The Concept of the Political', 1932) has been widely interpreted as an apologia for the 'Führer state'. He joined the Nazi Party in 1933 and was appointed a Prussian state councillor by GÖRING. Schmitt became the

Third Reich's principal legal and constitutional apologist. He accepted the ENABLING LAW and its implications as a valid constitutional starting point, promoted the notion of a 'legal revolution', argued that the will of the Führer was law, and approved of the anti-Semitic NUREMBERG LAWS. After the NIGHT OF THE LONG KNIVES of 1934 he justified the multiple murders of SA men and others as 'the highest form of administrative justice'. After World War II he was dismissed from his teaching post, and was imprisoned for a number of years. Schmitt enjoyed something of a rehabilitation in conservative circles during the 1980s.

Schmitz, Richard (1885–1954), Austrian conservative politician. Born in Müglitz (now Mohelnice), Schmitz made his career in the CHRISTIAN SOCIAL PARTY, and served as social security and education minister in the *'Bürgerblock'* coalitions of the 1920s. He became vice chancellor in 1930, and was appointed mayor of Vienna after the suppression of parliamentary democracy in the wake of the AUSTRIAN CIVIL WAR of 1934. He retained the post throughout the DOLLFUSS–SCHUSCHNIGG dictatorship, and was then imprisoned by the Nazis between 1938 and 1945. After the end of World War II he was director of a publishing company.

Schnee, Heinrich (1871–1949), German colonial administrator. Schnee was governor of GERMAN EAST AFRICA.

Schneider, Johann Georg (1756–94), revolutionary journalist known also by the pseudonym 'Eulogius'. The son of a poor vintner, Schneider was born near Würzburg and studied philosophy and law at the university there. He was ordained a priest in 1780, and taught philosophy at Augsburg from 1784. He was appointed to a chair at Bonn in 1789, but was later dismissed for his support of the French Revolution. In exile in Strasbourg he became the leader of a group of German-speaking Alsace Jacobins, and was the publisher of *Argos*, one of the most influential Jacobin journals in German. He occupied a number of offices in the service of France, including mayor of Hagenau (Alsace) in 1792, and public prosecutor, both in the *département* of the Lower Rhine and at the Alsatian Revolutionary Tribunal (1793). He also made enemies in Paris, and was arrested in December 1793. He was sentenced to death by the Revolutionary Tribunal and executed in 1794.

Schnitzler, Arthur (1862–1931), Austrian writer. Born in Vienna, the son of a Jewish doctor, Schnitzler began writing while still a schoolboy, and became one of the most widely performed German-speaking playwrights of his day. His best-known work is probably *Reigen* (*La Ronde* or *The Round Dance*), which was written in 1897 and banned as pornography. It was finally performed in 1920 in Berlin, and then in Vienna the following year, but caused such an uproar that it was defined as a threat to public order and further performances were banned.

Schoenberg, Arnold (1874–1951), Austrian modernist composer. Born in Vienna, Schoenberg was a pioneer of modern music, establishing his reputation with the late Romantic *Verklärte Nacht* (*Transfigured Night*, 1899). He went on to explore atonality in works such as *Pierrot Lunaire* (1912), and in the 1920s developed the twelve-note system of composition, which he used in such works as his unfinished opera *Moses und Aron* (1932–51). From 1910 he taught at the Vienna Academy, where his students included BERG and WEBERN. He fled to the United States in 1933 to escape the Nazis' anti-Semitism, and was appointed to a university chair in California. In the USA he changed the spelling of his name from Schönberg to Schoenberg.

Schöffel, Josef (1832–1910), early Austrian conservationist. Born in Brno in Moravia, Schöffel was a journalist who campaigned against the felling of trees in the Vienna woods. As mayor of the small town of Mödling he was also responsible for a number of progressive social measures in local politics.

Scholl, Hans (1918–43) and **Scholl, Sophie** (1921–43), anti-Nazi protesters, brother and sister. The Scholls were students at Munich University, where they were involved in organizing a Christian resistance group, the 'White Rose'. They were arrested, interrogated and severely beaten up by the Gestapo for their part in a demonstration against the regime in Munich in February 1943, and for dropping leaflets critical of the regime from a balcony in the university buildings. Both the Scholls were executed.

Scholtz-Klink, Gertrud (1902–99), leader of the Nazi Women's League. Scholtz-Klink was an early member of the Nazi Party, women's leader in her native Baden from 1929, and Reich women's leader from 1933. She was also head of the DEUTSCHES FRAUENWERK, and from 1934 head of the women's section of the DAF (the German Labour Front). She went into hiding after the war but was tried by the French in 1948 and sentenced to 18 months' imprisonment.

Scholz, Ernst (1874–1932), conservative politician. Scholz came from a middle-class Berlin family and studied law. He was appointed mayor of Kassel in 1912 and joined the Prussian HERRENHAUS (the upper chamber of the parliament) as a NATIONAL LIBERAL in the same year. After World War I Scholz joined the conservative DVP and served as Reich economics minister in the FEHRENBACH administration (1920–1). He was a member of the Reichstag from 1921 to 1932 and was chairman of the DVP parliamentary party from 1923. He was on the right of the party, and while STRESEMANN, the party chairman, favoured a strategy of opening up to the centre and left, Scholz successfully supported the participation of the nationalist DNVP in 'bourgeois bloc' coalitions in 1923 and 1925. He also got on well with HINDENBURG after the latter's election to the presidency in 1925. He was less successful in 1928, when Stresemann agreed to enter the last Weimar coalition of the 1920s under the leadership of Hermann MÜLLER, a Social Democrat. However, Stresemann's death and Scholz's own election to the party chairmanship signalled a move to the right by the DVP, a shift that left the Müller coalition in difficulties. In the elections of 1930, which followed the fall of the Müller government, the DVP lost almost half its share of the vote and a third of its seats. Scholz resigned the party chairmanship and declined the post of interior ministry in the BRÜNING government.

Schönaich, Franz, Freiherr von (1844–1916), Austrian officer. Schönaich was inspector general of the army from 1887. He was defence minister (1905–6) and then minister of war (1906–11) before World War I.

Schönberg, Arnold. See SCHOENBERG, ARNOLD.

Schönbrunn, treaty of (1809). See COALITIONS, WARS OF THE.

Schönerer, Georg, Ritter von (1842–1921), Austrian politician, the most prominent figure in the German nationalist movement in Austria before World War I. Born in 1842, the son of a railway engineer, he was elected to the Austrian parliament in 1873 for the constituency of Waidhofen-Zwettl, and joined the progressive club in the house of representatives (*ABGEORDNETENHAUS*). Schönerer was an anti-clerical liberal, but although he was ostensibly on the left he was also increasingly anti-Semitic, and was a co-founder of the Pan-German Nationalist Party in 1879. He argued for a reorientation of Austria away from the Balkans, and in favour of economic and political union with Germany. His involvement in political violence resulted in his losing his title, his officer rank and his seat in parliament. HITLER admired his ideological principles in *MEIN KAMPF*, but considered his more successful contemporary, Karl Lueger, a far more effective politician. Schönerer died in his castle in Lower Austria a few years after the end of World War I.

Schönheit der Arbeit ('beauty of labour'), an organization of the German Labour Front

(DAF), established on 27 November 1933 to encourage German employers to improve working conditions. The modernization of factory premises and facilities that was taking place as industry started to expand again and new branches developed was subsumed into a programme subordinate to *Schönheit der Arbeit*. There were thousands of minor improvements to canteens, staff rooms, washing and changing rooms and so on, and recreational facilities were also introduced or improved, often 'voluntarily' by workers themselves outside normal working hours. The whole programme was monitored by thousands of factory inspections.

Schönhuber, Franz (1923–), leader of the radical right-wing *REPUBLIKANER* movement. He was replaced as leader by Rolf Schlierer in 1994, and left the party in 1995.

Schreiber, Adele (1872–1957), politician. Schreiber was a member of the Reichstag for the SPD from 1920 to 1924, and again from 1928 to 1932.

Schröder, Gerhard (1944–), SPD politician; federal chancellor (1998–). Schröder joined the SPD in 1963 and was elected to the Bundestag in 1980. He was minister-president of lower Saxony from 1990 to 1998, and became chancellor following the SPD election victory of 1998.

Schröder, Kurt von (1889–1966), Nazi banker. Born in Hamburg, Schröder studied at Bonn, served in World War I and subsequently pursued a banking career in the Rhineland. He was an early contributor to the NSDAP, and also directed funds to the party from the business community. He arranged the meeting between PAPEN and HITLER in January 1933, at which the fall of Kurt von SCHLEICHER, the last Weimar chancellor, was planned. Schröder pursued a successful business career under the Nazis and received a nominal prison sentence in 1947.

Schrödinger, Erwin (1887–1961), Austrian physicist. Schrödinger was born in Vienna, the son of a well-to-do businessman. He studied at Vienna University and served in

World War I before taking up university teaching posts at Stuttgart and Kiel. In 1927 he succeeded PLANCK as professor of physics at Berlin, and was awarded the Nobel prize for physics in 1933 for his work on the aspect of quantum theory known as wave mechanics. He fled Germany for Oxford when the Nazis came to power, returning to Austria briefly (1936–8) before the ANSCHLUSS. He settled at the Institute of Advanced Studies in Dublin in 1939 and remained there until 1956, when he retired and returned to Vienna as professor emeritus.

Schubert, Franz (1797–1828), Austrian composer. Born in Vienna, the son of a Moravian schoolmaster, Schubert joined the Vienna Boys' Choir in 1808 and began to compose songs (*Lieder*) in 1811. He wrote his first symphony two years later, and then began work as a teacher in his father's school. The following year he set to music GOETHE's 'Gretchen at the Spinning Wheel', and then went on to compose 145 *Lieder* within a year, as well as two more symphonies and a number of other works. His success as a composer and the generosity of his friends and admirers eventually enabled him to give up teaching and to concentrate on composition. Schubert died in Vienna in 1828. Like that of the later Beethoven, his work marks the transition from the Classical period to Romanticism.

Schücking, Walther (1875–1935), diplomat and liberal activist. Schücking was a member of the Reichstag for the DDP from 1919 to 1928. He was also a member of the German peace delegation to VERSAILLES in 1919, and then a judge at the International Court of Justice in The Hague (1932). He was deputy president of the *Liga für Völkerbund*, a German pro-League of Nations organization, and president of the German branch of the Inter-Parliamentary Union. He was forced into retirement by the Nazis in 1933.

Schulenburg, Friedrich Werner von (1875–1944), diplomat. Schulenburg was German ambassador in Tehran (1922–31), Bucharest

(1931–4) and Moscow (1934–41). He was executed for his part in the JULY BOMB PLOT.

Schulte, Karl Joseph (1871–1941), Roman Catholic priest. Schulte was born in Oedingen and studied theology at Bonn, Munich and Tübingen. He was ordained as a priest in 1895. In 1920 he became cardinal archbishop of Cologne. He was a conservative opponent of the Nazis, and in particular of the anti-Christian ideology and propaganda of Alfred ROSENBERG, but was reticent in his public criticism of the regime.

Schultze, Walther (1894–1979), Nazi leader of the University Teachers' Association. A party member from 1919, Schultze participated in the BEER HALL PUTSCH and was elected to the Bavarian LANDTAG in 1936. He became leader of the University Teachers' Association in 1935. He was sentenced to four years in 1960 for complicity in the Nazi euthanasia programme.

Schulze-Gaevernitz, Gerhart von (1864–1943), liberal politician and economist. Schulze-Gaevernitz was a member of the Reichstag for the DEUTSCHE FORTSCHRITTSPARTEI (the Progress Party) from 1912 to 1918, and then for the DDP from 1919 to 1920.

Schumacher, Kurt (1895–1952), Social Democratic politician. Schumacher was born in Culm (Chełmno), West Prussia, into a middle-class family and studied law and economics at Halle, Berlin and Münster. He lost his right arm while serving in World War I, and made his career as a socialist journalist in Swabia during the 1920s. He joined the MSPD (Majority Social Democrats) in 1918 and was a member of the Workers' and Soldiers' Council (*RAT*) in Berlin. He was a member of both the Württemberg LANDTAG (1924–31) and the Reichstag (1930–33) for the SPD, and made his political reputation with his maiden speech in parliament in 1930. He was imprisoned by the Nazis in 1933 for ten years, and was arrested a second time following the failed JULY BOMB PLOT of 1944. After the war he became chairman of the SPD in the western zones of occupation (May 1946), and leader of the SPD in the Bundestag in 1949. He was opposed to the policy adopted by ADENAUER of integrating the Federal Republic into the Western alliance, and was a committed supporter of the reunification of Germany. His health had suffered during his imprisonment in CONCENTRATION CAMPS, however, and as a consequence he lost a leg after the war, and died in Bonn a few weeks before his 57th birthday.

Schuman plan (1950), plan proposed by the French foreign minister Robert Schuman, setting out the framework for the establishment of the European Coal and Steel Community. The plan was announced on 9 May 1950. The coal-mining and steel-working areas on either side of the Franco-German border lay in territories such as the SAARLAND, ALSACE-LORRAINE, the RHINELAND and the RUHR VALLEY, all of which had been contested, invaded, occupied and subjected to exceptional political arrangements for the best part of a century. Under the new plan all French and German coal and steel production was to be placed under a common 'High Authority', whose establishment was the first step towards European integration.

Schumpeter, Joseph A(lois) (1883–1950), Austrian economist and finance minister. Schumpeter was born in Triesch (now Třešt') in Moravia, the son of a successful businessman. He studied law and politics at Vienna University, and was appointed professor of economics at Czernowitz (1909) and then at Graz (1911). During World War I he worked on plans for the reorganization of the HABSBURG monarchy, and resisted the idea that Austria could effectively be annexed by Germany as part of a greater '*MITTELEUROPA*'. He was briefly finance minister of the Austrian First Republic under Karl RENNER after the end of the war (March to October 1919). He resigned his post and became director of a private bank. In 1925 he was appointed professor of public finance at Bonn, and in 1932 he emigrated to the United States and remained at Harvard University for the rest of his career. His major works included *Theorie der wirtschaftlichen Entwicklung* (*Theory of Economic Development*, 1912); *Konjunkturzyklen* (*Business Cycles*, 1939) and *Kapitalismus, Sozialismus und Demokratie* (*Capitalism, Socialism and Democracy*, 1942). He is remembered for his development of a theory of economic cycles, whose predictive value for the real economy he nevertheless doubted. Towards the end of his life he argued that capitalism would be replaced by socialism.

Schupo (abbreviation of *Schutzpolizei*), ordinary uniformed police.

Schuschnigg, Kurt von (1897–1977), Austrian conservative politician; chancellor from 1934 until the Nazi invasion (*ANSCHLUSS*) of 1938. Schuschnigg was born at Riva on Lake Garda, which was then in Austria, and served in the Austrian army during World War I. He was elected to parliament for the CHRISTIAN SOCIAL PARTY in 1927 and in 1930 founded a Christian defence unit, *Ostmärkische Sturmscharen*. After serving as minister of justice (1932) and minister of education (1933–4), he was appointed chancellor following the assassination of his predecessor Engelbert DOLLFUSS. (He remained education minister, and was also army minister throughout his chancellorship.)

Schuschnigg consolidated the authoritarian 'AUSTROFASCIST' dictatorship established by Dollfuss, and strengthened his own position within the regime after the effective marginalization of the paramilitary HEIMWEHR in 1936. He came under increasing pressure to make concessions to Germany and to the Austrian Nazis, however, and resigned on 11 March 1938 after an ill-fated attempt to rally the Austrian people behind him with plans for a plebiscite affirming Austrian independence.

Schuschnigg was imprisoned by the Germans after the *Anschluss* and pursued an academic career at the University of St Louis in the United States for twenty years after the end of the war. He returned to the Tyrol on his retirement in 1967 and died there ten years later.

Schutzhaft ('protective custody'), the term used by the Nazis to describe the detention of political opponents. Before the Nazi era, 'protective custody' was in the interests of the person detained, but the term lost this meaning during World War I when the authorities detained people they considered politically unreliable. It was also used by the Reichswehr to imprison Communist insurgents in Berlin and the Ruhr after the war, and during the suppression of the Bavarian 'soviet' republic of 1919. Under a Prussian law of 1931 the term *Schutzhaft* was used to describe police detention on the grounds of protecting law and order. The emergency decree 'for the protection of the German people' passed by the coalition government on 4 February 1933 prolonged the permissible period of detention. This was superseded after the REICHSTAG FIRE by the Decree for the PROTECTION OF PEOPLE AND STATE (28 February 1933), which freed the police (whose ranks now included auxiliaries from the SA and SS) from judicial investigation into their actions, and enabled them to make mass arrests in order to protect the state from the threat of political subversion.

Schutzpolizei (abbreviated to *Schupo*), ordinary uniformed police.

Schutzstaffel. *See* SS.

Schwarz, Franz Xaver von (1875–1947), treasurer of the NSDAP (Nazi Party). Schwarz joined the NSDAP in 1922 and became treasurer in 1925. He was elected to the city council in Munich in 1929, and became a member of the Reichstag in 1933. He was made a *Reichsleiter* in 1935. Schwarz died in an internment camp after the war.

Schwarze Front ('black front'), a breakaway Nazi movement based in Prague and led by Otto STRASSER and Walter Stennes in 1930, following their expulsion from the NSDAP.

Schwarze Korps, Das, the weekly newspaper of the SS.

Schwarzenberg, Felix, Fürst zu (1800–52), Austrian politician; minister-president (1848–52). Born in Böhmisch Krumau (now Český Krumlov) into a distinguished aristocratic family with large estates in Bohemia, Schwarzenberg was a career officer who joined a cavalry regiment at the age of 18. He was stationed in Italy at the time of the REVOLUTIONS OF 1848 and took command of a brigade under RADETZKY. In October 1848 he was appointed minister-president and foreign minister. Although his name is associated with the 'NEO-ABSOLUTISM' of the counter-revolution, he began his ministerial career by insisting on the abdication of the emperor Ferdinand, who was succeeded by the young FRANZ JOSEPH. Although he appointed liberal ministers, Schwarzenberg presided over an authoritarian regime that disregarded the Kremsier REICHSTAG and issued a constitution in March 1849 whose main purpose was to undermine the FRANKFURT PARLIAMENT and check Hungarian separatism. Under his leadership Austria led the move to thwart attempts by the Prussian minister RADOWITZ to enhance the position of Berlin with the creation of a new 'German union'. Schwarzenberg's own attempts to establish a new political system for Germany were equally unpopular, however, and the GERMAN CONFEDERATION was re-established by the OLMÜTZ agreement of 1850. Schwarzenberg died suddenly in Vienna in 1852, leaving the young emperor at the head of the new regime.

Schwarzenberg, Karl Philipp, Fürst zu (1771–1820), Austrian field marshal and diplomat. Born in Vienna, Prince Schwarzenberg took part in the last war against the Turks in 1789. He later served as ambassador in Paris (1809) and negotiated the French emperor's engagement to Archduchess Marie Luise. In 1812 he commanded Napoleon's Austrian army in Russia, and in 1813 led the Allied armies against Napoleon at the battle of LEIPZIG, entering Paris at the head of his victorious troops the following year.

Schwarzhaupt, Elisabeth (1901–86), conservative politician. Schwarzhaupt was born in Frankfurt am Main. She trained as a teacher and also studied law and politics. Her parents were committed (evangelical) Christians and politically active, and she was a member of the conservative DVP during the Weimar Republic. When the Nazis came to power she was compelled to give up her career as a judge, and to leave the public service altogether. After the war she was active both in the EVANGELICAL CHURCH and in the CDU, and was a member of the Bundestag from 1953 to 1969. She was the first women to serve as a federal minister when she took over the ministry of health (1961–6).

Schweitzer, Albert (1875–1965), doctor and missionary. Born in Kaysersberg, Alsace, the son of a pastor, Schweitzer studied theology and medicine at Strasbourg. He lectured in philosophy, and was influenced by Goethe, Schopenhauer and Nietzsche. He also made his name as a theologian and musician with a book on the eschatology of Christ and St Paul, and a study of Bach. In 1913 Schweitzer founded a hospital in Lambaréné in French Equatorial Africa (now in Gabon) and worked there more or less continuously until his death. After World War II he was a vociferous opponent of atomic weapons, and in 1951 he was awarded the *Friedenspreis des deutschen Buchhandels* ('peace prize of the German book trade'). The following year he received the Nobel Peace Prize.

Schwerin von Krosigk, Lutz, Graf (1887–1977), nationalist politician and civil servant. Born in Anhalt into a north German aristocratic family, von Krosigk acquired the name Schwerin when he was adopted by an uncle in 1925. He was educated at Oxford and Lausanne, and joined the Prussian public service in 1909. He was a reserve officer during World War I, and after the war was a supporter of the nationalist DNVP (although not a member). A successful (and anti-republican) career civil servant throughout the

1920s, he became head of the REPARATIONS section in the finance ministry in 1931, and was appointed finance minister in PAPEN's 'cabinet of barons' in 1932. Schwerin was an advocate of Nazi participation in government and remained in office throughout the Nazi dictatorship, becoming foreign minister in the short-lived DÖNITZ government at the very end of World War II. In 1949 he was sentenced to imprisonment for ten years at Nuremberg, but was released in 1951.

Schwitters, Kurt (1887–1948), artist. Born in Hanover, Schwitters was originally a draftsman and naturalistic painter, but turned increasingly to EXPRESSIONISM and DADA towards the end of World War I. He began to make collages from refuse, and this technique, which he called *Merz* (from *Kommerz*, 'commerce'), was his distinctive creative form. His own house became a *Merzbau* and he published a journal under the name *Merz* from 1923. In 1927 he organized a retrospective touring exhibition of his work. Clearly a 'degenerate' to the Nazis, he nevertheless remained in Hanover until 1937, when he moved to Norway. In 1940 he fled to England to escape the German invasion of Norway.

SD (*Sicherheitsdienst des Reichsführers SS*, 'security service of the Reich leader of the SS'), the Nazi Party's intelligence service. The role and activity of the SD emerged before the party came to power, and was foreshadowed by the gathering of information on political opponents and internal dissent first by the SA and then by HIMMLER. The SD itself was established in the autumn of 1931, and was placed under the leadership of Reinhard HEYDRICH. When the Nazis came to power the SD was able to invest its work with the authority of a quasi-state organization, and on 9 November 1933 the SD became an SS office with ten regional divisions.

As the police state grew, and came increasingly under the single authority of Himmler during the course of the 1930s, it was necessary to demarcate the respective spheres of interest of the SD and the GESTAPO. In a ruling of July 1937 Heydrich insisted that the two organizations were not – and should not be – in competition (although there were often tensions between them in practice). The SD would investigate opposition, and would concentrate on racial matters, the party, the state, education, science and the arts. The Gestapo on the other hand would be more directly involved in combating opposition and would be responsible for treason, for monitoring the activities of the underground left, and for emigrants. In a number of areas (including religious groups, the Jews, pacifists, the economy and the press) the SD would deal with general matters while the Gestapo would address specific cases that necessitated police measures. On 11 November 1938 the SD officially became an auxiliary to the security police (*Sicherheitspolizei*, SIPO), and on 27 September 1939 the Reich Security Head Office (*Reichssicherheitshauptamt*, RSHA) was established, embracing both the SD on the one hand and the main office of the security police, that is the Gestapo and criminal police (*Kripo*), on the other.

SD agents compiled detailed reports on a daily basis, which were then collected and edited at local, regional and national offices to produce a comprehensive survey of events and opinions at every level of German society. In the absence of free expression of public opinion these reports on the 'general situation' or 'reports from the Reich' (*Meldungen aus dem Reich*) were intended to give the regime some idea of developments in morale, popular responses to political and military developments, and the reception of propaganda, radio speeches and even feature films. The organization was also responsible for actions against partisans in occupied Europe. The SD was found to be a criminal organization at Nuremberg.

SDAP (*Sozialdemokratische Arbeiterpartei*), the Social Democratic Workers' Party, a fore-runner to the SPD established in 1869 at Eisenach by August BEBEL and Karl LIEBKNECHT, along with a number of former members of the General German Workers' Association (ADAV) of Ferdinand LASSALLE. The two parties differed on little other than their approach to the question of German unity, and eventually merged to form the SAPD (which subsequently became the SPD) at the 'unity conference' in Gotha in 1875.

SDAP (*Sozialdemokratische Arbeiterpartei*), the Social Democratic Workers' Party (the Austrian labour party), founded in 1889 at Hainfeld, Lower Austria. The Hainfeld conference brought together moderate and radical factions within the Austrian labour movement, and they agreed to settle their differences following the dissolution of workers' associations and the suppression of their newspapers in 1884. Although it was strongly influenced by the German Social Democratic movement, and both the organization and the political outlook of the party reflected that of the SPD, the SDAP was formed and developed in response to specifically Austrian political circumstances.

Before World War I the SDAP's agenda was dominated by the Habsburg monarchy's intractable nationalities problem, on which many of the party's senior theoreticians published at some length. An official nationalities' programme was published at Brünn (Brno in Moravia) in 1899. The party wanted to see the Austro-Hungarian empire transformed into a democratic federation of nationalities, but despite its avowedly internationalist position it was unable to prevent divisions based on national allegiances even within the ranks of the labour movement itself. The problem of nationalism was particularly acute in Bohemia and Moravia, where the Czech socialists preferred to form alliances with the liberal parties of their own bourgeoisie, while German workers founded breakaway right-wing organizations such as the DEUTSCHE ARBEITERPARTEI (DAP).

The SDAP was also, arguably, more radical

than its German sister party and ostensible model. Its 'Austromarxist' political outlook was an important factor in inhibiting the development of a significant Communist Party in Austria after World War I (at least until the 1930s, when the KPÖ became an important focus of opposition to AUSTRO-FASCISM and the CORPORATE STATE). The unity of the labour movement made the SDAP the strongest single political force in the new republic at the end of World War I, but far from ensuring the party a role in government, this fact and the party's overwhelming majorities in 'RED VIENNA' made it a threat to the beleaguered Austrian middle classes. A succession of right-wing 'bourgeois bloc' coalition governments of the CHRISTIAN SOCIAL PARTY and German Nationalists (the GREATER GERMAN PEOPLE'S PARTY) kept the SDAP perpetually out of office after 1920. The party was suppressed after the brief AUSTRIAN CIVIL WAR of 1934. It split into an exile organization (*Auslands-organisation Österreichischer Sozialisten*, ALÖS), and a more radical group of 'Revolutionary Socialists' who remained within Austria and formed an underground resistance movement against the dictatorship of DOLLFUSS and SCHUSCHNIGG. The two groups were reunited as the Socialist Party of Austria (*Sozialistische Partei Österreichs*, SPÖ) after the end of World War II. A moderate Social Democratic party, the SPÖ was in government for much of the remainder of the 20th century, first in coalition with the conservative ÖVP (Austrian People's Party) between 1945 and 1965, and then in sole power under Bruno Kreisky (1971–83). Its brief coalition with the then ostensibly liberal FPÖ (Freedom Party) came to an end in 1985, when the leadership of the latter party was taken over by extreme right-wing nationalists. However, the party remained in power, again in coalition with the ÖVP, until January 2000.

Sea Lion (*Seelöwe*), German code name for the planned invasion of Britain in 1940.

Secession (*Sezession*), the name given to various groups of artists in Vienna, Munich, Berlin and Darmstadt, all of whom broke away from their respective academic establishments. The Munich Secession was founded in 1892 by von Stuck, von Uhde and Trübner. The Berlin Secession was founded in May 1898 by Max LIEBERMANN and others. There were 65 founding members, and membership was open to both men and women. Liebermann became president, and Walter Leistikow was first secretary. The most significant group was the Vienna Secession, founded in 1897 by Gustav KLIMT and 19 other members of the Vienna *Künstlerhaus*. The Austrian Secession movement faced less hostility from the public authorities than its counterpart in Berlin. It had its own building near the centre of Vienna and its own journal (*Ver Sacrum*). The work of the Vienna Secession was dominated by the style known as JUGENDSTIL (Art Nouveau), which came to be known in Austria as *Sezessionsstil*.

SED (*Sozialistische Einheitspartei Deutschlands*), the Socialist Unity Party of Germany, the governing party of the GERMAN DEMOCRATIC REPUBLIC. The party was founded on 21 April 1946 when the SPD (Social Democrats) and KPD (Communists) were combined in a single party in the SOVIET ZONE OF OCCUPATION (SBZ). The KPD had rejected an SPD offer of unification in 1945, but election results in Austria and Hungary had been disappointing for the communist parties there, and there was in any case still some support among Social Democrats at local level for such a merger. According to official sources in East Germany, 47% of the delegates present at the founding conference were members of the KPD, and 53% percent were Social Democrats. These proportions were to be retained in the principle of equal representation for Social Democrats and Communists in organs and committees of the party at all levels, at least until 1949. By that time those Social Democrats who had not wholly adjusted to the new party were increasingly marginalized, as the SED set out to become a party of the Leninist type, based on the principle of 'democratic centralism'. Real power lay not with the party's Central Committee (ZK) but in the Politburo and the party Secretariat, which was divided into departments with responsibilities corresponding to those of the government, so that the party could effectively shadow and oversee the business of the state. This close relationship between party and state was often reinforced by a 'personal union': leading party functionaries also occupied important government posts. Many also had key posts in the mass organizations that were an important part of the political system of the GDR.

According to official figures the SED had 1,298,000 members in 1946, and 1,750,000 in 1950. In 1952, however, it expelled 150,000 members in a purge of Social Democrats along with some internal party dissidents from the old KPD. The official membership figure for the party in 1954 was 1,413,000. Members of the leadership were also expelled from the party from time to time. This happened to Franz Dahlem (ULBRICHT's second in command) in 1952, and (following the June uprising of 1953) to Wilhelm ZAISSER, the minister for state security, and to Rudolf HERRNSTADT, editor of the party newspaper *Neues Deutschland*. A number of senior figures were expelled in the late 1950s for advocating liberalization, including Karl Schirdewan, Fred Oelssner, and Ernst WOLL-WEBER.

The SED was always subject to pressure from Moscow, and was ultimately undermined by the politics of glasnost and perestroika introduced in the Soviet Union by Gorbachev during the late 1980s. The SED had generally been more resistant to liberalization than other ruling parties in the Soviet Bloc, and since June 1953 had not faced the frequent political upheavals experienced by Poland, or crises similar to those in Hungary (1956) or Czechoslovakia (1968). The détente and *OSTPOLITIK* of the 1970s had opened up the possibility of the discussion of reform, but it was only after 1985 that a real split developed between hardliners and 'renewers', with the party leadership under Erich HONECKER firmly set against any real measure of reform. Ultimately, however, the East German system was guaranteed only by the support of the Soviet Union, and by the ultimate threat of military intervention. When the promise of such support was withdrawn by Gorbachev, the party could no longer maintain its authority, and was faced with large-scale and unprecedented public demonstrations in the autumn of 1989. On 18 October Honecker was replaced by Egon KRENZ. On 8 November a mass demonstration of party members in Berlin demanded internal party democracy, an extraordinary congress and a new leadership, but these demands were overtaken by events when the border to the West was opened. Some 600,000 members had left the party by the end of the year, and its monopoly of state power ceased on 1 December. At an open conference of 8 December 1989 the party elected a new leader, Gregor Gysi, and adopted a new name, the Party of Democratic Socialism (PDS).

Sedan, battle of (1–2 September 1870), the decisive battle of the FRANCO-PRUSSIAN WAR. The French forces of General MacMahon were surrounded by Prussian troops under MOLTKE, and defeated in the biggest artillery battle of the war. Napoleon III was with the French troops, and BISMARCK and the king watched the battle from the Prussian camp. A second battle took place at Sedan during the German invasion of France in 1940.

Sedlnitzky, Josef, Graf (1778–1855), Austrian public servant. Sedlnitzky was METTERNICH's chief of police and head of the imperial censorship office from 1817 to 1848.

Seebohm, Hans-Christoph (1903–67), conservative politician. Seebohm was a member of the Bundestag for the *DEUTSCHE PARTEI*

(1949–60), and then for the CDU (1960–7). He was minister of reconstruction and labour in Lower Saxony (1947–9) and then federal minister of transport (1949–66). From 1959 he was also a spokesman on behalf of the *Sudetendeutsche Landsmannschaft*, an organization of Germans expelled from the SUDETENLAND at the end of World War II.

Seeckt, Hans von (1886–1936), general and conservative politician. Born in Schleswig, the son of an army general, Seeckt was a career officer who served in World War I. He was chief of staff to August von MACKENSEN in the GORLICE and Serbian offensives of 1915, and was promoted to major general. He was then appointed chief of staff to the 12th Austro-Hungarian Army, and took part in the Romanian campaign of 1916. He was also chief of staff to the Turkish army in 1917 and 1918. After the end of the war he was charged with the command of German forces in the approaches to East Prussia.

Seeckt was a member of the German delegation to Versailles, and was appointed head of the *TRUPPENAMT*, an office that fulfilled the function of the general staff (prohibited by the treaty of VERSAILLES). He was then commander of the Reichswehr from 1920 to 1926, and was instrumental in disbanding the FREIKORPS units and keeping the army out of politics as much as possible. He was dismissed in 1926 for offering a post to a member of the former royal family. Seeckt was a member of the Reichstag (1930–2) for the conservative DVP, and was a supporter of Hitler during the Depression. He led a German military mission to China in 1934, and acted as a military adviser to Chiang Kai-shek (1934–5) shortly before his death in Berlin.

Seghers, Anna (1900–83), East German writer. Born in Mainz as Netty Reiling, the daughter of an art dealer, Seghers studied the history of art, Chinese studies and philology at Cologne and Heidelberg. In 1925 she married a Hungarian communist, and in 1928 won the Kleist Prize for her story '*Der Aufstand*

der Fischer von St. Barbara' ('the uprising of the St Barbara fishermen'), which was made into a film in the USSR by PISCATOR in 1934. In 1928 Seghers also joined the KPD (the German Communist Party). In 1933 she was arrested and detained briefly by the Gestapo, and fled to Paris after her release (via Prague and Switzerland), and eventually, after the German invasion of France, to Moscow. In 1947 she returned to Germany and became a member of the SED (the Communist-dominated ruling party of East Germany). The following year she became vice president of the *Kulturbund zur demokratischen Erneuerung Deutschlands* (Cultural League for the Democratic Renewal of Germany). In 1952 she was a co-founder of the East German Writers' Association.

Seipel, Ignaz (1876–1932), Austrian priest and conservative politician; chancellor (1922–4 and 1926–9). Seipel was born in Vienna and studied theology at the university there. He joined the Benedictine order and was ordained as a priest in 1899. He received his doctorate in 1903, was professor of theology at Salzburg from 1909 to 1912, and then professor at Vienna from 1917. By 1918 he was a leading figure in the CHRISTIAN SOCIAL PARTY (CSP), and was important in reconciling differences between its monarchist and republican wings. In October and November 1918 he was minister of public works and social security in the LAMMASCH ministry, and after the end of the war he was elected to the parliament of the Austrian Republic for the CSP, over which he presided as leader from 1921 to 1929.

Seipel was chancellor and foreign minister at the head of a 'bourgeois bloc' coalition from 1922 to 1924, at the peak of the postwar crisis. He was responsible for successfully negotiating the Geneva Protocols (October 1922), which reaffirmed the political independence and territorial integrity of Austria, and helped to stabilize the country politically and economically through a combination of loans from Britain, France,

Italy and Czechoslovakia totalling 650 million gold crowns and draconian public expenditure cuts in Austria itself. The country's economy was placed under the control of a commissioner general of the League of Nations, and the terms of the agreement caused fury in Vienna. The financial burden of the agreement fell disproportionately on the poorest: 85,000 public employees were dismissed, indirect taxes raised rather than the socially more equitable direct taxes, and pensions were cut. Seipel's hostility to the SDAP (Social Democrats) – which had prevented him from taking up a ministerial position in Austria's first democratic government, and which was heartily reciprocated – soured the political atmosphere of the 1920s.

In June 1924 Seipel was wounded in an assassination attempt. He resigned and was succeeded as federal chancellor by Rudolf RAMEK, but returned to form a second administration when Ramek's government fell in the wake of financial scandals. From 1926 to 1929 he occupied the offices of both chancellor and foreign minister, and presided over the rapid erosion of parliamentary democracy in Austria. It was shortly after his return to office that a child and a war veteran were murdered by armed right-wing agitators during a socialist demonstration at SCHATTENDORF in the Burgenland, and Seipel's promotion of the violent radical right-wing HEIMWEHR movement as a means of containing and suppressing the labour movement is generally held to have strengthened fascism in Austria, and to have paved the way for the AUS-TROFASCIST dictatorship of the 1930s. Seipel himself was now also increasingly in favour of radical authoritarian solutions to Austria's political problems, and advocated a 'CORPORATIST' constitution with strong presidential powers.

Seipel retired from the chancellorship and from the leadership of the Christian Social Party in 1929, and although he served briefly as foreign minister under Vaugoin in 1930, his political career was effectively at an end: the German Nationalists (GREATER GERMAN PEOPLE'S PARTY) would no longer countenance participation in a coalition under his leadership (as proposed in 1931), despite his ostensible objective of moving closer to Germany with the long-term aim of a central European union of some kind. His influence continued to be enormous, however, until his death the following year.

Seitz, Karl (1869–1950), Austrian Social Democratic politician. Seitz was a member of parliament during the empire, and after World War I he was first president of the constituent national assembly and effectively head of state (1918–20). He was mayor of 'RED VIENNA' until 1934, when he was forcibly removed from office by the AUS-TROFASCIST regime that followed the short AUSTRIAN CIVIL WAR of that year. He was imprisoned in Ravensbrück concentration camp during World War II (1944–5). Seitz was honorary president of the SPÖ (Socialist Party of Austria) from 1945 until his death in Vienna in 1950.

Seitz, Theodor (1863–1949), colonial administrator. Seitz was governor of CAMEROON (1907), and German SOUTH-WEST AFRICA (1910).

Seldte, Franz (1882–1947), founder of the STAHLHELM (1918) and Reich minister of labour (1933–45). Born in Magdeburg, the son of an industrialist, Seldte studied chemistry and then took over management of the family chemicals business. He was a reserve officer, and enlisted enthusiastically in 1914, later losing an arm at the battle of the Somme. Seldte's pre-war sympathies were with the NATIONAL LIBERAL PARTY, but he was closer to the nationalist DNVP after the end of World War I. He founded the nationalistic veterans' organization known as the *Stahlhelm* on Christmas Day in 1918. Initially a pressure group formed on behalf of ex-combatants, the organization rapidly developed a right-wing political agenda, and became the largest of the FREIKORPS formations. From 1924 Seldte ran the *Stahlhelm* together with Theodor DUESTERBERG, who was elected second president with equal rights. The campaign against the YOUNG PLAN in 1929 brought him close to HITLER and HUGENBERG, and he was appointed Reich labour minister by Hitler in 1933. He became head of the German Veterans' Organization (*NSD-Frontkämpferbund*) the following year. Seldte was indicted at Nuremberg but died in an Allied military hospital before he could be brought to trial.

September programme (1914), the war aims of Chancellor BETHMANN HOLLWEG, expressed in his preliminary principles for an armistice with France of 9 September 1914. Central to the September programme was the notion of a German-dominated *MITTELEUROPA*, along the lines aspired to by some of the country's businessmen and bankers before the war: the chancellor had held discussions in August with Walther RATHENAU, director of AEG, Clemens von Delbrück, the minister of the interior since 1909, and Arthur von Gwinner, director of the Deutsche Bank. Rathenau was a forceful advocate of a German *Mitteleuropa*, without which the country would not, in his view, be able to compete as a world power with Britain, the United States or even Russia. He saw the war as a means of achieving this, and Delbrück and Gwinner were essentially in agreement.

In general terms the September programme sought to disable France as a rival power and to push Russia back as far as possible from Germany's eastern frontiers. In particular terms it suggested the possibility of demanding from France the cession of Belfort and the western slopes of the Vosges, and the cession of a strip of coastline from Dunkirk to Boulogne: the military was to decide whether such demands were essential. In any event the iron-rich Briey area of French-held Lorraine was to be annexed, and a war indemnity was to be imposed on France, along with other conditions that would make the country economically dependent on Germany. Liège and Verviers were to be annexed by Prussia, and a further Belgian border territory would be transferred to Luxembourg, which would become a federal state of the Reich. The remainder of Belgium was to be reduced to the status of a 'vassal state'. Along with France, the Netherlands, Denmark, Austria-Hungary and Poland (which would have gained a nominal independence), it was to be a member of a central European economic association under German leadership. (Italy, Sweden and Norway were also considered suitable for membership.)

In the context of German opinion during World War I the aims of the September programme were perceived as moderate – others, both in industry (KRUPP and STINNES) and politics (the PAN-GERMAN LEAGUE), were much more extreme. However, the September programme constituted the working basis of German war aims more or less until the end of the war.

serfs, emancipation of, JOSEPH II took steps towards the emancipation of the serfs in Austria in the later 18th century. An edict of 1807 abolished serfdom in Prussia: serfs were granted personal liberty, legal equality and the right to own property. A further edict of 1811 abolished labour service in exchange for the expropriation of a third of peasant land by the aristocracy.

Seven Weeks War. *See* AUSTRO-PRUSSIAN WAR.

Seven Years War (1756–63), conflict that involved a number of European powers. Austria was allied with Russia, France, Sweden, Spain and Saxony in an attempt to win back Silesia from FRIEDRICH II (Frederick the Great) of Prussia. He in turn was allied with Great Britain, Hanover and Hesse.

The Prussians attacked first. They invaded Saxony, occupied Dresden and went on to defeat the Austrians at the battle of Prague (1757), only to be defeated in turn at the battle of Kolín a few weeks later. After that the war went badly for Prussia. The Hanoverians were defeated by the French in the west, Sweden invaded Pomerania in the north, and East Prussia was occupied by the Russians. Despite victories against a Franco-German army at Rossbach, an Austrian army at Leuthen and a Russian army at Zorndorf, the odds were against Prussia. Friedrich's army was defeated very heavily at Kunersdorf in 1759, and Berlin was occupied.

It was only with British support and victories in the west on the one hand, and the death of Tsarina Elisabeth and the accession of Peter III on the other, that the tide of the war turned. The new tsar, Peter (originally Karl Peter, duke of Holstein-Gottorp, and a supporter of Prussia), changed sides and took Sweden out of the Austrian alliance along with him, and although he reigned for only six months before he was assassinated, Catherine II ('the Great'), his wife and successor, did not renew hostilities against Prussia. France too was compelled to abandon the war, and lost Canada and India to Britain. The peace of Hubertusburg confirmed the territorial status quo in central Europe, and established Prussia as a fifth great power.

Severing, Carl (1875–1952), Social Democratic politician and minister. Severing was born the son of working-class parents in Herford, Westphalia, and trained as a fitter. He joined the SPD at the age of 18 in 1893. He was also a member of the metalworkers' union. He edited the Social Democratic *Volkswacht* from 1912 and was elected to the Reichstag for the first time in 1907, serving as a deputy until 1912, and again from 1920 to 1933. He was Prussian interior minister from 1920 until 1926 and again from 1930 to 1932, and Reich interior minister in the intervening period (1928–30). Severing was on the right of the SPD: he supported the party's backing for the government during World War I, and as interior minister in Prussia was even-handed in dealing with radicals of left or right. Much of the political opposition to the elected government in

Prussia came from intransigently anti-democratic civil servants, and he won the support of his coalition partners in his attempts to get rid of them and democratize the public service. His attempts were undone in the end by the unconstitutional dismissal of the Prussian government – the so-called Prussian coup or PREUSSENSCHLAG – by Franz von PAPEN in 1932. Severing took no part in public affairs during the Nazi dictatorship, but became involved in politics and radical journalism again after World War II, and was a member of the LANDTAG of North Rhine-Westphalia.

Seyss-Inquart, Arthur (1892–1946), Austrian Nazi politician. Born the son of a schoolmaster in Stannern (now Stonařov), near Iglau in Moravia, Seyss-Inquart served in World War I and was wounded in battle. During the 1920s he made his career as a lawyer in Vienna, and although a supporter of ANSCHLUSS with Germany and a Nazi sympathizer, he did not join the NSDAP until 1938. Nevertheless he was the effective leader of the 'moderate' faction of Austrian Nazism during the 1930s, and was appointed to the Austrian State Council in 1937 by Chancellor SCHUSCHNIGG, who hoped to win their support for the government. The chancellor was then forced by Hitler to appoint him interior minister in February 1938, a position he used to undermine the Austrian state from within. He was briefly chancellor of Austria, a position he used merely to implement the *Anschluss* with Germany, and then a Nazi puppet governor of the 'OSTMARK' until April 1939. He was moved to occupied Poland in 1939, and subsequently became Reich commissioner of the occupied Netherlands. He was tried and executed at Nuremberg in 1946.

Sezession. See SECESSION.

Sicherheitsdienst. See SD.

Siebenbürgen, the German name for TRANSYLVANIA.

Siegfried Line (also known in German as the *Westwall*), a system of defensive fortifications on the western border of Germany built in 1938–9. It was superseded in 1942 by the Germans' Atlantic defences (*Atlantikwall*).

Siemens, Carl Friedrich von (1872–1941), industrialist. Siemens was born in Charlottenburg, the youngest son of Werner von SIEMENS, the founder of the family firm, and he took over as president of the Siemens–Schuckert works in 1912. He was elected to the Reichstag for the liberal DDP in 1920, but resigned his seat after four years.

Siemens, (Ernst) Werner von (1816–92), engineer and industrialist. After leaving school at 17, Siemens learned his trade as an engineer with the Prussian artillery, and in 1847 founded a telegraph works with Johann Georg Halske, which was the foundation stone of the Siemens industrial empire. Siemens was a gifted inventor, and played an important part in effecting the introduction of a German patent law. He was also an important figure in the founding of the *Physikalisch-Technische Reichsanstalt* (Reich Physical and Technical Institute). He was ennobled in 1888, and died in Charlottenburg four years later.

Silesia (German name: Schlesien), a central European province, now part of Poland, and historically one of the most disputed territories in the region. Germans settled in Silesia during the later Middle Ages, and the region became part of Bohemia in the 14th century. It came under the rule of the Austrian HABSBURGS with their acquisition of Bohemia in 1526. Most of Silesia was lost to Prussia during the early years of the reign of MARIA THERESIA, when Frederick the Great (FRIEDRICH II) invaded the province and annexed the greater part of it during the War of the AUSTRIAN SUCCESSION. A Prussian province of Silesia was created in 1807, and acquired further territory from Saxony in 1815.

Those districts of southern Upper Silesia that remained part of the Habsburg empire largely became part of Czechoslovakia after

World War I under the terms of the treaty of ST GERMAIN (1919). The treaty of VERSAILLES (1919) transferred some districts in German Silesia to Poland, and a plebiscite was held in 1921 to determine the fate of Upper Silesia: 59.6% voted for Silesia to remain part of Germany, but the plebiscite was followed by violence, and the province was divided between Poland and Germany. German Silesia was divided into two provinces of Prussia: Lower Silesia, with a population of some 3 million, had its capital in Breslau (now Wrocław in Poland); and Upper Silesia, with a population of 1.3 million, had its capital in Oppeln.

After the German invasion of Poland in 1939 the territories lost after World War I were reincorporated into the Reich, but almost all of Silesia became Polish after World War II. After the end of the war the German resettlement policy, which had sought to Germanize the province, was reversed, and over 3 million Germans were expelled from Silesia after 1945. The area was resettled by Poles from those regions that had been lost by Poland to the Soviet Union. After the treaty of Warsaw (1970) – part of Chancellor BRANDT'S OSTPOLITIK – more Germans left Silesia, and it was not until the reunification treaty of 1990 that Germany finally recognized the post-1945 frontier (the ODER–NEISSE LINE) between Germany and Poland.

Silesian Wars. *See* AUSTRIAN SUCCESSION, WAR OF THE.

Simmel, Georg (1858–1918), sociologist. Simmel was born in Berlin and studied at the university there. He began teaching at the university in 1885, and was appointed to a chair in sociology in 1900. He published his best-known work, *Philosophie des Geldes* (*Philosophy of Money*) in the same year. He became professor of philosophy at Strasbourg in 1914. Simmel was one of the founders of sociology as an academic discipline. His *Grundfragen der Soziologie* (*Fundamental Questions of Sociology*) appeared in 1917.

Simons, Walter (1861–1937), public servant and non-party politician. Simons was born in Elberfeld and studied law and history before entering the Prussian public service in Kiel in 1905, and then in Berlin later the same year. In 1918 he took over the legal department of the German foreign office and was ex officio secretary general of the German peace delegation to VERSAILLES from April to June 1919. He was foreign minister (non-party) in the FEHRENBACH administration (1920–1), and was president of the Reich court (1922–9). He resigned in protest following a dispute between the court and the Reich government in 1928, and took up a chair at Leipzig university.

Sipo (*Sicherheitspolizei*, security police), comprising the GESTAPO (*Geheime Staatspolizei*, secret state police) and the *Kripo* (*Kriminalpolizei*, criminal police).

Sippe, a rare archaic word, first revived by the conservative intellectual Stefan GEORGE, and widely used by the Nazis as a Germanic alternative to the Latinate word 'family'. The word and its derivations in official usage acquired the broader meaning of 'racial kinship'.

Sitzkrieg, a term used to describe the 'phoney war' of 1939–40 (*see* WORLD WAR II). The term is derived from the German words *sitzen* (to sit) and *Krieg* (war).

SMAD, abbreviation for Soviet Military Administration in Germany, the government in the Soviet zone of occupation in East Germany after World War II.

Smolensk, battle of (July–August 1941), one of the first battles during the German invasion of the Soviet Union. Smolensk was the principal objective of Army Group Centre, and Field Marshal von BOCK advanced rapidly, but the infantry lagged behind GUDERIAN's Panzer units, which reached the city on 16 July. Large numbers of Soviet troops were encircled in pockets – around 300,000 at Minsk and about the same number at Smolensk itself. They put up a stiff resistance to the advancing Germans, inflicted heavier losses than expected, and delayed the German advance. By the middle of July German infantry divisions in the Soviet Union had lost half to three-quarters of their strength, and motorized forces about half. The pocket of resistance at Smolensk was cleared on 5 August, opening the way for an advance on Moscow, but not before many more members of the Soviet forces had escaped.

Sobibor, Nazi extermination camp in eastern Poland, opened in May 1942 and closed after a rebellion of the Jewish prisoners on 14 October 1943. Some 200,000 Jews were killed there. Most of them were from Poland, but there were also 10,000 from the Reich, 34,000 from the Netherlands, and 24,000 from Slovakia, along with smaller numbers from France (2000) and Russia (1000).

Social Democratic Party of Germany. *See* SPD.

Social Democratic Workers' Party. *See* SDAP.

socialist cities (*sozialistische Städte*), new towns without private property built in the German Democratic Republic. The first was STALINSTADT, and the second was constructed next to the lignite combine *Schwarze Pumpe* (Black Pump) near Hoyerswerda.

Socialist Unity Congress/Unity Congress (1875), meeting in Gotha at which the ADAV and the SDAP agreed on the GOTHA PROGRAMME and merged to form the SPD.

Socialist Workers' Party of Germany. *See* SAPD.

Soden, Julius, Freiherr von (1846–1921), colonial administrator and politician. Soden was governor of CAMEROON and GERMAN EAST AFRICA (1891–3). He was succeded in that post by Friedrich Radbod Freiherr von Schele (1847–1904). Soden was also foreign minister of Württemberg.

SOE. *See* SPECIAL OPERATIONS EXECUTIVE.

Solf, Wilhelm (1862–1936), diplomat, colonial administrator and politician. Born in Berlin, Solf was governor of Samoa (1900–11), state secretary in the Reich colonial office (1911–18) and in the foreign office

(October–December 1918). He was then ambassador to Tokyo (1920–8). Solf was a political liberal. In 1919 he joined the DDP, and during the Nazi dictatorship he and his wife Johanna were at the centre of an anti-Nazi circle, the so-called *Solf-Kreis* (Solf circle).

Sollmann, Wilhelm (1881–1951), Social Democratic politician and journalist. Born into a middle-class family in Cologne, Soll-man studied business at the commercial college there. He started work on the *Rheinische Zeitung* in 1911 and was its editor from 1920 until 1933. Sollmann joined the SPD in 1906 and pursued a career in local politics. He was on the right of the party, and was in favour of cooperation with the middle-class parties, with the aim of establishing a cross-party democratic consensus in support of the Weimar Republic. In 1933 he was severely beaten up by Nazi stormtroopers and fled to the Saarland, then to Luxembourg, and eventually to the United States. He remained in America after the war.

Sombart, Werner (1863–1941), economist. Sombart was born in Ermsleben (Harz) and studied at Berlin and in Italy (Pisa and Rome) before taking up a teaching position in Breslau (now Wrocław in Poland) in 1890. He moved to the commercial university (*Handelshochschule*) in Berlin (1906–17), and then to Berlin University. Sombart was sympathetic to Marxism during the early years of his career, but distanced himself from his earlier position during the 1920s, and was initially supportive of Nazism after 1933. His best-known work is *Der moderne Kapitalismus* (*Modern Capitalism*), which was published in Leipzig in 1927.

Somme, battle of the (24 June–18 November 1916), a British-led offensive against the Germans in northern France. The battle began on 24 June with a week-long artillery barrage against the German lines, which failed to make sufficient impact. An infantry assault was launched on 1 July, resulting in 56,000 casualties among the British and empire troops on the first day for no particu-

lar advantage. The battle had no specific strategic purpose other than as a 'battle of attrition' and a diversion of German resources from the assault on VERDUN. By November British and empire losses numbered some 420,000 and French losses were 195,000. German losses were around 650,000. The Entente powers had advanced 13 km (8 miles) against the Germans along a 32-km (20-mile) strip of land that was of no real military significance.

Sonderaufgabe deutsche Roh- und Werkstoffe, an office established in 1934 in order to assist Germany in the pursuit of the goal of economic AUTARKY or self-sufficiency. It was run by Wilhelm KEPPLER, and was independent of the economics ministry.

Sonderweg, a term used by some historians to describe Germany's 'peculiar route' to modernity. It is an interpretation that maintains that Germany's history was skewed by the failure of the 1848 'bourgeois' revolution (*see* REVOLUTIONS OF 1848), and the survival of pre-modern elites such as the JUNKERS in positions of power into the 20th century. As a consequence, it is argued, Germany was unable to develop the civil society and political institutions characteristic of the Western democracies.

Sonnenberg, Max Liebermann von (1848–1911), right-wing politician and journalist. Born in Weisswasser (Beła Woda in Upper Lusatia, now in Poland), the son of an officer, Sonnenberg joined the Prussian army in 1866, and was wounded in the Franco-Prussian War. In 1881 he founded the *Deutsche Volkszeitung*, and in 1884 he left the army to work as a writer and journalist. From 1884 to 1911 he was editor of the ANTI-SEMITIC *Deutschsoziale Blätter*, and from 1885 to 1887 editor of the *Deutsche Volkszeitung*. In 1890 he was elected to the Reichstag, where he presented the 'anti-Semitic petition' of 1891, which demanded an end to Jewish immigration into Germany, and the exclusion of Jews from government office at all levels, and from the civil service and education system. In 1889 Sonnenberg had been instrumental in bringing STOECKER's CHRISTIAN SOCIAL PARTY together with other anti-Semitic groups to form the *Antisemitische Deutschsoziale Partei*. This in turn merged with BÖCKEL's *Deutsche Reformpartei* to form the *Deutschsoziale Reformpartei*. During the first decade of the 20th century Sonnenberg agitated for anti-British import tariffs.

Sonnenfels, Joseph von (1733–1817), Austrian lawyer, political economist and public servant. Born in Nikolsburg (now Mikulov), Sonnenfels was appointed to a chair at Vienna University in 1763. Sonnenfels was considered one of the most enlightened of the Josephinian reformers. He was the editor of the weekly journal *Der Mann ohne Vorurtheil* ('the man without prejudice') from 1765 to 1767. He advised the crown on the question of the emancipation of the serfs, and his proposals for the reform of the police were accepted by LEOPOLD II. He became theatre censor in 1810, and president of the Academy of Fine Arts in Vienna in 1811.

Sopade, acronym used by the SPD in exile after 1933. Reports on conditions in Germany were smuggled out to Prague, and later Paris, by the party's agents and formed the basis of published summaries.

South Tyrol (German name: Südtirol; Italian name: Alto Adige), territory transferred from Austria to Italy after World War I. It comprised that part of Tyrol that lies to the south of the Brenner Pass. The South Tyrol had a substantial German-speaking population, and some two-thirds of the region's population still gave German as their native language in the Italian census of 1991. Just over a quarter (27.6%), mainly in the larger towns, Bolzano (Bozen) and Merano (Meran) were native Italian speakers. The Italian Fascist regime attempted to Italianize the German-speaking population, although with little success. In 1939 a resettlement treaty was signed between Italy and Germany (which had recently annexed Austria) and the overwhelming majority of South Tyrol-

eans who claimed German citizenship were destined to be resettled. After World War II Austria demanded the return of the territory, but settled for the granting of regional autonomy by Rome, albeit in a province (Trentino-Südtirol/Trentino-Alto Adige) that put German and Ladin speakers in a minority. The issue continued to generate tension between Austria and Italy for half a century after the end of World War II, and the position of German speakers in the province generated enormous sympathy in both Austria and Germany.

South-West Africa, formerly a German colony, now Namibia. The region between the Cape Colony and Angola was annexed by Germany in 1884 after the acquisition of territory there by a Bremen merchant, F.A.E. Lüderitz. It had a surface area of some 835,000 square km (320,000 square miles) and a population of 86,000, including over 12,000 Germans. Although Britain had been reluctant to extend sovereignty over the region before Germany showed any interest, it initially opposed the acquisition of the territory. Nevertheless German annexation was formalized from 1885, and its borders with Angola were regulated in 1886 and those with the Cape in 1890. An uprising by the native Herero people in 1904–7 was brutally suppressed, and three-quarters of the population perished. During World War I the colony was taken by South African forces (1915). It was mandated to South Africa by the treaty of VERSAILLES.

Soviet zone of occupation (*Sowjetische Besatzungszone*, SBZ), one of the four zones of Allied-occupied Germany after World War II. The territory occupied by the Soviet Union became the GERMAN DEMOCRATIC REPUBLIC (GDR) in 1949.

Sowjetnik, East German term for a Soviet officer seconded to the Nationale Volksarmee (NVA) in a supervisory capacity. During the term of his secondment such an officer wore the uniform of the appropriate rank of the NVA.

Sozialdemokratische Arbeiterpartei. *See* SDAP.

Sozialdemokratische Partei Deutschlands. *See* SPD.

Soziale Reichspartei, ANTI-SEMITIC political party founded in 1881 by Ernst Henrici. It called for the exclusion of Jews from public life and an end to Jewish immigration. Its significance was in its insistence on racial anti-Semitism and rejection of the possibility of the assimilation of Jews into German society through conversion to Christianity.

Sozialistische Arbeiterpartei Deutschlands. *See* SAPD.

Sozialistische Reichspartei (SRP), a radical right-wing party formed in 1949 by Ulrich von Bothmer, Otto Ernst Remer, Fritz Dorls, Franz Richter, Gerhard Krüger and Wolf, Graf von Westarp, all of whom had belonged to other, earlier splinter groups on the extreme right immediately after World War II. In terms of both ideology and membership, it was effectively a successor party to the NSDAP (the Nazi Party). It dissolved itself on 12 September 1952, a few weeks before it was prohibited by the FEDERAL CONSTITUTIONAL COURT (23 October 1952). Most of the members joined the *DEUTSCHE REICHSPARTEI.*

Spann, Othmar (1878–1950), Austrian writer of the radical right. Spann was born in Vienna, and held a chair at Brünn (Brno) University until the fall of the Habsburg empire, when he was dismissed by the Czechs. A clerical proponent of the CORPORATE STATE and opponent of parliamentarism and Marxism, Spann was an unofficial philosopher of AUSTROFASCISM and, more broadly, an important influence on European fascist ideology. Nevertheless, his relationship with Nazism was ambiguous, and he was arrested and imprisoned after the *ANSCHLUSS.*

Spartacus League (*Spartakusbund*), a radical left-wing political group, led by Rosa LUXEMBURG and Karl LIEBKNECHT. It grew out of the left-wing opposition within the SPD to the party's support of the German government during World War I. Its members formed the basis of the KPD (*Kommunistische Partei Deutschlands*, German Communist Party), which was formed in December 1918, and many took part in the SPARTACUS UPRISING of January 1919.

Spartacus uprising (January 1919), a revolt of left-wing radicals in Berlin. The Independent Social Democrats (USPD) in Berlin, the Revolutionary Shop Stewards' Movement and the recently founded Communist Party (KPD) called for demonstrations against the government on 5 January 1919. Some newspaper buildings were occupied, a 'Revolutionary Committee' was appointed, representing the three radical groups, and a decision was taken to overthrow the government. In the event the action was unpopular, had no base of support among the working class of Berlin, and was thwarted by the lack of organization on the side of the revolutionaries, and their inability to assert their authority. The revolt was put down by Reich defence minister Gustav NOSKE, with the help of right-wing paramilitary FREIKORPS formations. The two leading members of the Communist Party, Karl LIEBKNECHT and Rosa LUXEMBURG, were abducted and murdered by Freikorps members.

SPD (*Sozialdemokratische Partei Deutschlands*), the German Social Democratic Party, formed in 1875 at the 'unity conference' in Gotha by the merger of the ADAV (the General German Workers' Association) and the SDAP (the Social Democratic Workers' Party). The new party, which was at first known as the SAPD (the Socialist Workers' Party of Germany), drew up the GOTHA PROGRAMME at the conference.

The Social Democrats constituted a new kind of party that sought not merely to mobilize support, but to integrate working-class voters and their families into a Social Democratic sub-culture, related to the FREE TRADE UNIONS of the workplace and based on a network of consumer cooperatives and educational and leisure associations.

There had been two Social Democrats in the first Reichstag of 1871, and twelve were elected in 1877. The ANTI-SOCIALIST LAWS hampered the growth of the party, but after they were allowed to lapse in 1890 the SPD went from strength to strength. There was only one setback in the party's electoral fortunes during the imperial period, and that was the so-called 'HOTTENTOT ELECTION' of 1907. The election of 1912 on the other hand was the party's greatest triumph yet: with 4,250,329 votes (34.8%) and 110 seats it became the largest party in the Reichstag. It had won more than twice as many votes as the second largest party (the CENTRE PARTY). The success of the party in elections to the Reichstag was also reflected in LAND-TAG and municipal elections. The party had 101 delegates in provincial diets in 1903 and 231 in 1912, and in 1913 almost 11,000 Social Democrats sat on local councils. Party membership also grew, from 384,000 in 1906 to just over 1 million in 1914.

The SPD supported the government by voting for war credits in 1914, but during the course of World War I the party's internal divisions widened. These divisions primarily arose out of the war and its conduct – but also reflected deeper disagreements – and in April 1917 the Independent Social Democratic Party (*Unabhängige Sozialdemokratische Partei Deutschlands*, USPD) broke away from the majority of the party (MSPD). As the war ended Prince Max von BADEN, who had been appointed head of a government responsible to the Reichstag on 5 October 1918, made Friedrich EBERT (leader of the Majority Social Democrats) chancellor, and Ebert's colleague Philipp SCHEIDEMANN declared Germany a republic. Ebert and Scheidemann joined USPD members in a COUNCIL OF PEOPLE'S REPRESENTATIVES, which assumed governmental authority pending elections to a constituent NATIONAL ASSEMBLY.

The SPD played a decisive role in the framing of the new constitution and the creation of the WEIMAR REPUBLIC, but it was rarely in power during the 1920s. The MSPD won 37.9% in the elections to 1919 National Assembly and Scheidemann formed a coalition government with the Centre Party and the liberals (DDP). This was followed by two further short-lived SPD-led administrations under Gustav BAUER (1919–20) and Hermann MÜLLER (1920). The latter's government failed to survive the first elections to the Reichstag, however, and was superseded by a centre–right administration. The party then spent most of the Weimar Republic in opposition at Reich level, although it was in power in Prussia until 1932 (see *PREUSSEN-SCHLAG*) and also in many of the major cities.

The SPD was the only party to oppose Hitler's ENABLING LAW in March 1933. The party was dissolved immediately afterwards and many of those leaders and functionaries who were unable to escape Germany were arrested and imprisoned in CONCENTRATION CAMPS. Social Democratic resistance to the Nazis was pragmatic. Although there were some groups of underground activists there was no network of cells comparable to that of the KPD (the German Communist Party), and although Social Democrats were present in some of the conspiratorial groups of the later war years, party members lacked the social and political connections of the aristocratic and military conspirators.

The SPD survived World War II to become one of the two major parties of the Federal Republic. In the Soviet zone it was quickly forced into the Socialist Unity Party (SED) along with the Communist Party. In the Federal Republic the SPD remained in opposition throughout the 1950s, and it abandoned its remaining Marxist rhetoric with the BAD GODESBERG PROGRAMME of 1959. Its electoral performance improved gradually during the 1960s and it formed a GRAND COALITION with the CDU in 1966. It then went on to form the reforming 'social–liberal' coalition of 1969 with the FDP, under the leadership of the Social Democratic chancellor Willy BRANDT. When Brandt resigned following a spy scandal in 1974, Helmut SCHMIDT took over as chancellor and led the coalition until the FDP decided to switch its allegiance to the conservatives in 1982. The party was re-elected to office in 1998 under leadership of Gerhard SCHRÖDER, forming a coalition with the GREENS.

Special Operations Executive (SOE), a unit formed by the British government to encourage and support guerrilla warfare against the Germans in occupied Europe during World War II. It was under the charge of Hugh Dalton, a junior minister in the Department of Economic Warfare. The SOE formed departments for each occupied country, and sent agents to set up cells and communications networks for sabotage operations. Its impact is difficult to assess, given the unquantifiable nature of its operations, but was probably greatest in morale terms. SOE also established branches in Africa and the Far East.

Speer, Albert (1905–81), architect and Reich minister for armaments and war production (1942–5). Born in Mannheim, Speer studied architecture and joined the NSDAP in 1931. He stage-managed the NUREMBERG RALLIES and designed the new Reich Chancellery in Berlin and Party Headquarters in Munich. He was appointed armaments minister on the death of Fritz TODT in 1942, and was responsible for a sharp increase in arms production during the later war years. Despite clashes with other centres of influence within the regime, his responsibilities were extended and his influence increased until his eclipse by GOEBBELS during the last twelve months of the war. He was sentenced to 20 years at Nuremberg, and was released in 1966. He published two volumes of apologetic memoirs before his death.

Spengler, Oswald (1880–1936), writer. Spengler was born in Blankenburg and studied at Munich, Berlin and Halle. He worked as a teacher of mathematics until 1911. In his major work, *Der Untergang des Abendlandes* (*The Decline of the West*, two volumes,

1918–22), Spengler elaborated a cyclical theory of history founded on the then fashionable pseudo-biological theories. The work was an emotive discussion of the imminent fall of modern European civilization, based on literary allusion and mixed metaphors rather than historical analysis. Nevertheless it was popular and influential on its publication after World War I. Spengler welcomed Nazism but remained a conservative elitist in his last years.

***Spiegel* affair** (1962), the arrest and imprisonment of the editor of the weekly news magazine *Der Spiegel*, Rudolf Augstein, and ten of his colleagues, including assistant editor Conrad Ahlers, on suspicion of treason, the ostensible reason for the arrests was a *Spiegel* article about NATO manoeuvres, which also suggested that West Germany was involved in NATO planning for nuclear warfare. Ahlers' arrest in Franco's fascist Spain added a symbolic dimension. The incident came at the end of a long period of conservative government under Konrad ADENAUER, and caused a public outcry. At home and abroad it was seen as the first real test of postwar democracy in West Germany, and parallels were drawn with the shallowness of Germany's attachment to democracy during the WEIMAR REPUBLIC. Adenauer and his right-wing defence minister, Franz-Josef STRAUSS denied any complicity in the arrests, but it was subsequently revealed that they had indeed been involved, but omitted to take the FDP minister of justice into their confidence. The episode lent the government a sinister authoritarian air, particularly when the charges, which were without foundation, were dropped, and the FDP withdrew from the coalition until Strauss was dismissed from the administration.

Springer, Axel (Caesar) (1912–85), publisher and right-wing press baron. The son of a publisher, Springer built up his publishing group after World War II. The Springer company (*Springer-Konzern*) was founded in 1945. It was based in Hamburg until 1967, and then moved to West Berlin, where Springer wanted to establish a symbolic presence. Both *Die Welt*, a popular conservative broadsheet (originally established by the British occupation authorities and bought by Springer in 1950), and the notoriously populist right-wing tabloid *Bild-Zeitung* were Springer titles, and the group attracted protests from the radical left-wing political groups of the 1960s and 1970s. The *Springer-Konzern* also acquired the old ULLSTEIN publishing house, and diversified into television and satellite broadcasting with the channel SAT 1.

Srbik, Heinrich, Ritter von (1878–1951), Austrian historian and collaborator. Educated at the Theresianum and Vienna University, Srbik taught at the Austrian Institute of History and at Vienna University before World War I and held chairs at Graz and Vienna. He was education minister (1928–32) during the First Austrian Republic. He welcomed the ANSCHLUSS, and was elected to the Reichstag and appointed head of the German Historical Commission in 1938. He died in retirement in the Tyrol.

SS (*Schutzstaffeln*, 'guard units'), Nazi organization founded in 1925 to protect leading Nazis. They were under Hitler's direct command and functioned as guards for meetings and bodyguards for leading party personnel. Under HIMMLER (Reich Leader of the SS from 1929) the SS organization grew rapidly from a membership of 280 in 1929 to some 240,000 ten years later. Nevertheless it remained an exclusive order, with strict rules for admission based on racial origin and political reliability. It was intended to constitute the kernel of a 'new aristocracy' for a German-dominated Europe. Its first decisive intervention as an instrument of coercion was during the Röhm purge ('NIGHT OF THE LONG KNIVES') of 1934, and it subsequently became the most powerful affiliated organization of the NSDAP, establishing control over the entire police and security systems in the course of the 1930s,

and forming the basis of the Nazi police state. In 1931 Himmler founded an internal party intelligence service, which became the SD (*Sicherheitsdienst*, Security Service) a year later. In 1939 this organization was united with the security police (*SIPO*) and criminal police (*KRIPO*) in the Reich Security Head Office (RSHA). The SS guards who had formed Hitler's bodyguard expanded to become the special duty troops that would form the basis of the WAFFEN-SS. Some were designated special guard groups for concentration camps, the Deaths-Head units. By 1939 there were about 9,000 of these, and they too were incorporated into the Waffen-SS, and replaced by men of the general SS.

The SS was the major instrument of racial policy in the camps and in occupied Europe. Special units of SS and *Sipo* men (*EINSATZ-GRUPPEN*) followed German troops into Poland and the Soviet Union and carried out mass killings of Jews and local political leaders. The SS also ran the EXTERMINATION CAMPS in which the mass murder of European Jews took place. The camp system developed its own economy, based on slave labour, and a bureaucracy which paralleled that of the state. This enabled it to develop a quasi-autonomous existence within the Third Reich, and play a major role in the cartel of competing interests within the regime.

Staatsbibliothek (Berlin), from 1992 the name given to the merged libraries of East and West Berlin. Its origins are in the electors' library (*Churfürstliche Bibliothek*), which was founded in Berlin in 1661. It became the royal library in 1701 with the establishment of the kingdom of Prussia, and then the state library after World War I (1918) – it never became a national library for Germany. The library was divided along with the city at the end of World War II, and those collections in the West at the time of the erection of the Berlin Wall were kept under the auspices of the Prussian Cultural Property Foundation (*Stiftung Preussischer Kulturbe-*

sitz). The East German collections became the *Deutsche Staatsbibliothek* in 1954.

Staatspartei, Deutsche. *See* DDP.

Staatsrat (Austria), the council of state established in 1760 to oversee the government of the HABSBURG hereditary lands. It survived until 1848.

Staatsrat (East Germany), the state council that constituted the 'collective head of state' of the GERMAN DEMOCRATIC REPUBLIC from 1960 to 1990, on a model analogous with similar bodies in other Soviet Bloc states. The Staatsrat was elected by the *VOLKSKAMMER* at the beginning of each legislative period.

Staatssicherheitsdienst (state security service). See STASI.

Staatsstreich, German term for a coup d'état carried out by those in power or by those holding other high political office.

stab-in-the-back myth. *See* DOLCHSTOSS-LEGENDE.

Stadion-Warthausen, Johann Philipp, Graf von (1763–1824), Austrian foreign minister during the Napoleonic Wars (the later Wars of the COALITIONS). Stadion was born in Mainz, into an old Swabian aristocratic family. He was Austrian foreign minister from 1805 to 1809, and planned to rally the whole of Germany against the French. Following the defeat of Austria in 1809 he was replaced by Clemens von METTERNICH. After the end of the Napoleonic Wars Stadion was appointed finance minister (1816) and founded the National Bank.

Staël, Madame de (full name: Anne Louise Germaine Necker, Freiin von Staël-Holstein; 1766–1817), one of the most celebrated observers of German cultural life at the beginning of the 19th century. Born in Paris, the daughter of a financier, she left France in 1803 and visited Berlin, Vienna and the then fashionable literary centre of Weimar. Her best-known work, *D'Allemagne* (*On Germany*) was published in 1810.

Stahlhelm (literally, 'steel helmet'), the largest and most important FREIKORPS formation in the Weimar Republic. *Der Stahlhelm, Bund der Frontsoldaten e.V* (BdF) was founded on 25 December 1918 by Franz SELDTE, and non-veterans were permitted to join from 1924. The organization joined the right-wing HARZBURG FRONT in 1931, and in 1933 the *Wehrstahlhelm*, comprising those members up to 35 years of age, was subsumed in the SA. The *Stahlhelm* was absorbed into the NSDAP on 28 March 1934 as the *Nationalsozialistischer Deutscher Frontkämpferbund* (National Socialist German Veterans' League), and was dissolved on 7 November 1935. It was refounded in 1951.

Stalag (*Stammlager*), a permanent prisoner-of-war camp.

Stalinallee, former name of a street in the East Berlin district of Friedrichshain that became a prestigious ceremonial avenue under the Soviets. Prior to the Soviet occupation it was known as the Frankfurter Allee. The housing blocks built there were considered representative examples of collective living. It was among the construction workers on the Stalinallee that the strike broke out that led to the June uprising of 1953 (*see* GERMAN DEMOCRATIC REPUBLIC; NEW COURSE). In 1961, after the XXII Party Conference of the Soviet Communist Party (CPSU), the eastern part of the street was renamed Frankfurterallee, and the western part, nearer to Mitte, became Karl-Marx-Allee.

Stalingrad, battle of (1942–3), the most important battle on the Eastern Front during World War II, and a turning point in German military success and civilian morale. The city of Stalingrad (formerly Tsaritsyn, subsequently Volgograd) became an objective for the German 6th Army under General Friedrich PAULUS during the summer of 1942, as the Germans advanced towards the Caucasus. The advance on Stalingrad was intended to be a straightforward operation, subsidiary to the main thrust towards the Caucasian oil fields, but the Germans encountered such fierce resistance there that the 4th Panzer Army was transferred back from the Caucasus and committed to Stalingrad. The battle for the city started on 19 August, and was exceptionally bitter. The city was defended street by street and more German units were brought in from the north and south to strengthen the attack. As a result the thrust towards the Caucasus was weakened, and the defence of the German flanks was left to the poorly trained and poorly equipped 3rd and 4th Romanian Armies. While Soviet forces continued to resist the Germans within the city, massive Soviet reinforcements arrived outside the city. Led by General Zhukov they launched an attack on the Germans in November, and encircled them within days. Hitler refused to accept defeat, or to allow Paulus to break out, ordering him to remain at Stalingrad until he could be relieved by Field Marshal von MANSTEIN. In the event, however, Manstein himself was repulsed by a Soviet counterattack some kilometres from the city, and Paulus and his men were left to their fate. The last messages from the 6th Army were received on 31 January and 2 February. The Germans and their allies had lost 200,000 men in the battle, and a further 94,000 surrendered with Paulus. The news of the defeat had an enormous impact on German civilian morale, and was considered a turning point in the course of the Soviet campaign and of World War II.

Stalinstadt, former name of an urban district in Brandenburg on the Oder–Spree canal. The town was built as living quarters for the 'eastern iron-processing combine' (*Eisenhüttenkombinat Ost*, EKO). It was designated the first 'SOCIALIST CITY' in Germany. In 1961 it was renamed Eisenhüttenstadt.

Stangl, Franz (1908–71), commandant of the TREBLINKA extermination camp (1942–3). An Austrian policeman from 1931, Stangl joined the Euthanasia Institute in 1940 and was appointed to run the death camp at SOBIBOR in 1942. He was transferred to Treblinka the same year, where he remained until the camp revolt of August 1943, when he was

transferred to Trieste. After the war he was sent to an open prison by the Austrians and escaped with the assistance of the Vatican to Syria and then to Brazil. Despite his active leading role in the HOLOCAUST he was not pursued by the Austrian authorities until 1961. He was finally arrested in 1967, and in 1970 was tried and sentenced to life imprisonment by a German court for the murder of 900,000 Jews.

Stapo (*Staatspolizei*, state police), the Prussian political police before 1933. The *Stapo* was absorbed into the GESTAPO.

Stapostellen (*Staatspolizeistellen*), regional offices of the GESTAPO established in Prussia in 1933.

Stark, Johannes (1874–1957), physicist. Stark was born in Schickenhof in the Upper Palatinate and was a student at Munich. He quickly established a research reputation, and was awarded the Nobel prize for physics in 1919. He was professor at both Greifswald and Würzburg, but was forced to give up his university career in 1922 after differences with colleagues. He became involved in politics and agitated against 'dogmatic Jewish physics'. After the Nazis came to power he was appointed president of the Reich Physical-Technical Institute (*Physikalisch-Technische Reichsanstalt*), and used his position to persecute his Jewish colleagues. After the war he was sentenced to four years in a labour camp.

Stasi (*Staatssicherheitsdienst*), political police in the GERMAN DEMOCRATIC REPUBLIC (GDR). The origins of the political police in East Germany lie in the *Kommissariate 5* (K5) of the regional and district police authorities in the Soviet zone of occupation. At the end of 1946 a central K5 department was established within the provisional interior administration (*Deutsche Verwaltung*) to deal with political crimes on behalf of the occupying power. Alongside this a 'Committee for the Protection of the People's Property' (*Ausschuss zum Schutz des Volkseigentums*) was established on 12 May 1948, which was charged with the administrative control of all state-owned property. With the founding of the GDR in 1949 the two departments were combined, initially within the interior ministry but shortly afterwards (by a law of 8 February 1950) as a separate ministry of state security. The first minister was Wilhelm ZAISSER. After the June uprising of 1953 (*see* GERMAN DEMOCRATIC REPUBLIC; NEW COURSE) the ministry was briefly renamed the state secretariat for state security (*Staatssekretariat für Staatssicherheit*). From 1955 it reverted to its former title. Erich MIELKE was minister of state security from 1957 until the collapse of the GDR in 1989.

Statute of Limitations (for war crimes), legislation that specified that proceedings against suspected war criminals could not be brought after 1969. In that year it was extended for a further ten years. In 1979, however, it was abolished, which meant that newly discovered evidence of Nazi atrocities could be investigated and those responsible prosecuted and punished.

Staudinger, Hermann (1881–1965), chemist. Staudinger was born in Worms, the son of a university professor, and was educated at Halle. He was opposed to the use of science for military purposes, in particular the use of gas during World War I. As a result he was regarded with suspicion by many Germans after the end of the war, and there were protests from some quarters when he was appointed to a chair at Freiburg in 1926. He was awarded the Nobel prize for chemistry in 1953.

Stauffenberg, Berthold, Graf (Schenk) von (1905–44), officer and anti-Nazi conspirator. He was the brother of Claus von STAUFFENBERG, and was directly involved in the JULY BOMB PLOT of 1944. Like his brother he was arrested and executed for his part in the conspiracy.

Stauffenberg, Claus, Graf (Schenk) von (1907–44), officer and leader of the 1944 JULY BOMB PLOT (the 'Stauffenberg plot') by senior officers to assassinate Hitler.

Stauffenberg was born in Jettingen, attended military schools, and was commissioned as an officer in 1930. In World War II he served in North Africa, where he was wounded. Posted back to Berlin he recruited support for an assassination attempt on Hitler, to be followed by a coup. The plotters failed to win Allied support, not least because they proposed to retain many of Hitler's territorial gains and an authoritarian system of government within Germany. The assassination attempt itself failed, and Stauffenberg and others were arrested and executed after show trials.

Stegerwald, Adam (1874–1945), Christian trade unionist and CENTRE PARTY politician. Stegerwald was born in Greussenheim, near Würzburg, into a family of small farmers and artisans. He became secretary general of the Christian trade-union movement in 1902, was a staunch nationalist during World War I and entered the upper house (*HERRENHAUS*) of the Prussian parliament in 1917. After the war he was a member of the NATIONAL ASSEMBLY (1919) and the Reichstag (1920–33) for the Centre Party, and was appointed transport minister in 1929. He was subsequently minister of labour (1930–2). He was a co-founder of the CDU after World War II, shortly before his death.

Stein, Charlotte von (1742–1827), writer. Stein was born in Eisenach and married Friedrich, Freiherr von Stein in 1764. She was a close friend of GOETHE from 1775 until the end of his first journey to Italy (1788), when Goethe began a relationship with Christiane Vulpius (whom he later married). Some of her letters to Goethe were published, and a novel, *Dido* (1794), was published posthumously (1867).

Stein, Edith (1891–1942), philosopher and theologian. Edith Stein was born into a middle-class Jewish family in Breslau (now Wrocław in Poland) and studied for a doctorate with Edmund HUSSERL. She converted to Roman Catholicism in 1922 and became a Carmelite nun in 1933. Her philosophical and theological work was concerned with the application of phenomenology to the ideas of Thomas Aquinas. She was murdered at AUSCHWITZ.

Stein, (Heinrich Friedrich) Karl, Reichsfreiherr vom und zum (1757–1831), Prussian politician and reformer. Freiherr vom Stein was born in Nassau and studied law at Göttingen before entering the Prussian public service in 1780. He was effectively prime minister of Prussia in 1807–8, and instituted a series of major reforms in government, the armed forces and the economy, including the emancipation of the peasants from hereditary serfdom (begun in 1807 and finally completed in 1850), and the emancipation of the Jews (1812). He was responsible for the introduction of commercial freedom (1811) and municipal self-government (1808), but was unable to introduce self-government for rural communities. He reorganized the government of the state on the basis of five ministries (interior, foreign, war, justice and finance) represented in a state council presided over by a state chancellor. Military reforms were introduced from 1807, including a system of short-term training to create a reserve army (the *Krümpersystem*) and the introduction of general conscription in 1814. Education reforms at all levels began in 1809 under the direction of Wilhelm von HUMBOLDT.

Stein was an adviser to Alexander I of Russia during the last years of the Napoleonic Wars (1812–15), and negotiated the Tauroggen alliance between Prussia and Russia in 1813 (*see* LIBERATION, WARS OF). He was a member of the Russian delegation at the Congress of VIENNA, and then retired from public life. Stein was founder of the *Gesellschaft für deutsche Geschichtskunde* (Society for German History), which began the publication of the *Monumenta Germaniae Historica*.

Steinernes Haus, a conservative grouping at the 1848 FRANKFURT PARLIAMENT. As with other political factions in the parliament, it was named after its meeting place.

Steller, Georg Wilhelm (1709–46), scientist and explorer. Steller studied theology at Wittenberg, and then moved to the Academy of Sciences at St Petersburg. He took part in expeditions to Kamchatka, Siberia and Alaska in the 1730s and 1740s. His work on marine zoology was published after his death.

Sternberg, Josef von (1894–1969), Austrian film director. Sternberg was born in Vienna, emigrated to the United States with his parents in 1908, and worked in Hollywood before returning to Europe in 1930, where, in Germany, he directed his most famous film, *Der blaue Engel (The Blue Angel)*, starring Marlene DIETRICH. He subsequently returned to Hollywood, and made several other films with Dietrich.

Sternheim, Carl (1878–1942), EXPRESSIONIST dramatist. Sternheim was born in Leipzig and moved to Brussels in 1924 after marrying the wealthy Thea Bauer. He established his reputation as a writer of satirical comedy before World War I, lampooning the middle classes of imperial Germany. Sternheim was one of the most frequently performed playwrights of his day. All his work was banned by the Nazis in 1933.

Stettin, formerly a German city, now Szczecin in Poland. Stettin was the capital of the former Prussian province of POMERANIA.

Stinnes, Hugo (1870–1924), industrialist. Stinnes was a Ruhr businessman who was born in Mülheim and whose interests included coal, iron, steel, energy, catering and the press. An annexationist during WORLD WAR I, he supported the territorial demands of the PAN-GERMAN LEAGUE, and went further in demanding the cession of iron and coal fields in Normandy. With the support of CLASS and HUGENBERG he secured the general acceptance of the League's ideas by Pan-German leaders in October 1914. He was chief negotiator for the industrialists in the drawing up of a social and economic settlement with the trade unions after World War I (the STINNES–LEGIEN AGREEMENT).

Although Germany's territorial losses were a blow to Stinnes' business interests, he profited immensely from both the war and the post-war INFLATION, which he successfully used to expand and diversify his business interests. The extensive conglomerate he brought together during the early 1920s (the Siemens-Rheinelbe-Schuckert-Union) survived for only two years after his own death.

Stinnes–Legien agreement (1918), agreement that established the relationship between employers and workers during the Weimar Republic. It was named after the industrialist Hugo STINNES and Carl Legien, the leader of the FREE TRADE UNIONS. Employers recognized the unions as legitimate bargaining partners and agreed to refrain from sponsoring their own 'yellow' unions. Mandatory collective bargaining and wage contracts were introduced, and the working day was reduced to eight hours (without loss of earnings). Workers' committees were set up in firms with more than 50 employees, and the employers agreed to cooperate with the demobilization process and in particular to re-employ soldiers returning from the front in their old jobs. A 'working community' (*Zentralarbeitsgemeinschaft*, ZAG) was established as a forum for cooperation between employers and the representatives of labour in the implementation of the agreement.

Stockhausen, Karlheinz (1928–), composer. Stockhausen was educated at the universities of Cologne and Bonn. He is known for his experimentation with electronic music. He was a co-founder (1953) and later director (1963–77) of the electronic music studio in Cologne, and was appointed to a chair at the university there in 1971.

Stoecker, Adolf (1835–1909), ANTI-SEMITIC politician. Stoecker was born in Halberstadt, in the Harz mountain area, the son of a blacksmith turned soldier and eventually prison warder. He studied theology in Berlin and Halberstadt (1854–7), and was then employed as a private tutor to an aristocratic family in Courland. He was appointed pastor in an industrial town near Magdeburg before serving as an army chaplain during the Franco-Prussian War. After the war he became a court preacher at Berlin cathedral. In 1874 he took over the Berlin *Stadtmission* (city mission) with the aim of reversing the secularization of society, and agitated for social reform within a conservative and religious framework.

In 1878 Stoecker founded the Christian Social Workers' Party (later the CHRISTIAN SOCIAL PARTY), but the 'Stoecker movement' as it was sometimes called was an outright failure. Stoecker aimed to win over the workers from the irreligious SPD with a mixture of anti-Semitic propaganda and proposals for social welfare. When it won only 1422 votes in the election of that year the emphasis of the party moved very firmly to anti-Semitism, and the dropping of 'workers' from the title in 1881 suggested a reorientation of appeal to a different constituency. In 1880 Stoecker founded the 'Berlin movement' as an umbrella organization for anti-Semitic splinter groups in Berlin, and directed his appeal towards the lower middle class and to university students, with greater success.

From 1879 to 1898 Stoecker sat in the Prussian house of representatives (*ABGEORD-NETENHAUS*) for the German Conservative Party (*DEUTSCHKONSERVATIVE PARTEI*), and from 1880 to 1893 he was a conservative member of the Reichstag. In 1889 Chancellor BISMARCK, whom he and his movement had antagonized, succeeded in getting him to withdraw from public affairs, but with the accession of WILHELM II, who favoured him, and the dismissal of the chancellor, his fortunes rose again. In 1890 he founded the Evangelical Social Congress for research into social reform, but left it when liberals became a majority. Although he managed to persuade the German Conservative Party to adopt a more anti-Semitic stance in 1892, he was eventually marginalized by agrarian interests in the party. He died in Bozen in the South Tyrol (now Bolzano in Italy).

Stohrer, Eberhard von (1883–1953), diplomat. Stohrer was minister in Cairo (1927–35) and in Bucharest (1935–7). He was ambassador to Franco's Spain from 1937 to 1943.

Stoph, Willi (1914–99), East German politician. Stoph was born into a working-class family in Berlin and joined the Communist youth movement and the Communist Party (KPD) during the Weimar Republic. He was involved in the underground resistance against the Nazis during the 1930s and was wounded in action during World War II He joined the East German Socialist Unity Party (SED) after the war and occupied important positions in the party leadership during the late 1940s. During the early 1950s Stoph was involved in the establishment of the state security ministry (STASI) and the development of East Germany's proto-military force, the *Kasernierte Volkspolizei* (KVP). He was a member of the East German parliament (the *VOLKSKAMMER*) and of the Central Committee (ZK) of the SED from 1950 until the demise of the German Democratic Republic in 1989. He was appointed interior minister in 1952, and became a member of the party's Politburo in 1953. From 1954 to 1962 he was a deputy president of the COUNCIL OF MINISTERS (*Ministerrat*). In 1964 he joined the council of state (STAATSRAT). Stoph succeeded Otto GROTEWOHL as president of the council of ministers – effectively prime minister – from 1964 to 1973. Following the death of Walter ULBRICHT, Stoph was elected chairman of the council of state (1973–6), a post which effectively made him head of state. In 1976 the East German leadership was restructured along Soviet lines and Erich HONECKER, as head of the party, became head of state. Stoph returned to his former position as president of the state until 1989, when he resigned along with the entire government. In December 1989 he was expelled from the party. He was subsequently charged with corruption and arrested, first in 1989 for abuse of office, and then in 1991 for his responsibility for shootings on the East–West German border. He was released on health grounds on both occasions, but his assets were confiscated. Stoph died in Berlin in 1999.

Storm, Theodor (1817–88), writer. Storm was born in Husum in SCHLESWIG-HOLSTEIN, the son of a lawyer, and studied law in Kiel and Berlin. He returned to practise in his native town, but was compelled to leave when his licence was revoked by the Danish authorities in 1848. He returned as an official of the Prussian government when Schleswig was annexed by Prussia. Storm wrote poetry and a large number of novellas, the best-known of which is his last, *Der Schimmelreiter* (1888, translated in 1917 as *The Rider on the White Horse*).

Storm and Stress. See STURM UND DRANG.

stormtroopers, term originally applied to heavily armed shock troops used in the 'infiltration tactics' developed by the German army in the last year of World War I. Subsequently the term was applied to members of the Nazi paramilitary organization, the SA.

Strandes, Justus (1859–1930), businessman and politician. Strandes was civil governor of Antwerp during the German occupation of Belgium in World War I.

Strasser, Gregor (1892–1934), leading Nazi politician. Strasser joined the party after serving in World War I and participated in the BEER HALL PUTSCH of 1923. As leader of the north German wing of the NSDAP during the 1920s he attempted to propagate a populist 'anti-capitalism' he considered appropriate to the mobilization of the industrial workers of the north. This earned him a reputation as the leader of a supposedly 'left-wing' faction within the party. He came into conflict with Hitler when he negotiated with SCHLEICHER (the last Weimar chancellor) for the post of vice chancellor in 1932, and was forced to withdraw from active politics. He was arrested and murdered during the NIGHT OF THE LONG KNIVES, the 1934 purge of the SA.

Strasser, Otto (1897–1974), Nazi politician. The brother of Gregor STRASSER, he became head of propaganda of the north German wing of the NSDAP. He was expelled from the party in 1930 following ideological differences with Hitler. He went into exile during the Nazi dictatorship, but returned to fascist politics in postwar West Germany.

Strauss, Franz-Josef (1915–88), right-wing politician; leader of the CSU (1961–88) and minister-president of Bavaria (1978–88). Strauss was born in Munich and studied at the university there. He served in World War II, joined the CSU in 1945, and became party leader in 1961. He was elected to the Bundestag in 1949, and was federal minister for nuclear energy under ADENAUER (1955–6) before taking over the defence portfolio (1956–62). His involvement in the *SPIEGEL AFFAIR* compelled him to leave the government. He returned to ministerial office as finance minister in the GRAND COALITION (1966–9), and worked closely with the SPD economics minister Karl Schiller to overcome Germany's economic recession by lowering taxes – despite the country's empty coffers.

In opposition Strauss was an outspoken critic of the social–liberal coalition of 1969–82, and was particularly strident in his opposition to the *OSTPOLITIK* of Willy BRANDT – despite the more conciliatory position taken by Rainer Barzel, then leader of the CDU/CSU group in the Bundestag. Disappointed by the defeat of the conservatives in the general election of 1976, Strauss threatened to take the CSU out of the joint parliamentary group in protest at the hesitancy of the CDU leadership's opposition to the government. The threat was only withdrawn when the CDU – led by Helmut KOHL – threatened in turn to organize alongside the CSU in Bavaria.

Strauss became minister-president in Bavaria in 1978, and was the unsuccessful candidate of the CDU/CSU for the federal chancellorship in 1980. Although he did not join the conservative–liberal coalition formed by Helmut Kohl in 1982 he remained active in politics, and was particularly vociferous on matters concerning relations between the Federal Republic and East Germany. He continued as leader of the CSU and Bavarian minister-president until his death.

Strauss, Johann (the elder; 1804–49), popular Austrian composer and musician. The elder Strauss was born in Vienna and toured Europe with his orchestra. He composed marches, including *The Radetzky March*, and is considered, along with Joseph Lanner (1801–43), one of the founders of the traditional Viennese waltz. Strauss fathered six children, of whom the younger Johann STRAUSS was the eldest. He became estranged from his wife and family towards the end of his life, and died of scarlet fever and meningitis in 1849.

Strauss, Johann (the younger; 1825–99), popular Austrian composer, and son of Johann STRAUSS the elder. Strauss was born in Vienna, and attended the *Schottenstift-Gymnasium* and the Polytechnic Institute, where he studied commercial law. Although his father was against a musical career for his son, his mother arranged lessons for him and he abandoned his law studies to pursue a musical career. Strauss wrote 550 musical works, including the waltzes *The Blue Danube* (*An der schönen blauen Donau*, 1867), and *Tales from the Vienna Woods* (*Geschichten aus dem Wienerwald*, 1868). He is also well known for his contribution to the development of Vienna operetta, his works in this genre including *Die Fledermaus* ('the bat', 1874) and *Der Zigeunerbaron* (*The Gypsy Baron*, 1885).

Strauss, Richard (1864–1949), composer and conductor. Strauss was born in Munich, the son of a musician in the court opera orchestra. He moved to Berlin in 1898, and was musical director of the opera there from

1908 until 1919. He then moved to Austria as director of the Vienna State Opera (1919–24), after which he devoted his time largely to composition. His works, in a rich, late Romantic style, include the tone poems *Till Eulenspiegel* (1895) and *Also sprach Zarathustra* (1896), and the operas *Salome* (1905), *Elektra* (1908), *Der Rosenkavalier* (1910) and *Ariadne auf Naxos* (1912) – the last three with librettos by Hugo von HOF-MANNSTHAL. Arguably the leading figure in German music of his period, Strauss not only remained in Germany in 1933 but also accepted the post of president of the Reich Chamber of Music. He held this post until 1935 when he was dismissed because of his collaboration with the Jewish librettist Stefan ZWEIG on the opera *Die schweigsame Frau* ('the silent woman', 1935), which was banned. He was also considered suspect because of his Jewish daughter-in-law. However, his next opera, *Friedenstag* (1938), met with Hitler's approval. In 1945 Strauss composed *Metamorphosen* for strings, a work interpreted by some as a lament for the destruction of German cultural life, but by others as a threnody for Hitler – it was banned in the Netherlands after the war. Strauss moved to Switzerland after the war, and did not return to Germany until he was cleared by a DENAZI-FICATION tribunal in 1949, shortly before his death.

Streicher, Julius (1885–1946), Nazi politician. Streicher was born in Fleinhausen, near Augsburg in Bavaria, and was a schoolmaster in Nuremberg before serving in World War I. He formed the *Deutschsozialistische Partei* in 1919, before joining the NSDAP along with the rest of his own party in 1922. In 1923 he founded *Der Stürmer*, a virulently anti-Semitic journal, and became *Gauleiter* of Franconia in 1925. He was dismissed from his job for anti-republican activity in 1928 and was elected to the Bavarian LANDTAG in 1929. He was then a member of the Reichstag from 1932 to 1945. *Der Stürmer* led the campaign for anti-Semitic legislation, which

culminated in the NUREMBERG LAWS. His unpopularity with other leading Nazis led to his being brought before the supreme party court in 1940 on charges of corruption. He was dismissed from his party posts, and was succeeded as *Gauleiter* of Franconia by Hans Zimmermann. Streicher was tried and hanged at Nuremberg in 1946.

Strength through Joy (*Kraft durch Freude*, KdF), Nazi leisure organization. Originally called *Nach der Arbeit* ('after work'), Strength through Joy (usually abbreviated to KdF) was modelled on its Italian Fascist counterpart *Dopolavoro*. It was established in 1934 as a subsidiary organization of the German Labour Front (*Deutsche Arbeitsfront*, DAF), and the programme was heavily subsidized: almost a quarter of its budget was covered by DAF subventions between 1934 and 1942. The subsidy covered the greater part of the organization's administrative costs, and by the end of 1939 the KdF had a full-time staff of 7500 and a much larger work-force of 'honorary' volunteers.

Among the organization's first ventures were a production of SCHILLER's *Die Räuber* at the KdF People's Theatre (*Theater des Volkes*) in Berlin, and excursions from large industrial cities to areas such as the Black Forest and Upper Bavaria. As the KdF became established, new parts of rural Germany were opened up to working-class tourism by the organization, including the Eifel district and the Masurian Lakes. After the ANSCHLUSS with Austria there were trips further afield, to the Tyrol, Carinthia, the Salzkammergut and Styria. An agreement with *Dopolavoro* in 1937 made possible an exchange of holidaymakers between Fascist Italy and Nazi Germany, and KdF ships sailed from Hamburg and Bremerhaven to Norway and Madeira. Such sea cruises were in practice very exclusive affairs, however: only 1% of German workers ever took one, and only one-fifth of cruise passengers were workers. Most people only took short local breaks, and Lake Constance, the Harz mountains and the Munich Beer Festival were among the most popular destinations. Strength through Joy accounted for some 10% of the German tourist market, and 8.5 million people took KdF trips in the last year before the war (the majority of them – some 6 million – only for one or two days in resorts close to home).

Strength through Joy sought to appeal to aspirations towards upward social mobility ('embourgeoisement') among workers, and many of its activities recalled Social Democratic attempts to direct and structure workers' leisure time (*see* SPD): there were theatre and concert visits, and educational lectures on subjects ranging from photography to cancer. There were also riding, sailing and tennis lessons.

Stresa Front, term used for the agreements reached on 11 April 1935 at the Stresa Conference by Britain, France and Italy. The last common front against German rearmament and Nazi expansionism, it was undermined by the separate naval agreement between Britain and Germany (the ANGLO-GERMAN NAVAL AGREEMENT) signed on 18 June, and by Italy's invasion of Ethiopia in October.

Stresemann, Gustav (1878–1929), Weimar conservative politician; chancellor (1923) and foreign minister (1923–9). Stresemann was born in Berlin into a lower middle-class family, studied economics and was a successful businessman and legal adviser to the League of Saxon Industrialists from 1902. Before and during World War I he was a member of the NATIONAL LIBERAL PARTY, which he represented in the Reichstag (1907–12 and 1914–18). He was the youngest deputy in parliament when he was first elected, and became parliamentary leader of the party in 1917. During World War I Stresemann was an annexationist nationalist and a member of the PAN-GERMAN LEAGUE, and played a part in the downfall of Chancellor BETHMANN HOLLWEG in 1917. After the war he was a co-founder of the conservative DVP (1918), which he also represented in the

constituent NATIONAL ASSEMBLY (1919) and the Reichstag (1920–9). He was chancellor at the height of the INFLATION crisis of 1923, and subsequently foreign minister until his death in 1929. The 1920s has come to be known as the Stresemann era.

Although the DVP had initially been an anti-republican party, Stresemann and his colleagues were increasingly prepared to work with the republic and its institutions in the interests of establishing a liberal political and economic order in Germany. The LOCARNO TREATIES, which he negotiated (1925), helped considerably to stabilize Germany's relations with the West. Stresemann was a pragmatic politician, who acknowledged that Germany's sovereignty and international status could only be enhanced through negotiation, and he was as concerned to prevent a permanent Anglo-French coalition against Germany in the west as he was to address French concerns. His approach to Germany's eastern frontiers was more ambiguous, and his revisionist approach to the eastern territorial provisions of the treaty of VERSAILLES was more persistent. Nevertheless, he proceeded by negotiation here too, and his approach to foreign policy was markedly different from that of his predecessors of the imperial era, and his successors in the 1930s. In 1926, together with his French counterpart, Aristide Briand, he was awarded the Nobel Peace Prize.

Stroop, Jürgen (1895–1951), SS officer. Stroop served in World War I and was promoted through the ranks of the SS after 1933. He served with the SS in eastern Europe and the USSR after the outbreak of war and commanded the suppression of the revolt in the WARSAW GHETTO of 1943. His report on the suppression of the uprising, entitled 'The Warsaw Ghetto Is No More' was produced as evidence at the Nuremberg trials. He was also SS leader in occupied Greece (1943–4). Stroop was tried at Dachau and executed in Poland in 1951.

structuralists, in the narrow sense in which it is applied to the historiography of Nazi Germany, the term refers to those historians espousing a 'structural' or 'functional' interpretation of the political system of the Third Reich. They have emphasized the polycratic nature of the regime, and the unwillingness of Hitler to make clear decisions, as opposed to the 'INTENTIONALISTS', who emphasize the dominant role of Hitler and his ideology and political programme. Disagreements between structuralists and intentionalists were at the centre of historiographical debates on the nature of Nazi Germany during the 1970s and early 1980s.

Stülpnagel, Karl-Heinrich von (1886–1944). German officer, and cousin of Otto von STÜLPNAGEL. Born in Darmstadt, Stülpnagel was a career soldier, who was military governor of France from 1942 to 1944, during which he time he ordered violently repressive measures against the Resistance. He was a leading member of the 1944 JULY BOMB PLOT against the Nazi regime. After the failure of the plot he unsuccessfully tried to commit suicide and was arrested and hanged in Berlin.

Stülpnagel, Otto von (1878–1948). German officer. Stülpnagel earned a reputation for brutality during World War I, which he consolidated as military governor of France between 1940 and 1942, with reprisal executions and the mass murder of Jews and Communists. He was extradited to Paris after the war and committed suicide while awaiting execution.

Stürgkh, Karl, Graf von (1859–1916), Austrian politician; minister-president (1911–16). Stürgkh was born in Graz, Styria, and was a member of the Austrian parliament (Reichsrat) from 1891. He aligned himself with those landowners who supported the constitution, and was minister of education from 1909 to 1911. He became minister-president in 1911, adjourned the parliament indefinitely at the outbreak of World War I, and instituted a period of authoritarian rule,

despite requests to reconvene the house. He was assassinated by Friedrich ADLER in 1916.

Sturmabteilung. See SA.

Sturm und Drang ('storm and stress'), early Romantic cultural movement of the late 18th century, also referred to as the 'age of genius' (*Geniezeit*). The movement was a reaction against French classicism, and among its heroes were Rousseau and Shakespeare. The Young Romantics of the *Sturm und Drang* movement were preoccupied with history, and increasingly 'national' history and the idea of the 'cultural nation' (*Kulturnation*), folklore and language. The writing of HERDER, and of the young GOETHE (*Die Leiden des jungen Werthers*) and SCHILLER (*Die Räuber*) is characteristic of the movement. The term is also applied to some of the romantically expressive German and Austrian music of the period, such as Haydn's symphonies of the 1760s and 1770s.

successor states (sometimes 'succession states'), a term that generally refers to those new countries in central Europe formed from the territory of the defeated HABSBURG empire after WORLD WAR I. They included 'rump' or 'German' Austria, Hungary, Czechoslovakia, Yugoslavia, Poland, and also Romania, which, although not a new state, acquired much new territory. Although they were constructed with the ostensible intention of freeing small nations from 'foreign' rule, none of them was in fact ethnically homogeneous (except perhaps the new republic of Austria).

Südekum, Albert (1871–1944), Social Democratic politician. Südekum was Prussian finance minister (1919–20).

Sudetenland, former German-speaking territories in Bohemia that were part of the HABSBURG empire before World War I, and were incorporated into Czechoslovakia by the treaty of ST GERMAIN. The Nazis financed a Sudeten German Party (led by Konrad HENLEIN) from 1935. This agitated for secession from Czechoslovakia, and provided popular support for Hitler's irredentist claim on the region. The Sudetenland was transferred to Germany in 1938 by the MUNICH AGREEMENT, an act that considerably weakened Czechoslovakia's border defences and industrial strength. Most Germans were expelled from the region by Czechoslovakia when the region was recovered after World War II.

Sunflower, German code name for the intervention of German troops under ROMMEL in support of the Italians in North Africa in 1941.

Sybel, Heinrich von (1817–95), historian. Born in Düsseldorf, Sybel was a student of Leopold von RANKE, and professor of history at Munich University from 1854. He founded the *Historische Zeitschrift* in 1859, and was appointed director of the Prussian state archives in 1875. Sybel was a member of the Prussian LANDTAG from 1862 to 1864, and again from 1874 to 1880. His historical writing was important in shifting the focus of German historical writing towards the Protestant northeast, and in particular towards the rise of Prussia. His best-known work, *Die Begründung des Deutschen Reiches durch Wilhelm I (The Foundation of the German Empire by William I)* appeared in seven volumes between 1890 and 1894.

System, a disparaging term for parliamentary democracy used by the radical right during the first half of the 20th century. The Nazis looked back scathingly on the WEIMAR REPUBLIC as the 'time of the system' (*Systemzeit*).

T

Taaffe, Eduard, Graf von (1833–95), Austrian politician; minister-president (1868–70 and 1879–93). Taaffe was born in Vienna, and was a friend of the young Emperor FRANZ JOSEPH. He was minister of the interior in CISLEITHANIA – the Austrian part of the Dual Monarchy – in 1867, 1870–1 and 1879. His long term as minister-president marked the end of the liberal era in Austrian politics. He formed a coalition of conservatives, German clericals and Slav national groups (the so- called 'Iron Ring') and pursued a conservative, pro-Slav policy at home. He modified the liberal education legislation of his predecessors in order to mollify his Catholic supporters, and made some concessions to the Czechs in linguistic matters: the 'Stremayr ordinances' of 1880 allowed the use of Czech in dealings with the authorities in Bohemia.

Taaffe introduced moderately progressive social legislation, regulating working hours and prohibiting child labour below the age of 12. Accident and sickness insurance similar to that in Germany was also introduced. At the same time the government cracked down on the labour movement, and suspended civil rights in Vienna and elsewhere during the 1880s. In 1882 the property qualification for voting for was reduced from 10 to 5 gulden, but attempts to introduce a quasi-universal suffrage failed when they were resolutely opposed by radical nationalists. Taaffe's government fell in the autumn of 1893. Taaffe died at Ellischau (now Nalzovy in the Czech Republic) in 1895.

taler, an old German coin. It was first minted in 1500 in Joachimsthal im Erzgebirge. It was a silver equivalent of the GULDEN prevalent in central, northern and western Germany. It remained in circulation until 1907 (when it was worth three marks). The name 'dollar' derives from the word *Taler*.

Tandler, Julius (1869–1936), Austrian Social Democratic politician. Tandler was born in Iglau (now Jihlava in the Czech Republic). A doctor by profession, he was a professor at Vienna University from 1910 and undersecretary of state in the ministry of public health in 1919–20. He is best-known for his work as a social reformer in 'RED VIENNA', where he directed the establishment of welfare and medical services and kindergartens during the 1920s, and promoted sports for workers. After the AUSTROFASCIST coup of 1934 he was stripped of his professorial title and left Austria, first for China, and then for the Soviet Union. He died in Russia in 1936 after being invited to Moscow as a consultant for Soviet hospital reforms.

Tanganyika, the main part of GERMAN EAST AFRICA, mandated to Britain after World War I.

Tannenberg, battle of (26–31 August 1914), decisive victory for Germany against Russia at the beginning of WORLD WAR I. The battle at Tannenberg (Stębark in Poland) was one of the biggest defeats in military history. Some 30,000 Russians were killed or wounded and 92,000 taken prisoner; only 60,000 escaped. It established the reputation of General HINDENBURG, who, along with LUDENDORFF, had replaced General Max von Prittwitz, commander of the German 8th Army, after he had lost his nerve and ordered the abandonment of East Prussia in the wake of Russian attacks. After his victory at Tannenberg, Hindenburg turned north to engage in the battle of the MASURIAN LAKES. (An earlier battle had taken place at Tannenberg in the Middle Ages. In 1410 a Polish-Lithuanian army defeated the Germans.)

Tannenberg League (*Tannenberg-Bund*), a right-wing religious and political organization in Weimar Germany founded in 1925 by General LUDENDORFF and Konstantin Hierl (1875–1955). Its aim was the establishment of a militaristic 'GREATER GERMANY' and a 'racially appropriate' German religion. The Tannenberg League was opposed to the (perceived) influence of Jews, Marxists, Freemasons and Jesuits, who were held responsible for the German defeat in 1918 (*see DOLCHSTOSSLEGENDE*).

Tat, Die ('the deed'), a conservative monthly journal founded in 1909 and edited by Eugen Diederichs (1867–1930). After World War I it was the organ of the radical right-wing TATKREIS. *Die Tat* had a circulation of up to 30,000 at the end of the 1920s. After 1939 it became *Das 20. Jahrhundert*, and was published until 1944.

Tatkreis ('action circle'), a radical-right wing splinter group of the Weimar Republic. Many of the organization's members subsequently joined the Nazi Party.

Tehran Conference (28 November–1 December 1943), the first meeting of the 'big three' Allied wartime leaders (Churchill, Roosevelt and Stalin) in Tehran, Persia. It was agreed that the invasion of northern France would take place on 1 May 1944 (a date that was later revised), and that the Soviet Union would declare war on Japan in the Far East once Germany had been defeated in the west. The future of Poland and Germany was also discussed in the context of Western anxiety about the possibility of a separate peace between Germany and the Soviet Union. Churchill indicated to Stalin that he was ready to accept the Soviet annexation of eastern Poland, and Roosevelt – despite the professed antipathy of the United States to territorial gains by the Allies – did not oppose it, and nor was he prepared to go to war with the USSR on behalf of the occupied Baltic states. The West also accepted the claim of the Soviet Union to the MEMEL district and to a part of East Prussia, including the old German university town of KÖNIGSBERG (which was to be renamed Kaliningrad). In exchange for the loss of its eastern territories Poland was to be compensated with German territory east of the ODER–NEISSE LINE. These territorial arrangements were further discussed at the YALTA CONFERENCE in February 1945.

Terboven, Josef (1898–1945), Nazi politician. Born in Essen, Terboven served in World War I and studied at Freiburg and Munich. A member of the SA, he was elected to the Reichstag for Düsseldorf-West at the time of the Nazi electoral breakthrough in 1930. He was *Gauleiter* of Essen from 1933, *Oberpräsident* of the Rhineland from 1935 and Reich defence commissioner for District VI (Münster) from 1939. He became Reich commissioner in Norway in 1940, a position in which he was designated guardian of the interests of the Reich, and responsible directly to Hitler. He was responsible for the arrest and deportation of Norwegian Jews to the Reich in 1941 and 1942. After 1942 Terboven carried out much of his business through the puppet government led by the Norwegian collaborator Vidkun QUISLING. He committed suicide in Norway in 1945.

Terezin, Czech name for THERESIENSTADT.

Thalheimer, August (1884–1948), Communist politician. Born into a middle-class Jewish family in Affaltrach, Württemberg, Thalheimer studied linguistics. He joined the SPD in 1904 and pursued a career in journalism, first as editor in chief of the Göppingen *Freie Volkszeitung* from 1909 and then of the Braunschweig *Volksfreund* from 1914 to 1916. Thalheimer was on the left of the party, and was active in the SPARTACUS group around Karl LIEBKNECHT and Rosa LUXEMBURG during World War I. He was called up in 1916, and was wounded in action. He moved to Stuttgart in 1918, and was a founder member of the KPD (German Communist Party) at the end of the year. He was elected to the Central Committee (ZK) of the party, and was its leading theoretician. Thalheimer was an orthodox Marxist in a rather pragmatic way, and a defender of Leninism and the Soviet Union. He recommended a strategy of 'revolutionary offensive' to the KPD, and when this failed he was severely criticized, and in 1924 was eventually expelled from the party. He then moved to the Soviet Union, where he joined the CPSU (Soviet Communist Party) and taught philosophy at the Marx–Engels Institute in Moscow. He returned to Germany in 1928, and he fled to France in 1933. He was refused entry to Germany by the Allies after the war, and died in Cuba.

Thälmann, Ernst (1886–1944), leader of the German Communist Party (KPD) from 1925. Thälmann was born in Hamburg, into a lower middle-class family. His father was a small shopkeeper and he worked in the family business for two years after leaving school in 1900. He left home at 16 and went to sea, worked briefly as an agricultural labourer in New York State, but returned to Hamburg and joined the SPD as a dock worker in 1903. He served during World War I as an ordinary soldier on the Western Front. He deserted in 1918. He left the SPD for the breakaway USPD, was elected to the Hamburg BÜRGERSCHAFT in 1919, and stood unsuccessfully in the Reichstag elections of that year. He joined the KPD in December 1920 when it merged with the left wing of the USPD, was re-elected to the Bürgerschaft

as a Communist, and was a Communist member of the Reichstag from 1924 to 1933. He became president of the KPD in 1925. He ran unsuccessfully for the office of Reich president in 1925 and 1932. Thälmann was on the left of the KPD and a loyal supporter of Stalin and the Soviet Union. He was a member of the executive committee of the Comintern, and joined the Presidium in 1931. He was arrested in 1933 and was murdered in Buchenwald after eleven years in CONCENTRATION CAMPS.

Thälmann Pioneers. *See* YOUNG PIONEERS.

Theresienstadt (Czech name: Terezin), 'model' Jewish GHETTO in Nazi-occupied Czechoslovakia. Established in early 1942 outside Prague, Theresienstadt was not a sealed section of an ordinary town, but rather an 18th-century Austrian garrison complex. It became a Jewish town, governed and guarded by the SS. When the deportations from central Europe to the EXTERMINATION CAMPS began in the spring of 1942, certain groups were initially excluded: invalids, partners in a mixed marriage and their children and prominent Jews with special connections. These were sent to the ghetto in Terezin. They were joined by old and young Jews from the Protectorate of Bohemia and Moravia, and, later, by small numbers of prominent Jews from Denmark and the Netherlands. Its large barracks served as dormitories for communal living; they also contained offices, workshops, infirmaries and communal kitchens. The Nazis used Terezin to deceive public opinion. They tolerated a lively cultural life of theatre, music, lectures and art. Thus it could be shown to officials of the International Red Cross. Terezin, however, was only a station on the road to the extermination camps; about 88,000 Jews were deported from Terezin to their deaths in the east. In April 1945 only 17,000 Jews remained in Terezin, where they were joined by 14,000 Jewish concentration camp prisoners, evacuated from camps threatened by the Allied armies.

On 8 May 1945 Terezin was liberated by the Red Army.

Thierack, Otto (1889–1946), Nazi politician. Born in Wurzen, Saxony, into a middle-class family, Thierack studied law at Marburg and Leipzig, served in World War I and then practised as a lawyer. Thierack joined the NSDAP in 1932 and became head of the Nazi lawyers' organization (*NS-Rechtswahrerbund*) the same year. He was appointed Saxon justice minister in 1933, and was president of the VOLKSGERICHTSHOF, the 'people's court' (1936–42). Thierack was instrumental in the murderous exploitation of slave labour during the Third Reich. After the war he was captured by British forces, but committed suicide before he could be brought to trial for war crimes.

Thingspiel, Nazi form of light entertainment that included mock medieval battle scenes with pagan overtones. The *Thingspiel* was a propaganda display, frequently in a rural setting, which was intended to evoke ancient Teutonic tribal custom.

Third Germany, term used during the discussions about reform of the Reich in the early 19th century to describe those German states outside Prussia and Austria. In 1806 HARDENBERG, the Prussian reformer, suggested the reorganization of the HOLY ROMAN EMPIRE into six *Kreise* (imperial 'circles') around Austria, Prussia, Bavaria, Saxony, Hesse and Württemberg, with all other princes effectively subordinated to these states, while otherwise retaining their prerogatives. These six *Kreise* would in turn be allocated to one of three larger groupings: Austria, Prussia (with Hesse and Saxony), and a 'Third Germany' comprising the southern states of Bavaria, Baden and Württemberg. Hardenberg's proposals were seen by many outside Berlin as a pseudo-constitutional cover for the expansion of Prussia in northern Germany.

Third Reich, popular term for the Nazi dictatorship. The Nazi regime was portrayed as the successor to the medieval German empire (the First Reich) and the GERMAN EMPIRE founded in 1871 (the second Reich). The term was popularized on the German right by Moeller van den Bruck's book of the same name, published in 1923. Van den Bruck emphasized the cultural separateness of the Germans, and their mission to pioneer a 'third way' between the prevailing ideologies of economic liberalism in the West and Soviet communism in the East. The idea, and the term, was adopted by the Nazis.

thousand-mark barrier, a financial penalty imposed on Germans travelling to Austria from 1933 to 1936. Following the expulsion from Austria of the Bavarian Nazi minister of justice, Hans FRANK, Germany passed a law requiring all German citizens visiting Austria to pay 1000 marks. The measure was the beginning of a diplomatic conflict between the Nazi regime, which had recently come to power in Germany, and the Austria of DOLLFUSS, which was trying to contain the activities of its own Nazi agitators. The measure was rescinded as part of the July agreement of 1936 between Hitler and SCHUSCHNIGG, Dollfuss's successor as chancellor.

three-class voting system, Prussian electoral system introduced in 1849 by FRIEDRICH WILHELM IV, and retained until 1918 – despite the more progressive suffrage introduced at Reich level with the establishment of the GERMAN EMPIRE in 1871. Voters were divided according to the amount of direct tax they paid. In 1908, 4% were in the first class, and elected as many representatives as the 82% in the third class. Moreover, the constituency boundaries for the Prussian LANDTAG consistently favoured the sparsely populated rural areas east of the Elbe, and this served to exacerbate the already heavy bias against the SPD. Despite the promises of electoral reform in Prussia during World War I, the system was abolished only after the defeat of the Reich and the NOVEMBER REVOLUTION of 1918.

Three Emperors, battle of the. *See* AUSTERLITZ, BATTLE OF.

Three Emperors' League (*Dreikaiserbund*), formal agreement between Germany, Austria-Hungary and Russia, signed on 18 June 1881. The agreement was originally an informal understanding between Germany and Austria in 1872; in the following year Russia was also drawn in. It was a German initiative and reflected BISMARCK's policy of maintaining the new international order after the FRANCO-PRUSSIAN WAR of 1870–1, and thereby consolidating and defending Germany's territorial gains from France. France was isolated by the agreement and prevented from gaining the allies that would make a war of revenge possible. The Balkan crisis of the late 1870s persuaded Bismarck of the necessity of a more formal agreement, which was negotiated in 1881 and was valid for three years in the first instance (it was re-negotiated in 1884). Should any of the contracting powers be attacked by a fourth power, the others pledged to observe a benevolent neutrality and to help ensure that the conflict remain localized. If there were to be a war between one of the powers and Turkey, however, the stipulations of the treaty would only apply if a previous agreement had been reached between the three powers. Russia agreed to respect Austria-Hungary's new interests arising from the treaty of Berlin (1878; see BERLIN, CONGRESS OF), and all three parties expressed their desire to avoid discord and their intention to engage in consultations, especially if the territorial status quo of Turkey in Europe were to be affected. In a separate protocol it was agreed that Austria-Hungary had the right to annex BOSNIA-HERZEGOVINA at any time. These qualifications reflected a recognition that potential difficulties between the contracting powers lay in the Balkans, and in the event political tension between Austria-Hungary and Russia in the Balkans prevented the renewal of the treaty in 1887. Germany then pursued its common interests with Russia on the basis of the REINSURANCE TREATY.

Thugut, Johann (Amadeus Franz), Freiherr von (1736–1818), Austrian diplomat, also referred to as Franz Maria von Thugut. He was born a commoner in Linz and pursued a career at court and in the diplomatic service. He was appointed court interpreter at Constantinople by KAUNITZ in 1757 with the rank of chancellery secretary. He worked as an agent for the Bourbons during the 1760s, and received a pension from the French crown up to the Revolution. He was Austria's diplomatic representative in the Ottoman empire from 1769 and negotiated the cession of Bukovina from Turkey to Austria in 1775. He was ennobled in 1771, and named a councillor of state by JOSEPH II in 1783. He was then posted as ambassador to Naples, Berlin and Warsaw before taking on the post of high commissioner of the principalities of Moldavia and Walachia (1788–90). After the outbreak of the French Revolution he travelled to Paris in order to try to retrieve his personal fortune, and was in contact with Mirabeau.

Thugut was at the head of the war party against Revolutionary France, and from 27 March 1793 until 16 January 1801 he effectively directed Austrian foreign policy. He was appointed foreign minister after the death of Kaunitz in 1794. In 1798 he refused to accept the legitimacy of the French ambassador to Vienna, General Bernadotte, because he was a revolutionary, and refused to meet him personally. He was also suspicious of Prussia. In 1795 Thugut brought about the coalition between Austria, England and Russia, but fell from power as a consequence of the difficult negotiations at the end of the War of the Second COALITION against France (1799–1802). He retired to Pressburg (now Bratislava in Slovakia) and died in Vienna in 1818.

Thule Society, radical right-wing organization founded in Munich during World War I by Rudolf, Freiherr von Sebottendorff. Among its members were Gottfried FEDER, one of the first members of the Munich

DEUTSCHE ARBEITERPARTEI, Rudolf HESS and Alfred ROSENBERG. The organization is considered one of the organizational predecessors of Nazism. It used the swastika as a symbol, along with Germanic runes and other paraphernalia of a supposed medieval Germandom. Despite the organization's mystic inclinations it was also involved in more down-to-earth political violence, especially during the suppression of the 1919 Bavarian councils' republic (see BAVARIA).

Thun-Hohenstein, Austrian aristocratic family. Originally from the South Tyrol, the Thun-Hohensteins were associated with Bohemia, where they had acquired land in the 17th century. They became barons in 1495, held the title of imperial count from 1629 and became princes in 1911.

Thun-Hohenstein, Franz Anton, Fürst (1847–1916), Austrian politician. Born in Tetschen (now Decín in the Czech Republic), Thun-Hohenstein was governor of Bohemia (1889–96 and 1911–15), and minister-president of Austria and interior minister (1898–9). The BADENI language decrees were repealed during his period of office.

Thun-Hohenstein, Leo, Graf (1811–88), Austrian politician. Born in Tetschen (now Decín in the Czech Republic), Thun studied law and philosophy at Prague University and then travelled abroad, before being elected to the Bohemian diet. He was effectively appointed ruler of Bohemia when the revolution broke out in 1848 (see REVOLUTIONS OF 1848), and was captured and imprisoned by the revolutionaries. He supported the suppression of the revolution by military force. Thun was education minister in Austria from 1849 to 1860, and is remembered for his reform of the education system. The status of the *Gymnasium* (grammar school) was raised by making it an eight-year (rather than six-year) institution, with a final examination for university entrance (*Matura*). Despite his own strong Catholic convictions, many of his reforms were liberal in spirit. He extended academic freedom for university

teachers, allowing them to teach what they wanted, and students to attend the courses of their choosing. The Protestant College of Divinity became a faculty in 1850, the number of scientific disciplines was increased, and professorial appointments were also opened up to Protestant and Jewish applicants. Thun hoped that liberalization would revitalize Catholicism and broaden its appeal among intellectuals who had been put off by the sterile authoritarianism of the VORMÄRZ (pre-1848) period. In the event the Josephinian bureaucrats and Austrian Catholics Thun had hoped to recruit to his cause defended the pre-revolutionary university system. Moreover, many of Thun's supporters were Germans, and the reforms had a German orientation that was intended not least to reinforce Austria's claim to leadership within Germany. This alienated many of the monarchy's non-German intellectuals. After 1860 Thun tried unsuccessfully to promote a federalist concept of the state with the help of his Catholic Conservative group and the journal *Das Vaterland* (1865–88).

Thuringia, one of the NEW FEDERAL STATES. Modern Thuringia was created in 1920, and its borders were altered in 1944 when Erfurt and the district of Schmalkalden were transferred to Thuringia. After the Soviet occupation it became one of the states of the GERMAN DEMOCRATIC REPUBLIC, and its borders were simplified: the territorial enclaves that had existed within Thuringia during the Weimar Republic were absorbed. Its capital city was at first Weimar (until 1947), then Erfurt. In 1952 the state was replaced by the administrative districts of Erfurt, Gera and Suhl, and after reunification the present state was reconstituted from those districts, along with parts of the Halle and Leipzig districts.

In the LANDTAG election of 1929 the Nazis won 11.3% of the vote in Thuringia, and formed a coalition with the conservatives; it was their first opportunity to exercise ministerial power, albeit at regional level. Since 1990 the Christian Democrats have been the strongest party in Thuringia, and won 51% of the vote and a majority of seats in the 1999 Landtag election. At the end of the 20th century Thuringia had a population of about 2.6 million.

Thyssen, Fritz (1873–1951), German nationalist businessman. The eldest son of August Thyssen, founder of the Thyssen iron-and-steel company, Fritz Thyssen was born near Mülheim an der Ruhr, studied engineering, and then joined the family business. He volunteered for military service when war broke out in 1914, but returned to his civilian occupation after two years. A political conservative who hoped for the restoration of Germany's international position, Thyssen organized passive resistance during the 1923 French and Belgian occupation of the Ruhr (*see* REPARATIONS) and was an early financial backer of the NSDAP (the Nazi Party). He joined the party in 1931, by which time he was at the head of the family firm, president of the supervisory council of the Vereinigte Stahlwerke (United Steelworks) and one of the country's leading businessmen. He mediated between the Nazis and the Rhineland business community, and was rewarded in 1933 by election to the Reichstag in the plebiscite of November of that year. He was also appointed as a Prussian state councillor by GÖRING. In 1933 he was charged with the establishment of an institute (*Institut für Ständewesen*) which served as a forum for the development of his CORPORATIST ideas, but he fell out of favour with Hitler, fled from Germany to Switzerland in 1939 after resigning from the Prussian Council of State in 1938, denouncing Robert LEY, the leader of the German Labour Front (DAF), and criticizing the regime's foreign policy. He repudiated the regime from abroad and was stripped of his German citizenship. He was arrested by the Vichy French and turned over to the Germans during World War II, and he and his wife were both imprisoned in CONCENTRATION CAMPS. The Thyssens survived until 1945, however, and after being fined by a denazification court Fritz Thyssen died in Buenos Aires while visiting his daughter.

Tietz, Oskar (1858–1923), industrialist. Born in Birnbaum into a Jewish business family, Tietz founded the first significant German department store company before World War I. It later became Hertie, with large stores in Berlin, on the Alexanderplatz and in the Leipziger Strasse. Tietz was a committed republican and was actively engaged in the liberal DDP after 1918. He persuaded other employers to pay half-wages to their workers during the general strike against the 1920 KAPP PUTSCH. Tietz and his department stores, which revolutionized German retailing, were targets of persistent anti-Semitic campaigns.

Tillich, Paul (Johannes) (1886–1965), Protestant theologian. Born in Starzeddel (now Starosiedle), Tillich was appointed to the chair of theology and philosophy at Marburg in 1924, and subsequently moved to chairs at Dresden, Leipzig and Frankfurt am Main (1929). He founded the League of Religious Socialists in 1920, thereby placing himself on the margins of German Protestantism in the 1920s. He contributed to the journal *Blätter für den religiösen Sozialismus* (1920–7) and was an editor of the *Neue Blätter für den Sozialismus*, which was established in 1929. At Frankfurt University he got to know Theodor ADORNO and Max HORKHEIMER before emigrating to the United States in 1933. In 1944 he was elected president of the Council for a Democratic Germany and broadcast against the Nazi regime from the United States. He remained in America, however, where he taught at the Union Theological Seminary in New York until 1955, when he was appointed professor at Harvard. He died in Chicago.

Tilsit, treaty of (1807), peace agreement made by Napoleon on behalf of France with Friedrich Wilhelm III of Prussia and Alexander I of Russia during the Wars of the COALITIONS. Prussia was forced to cede territories to the west of the Elbe, most of which (along with other German territories) went to form the basis of the new kingdom of WESTPHALIA. Prussian territories in Poland became the grand duchy of Warsaw. Prussia was reduced to four territories occupied by the French, and an indemnity was imposed. Russia was required to join the continental system and to recognize the CONFEDERATION OF THE RHINE.

Tirpitz, Alfred von (1849–1930), admiral. Tirpitz joined the navy in 1865. His enthusiasm for torpedo squadrons was supported by Kaiser WILHELM II, who charged him with the development of a battle fleet. He was state secretary of the navy and Prussian minister of state (1898–1916), and, supported by the NAVY LEAGUE, he oversaw an enormous expansion of German naval construction in the wake of the navy bills of 1898 and 1900. The scale and pace of naval expansion did much to undermine relations with Great Britain, particularly after 1906, but the German fleet was not ready for war when it eventually broke out in 1914. Tirpitz was frustrated when the navy – ostensibly planned for defence – was not used in offensive action, and when his advice to adopt unrestricted submarine warfare went unheeded. Tirpitz was on the radical right of German politics. A founder member of the authoritarian, annexationist Fatherland Party (*VATERLANDSPARTEI*), he sat in the Reichstag as a DNVP deputy from 1924 to 1928.

Tisch, Harry (1927–95), Communist politician. Tisch was born in Heinrichswalde in Ueckermünde district into a working-class family. He was interned in Flensburg for several months after World War II, and then made his career as a politician in the Soviet zone of occupation and the GERMAN DEMOCRATIC REPUBLIC. He joined the German Communist Party (KPD) and the FDGB (the East German trade-union association) in 1945. From 1948 to 1953 he was a senior union official, and in 1950 he was elected to the Mecklenburg LANDTAG. During the 1950s he was a member of Rostock district council and in 1963 he was elected to the *VOLKSKAMMER* (the 'People's Chamber' of the GDR), and became a candidate for membership of the Central Committee of the SED (Socialist Unity Party). He was a member of the Central Committee and a candidate for membership of the Politburo from 1971. He became a member of the Politburo in 1975. In the same year he became president of the federal council of the FDGB, an office he retained until 1989; he also joined the State Council (STAATSRAT) and the Presidium of the National Council (Nationalrat) of the National Front. He resigned from his party, state and trade-union offices in November 1989, and – along with Erich HONECKER and other leading members – was expelled from the party in December. He was arrested (twice) in the aftermath of the collapse of the East German state, and although he was sentenced to 18 months his time in custody awaiting trial was counted towards his sentence and he was released in June 1991. In 1995 the Berlin public prosecutor then brought fresh charges against Tisch and others for collective manslaughter on the 'internal German border', but he died shortly afterwards of a heart attack at the age of 68.

Todt, Fritz (1891–1942), Nazi minister for armaments and munitions (1940–2). Born in Baden into an upper middle-class family, Todt served in World War I, and studied civil engineering at Karlsruhe. He joined the Nazis in 1922 and became an SS colonel in 1931. In 1933 he was appointed inspector general of German roads, a post that gave him responsibility for the construction of the AUTOBAHNS (motorways) and military fortifications. He was appointed armaments minister in 1940, and inspector general of roads, water and power in 1941. He died in an air crash and was succeeded by SPEER.

Togoland, German colony in west Africa acquired in 1884 along with CAMEROON. The territory had a population of just over 1 million, of whom about 300 were German.

Togoland was occupied by British and French forces in 1914, and both Togoland and Cameroon were mandated to Britain and France in the treaty of VERSAILLES. The French part of Togoland became independent as the Republic of Togo in 1956, while the British part joined Ghana in 1957.

Toller, Ernst (1893–1939), EXPRESSIONIST playwright. Toller was born into a middle-class German Jewish family in Samotschin in the Prussian province of Posen, now in Poland. He volunteered to serve in World War I, but was discharged from the army in 1916 following a breakdown. He studied law at Heidelberg and Münster and met Kurt EISNER in Berlin in 1917. Toller was a member of the left-wing USPD, and was involved in the NOVEMBER REVOLUTION and in the Councils Republic in BAVARIA after the war. He was imprisoned there for five years for his involvement with the revolutionary government, and much of his important work was written in prison, including *Die Wandlung (The Transfiguration)*, which was performed in Berlin in 1919 and considered one of the greatest works of contemporary German theatre. Toller's work is characterized by scenes of grotesque violence and suffering, and presents a pessimistic view of the human condition. *Der deutsche Hinkemann* (1924, translated as *Brokenbow*, 1926) tells the story of a soldier emasculated at the front, who returns to a life of humiliating poverty and hangs himself after his wife commits suicide. His biography *Eine Jugend in Deutschland* (translated as *I Was a German*) was published in 1933. Toller fled Germany in the same year, and undertook lecture tours in Europe before moving to the United States. He committed suicide in New York in 1939.

Tönnies, Ferdinand (1855–1936), sociologist. Tönnies was born in Oldenswort in northern Friesland, Schleswig-Holstein, into an affluent farming family and studied philology and history. He travelled to England several times as a young man, and was impressed by the work of the conservative political philosopher Thomas Hobbes. In his most famous work, *Gemeinschaft und Gesellschaft* (1887) he contrasted the primary, intimate relationships of what he perceived to be the traditional 'community' (*Gemeinschaft*) – based on family, extended kinship and an informal code of laws and customs based on religious belief – with the impersonal relationships of urban 'society' (*Gesellschaft*). For Tönnies, 'community' reinforced 'identity' through a shared language, system of values, an organic, homogeneous view of the world and a recognized unitary, patriarchal authority. The 'society' of modern industrial civilization on the other hand dissolved such organic ties and replaced them with formal bonds of contract, which served to instrumentalize personal and social relationships. Tönnies repeatedly emphasized that these models were ideal types envisaged as part of a general theory of sociology, and distanced himself from the VÖLKISCH anti-urbanism of some of his contemporaries. Before World War I he became involved in campaigns for land reform, and for the establishment of consumer cooperatives. In 1909 he was appointed to a chair at Kiel University. Towards the end of his life he became a member of the SPD, and although his vision of social democracy contained CORPORATIST elements, he warned against the rise of the NSDAP (Nazi Party), and was dismissed from his chair and his teaching post when the Nazis came to power in 1933. He died in Kiel in 1936.

Torgler, Ernst (1893–1963), Communist politician. Torgler was born into a poor working-class family in Berlin. He was educated at a commercial college and took a clerical job after graduating. He joined the Social Democratic youth movement and was a trade-union member. He served in the infantry during World War I, and as a radio operator in the air force. In 1917 he left the SPD for the breakaway USPD, and later joined the KPD (the German Communist Party). He was elected to the Reichstag in 1924, and was leader of the KPD in parliament from 1929 until the party was banned by the Nazis in 1933. He presented himself to the police with an alibi after the REICHSTAG FIRE, knowing that he was a suspect. He was arrested nevertheless, and imprisoned for five months before his trial (during which time he was bound hand and foot in his cell). The case against Torgler was dismissed on grounds of insufficient evidence, but he was kept in prison until 1936. When he was released he returned to the SPD, having been expelled from the KPD for 'disloyalty'. Torgler survived the war and died in Hanover in 1963.

Transleithania (German name: Translei-thanien), term used to describe the territories of the kingdom of Hungary after the *AUSGLEICH* of 1867. The agreement with Austria more or less conceded home rule to the Hungarians. The River Leitha was the boundary between the two halves of the HABSBURG empire – the other half was known as CISLEI-THANIA.

Transylvania (German name: Siebenbürgen; Hungarian name: Erdély), a wooded mountain region in the Carpathians, formerly a part of Austria-Hungary and now a part of Romania. Germans (the so-called *Siebenbürger Sachsen*) settled in Transylvania in the 12th and 13th centuries. The territory came under Turkish rule after the battle of Mohács (1526), and was reconquered during the Habsburgs' wars against the Turks in the late 17th century. There was further German settlement during the 18th century. At the end of the 20th century two-thirds of the region's population were ethnically Romanian, and the rest, mainly in the west, were of Hungarian or German descent.

Traub, Gottfried (1869–1956), Protestant theologian and conservative politician. Traub was born, the son of a pastor, in Riel-inghausen, Württemberg. He was educated in seminaries, studied theology at Tübingen (1887–91) and became a pastor in Dortmund before World War I. He was a follower of Friedrich NAUMANN, and a member of the left-liberal Progressive People's Party (*FORT-SCHRITTLICHE VOLKSPARTEI*, FVP) from 1910 to 1917. He was elected to the Prussian LAND-TAG in 1913 for a constituency in Berlin. He moved to the right during the war, and was expelled from the FVP in 1917. Traub was an annexationist, a founder member of the Fatherland Party (*VATERLANDSPARTEI*), and after the war a co-founder of the nationalist DNVP. He was involved in the KAPP PUTSCH of 1920, and was the intended culture minister in the putative Kapp government. He fled to Austria after the putsch failed, but quickly returned to Germany. He remained active in right-wing politics, and wrote for HUGENBERG's *München-Augsburger Abendzeitung*. He kept his distance from Hitler and the Nazis, and survived the dictatorship and the war.

Trauttmansdorff(-Weinsberg), Ferdinand, Graf von (1749–1827), Austrian politician and imperial public servant. Trauttmansdorf was minister plenipotentiary and effectively governor (president of the *Gubernium*) of the AUSTRIAN NETHERLANDS (modern Belgium) during the political upheavals there at the end of the reign of JOSEPH II. He was then imperial chancellor of the Netherlands (1793–4), and from 1801 he was deputy foreign minister in Vienna. He was lord chamberlain (*Obersthofmeister*) to Emperor FRANZ II from 1807 to 1827.

Treblinka, Nazi EXTERMINATION CAMP on the River Bug in northeast Poland, established in May 1942 along with the Warsaw–Bia-lystok railway line. Some 870,000 people were murdered before the autumn of 1943, when the Nazis themselves destroyed and attempted to conceal evidence of the mass murders that had taken place there. Most of the victims were Polish Jews, some 300,000 of them from the WARSAW GHETTO.

Treitschke, Heinrich von (1834–96), German nationalist historian, journalist and politician. Treitschke was born in Dresden. He was appointed professor of government at Freiburg University in 1863, and professor of history at Kiel (1866), then at Heidelberg (1867) and Berlin (1874). He was a member of the Reichstag for the NATIONAL LIBERAL PARTY from 1871 and 1879, and then as an independent until 1884. Treitschke was one of the most influential historians of his time, but is remembered as much for his stridently nationalistic political interventions and his anti-Semitic prejudices as for his principal work. This was a five-volume history of Germany in the 19th century, which appeared between 1879 and 1894, and did much to shape the German middle classes' understanding of their history. He died in Berlin.

Trenck, Friedrich, Freiherr von der (1726–94), Prussian officer. Von der Trenck was born in Königsberg, East Prussia, and was a cousin of the Austrian officer Franz, Freiherr von der Trenck (1711–49). He was *Ordonnanz-offizier* to Frederick the Great (FRIEDRICH II) and was arrested on suspicion of espionage in 1745. He was arrested again in 1754, and executed as a suspected Austrian spy in Paris in 1794.

Trendelenburg, Ernst (1882–1945), civil servant and politician. Trendelenburg was born into an academic family in Rostock. His grandfather was the philosopher Friedrich Trendelenburg, and his father was a surgeon. He studied law at Bonn and Leipzig, and then joined the justice ministry in 1908. In 1919 he became Reich commissioner for imports and exports, and he moved to the economics ministry in 1922. He was closely involved in trade negotiations with France, and was a supporter of the policy of 'FULFILMENT' and of building a planned economy in Germany in order to assist recovery from the economic dislocation caused by the war. In June 1930 Trendelenburg joined the BRÜNING government as economics minister. He was brought into political office as a non-party economic 'expert', and supported the chancellor's deflationary wages and prices policies. He served until October 1931

when he was replaced by Hermann Warmbold. He was economic minister again for a matter of weeks in May 1932, shortly before the fall of the Brüning government. He represented Germany as deputy secretary general at the League of Nations in Geneva. He returned to Germany after the Reich's withdrawal from the League, and became chairman of the supervisory board of the industrial conglomerate VIAG. Although he was not a supporter of the Nazi Party, he was not a committed opponent either, and was able to work with GÖRING. He committed suicide with his wife and family in Berlin at the end of April 1945.

Treviranus, Gottfried (1891–1971), conservative politician. Treviranus was born into a middle-class family in Schieder, Lippe, pursued a career as an officer in the navy and served in World War I. By the time he retired in 1918 he had attained the rank of lieutenant captain. He was director of the Chamber of Agriculture in Lippe from 1921 to 1930, and was a member of the Reichstag for the nationalist DNVP from 1924 to 1930. His conservatism was too progressive for the chauvinistic nationalist party leader Alfred HUGENBERG, and Treviranus left the DNVP with several of his colleagues at the end of 1929. After their departure he and his colleagues joined forces with the tiny Christian National Peasants' and Agrarian People's Party (*Christlich-Nationale Bauern- und Landvolkpartei*, or more briefly *Christliches Landvolk*) in a Christian National Coalition. Their plans to build a broader alliance of moderate conservatives came to little, however, and the small *Volkskonservative Vereinigung* (Popular Conservative Union), of which Treviranus was the leading figure, remained an insignificant political force, even after it joined forces with the supporters of Kuno von WESTARP in the *Konservative Volkspartei* (Conservative People's Party). In 1930 Treviranus was appointed 'minister for the occupied territories' in the BRÜNING cabinet, but got the government into diplomatic difficulties by causing a row with Poland over the Reich's 'lost territories' in the east. The post was abolished but Treviranus remained in the government as minister without portfolio, and from September 1930 became Reich commissioner for the government's OSTHILFE ('eastern aid') programme. He concluded his ministerial career with a brief spell as transport minister (1931–2). After the fall of the Brüning government Treviranus went back to his job as director of the Chamber of Agriculture in Lippe, where he remained until he was dismissed by the Nazis in 1933. His *Volkskonservative Vereinigung* scarcely withstood the haemorrhage of votes from all conservative parties to the Nazis in 1932, and was banned after Hitler came to power in 1933. Treviranus emigrated in 1934, and although he advised the US military authorities in Germany after the end of World War II, he did so from abroad. He spent his declining years in Italy, and died in Florence in 1971.

Trianon, treaty of (1920), peace treaty following WORLD WAR I between the Allies and Hungary, signed at the Trianon Palace, Versailles. Along with the treaty of ST GERMAIN with Austria, the treaty of Trianon provided for the dismemberment of the HABSBURG empire.

Triepel, Heinrich (1868–1946), lawyer and academic. Triepel was born in Leipzig and studied and taught at the university there. In 1900 he was appointed to the chair of government at Tübingen, and then moved in 1908 to Kiel, where he also taught international law at the Naval Academy. In 1913 he moved to the Berlin law faculty, and was rector of the Friedrich-Wilhelm University (1926–7). He was a supporter of the nationalist DNVP until HUGENBERG became leader, and was an influential opponent of parliamentary democracy. He was dismissed by the Nazis in 1935 and died in Grainau, Upper Bavaria, shortly after the end of World War II.

Tripartite Pact (1940), military agreement between Germany, Japan and Italy, signed in Berlin (27 September 1940) for ten years. It formalized the AXIS but was not a full military alliance, in that none of the members were obliged to declare war on the enemy of another.

Triple Alliance (1882), defence treaty signed in secret in Vienna on 20 May 1882 by Germany, Austria-Hungary and Italy. Germany and Austria-Hungary (earlier signatories to the DUAL ALLIANCE of 1879) were to support Italy in the case of an attack by France, and Italy would reciprocate if France attacked Germany. The treaty was to be valid for five years in the first instance, but was renegotiated and expanded. In the event Italy considered Germany the aggressor in 1914 and remained neutral, until joining the war on the Allied side in 1915.

Trizone, unified economic area in postwar western Germany. The Trizone was the name given to the three western zones of occupation after effective economic unification when the French zone joined the British and American zones (the BIZONE) on 8 April 1949. It was quickly superseded by the FEDERAL REPUBLIC OF GERMANY, which was founded later the same year.

Troeltsch, Ernst (1865–1923), Protestant theologian and historian. Troeltsch was born into a middle-class family in Haunstetten near Augsburg in Bavaria. He was a student at Bonn, and in 1894 he was appointed to a chair in theology at Heidelberg, where he was a close associate of Max WEBER. In 1915 he was appointed successor to Wilhelm Dilthey as professor of philosophy at Berlin, and established a reputation as one of the leading theologians of liberal Protestantism, and also as Germany's foremost historian of religion and philosopher of historicism. Along with other historians from Berlin he attempted to influence the country's political leadership towards a more moderate war-aims policy during World War I. After the war was over he was a co-founder of the liberal German Democratic Party (DDP), and was elected to the Prussian LANDTAG.

Troppau, Congress of (1820), a meeting of the major European powers to coordinate responses to the outbreak of revolutions in Spain, Portugal and Naples. The affairs of the Congress were dominated, however, by the so-called HOLY ALLIANCE (Russia, Austria and Prussia), who favoured intervention, and marked the beginning of withdrawal of support by Great Britain for the suppression of liberal and national movements in continental Europe.

See also CONGRESS SYSTEM.

Truppenamt (literally 'troops office'), a department of the ministry of defence during the Weimar Republic. It was intended to take over the work of the Great General Staff, which had been dissolved under the terms of the treaty of VERSAILLES.

Tschabuschnigg, Adolf Ignaz, Ritter von (1809–77), Austrian writer and politician. Born in Klagenfurt into a Carinthian noble family, von Tschabuschnigg joined the civil service in 1835 and was elected to the Carinthian diet in 1848. In 1859 he became a court counsellor at the Austrian supreme court, and in 1861 he joined the imperial council (REICHSRAT). After the *AUSGLEICH* of 1867 he was justice minister in the POTOCKI administration (1870–1).

Tschirsky und Bögendorf, Heinrich von (1858–1916), diplomat. He was state secretary in the foreign office (1906–7), then German ambassador to Vienna (1907–16).

Tucher von Simmelsdorf, Heinrich, Freiherr von (1853–1925), diplomat. He was Bavarian ambassador to Vienna from 1896 to 1918.

Tucholsky, Kurt (1890–1935), writer and journalist. Born in Berlin into a middle-class Jewish family, Tucholsky studied law and served in World War I. He moved to Paris in 1924, and to Sweden in 1929. Tucholsky was a prolific writer who published satirical essays and poems (many of which became cabaret songs) under his own name, but also wrote under a number of pseudonyms: Peter Panter, Theobald Tiger, Ignaz Wrobel and Kaspar Hauser. His first published work appeared before World War I, and after the publication of *Bilderbuch für Verliebte* ('picture book for lovers', 1912), he began writing for the magazine *Die Schaubühne* (which became *Die WELTBÜHNE* in 1918) and was briefly its editor (1926–7). He was also Paris correspondent for the *Vossische Zeitung* and wrote for the Social Democratic paper *Vorwärts*, aligning himself with the radical left. He was a member of the Independent Social Democratic Party (USPD), but found it difficult to establish a clear relationship with the KPD (German Communist Party) when the USPD was wound up. His antipathy towards the German right, and particularly the increasingly strident nationalist and militarist right, were expressed in his book *Deutschland Deutschland über alles* (1929). Tucholsky's books were burned by the Nazis, and he was stripped of his citizenship. He committed suicide in Sweden in 1935.

Turnbewegung, gymnastics movement. During the 19th century the German gymnastics movement was often closely associated with German nationalism. It grew up in the early 19th century under the leadership of Friedrich Ludwig JAHN ('Turnvater Jahn'), who established a gymnastics ground on the Hasenheide in the south of Berlin in 1811. The first gymnastics association was established in Hamburg in 1816. Gymnastics had developed strong associations with nationalism and liberalism, and was effectively banned in Germany during the METTERNICH era. Gymnastics was banned in public places in Prussia from 1819, and gymnastics associations were closed down in 1820. Jahn himself was arrested. The ban was lifted in 1842, and the movement grew rapidly. Gymnastics festivals (*Turnfeste*) were held in a number of German towns during the 1840s, and a national meeting was held for the first time in Coburg in 1860. The German gymnastics association (*Deutsche Turnerschaft*) was founded in 1868. The gymnastics movement retained its politically subversive reputation during the 1840s, when it was associated with the REVOLUTIONS OF 1848, but despite the establishment of a workers' gymnastics association the movement came to be associated increasingly with the nationalist right after the founding of the empire in 1871. The *Deutsche Turnerschaft* was superseded by a section of the Nazi *Reichsbund für Leibesübungen* (National Association for Physical Exercises). Associations were re-established after World War II in 1950 in the Federal Republic and in 1958 in East Germany.

Two-plus-Four Treaty (1990), treaty signed by the FEDERAL REPUBLIC OF GERMANY and the GERMAN DEMOCRATIC REPUBLIC, plus the former Allied occupying powers (the USA, USSR, Great Britain and France) that paved the way for the reunification of Germany.

Tyrol (German name: Tirol), a province of Austria. The area was settled by Germanic tribes from the 6th century, and was incorporated into the Carolingian empire in 788. The counts of Tirol extended their rule over the area during the Middle Ages. Duke Friedrich IV moved his seat to Innsbruck in 1420. The incorporation of the Tyrol into Bavaria by Napoleon in 1805 precipitated a local uprising, led by Andreas HOFER, which was eventually put down by the French, but as the 'Tyrolean War of Liberation' (*Tiroler Befreiungskrieg*) became an important formative episode in modern Tyrolean history and identity. In 1809 the French divided the Tyrol between Bavaria, Italy and the Illyrian provinces, but the whole county became a part of the Austrian empire after the Wars of LIBERATION. After World War I the SOUTH TYROL was ceded to Italy by the treaty of ST GERMAIN, and the remainder of the Tyrol became a federal state of the Austrian Republic. After the *ANSCHLUSS* the Nazis incorporated the neighbouring province of Vorarlberg into the Tyrol as a district administered from Innsbruck, but the two were separated again after World War II. The Tyrol had almost 700,000 inhabitants at the end of 20th century. It is a rural province with a strong Catholic tradition, and its electoral allegiances have been staunchly conservative since the introduction of the universal suffrage.

U

U-Bahn (*Untergrundbahn*), underground railway.

U-boat (*Unterseeboot, U-Boot*), submarine. After unsuccessful attempts in America and Germany, and a successful attack by a semi-submersible vessel during the American Civil War, the first practical submarine was developed at the end of the 19th century by John Holland.

U-boats were used by Germany during World War I in an attempt to blockade the Entente powers, and then (from 1917) for unrestricted attacks on allied shipping. The development of sonar (sound navigation and ranging) in 1918 by the British and French to detect underwater objects seemed to suggest the end of the use of submarines in warfare, until imperfections in the system were revealed when British destroyers used sonar during the Spanish Civil War.

In World War II U-boats under the command of Admiral DÖNITZ played a significant part in the battle of the ATLANTIC during World War II. After the fall of France in 1940 British shipping was attacked in the Atlantic by both aircraft and surface vessels, but the disabling of a number of German ships and the sinking of the battleship *Bismarck* made submarine warfare a more promising option. Dönitz deployed U-boats in packs controlled by radio, and 1299 ships were lost in the twelve months from September 1941 (at a cost of only 51 submarines). Thereafter submarine warfare proved more difficult for the Germans, not least as a result of the development of radar, but the reluctance of the Americans to use convoys enabled the Germans to sink unprotected ships off the coast of the United States. The tide turned in 1943 with the introduction of escort aircraft carriers for the mid-Atlantic gap and improved communications technology (above all the cracking of the German ENIGMA codes by British intelligence). Increasingly from this point, submarine losses were disproportionately high relative to the losses imposed on Allied shipping, and Dönitz was forced to withdraw his U-boats from the North Atlantic. New developments in U-boat technology enabled the Germans to attempt a resumption of submarine attacks in the Atlantic in 1944, but the loss of French ports in the English Channel and on the Atlantic coast after the invasion of France meant that it was too late to affect the outcome of the war.

UFA (Universum Film AG), film production company founded on 18 December 1917 with a Reich subvention at the prompting of the army. It was formed by combining a number of smaller companies. UFA became a major film production company and was associated with some of the best-known performers, directors and films in Germany between the wars. The company was taken over by the HUGENBERG media group in 1927, and in 1937 the state became a majority shareholder, after which the company effectively came under the control of GOEBBELS' Reich ministry of popular enlightenment and propaganda. The organization was broken up at the end of World War II, and separate new companies founded in East and West Germany. In the German Democratic Republic the Deutsche Film AG (DEFA) occupied the company's premises in Potsdam-Babelsberg, while in the Federal Republic the Bavaria Filmkunst GmbH was set up in Munich, Ufa-Theater in Düsseldorf, and Universum-Film AG in Berlin. The latter was taken over by the Bertelsmann concern in 1964. In 1997 Bertelsmann merged its UFA film and television interests with Luxembourg television to form CLT-UFA.

Uhland, Ludwig (1787–1862), writer. Uhland was born in Tübingen, and was a lawyer in Stuttgart during the *VORMÄRZ* period (from 1814). He was a professor of literature at Tübingen university (1830–3) and a liberal member of the Württemberg diet (1833–8). He was a member of the FRANKFURT PARLIAMENT in 1848–9, and supported a 'greater German' resolution of the problem of national unification. His poetry was set to music by Brahms, Liszt, Schubert and Schumann. He also wrote works dealing with history and mythology, and published a monograph on the medieval poet Walther von der Vogelweide.

Ulbricht, Walter (1893–1973), Communist politician; leader of East Germany (1950–71). Born in Leipzig, the son of a tailor, Ulbricht joined the SPD in 1912, and then became a member of the SPARTACUS LEAGUE in 1918. He was a co-founder of the German Communist Party (KPD). He spent some time at the Lenin School in the USSR, and then as a Comintern agent in Prague and Vienna before his election to the Saxon LANDTAG in 1926. He was elected as a Reichstag deputy in 1928. He fled to the Soviet Union when the Nazis came to power in 1933, and commanded a Republican army unit in Spain between 1936 and 1938. He returned to Germany with the Red Army at the end of World War II and played an important part in the setting up of the Socialist Unity Party (*Sozialistische Einheitspartei Deutschlands*, SED), and took on the newly-created post of General Secretary in 1950. Although nominally only a deputy to the minister-president after the founding of the GERMAN DEMOCRATIC REPUBLIC in 1949, Ulbricht became the effective leader of East Germany. He reinforced his power in 1960, when he became chairman of the new STAATSRAT (state council). Under Ulbricht's leadership a Soviet-style planned economy was introduced. He survived the Berlin uprising of 1953 (*see* NEW COURSE), and was responsible for the building of the BERLIN WALL in 1961. Although he introduced some limited reforms to the economy during the 1960s, he was unable to change with the times. In particular he was wrong-footed by the successful *OSTPOLITIK* of West German chancellor Willy BRANDT, and attempted to sabotage the détente between the Soviet Union and the Federal Republic. As a result he lost the support of Moscow, and ultimately his position as first secretary of the party, which he was forced to cede to HONECKER in 1971. He remained president of the Staatsrat until his death, after an illness, in Berlin in 1973.

Ullstein Verlag, one of Germany's most distinguished publishing houses between the wars. It was founded in 1877 by Leopold Ullstein (1826–99) with the publication of *Die Deutsche Union*. It was associated with the metropolitan liberal press, and published both the *Berliner Zeitung* (from 1878) and the *Vossische Zeitung*. Ullstein also founded the *Berliner Abendpost* and the *Berliner Morgenpost* (1898). The firm took over the *Berliner Illustrirte Zeitung* in 1894, and Ullstein was the dominant force in the capital's press in late imperial and Weimar Germany. The press was taken over by the Nazis in 1934 and became part of the NSDAP-Verlag. After World War II the firm was absorbed into the publishing empire of the right-wing press baron Axel SPRINGER.

Ulm, battle of (1805). *See* COALITIONS, WARS OF THE.

Ultra, code name for the information obtained during World War II through the decryption at Bletchley Park in England of the German ENIGMA signals traffic.

Umschlagplatz, 'collection point', a square in the WARSAW GHETTO where Jews were rounded up for deportation to TREBLINKA.

Unabhängige Sozialdemokratische Partei Deutschlands (Independent Social Democratic Party of Germany). *See* USPD.

Unger, Georg Christian (1743–99), architect. Born in Bayreuth in Bavaria, Unger was a student of the baroque architect Karl von Gontard, and designed a number of important buildings in Berlin and Potsdam for FRIEDRICH II (Frederick the Great) of Prussia.

unification, in German history, term generally referring to the political unification of most of the states of the GERMAN CONFEDERATION, led by PRUSSIA under BISMARCK. The process began with the SCHLESWIG-HOLSTEIN crisis of the early 1860s, and continued during the AUSTRO-PRUSSIAN WAR (1866), which led to the effective expulsion of Austria from Germany. States north of the River Main were either annexed by or united with Prussia in a NORTH GERMAN CONFEDERATION. This in turn was replaced by the GERMAN EMPIRE, which was proclaimed at the end of the FRANCO-PRUSSIAN WAR (1870–1), and brought the remaining south German states within the new Germany.

This process resolved the problem of German national unity with a 'little German solution' (*kleindeutsche Lösung*) rather than a 'greater German solution' (*grossdeutsche Lösung*) to the question of German political unification, which had preoccupied politicians and German nationalists in all the German states for much of the 19th century. It left unresolved the position of the Austrian and Bohemian Germans in relation both to the new state and to their own. It was an issue that preoccupied German nationalists in Austria and Germany alike, and remained central to the concerns of the PAN-GERMAN movement. The issue resurfaced after World War I with the fragmentation of the HABSBURG empire and the pressure from both sides for the ANSCHLUSS of the 'rump' Austrian Republic with Germany.

Germany was united for a second time in 1990, after 45 years of division following defeat in World War II (*see* FEDERAL REPUBLIC OF GERMANY; GERMAN DEMOCRATIC REPUBLIC).

United Diet, Prussian assembly of 1847. Although many of the smaller German states had introduced constitutions either during the Napoleonic period or after the Congress of VIENNA, both Austria and Prussia – the two largest states in the GERMAN CONFEDERATION – strongly resisted constitutionalism, and both the HABSBURGS and the HOHENZOLLERNS continued to rule effectively as autocrats. In Prussia the assemblies of the states in the provinces were convened in 1841 and then met regularly, but no constitution was granted, nor was a diet called for the whole country until 1847. The diet's members, however, were not satisfied with the prospect of being called on an irregular basis as a consultative body, and asserted themselves by voting against the measures proposed by the government (which needed a loan). Instead the diet proposed to accuse the king of infringing the laws pertaining to the arrangements for assemblies, and to make a number of demands. In the event the draft address was toned down substantially.

Unity Congress. *See* SOCIALIST UNITY CONGRESS.

Unruh, Fritz von (1885–1970), EXPRESSIONIST writer. Born in Koblenz in the Rhineland into an old aristocratic family, Fritz von Unruh was an officer in Berlin before serving in World War I, which made him a convinced pacifist. With Carl von OSSIETZKY he was a co-founder in 1924 of the unsuccessful Republican Party. His plays provoked the hostility of the radical political right, and he left Germany for Italy (and then France and the United States) after a riot by Nazis during a performance in Frankfurt in 1932. He remained abroad after the war, but returned to Germany in 1962.

Untermensch, 'subhuman', a term used by the radical right in early 20th-century Germany and Austria, and popularized by the Nazis, to refer to those considered racially inferior.

Unzer, Johann Christoph (1747–1809), radical writer and journalist. Born in Wernigerode, the son of a doctor, Unzer studied medicine at Göttingen and then settled in Altona, where he was editor of the daily newspaper *Altonaer Mercurius*, and wrote plays for the radical Altona National Theatre. He was a leading figure in local revolutionary circles, and two volumes of his political writings appeared shortly after his death (1811).

Urania (Berlin), scientific society, named after the Greek muse of astronomy, and founded in 1888 by Werner von Siemens for the dissemination of scientific education. A similar organization of the same name existed in the German Democratic Republic from 1966. Since the reunification of Germany in 1990 the two traditions of scientific association have merged in a single associational network.

USCHLA (*Untersuchungs- und Schlichtungs-Ausschüsse*), Investigation and Arbitration Committees. These committees, introduced in 1926, functioned as internal party courts of the NSDAP, resolving differences between party members and keeping internal discipline.

USPD (*Unabhängige Sozialdemokratische Partei Deutschlands*), the Independent Social Democratic Party of Germany. The USPD was formed by a radical group of Social Democrats in April 1917, when they broke away from the SPD in frustration at the party's compromises and continuing support for the imperial government. The remainder of the party was referred to as the Majority SPD (or MSPD) for the duration of the split. The USPD began as a party of antiwar dissidents, but became a significant political party in its own right, and the most radical party on the political spectrum during the last months of imperial Germany and the first years of the Weimar Republic.

In November 1918, together with the MSPD, the USPD formed the COUNCIL OF PEOPLE'S REPRESENTATIVES, the first (provisional) government of the republic, although it left after a matter of weeks in frustration at the slow progress made towards the democratization of Germany. Although it won only 7.6% of the vote in the elections to the constituent NATIONAL ASSEMBLY in 1919, the USPD's share of the vote rose to 17.9% in the first elections to the new democratic Reichstag the following year, as working-class voters became increasingly disillusioned with the more moderate mainstream Social Democrats in the MSPD. The USPD itself broke apart in October 1920 when the majority of its members joined the KPD (the German Communist Party). Most of the remaining members returned to the SPD in 1922.

Usteri, Paul (1768–1831), Swiss politician. Born in Zurich into a well-to-do family, Usteri studied science and medicine at Zurich and Göttingen, taught natural history at the Zurich Institute and published several works on zoology. He supported revolutionary causes and publications in Switzerland and Germany during the 1790s, including *Klio* and *Beiträge zur Französischen Revolution*, which were published in Leipzig. He was a member of the Zurich Greater Council from 1797, where he recommended social reforms in order to avoid a French occupation. He was a co-founder of the *Schweizer Republikaner* with Hans Conrad Escher von der Linth (1767–1823), the president of the Great Council of the Helvetic Republic (1798–9), and was himself a senator of the Helvetic Republic. He conspired with others to depose the pro-French Frédéric-

César de la Harpe, and was a leading liberal figure in Swiss politics during the Revolutionary period, but retired from public life except for his journalism during the Napoleonic period. He was an important contributor to the *Zürcher Zeitung* (which was refounded as the *Neue Zürcher Zeitung* in 1821), and helped to establish the paper's international reputation. In 1830 Usteri headed a reform commission for Zurich, and was elected mayor the following year, but died almost immediately after taking office.

Utrecht, peace of, peace settlement, based on two treaties (1713 and 1715), which brought to an end the War of the Spanish Succession. Spain lost possessions in Italy and the Netherlands to Austria.

V

Vaterländische Front, the Fatherland Front, the 'mass' movement of AUSTROFASCISM, founded by Engelbert DOLLFUSS in 1933. It was the only political organization permitted in Austria between the promulgation of the fascist constitution of 1934 and its dissolution with the ANSCHLUSS of 1938. Its attempts to mobilize the unenthusiastic Austrian people in support of the dictatorship met with only limited success.

Vaterlandspartei, the Fatherland Party, a political party of the extreme right formed in 1917 to oppose the Reichstag PEACE RESOLUTION. It disbanded in December 1918. The *Vaterlandspartei* attracted members from among the conservatives and right-wing liberals of late imperial Germany, and drew support from the propertied middle classes. It was also supported by the Army High Command, and in particular by LUDENDORFF and HINDENBURG, albeit more covertly. By the summer of 1918 it had a million members, and after it disbanded itself in December 1918 many of them went on to join the fascist parties on the right-wing margins of Weimar politics before gravitating towards the NSDAP (the Nazi Party).

VDA (*Verein für das Deutschtum im Ausland*), the Association of Germans Abroad or 'Union of Germanism Abroad'. The VDA was founded in 1881 on the model of an Austrian predecessor of the previous year in order to provide suitable schooling for Germans where it was not provided by the local authorities. The association was discredited by its association with the Nazi regime, but was refounded in 1955.

VdU (*Verband der Unabhängigen*), the League of Independents, one of the so-called 'fourth parties' that grew up in occupied Austria after World War II as 'voter-soliciting groups' alongside the officially licensed Austrian People's Party (ÖVP), the Socialist Party (SPÖ) and the Communist Party (KPÖ). It openly campaigned for the votes of former Nazis, and eventually became the right-wing Freedom Party (*Freiheitliche Partei Österreichs*, FPÖ).

VEB (*volkseigener Betrieb*), the generic term for a state-owned enterprise in the GERMAN DEMOCRATIC REPUBLIC. About 80% of all East Germans worked in such enterprises at the time of the fall of the German Democratic Republic in 1989. Some 8000 such enterprises were privatized in 1990.

VEBA (*Vereinigte Elektrizitäts- und Bergwerks-AG*), an electricity and mining conglomerate, founded as a Prussian state enterprise in 1929. It was sold off in a series of privatizations in 1965 and during the 1980s. It was completely privatized by 1997, and shed some of its activities shortly afterwards. It merged with VIAG in June 2000.

Veesenmayer, Edmund (1904–77?), SS officer. An early member of the Nazi Party, Veesenmayer pursued a career in the SS and the German foreign service. He had business interests and diplomatic postings in the

Balkans, where he became involved in the deportation of local Jewish populations. He was appointed Reich plenipotentiary in Hungary in 1944, where he organized the deportation of Hungarian Jews. He was sentenced to 20 years at Nuremberg in 1949, but released after two years following US intervention on his behalf.

VEG (*Volkseigenes Gut*), a state-owned agricultural enterprise in the GERMAN DEMOCRATIC REPUBLIC.

Veidt, Konrad (or **Conrad**) **(Hans Walter)** (1893–1943), film actor. Veidt was born in Berlin and attended Max REINHARDT's stage school there from 1913. He made a successful career as a stage actor, and also appeared in films from 1916. His film career flourished following the revision of the imperial censorship laws after the end of World War I, and he is best known for the role of Cesare in *The Cabinet of Dr Caligari* (1919). He left Germany for Britain in 1932, continuing his career in films there and in Hollywood, where he moved in 1940 and died three years later.

VELKD (*Vereinigte Evangelisch-Lutherische Kirche Deutschlands*), the United Evangelical Lutheran Church of Germany. It was formed in 1948 from the union of nine regional Protestant churches. In 1968 the provincial Protestant churches of Saxony, Thuringia and Mecklenburg formed a separate East German organization, but rejoined the VELKD in 1992.

Verdun, battle of (February–September 1916), one of the major battles on the Western Front during WORLD WAR I. Verdun had been the object of a siege during the FRANCO-PRUSSIAN WAR, and was refortified as a critical point near to the German border. It was the objective of General FALKENHAYN to force France into a debilitating battle of attrition, in the hope that he could 'bleed the French army white' and perhaps inflict a victory that would seriously undermine French civilian morale.

The battle did indeed continue for some months, with losses of over 542,000 men on the French side, and almost as many (434,000) on the German side, but Falkenhayn had made a number of incorrect assumptions, and it quickly became clear that the offensive was proving to be counterproductive. The system of forts at Verdun was less vital to French strategy than he had thought, and he had not sufficiently considered the effects of attrition on his own men. Despite these mistakes Falkenhayn pressed on with the assault for reasons of prestige. In the end the French were relieved by the opening of the Russian Brusilov offensive on the Eastern Front, and by the opening of the British offensive on the SOMME. Falkenhayn was replaced by HINDENBURG in July, and the Germans went on to the defensive while the French managed to recapture lost ground. The French tactical victory made the reputations of Generals PÉTAIN and Nivelle, but damaged French morale as well as German.

Vergangenheitsbewältigung, 'mastering the past', a term used to denote postwar Germany's attempts to deal with the Nazi past. The formulation of the term implies an attempt to overcome and even suppress the difficulties arising from a compromised national history rather than come to terms with them. During the 1980s some Germans argued the necessity of constructing a history that present-day Germans could live with. Their critics charged them with trying to create a 'usable' past.

See also HISTORIKERSTREIT.

Vernichtungslager. See EXTERMINATION CAMPS.

Vernunftrepublikaner, 'pragmatic republican', a term applied to those who were instinctively opposed to the WEIMAR REPUBLIC politically, but either came to terms with its existence or chose to work with it for pragmatic reasons to further their own ends.

Verona, Congress of (1822), a meeting of Austria, France, Great Britain, Prussia and Russia to discuss the situation in Greece, where there had been an uprising against the Ottoman empire. In the event the agenda was taken over by developments in Spain, where the French wanted to overthrow the constitutional system established in 1820. The powers of the HOLY ALLIANCE effectively agreed to back France, but Great Britain now withdrew entirely from the CONGRESS SYSTEM, which effectively broke down, and Britain's representative, the Duke of Wellington, left the Congress before it concluded. METTERNICH and the other leaders of the Holy Alliance wrote to the Spanish government to convey their conclusions, and France invaded Spain and restored the king in 1823.

Versailles, treaty of (1919), peace settlement between Germany and the 'Allied and Associated Powers', signed on 28 June 1919 to come into effect on 10 January 1920. After several months of difficult negotiations the treaty was imposed on the German government, which was forced to accept it without alteration. It was subsequently demonized in Germany as the '*Diktat*' of Versailles, and provoked opposition not only on the political right, but in all political quarters and among all sections of the population.

Part I of the treaty incorporated the covenant of the LEAGUE OF NATIONS. Parts II and III dealt with the new frontiers of the German state, the future of the SAARLAND and arrangements for plebiscites in disputed territories. Germany was compelled to cede a substantial amount of territory – about one-tenth of its total area and population. In the west ALSACE-LORRAINE was returned to France, Eupen-Malmédy went to Belgium (confirmed by a plebiscite in 1920) and northern SCHLESWIG to Denmark (also confirmed by plebiscite in the same year). Germany was forbidden to maintain or construct any fortifications on the left (western) bank of the Rhine, or within a 50-km (30-mile) strip on the right bank. No armed forces were to enter this demilitarized zone, no military manoeuvres of any kind were to take place there, and the maintenance of

works essential to mobilization was forbidden. Germany was to accept an army of occupation on the left bank of the Rhine, and bridgeheads at Cologne, Koblenz and Mainz (*see* RHINELAND, DEMILITARIZATION OF THE). HELIGOLAND was also to be demilitarized. In compensation for the destruction of coal mines in northern France, Germany was forced to surrender the coal mines of the Saar basin, and compelled to abdicate the government of the Saarland. After 15 years a plebiscite was to be held to determine the future of the province. (It was duly held in 1935, and was a foreign policy triumph for the Nazi regime.)

In the east the province of Posen (Poznań) went to Poland, as did West PRUSSIA. Upper SILESIA also became part of Poland, and a plebiscite held in 1921 confirmed this. The city of DANZIG (Gdańsk) was placed under the control of the League of Nations. The loss of territory to Poland created the 'Polish Corridor', which gave the new state access to the sea and cut off East Prussia from the rest of Germany. The districts of Allenstein and Marienwerder were to be allocated according to a plebiscite. MEMEL, on the farthest northeastern border of the Reich, was placed under League of Nations control, and then transferred to Lithuania. Germany also accepted the abrogation of the treaty of BREST-LITOVSK. A further grievance was created by the prohibition of union (*ANSCHLUSS*) between Germany and 'rump AUSTRIA', the newly created, almost homogeneously German 'Alpine republic' that was left over after the dismemberment of the Habsburg empire.

Part IV of the treaty dealt with Germany's rights and interests abroad. Germany renounced all its overseas territories, and German colonies became mandated territories of the League of Nations. GERMAN EAST AFRICA was mandated to Britain, apart from Rwanda and Burundi, which went to Belgium; German SOUTH-WEST AFRICA (now Namibia) to South Africa; CAMEROON and TOGOLAND jointly to Britain and France;

Western Samoa to New Zealand; German New Guinea to Australia; and the Marshall Islands and Germany's Pacific Ocean island territories north of the equator to Japan. Germany also lost trading rights and concessions in China and the Middle East.

In addition all war material was to be surrendered, and imports of such material into Germany were banned. The general staff was to be dissolved and conscription done away with. The army was to be devoted exclusively to the maintenance of order within Germany and the defence of the state frontiers. The size of the German navy was to be reduced. The numbers of battleships and light cruisers were each limited to six, destroyers and torpedo boats to twelve, and submarines were banned. There was to be no German air force.

Part VI contained conditions relating to prisoners of war and war cemeteries, and Part VII contained conditions relating to war criminals and charges against Kaiser WIL-HELM II. Part VIII dealt with the question of REPARATIONS. Germany was compelled to accept responsibility for the war by article 231 (the 'WAR-GUILT CLAUSE'), and while the Allies accepted that Germany could not pay for the whole cost of the war, there were to be payments of reparations, to be determined by an inter-Allied Reparation Commission. For the time being (1919, 1920 and the first four months of 1921), and pending the outcome of the deliberations of the Reparation Commission, Germany was to pay the equivalent of 20 billion gold marks (either in gold or in kind).

The treaty of Versailles was a permanent thorn in the side of all the governments of the WEIMAR REPUBLIC. The parties of the right refused to take part in government rather than be a party to it, and the Weimar coalition that signed it did so only against its collective will and in order to prevent the international situation and the political condition of Germany deteriorating even further. The adoption of this 'Erfüllungspolitik'

(FULFILMENT POLICY) made the democratic parties an easy target for the populist right.

VIAG (*Vereinigte Industrie-Unternehmungen AG*, 'united industrial enterprises'), a utilities and industrial conglomerate founded by the German government in 1923 to manage its industrial holdings. It was partially privatized in 1986, and the remaining government shares were sold in 1988. It became increasingly involved in the telecommunications sector and merged with VEBA in 2000.

Vichy France, authoritarian German-controlled puppet state in unoccupied France during World War II. It comprised mainly south-central France, and its seat of government was in the small spa town of Vichy in the Auvergne. The French state governed from Vichy under the leadership of Marshal PÉTAIN was reformed along fascist lines: civil liberties were suppressed, political parties and trade unions banned, and government was by decree. Anti-Semitic legislation was passed very quickly (in October 1940), Jewish property was expropriated in 1941, and 350,000 French Jews were deported to the Reich and beyond between 1942 and 1944. The Germans demanded heavy reparations payments, charged burdensome occupation costs, and undertook widespread requisitioning. In addition the Germans drafted French workers for forced labour in the Reich. The so-called 'free zone' under the Vichy government was occupied by the Germans in November 1942 immediately after the Allied landings in North Africa.

Vienna, Congress of (1814–15), international conference at which the peace settlement concluding the Napoleonic Wars was arranged. The leading figures were Prince METTERNICH, the Austrian foreign minister; Alexander I of Russia; FRIEDRICH WILHELM III of Prussia; Talleyrand, the French representative; and Castlereagh and Wellington representing Britain. Although France attended the Congress, whose first session was held in the Austrian capital between October and June

1814, only the victorious powers, Great Britain, Russia, Austria and Prussia had any real say in the provisions of the peace.

The powers initially concluded a relatively mild peace settlement (the first treaty of PARIS, 30 May 1814), but after Napoleon's return from Elba and the battle of WATER-LOO, the Congress reconvened and a harsher peace was concluded (the second treaty of PARIS, 20 November 1815). There was, however, no attempt to restore the HOLY ROMAN EMPIRE and the multiplicity of German states abolished by Napoleon. Instead, the GERMAN CONFEDERATION was established under the leadership of Austria and Prince Metternich. Austria gave up the Austrian Netherlands (modern Belgium), which were absorbed with the former Dutch Republic into the United Kingdom of the Netherlands. Austria also lost its possessions in southwestern Germany. In exchange Austria expanded in Italy, acquiring Lombardy and Venetia, and also acquired the Dalmatian coast. Modena, Parma and Tuscany also came under Austrian rule. From the perspective of London, Austria's role was to stabilize central Europe and to protect it from the possibility of incursions from either France or Russia. To this end Britain (and France) successfully supported Austria's objections to Russia acquiring the whole of Poland, and to Prussia acquiring the whole of Saxony. Prussia nevertheless gained two-fifths of Saxony, part of Pomerania, Posen (Poznań) province, Westphalia and the Rhineland.

The Congress established the so-called 'CONGRESS SYSTEM' of collaboration between the victorious powers, intended to police Europe and to keep it free of revolution. The Congress also produced the HOLY ALLIANCE between Russia, Austria and Prussia (26 September 1815), whose pious aim was to reinforce Christian ethics in government, and solidarity between Christian governments in international affairs. The QUADRUPLE ALLIANCE (which also included Britain) was concluded on the same day as the second treaty of Paris, with the purpose of providing the diplomatic means necessary for the enforcement of the treaty and the maintenance of the peace. This alliance also provided for further regular meetings of the Congress.

Vienna awards (2 November 1938 and 30 August 1940), a term used to describe the territorial revisions imposed on eastern Europe by Nazi Germany. The first Vienna award transferred the Feldvidek region from Slovakia to Hungary after the Nazi occupation of Bohemia and Moravia. The second Vienna award transferred the greater part of TRANSYLVANIA (Siebenbürgen) from Romania to Hungary, thereby reversing in part the work of the Allies at the end of World War I.

Vimy Ridge, battles of (1916), series of engagements on the Western Front during WORLD WAR I. The Germans captured the Vimy Ridge escarpment near Arras in August 1914, and the French fought to win it back in battles in May, June and September 1915. The ridge was won back in a Canadian offensive of April 1917 and remained in Allied hands for the rest of the war.

Virchow, Rudolf (1821–1902), doctor, anthropologist and liberal politician. Virchow was born in Schievelbein, Pomerania (now Swidwin in Poland), the son of a master butcher. His medical studies were sponsored by the army, and when he graduated he was appointed to a position in the Military Medical Academy in Berlin. During the REVOLUTIONS OF 1848 he was politically active as a democrat, and took part in the Democratic Congress in Berlin. As a consequence he lost his position as a pathologist at the Academy. He was appointed to a chair at Würzburg in 1849, but only on the understanding that he would refrain from radical political activity. In 1856 he was appointed to a new chair at Berlin. In 1859 he was elected to the Berlin city council, and argued there for the building of hospitals and for the collection of medical statistics. In 1861 he was a co-founder of the *DEUTSCHE FORTSCHRITTSPARTEI* (the Progess Party) and represented it in the Prussian house of representatives (*ABGEORD-NETENHAUS*) from 1862 to 1867, using his position to promote the installation of a water supply and sewage system in Berlin. From 1880 to 1884 he sat in the Reichstag for the *Fortschrittspartei*, and from 1884 to 1893 for the liberal *DEUTSCHE FREISINNIGE PARTEI*. In 1866 he founded the *Zeitschrift für Ethnologie* ('journal of ethnology'), and in the late 1880s was involved in the establishment of an ethnological museum in Berlin.

Vlasov Army, a force made up of Soviet prisoners of war, which was formed by Nazi Germany and fought against the USSR on the Eastern Front in the spring of 1945. It took its name from a captured Soviet general, Andrei Vlasov, who was persuaded by the Germans to incite members of the Soviet armed forces to desert. He was handed over to the Soviet authorities and executed in 1946.

V-Mann (*Vertrauensmann*), informer or intelligence agent.

Vögler, Albert (1877–1945), industrialist and conservative politician. Born in Borbeck near Essen, Vögler studied engineering at a technical university. He was a protégé of Hugo STINNES, who appointed him director of a mining and steel company in 1915. Vögler was one of the founders of the conservative, business-orientated German People's Party (DVP) after World War I. He was elected to the 1919 NATIONAL ASSEMBLY, and sat in the Reichstag until 1924. He was on the right of the party, opposed to the government's 'FULFILMENT POLICY', and in favour of collaboration with the German nationalist DNVP. He was also an anti-union employer, and was a co-founder of the *Deutsches Institut für technische Arbeitsschulung* ('Dinta', 'German institute of technical training). Vögler was involved in negotiations with the French over the end of the occupation of the RUHR VALLEY in 1923. He was general director of Vereinigte Stahlwerke (United Steelworks),

which was founded in Düsseldorf in 1926 through the merger of seven companies (including THYSSEN). The company became the largest concern of its kind in Europe until it was broken up after the end of World War II. Although Vögler never joined the NSDAP, he supported the participation of the Nazis in government after the resignation of BRÜNING, and was appointed plenipotentiary for munitions production in the Ruhr by SPEER. He committed suicide in April 1945 when threatened with arrest by Allied soldiers.

Völckers, Hans Hermann (1886–1977), diplomat. Völckers was embassy counsellor in Madrid (1933–7) before and during the Spanish Civil War, then ambassador to Cuba (1937–9). From 1940 he was head of the Reich protector's office in Prague.

Volhynia, a province of Ukraine with a substantial ethnic German minority. From 1915 some 200,000 Volhynian Germans were forcibly resettled in Siberia. About 100,000 returned and many of these were resettled in Germany and Nazi-occupied Poland during World War II. Most of the Jewish population was murdered during the German occupation of Ukraine (1941–4).

Volk, literally 'people', a term that also acquired the meaning of 'nation' or 'race'.

völkisch, term used to describe the racist nationalist movements of German-speaking Europe and their ideology. The radical right in German-speaking Europe was for many years prior to World War I organizationally fragmented, but shared common assumptions and demands. Among these was a militant xenophobic nationalism related to a new kind of 'scientific' racism, which claimed be founded on ethnological principles and scholarship.

A racial hierarchy was assumed, at the top of which were 'ARYANS', an imprecisely defined term (borrowed from linguistics), which when used broadly referred to the 'white races', and more specifically meant non-Jews. Within the 'Aryan' category finer distinctions were made between Germanic or Nordic peoples and the rest. These were based on superficial characteristics such as hair, eye colour, the shape of the head and height, which popular ideologues then attributed to 'nations', despite the overwhelming empirical evidence that there was no such relationship. Despite the range of strengths attributed to 'Aryans' and the weaknesses attached to 'inferior' races (*UNTERMENSCHEN*), the former were perceived to be threatened by the latter in a number of ways (economic, political and even sexual), reflecting popular anxieties at a time of social upheaval and change. *Völkisch* racism was most virulent when it was directed against the Jews, but other racial minorities, particularly Slavs and Gypsies (ROMA AND SINTI), were also targets.

The appeal of *völkisch* ideology in the late nineteenth and early twentieth centuries was strongest in situations where German identity was less self-assured, in the border regions of Austria (such as the SUDETENLAND, Styria and CARINTHIA), in northeastern Germany and SCHLESWIG-HOLSTEIN, and in cities or regions with large numbers of exotic immigrants, such as Vienna. In Austria and Bohemia the insecurities of German nationalists were compounded by the exclusion of Austrian Germans from the Reich.

Ideological assumptions about the *Volk* and racial purity were also nostalgic, and there was a general antipathy to modern industrial society in all its manifestations, whether political (liberalism, parliamentary democracy, Marxism and the labour movement), economic (whether big business or workers' cooperatives), social (urbanization, women's emancipation, ethnic diversity) or cultural (the 'degeneracy' of modern art and 'falling standards' encouraged by popular culture). The response of the radical right – couched in the 'organic' and even medicinal figures of speech that were currently modish – was to call for the purging of society of all its 'unhealthy' elements, the

rejuvenation of the nation, the restoration of 'traditional values', and ultimately the re-establishment of a stable and 'organic' rural society that approximated to the communities of a mythical Germanic past.

Elements of this arguably 'proto-fascist' ideology came from many quarters, ranging from the pamphleteering of university-educated academics, schoolteachers and journalists to the anti-Semitic pornography of street pedlars. In organizational terms the movement embraced hundreds of tiny ephemeral groups, but many of those active in the *völkisch* movement eventually came together in the *VATERLANDSPARTEI* at the end of World War I, afterwards in the DNVP, and ultimately in the NSDAP – the Nazi Party.

Völkischer Beobachter, Nazi newspaper from 1920 to 1945.

Volksdeutsche, German minorities abroad. During World War II the Reich insisted that ethnic Germans in its satellite states be allowed a separate corporate existence with their own local government. Several separate agreements were signed in 1940 between Germany and states with substantial German minorities in southeastern Europe.

volkseigen, a term originally proposed by linguistic purists of the 19th century as an alternative to the Latinate 'national'. It was also defined in a dictionary of 1885 as 'belonging to the country or state'. The Nazis adopted the first meaning, and used it loosely (though not prominently) as a synonym for 'national'. In the GERMAN DEMOCRATIC REPUBLIC on the other hand it was used to describe state-owned or nationalized property or enterprises (*see* VEB).

Volksgemeinschaft ('national community'), Nazi term for a harmonious society transcending class conflict and founded on racial exclusivity.

Volksgenossen ('national comrades'), a term used to describe members of the *VOLKSGE-MEINSCHAFT*. It was intended to convey the sense of belonging to the race or nation, as opposed to citizenship in a formal constitutional sense. The word had been used occasionally in the late 18th and 19th centuries, among others by HERDER, JAHN and LAGARDE. In the 20th century it was used as a synonym for 'compatriot', and also acquired the racist sense that became its predominant usage under the Nazis, who distinguished between 'racial comradeship' and mere 'citizenship'.

Volksgerichtshof, 'people's court', a special court set up in Berlin by the Nazis in 1934, initially to deal mainly with cases of treason. It came to deal with a range of activities that were criminalized by the regime. Under the presidency of Roland FREISLER (from 1942) it became an institution for the suppression of political opposition. Between 1937 and 1944 it passed some 5000 death sentences, including those passed on the conspirators involved in the JULY BOMB PLOT of 1944. The court's sentences were not recognized as invalid until 1985.

Volkskammer (people's chamber), parliament of the GERMAN DEMOCRATIC REPUBLIC. According to the East German constitution it was the highest representative organ of the republic, but its members were elected by means of a so-called unity list (*Einheitsliste*), a single list of candidates which also included members of the Liberal Democratic Party (LDPD) and (East German) CDU, but effectively ensured a working absolute majority in the chamber for the ruling SED.

Volkspolizei, the police force of the GERMAN DEMOCRATIC REPUBLIC, popularly known as the *Vopo*. It was established on 1 June 1945, and encompassed the uniformed and criminal police.

Volkssturm, militia of all able-bodied German males between the ages of 16 and 60, formed in September 1944 and deployed, without training or adequate arms, against the invading Allied armies.

Volkswagen, 'people's car'. The Volkswagen was to be a mass produced people's car for the citizens of the Third Reich. The project was initiated by the German Labour Front (DAF) in 1937, and the car was originally called the KdF-Wagen after the leisure section of the DAF (*Kraft durch Freude*, STRENGTH THROUGH JOY). A new town was founded in 1938 and Ferdinand PORSCHE was appointed director of the project. In practice the new factory produced vehicles for the war rather than mass consumption, and increasingly depended on foreign slave labour. The famous Volkswagen beetle (*Käfer*) was mass-produced only after the war, and came to be a symbol of Germany's economic recovery.

vollgenossenschaftlich, 'fully collective', a term used in the GERMAN DEMOCRATIC REPUBLIC to describe the nature of social and economic relations in a community that had undergone collectivization, or where all the population worked for an agricultural collective. It was perceived by West German propagandists as an evasion of the term 'socialist'.

Vollzugsrat, 'executive council', a committee of 28 members, elected by the Berlin workers' and soldiers' councils (*RÄTE*) during the NOVEMBER REVOLUTION of 1918. On 9 November 1918, Berlin workers' and soldiers' councils convened in the Reichstag and agreed that delegates should meet the next day at the Busch Circus. Here left-wing radicals among the delegates demanded a more revolutionary political structure than the coalition cabinet of Majority Social Democrats (MSPD) and Independent Social Democrats (USPD) that Friedrich EBERT reported had been agreed. After some heated discussion the meeting eventually agreed that workers' and soldiers' councils in Berlin should elect an executive committee of 28 (later 40) members. This committee asserted its leadership of the German councils' movement. The powers of the *Vollzugsrat*, as distinct from those of Ebert's cabinet, were never clearly enough defined and there was some tension between the two.

Vopo. See *VOLKSPOLIZEI*.

Vorarlberg, westernmost federal province (*Land*) of the Austrian Republic. It was separated from the TYROL in 1918, and some

80% of its inhabitants voted in a plebiscite to secede to Switzerland the following year. It nevertheless became a constituent federal state of the new Austrian Republic. After the ANSCHLUSS it was reduced to an administrative district governed from the Tyrolean capital Innsbruck, but was restored as a separate state in 1945. It has around 350,000 inhabitants, and the provincial capital is Bregenz.

Vormärz (literally 'pre-March'), term used to designate the period between the Congress of VIENNA (1814–15) and the March REVOLUTIONS OF 1848. It is generally thought of as a politically uneventful period of authoritarian conservatism.

Vorparlament. *See* PRE-PARLIAMENT.

Vorpommern ('hither Pomerania'), the western part of the old German province of POMERANIA, now part of the federal state of MECKLENBURG-Vorpommern. Hinterpommern (eastern Pomerania) became part of Poland after World War II.

Vosberg, Fritz (1872–1957), general secretary of the *OSTMARKENVEREIN* (Eastern Marches Association), a radical right-wing pressure group in imperial Germany.

Voss, Johann Heinrich (1751–1826), writer. Voss was a member of the Göttinger Hain, a group of Romantic writers associated with Göttingen University (the word *Hain* – grove – reflects the Romantic preoccupation with nature). Voss was also editor of the literary journal *Göttinger Musenalmanach*.

Vossische Zeitung, Berlin newspaper. The paper was originally founded in 1617 as *Berlinische Priviligierte Zeitung*. It derived its subsequent name from the publisher Christian Friedrich Voss (1724–95), who acquired it in 1751. Both LESSING and FONTANE were among its contributors. It was shut down by the Nazis in 1934.

V-weapons (*Vergeltungswaffen*), 'revenge weapons', secret weapons developed and deployed by the Nazis partly in retaliation for the Allied bombing of German cities during WORLD WAR II. The V-1, or 'flying bomb', was an unmanned aircraft that could carry an explosive warhead up to 240 km (150 miles) at a speed of up to almost 640 km (400 miles) per hour. Over 30,000 V-1s were produced and some 20,000 were fired from June 1944, 13,000 of them against Britain after (and ostensibly as revenge for) the D-Day landings in June of that year. Over half of these were shot down by British fighter planes or anti-aircraft guns, and the majority of the launch sites were in any case overrun by the end of the year. The V-2 (or A4, officially) rocket was a much more sophisticated weapon. Developed by Wernher von BRAUN at Peenemünde, it was first tested successfully in October 1942, and was used against Britain, Belgium and France from September 1944. The V-2 carried a 1-ton warhead, and flew at altitudes up to 80 km (50 miles). There was little defence against them, and some 5000 were launched, although many of these suffered mechanical problems or exploded deep underground. There was also the V-3 long-range gun. Von Braun and many of the other German rocket engineers were subsequently employed either by the United States or the Soviet Union on the development of intercontinental and medium-range missiles during the Cold War.

W

Waffen-SS, armed SS. There had been armed formations in the SS since the 1930s – the so-called *Verfügungstruppe*, troops to be deployed according to necessity. The term Waffen-SS was introduced in 1940 to designate militarized SS units during the war. The Waffen-SS effectively constituted a separate independent armed force during World War II. Waffen-SS troops were also recruited abroad, from France, the Low Countries, Scandinavia, the Baltic states, Hungary, Romania and Spain, and were supposedly selected according to criteria of racial purity. Some of the 40 Waffen-SS units deployed during World War II were self-consciously elite formations, and many units were involved in atrocities.

Wagner, Adolf (1890–1944), Nazi politician. Born in Lorraine, Wagner was an officer in World War I and joined the NSDAP in 1923. He was elected to the Bavarian LANDTAG in 1929 and was appointed *Gauleiter* of Munich-Upper Bavaria in the same year. He went on to become Bavarian interior minister from 1933, Bavarian education minister from 1936 and defence commissioner of Districts VII and XIII (Munich and Nuremberg) in 1939. He lost influence after the outbreak of war.

Wagner, Cosima (1837–1930), the daughter of Franz Liszt and wife of Richard WAGNER. After the death of her husband she took over the direction of the Bayreuth festivals until 1906 when the job passed to their son Siegfried WAGNER.

Wagner, Gerhard (1888–1938), Nazi functionary. A former FREIKORPS member, Wagner was head of the Nazi Doctors' League from 1932, and was elected to the Reichstag in the 1933 election. Wagner was an early supporter of euthanasia for the disabled.

Wagner, Richard (1813–83), Romantic composer. Wagner was born in Leipzig, the youngest of nine children, and studied music there. He married the actress Minna Planer in 1836. In order to escape creditors they moved to Paris (1839–42). Following the premiere of *Rienzi* (20 October 1842) in Dresden Wagner was appointed *Hofkapellmeister* in Saxony and during the 1840s he wrote his first three mature operas. In 1841 he completed *Der fliegende Holländer* (The Flying Dutchman); *Tannhäuser* followed in 1845 and in 1847 he completed *Lohengrin*, which had its premiere in 1850. In 1849 he fought on the side of the insurgents in the May uprising (*see* REVOLUTIONS OF 1848), and had to flee to Switzerland. He lived in Zurich until 1858, and then travelled, staying in Venice, Lucerne, Vienna and Berlin. After a short spell in Bavaria, where LUDWIG II paid off his debts, Wagner moved again to Switzerland, and from 1866 to 1872 lived in Tribschen near Lucerne. He completed *Die Meistersänger von Nürnberg* (The Master Singers of Nuremberg) in 1867, and married Liszt's daughter Cosima in 1870, returning to Bavaria in 1872. Wagner's major work was the 'Ring cycle', a series of operas written over three decades. *Das Rheingold* was completed in 1854; *Die Walküre* in 1856; *Siegfried* in 1871 and *Götterdämmerung (Twilight of the Gods)* in 1874. In Bayreuth he built the Festspielhaus, an opera house dedicated to the performance of his own works, where the complete Ring cycle was performed in 1876. The annual Bayreuth festivals were directed after Wagner's death by his wife Cosima and subsequently by their son Siegfried WAGNER. Wagner's last opera, *Parsifal*, was completed in 1882. In addition to his operas he wrote a number of works for orchestra and published essays on aesthetics. In 1882 he travelled to Venice, and died there the following year.

Wagner is remembered as an innovative composer, whose proposal for a fusion of drama and music in the *Gesamtkunstwerk* (total work of art) was his major contribution to musical theory. His political views, and particularly the outspoken anti-Semitism in a number of his essays, have made him a controversial figure in German cultural history.

Wagner, Robert (1895–1946), Nazi politician. Wagner served in World War I and participated in the 1923 BEER HALL PUTSCH while still a Reichswehr officer. He was *Gauleiter* of Baden from 1925, and a member of the Baden LANDTAG from 1929 to 1933, when he became Reich governor of Baden. He acquired responsibility for Alsace after the fall of France, initially as chief of the civil administration. He was tried by the French and executed in Strasbourg in 1946.

Wagner, Siegfried (1869–1930), composer and conductor. Siegfried Wagner, who was born in Tribschen (now part of Lucerne), was the son of the composer Richard WAGNER. Although he was undecided whether to pursue a career in music or architecture, Wagner studied composition with Humperdinck and composed his own works. He conducted at the Bayreuth festivals from 1894, and in 1906 took over the management of the festivals from his mother Cosima Wagner. In 1915 he married Winifred Williams,

the adopted daughter of the Wagner enthusiast Karl Klindworth. When the festivals were relaunched after World War I (1924), visits to Bayreuth became a form of pilgrimage for the radical German nationalist right. Hitler visited the festival for the first time in 1925. Wagner persuaded Hitler to stay away from the festival for political reasons, and it was not until after Wagner's death that he visited again. Winifred took over the direction of the festival after her husband's death, and was much closer to the Nazis. After World War II their sons Wieland and Wolfgang took over the management of the festival, and purged it of its Nazi associations.

Wagram, battle of (5–6 July 1809), Napoleon's revenge for his first defeat in battle at ASPERN in May, during the Wars of the COALITIONS. The battle was fought around the village of Wagram, near the Danube north of Vienna. It was the largest artillery battle yet fought, and Napoleon commanded 154,000 troops against 158,000 Austrians led by Archduke Karl, with the expectation of reinforcements on the Austrian side. Casualties were proportionately great: 42,000 on the Austrian side, compared with 37,500 on the French side. Archduke Karl signed an armistice on 12 July at Znaim.

Walde, Werner (1926–), East German politician. Walde served an apprenticeship as an administrative clerk during World War II (1940–3) and joined the Socialist Unity Party (*Sozialistische Einheitspartei*, SED) in the Soviet zone of occupation in 1946. He pursued a career within the SED in the Cottbus district, and was a candidate for Politburo membership when the GERMAN DEMOCRATIC REPUBLIC collapsed in 1989.

Walden, Herwarth (1878–1941), journalist and patron of the arts. Born in Berlin, the son of a doctor, Walden studied at Florence and at the Berlin Conservatory. He founded the *Verein für Kunst* ('association for the arts') in Berlin in 1904, where readings were organized featuring a number of well-known contemporary writers, including the poet Rainer Maria Rilke (1875–1926) and Heinrich and Thomas MANN. Walden edited a number of cultural journals before founding *Der Sturm*, the 'house journal' of German EXPRESSIONISM in 1910. He was editor until 1932. During the 1920s he became a Communist, and emigrated to the Soviet Union in 1932. He was arrested there in 1941, and was reported to have died in prison.

Waldheim, Kurt (1918–), president of Austria (1986–92). Waldheim attracted controversy as a result of his military and political career during the German occupation of Austria. He served a year's military service in the Austrian army before the ANSCHLUSS, and then enrolled as a law student at Vienna University. He took part in the German occupation of the SUDETENLAND in the autumn of 1938, and during World War II served in France and on the Eastern Front before being posted to Belgrade as an interpreter. At the time of his election to the Austrian presidency he denied that he had joined the National Socialist Student League during the 1930s or that he had become a member of the *SS-Reitersturm* in 1938. His own statements about his second period of service in the Balkans (from March 1943) were inconsistent. DENAZIFICATION proceedings were opened against him after the end of the war but, as in many cases, were never concluded, and did not impede his postwar career. He was foreign minister of Austria from 1968 to 1970, and general secretary of the United Nations from 1972 to 1981. Charges of dishonesty about his past did not prevent him being successfully elected in 1986 to the presidency with the support of Austria's principal conservative party, the ÖVP (Austrian People's Party).

Walter, Bruno (1876–1962), conductor. Walter was born in Berlin and met Gustav MAHLER in Hamburg in 1894. After visiting Pressburg (now Bratislava), Riga and Berlin, he returned to the court opera in Vienna with Mahler and became one of the most important interpreters of the composer's work. Walter supervised the first performances of the Ninth Symphony and *Das Lied von der Erde* after the composer's death. In 1912 he moved to Munich. In 1918 the first Bruno Walter concerts were held in Berlin, and in 1925 he took over as director of the *Städtische Oper* there. In 1933 he was dismissed from all his posts, and left Germany for Austria, and then in 1938 for France. He eventually settled in the United States, and died in California.

Wannsee Conference (20 January 1942), conference held at a lake near Berlin to discuss and coordinate the 'final solution' (*see* HOLOCAUST). It was attended by many high-ranking Nazis, including Reinhard HEYDRICH and Adolf EICHMANN.

Warburg, Max (1867–1946), banker. Warburg was born into a Jewish banking family in Hamburg. He was an adviser to Prince Max von BADEN, and was involved in the VERSAILLES peace negotiations. He was reluctant to enter politics himself but was an adviser to WIRTH and to RATHENAU. His international connections, particularly in America, were especially useful to Germany during the world economic crisis of the early 1930s. During the 1930s Warburg concentrated his efforts on his work for the Palästina-Treuhand GmbH, which helped Jews emigrate to Palestine. He himself fled to New York in 1938.

war-guilt clause, article 231 of the treaty of VERSAILLES. It stipulated that Germany and its allies accept responsibility for WORLD WAR I, 'for causing all the loss and damage to which the Allied and Associated Governments and their nationals have been subjected as a consequence of the war imposed upon them by the aggression of Germany and her allies'. Article 227 picked out Kaiser WILHELM II himself for particular blame: 'The Allied and Associated Powers publicly arraign William II of Hohenzollern, formerly German Emperor, for a supreme offence against international morality and the sanctity of treaties'. The 'war-guilt clause' was repudiated by German public opinion, and with particular vehemence by the political right. Following the publication of Russia's secret treaties the German government published 39 volumes of diplomatic documents during the 1920s (*Die Grosse Politik der Europäischen Kabinette*) in order show that the diplomacy of secret treaties had involved all European governments. When the question of war guilt was revived after World War II it remained an article of faith among conservative historians in Germany that the Reich was no more to blame for the outbreak of World War I than the other belligerents, and it was only with the FISCHER CONTROVERSY, and the assertion that Germany had deliberately gone to war in 1914 in order to annex territory, that the far-reaching consensus among German historians was disturbed.

Warnke, Herbert (1902–75), Communist activist and politician. Warnke was involved in trade-union politics during the Weimar Republic and was briefly a member of the Reichstag (1932–3) before joining the KPD underground resistance (1933–6). He fled to Denmark, and then to Sweden, where he was interned. After the end of World War II he occupied a number of posts in the trade-union movement in the Soviet zone of occupation and became chairman of the FDGB in 1948. In 1950 he became a member of the Central Committee (ZK) of the Socialist Unity Party (*Sozialistische Einheitspartei*, SED). From 1953 he was a candidate for the Politburo, and from 1958 he was a full member.

Warsaw, battles of (1914–15, 1939, 1944), three battles to capture the Polish city during World War I and World War II. The first battle of Warsaw, during World War I, followed the German victory at TANNENBERG (August 1914), when HINDENBURG advanced on Warsaw with a view to relieving the Austro-Hungarian army, which had been defeated in Galicia. The advance was repulsed by the Russians. The Germans were thrown back

again in November, but the city was forced to capitulate when the Russians withdrew all along the Eastern Front in 1915. The battles of Warsaw in World War II were far more brutal. The city was bombed and attacked by German artillery in September 1939, and resisted for three weeks. In 1944 the Polish 'Home Army' rose against the Germans but they were heavily defeated when the Soviets, who were camped near the city, failed to intervene. The city was destroyed and around 100,000 Poles were killed.

Warsaw ghetto, a Jewish GHETTO created in the former Polish capital by the Nazis in November 1940. Half a million people were confined within it, and thousands died from overcrowding, starvation and forced labour. The systematic deportation of Jews from the ghetto to the Nazis' EXTERMINATION CAMPS began in July 1942, and it is estimated that only 70,000 remained by October of that year. When the SS and army under Jürgen STROOP attempted to demolish the ghetto and deport the last remaining inhabitants to TREBLINKA, there was a revolt of the surviving inhabitants, led by Mordecai ANIELEWICZ. The revolt, which broke out on 19 April 1943, was finally ended on 16 May. The poorly armed resisters fought for every inch of ground, and it is estimated that only 100 Jews survived the revolt. The uprising was one of a number of acts of collective resistance by Jews in ghettos and extermination camps.

Warsaw Pact, the military and political alliance that bound together the Soviet Union and its satellite states in the Eastern Bloc. It was signed on 14 May 1955, and was prompted by Soviet concern at the entry of the Federal Republic into NATO. The GERMAN DEMOCRATIC REPUBLIC was a founding member, but left in 1990, and the following year the remaining members dissolved the organization.

Wartburg rally, a gathering of nationalist students in 1817. The meeting was called by students from Jena University, and its ostensible purpose was to celebrate the 300th anniversary of the Reformation and to commemorate the anniversary of the battle of LEIPZIG. Nationalist speeches were made, but books were also burned, including a copy of the Napoleonic Code. The rally is seen as one of the most significant events in the early history of German nationalism.

Wartheland (also called Warthegau), part of Poland incorporated directly into the Reich after the defeat of Poland in 1939. It was constituted as a *Reichsgau* by a decree of Hitler and comprised the districts Posen, Hohensalza and Litzmannstadt (Łódź in Poland). It was originally called Reichsgau Posen and was renamed Warthegau on 29 January 1940. It had a population of 4.2 million, 85% of whom were Poles (3.96 million), 7% Germans (327,000) and 8% Jews (366,000). The Warthegau was the site of extensive Nazi racial 'resettlement' policy involving an attempt to move out as many Poles as possible and replace them with Germans.

Wassilko, Nikolaj, Ritter von (1868–1924), Austro-Ukrainian politician. Wassilko was born in Czernowitz in the Bukovina, and was a member of both the REICHSRAT and the provincial diet. He was chairman of the Ukrainian group in the Bukovina diet and vice president of the Ukrainian national assembly. He played an important role in the peace talks and treaty of BREST-LITOVSK (1918) between Germany and Russia.

Waterloo, battle of (18 June 1815), the final battle of the Wars of LIBERATION at the end of the Napoleonic Wars, fought near the village of Waterloo in Belgium, just south of Brussels. The 72,000 French troops faced a slightly smaller allied army of 68,000 men under the Duke of Wellington and 45,000 Prussian troops commanded by BLÜCHER. Prior to the main engagement Blücher had been beaten on 16 June at Ligny, and Wellington held at Quatre Bras, but neither army was completely defeated. Blücher's army escaped pursuit by Marshal de Grouchy,

and managed to rejoin the main battle of Waterloo, where his intervention was decisive in the outcome of the battle. Blücher lost about 8000 men and Wellington almost twice as many in the battle, but the French losses were greater: 25,000 were killed or wounded, and 9000 more taken prisoner. The battle of Waterloo marked the final defeat of Napoleon.

Weber, Alfred (1868–1958), economist. Weber was born in Erfurt, the younger brother of Max WEBER, and grew up in an educated middle-class family with NATIONAL LIBERAL political affiliations. He was professor at Prague from 1904, and from 1907 to 1933 at Heidelberg. His work was concerned with the social and economic history of industrialization, and in particular with the geographic location of industrial activity. Along the lines of the early 19th-century work of Johann Friedrich von Thünen on the location of agricultural activity, he developed a theory of industrial location, which was set out in his *Über den Standort der Industrien* ('on the location of industries', 1909). After World War I Weber was a co-founder of the liberal DDP and concentrated increasingly on the contemporary problems facing Germany and Europe. He retired in 1933.

Weber, Carl Maria von (1786–1826), composer. Born in Eutin, Weber studied music at Salzburg and Vienna, and became opera conductor in Breslau (now Wrocław in Poland) in 1804. In 1813 he moved to Prague as opera *Kapellmeister* and in 1817 he went to Dresden at the invitation of the king of Saxony to direct the newly founded *Deutsche Oper* (German Opera). He was one of the most important of German Romantic composers, and his best-known works, *Der Freischütz* ('the marksman', 1821), *Euryanthe* (1823) and *Oberon* (1826), reflect the themes of the Romantic era, from popular national sentiment and folklore to the celebration of nature.

Weber, Helene (1881–1962), conservative politician. Weber was born in Elberfeld in

1881 and trained as a teacher. She taught in a primary school in Aachen until 1905, and then moved to university posts first at Bonn and then at Cologne. In 1916 she took over as director of the *Soziale Frauenschule* of the *Katholischer Deutscher Frauendbund* (German Catholic Women's League). After World War I she moved to Berlin to a post in the welfare ministry, remained active in the Catholic Women's League, and became politically engaged in the CENTRE PARTY. Weber was a specialist in women's education, youth welfare and family law. She was a firm opponent of any relaxation to the abortion laws. Weber was dismissed from all her posts when the Nazis came to power. Although she was against the ENABLING LAW in the Centre Party caucus she voted for it in the Reichstag. After World War II she was a member of the 1949 *Parlamentarischer Rat* (PARLIAMENTARY COUNCIL) that set up the constitution of the Federal Republic, and then sat in the Bundestag for the CDU from 1949 until her death in Bonn in 1962.

Weber, Marianne (née Schnitger; 1870–1954), campaigner for women's rights. Born in Oerlinghausen, Lippe, Marianne Schnitger married Max WEBER in 1892. She was active in the women's movement from 1898, was elected to the constituent assembly in Baden in 1919, and was president of the League of German Women's Associations (*Bund Deutsche Frauenvereine*) from 1919 to 1923. She organized the publication of Max Weber's papers after his death in 1920, and published a biography of him in 1926.

Weber, Max (1864–1920), economist and social philosopher. Weber was born into an educated, liberal middle-class family in Erfurt, Thuringia, then under the jurisdiction of Prussia. His father was a member of both the Reichstag and the Prussian house of representatives (*ABGEORDNETENHAUS*), and his mother Helene (born Fallenstein) came from a family of teachers and intellectuals originally from the Rhineland. The Weber family lived in Charlottenburg, and Weber attended a *Gymnasium* (grammar school) there, then studied law at Heidelberg, and later at Berlin and Göttingen. He completed his doctorate on medieval trade in 1889 and his *Habilitationsschrift* (thesis) on the significance of Roman agrarian law was completed in 1891. He married Marianne Schnitger (*see* WEBER, MARIANNE) in 1892. He was appointed to chairs at Freiburg (1894) and Heidelberg (1897) before publishing his best-known work, *The Protestant Ethic and the Spirit of Capitalism* in the *Archiv für Sozialwissenschaft und Sozialpolitik* (of which he was a co-editor) in 1904 and 1905. In this work he defined capitalism as a relatively recent phenomenon distinguished from the drive for gain or profit in ancient and non-Western societies by the rational organization of labour and consistent investment of capital in continuously existing enterprises. In capitalism, he argued, the acquisition of wealth becomes the supreme aim in life, and he explained the capitalistic drive for gain, combined with the frugal lives of many capitalists, with reference to Protestant theology. This, he argued, promoted the idea that the highest calling of a Christian in this world is to fulfil his professional duties; acquisition, in these conditions, was to be celebrated and should not cause guilt or prompt condemnation. His critics – who were many, and with whom he argued in the pages of the *Archiv* – had many valid objections to his thesis as they understood it: that he had misunderstood the meaning of Protestantism, and of the Reformation, on many levels; that he had similarly misunderstood Catholic doctrine on these issues; that the causal relationships he implied between religious belief and secular activity were misleading and based on unreliable and incomplete sources; and that he had exaggerated the differences between modern Western capitalism and other, similar types of capitalistic activity in earlier or in non-European societies.

Weber volunteered for military service at the age of 50 in 1914, but was turned down and served in hospital administration during World War I. He spoke out against an annexationist peace during the war and he campaigned for a reform of the Reichstag. He was a co-founder of the liberal DDP after the war, and participated in the drafting of the Weimar constitution. He died of a lung infection, a late victim of the postwar influenza epidemic. His younger brother was the economist Alfred WEBER.

Webern, Anton (1883–1945), Austrian composer. Webern was born in Vienna and studied music with Arnold SCHOENBERG. He was one of the most important representatives of EXPRESSIONISM in music, and latterly adopted Schoenberg's twelve-note system of composition. His music was declared 'degenerate' by the Nazis, and he struggled to make a living after the ANSCHLUSS. He was accidentally shot by a US sentry during the postwar occupation of Austria. Webern's music has had a considerable influence on the younger generation of composers, including Boulez and STOCKHAUSEN.

Wedding, district of Berlin, to the north of the centre of the city. 'Red Wedding' was traditionally an industrial working-class district with a reputation for political radicalism.

Wedekind, Frank (1864–1918), writer. Wedekind was born in Hanover, but grew up in Switzerland, where he worked on advertising copy for Maggi, the food company. He contributed to the humorous magazine *Simplicissimus*, and was arrested in 1899 for lese majesty. His dramatic works, such as *Frühlings Erwachen* (*Spring Awakening*, 1891), were directed against conventional bourgeois morality, and their sexual explicitness led to them being censored and banned. His 'Lulu' plays – *Der Erdgeist* (*Earth Spirit*, 1895) and *Die Büchse der Pandora* (*Pandora's Box*, 1904) – formed the basis of Alban BERG's opera *Lulu*. Wedekind died in Munich in March 1918.

Wedel, Botho, Graf von (1862–1943), public servant and diplomat. He was a privy councillor in the foreign office, and then ambassador to Vienna from 1914 to 1919.

Wedel, Karl, Graf von (1842–1919), diplomat. Wedel was military attaché in Vienna (1877–88), and ambassador in Stockholm (1892–4), Rome (1899–1902) and Vienna (1903–7) before becoming governor of Alsace-Lorraine (1907–14). He became Fürst von Wedel in 1914.

Wednesday Club (*Mittwochsgesellschaft*), a society founded in 1863 for the promotion of scholarly or scientific knowledge. It met in Berlin on the second Wednesday of every month until 1944, and came to comprise a group of leading figures from the worlds of politics, business and culture.

Weerth, Georg (1822–56), political journalist. Weerth was the editor of the cultural section (*Feuilleton*) of Karl MARX's *Neue Rheinische Zeitung* in Cologne during the REVOLUTIONS OF 1848. He was imprisoned briefly for a satirical depiction of the Prussian aristocracy. Weerth died in Havana.

Wehberg, Hans (1885–1962), journalist. Born the son of a doctor in Düsseldorf, Wehberg was a pacifist who was active before the outbreak of World War I, and from 1912 was one of the editors of the journal *Zeitschrift für Völkerrecht*, a journal of international law. He resigned when he was unable to publish a protest against the German violation of Belgian neutrality at the beginning of World War I. During the war he campaigned for a just peace and for internal political reforms, and after the war demanded a clear recognition of war guilt. In 1928 Wehberg was appointed to a position at the Institut Universitaire des Hautes Etudes Internationales in Geneva, and spent the rest of his life in Switzerland.

Wehner, Herbert (1906–90), Social Democratic politician. Wehner was born in Dresden and joined the Communist Party (KPD) in 1927. After 1933 he worked for the underground Communist resistance movement, and then fled to the West, before moving on to Moscow in 1937, where he worked for the Comintern. In 1941 he was sent to Sweden to interview German Communists and was imprisoned there by a Swedish court. He was accused of having betrayed the party and expelled. He returned to Germany in 1946 and joined the SPD. He was a member of the Bundestag from 1949 to 1983, and deputy president of the party from 1949 to 1973, supporting party reform at BAD GODESBERG (1959). He had ministerial responsibility in the GRAND COALITION (1966–9) for relations with the German Democratic Republic, and chaired the SPD parliamentary party from 1969 to 1983. He was also an enthusiast for the reunification of Germany.

Wehrmacht ('defence force'), official designation of the armed forces of the Third Reich from 1935 to 1945. (The term is also often used more loosely to refer to the army alone.) Supreme commander (*Oberster Befehlshaber*) was HITLER himself. Overall commander of all the armed forces directly beneath Hitler was Werner von BLOMBERG (war minister from 1935), and Werner von FRITSCH was supreme commander of the army. Both were dismissed in 1938, and Hitler took command of the armed forces directly. Fritsch was replaced by Walther von BRAUCHITSCH until 1941, when Hitler himself assumed direct command. Erich RAEDER was supreme commander of the navy until 1943, when he was replaced by Karl DÖNITZ, and Hermann GÖRING was supreme commander of the air force (LUFTWAFFE) until the end of World War II. The supreme command of the armed forces was reorganized in 1938 in the OKW (*Oberkommando der Wehrmacht*) under Field Marshal Wilhelm KEITEL.

Wehrwirtschaft, defence economy. The term was used during the Nazi era to refer to mobilization of the nation's resources for war during peacetime.

Weill, Kurt (1900–50), German Jewish composer best known for his collaborations with Bertolt BRECHT. Weill was born in Dessau and began his study of music there with Albert Bing, the *Kapellmeister* of the Dessau Opera. He then studied at the Berlin High School of Music, and after composing a symphony (1921) he began to work with opera. He collaborated with the expressionist playwright Georg KAISER on *Protagonist* (1925), but his reputation was established by his work with Brecht on *Aufstieg und Fall der Stadt Mahagonny* (*The Rise and Fall of the City of Mahagonny*, 1927), and particularly on *Die Dreigroschenoper* (*The Threepenny Opera*, 1928). When the Nazis came to power he fled abroad, initially to Paris (1933), and then to London and finally New York (1935), where he re-established himself as a composer of Broadway musicals. He was married to the singer Lotte LENYA.

Weimar Republic, term generally used to refer to the German Republic of 1919–33. It takes its name from the town of Weimar in Thuringia, where the members of the NATIONAL ASSEMBLY fled in February 1919 to avoid the violent political unrest in Berlin (*see* SPARTACUS UPRISING).

It was in Weimar that a constitution was drawn up and approved for the successor state to the defeated GERMAN EMPIRE. The Weimar constitution was formally adopted by the National Assembly in July, and made Germany arguably the most progressive parliamentary democracy in Europe. The Kaiser (emperor) was replaced by a president, who was directly elected for a period of seven years. The office was held first by Friedrich EBERT, the Social Democratic leader of the provisional government (the COUNCIL OF PEOPLE'S REPRESENTATIVES). Ebert held the post until his death in 1925. The presidency was then contested, and the successful candidate, Field Marshal Paul von HINDENBURG, held the post until his death in 1934. The president appointed the CHANCELLOR, who was accountable to parliament (the REICHSTAG), which was elected by a system of proportional representation every four years.

The Weimar Constitution also introduced universal adult suffrage for the first time. The upper house of parliament (the REICHS-RAT) represented the interests of the country's constituent federal states (*Länder*), which survived the collapse of the empire with a high degree of autonomy, despite strong arguments for a greater centralization of the nation-state.

The party system that emerged from World War I reflected a fragmented, sectional politics where no single party had much prospect of gaining an overall majority in parliament. Stable coalitions proved difficult to sustain: there were 21 governments during the Weimar Republic, with an average life expectancy of eight months. Most parties represented sectional interests, and were unable to transcend a relatively narrowly defended constituency – until the Nazi Party (NSDAP) presented itself as a *Volkspartei*, that is a party that directed its appeal to the whole people. However, broad political alignments were relatively stable. The combined vote for the left consistently accounted for 35–40% of the vote, but the mutual hostility of the Social Democrats (SPD) and Communists (KPD) prevented any cooperation. The CENTRE PARTY also drew on a relative stable constituency of Roman Catholic voters (15–20%). The most fragmented and volatile electorate was made up of the Protestant middle classes, whose loyalties were divided between the liberal German Democratic Party (DDP), the bourgeois, business-orientated German People's Party (DVP) and the radical right-wing German Nationalist People's Party (DNVP). There was also a host of smaller splinter parties. All of these parties more or less collapsed with the rise of Nazism during the political crisis of the early 1930s. (Without proportional representation the collapse of these parties would have been swifter and more complete, and the Nazis would have had a larger presence in the Reichstag.)

Nevertheless the problem of the Weimar party system was not the smaller splinter parties, but the problem of forming a coalition among the larger ones. For the purposes of everyday politics two ideal types of coalition presented themselves during the 1920s. The first of these was the so-called 'Weimar coalition' of democratic parties (SPD, DDP and Centre), which effectively established the republic, designed the political system, and set up its relatively progressive welfare state. The 'Weimar coalition' parties also accepted the punitive peace terms of the treaty of VERSAILLES, enabling the parties of the right largely to escape the opprobrium associated with it, and to attack the 'Weimar coalition' parties for their 'FULFILMENT POLICY'.

The typical coalition during the Weimar Republic, however, was a centre–right 'bourgeois bloc', aimed more or less explicitly at keeping the SPD out of office, in keeping with a widespread antipathy to social democracy, however moderate or compromising, among all parties of the right. Moreover, many party politicians on the right – along with powerful figures in the armed forces, the bureaucracy, big business and among the landed aristocracy – simply refused to accept the legitimacy of parliamentary democracy itself, and were engaged long before 1933 in exploring the possibilities for an authoritarian state of some kind. Many others on the conservative right, although not instinctive republicans, were 'rational' or 'pragmatic' republicans' (*VERNUNFTREPUBLIKANER*) who persuaded themselves of the merits of the republic.

The Weimar Republic suffered not so much from flaws in the original design, but from a variety of contingent factors: the circumstances of its birth; the hostility of an imperial ruling class that perceived itself to be politically dispossessed; Germany's vulnerable international position; and the extraordinarily acute experience of political and economic crisis both during the early years of the republic and at its demise during the Depression. Between the postwar political crisis (1919–23) and the final crisis (1929–33) there was a brief period of illusory stability during the mid-1920s.

The first of these periods (1919–23) was characterized by attempts to stabilize the republic politically and economically against a background of putsch attempts from the right (the KAPP PUTSCH of 1920 and the BEER HALL PUTSCH of 1923) and political unrest on the left. The governments of this period also had to try to deal with the economic dislocation resulting from the loss of territory, war damage, the burden of REPARATIONS, the problems of demobilization and readjustment to a peacetime economy, and the gathering pace of price INFLATION. The parties of the right refused to take part in government at all until the hyperinflation of 1923, when the DVP under Gustav STRESEMANN joined the government. Stresemann's administration brought the crisis to an end with the stabilization of the currency (see RENTENMARK).

During the years that followed, Germany was governed by rather unstable centre–right governments, but they were administrations that included the DVP, and they reflected a broader political consensus behind the republic than had hitherto existed. Although the world slump in agricultural prices had serious consequences for the German agrarian sector, the industrial economy recovered. Germany also broke out of the international isolation of the postwar crisis years, not least with the LOCARNO TREATIES of 1925. Germany joined the LEAGUE OF NATIONS in 1926.

The collapse of the Weimar Republic began with the fall of the 'grand coalition' government (SPD–DDP–Centre–DVP) of 1928–30, headed by Hermann MÜLLER. The ostensible reason for the collapse of the government was a disagreement between the DVP, representing business interests, and the SPD, representing the interests of labour, over the rate of unemployment benefit contributions. Although such issues were to become increasingly important as the slump began to take its toll, the immediate disagreement reflected a broader inability to reconcile the interests of capital and labour.

A new minority government was formed under Heinrich BRÜNING, and elections were held. The outcome of the elections provided the extra-parliamentary opposition around President Hindenburg with an opportunity to move towards an authoritarian solution to the political impasse. The Nazis increased their share of the vote from 2.6% to 18.3%, almost wholly at the expense of the two conservative parties (DVP and DNVP) each of which lost half their share of the vote. The Brüning government continued to be dependent on presidential decrees rather than a parliamentary majority for its survival. The Reichstag could have overturned presidential rule, but the SPD, fearing that new elections would make matters worse by increasing the number of Nazis in the Reichstag even further, tolerated the government rather than challenging the president's use of ARTICLE 48. Brüning's government fell, appropriately enough, not by being defeated in the Reichstag, but by the withdrawal of the president's support. Against a background of increasing political tension (and recent Nazi gains in regional elections), the president refused his assent to a decree that aimed to break up the large and uneconomic landed estates of eastern Germany.

Brüning was replaced by Franz von PAPEN, a Westphalian aristocrat, and his so-called 'cabinet of barons'. He immediately dissolved the Reichstag, and called the Reichstag election (July 1932) that saw the Nazis win their largest share of the vote and largest number of seats in the Reichstag. HITLER, however, refused not only to 'tolerate' the government, but even to join it unless he were appointed chancellor himself. Nevertheless, the president and his associates were reluctant to set a date for further new elections, and were prepared to impose an authoritarian system by force if necessary.

In the event they were thwarted: two major opposition parties (the Centre Party and the Nazis) joined forces to defeat Papen's government overwhelmingly in a no-confidence vote on 12 September and new elections were called for November. Although the Nazis now lost some support, they remained strong enough to bring down the government if they again joined forces with another major party. Kurt von SCHLEICHER'S opposition blocked the possibility of a coup d'etat, and Papen was dismissed on 17 November and replaced by Schleicher. The new chancellor lasted only a matter of weeks. His attempts to bring the Nazis into government by appointing Gregor STRASSER vice chancellor were blocked by Hitler and other Nazi leaders. His own attempts to win popular support for himself served only to alienate the right. With virtually no support in parliament the government fell to a DNVP censure motion in January, and Hitler was appointed chancellor.

It is conventional to date the end of the Weimar Republic from Hitler's appointment on 30 January 1933. As an effective parliamentary democracy, however, the republic had more or less ceased to function in 1930. The constitution was never repealed by the Nazis, and remained in force until 1945. The FEDERAL REPUBLIC OF GERMANY claimed to be its successor.

Weishaupt, Adam (1784–1830), founder of the ILLUMINATI, a radical secret society. Born in Ingolstadt in Bavaria, Weishaupt was professor of law and philosophy at the university there from 1772 to 1785, and became involved in wrangles with local Jesuits. He founded the Illuminati order in 1776. After the dissolution of the order in 1786 he was employed at the court of the duke of Gotha. He died in Gotha in 1830.

Weiss, Wilhelm (1892–1950), Nazi journalist. A former student at Munich University, FREIKORPS member and participant in the BEER HALL PUTSCH, Weiss joined the Nazi newspaper, the *Völkischer Beobachter*, in 1927

and became its editor in 1938. He was elected to the Reichstag in March 1933 and appointed head of the Reich Association of the German Press by GOEBBELS in 1934.

Weizsäcker, Ernst, Freiherr von (1882–1951), diplomat. A naval officer in World War I, Weizsäcker joined the German foreign office in 1920 and received a number of diplomatic postings before his promotion by RIBBENTROP to chief state secretary. He was ambassador to the Vatican from 1943 until the end of the war. He was sentenced to five years at Nuremberg, but released after 18 months, and published apologetic memoirs shortly before his death.

Weizsäcker, Richard, Freiherr von (1920–), conservative politician; federal president (1984–94). Weizsäcker was born in Stuttgart, the son of the diplomat Ernst von WEIZSÄCKER, and studied at Oxford and Grenoble before serving in World War II. After the war he studied law and history at Göttingen. He joined the CDU in 1950, and was a member of the Bundestag from 1969 to 1981. He was also actively involved in the Evangelical Church, and was a member of the World Council of Churches. From 1981 he was mayor of West Berlin, and from 1984 federal president, following an unsuccessful candidature against SCHEEL in 1974. He was elected for a second term in 1989, and was succeeded by Roman Herzog in 1994.

Welf, originally a medieval German dynasty. The term is more recently associated with the house of Hanover. The *Deutschhannoversche Partei* in imperial Germany sought a restoration of the kingdom of Hanover, and was popularly known as the Welf Party.

Wels, Otto (1873–1939), Social Democratic politician. Wels was born in Berlin into a family already engaged in Social Democratic politics. He joined the SPD in 1891 after four years in the socialist youth movement, and was party secretary for Brandenburg province from 1907 to 1918. From 1908 he was chairman of the party's *Vorwärts* press organization. Wels was elected to the Reichstag for the SPD in 1912, and remained a deputy until the party was suppressed by the Nazis in 1933. He joined the party executive in 1913 as a protégé of August BEBEL. He supported the party line at the beginning of World War I, and was a close associate and political ally of Friedrich EBERT, whom he assisted in tightening party discipline in the wake of defections by the left and the establishment of the USPD in 1917.

During the revolutionary upheaval that immediately followed the war Wels proved to be a stalwart of the right of the party, and used his positions as city commandant of Berlin (from 10 November 1918) and head of the *Republikanische Soldatenwehr* (a paramilitary formation whose purpose was to protect the COUNCIL OF PEOPLE'S REPRESENTATIVES) to take on the radical left on the streets. As a consequence he was hated by the left, and briefly held hostage in the royal palace by a division of radical sailors. In 1920 he helped Carl Legien to organize the general strike that defeated the KAPP PUTSCH. He advised against a similar uprising against the Papen coup of 1932 in Prussia (the *PREUSSEN-SCHLAG*), on the grounds that mass unemployment would make a strike difficult and the labour movement would be easily defeated.

Wels was chairman of the SPD from 1931 to 1933. In March 1933 he spoke against Hitler's ENABLING LAW, as the leader of the only party to oppose it. He fled to Prague shortly afterwards and there took charge of the party in exile (SOPADE). He fled with the Sopade to Paris in 1938, and died there the following year.

Weltanschauung ('view of the world'), a term loosely corresponding to 'ideology'. It was used in a literal sense by natural scientists at the beginning of the 19th century, but had acquired the meaning 'outlook' or 'world view' by the 1850s. The Nazis used it in this sense to convey the sense of an outlook on the world rooted in the deepest convictions, and the struggle between *Weltan-schauungen* implied a more profound conflict than the superficial contest for formal political power.

Weltbühne, Die, a cultural and political journal of the Wilhelmine empire and Weimar Republic. It was founded in 1905 as *Die Schaubühne* and edited by Siegfried Jacobsohn (1881–1926) until his death. The journal extended its repertoire during World War I from theatrical criticism to political satire and articles on economics. It changed its name to *Die Weltbühne* in 1918 and became one of the leading organs of the left-wing intelligentsia during the Weimar Republic. Among its contributors were Kurt TUCHOLSKY, who became editor briefly in 1926, and Carl von OSSIETZKY, who succeeded him in 1927. It was suppressed by the Nazis in 1933, but refounded after World War II by Maud von Ossietzky, and appeared from 1946 to 1993.

Werefkin, Marianne von (1860–1938), Russian-born painter. Werefkin was born in Tula, south of Moscow, and studied in St Petersburg before moving to Munich in 1896. She was one of the founders of the BLAUE REITER group of EXPRESSIONIST artists. In 1914 she moved to Switzerland, where she painted her later, more abstract pieces.

Werfel, Franz (1890–1945), Austrian writer. Werfel grew up in Prague, where he belonged to the same circle as Franz KAFKA, and published some of his first work in *Die Fackel*, the Vienna journal edited (and largely written) by Karl KRAUS. Werfel's early work was EXPRESSIONIST and unpolitical, but he became increasingly politicized by World War I, and was involved in revolutionary activity in Vienna during the Austrian revolution of November 1918. He left Austria for Capri in 1938, and eventually emigrated to the United States. He died in California less than three weeks after the end of World War II.

Werkbund. *See DEUTSCHER WERKBUND.*

Wertheimer, Max (1880–1943), Austrian psychologist. Wertheimer was born in Prague, qualified at Würzburg and worked at the *Psychologisches Institut* in Frankfurt from 1910. His experiments formed the basis for Gestalt psychology, on which he worked with Wolfgang Köhler and Kurt Koffka between 1912 and 1920. In 1916 Wertheimer moved to the *Psychologisches Institut* in Berlin, which became a centre for research in Gestalt psychology during the Weimar Republic. Wertheimer was dismissed from his subsequent position in Frankfurt in 1933 and left for New York, where he taught at the New School for Social Research.

Werther, Karl, Freiherr von (1809–1904), Prussian diplomat. Werther was appointed ambassador to Russia (1854), to Austria (1859) and to France on the eve of the FRANCO-PRUSSIAN WAR (1869–70). He was subsequently ambassador in Constantinople (1874–7). He was the son of Heinrich von Werther, Prussian ambassador to Paris (1824–37) and foreign minister (1837–41).

Weser Exercise, German code name for operations against Denmark and Norway in 1940.

Wessel, Horst. *See* HORST WESSEL SONG.

Westarp, Kuno, Graf von (1864–1945), nationalist politician. Count von Westarp was born into the Junker aristocracy of Prussia at Ludom, near Piła (German Schneidemühl), in what is now the Polish province of Poznań. He studied law and joined the Prussian public service as a local *Landrat* (magistrate) before becoming police president of the Berlin district of Schöneberg in 1902. He was appointed to a senior judicial position in 1908, and was elected to the Reichstag for the DEUTSCHKONSERVATIVE PARTEI the same year. He was chairman of the parliamentary party from 1912 until the end of World War I. He was a founder member of the nationalist DNVP, and was elected to represent it first in the 1919 NATIONAL ASSEMBLY and then in the Reichstag (1920–30). Westarp was on the relatively moderate wing of the party; he was persuaded, if somewhat belatedly, to accept the

republic, and tried to persuade his colleagues to work with the other Weimar parties. In March 1926 he became party leader, but was challenged by right-wing radicals after the party's losses in the 1928 elections and was replaced by HUGENBERG. Despite increasingly acrimonious differences with the new party leadership, Westarp remained in the DNVP until 1930, when he resigned his membership to form the Conservative People's Party (*Konservative Volkspartei*, KVP) along with other dissident former party members. He was re-elected to the Reichstag for the KVP and remained a member until 1932, when the new party collapsed. Westarp remained a close associate of President HINDENBURG, but his public political career was effectively over. He remained in retirement throughout the Nazi dictatorship, and died in Berlin shortly after the end of the war.

Westendhall, a centre–left faction at the FRANKFURT PARLIAMENT of 1848.

West Germany. *See* FEDERAL REPUBLIC OF GERMANY.

Westphalia (German name: Westfalen), historic German land, now part of North Rhine-Westphalia (Nordrhein-Westfalen). A duchy in the Middle Ages, Westphalia was divided and governed by several different jurisdictions, some of which were acquired by Brandenburg-PRUSSIA. In 1807 Napoleon created a kingdom of Westphalia under his brother Jérôme. In 1815 it became a province of Prussia, and was integrated into the new state of Nordrhein-Westfalen in 1946.

WHW. *See* WINTERHILFSWERK.

Wiene, Robert (1880–1938), film director. Wiene was born in Dresden and began his film career making comedies during and after World War I. He made his name with the EXPRESSIONIST film *Das Kabinett des Dr. Caligari* (*The Cabinet of Dr Caligari*, 1919), which was originally to be directed by Fritz LANG. Expressionist artists were hired for the set design, and the striking results made the film a worldwide success. Wiene tried to repeat his success, but none of his subsequent films achieved the same status. After the Nazis came to power he emigrated to France. Plans to remake *Caligari* in cooperation with Jean Cocteau came to nothing, and Wiene died in Paris in 1938.

Wiener, Alfred (1885–1964), leader of the German Jewish community. Born in Potsdam, Wiener studied at Berlin and Heidelberg and wrote a doctorate on Arabic literature. After World War I he became head of the *Centralverein*, Germany's most important Jewish organization. He fled to the Netherlands in 1933 and documented the Nazi persecution of the Jews at the Jewish Central Information Office, whose collection formed the basis of the Wiener Library in London. The collection is now in Tel Aviv.

Wiener Werkstätte, a design group founded in 1903 in Vienna by the architect and designer Josef HOFFMANN, the artist Koloman Moser (1868–1918) and the collector Fritz Waerndorfer. It was in some ways similar to the British Arts and Crafts movement. The group specialized in the production of objects based on designs by SECESSION artists, ranging from jewellery to furniture. It was closed down in 1932.

Wiesenthal, Simon (1908–), Jewish writer and 'Nazi-hunter'. Born in Buczacz (now in Ukraine), Wiesenthal was arrested in Lemberg (now Lviv) in 1941 and remained imprisoned in a concentration camp until 1945. He has been involved in the tracking down of hundreds of Nazi war criminals, including Adolf EICHMANN, and founded the Simon Wiesenthal Centre in Vienna in 1961.

Wildermuth, Eberhard (1890–1952), officer and liberal politician. Wildermuth was a member of the Bundestag for the FDP and federal minister of housing (1949–52).

Wilhelm I (1797–1888), HOHENZOLLERN king of Prussia (1861–88) and Kaiser (emperor) of Germany (1871–88). Born in Berlin, the second son of FRIEDRICH WILHELM III, he was a fierce opponent of the REVOLUTIONS OF 1848, and as crown prince of Prussia put down rebellions in Baden and the Palatinate in 1849. He acted as regent for his brother FRIEDRICH WILHELM IV from 1858, and established a 'New Era' of relatively liberal policies. He came to the throne in his own right in 1861, and despite his early moderation he came into conflict with the Prussian diet over the reform of the army. In 1862 he appointed BISMARCK minister-president of Prussia in order to break the deadlock in the dispute. From then on he was carried along by the aggressive policy of the new minister-president during the wars of German UNIFICATION. He presided over the NORTH GERMAN CONFEDERATION from 1867, and in 1871, after the Prussian victory in the FRANCO-PRUSSIAN WAR, he was proclaimed at Versailles as Kaiser Wilhelm I of the GERMAN EMPIRE.

Wilhelm II (1859–1941), HOHENZOLLERN king of Prussia and Kaiser (emperor) of Germany (1888–1918); frequently referred to simply as the 'the Kaiser' in discussions of the period. Wilhelm II was the son of Friedrich III, who assumed the throne on the death of his father WILHELM I in 1888, but reigned for only three months before dying of throat cancer (making 1888 the 'year of the three emperors'). Wilhelm's mother was Victoria (daughter of Queen Victoria). He married Princess Auguste Viktoria of Schleswig-Holstein-Sonderburg-Augustenburg in 1881, and together they had six sons and a daughter.

Wilhelm's approach to the government of Germany was more interventionist than that of his grandfather Wilhelm I, and he began his reign by ensuring the fall of BISMARCK (1890). Wilhelm intervened very decisively in matters of state from the later 1890s, and proved to be an obstacle to the constitutional development of Germany towards a parliamentary democracy. The Kaiser was known for his instability, vacillation and lack of judgement, which was reflected in particular in his erratic interventions in foreign policy. Towards the end of World War I real political power was increasingly concentrated in the hands of

HINDENBURG and LUDENDORFF, who had established a virtual military dictatorship in Germany. The emperor abdicated in November 1918, following the NOVEMBER REVOLUTION and the declaration of a republic. Attempts by the Allies to arraign him for war crimes were unsuccessful, and he spent the rest of his life on his estate at Doorn in the Netherlands.

Wilhelmstrasse, street in Berlin named after Friedrich Wilhelm I. It was the site of the German foreign office, Reich Chancellery and other ministries in Berlin.

William. *See* WILHELM.

Wimpffen, Felix, Graf (1827–82), Austrian diplomat. Wimpffen occupied important positions during a difficult period in Austrian foreign policy. Following minor postings in Naples (1854–9) and London (1859–66), he was appointed Austrian ambassador in Copenhagen (1866), political commissioner in Verona (1866) and then Austrian ambassador in Berlin (1866–71). He was subsequently ambassador in Rome (1871–6), Paris (1876–8) and Rome again (1880–2). Wimpffen was one of the most important Austrian diplomats of the FRANZ JOSEPH period.

Winckelmann, Johann (Joachim) (1717–68), archaeologist and cultural historian. Winckelmann was born in Stendal, Prussia, and was educated in Latin and later in Greek at a *Gymnasium* (grammar school) in Berlin. He studied theology and philosophy at Halle, and then moved on to Jena. He began work as a teacher, but secured a position with an aristocrat near Dresden. He converted to Catholicism in 1754, and published *Gedanken über die Nachahmung der griechischen Werke in der Malerei und Bildhauerkunst* (*Thoughts on the Imitation of the Painting and Sculpture of the Greeks*), his most important work, the following year. In 1755 he moved to Rome and consolidated his reputation as an expert in Greek art. He was appointed prefect of antiquities in 1763. Winckelmann exercised an enormous influence on German think-

ing about classical culture, and his ideas were taken up by LESSING, GOETHE and SCHILLER. He was murdered in Trieste.

Windischgrätz, Alfred, Fürst zu (1787–1862), Austrian field marshal. Winidischgrätz commanded the troops that suppressed the uprising in Prague on 31 October 1848 and went on to lead the Austrian military action against the Hungarian revolutionaries.

Windischgrätz, Alfred, Fürst zu (1851–1927), conservative Austrian politician; minister-president of Austria (1893–5). Born in Prague, Windischgrätz was the grandson of the first Alfred, Prince WINDISCHGRÄTZ, the field marshal who helped to suppress the REVOLUTIONS OF 1848. He presided over a governing coalition of conservatives, Poles and left-wingers from 1893 to 1895. He entered the *HERRENHAUS* (upper house) in 1879, and was president of the chamber from 1897 to 1918.

Winnig, August (1878–1956), trade unionist, politician and writer. Born in Blankenburg in the Harz into a working-class family, Winnig was active in the construction workers' union and the SPD before World War I, and supported the nationalist right wing of the SPD during the war. He was appointed German plenipotentiary in the Baltic after the collapse of the empire, Reich commissioner for the east in January 1919 and *Oberpräsident* of East Prussia in June. He was increasingly estranged from the SPD, not least as a result of his close association with right-wing radicals, and was expelled from the party after declaring his support for the 1923 KAPP PUTSCH. He settled in Potsdam and pursued a successful career as a journalist and writer of radical right-wing cultural and political commentary. He was briefly associated with populist splinter parties during the later years of the Weimar Republic, and later supported the NSDAP (Nazi Party), albeit without joining the party. He survived the war and resumed his career as a successful writer.

Winter Aid. *See* WINTERHILFSWERK.

Winterhilfswerk, Winter Aid, a Nazi fundraising organization founded on 13 September 1933. It provided much of the finance for the activities of the Nazi welfare organization (*Nationalsozialistische Volkswohlfahrt,* NSV). It sold badges and undertook street collections. It promoted the idea of the 'Sunday stew' (*Eintopfsonntag*): once a month families should forgo Sunday lunch for a simple stew and donate the money saved to the NSV. The initiative was seen as a morale and consciousness raising exercise as well as a source of money, and one that absorbed the energies of rank-and-file Nazi Party members, particularly members of the women's organizations.

Winzer, Otto (1902–75), Communist politician. Winzer joined the German Communist Party (KPD) in 1919. After the Nazis came to power he left Germany for France (1935), then moved to the Netherlands and eventually found his way to the Soviet Union. After the end of World War II he was a member of the Central Committee (ZK) of the KPD with responsibility for education in Berlin. He pursued a political career within the Socialist Unity Party (SED), and became state secretary and first deputy minister for foreign affairs in 1958. He was foreign minister from 1965 to 1975.

Wirth, Christian (1885–1944), SS officer. Wirth served in World War I before pursuing a career in the Württemberg police and subsequently the *KRIPO*. He was appointed head of a euthanasia institute in 1939 and transferred to Poland in 1941, where he was head of the death-camp organization and first camp commandant of the extermination camp at BELZEC. He was transferred to Trieste in 1943. He was shot by partisans in Fiume (now Rijeka in Slovenia).

Wirth, Joseph (1879–1956), CENTRE PARTY politician; chancellor (1921–2). Born into a lower middle-class family in Freiburg im Breisgau, Wirth studied mathematics and was a grammar school teacher during World War I. He was a member of the Baden LAND-TAG for the Centre Party from 1913, and of the Reichstag from 1914 to 1933. From November 1918 until 1920 he was finance minister in Baden, and was appointed Reich finance minister in 1920, an office he held under MÜLLER and FEHRENBACH. Wirth was on the left of the party, and sought to pursue an economic policy that would enable Germany to pay off its REPARATIONS debts.

Wirth developed this 'FULFILMENT POLICY' when he became chancellor himself in May 1921. He resigned in October when Germany was forced to hand over territory in Upper SILESIA to Poland, but immediately formed another government. With Walther RATHENAU, his foreign minister, he negotiated the treaty of RAPALLO with the Soviet Union. Both men attracted intense opposition from the radical right. His efforts to appease the Allies went unrewarded, in so far as a request for a temporary moratorium on reparations payments was turned down in 1922. At the same time he had to contend with domestic difficulties: the territorial issue in Silesia and the crisis in Bavaria following the dissolution of the right-wing paramilitary FREIKORPS units, and political insurgency from both right and left. Rathenau was murdered by nationalists (24 June 1922), and Wirth took over as foreign minister until November, when the government fell following a crisis prompted by the reunification of the SPD and USPD. Wirth was a co-founder of the REICHSBANNER *SCHWARZ-ROT-GOLD* in 1924 and continued to be active in politics as a committed republican. He was interior minister in the first BRÜNING administration from March 1930 to October 1931. He emigrated to Switzerland in 1933 but returned to Germany after the war and died in his native Freiburg.

Wirtschaftswunder, 'economic miracle', the colloquial term for the rapid economic growth of the 1950s in the FEDERAL REPUBLIC OF GERMANY, following the currency reform of 1948 and the reconstruction boom of the late 1940s.

Wischnewski, Hans-Jürgen (1922–), Social Democratic politician. Born in Allenstein, Wischnewski was a member of the Bundestag for the SPD from 1957 to 1990. He was minister for development aid (1966–8) in the GRAND COALITION and minister of state in the foreign office (1974–9) under SCHMIDT. He was subsequently deputy leader of the party (1979–82) and party treasurer (1984–5).

Wissell, Rudolf (1869–1962), Social Democratic politician. Wissell was born into a lower middle-class family in Göttingen, and completed an apprenticeship in machine construction. He was active in the metalworkers' union and in the SPD in Bremen, and was elected to the BÜRGERSCHAFT in 1905. In 1908 he moved to Berlin to work in the union's national offices, and contributed to *Sozialistsische Monatshefte* before taking over the editorship of a union journal in 1916. He was a member of the Reichstag for the SPD from 1918 to 1933, and joined the COUNCIL OF PEOPLE'S REPRESENTATIVES following the withdrawal of the USPD at the end of 1918. He was Reich economics minister under both SCHEIDEMANN and BAUER in 1919, and promoted a socialized planned economy. He was also labour minister from 1928 to 1930. Wissell was arrested and imprisoned briefly in 1933, but remained in Germany throughout the Nazi dictatorship and resumed his political engagement and union activity after the end of the war.

Wissenschaftlich-humanitäres Komitee (WhK, 'scientific humanitarian committee'), a pressure group set up by the psychologist Magnus HIRSCHFELD to press for decriminalization of HOMOSEXUALITY. The group was established at a meeting in Hirschfeld's house in Charlottenburg in May 1897, and among the other founding members present were the Leipzig publisher Max Spohr, the writer Franz Josef von Bülow and Eduard Oberg, a lawyer. Their aim was to petition the Reichstag to repeal the PARAGRAPH 175 of the Reich criminal law. The campaign was unsuccessful.

Wissmann, Hermann von (1853–1905), officer and explorer. He undertook an exploratory expedition in equatorial Africa in 1880, and was later governor of GERMAN EAST AFRICA (1895–6).

Wittelsbach, ruling dynasty of BAVARIA, named in 1115 after the family fortress in Upper Bavaria. The Wittelsbachs became dukes of Bavaria in 1180, and kings of Bavaria in 1806 as a consequence of Napoleon's strategy of building up the 'middling powers' (*Mittelstaaten*) of central Germany as a buffer against Austria and Prussia. Bavaria was declared a republic in 1918.

See also BAVARIAN SUCCESSION, WAR OF THE.

Wochenblattpartei, liberal conservative party in Prussia during the 1850s. The party was led by Moritz August von Bethmann Hollweg (1795–1877) of the Frankfurt banking family, who was a lawyer and a former student of Friedrich Carl von Savigny (1779–1861), the most influential legal theorist in 19th-century Germany. The party had split from the main conservative grouping in Prussia and supported the constitution against arbitrary interference from the crown. It also supported the idea of German national unity, and was in many ways a forerunner of the Free Conservative Party (*FREIKONSERVATIVE PARTEI*). The group advocated support for Britain during the Crimean War, breaking with traditional German conservative support for Russia. Bethmann Hollweg was Prussian minister of education and culture from 1858 to 1862.

Wolf, Christa (1929–), East German writer. Wolf was born in Landsberg an der Warthe. Her best-known works are *Nachdenken über Christa T.* (*The Quest for Christa T.*, 1968) and *Kassandra* (1983). She was awarded the Georg Büchner Prize in 1980. After the fall of the GERMAN DEMOCRATIC REPUBLIC she was accused of association with the STASI, the East German security service.

Wolf, Konrad (1925–82), film-maker. Wolf

was the son of a doctor and Communist Party member, and brother of Markus WOLF. He fled with his family to the USSR in 1933, served as an officer in the Soviet army and returned to Moscow after the war (1949) to study film. From 1965 he was president of the East German Academy of Arts.

Wolf, Markus (1923–), East German politician. The brother of Konrad WOLF, he was educated in the USSR. He was head of the military intelligence service in the GERMAN DEMOCRATIC REPUBLIC and a deputy minister of state security. Wolf was brought to trial twice (1995 and 1997) after the collapse of the GDR.

Wolff, Karl (1900–84?), SS officer. Born in Darmstadt into an upper middle-class family, Wolff served in World War I and joined the Nazi Party in 1931. He was promoted through the SS ranks and became a lieutenant general in the WAFFEN-SS in 1940. He was appointed military governor of occupied northern Italy in 1943. Wolf went over to the Allies at the end of the war, and played a key role in negotiating the early surrender of German forces in Italy, thereby avoiding prosecution as a war criminal, and although he was later sentenced to four years by a German court, he was released after a week. He was tried again in 1964 for war crimes and sentenced to 15 years, but was again released early (in 1971).

Wolff, Kurt August Paul (1887–1963), publisher. Wolff was born in Bonn into an affluent and educated upper middle-class family. He was an adviser to the publishing firm Rowohlt while still a literature student. He took over the firm in 1912, and made it the most influential publisher of EXPRESSIONIST and avant-garde literature. The firm sprouted a number of subsidiaries in Germany and abroad, but got into financial difficulties and finally had to be sold in 1930. Wolff moved to France in 1933, and then emigrated (penniless) to New York in 1941.

Wolff, Otto (1881–1940), industrialist. Wolff was born in Cologne and opened his first

business there in 1904. With profits made during the war and the postwar INFLATION he bought his way into the leading heavy industrial concerns of the Ruhr during the 1920s, including the steel companies *Rheinische Stahlwerke* and *Vereinigte Stahlwerke*. He was quick to trade with foreign clients who were regarded as pariahs in some quarters, doing business with both the French and Belgian control authorities after the occupation of the Ruhr (*see* REPARATIONS), and with the Soviet Union. He was well connected to influential politicians in Berlin, including STRESEMANN, BRÜNING and SCHLEICHER, but kept his distance from the Nazis.

Wolff, Theodor (1868–1943), liberal journalist. Wolff was born in Berlin into a middle-class Jewish family, and reported for the *Berliner Tageblatt* as Paris correspondent from 1894. In 1906 he became the paper's editor, and was one of the first senior journalists to speak out against a war of conquest during World War I. He was a co-founder of the liberal DDP in 1918, but left the party in 1926 when some of its members supported a censorship law (the *Schmutz- und Schundgesetz*) in the Reichstag. In 1933 his work was publicly burned, and he emigrated to Nice, where he was arrested by the Italian occupation police in May 1943 and handed over to the Germans. After some months in a concentration camp Wolff died in the Jewish hospital in Berlin in September 1943.

Wölfflin, Heinrich (1864–1945), Swiss art historian. His best-known work *Kunstgeschichtliche Grundbegriffe* (1915, published in English in 1932 as *Principles of Art History*) was very influential within his field. He also wrote *Renaissance und Barock* (1888), and works on Michelangelo and Dürer.

Wolfsschanze, the Wolf's Lair, the name of Hitler's headquarters near Rastenburg in East Prussia (now in Poland). It was here that the failed assassination attempt of July 1944 took place (*see* JULY BOMB PLOT).

Wollweber, Ernst (1898–1967), Communist activist and politician. Wollweber took part in the KIEL MUTINY during the NOVEMBER REVOLUTION of 1918. He joined the KPD (German Communist Party) in 1919 and was a member of both the Prussian LANDTAG (1928–32) and the Reichstag (1932). During the Nazi dictatorship he was a member of the Communist underground resistance movement, then fled to Sweden, where he was imprisoned for sabotage in 1940. He was released following representations by Moscow. After the war he pursued a political career in the GERMAN DEMOCRATIC REPUBLIC, and was state secretary for security and deputy interior minister in 1953. He was state security minister from 1955 to 1957, and a member of the Central Committee (ZK) of the Socialist Unity Party (*Sozialistische Einheitspartei*, SED) from 1954 to 1958. He was removed for 'factionalism' – in effect for advocating liberalization.

Workers' and Soldiers' Councils (*Arbeiter- und Soldatenräte*), popular assemblies formed spontaneously during the revolutions of 1918 in central Europe. *See* RÄTE.

Working Group for the Education of Girls and Women (*Arbeitsgemeinschaft für Frauen- und Mädchenbildung*), organization founded in Hamburg on 8 October 1947 by Emmy Beckmann. Beckmann had been the last president of the General Association of German Women Teachers (*Allgemeiner Deutscher Lehrerinnenverein*), which had been dissolved in 1933 by the Nazis. Declining membership forced the group to disband in 1969.

Works Council Law (1920), legislation providing for the annual election of works councils in firms with more than 20 employees. The works council was charged with the defence of the collective interests of all employees, while supporting the employer in carrying out the company's business. Council members had voting rights on boards of directors, and access to company accounts. Employers were frequently hostile, however, to the perceived interference in their business, and council members were poorly trained.

World War I (1914–18), a conflict on an unprecedented scale that originated in Europe but also involved the colonies of the European imperial powers and eventually drew in the United States and other non-European countries. The origins of the war have been debated among politicians and historians since it broke out, and not least since the insertion into the treaty of VERSAILLES of the 'WAR-GUILT CLAUSE', which compelled the defeated Germans to accept responsibility.

The outbreak of hostilities was preceded by a prolonged antagonism between the principal European belligerents, which was characterized by frequent sabre-rattling, periodic international crises, secret diplomacy and the development of chauvinistic nationalisms. As in the Cold War that followed World War II, the tense international situation that preceded World War I was accompanied by extensive rearmament by the European powers, and a degree of ideological rivalry.

In 1914 there were two broad alliances in Europe: the CENTRAL POWERS, principally Germany and Austria-Hungary; and the Triple Entente (France, Great Britain and Russia). The German alliance with Austria dated from the DUAL ALLIANCE of 1879. (Italy had become a third member, making it a TRIPLE ALLIANCE, in 1882, but had only agreed to support Germany in the case of French aggression, and stayed out of the war in 1914.) On the outbreak of war, Serbia, Montenegro and Belgium joined the Entente, and in October 1914 the Ottoman (Turkish) empire joined the war on the side of the Central Powers. Hostilities were prompted by the assassination on 28 June 1914 of the heir to the Austrian throne, FRANZ FERDINAND. This incident prompted the JULY CRISIS, a flurry of diplomatic activity that failed to prevent the outbreak of hostilities. Austria-Hungary declared war on Serbia on 28 July, prompting the other powers to declare war in turn, beginning with Germany, which declared war on Russia on 1 August.

The course of the war unfolded initially on three fronts. The war on the Western Front began on 2 August with the occupation of Luxembourg by Germany (without a formal declaration of war). The following day Germany invaded neutral Belgium in order to facilitate the implementation of the SCHLIEFFEN Plan for the rapid defeat of France. The strategically positioned city of Liège (Lüttich in German) was taken on 3–4 August by a brigade led by Erich LUDENDORFF. The French concentrated their counter-attack on Alsace-Lorraine, taking on the Germans at MÜLHAUSEN (Mulhouse) (19 August) and in further battles in Lorraine and the Vosges. The French offensive was halted, however, and by the end of August the Germans, who had not reached the Channel coast as foreseen in the Schlieffen plan, had swung south and reached the Marne, and the French government fled from Paris to Bordeaux. At the Marne the Germans encountered an Anglo-French force whose purpose was to block the advance on the French capital. The Germans were forced to retreat during the battle of the MARNE (5–9 September), and the failure of either side to win a decisive victory led to a much longer conflict than had been anticipated.

On the Eastern Front the Russians attacked early, crossing the southern border of East Prussia and threatening the German rear, but the Germans won early battles at TANNENBERG (August) and the MASURIAN LAKES (September) under the leadership of General von HINDENBURG. The Russians then won twice before WARSAW, and the conflict on this front too developed into something of a stalemate.

On the Balkan Front, the Austrians advanced into Serbia (albeit at a numerical disadvantage after transferring some of their troops to Galicia on the Eastern Front), and the Serbs were compelled to evacuate Belgrade on 30 November after the battle of Kolubara. The Serbs managed to retake their capital by 15 December, although without repelling the Austrians decisively.

Modern military technology on land impeded infantry advances and, on the Western Front especially, forced the opposing sides to build long lines of trenches, from where they fought a war of attrition. Similarly at sea, mines, torpedoes and submarines impeded the free movement of ships. Naval engagements between surface fleets were superseded by blockade and the warfare of economic attrition. There were few remotely decisive initiatives. The Germans developed a strategy of defence in depth in the trenches, and the Allies responded with longer and heavier artillery attacks.

There was little movement on the Western Front, where thousands died in order to advance a few thousand metres in battles such as VERDUN (February–September 1916) and the SOMME (June–November 1916). The situation was similar on the Eastern Front, except for the GORLICE offensive of 1915, where the Russians were forced to retreat and the Germans went on to take Warsaw (5 August), Kovno (18 August), Brest-Litovsk (25 August) and Vilnius (18 September), before they were halted in eastern Galicia. Action in the other theatres of war – initially the Balkans, Italy and the Middle East – similarly had little impact on the balance of forces. Japan profited from its entry into the war by consolidating its position in the Pacific, and in Africa the German colonies fell to Allied forces. The entry of Italy (23 May 1915) followed by Romania (27 August 1916) and Greece (27 June 1917) into the war on the side of the Allies, and the entry of Bulgaria (6 September 1915) on the side of the Central Powers, made less difference than the economic impact of blockade warfare. Britain had declared the North Sea a war zone, and the battles of Dogger Bank (1915) and JUTLAND (1916) did little to affect the supremacy of the Royal Navy. Most of the German ships operating were sunk by the Allies.

The end of the war was heralded by a

series of events in 1917 that combined to break the deadlock. The Russian army was exhausted after the three Brusilov offensives, and the 1917 February Revolution broke out in Petrograd shortly after the third and final one came to an end. The collapse of Russia was followed by political crisis in Germany, with BETHMANN HOLLWEG being ousted from the chancellorship during the debate on the PEACE RESOLUTION; this in turn was followed by massive industrial unrest in Germany and Austria-Hungary at the beginning of the following year. Other critical events in 1917 included mutinies in the French army and the entry of the United States into the war (6 April 1917), prompted by the leaking of the ZIMMERMANN TELEGRAM and the U-BOAT attacks on American shipping. The breaking of the impasse seemed at first to favour Germany, especially on the Eastern Front, where Galicia and the Bukovina were won back by German troops and the new Russian revolutionary government was forced to conclude an armistice (15 December) and begin the peace talks that led to the treaty of BREST-LITOVSK (3 March 1918). On the Western Front, however, the use of British tanks at the battle of CAMBRAI (November–December 1917) failed to achieve the hoped-for breakthrough. Similarly, the 1918 Hindenburg offensives, although they pressed the Allies hard, failed to achieve their aims. The launching of a surprise French counterattack on the MARNE (July) and the launching of a further Allied counterattack at AMIENS (8–11 August) proved decisive. The Allies used 450 tanks to break the German resistance, and after the battle a further German offensive was unthinkable. The Allies continued on the offensive, and an armistice was concluded at Compiègne on 11 November 1918.

The impact of World War I on Germany was immense. Of the 11 million troops that had been mobilized 1,774,000 had died in combat or later from their wounds, and many others were permanently disabled.

The war was followed immediately by the NOVEMBER REVOLUTION of 1918, and a prolonged economic and political crisis (see WEIMAR REPUBLIC). The treaty of VERSAILLES (1919) imposed punitive and humiliating conditions, which were to exacerbate the political instability of the years between the wars.

World War II (1939–45), global conflict between the AXIS powers (principally Germany, Italy and Japan) and the Allies (principally Great Britain, the Commonwealth, France, the Soviet Union and the USA). World War II is seen by many historians as 'Hitler's war' despite the case for continuities in German foreign policy from WORLD WAR I (see FISCHER CONTROVERSY). The treaty of VERSAILLES following the end of World War I generated enormous resentment in Germany, and there was always a large constituency of support for revisionism during the interwar years. Hitler's MEIN KAMPF, which set out his foreign-policy ambitions in 1923, articulated the prevalent mood and has been taken by so-called INTENTIONALIST historians as evidence of a plan or programme for aggressive expansion. Most historians agree that there was certainly a primacy of foreign policy in the decision-making process that led to war in 1939.

The programme of rearmament on which the Nazis embarked on coming to power and which violated the Versailles treaty, was accelerating by 1936, when the demilitarized RHINELAND was reoccupied by German troops. The first expansionist moves undertaken by Nazi Germany came shortly afterwards, and marked a general radicalization of the regime. First came the invasion and annexation (ANSCHLUSS) of Austria in March 1938, then the occupation first of the SUDETENLAND in the autumn of 1938 following the MUNICH AGREEMENT. The German occupation of the rest of Czechoslovakia in the spring of 1939 went beyond Hitler's professed aim of righting the wrongs of Versailles and uniting all Germans in one nation state. The public response in Britain to the Czech crisis marked the effective end of Britain's appeasement of Nazi Germany.

The war began with Germany's invasion of Poland on 1 September 1939 following staged border incidents. Britain and France declared war two days later. Poland was quickly overrun using BLITZKRIEG tactics and the country was divided between Germany and the Soviet Union as agreed in the MOLO-TOV–RIBBENTROP PACT (23 August 1939). The victory was followed by the wholesale massacre of Polish Jews and members of the ruling intelligentsia by SS EINSATZGRUPPEN. Britain and France undertook no retaliatory action against Germany, however, and there followed a period of 'phoney war' (SITZKRIEG), which ended with the German invasion of Norway and Denmark on 8 April 1940. Whereas Denmark was subdued within hours, there was stiffer resistance in Norway, but the campaign was another successful Blitzkrieg, which ended with the capitulation of Norway. This enabled Hitler to turn his attention to the west. German troops invaded Belgium, the Netherlands and Luxembourg on 10 May. The offensive against France was launched on 13 May, and led to a German victory within weeks. An armistice was signed by General PÉTAIN on 22 June at Compiègne. By this time Italy had entered the war on the Axis side (10 June).

The swift Blitzkrieg victories – which did much to reinforce Hitler's authority at home despite popular anxiety about the war – were unexpected, and succeeded not least as a result of the element of surprise in the German attacks and the lack of preparedness of Germany's enemies. In the Reich the fall of France prompted public discussion of the anticipated Nazi NEW ORDER in Europe, but the failure to win the battle of BRITAIN in the summer of 1940 was the first setback for Germany since the beginning of the war. Germany now not only tried to keep up the pressure on Britain with continued aerial bombardment in the BLITZ and naval warfare in the battle of the ATLANTIC, but immediately started planning for the confrontation with the Soviet Union that was the centrepiece of Hitler's policy. In addition German troops were drawn into Italy's campaigns in North Africa and the Balkans, and although the German invasion of Yugoslavia and Greece in April 1941 brought further swift victories, Germany's military capacity and resources were seriously overstretched by the time of the invasion of the USSR (22 June 1941).

The invasion of the Soviet Union seemed to go well at first. The Baltic states and large areas of Belarus and Ukraine were occupied during the late summer of 1941. Against the advice of the Field Marshal BRAUCHITSCH, the supreme commander of the army, and General HALDER – both of whom advocated concentrating on a push towards Moscow by Army Group Centre – Hitler now insisted on delivering the final blow against the Soviet army from the flanks rather than the centre. He despatched Army Group North to Leningrad, whose capture he deemed necessary to secure supply communications with Scandinavia and the continuing supply of Swedish iron ore, and Army Group South towards the agriculturally rich Ukraine, the industrial Donetz basin and the Caucasus oil fields. It was only in October that an attempt was made to move in on Moscow, and the campaign ended in disaster for the Germans, who were insufficiently equipped for the extremes of the Russian winter. Nevertheless Hitler ensured the globalization of the war on 11 December 1941 with his declaration of war on the United States following the Japanese attack on Pearl Harbor.

The following year, 1942, was a crucial year in the course of the war, and one in which the Axis powers came close to winning. The Soviets were driven back to the Caucasus, the Japanese took control of Hong Kong, the Philippines, Malaya, the Dutch East Indies and Burma, and the British were driven back into Egypt by ROMMEL and his Afrikakorps. By the end of the year, however, the tide of the war was turning. The Germans were halted at STALINGRAD and the British victory at El ALAMEIN (23 October–4 November) marked the beginning of the end in North Africa. Allied troops landed in Morocco and Algeria on 7 November to open a second front. In Europe itself the RAF stepped up its bombardment of German cities in an attempt to undermine German civilian morale. Popular opinion in Germany, which had understood that the invasion of the Soviet Union had marked a qualitatively different stage of the war, was at best subdued and increasingly panic stricken as Stalingrad fell in the New Year and the Red Army advanced west, albeit not without reverses. The mood became further depressed with the Allied invasion of Sicily on 9 and 10 July and the overthrow of Mussolini later in the month.

On 18 February 1943 GOEBBELS appealed to the Germans to commit themselves to a total war at a time when aerial bombardment of German cities was taking an increasingly heavy toll. Soviet successes at Kursk in July 1943 and the recapture of Leningrad (26 January 1944) prompted the Nazis to extend this appeal and to portray their war of subjugation and plunder – in reality characterized by the genocide of the HOLOCAUST and the impressment of slave labour from the whole of occupied Europe – as a united crusade undertaken by civilized Christian Europe against the barbarism of Bolshevik Russia. If it is not surprising that few Germans, still less other Europeans, were persuaded by this new propaganda, it is a measure of the extent of pro-Nazi sympathy in Europe as a whole that many local collaborators persisted in their support for Nazi Germany.

With the Allied landings in Normandy (6 June 1944) a second front was opened and the Allies advanced quickly, taking Paris on 25 August and Brussels on 3 September.

Aachen was the first German city to fall to Allied troops in October but they failed to advance further into Germany. The Germans launched a last counter-offensive in the ARDENNES on 16 December, but it was driven back by an Allied counter-offensive (3 January 1945), and the Germans suffered 100,000 casualties and lost 800 tanks. When the Soviets launched a new offensive of their own on the Eastern Front on 12 January, the Germans had effectively no reserves with which to oppose it. In the west the Allies crossed the Rhine in March, while the Soviet assault on Berlin began in April. Hitler committed suicide on 30 April, and General JODL and Admiral von FRIEDEBURG signed an unconditional surrender at Rheims on 7 May 1945, bringing the war to an end.

By the time hostilities ended, over 6 million Germans had been killed (9.5% of the pre-war population), and 55 million service personnel and civilians had been killed altogether in the conflict. In addition, German cities were in ruins, and the country's economy had ground to a halt. The Allied insistence on unconditional surrender meant that there was no question of negotiating with the defeated enemy about the future of Germany as at Versailles. Germany was divided into four zones of occupation in which the Allied powers had supreme authority.

Worpswede, village in Lower Saxony, near Bremen. It was the location of an artists' settlement in the late 19th century. Among its members were Fritz Mackensen (1866–1953), Otto Modersohn (1865–1943) and Paula Modersohn-Becker (1876–1907). Mackensen arrived in 1884 and was followed by Modersohn and others. They came to public attention at an exhibition in Munich in 1895. The poet Rainer Maria Rilke (1875–1926) was also associated with the artists' colony in Worpswede.

Wrocław. *See* BRESLAU.

Wunderlich, Carl August (1815–77), doctor. Wunderlich was professor of medicine at the

University of Leipzig. He introduced into hospitals the practice of recording the temperature of patients with fever, maintaining that it was a symptom rather than a condition per se.

Württemberg, historical German *Land,* now part of the state of BADEN-WÜRTTEMBERG. The Württembergs were an aristocratic family in medieval Swabia whose territory became a duchy in 1495. It became an electorate in 1803, shortly before the dissolution of the HOLY ROMAN EMPIRE, and made substantial territorial acquisitions as an ally of France during the Napoleonic Wars, including Heilbronn, Ulm, Rottweil and parts of Upper Swabia and of the Allgäu. It was a member of the CONFEDERATION OF THE RHINE from 1806 to 1813, and became kingdom. Building on earlier involvement of the estates in the government of the country, Württemberg had a relatively strong liberal parliamentary tradition in the 19th century, and a bicameral parliament was established by the constitution of 1819. Württemberg joined the *ZOLLVEREIN* in 1834 and became a part of the German empire in 1871. It retained a great deal of autonomy over its own affairs during the imperial period, including rights over taxation and the army. This degree of independence disappeared with the establishment of the WEIMAR REPUBLIC, and, after some uncertainty about the shape of regional government in southwest Germany, Württemberg was absorbed into the state of Baden-Württemberg in 1952.

Württemberger Hof, a faction of 41 moderate democrats at the 1848 FRANKFURT PARLIAMENT. The group stood between the centre–right and the left-wing factions, both in terms of political proposals and in terms of social background.

WVHA (*Wirtschafts- und Verwaltungshauptamt*), Head Economic and Administrative Office (of the SS).

Y

Yalta Conference (4–11 February 1945), the most important Allied conference of World War II. Churchill, Roosevelt and Stalin met at Yalta in the Crimea to discuss the postwar order. It had already been decided that Germany would be divided into Allied zones of occupation. France was to be an equal member of the ALLIED CONTROL COUNCIL and to occupy a zone carved out of the British and American zones. Germans were to be provided with the minimum resources necessary for subsistence, and such German industry as might be used for rearmament and a future war of aggression was to be dismantled. It was agreed in principle that reparations in kind, including the use of German labour, were to be extracted from Germany, but the question of the scale and details of reparations payments was left to a separate commission. The future of Poland was also tentatively agreed, and this had territorial implications for postwar Germany: eastern Poland was to be ceded to the Soviet Union, and in return Poland was to gain territory from Germany in the west, where the frontier would be moved to the ODER–NEISSE LINE, as discussed at the TEHRAN CONFERENCE. Yugoslavia and the relationship between the Soviet Union and China were also discussed. The future of postwar Germany was discussed in more detail at the POTSDAM CONFERENCE (July–August 1945).

Yorck von Wartenburg, Hans (David Ludwig), Graf (1759–1830), Prussian general. Yorck was born in Potsdam and joined the Prussian army in 1772. Disciplined and dismissed for insubordination in 1779 he went to the East Indies in the service of the Netherlands. He returned to Germany in 1787, and fought in the Napoleonic Wars. He was commander of the Prussian forces with Napoleon's army of invasion in Russia in 1812, and when it retreated he took the initiative of changing sides by concluding the Tauroggen Convention with Russia, which declared his army neutral. Prussia then entered the war on the Coalition side, initiating the Wars of LIBERATION, in which he also fought. He became Count von Wartenburg in 1814.

Yorck von Wartenburg, Peter, Graf (1904–44), anti-Nazi conspirator. Born in Klein Oels (now Olesniczka in Poland), the great grandson of Count Hans YORCK VON WARTENBURG, he entered the public service in 1927. He was a founder member of the KREISAU CIRCLE in 1942 and a close associate of STAUFFENBERG. He was executed after the failed JULY BOMB PLOT of 1944.

Young Germany (*Das junge Deutschland*), a cultural and political movement of the mid-19th century associated with the radical YOUNG HEGELIANS. It comprised a group of young intellectuals, mainly poets, who eschewed the excesses, as they perceived them, of German Romanticism in favour of greater realism. The group's members were committed liberals and nationalists, who also agitated in support of social justice. The name *Junges Deutschland* had already been used in the journal *Aesthethische Feldzüge* in 1834. It was reinforced as a designation for the group, however, by a law passed at METTERNICH's insistence by the diet of the GERMAN CONFEDERATION the following year. The law listed the journal's editor, Ludolf Wienbarg (1802–72), Heinrich HEINE, Karl Gutzkow (1811–78), Theodor Mundt (1808–61) and Heinrich Laube (1806–84) as members. In its broader sense the term has also been applied to a larger group of radical activists not especially mentioned in Metternich's decree, including Karl MARX, Georg Herwegh (1817–75) and Ludwig Börne (1786–1837).

Young Hegelians, radical followers of the philosopher HEGEL. They were at first primarily concerned with philosophical and religious issues, but the accession of FRIEDRICH WILHELM IV in 1840, and the subsequent relaxation of censorship permitted them to engage in a more open discussion of radical political ideas, albeit briefly. Karl MARX and Friedrich ENGELS were associated with the group.

Young Lithuania (*Jung-Lithauen*), a group of left-wing liberals, so called because of their East Prussian base, who broke away from the Prussian liberals during the constitutional crisis of 1861–2. The group formed a separate faction in February 1861. Its members formed the Progress Party (*DEUTSCHE FORTSCHRITTSPARTEI*), which was founded on 6 June 1861.

Young Pioneers (*Junge Pioniere*, JP), also called the THÄLMANN Pioneers, a subdivision of the East German state's youth organization, the *FREIE DEUTSCHE JUGEND* (FDJ). The organization was founded on 13 December 1948, and dissolved in 1989.

Young Plan, an attempt to reach a definitive settlement of the question of German REPARATIONS after World War I. A committee was set up under the chairmanship of Owen D. Young in Paris in 1929 to find a settlement to replace the DAWES PLAN, with which both the Germans and the Allies were unhappy. The Young Plan reduced the total amount of reparations by about three-quarters, and brought to an end the surveillance of Germany's budget by the Reparations Agency. Annual payments were to be made until 1988, starting at 1.65 billion gold marks and increasing on a sliding scale. Hjalmar SCHACHT, the president of the Reichsbank and future Nazi economics minister, resigned in protest. Payments were suspended by the Hoover moratorium of 1931, and never resumed.

Ypres, small town of about 35,000 in western Flanders, and site of battles during World War I. The first came when General von Falkenhayn set out to reach the coast and capture Calais in early October 1914. Ypres was a route centre and the Germans' first objective. It was defended by the Belgians, French infantry, four British infantry corps, the Indian infantry corps and French and British cavalry, under the leadership of General Foch. Both sides suffered heavy losses, and the Germans failed in their objective. The second battle (22 April 1915) involved the first use of poison gas (by the Germans). Again there were heavy losses, but the outcome was that there was no discernible advance on either side. A British and Canadian offensive took place at Ypres between July and November 1917, resulting in the capture of the insignificant village of Passchendaele at great cost to both sides. The Germans tried to encircle the town in April 1918 and there was further fighting in September.

Z

Zabern affair (1913), unlawful action taken by the military against the people of Zabern (French name: Saverne) in ALSACE. Provocative and insulting behaviour on the part of some German officers towards the local population prompted hostility and rioting, in the wake of which arbitrary arrests were made by the German authorities. Disciplinary measures taken against the principal officer concerned, the 20-year-old Lieutenant Günter Forstner, remained largely unknown to the public. The incident prompted a cross-party vote of no confidence in Chancellor Bethmann Hollweg in the Reichstag and led to a constitutional crisis. The affair and its consequences were widely reported abroad as a reflection of the unreformability of the constitution of imperial Germany, and the undue influence of the military in the public affairs of the empire.

ZAG (*Zentralarbeitsgemeinschaft*, 'central working association'), the formal forum for negotiation of agreements between employers and workers in German industry during the WEIMAR REPUBLIC. Agreements negotiated in November 1918, and subsequent legislation, introduced a modern, liberal industrial-relations system into German industry.

Zaisser, Wilhelm (1893–1958), Communist activist and East German politician. Zaisser was born in Rotthausen near Gelsenkirchen, and was a primary-school teacher in Essen before serving in World War I. He joined the USPD in 1918 but left to join the newly-founded KPD (German Communist Party) in 1919, and was one the leaders of the so-called 'Red Army of the Ruhr' during the 1920 KAPP PUTSCH. He was imprisoned for four months for his political activities, lost his teaching post and became an employee of the Communist Party. He worked as a journalist and pursued a political career within the KPD in the Ruhr valley. By the late 1920s he was a national leader, with responsibility for military-political schooling, and from 1927 to 1939 he was attached to the Communist International (Comintern). He worked in China from 1927 to 1930 under the auspices of the Executive Committee (EKKI) of the Comintern. From 1932 to 1936 Zaisser was deputy director of the military-political school outside Moscow, and from 1936 to 1938 he was a military adviser in Spain, where he was known as 'General Gomez'. He returned to Moscow in 1938 and received Soviet citizenship in 1940. From the time of the German invasion of the Soviet Union in 1941 Zaisser was a political adviser in the central administration of the Red Army, and from 1943 was responsible for the 'anti-fascist' schooling of German prisoners of war. In 1947 he returned to the Soviet zone of occupation, joined the Socialist Unity Party (*Sozialistische Einheitspartei*, SED) and was briefly interior minister of Saxony-Anhalt. From 1950 to 1953 he was minister for state security in the GERMAN DEMOCRATIC REPUBLIC and a member of the

Politburo and Central Committee of the SED. In 1953 he was removed from both bodies, and dismissed from his ministerial office. His long-standing political rival Walter ULBRICHT maintained that the state had deployed insufficient force during the June uprising of 1953 (*see* NEW COURSE), and blamed Zaisser. In 1954 Zaisser was expelled from the party. During the four years until his death in 1958 he worked as a translator at the Dietz publishing house and at the Institute for Marxism-Leninism.

ZDF (*Zweites Deutsches Fernsehen*), the second public-service broadcasting channel to be set up in the Federal Republic of Germany. The ZDF was established in 1961 by a contract between the constituent federal states. It is based in Mainz, and its first transmission was on 1 April 1964. The ZDF transmits its television programmes nationwide.

See also ARD.

Zechlin, Erich (1883–1954), diplomat. Zechlin was consul general in Leningrad (1928–33), ambassador to Lithuania (1933–41) and ambassador to Finland (1941–4).

Zeigner, Erich (1886–1949), Social Democratic politician. Zeigner was born into a middle-class family in Erfurt, then in the Prussian province of Saxony. He studied law and economics, and then entered the public service in Saxony. He joined the SPD in 1919 and was appointed Saxon justice minister in 1921, a position he used to replace the judicial old guard with republican judges and officials. In 1923 he became minister-president of the Saxon government, and although the cabinet was exclusively made up of Social Democrats, it was supported by the KPD (German Communist Party) – together the two parties had a majority in the LANDTAG. In October three Communists joined the government, and the increasing tension between Saxony and the Reich culminated in the removal of Zeigner from office, and the appointment of a governor, Rudolf Heinze, a member of the conservative DVP. The Saxon Landtag elected a new SPD cabinet almost immediately, but the repercussions had spread to Berlin, where the SPD ministers had left the STRESEMANN coalition in protest, effectively bringing down the government. Zeigner's enemies on the right then had him imprisoned on charges of petty corruption. After he had served most of his three-year sentence he secured a teaching post in a local college. He was arrested again, several times, during the Nazi dictatorship, but was able to resume his political career after the war in the Soviet occupation zone. He was mayor of Leipzig from 1945 until 1949.

Zeit, Die, a liberal political weekly newspaper established in Hamburg in 1946. The former SPD chancellor Helmut SCHMIDT is one of its editors. Its circulation in 2001 was 438,000.

Zelinka, Andreas (1802–68), mayor of Vienna. Born in Wischau (now Vyskov in the Czech Republic), Zelinka was a lawyer. He was elected to the city council of Vienna in 1848 and was mayor from 1861 to 1868, during the so-called 'Ringstrasse' era, when the city's fortifications were demolished and replaced with a boulevard lined by public buildings. The 1860s saw enormous changes in the city, including the provision of piped water from the neighbouring countryside, the regulation of the Danube and the founding of the *Zentralfriedhof* (central cemetery). Zelinka was also a member of the Lower Austrian LANDTAG from 1872, and of the upper chamber of parliament (the Reichsrat) from 1867.

Zentralrat, central committee of the CONGRESS OF WORKERS' AND SOLDIERS' COUNCILS during the NOVEMBER REVOLUTION of 1918. The central council was given the authority to oversee the activities of the COUNCIL OF PEOPLE'S REPRESENTATIVES and the Prussian cabinet. After disagreement between the Majority Social Democrats (MSPD) and the Independent Social Democrats (USPD), the latter decided not to participate in a central body for the whole of Germany.

Consequently all those elected to the Central Council were MSPD delegates.

Zentrum. *See* CENTRE PARTY.

Zeppelin, Ferdinand, Graf von (1838–1917), army officer. Born in Konstanz, Zeppelin served in the Franco-Prussian War, and between 1897 and 1900 constructed the first of the dirigible airships that made his name famous. The launch of the first Zeppelin took place at Friedrichshafen, Lake Constance, on 2 July 1900. It was 127 m (416 feet) long and was filled with hydrogen gas. It had a maximum speed of 27.7 km (17.3 miles) per hour. By the outbreak of World War I, the German army owned seven Zeppelin Z1 airships, which had a maximum speed of 136 km (84.5 miles) per hour and were equipped with five machine guns and 2000 kg (4,400 lbs) of bombs. For the first three years of the war these airships were used in bombing raids on the Western Front and over England – the first attack on London occurred in May 1915. Their susceptibility to ground fire brought their use in bombing raids to an end in June 1917; of the 115 Zeppelins deployed over Europe, 77 were destroyed or put beyond use.

Zernatto, Guido (1903–43), Austrian politician. Zernatto was involved in the radical right-wing HEIMWEHR movement between the wars, and was secretary to the *HEIMATSCHUTZ* from 1929 and the *Heimatblock* from 1930. From May 1936 he was secretary to the AUSTROFASCIST Fatherland Front (*VATERLÄNDISCHE FRONT*), and from February 1938 he was briefly minister without portfolio. He fled to France in 1938, and then to the USA, where he took up a university teaching post.

zero hour (*Stunde null*), a term used to designate the end of World War II. Its emphasis on the discontinuity between the Nazi period and the years of postwar reconstruction is widely considered to be misleading.

Zetkin, Clara (née Eissner; 1857–1933), Communist politician. Born in Wiederau, Saxony, the daughter of a schoolteacher, Eissner

moved to Leipzig with her family in 1873. She was a student at the Leipzig teaching college for women. She met the Russian émigré Osip Zetkin and married him in Switzerland. A socialist and feminist, Zetkin was present at the founding of the Second (social democratic) International in 1889, contributed to the journal *Der Sozialdemokrat*, and was editor of the women's paper *Die Gleichheit* ('equality'). She was a member of the SPD from 1881 to 1917, and was one of the founders of the SPARTACUS LEAGUE (1916), of the USPD (1917) and of the German Communist Party (KPD) (1919). She was a member of the Reichstag for the KPD from 1920 to 1933, left for Moscow before the Nazis came to power and died there shortly afterwards.

Zille, Heinrich (1858–1929), artist. Born into a poor family in Radeburg, Saxony, Zille grew up in Berlin and took evening classes in art while learning his trade as a lithographer during the day. From 1878 he worked in a photographic workshop, and from 1900 he published drawings in newspapers and magazines, including *Jugend* and *Simplicissimus*. He exhibited at the Berlin SECESSION in 1901. Zille lost his job at the age of fifty in 1908, and made his living from selling his sketches of 'typical' figures from the Berlin working class. His work, which frequently depicted the miseries and injustices of the life of the poor, was initially unpopular, but found greater acceptance during the Weimar Republic.

Zimmermann telegram, an encoded message sent by Arthur Zimmermann (1864–1940), foreign minister of Germany (1916–17), to the German minister in Mexico on 19 January 1917 via the German ambassador in Washington, Count BERNSTORFF. It discussed the possibility of an alliance between Germany and Mexico, should war break out with the United States when Germany resumed unrestricted submarine warfare on shipping, as intended, on 1 February. In exchange for such an alliance Mexico would be offered the possibility of recovering her 'irredenta' in the southern United States (Arizona, New Mexico and Texas, which had been ceded to the USA in 1848). The telegram was intercepted by British intelligence and passed on to President Wilson. The contents were revealed to the American press on 1 March. Wilson attempted to avoid declaring war on Germany even so, and requested that American shipping be allowed to pass freely to Britain. It was only when this request was rejected by Berlin that the United States declared war on Germany on 17 April.

Zinnemann, Fred (1907–97), Austrian-born film director. Zinneman was born in Vienna and studied law there (1925–7). He then went to Paris to study cinematography, and emigrated to the United States in 1929. His films include *High Noon* (1952), *From Here to Eternity* (1953), which won him an Oscar, *A Man for All Seasons* (1966) and *The Day of the Jackal* (1973).

Zisleithanien. *See* CISLEITHANIA.

Zitz-Halein, Kathinka (1801–77), writer and political activist. Zitz-Halein was born into a prosperous middle-class family in Mainz, published her first work at the age of 16, married in 1837 and had separated from her husband within two years. She became politically active during the 1840s and, in the wake of the REVOLUTIONS OF 1848, she became president of *Humania*, a women's group formed in 1849 to defend the achievements of the revolution. Zitz-Halein believed women could make their contribution in their own sphere, and returned to literary writing within a few years.

ZK (*Zentralkomitee*), the Central Committee of the East German Socialist Unity Party (SED), regarded as the party's 'highest organ'.

Zollverein, German customs union founded in 1834. The development of a free-trade area within Germany began with the abolition of internal trade barriers within states: Prussia abolished its internal trade barriers in 1818, and then began to establish bilat-

eral agreements with other members of the GERMAN CONFEDERATION. Smaller states made such agreements with Prussia very quickly, while the middling states attempted to emulate Prussia and create their own customs unions. In 1828 Bavaria and Württemberg established a bilateral agreement, and Saxony joined forces with neighbouring states in the same year.

However, the largest single advance towards a common German market was the union of 1834, in which 18 states joined Prussia. (Others joined later, although the 'free and Hanseatic' ports of Bremen and Hamburg remained outside the union until 1888.) The Prussian tariff was levied against external trade, while there were no tariffs at all within the union. There was clearly a political dimension to the *Zollverein*. It excluded Austria from the outset, and strengthened Prussia's position. This state of affairs was challenged after the REVOLUTIONS OF 1848 by Karl Ludwig Bruck, the Austrian commerce minister, who wanted to modernize the Austrian economy on the one hand and to challenge Prussia's emerging leadership role on the other. He proposed that Austria (with Hungary) join the *Zollverein* along with the remaining states of northwestern Germany. The proposal was well received in the middling states of southern Germany but opposed by Berlin. The Prussian commerce minister Rudolf Delbruck outmanoeuvred Bruck by inviting Hanover to join separately and by winning back the support of the south Germans. Austria remained excluded from the agreement when the customs union was renewed for a further twelve years in 1854. The *Zollverein* continued to be dominated by Prussia, whose area, population and economy were all incomparably greater than those of the other members. Moreover Berlin pursued its international trade policy more or less independently, and expected the smaller states simply to fall into line. Increasingly, and despite expressions of dissent, this reflected the political domination of Germany by Prussia, and with the defeat of Austria in the AUSTRO-PRUSSIAN WAR of 1866 the management of the customs union passed to the federal council (BUNDESRAT) of the NORTH GERMAN CONFEDERATION and a *Zollparlament*, a quasi-parliamentary arrangement that foreshadowed the two chambers of the 1871 Reich, and which served to bind the states of southern Germany to Prussia.

Zuckmayer, Carl (1896–1977), writer. Born in Nackenheim, the son of a businessman, Zuckmayer started out by writing expressionist poetry. He served in World War I, was decorated, and became a member of a workers' and soldiers' council in Mainz (*see RAT*). He is best known for his dramatic works, above all *Der Hauptmann von Köpenick (The Captain of Köpenick*, 1931) and *Des Teufels General (The Devil's General*, 1946). He left Germany in 1933 for Austria, and spent the war in the United States. After the war he returned to Europe and lived in Switzerland.

Zweig, Stefan (1881–1942), Austrian-Jewish writer. Born in Vienna, the son of a Bohemian textiles manufacturer, Zweig began his career as a poet, before turning to short stories and novels. In 1916 he composed a dramatic poem directed against the war, *Jeremias*. Zweig became a best-selling author during the 1920s. He emigrated to London in 1934 and to Brazil in 1940, where he and his wife committed suicide. His best-known work is probably his autobiography, *Die Welt von Gestern* ('the world of yesterday'), a nostalgic evocation of the last years of the Habsburg empire. It was published posthumously in 1943.

Zyklon-B, gas that was used in the mass murder of the Jews by the Nazis.

MAPS AND APPENDICES

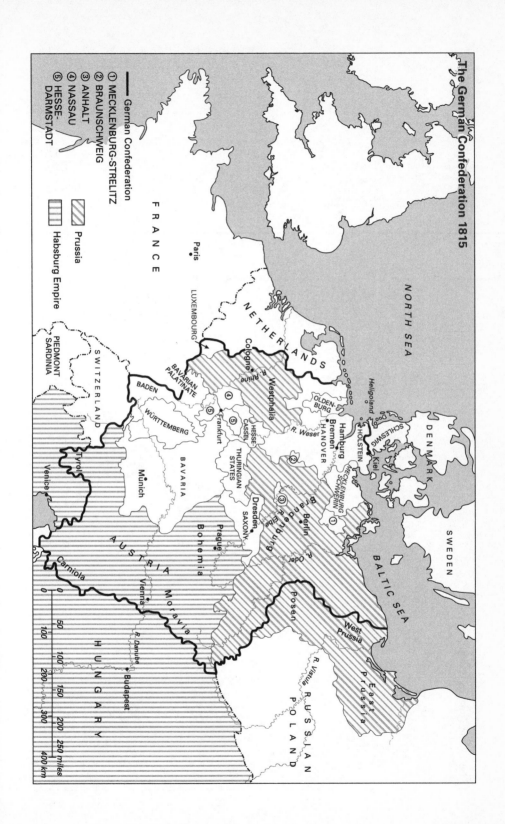

The German Confederation 1815

Legend:

— German Confederation
① MECKLENBURG-STRELITZ
② BRAUNSCHWEIG
③ ANHALT
④ NASSAU
⑤ HESSE-DARMSTADT

Prussia

Habsburg Empire

Places and regions labelled on the map:

FRANCE
Paris
LUXEMBOURG
NETHERLANDS
NORTH SEA
SWITZERLAND
PIEDMONT SARDINIA
Tirol
Venice
Carniola
BADEN
WÜRTTEMBERG
BAVARIA
Munich
BAVARIAN PALATINATE
Cologne
R. Rhine
Westphalia
OLDEN-BURG
Bremen
Hamburg
Heligoland
SCHLESWIG
HOLSTEIN
Kiel
DENMARK
SWEDEN
BALTIC SEA
MECKLENBURG-SCHWERIN
Berlin
Brandenburg
R. Oder
R. Elbe
HANOVER
R. Weser
HESSE-CASSEL
Frankfurt
THURINGIAN STATES
SAXONY
Dresden
Prague
Bohemia
Moravia
AUSTRIA
Vienna
R. Danube
HUNGARY
Budapest
Posen
West Prussia
East Prussia
R. Vistula
RUSSIAN POLAND

Scale:

0   50   100   150   200   250 miles
0   100   200   300   400 km

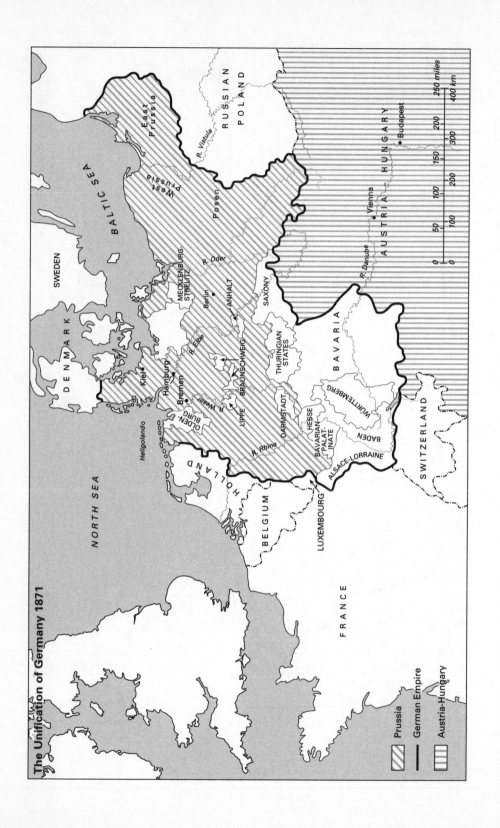

The Unification of Germany 1871

BALTIC SEA

SWEDEN

DENMARK

NORTH SEA

Heligoland

Kiel

Hamburg

Bremen

OLDEN-BURG

MECKLENBURG-STRELITZ

R. Elbe

R. Weser

LIPPE

BRAUNSCHWEIG

Berlin

ANHALT

R. Oder

SAXONY

THURINGIAN STATES

DARMSTADT

HESSE

BAVARIAN PALAT-INATE

ALSACE-LORRAINE

R. Rhine

BADEN

WÜRTTEMBERG

BAVARIA

East Prussia

West Prussia

Posen

R. Vistula

RUSSIAN POLAND

AUSTRIA — HUNGARY

Vienna

Budapest

R. Danube

SWITZERLAND

HOLLAND

BELGIUM

LUXEMBOURG

FRANCE

0 50 100 150 200 250 miles
0 100 200 300 400 km

Prussia

German Empire

Austria-Hungary

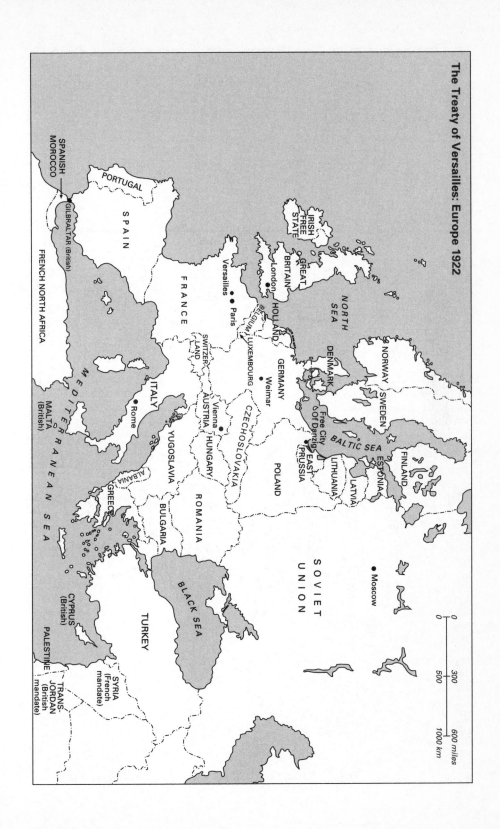

The Treaty of Versailles: Europe 1922

SPANISH MOROCCO

PORTUGAL

GILBRALTAR (British)

SPAIN

FRENCH NORTH AFRICA

IRISH FREE STATE

GREAT BRITAIN

London

NORTH SEA

Versailles

Paris

BELGIUM

HOLLAND

LUXEMBOURG

SWITZER-LAND

FRANCE

DENMARK

NORWAY

SWEDEN

Free City Of Danzig

EAST PRUSSIA

BALTIC SEA

ESTONIA

FINLAND

LATVIA

LITHUANIA

GERMANY

Weimar

AUSTRIA

Vienna

CZECHOSLOVAKIA

HUNGARY

POLAND

ITALY

Rome

YUGOSLAVIA

ALBANIA

GREECE

BULGARIA

ROMANIA

S O V I E T   U N I O N

Moscow

MEDITERRANEAN SEA

MALTA (British)

CYPRUS (British)

BLACK SEA

TURKEY

PALESTINE (British mandate)

TRANS-JORDAN (British mandate)

SYRIA (French mandate)

0   300   600 miles
0   500   1000 km

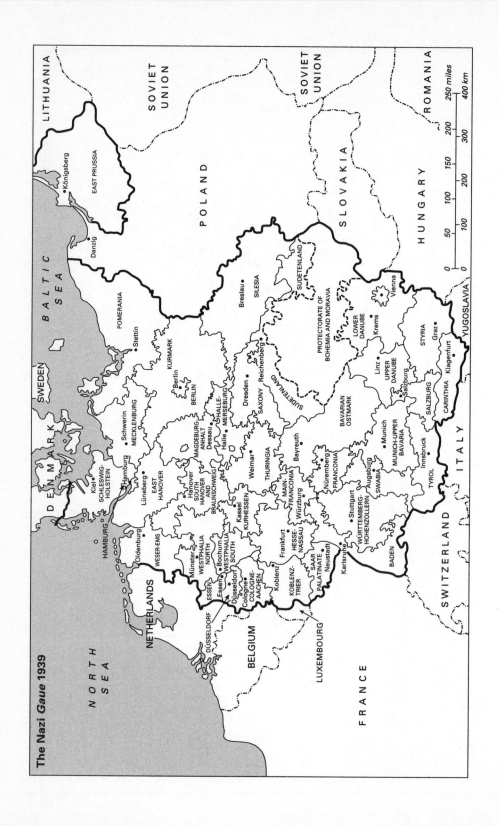

The Nazi *Gaue* 1939

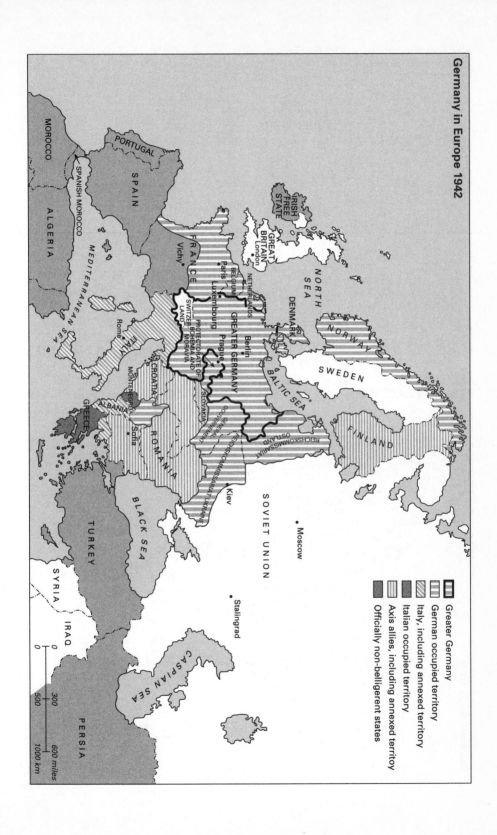

Germany in Europe 1942

Greater Germany
German occupied territory
Italy, including annexed territory
Italian occupied territory
Axis allies, including annexed territory
Officially non-belligerent states

MOROCCO
SPANISH MOROCCO
ALGERIA
PORTUGAL
SPAIN
MEDITERRANEAN SEA
FRANCE
Vichy
Paris
Luxembourg
BELGIUM
NETHERLANDS
GREAT BRITAIN
London
IRISH FREE STATE
NORTH SEA
DENMARK
NORWAY
SWEDEN
BALTIC SEA
FINLAND
GREATER GERMANY
Berlin
SWITZER-LAND
PROTECTORATE OF BOHEMIA AND MORAVIA
Prague
Rome
ITALY
SLOVAKIA
CROATIA
MONTENEGRO
ALBANIA
GREECE
Sofia
ROMANIA
GENERAL-GOUVERNEMENT
REICHSKOMMISSARIAT UKRAINE
REICHSKOMMISSARIAT OSTLAND
Kiev
BLACK SEA
TURKEY
SOVIET UNION
Moscow
Stalingrad
CASPIAN SEA
SYRIA
IRAQ
PERSIA

0   300   600 miles
0   500   1000 km

The Federal Republic of Germany 2000

DENMARK

NORTH
SEA

BALTIC
SEA

Kiel

SCHLESWIG-
HOLSTEIN

MECKLENBURG-
VORPOMMERN

Schwerin

HAMBURG

BREMEN

Lüneberg

BRANDENBURG

POLAND

Weser-Ems

LOWER SAXONY

Magdeburg

Hanover

Magdeburg   Potsdam   BERLIN

NETHER-
LANDS

Münster

Hanover

Detmold

Braun-
schweig

SAXONY-ANHALT   Dessau

Düsseldorf

Arnsberg

Halle

Leipzig

Dresden

Düsseldorf

NORTH RHINE-
WESTPHALIA

Kassel

Erfurt

SAXONY

Dresden

Cologne

Bonn

Giessen
HESSEN

THURINGIA

Chemnitz

BELGIUM

Darmstadt
Wiesbaden

Lower
Franconia

Upper
Franconia

CZECH REPUBLIC

RHINELAND-
PALATINATE

LUXEMBOURG

Mainz

SAARLAND

Saarbrücken

Central
Franconia

Upper
Palatinate

Stuttgart

Karlsruhe   Stuttgart

BAVARIA

Lower
Bavaria

FRANCE

Tübingen   Swabia

BADEN-
WÜRTTEMBERG

Freiburg

Upper Bavaria

Munich

AUSTRIA

SWITZERLAND

▪▪▪▪ Former border between East
and West Germany

ITALY

0   50   100   150 miles

0   100   200 km

CHRONOLOGY

1683
~ Turkish siege of Vienna

1685
~ Birth of Johann Sebastian BACH

1701
~ Friedrich, elector of Brandenburg becomes king of Prussia

1701–14
~ War of the Spanish Succession

1702
~ Founding of Breslau university

1705
~ Accession of Emperor Joseph I

1711
~ Accession of Emperor KARL VI

1713
~ Accession of Friedrich Wilhelm I of Prussia
~ PRAGMATIC SANCTION

1713–15
~ Treaties establish peace of UTRECHT

1714
~ HELIGOLAND ceded to Denmark

1716–18
~ War between Austria and Turkey

1718
~ Founding of the Vienna porcelain manu-factory

1719
~ Foundation of the Austrian Oriental Company in Trieste; it was dissolved, along with Austria's other overseas trading companies, in 1731 following conflicts with Britain

1723
~ GENERAL DIRECTORY established in Berlin as central Prussian governmental apparatus

1724
~ Pragmatic Sanction proclaimed as law in Vienna

1736
~ Founding of Göttingen University

1740
~ Accession of MARIA THERESIA; beginning of the War of the AUSTRIAN SUCCESSION
~ Accession of FRIEDRICH II (Frederick the Great) of Prussia; he invades SILESIA and captures BRESLAU (now Wrocław)

1742
January With the accession of the elector of Bavaria as Emperor KARL VII, the imperial crown passes away from the HABSBURGS for the first time in centuries

17 May Narrow Prussian victory at the battle of Chotusitz

1743

~ Founding of Erlangen University

1744–7

~ Building of SANSSOUCI palace in Potsdam

1745

April Peace concluded between Austria and Bavaria

4 June Prussian victory at Hohenfriedberg

30 September Prussian victory at Soor

15 December Prussian victory at Kesselsdorf

25 December Peace of DRESDEN confirms the cession of Prussian Silesia, agreed in the truce of 1742

~ Accession of Emperor FRANZ I

1748

~ Peace of AACHEN ends the War of the Austrian Succession

1749

~ Birth of GOETHE

1756–63

~ SEVEN YEARS WAR

1756

29 August Friedrich II invades Saxony

~ Birth of MOZART

1757

6 May Prussian victory at Prague

18 June Austrian victory over Prussia at Kolin

30 August Russia defeats Prussian army defending East Prussia at Gross Jägersdorf

5 November Prussian victory over French and imperial troops at the Battle of Rossbach

5 December Prussian victory over Austrian troops at the battle of Leuthen (Lutynia in Poland)

1758

January Russian occupation of East Prussia

25 August Prussian victory at Zorndorf compels Russia to evacuate Neumark and Pomerania

14 October Austrian victory over Prussia at Hochkirch

1759

23 July Prussia defeated at the battle of Kay (Paltzig)

12 August Prussia defeated by Russia at the battle of Kunersdorf

1760

15 August Austria defeated at Liegnitz

3 November Austria defeated by Prussia at Torgau

1762

5 January Death of Elizabeth, empress of Russia; her successor, Peter III, concludes peace with Prussia (5 May)

22 May Prussia concludes a separate peace with Sweden

21 July Prussian defeat of Austria at Burkersdorf

16 August Prussian defeat of Austria at Reichenbach

29 October Prussian victory over Austrian and imperial troops at Freiberg (Saxony)

3 November Preliminary peace of Fontainebleau

1763

15 February Peace of Hubertusberg: the territorial arrangements of 1756 remain unaltered

~ Implementation of a system of primary schooling in Prussia

1764

~ Founding of universities of Dresden and Leipzig

1765

~ Accession of Emperor JOSEPH II

1770

~ Birth of BEETHOVEN

1772

~ First partition of Poland: Austria obtains Galicia, which becomes a Crown land under the title of Kingdom of Galicia and Lodomeria; Friedrich II acquires West Prussia, with the exception of DANZIG and Thorn

~ *Seehandlungsgesellschaft* (predecessor of the Prussian State Bank) founded in Berlin by FRIEDRICH II

1778–9

~ War of the BAVARIAN SUCCESSION

1781

~ JOSEPH II's EDICT OF TOLERATION grants freedom of worship to non-Catholics

1786

17 August Death of FRIEDRICH II (Frederick the Great) of Prussia; accession of FRIEDRICH WILHELM II of Prussia

1788–91

~ Building of BRANDENBURG GATE in Berlin

1789

~ Revolt of the AUSTRIAN NETHERLANDS

~ French revolution

1790

~ Accession of Emperor LEOPOLD II

1792

20 April France declares war on Austria and Prussia beginning the War of the First COALITION (1792–7)

20 September Battle of Valmy; the Prussian army retreats

~ Accession of FRANZ II, last Holy Roman Emperor

1793

17 March Rhenish–German Convention in Mainz declares a republic which later (*23 July*) votes to merge with France

~ Declaration of war on France by the REICHSTAG

~ French occupation of the Austrian Netherlands and the Rhineland

~ Second partition of Poland: Prussia, under Friedrich Wilhelm II, acquires DANZIG and Thorn and a new province of South Prussia

1794

26 June France defeats Austria at Fleurus

~ Prussian legal code (*Allgemeines Landrecht*) is promulgated

~ Regulations introduced restricting the organization of labour and enforcing industrial discipline

1795

~ Third partition of Poland: Friedrich Wilhelm II acquires New East Prussia

~ Peace between France and Prussia

1797

~ War of the First COALITION ends with the treaty of CAMPO FORMIO between France and Austria

~ Accession of FRIEDRICH WILHELM III of Prussia

1799–1804

~ Alexander von HUMBOLDT's journeys in South and Central America

1800

~ Battle of Hohenlinden

1801

9 February Treaty of Lunéville is signed ending the War of the Second COALITION

1803

6 August Final decree of the Reich Deputation (*REICHSDEPUTATIONSHAUPTSCHLUSS*)

~ German ecclesiastical states are secularized

1804

12 February Death of Emmanuel KANT

~ Emperor FRANZ II takes the title emperor of Austria

1805

9 May Death of Friedrich von SCHILLER

17 October Defeat of Austria by France at the battle of Ulm

2 December Battle of the Three Emperors at AUSTERLITZ

26 December Peace of Pressburg ends the War of the Third COALITION

1806

12 July Establishment of the CONFEDERATION OF THE RHINE

6 August Abolition of the HOLY ROMAN EMPIRE; Franz II abdicates

14 October Defeat of Prussia by France at the battles of JENA and Auerstedt

1807

7–9 July Treaty of TILSIT

September Freiherr vom STEIN takes over the leadership of the Prussian government and begins to institute major reforms

9 October Emancipation of the SERFS in Prussia

1808

19 November Introduction of limited male franchise (with property qualification) in Prussian towns and cities

1809

April Rising of Austria and the TYROL against Napoleon

1 May Bavarian constitution is promulgated

21–2 May Battle of ASPERN: Napoleon is defeated for the first time during the Wars of the COALITIONS

5–6 July Defeat of Austria by Napoleon at the battle of WAGRAM

8 October Prince METTERNICH becomes foreign minister of the HABSBURG hereditary lands and effectively takes over leadership of Austrian government

14 October Treaty of Schönbrunn ends the War of the Fifth COALITION

~ Saxony-Weimar consitution is promulgated

1810

~ Founding of Berlin University

1811

~ Abolition of feudal labour service (corvée) in Prussia

~ Austrian legal code (*Allgemeines Bürgerliches Gesetzbuch*) is promulgated

~ KRUPP works founded in Essen

1812

30 December Convention of Tauroggen permits Russia to levy troops from East Prussia and thus provides the wherewithal for the Wars of LIBERATION

~ Emancipation of the Jews in Prussia; establishment of the secondary school system in Prussia, based on humanistic education in the *Gymnasium*

1813

16–19 October 'Battle of the Nations' at LEIPZIG marks the end of Napoleon's ambitions in the east

October Dissolution of the CONFEDERATION OF THE RHINE

1814

14 January HELIGOLAND ceded to Great Britain

Spring Occupation of Paris and exile of Napoleon on Elba

30 May First treaty of PARIS

~ Nassau constitution is promulgated

1814–15

~ Congress of VIENNA

1815

9 June Promulgation of the BUNDESAKTE ('federal acts'); establishment of the GERMAN CONFEDERATION

18 June Battle of WATERLOO

26 September HOLY ALLIANCE formed between Austria, Prussia and Russia

20 November Second treaty of PARIS; QUADRUPLE ALLIANCE is formed between Austria, Prussia, Russia and Great Britain to enforce the provisions of the treaty

1816

6 November Opening of Federal Assembly of the German Confederation at Frankfurt

15 November Concluding protocol of Congress of AACHEN

1817

17–18 October WARTBURG RALLY

1818

26 May Bavarian constitution is promulgated

22 August Baden constitution is promulgated

18 October Founding of German student corporation (*see BURSCHENSCHAFTEN*) in Jena

~ University founded at Bonn

1819

23 March Murder of August von KOTZEBUE

20 September KARLSBAD DECREES promulgated in response to student unrest

25 September Württemberg constitution is promulgated

1820

15 May Final Acts of Vienna (*Wiener Schluss-akte*) extending the BUNDESAKTE of 1815

~ Congress of TROPPAU

1821

~ Congress of LAIBACH

1822

~ Congress of VERONA

1823

~ First performance of BEETHOVEN's Ninth Symphony

1826

~ Founding of Munich University

1828

~ Customs agreement between Prussia and Hessen-Darmstadt

~ Central German customs union

1829

~ Alexander von HUMBOLDT's journey to northern Asia

1830

September Riots in many parts of Germany following the July revolution in France

November Uprising in Poland

24 December Student unrest in Munich

1831

5 January Hesse constitution is promulgated

4 September Constitution in Saxony

~ Saxon constitution is promulgated

1832

29 January Founding of liberal German Press and Fatherland Association

22 March Death of GOETHE in Weimar

27 May HAMBACH FESTIVAL

~ Founding of liberal nationalist *Deutscher Volksverein* by refugees in Paris

1833

4 April Guard positions in Frankfurt are stormed by insurgents

~ Hanover constitution is promulgated

~ First workers' educational associations founded in Leipzig and Erlangen

1834

1 January Customs Union (*ZOLLVEREIN*) comes into force

April YOUNG GERMANY founded in Switzerland

1835

March Accession of FERDINAND I, emperor of Austria

7 December Opening of the first German railway from Nuremberg to Fürth

1837

~ Protest of the GÖTTINGEN SEVEN against the suspension of the Hanover constitution

1842

~ Karl BAEDEKER publishes his *Handbuch für Reisende in Deutschland und das österreich-ischen Kaiserreich* ('Handbook for Travellers in Germany and the Austrian Empire')

1844

4–6 June Uprising of Silesian weavers in the villages of Langenbielau and Peterswaldau

9 October Founding of the Central Association for the Welfare of the Working Classes by liberal social reformers

1845

~ First workers' consumer co-operative founded in Chemnitz

1847

21 April Hunger riots across Germany; attacks on butchers, bakers and markets in Berlin

12 September OFFENBURG MANIFESTO of the south-west German radicals

10 October HEPPENHEIM PROGRAMME of south-west German liberals

~ Prussian UNITED DIET

~ Founding of the Communist League

~ First Catholic workers' association founded in Regensburg

1848

See REVOLUTIONS OF 1848

February Publication of *Communist Manifesto*

27 February–13 March Outbreak of revolution in Vienna; METTERNICH flees to England

3 March Mass demonstration of workers in Cologne

5 March Meeting of prominent south-west German liberals at Heidelberg

8 March Outbreak of revolution in Berlin

20 March Abdication of Ludwig I of Bavaria

21 March–3 April PRE-PARLIAMENT in Frankfurt am Main

23 March Uprising in Kiel leads to Prussian military intervention in Schleswig-Holstein

April Republican uprising in Baden

15 May Second uprising in Vienna

18 May First session of the FRANKFURT PARLIAMENT

29 June Archduke Johann appointed REICHSVERWESER (imperial regent)

23 August–3 September General German Workers' Congress meets in Berlin

26 August Armistice of Malmö ends German–Danish War

18 September Uprising in Frankfurt

21–25 September Second republican uprising in Baden

6–31 October Third uprising in Vienna

10 November Troops occupy Berlin

2 December Abdication of FERDINAND I; accession of FRANZ JOSEPH

27 December Promulgation of basic civil rights by Frankfurt Parliament

1849

28 March Promulgation of Reich constitution

3 April FRIEDRICH WILHELM IV of Prussia rejects imperial crown

April–May Uprisings in Dresden and elsewhere in support of the constitution

12–16 May Third republican uprising in Baden

26 May ERFURT UNION is formed

30 May Electoral law in Prussia introduces the three-class voting system

6–18 June 'Rump' parliament held in Stuttgart

~ First German postage stamps introduced in Bavaria

~ First Reuter press office founded in Aachen (later re-established in London)

1850

20 March–29 April ERFURT UNION parliament

1 September Reopening of the federal diet of the GERMAN CONFEDERATION in Frankfurt

29 November Treaty of OLMÜTZ

1851

~ Repeal of the basic rights agreed at the FRANKFURT PARLIAMENT

1852

~ GRIMM BROTHERS begin their work on a German dictionary

1853

~ Dissolution of the German federal navy

1855

~ Concordat between Austria and the Catholic church gives the church far-reaching powers

1857

~ First international economic crisis affects Germany in the wake of industrialization during the 1850s

1858–61

~ WILHELM I rules as regent on behalf of his brother FRIEDRICH WILHELM IV

1859

~ Prussian army reforms are instituted by war minister Albrecht von ROON

~ Austria loses Lombardy after defeat by France and Piedmont in Italy

1860

October 20 Austrian October Diploma granted

1861

June DEUTSCHE FORTSCHRITTSPARTEI (Progress Party) is founded by breakaway Prussian liberals

1862

~ Constitutional crisis in Prussia; BISMARCK becomes minister-president and foreign minister

1863

~ LASALLE founds the General German Workers' Association (ADAV)

~ Hoechst is founded in Frankfurt, and Bayer in Leverkusen; two companies which in 1916 will form part of the industrial cartel IG FARBEN

1864

~ Second GERMAN–DANISH WAR

30 October Peace of Vienna between Austria, Prussia and Denmark: Schleswig is ceded to Prussia and Holstein to Austria

1865

14 August Gastein agreement regulates the occupation of Schleswig and Holstein

16 October Founding of the *Allgemeiner Deutscher Frauenverein* (General German Women's Association) at a women's conference in Leipzig under the leadership of Luise OTTO

~ BASF (Badische Anilin- und Sodafabrik) is founded in Mannheim

~ First performance of WAGNER's *Tristan und Isolde*

1866

June–July AUSTRO-PRUSSIAN WAR (Seven Weeks War)

3 July Battle of SADOVÀ (Königgrätz): Austria is defeated by Prussia

26 July (Preliminary) Peace Treaty of Nikolsburg

19 August Founding of Saxon People's Party in Chemnitz by August BEBEL and Wilhelm LIEBKNECHT

23 August Peace of Prague, dissolution of the GERMAN CONFEDERATION: Schleswig and Holstein become Prussian, Austria loses Lombardy and Venetia to Italy but retains

Istria and Dalmatia, together with Ragusa

14 September Prussian INDEMNITY LAW settles the constitutional conflict between the crown and the diet

20 September Prussian annexations in northern Germany

1867

February AUSGLEICH ('compromise') between Austria and Hungary

12 February Elections to the constituent Reichstag of the NORTH GERMAN CONFEDERATION

12 June NATIONAL LIBERAL PARTY publishes its founding programme

14 June Constitution of the North German Confederation is accepted; BISMARCK becomes federal chancellor and foreign minister

~ First volume of *Das Kapital* is published by Karl MARX

1868

~ Discovery of Troy by Heinrich Schliemann

1869

~ Founding of the Social Democratic Workers Party (SDAP) in Eisanach by August BEBEL and Wilhelm LIEBKNECHT

1870–1

~ FRANCO-PRUSSIAN WAR

1870

13 July EMS TELEGRAM sent

1–2 September Battle of SEDAN

December Founding of the CENTRE PARTY

~ Founding of Deutsche Bank

1871

January Prussian occupation of Paris leads to French capitulation

18 January GERMAN EMPIRE is proclaimed at Versailles; WILHELM I becomes Kaiser

10 May Treaty of Frankfurt: Germany annexes Alsace and half of Lorraine and

France is compelled to pay occupation costs

~ Catholic section of Prussian culture ministry is closed

1872

~ Jesuit activity is forbidden in Germany

~ Friedrich NIETSZCHE publishes *Birth of Tragedy*

1873

~ *May* Stock market crashes in Vienna, marking the beginning of the 'Great Depression'; 'May Laws' directed against the influence of the Catholic church in Prussia

~ World exhibition in Vienna

1874

~ Reichstag elections: Conservatives lose 35 of their 57 seats; NATIONAL LIBERAL PARTY and CENTRE PARTY gain seats

1875

~ Founding of the SAPD (Socialist Workers' Party of Germany) at Gotha by a merger of the SDAP and ADAV

1876

15 February Founding of the Central Union of German Industrialists

~ Founding of the REICHSBANK

~ First performance of WAGNER's *Siegfried* and *Götterdämmerung*

1877

~ Reichstag elections: NATIONAL LIBERAL PARTY lose seats

1878

11 May and 2 June Assassination attempts on emperor WILHELM I

13 June–13 July Congress of BERLIN held with a view to creating stability in the Balkans

13 July Treaty of Berlin makes Austria-Hungary administrator of BOSNIA AND HERZEGOVINA

19 October ANTI-SOCIALIST LAWS passed by the Reichstag

~ Reichstag elections: *DEUTSCHKONSERVATIVE PARTEI* and *FREIKONSERVATIVE PARTEI* gain seats

1879

12 July Passing of protectionist legislation by the Reichstag marks a change in the direction of Bismarck's domestic policy

7 October DUAL ALLIANCE concluded between Germany and Austria-Hungary

~ Technical universities founded in Berlin and Hanover

1880

4 May Right wing of CENTRE PARTY supports renewal of ANTI-SOCIALIST LAWS

~ Legislation is passed to moderate the anti-Catholic laws of 1870s *KULTURKAMPF*

1881

18 June THREE EMPERORS' LEAGUE agreement signed by Germany, Austria-Hungary and Russia

~ Reichstag elections: CENTRE PARTY becomes largest single party

1882

20 May TRIPLE ALLIANCE signed by Germany, Austria-Hungary and Italy

~ *DEUTSCHER KOLONIALVEREIN* (German Colonial Association) formed

~ First territory is acquired in SOUTH-WEST AFRICA by the Bremen merchant F.A.E. Lüderitz

1883

~ Sickness Insurance Law is passed

1884

~ Germany annexes SOUTH-WEST AFRICA, TOGOLAND and CAMEROON

~ German New Guinea Company formed

~ Accident Insurance Law is passed

~ Establishment of the Society for German Colonization by Karl PETERS

1884–5

~ Conference of BERLIN held to discuss territorial disputes in West Africa

1885

~ German annexation of Pacific islands

~ German East Africa Company formed (*see* GERMAN EAST AFRICA)

1886

~ Treaty with Angola determines the border with German South-West Africa

~ NIETSCHE publishes *Beyond Good and Evil*

1887

21 February Reichstag elections: SPD increases its share of the vote (to 10.1%) but loses 13 seats; CENTRE PARTY remains the largest single party

18 June REINSURANCE TREATY is signed by Germany and Russia

~ Work begins on the KIEL CANAL

1888

9 March–15 June Reign of emperor FRIEDRICH III; he is succeeded by Kaiser WILHELM II

1889

~ Old Age and Invalidity Insurance Law is passed

1890

20 February Reichstag elections: Conservative and NATIONAL LIBERAL losses; the SPD and CENTRE PARTY both gain, but the SPD, with over 1.4 million votes (10.1%) becomes the single most popular party, overtaking the Centre

20 March BISMARCK is dismissed by WILHELM II; Leo von CAPRIVI becomes Reich chancellor

27 March REINSURANCE TREATY lapses

1 July HELIGOLAND–Zanzibar Treaty: Heligoland is transferred to Germany by Britain in return for Zanzibar

8 August *Freie Volksbühne* theatre is founded in Berlin

24 October Founding of the popular Catholic association *Volksverein für das katholischer Deutschland* in Cologne

1891

21 October ERFURT PROGRAMME of the SPD

~ Founding of the General German League (the future PAN-GERMAN LEAGUE)

1892

~ First issue of the art journal *Blätter für die Kunst*

~ Munich SECESSION founded

1893

15 June Reichstag elections: SPD vote increases by 350,000 to 1.7 million, confirming its position as most popular party, but winning fewer than half the seats of its nearest rival (CENTRE PARTY); the vote for anti-Semitic parties increases five-fold

1894

~ *OSTMARKENVEREIN* (Eastern Marches Association) formed to combat 'Polonism'

~ General German League changes its name to PAN-GERMAN LEAGUE

~ Chlodwig Fürst zu HOHENLOHE-SCHILLINGSFÜRST becomes Reich chancellor

~ Reichstag building is completed

~ Work starts on Berlin cathedral

1895

8 November Wilhelm Conrad Röntgen discovers X-rays

~ KIEL CANAL is opened

1896

~ Unified legal code (*Bürgerliches Gesetzbuch*) is established for the German empire

~ Werner von SIEMENS and Johann Georg Halske begin work on a metropolitan railway system for Berlin, combining underground and overhead railways

1897

~ Vienna SECESSION is founded by Gustav KLIMT

~ Bernhard von BÜLOW becomes foreign minister

1898

30 July Death of BISMARCK at Friedrichsruh

~ Berlin SECESSION is founded

~ Germany acquires KIAOCHOW in eastern China

~ Founding of the NAVY LEAGUE

1898–1900

~ Navy Laws authorize massive expansion of the navy

1899

~ Germany purchases Caroline, Pelew and Mariana Islands in the South Pacific

~ First issue of Karl KRAUS's journal *Die Fackel* in Vienna

1900

28 January German football league (*Deutscher Fussball Bund*, DFB) founded in Leipzig

28 February In Baden women are allowed unrestricted access to higher education for the first time in Germany

22 May *Lex Heinze* strengthens and extends censorship law

June BOXER REBELLION

2 July First test flight of a ZEPPELIN airship at Lake Constance

25 August Death of NIETZSCHE in Weimar

10 October HOHENLOHE-SCHILLINGSFÜRST resigns; his successor as chancellor is BÜLOW

~ FREUD publishes *The Interpretation of Dreams*

1901

17 June German and Austro-Hungarian delegates at a conference in Berlin agree a common German spelling system based on Konrad Duden's dictionary of 1880

14 November Austrian doctor Karl Landsteiner publishes the results of his research on blood, revealing the discovery of three distinct types, A B and O

1902

15 February Opening of the first stretch of Berlin's metropolitan railway, between Warschauer Strasse and Zoo station

1903

13 April Baghdad railway company founded in Berlin

24 May German motorcyclists' organization (*Deutscher Motorradfahrer Vereinigung*) founded in Stuttgart

16 June Reichstag elections: CENTRE PARTY remains the largest party in the Reichstag with almost 1.9 million votes but has less than two-thirds of the votes cast for the SPD (3 million), which is the most popular party for the fourth successive general election

1 September First conference of municipal authorities (*Deutscher Städtetag*) meets in Dresden

20 November Landtag elections in Prussia: SPD wins 19% of the vote but no seats

15 December German Artists' League (*Deutscher Künstlerbund*) founded in Dresden

1904

12 January Herero uprising begins in German SOUTH-WEST AFRICA

23 March Police confiscate copies of Frank WEDEKIND's *Büchse der Pandora* (*Pandora's Box*)

8 April Entente Cordiale is agreed between Great Britain and France

4 May Founding of Schalke 04 football club

9 May *Reichsverband gegen die Sozialdemokratie* (Reich Association against Social Democracy) is founded

23 June Rosa LUXEMBURG is sentenced to three months' imprisonment for lese majesty

12 July International Women's Congress in Berlin

11 August Brutal suppression of Herero rising

1905

17 January–9 February Ruhr miners' strike against employers' attempts to extend

working hours is supported by 80% of the workforce

20 March BETHMANN HOLLWEG becomes Prussian interior minister

31 March WILHELM II visits Tangier (*see* MOROCCAN CRISIS OF 1905)

7 June Die BRÜCKE artists' community is founded in Dresden

22 June German Society for Racial Hygiene is founded in Berlin by Alfred Ploetz

~ Heinrich MANN publishes *Professor Unrat*, the novel on which the film *Der Blaue Engel* (*The Blue Angel*) was later based

~ Max WEBER publishes *The Protestant Ethic and the Spirit of Capitalism*

1906

16 January–7 April ALGECIRAS CONFERENCE

1 December Austrian parliament introduces universal manhood suffrage

1907

25 January 'HOTTENTOT ELECTION': despite the nationalistic tenor of the election campaign, SPD gains a quarter of a million extra votes; but loses almost half its seats

11 May Parliamentary elections in Austria: Social Democrats form the largest group in parliament

6 October DEUTSCHER WERKBUND is founded in Munich

~ Creation of German Colonial Office

~ Rainer Maria Rilke publishes *Neue Gedichte*

1908

15 May In accordance with a law of 8 April German women are allowed to join associations and political parties for the first time

16 June Prussian Landtag elections: Seven SPD candidates (including LIEBKNECHT, who was imprisoned for treason in 1907) win seats

5 October Austria annexes BOSNIA AND HERZEGOVINA

7 October Women are allowed to study in Prussian universities

28 October Interview with the Kaiser published in the British *Daily Telegraph* leading to the DAILY TELEGRAPH AFFAIR

1909

4 January German Judges Association (*Deutscher Richterbund*) is formed in Berlin to preserve independence of judiciary from executive

3 May German Doctors' Association (*Reichsverband deutscher Ärzte*) is founded in Berlin

2 June Karl LIEBKNECHT is released from jail and takes up the Landtag seat to which he was elected while imprisoned

24 June DEUTSCHKONSERVATIVE PARTEI votes against the government on the issue of inheritance tax; this marks the end of the chancellor's coalition (the so-called BÜLOW block)

30 June German Farmers' League (*Deutscher Bauernbund*) founded in Berlin to represent the interests of smaller farmers neglected by the AGRARIAN LEAGUE

14 July BETHMANN HOLLWEG replaces Bülow as chancellor

23 October Saxon Landtag elections: SPD wins a majority (53.8%) of the vote, but only 25 of the 91 seats

7 December German scientists Karl Ferdinand Braun and Wilhelm Ostwald win Nobel prizes for physics and chemistry (the former with Marconi)

1910

6 March Founding of the FORTSCHRITTLICHE VOLKSPARTEI (Progressive People's Party) through the merger of left liberal groups

12 September First performance of MAHLER's eighth symphony in Munich

1911

13 March BETHMANN HOLLWEG rejects British proposal for an arms limitation agreement

1 July German gunboat 'Panther' sent to AGADIR (second Moroccan crisis)

18 December First BLAUE REITER exhibition in Munich

1912

12 January Reichstag elections: SPD becomes the largest party

~ Thomas MANN publishes *Death in Venice* (*Der Tod in Venedig*)

1913

23 April Reichstag approves Law for the Strengthening of Germandom in Posen and West Prussia

6 November Protests against the German military by Alsatian civilians in the ZABERN AFFAIR

8 November First performance of BÜCHNER's *Woyzeck* in Munich

1914

16 March Parliamentary crisis in Austria leads to the dissolution of parliament and rule by emergency imperial decree

28 June Archduke FRANZ FERDINAND assassinated at Sarajevo

23 July Austria issues an ultimatum to Serbia

1 August Germany declares war on Russia

3 August Germany declares war on France

13 August Raw materials section (*Kriegsrohstoffabteilung*) of Prussian war ministry is established under Walter RATHENAU

26–31 August Battle of TANNENBERG

6–9 September Battle of the MARNE

9 October German troops take Antwerp

12 October–11 November First battle of YPRES

1 November HINDENBURG is appointed supreme commander on the eastern front

2–5 November Entente powers declare war on Turkey

2 December Austrian troops take Belgrade; Karl LIEBKNECHT breaks ranks with the SPD and votes against further war credits

1915

February Russians retreat from East Prussia

22 February Beginning of submarine warfare

22 April–24 May Second battle of YPRES: Germans use poison gas for the first time

2–4 May CENTRAL POWERS achieve breakthrough in Carpathian offensive

4 May Italy leaves the TRIPLE ALLIANCE

5 May PAN-GERMAN LEAGUE urges annexation of the Baltic

7 May German submarines sink the British passenger ship *Lusitania*

23 May Italy joins the war on the side of the Allies

22 June Austria retakes Lemberg (Lviv)

4–5 August Germans enter Warsaw

9 October Central Powers take Belgrade

14 October Bulgaria officially enters the war on the side of the Central Powers

24 November Central Powers' conquest of Serbia is complete

21 December 20 SPD members vote against further war credits and a further 22 abstain

1916

13 January Chancellor BETHMANN HOLLWEG announces intention to reform the Prussian THREE-CLASS VOTING SYSTEM

15 January First 'Balkan express' train from Berlin to Constantinople

5 February Dadaist Cabaret Voltaire opens in Zürich

21 February–18 December Battle of VERDUN

15 March Admiral TIRPITZ resigns following unsuccessful demand for unrestricted submarine warfare

11 May Reich interior minister Clemens von Delbrück resigns

31 May–1 June Battle of JUTLAND

June Mass strikes in Berlin, Bremen and Braunschweig

27 August Romania joins the war on the Allied side and invades Transylvania

21 October Austrian minister-president STÜRGKH is assassinated by Friedrich ADLER

5 November Germany and Austria declare an independent Poland

21 November Death of Austrian emperor FRANZ JOSEPH

12 December Central Powers make a peace offer (rejected by the Allies on 30 December)

1917

1 February Unrestricted submarine warfare begins

March Revolution breaks out in Russia

April USPD is founded by dissident members of the SPD

6 April USA enters the war

9 April–3 May Battle of Arras: Canadians take VIMY RIDGE

3 July BETHMANN HOLLWEG resigns as chancellor under pressure from generals HINDENBURG and LUDENDORFF

19 July PEACE RESOLUTION is proposed in the Reichstag

31 July–6 November Third battle of YPRES

2 September Founding of the extreme right-wing VATERLANDSPARTEI (Fatherland Party)

31 October Chancellor MICHAELIS resigns

5 November Austro-German war aims conference takes place in Berlin

7 November Bolshevik revolution in Russia

20 November–7 December Battle of CAMBRAI: first mass use of British tanks

2 December Fighting ends on the Russian front

3 December Austria and Germany end their Italian campaign

7 December USA declares war on Austria-Hungary

18 December UFA (Universum Film AG) founded

1918

January Strike movement in Austria-Hungary; strikes in Germany organized by Revolutionary Shop Stewards

8 January US president Woodrow Wilson delivers 'Fourteen Points' speech proposing an end to the war

9 February Separate peace with Ukraine

3 March Treaty of BREST-LITOVSK

7 March Separate peace with Finland

21 March German spring offensive on the Somme

7 May Treaty of BUCHAREST

8–11 August Battle of AMIENS

29 September German military leaders request armistice negotiations

30 September Chancellor HERTLING resigns

3 October Prince Max von BADEN becomes Reich chancellor

23 October USA refuses to conclude peace with an authoritarian German government

26 October Reform of constitution: LUDEN-DORFF is effectively dismissed; GROENER is appointed as his successor

November See NOVEMBER REVOLUTION

3 November KIEL MUTINY is suppressed and escalates to armed revolt; workers and sailors' councils (*RÄTE*) are established

6 November Revolution spreads to Hamburg, Bremen and Lübeck

7 November Revolution in Munich: BAVARIA is declared a republic

8 November Government of Workers' Peasants' and Soldiers' Councils set up in Bavaria under Kurt EISNER

9 November Declaration of the German republic by Philipp SCHEIDEMANN; Emperor WILHELM II abdicates; Prince Max von BADEN resigns and Friedrich EBERT becomes chancellor

10 November Formation of the COUNCIL OF PEOPLE'S REPRESENTATIVES; WILHELM II flees to the Netherlands

11 November Armistice is concluded at Compiègne

12 November Declaration of the Republic of German Austria and its *ANSCHLUSS* with the Reich, which is prohibited by the Allies

15 November STINNES–LEGIEN AGREEMENT: establishment of *Zentralarbeitsgemeinschaft* (ZAG), a co-operative forum for workers and employers

16–20 December CONGRESS OF WORKERS' AND SOLDIERS' COUNCILS meets in Berlin

25 December STAHLHELM veterans' association is formed

30 December Opening of the founding conference of the German Communist Party (KPD)

1919

5 January Founding of the radical right-wing *DEUTSCHE ARBEITERPARTEI* (German Workers' Party), which subsequently became the Nazi Party (NSDAP)

5–11 January General strike and Communist SPARTACUS UPRISING in Berlin

15 January Murder of SPARTACUS LEAGUE leaders Karl LIEBKNECHT and Rosa LUXEMBURG

6 February Opening of the NATIONAL ASSEMBLY in Weimar

11 February Friedrich EBERT is elected Reich president

13 February–20 June Scheidemann administration

21 February Kurt EISNER is assassinated by right-wingers

6 April Councils' Republic (*Räterepublik*) is established in BAVARIA

2 May Bavarian republic is suppressed by the army and FREIKORPS units

21 June Gustav BAUER becomes chancellor

28 June Signing of the treaty of VERSAILLES

11 August Weimar constitution comes into force

21 August Ebert takes the oath as Reich president without further confirmation by election

September Beginning of financial reforms of Matthias ERZBERGER

8 October Hugo HAASE, leader of the USPD, is shot; he dies on 17 November

1920

10 January Treaty of VERSAILLES comes into force

13 January 42 killed when a USPD–KPD

demonstration in front of the Reichstag is dispersed by machine-gun fire

4 February WORKS COUNCIL LAW ratified setting up joint committees of employers' and workers' representatives in German industry

10 February Plebiscite in northen zone of North Schleswig: 75% vote to become part of Denmark

24 February Programme of the DEUTSCHE ARBEITERPARTEI (German Workers' Party) adopted

27 February Première of WIENE's *The Cabinet of Dr Caligari*

12–17 March KAPP PUTSCH

14 March Plebiscite in the southern zone of North Schleswig: 80% vote to remain part of Germany

15 March–20 May Communist insurrection in the RUHR VALLEY

27 March Formation of MÜLLER government ('Weimar coalition')

5 June First international DADA fair in Berlin

6 June Reichstag elections: 'Weimar coalition' parties lose heavily and gains are made by the USPD and by the conservative (DVP) and nationalist (DNVP) parties

25 June New centre–right (minority) government is formed under Konstantin FEHRENBACH

11 July Plebiscites in the districts of Allenstein (East Prussia) and Marienwerder (West Prussia): 98% and 92% vote to remain part of Germany rather than become part of Poland

20 September Transfer of Eupen and Malmédy to Belgium is resolved by LEAGUE OF NATIONS

16 October USPD splits; the left wing (majority) later joins KPD

27 October Allies resolve to establish the Free City of DANZIG

1921

24–29 January Paris Conference on REPARATIONS

20 February Prussian Landtag elections: 'Weimar coalition' parties lose support

21 February–14 March London Conference on REPARATIONS

8 March Allied occupation of Düsseldorf and Duisburg

20 March Plebiscite in Upper Silesia: 60% vote to remain part of Germany rather than become part of Poland

29 March Special courts set up in the wake of Communist disturbances in central Germany

April First branch of the NSDAP is established outside Munich (Rosenheim, Bavaria)

16 April Pro-ANSCHLUSS demonstrations in Vienna

27 April Allied Reparations Commission sets the total reparations bill at 132 billion gold marks

4 May Resignation of FEHRENBACH government in order to avoid the responsibility for fulfilment of Allied reparations demands

5 May 'London Ultimatum': the Allies threaten to occupy the Ruhr if their demands are not met

7 May Konrad ADENAUER is elected president of Prussian state council

10 May Formation of new Weimar coalition government led by Joseph WIRTH

11 May Reichstag accepts London reparations plan unconditionally by 220 votes to 172

29 May 99% vote for *Anschluss* in an unofficial plebiscite in Salzburg

9 June USPD leader Karl Gareis is assassinated

29 July HITLER becomes the first chairman of the NSDAP

3 August Nazi paramilitary formation established (later the SA)

26 August Assassination of Matthias ERZBERGER by right-wing naval officers

1 November Resignation of CENTRE PARTY–DDP minority government in Prussia

5 November Formation of grand coalition in Prussia (SPD–DDP–CENTRE–DVP) under (Carl) Otto BRAUN, with Carl SEVERING as interior minister

10 December Albert EINSTEIN wins Nobel prize for physics

1922

5 March Première of F.W. Murnau's film *Nosferatu*

1 April Death of the last Habsburg emperor KARL I

16 April Treaty of RAPALLO establishes economic cooperation between Germany and the Soviet Union

24 June Murder of foreign minister Walter RATHENAU by members of the radical right-wing terrorist group CONSUL

18 July Law for the Protection of the Republic, banning anti-republican associations, is passed by the Reichstag against opposition from KPD, DNVP and BVP

2 September DEUTSCHLANDLIED becomes the national anthem

14 November Resignation of WIRTH administration over reparations issue

22 November Centre–right minority government is formed by Wilhelm CUNO

1923

11 January Occupation of the Ruhr by French and Belgian troops in an attempt to enforce REPARATIONS payments; payments are halted on 12 January

13 January Government announces policy of passive resistance, which effectively halts the economy and forces up the rate of inflation

18 January US dollar is worth 23,000 German marks

22 March DEUTSCHVÖLKISCHE FREIHEITSPARTEI is banned in Prussia

29 April NSDAP is prohibited in Hesse

13 May 'Mother's Day' is introduced into Germany

30 July US dollar is worth 1 million marks

13 August Formation of a grand coalition cabinet by Gustav STRESEMANN (DVP), following resignation of CUNO

15 August First BAUHAUS exhibition in Weimar

26 September Conflict between Bavaria and the Reich: Bavarian government responds to the end of the 'passive resistance' in the Ruhr with declaration of a state of emergency

27 September Reich government declares a national state of emergency as a counter-measure

October SPD and KPD form a 'government of republican and proletarian defence' in Saxony, which is deposed by the *Reichswehr*, 28 October

October–November Disturbances spread to Thuringia and Hamburg

21 October Declaration of the French-sponsored Rhenish Republic in Aachen

29 October Reich commissioner installed in Saxony; First German radio transmission in Berlin

3 November SPD ministers leave the government in protest at government policy in Saxony; and Bavaria

8 November BEER HALL PUTSCH

11 November US dollar is worth 631 billion marks

15 November New currency (RENTENMARK) is introduced (at 4.2 marks to the dollar)

23 November Banning of KPD and NSDAP

30 November STRESEMANN government resigns; new centre–right government is formed under Wilhelm MARX

1924

22 February Founding of REICHSBANNER *SCHWARZ-ROT-GOLD*

26 February BEER HALL PUTSCH leaders are tried for high treason

1 April HITLER is sentenced to five years in the Landsberg prison in Bavaria

6 April Bavarian Landtag elections: Conservative coalition (BVP–DNVP) suffers heavy losses; Nazis (campaigning as *Völkischer Block*) win 17.1% and 23 seats

9 April DAWES PLAN issued

4 May Reichstag elections: Gains for KPD and

the far right; the Nazis repeat their regional success in Bavaria (with 15% of the vote there, largely at the expense of BVP and DVP)

3 June Wilhelm MARX forms a new centre–right coalition government

29 August Reichstag approves DAWES PLAN

11 October Introduction of Reichsmark

15 October DDP refuses to work in a coalition with DNVP thereby preventing the formation of a grand coalition.

7 December Reichstag elections: Gains for SPD and moderate right at the expense of the KPD and nationalists; Prussian Landtag elections: Grand coalition (SPD–DDP–CENTRE –DVP) is returned with a decisive majority

15 December Resignation of MARX government

20 December Hitler is released from Landsberg prison

1925

15 January Formation of new centre–right government under non-party chancellor Hans LUTHER

27 February NSDAP refounded

28 February Death of President EBERT

25 April HINDENBURG is elected president

14 July–1 August Allied evacuation of Ruhr

16 October LOCARNO TREATIES are agreed, regulating German relations with the rest of western Europe; DNVP ministers resign in protest 25 October

5 December Resignation of LUTHER administration

8 December Official publication of first part of Hitler's MEIN KAMPF

1926

20 January Hans LUTHER forms a minority centre–right government; he resigns 12 May

14 February Hitler reimposes his authority on the NSDAP at the BAMBERG CONFERENCE

16 May Wilhelm MARX becomes chancellor; other ministers remain in place

8 September Germany joins the LEAGUE OF NATIONS

1 November Joseph GOEBBELS becomes *Gauleiter* of Berlin

17 December MARX government is defeated in a vote of no confidence

1927

29 January Marx forms new centre–right government (without the DDP)

6 May NSDAP is banned in Berlin and Brandenburg after street violence

16 July Unemployment Insurance Law is passed

1928

20 May Reichstag elections: decisive shift to the left

28 June Hermann MÜLLER forms a broad coalition government (SPD–DDP–CENTRE–DVP– BVP)

31 August Première of *The Threepenny Opera* by Bertolt BRECHT and Kurt WEILL

1929

6 January Heinrich HIMMLER is appointed *Reichsführer SS*

1 May Street violence erupts in Berlin during May Day demonstrations

12 May Saxon Landtag elections: NSDAP wins 5 seats; DNVP loses 6 of its 14 seats

7 June Publication of YOUNG PLAN, revising German reparations payments

23 June Nazi–Conservative joint electoral list wins an overall majority in municipal elections in Coburg

9 July NSDAP and DNVP join forces in opposition to Young Plan

6 August Young Plan is agreed

24–29 October US stock market crash

8 December Landtag elections in Thuringia: Heavy losses for the middle-class conservative parties (*Reichslandbund*, DNVP, DVP) and gains for NSDAP

~ Alfred DÖBLIN publishes *Berlin Alexanderplatz*

1930

23 January In Thuringia Wilhelm FRICK (NSDAP) becomes the first Nazi minister (interior and education) as part of a centre–right coalition under the leadership of Erwin Baum (*Reichslandbund*)

23 February All Quiet on the Western Front by Erich Maria REMARQUE is banned in all schools in Thuringia by Frick

27 March Fall of MÜLLER government

29 March Thuringian Landtag passes an 'Enabling Law' introduced by Frick to restructure the state's institutions

30 March Heinrich BRÜNING becomes Reich chancellor at the head of a minority right-of-centre government

22 June NSDAP becomes the second biggest party in the Saxon Landtag

30 June French troops withdraw from the Rhineland

16 July Government by presidential decree begins with measures on the economy

18 July Reichstag is dissolved following a successful SPD motion to rescind the presidential decree

12 September Newsreel with sound is introduced into German cinemas

14 September Reichstag elections: large NSDAP gains; the party's share of the vote increases from 2.6 to 18.3%, while that of both DNVP and DVP is halved; KPD also increases its vote but all other parties make small losses; with 107 seats the NSDAP is the second largest party in the Reichstag

1931

5 January Ernst RÖHM is appointed head of SA

15 January Nazis form factory cells in an attempt to recruit industrial workers

9 February Withdrawal of 'national opposition' (DNVP, NSDAP) from Reichstag

13 March Conservative–Nazi coalition collapses in Thuringia

20 March Announcement of proposed Austro-German customs union

1 April SPD in Thuringia wins a vote of no confidence in FRICK, who resigns his post as interior minister

20 June Hoover moratorium on reparations

13 July Collapse of Darmstädter und Nationalbank

3 August Labour service is introduced

12 September Jewish new year is accompanied by violent anti-Semitic rioting by Nazis in Berlin

27 September Elections to the BÜRGERSCHAFT (160 seats) in Hamburg, reflect political polarization: NSDAP seats increase from 3 to 43, DNVP loses 13 of its 22 seats, DVP 13 of its 20 seats and DDP 7 of its 14 seats; KPD gains at the expense of SPD, which remains, however, the largest party

7 October BRÜNING government resigns; HINDENBURG makes clear his preference for a more right-wing cabinet

9 October Brüning announces his new administration

11 October HARZBURG FRONT, right-wing anti-government coalition, is formed

23 November Carl von OSSIETZKY is imprisoned in Leipzig for publishing details of illegal German rearmament

1932

January Violent attacks by Nazi students on Jewish students in Berlin and Vienna

6 January Brüning informs Britain and France that Germany will be unable to afford REPARATIONS payments even after the expiry of the Hoover moratorium

27 January Speech by Hitler to Rhineland industrialists in Düsseldorf

15 February Unemployment reaches 6.127 million according to Reich labour ministry

10 April HINDENBURG is re-elected in second round of presidential elections

13 April Prohibition of SA and SS

20 May DOLLFUSS government takes office in Austria

21 May Nazi Alfred Freyberg is elected minister-president in Anhalt

24 May In Landtag elections in Prussia, Württemberg and Anhalt and in Bürgerschaft elections in Hamburg, NSDAP becomes the largest party in the respective diets; only in Bavaria, where the Nazis make equally substantial gains, does it remain the second party

29 May Oldenburg Landtag elections: NSDAP wins an absolute majority

30 May BRÜNING cabinet is effectively dismissed when HINDENBURG withdraws his support over the issue of East Elbian land reform

1 June Formation of PAPEN government

3 June Papen resigns from the CENTRE PARTY

5 June Mecklenburg-Schwerin Landtag elections: NSDAP win half the seats

14 June Lifting of the ban on the SA and SS

20 July PREUSSENSCHLAG: Prussian government is deposed by Papen for its continuing suppression of the SA

31 July Reichstag elections: NSDAP is now the largest party in Reichstag

12 September Reichstag is dissolved

6 November Last genuinely free Reichstag elections: German nationalist and Communist gains; NSDAP loses 34 seats

3 December Franz von PAPEN resigns; Kurt von SCHLEICHER becomes chancellor

1933

4 January Secret meeting of HITLER and Papen

30 January Hitler is appointed chancellor; first cabinet meeting of the new administration is held

1 February Reichstag is dissolved

2 February Hermann GÖRING bans all Communist demonstrations in Prussia

4 February Presidential 'Decree for the Protection of the German People' qualifies freedom of the press and freedom of assembly

17 February Prussian interior ministry (under Göring) permits shooting of 'enemies of the state' with impunity

22 February Formation of auxiliary police forces in Prussia composed of SA, SS and *STAHLHELM* members

23 February Homosexual rights groups are proscribed

27 February REICHSTAG FIRE

28 February Decree of the Reich President for the PROTECTION OF PEOPLE AND STATE gives Hitler emergency powers; SPD newspaper *Vorwärts* is banned

3 March Arrest of Ernst THÄLMANN and other KPD members

4 March End of parliamentary government in Austria

5 March Reichstag elections: NSDAP wins 288 seats, but fails to gain an overall majority despite widespread terror and intimidation during the election campaign; GLEICH-SCHALTUNG ('co-ordination') of Hamburg state government

6 March Gleichschaltung of Hesse, Lübeck and Bremen

7 March Gleichschaltung of Baden, Saxony and Württemberg; Government of Schaumburg-Lippe resigns

8 March Interior Minister Wilhelm FRICK announces the establishment of CONCENTRATION CAMPS

9 March HIMMLER becomes police president of Munich; Ritter von EPP is appointed governor of Bavaria

13 March GOEBBELS becomes Reich minister of public enlightenment and propaganda

16 March Hjalmar SCHACHT succeeds Hans Luther as president of the Reichsbank

17 March Hitler's 'bodyguard' (*Leibstandarte Adolf Hitler*) of 120 is established under the leadership of Sepp DIETRICH

21 March Reichstag is convened in a garrison church in Potsdam: Communist deputies are forbidden to take their seats; 'Special Courts' are established

22 March Establishment of a racial hygiene department in the Interior Ministry

23 March ENABLING LAW is ratified 444 votes to 94 (SPD); all KPD and 26 SPD deputies are absent, CENTRE PARTY support is nevertheless crucial in winning the necessary two-thirds majority

31 March First Law for the Coordination (*GLEICHSCHALTUNG*) of the Federal States

1 April Himmler becomes 'political police commander of Bavaria; Nationwide boycott of Jewish businesses; Literature by JEHOVAH'S WITNESSES is banned

7 April Law for the Restoration of a Professional Civil Service; second Law for the Coordination of the Federal States: office of *REICHSSTATTHALTER* (Reich governor) is created; PAPEN resigns as Reich commissioner for Prussia

1 May NSDAP membership is frozen

2 May Police and Nazis raid trade-union offices; FREE TRADE UNIONS are dissolved

6 May Robert LEY announces establishment of German Labour Front (DAF) to replace the trade unions; Magnus HIRSCHFELD's Institute of Sexual Research is ransacked and its library burned

19 May Law enacted providing for the regulation of employment contracts by 'Reich trustees of labour' (*REICHSTREUHÄNDER DER ARBEIT*)

1 June Law for the Reduction of Unemployment is passed, including MARRIAGE LOANS legislation; German firms begin to contribute 0.5% of wages costs to NSDAP

5 July CENTRE PARTY disbands

6 July Hitler announces the end of the NATIONAL REVOLUTION

8 July CONCORDAT between Germany and the Vatican

14 July NSDAP is formally declared the only political party in Germany, which thereby becomes a one-party state

13 September Law concerning the Provisional Establishment of the Reich Food Estate (*REICHSNÄHRSTAND*)

22 September REICH CHAMBER OF CULTURE is established

29 September REICH ENTAILED FARM LAW is passed to ensure that farmland and forest can only be inherited by a 'peasant' of German blood

12 November Reichstag elections and plebiscite

27 November Establishment of 'Beauty of Labour' (*SCHÖNHEIT DER ARBEIT*) and 'STRENGTH THROUGH JOY' (*Kraft durch Freude*) organizations by German Labour Front

30 November GESTAPO created by GÖRING

1 December Law to ensure the Unity of Party and State; Rudolf HESS and Ernst RÖHM are appointed ministers without portfolio

20 December Law against MALICIOUS ATTACKS ON THE STATE AND PARTY (*Heimtückegesetz*) prohibits outspoken criticism of the regime

1934

22 January German–Polish non-aggression pact

30 January Law for the Reconstruction of the Reich

February AUSTRIAN CIVIL WAR

12 February Suppression of workers' uprising by AUSTROFASCIST regime of Engelbert DOLLFUSS in Austria; council flats in Vienna are shelled

20 April HIMMLER appointed 'inspector of the Gestapo'

29 May Confessing Church (*BEKENNENDE KIRCHE*) formed

17 June PAPEN delivers his MARBURG SPEECH criticizing the violent conduct of the Nazi NATIONAL REVOLUTION

20 June HINDENBURG demands the dissolution of the SA

30 June NIGHT OF THE LONG KNIVES: Purge of stormtroopers initiates the liquidation of opposition both within and outside the party; 170 leading Nazis are killed, including SA leader Ernst RÖHM

20 July SS established as an organization independent from SA (under HIMMLER)

25 July Assassination of DOLLFUSS by Austrian Nazis

1 August Law concerning the Head of State of the German Reich provides for the combination of the offices of chancellor and president

2 August Death of President Hindenburg; Hitler becomes president and army swears oath of allegiance to him; Hjalmar SCHACHT is appointed minister of economics

19 August Hitler proclaims himself '*FÜHRER* and Reich chancellor'

September Schacht introduces his NEW PLAN

26 October Reich Central Office for the Combating of Homosexuality and Abortion is set up in Berlin under Joseph Meisinger leading to nationwide arrests of homosexuals in October and November (*see* HOMOSEXUALS, PERSECUTION OF)

1935
13 January SAARLAND plebiscite returns majority in favour of reunification with Germany

17 March Reintroduction of military service; several hundred Protestant pastors are arrested, including Martin NIEMÖLLER

27 March Arrest of underground leadership of KPD

28 March Première of Leni RIEFENSTAHL's film *The Triumph of the Will*

April Prohibition of employment of Jehovah's Witnesses in civil service is followed by nationwide wave of arrests

7 April NSDAP win absolute majority in elections to Danzig parliament

18 June ANGLO-GERMAN NAVAL AGREEMENT allows for the expansion of Germany's naval capacity

26 June Reich LABOUR SERVICE LAW comes into force

15 July Violent attacks on Jews by stormtroopers in Berlin

16 July Ministry of Churches created under Hanns KERRL, formerly minister without portfolio

24 July Dissolution of FREIKORPS organizations

August Arrest of members of SPD resistance group NEU BEGINNEN

10 August Jews forbidden civil marriages

15 September NUREMBERG LAWS are announced at the party conference

12 October Broadcasting of jazz music banned

13 December LEBENSBORN ('Fountain of Life') organization founded

1936
6 February Winter Olympics open in Garmisch-Partenkirchen

10 February GESTAPO actions placed above the law

7 March Military reoccupation of Rhineland leads to a plebiscite (28 March) affirming Hitler's policy

4 April GÖRING appointed commissioner of raw materials

24 April ORDENSBURGEN (Nazi elite schools) founded

17 June HIMMLER appointed head of the German police

19 June Swastika flag becomes new German national flag

26 June Himmler merges the Gestapo and the Criminal Police (*Kripo*) in the Security Police (*Sipo*), under the command of Reinhard HEYDRICH; all uniformed police similarly combined as *Ordnungspolizei* (ORPO) under Kurt DALUEGE

July First group of Gypsies (ROMA AND SINTI) sent to DACHAU

1 August Olympic Games open in Berlin

28 August Mass arrests of Jehovah's Witnesses

19 October Announcement of FOUR-YEAR PLAN under leadership of Göring

1 December HITLER YOUTH membership becomes compulsory for boys

24 December Catholic bishops declare their support for Hitler's 'struggle against Communism'

1937
30 January Reichstag extends Enabling Law for a further four years

9 March Mass arrests of persons designated 'habitual criminals'

14 March Publication of the Papal Encyclical *MIT BRENNENDER SORGE* denouncing Nazi persecution of the Church and clergymen

19 April First ADOLF HITLER SCHOOL opens

18 June Dual membership of Hitler Youth and Roman Catholic youth organizations is prohibited

1 July Arrests of members of the Confessing Church (*BEKENNENDE KIRCHE*), including NIEMÖLLER

15 July Construction of BUCHENWALD begins

18 July Exhibition of German Art opens in the House of German Art in Munich

19 July DEGENERATE ART exhibition opens in Munich

5 November Hitler sets out his plans for the annexation of Austria and Czechoslovakia at a meeting with military leaders

26 November Hjalmar SCHACHT compelled to resign as economics minister

1938

19 January Establishment of *GLAUBE UND SCHÖNHEIT* ('faith and beauty') organization for young women aged between 17 and 21

25 January General Werner von BLOMBERG resigns

4 February Political shift within the leadership of the regime is marked by the appointment of RIBBENTROP as foreign minister and the dismissal of FRITSCH as commander in chief of the Army; War Ministry is abolished and replaced by OKW; Hitler assumes personal command of the armed forces

5 February Last meeting of Reich cabinet

12 February Hitler meets Austrian chancellor SCHUSCHNIGG and threatens invasion unless Nazis join the Austrian government

16 February Austrian Nazi leader Arthur SEYSS-INQUART is appointed interior minister in Vienna

11–12 March German occupation of Austria is followed by annexation confirmed by plebiscite on 10 April

13 March Law for the 'Reunification of Austria with the German Reich' effects ANSCHLUSS

8 August Construction of MAUTHAUSEN concentration camp begins near Linz in Upper Austria

16 September Sudeten German Party is banned in Czechoslovakia

28–30 September Munich conference (*see* MUNICH AGREEMENT): Britain, France and Italy give in to Hitler's demand for a partition of Czechoslovakia

1 October Occupation of SUDETENLAND

28 October Germany attempts to expel 15,000 Jews to Poland

9–10 November KRISTALLNACHT: anti-Semitic pogroms organized by the Nazi leadership and carried out by stormtroopers throughout Germany

8 December All Gypsies (ROMA AND SINTI) are required to register with the police

1939

21 January Purge of leading Conservatives continues with SCHACHT's dismissal from the presidency of the Reichsbank

13 March PAN-GERMAN LEAGUE finally disbanded

15 March Occupation of Czechoslovakia

16 March RIBBENTROP declares the PROTECTORATE OF BOHEMIA AND MORAVIA a part of the Reich

20 March Burning of 'degenerate' works of art in Berlin

23 March MEMEL is annexed by agreement with Lithuania

7 June Germany concludes non-aggression pacts with Estonia and Latvia

23 August MOLOTOV–RIBBENTROP PACT is signed in Moscow

27 August Food rationing introduced

1 September German invasion of Poland

3 September Britain and France declare war on Germany

4–5 September War Economy Decrees abolish overtime payments and reduce holiday entitlements

13 September Germans take Warsaw

21 September Reinhard HEYDRICH draws up guidelines for EINSATZGRUPPEN in Poland

27 September Unification of SIPO and the office of the *Reichsführer SS* to form *Reichssicherheitshauptamt* (RSHA)

7 October HIMMLER becomes Reich commissioner for the consolidation of German nationhood, responsible for the Reich's 'resettlement' plans in Poland

26 October Direct incorporation of western Poland into Reich as Reichsgaue Danzig-Westpreussen, Posen (later WARTHELAND); other Polish administrative districts are incorporated into East Prussia and Silesia

8 November Failure of the attempt of Johann Georg Elser to assassinate Hitler in Munich

1940

9 April Invasion of Denmark and Norway

30 April Establishment of ghetto in Łodz

10 May Offensive against the West begins: Germany invades Belgium, the Netherlands and Luxembourg; British prime minister Neville Chamberlain resigns and is succeeded by Winston Churchill

14 May Dutch surrender

28 May Belgian surrender

29 May SEYSS-INQUART is appointed Reich commissioner for the Netherlands

29 May–3 June British forces are evacuated from DUNKIRK

June–September Battle of BRITAIN

10 June Italy declares war on Britain and France

14 June Germans enter Paris

17 June Soviet Union begins occupation of Baltic states

22 June France concludes armistice with Germany

3 July Britain sinks French fleet

7 August Baldur von SCHIRACH appointed *Gauleiter* of Vienna

12 October Operation SEA LION cancelled

21 November Cinema newsreel (*Wochenschau*) is nationalized by Goebbels

1941

29 January State secretary Franz Schlegelberger becomes justice minister following the death of Franz GÜRTNER

6 April Invasion of Yugoslavia and Greece

12 April Germans take Belgrade

21 April 'Reich Coal Organization' (*Reichsvereinigung Kohle*) founded to manage raw materials shortages

May Reich Press Chamber closes down 550 newspapers

10 May HESS flies alone to Scotland and is taken as a prisoner of war; Hitler dismisses him from all official party positions

27 May 'Bismarck' sunk by the Royal Navy in the ATLANTIC

29 May Martin BORMANN, takes over Hess's position as head of the Party Chancellery (*PARTEIKANZLEI*) and is appointed a minister

22 June German invasion of the Soviet Union; Finnish forces also attack in Karelia

2 July 7000 are murdered in an SS massacre at Lviv (Ukraine)

16 July Germans take SMOLENSK

15 August Bialystok incorporated into East Prussia under chief of civilian administration Erich KOCH

3 September ZYKLON-B gas used for the first time to murder Jewish prisoners in Auschwitz

19 September Germans take KIEV

28 September BABI YAR massacre

16 October Soviet government leaves Moscow

11 December Germany and Italy declare war on USA

1942

2 January Allies agree not to make a separate peace with Germany

20 January WANNSEE CONFERENCE is held by top-ranking Nazis to discuss the FINAL SOLUTION

1 February Nazi collaborator Vidkun QUISLING becomes prime minister of Norway

9 February Party ideologue Alfred ROSEN-

BERG joins the government as minister for the Occupied Eastern Territories

Spring Revolutionary Socialist resistance movement in Bavaria and Austria is suppressed

28 March Area bombing of Lübeck by RAF destroys much of the town centre

20 April German women are conscripted for munitions work

22 April Establishment of 'Central Planning' to co-ordinate allocation of raw materials and energy

27 May Assassination attempt on Reinhard HEYDRICH in Prague; he dies from his wounds eight days later

June Systematic mass murder of Jews begins in gas chambers at AUSCHWITZ

6 June Germans wipe out LIDICE as a reprisal for the assassination of Heydrich

20 August Otto Georg THIERACK becomes justice minister; Roland FREISLER replaces him as president of *VOLKSGERICHTSHOF*

5 September Germans enter STALINGRAD

11–12 November Germans occupy VICHY FRANCE

1943

14–24 January Roosevelt and Churchill meet at the Casablanca Conference and demand Germany's unconditional surrender

2 February Surrender of last German forces ends the battle of Stalingrad

18 February Goebbels delivers 'Total War' speech in Berlin

20 April WARSAW GHETTO massacre

12 May Surrender of Axis armies in Tunisia

17 May RAF bombs Ruhr dam

10 July Allied landings in Sicily

24 July Mussolini is deposed

1 August Germans enter northern Italy

20 August HIMMLER replaces FRICK as interior minister

3 September Italy surrenders unconditionally

10 September German troops occupy Rome

25 September Soviets liberate Smolensk

13 October Italy declares war on Germany

6 November Red Army liberates Kiev

1944

January Gestapo breaks up the KREISAU CIRCLE, a focus of conservative opposition

27 January Relief of Leningrad

19 March SS units occupy Hungary

6 June D-DAY: Allied landings in Normandy

10 June French village of ORADOUR-SUR-GLANE is destroyed as German reprisal against the French resistance

July Destruction of Communist resistance centres

20 July Abortive assassination attempt on Hitler by STAUFFENBERG and fellow conspirators (*see* JULY BOMB PLOT)

23 July Red Army liberates death camp at MAJDANEK

6 October Red Army enters Hungary

14 October British troops liberate Athens

16 October Soviets enter East Prussia

21 October Allies occupy Aachen

23 November Americans liberate Strasbourg

16 December Germans begin ARDENNES OFFENSIVE (battle of the Bulge)

1945

30 January Hitler's last radio speech is broadcast

4–11 February YALTA CONFERENCE

13–14 February Dresden is destroyed by Allied bombing

19 March Hitler orders destruction of all industry useful to the enemy

30 March Soviet troops take Danzig

2 April Red army enters Austria

14 April Red Army takes Vienna

24 April US and Soviet troops meet on the Elbe

30 April Hitler commits suicide in Berlin; Admiral DÖNITZ becomes head of state

1 May GOEBBELS commits suicide; Dönitz announces Hitler's death and his own succession to the leadership of the Reich

2 May Capitulation of Berlin

7 May End of World War II in Europe with German surrender

8 May Germany issues formal unconditional surrender

14 May Allies establish a separate government in Austria

23 May Dissolution by the Allies of the last Reich government

5 June Berlin Declaration: the Allies take over the government of Germany

9 June Soviet Military Occupation in Germany (SMAD) set up in Berlin

1–4 July British and American troops withdraw from Saxony, Thuringia and Mecklenburg

17 July–2 August POTSDAM CONFERENCE

30 July First session of the ALLIED CONTROL COUNCIL in Berlin

3–10 September Beginning of land reform in the Soviet Zone

10 September–2 October London Conference of Allied foreign ministers

20 November NUREMBERG TRIALS begin

1946

7 March FREIE DEUTSCHE JUGEND is founded in Berlin

21–22 April Merger of SPD and KPD in Soviet Zone to form SED

25 April–12 July Paris Conference of Allied foreign ministers

15 October GÖRING commits suicide

16 October Execution of ten major war criminals at NUREMBERG

20 October Landtag elections in the Soviet Zone: SED wins an average of 47.5% of the vote

4 November–11 December New York Conference of Allied foreign ministers

2 December Washington Treaty on the economic unification of the British and US zones

22 December SAARLAND is incorporated into French economic area

1947

1 January Inauguration of the BIZONE

25 February Formal dissolution of Prussia

10 March–24 April Moscow Conference of Allied foreign ministers

22–25 April Founding congress of DGB takes place in Bielefeld

5 June Announcement of the MARSHALL PLAN

6–8 June Minister-presidents' conference in Munich

25 June Constitution of the Economic Council (*Wirtschaftsrat*) of the Bizone

5 October Election of Saar Landtag

25 November–15 December London Conference of Allied foreign ministers

1948

20 March Last session of the ALLIED CONTROL COUNCIL

20–21 June Introduction of the Deutsche Mark in the western zones of occupation

24 June Beginning of the Berlin blockade (*see* BERLIN AIRLIFT)

25 June Introduction of the Deutsche Mark into West Berlin

1 September Constitution of the Parliamentary Council (*Parlamentarischer Rat*) in Bonn

10 November–10 December First reading of the draft constitution of the FEDERAL REPUBLIC OF GERMANY

11–12 December Merger of West German liberal parties to form FDP

15 December–20 January 1949 Second reading of the draft constitution of the Federal Republic

~ Free University founded in Berlin

1949

8–10 February Third reading of the draft constitution of the Federal Republic

4 April NATO is founded in Washington

22 April RUHR STATUTE comes into force

8 May Adoption of constitution (BASIC LAW) of Federal Republic of Germany

12 May End of the Berlin blockade; Military governors approve the constitution of the Federal Republic

18–21 May Ten LANDTAGE (all except Bavaria) ratify the constitution of the Federal Republic

23 May–20 June Paris conference of Allied foreign ministers

14 August Elections to the first BUNDESTAG

7 September Constituent session of the Bundestag and BUNDESRAT

12 September Theodor HEUSS elected first president of the Federal Republic of Germany

15 September Konrad ADENAUER elected first chancellor of the Federal Republic of Germany

21 September Statute of occupation for the Federal Republic of Germany comes into force limiting the role of Allied occupation authorities

7 October Establishment of the GERMAN DEMOCRATIC REPUBLIC

~ University founded at Nuremberg

1950

6 January End of food rationing in the Federal Republic of Germany

8 July The Federal Republic of Germany becomes an associate member of the Council of Europe

12–18 September New York Conference of Allied foreign ministers

1 October German Democratic Republic becomes a member of COMECON alliance of Soviet-Bloc states

1951

31 January Alfried KRUPP is released by the Americans and his property restored

15 March Adenauer becomes acting West German foreign minister

18 April Founding treaty of the European

Coal and Steel Community is signed (*see* SCHUMAN PLAN)

2 May Federal Republic becomes a member of the Council of Europe

9 July United Kingdom formally ends its state of war with Germany, along with Australia, New Zealand and South Africa

13 July France formally ends its state of war with Germany, along with Cuba, Denmark and Norway

14 September Washington Conference of the Allied foreign ministers

24 October United States formally ends its state of war with Germany

1 November East Germany's first Soviet-style Five Year Plan begins

1952

10 March Soviet note proposes a peace treaty with Germany

25 March In responses to Stalin's note of 10 March the Western Allies demand free elections throughout Germany as a precondition for a peace treaty

9 April Stalin agrees to free elections, but under four-power rather than UN supervision; stalemate ensues

24 August Purge of SED party members, largely former émigrés in the West

10 September Reconciliation Treaty between Israel and the Federal Republic of Germany; a reparations plan is agreed

1953

11 March GDR announces that a range of repressive measures will be repealed in order to correct policy errors of the past; increased norms for workers are not included

28–29 May Soviet Control Commission becomes the High Commission of the Soviet Union in Germany

9 June German Democratic Republic announces the NEW COURSE

14 June GDR announces the release of 4000 political prisoners

17 June Uprising in the GDR begins with a construction workers' strike in East Berlin

23 July East German state security minister Wilhelm ZAISSER dismissed along with Rudolf HERRNSTADT, editor of *Neues Deutschland*

3 September SPD responds sharply to US intervention in the West German election campaign (the American secretary of state had asserted that the defeat of Adenauer would be 'disastrous' for Germany)

6 September Bundestag elections: CDU and CSU increase their combined shares of the vote from 31% to 45.2%, consolidating the government's position in parliament

1954

25 March Soviet Union declares the German Democratic Republic a sovereignty state

30 March–6 April Fourth Party Conference of the SED proclaims a collective leadership

8 April Western Allies refuse to recognize East German sovereignty

1955

25 January Soviet Union ends its state of war with Germany

1 April Resumption of Lufthansa passenger flights discontinued since 1945

5 May Allied occupation of the Federal Republic of Germany ends; Berlin is excluded from the provisions of the agreement

14 May German Democratic Republic is a founding signatory to the WARSAW PACT

8–13 September State visit by Adenauer to Moscow: diplomatic relations are established between the Federal Republic and the Soviet Union

23 October SAARLAND plebiscite decides in favour of union with the Federal Republic of Germany

1956

5 January First Italian GASTARBEITER arrive in the Rhineland

18 January East German army (*NATIONALE VOLKSARMEE*) is formed

17 August KPD is declared illegal in the Federal Republic of Germany

1957

1 January Incorporation of the Saarland into the Federal Republic of Germany

25 March Treaty of Rome establishes the European Economic Community; Federal Republic of Germany is a founding member

5 July First West German divisions placed under the command of NATO

15 September Bundestag elections: CDU/CSU wins an absolute majority with 50.2% of the vote

3 October Willy BRANDT becomes mayor of West Berlin

10 October German Democratic Republic and Yugoslavia agree to establish diplomatic relations

19 October Federal Republic of Germany breaks off diplomatic relations with Yugoslavia in accordance with the HALLSTEIN DOCTRINE

11 December VOLKSKAMMER (People's Chamber) legislates to impose fines and prison terms on citizens of the German Democratic Republic who leave the country without official permission

1958

27 November Second Berlin crisis: The Soviet Union announces its withdrawal from the four-power agreement on Berlin and demands the demilitarization of West Berlin, and the establishment of the western sectors as a free city

1959

1 July Heinrich Lübke is elected president of the Federal Republic of Germany

1 October German Democratic Republic decides on Seven Year Plan to replace the interrupted second Five Year Plan; East Germany also modifies its flag (hitherto the same as that of the Federal Republic) to incorporate symbols of workers and peasants

24 December Nazis deface recently rebuilt

Cologne synagogue; this desecration is followed by a wave of anti-Semitic graffiti across West Germany

1960

27 January Neo-Nazi DEUTSCHE REICHSPARTEI, which is implicated in the wave of anti-Semitic activity, is banned in the Rhineland Palatinate

17 February Publication of the 'White Book': the federal government finds no evidence of organized anti-Semitic activity in West Germany

14 April Completion of collectivization of East German agriculture

7 September Death of Wilhelm PIECK, president of the German Democratic Republic

1961

18 March Franz-Josef STRAUSS is elected president of CSU

11 April Trial of Adolf EICHMANN begins in Jerusalem

13 August Building of the BERLIN WALL

17 September Bundestag elections: CDU/CSU loses its absolute majority

18 December East Germany recalls its ambassador to Albania

~ Günter Grass publishes *Katz und Maus*

1962

31 May Eichmann is executed in Israel

26 October 'SPIEGEL AFFAIR' erupts

19 November FDP ministers leave the government in the wake of the *Spiegel* affair, demanding resignation of Franz-Josef STRAUSS

30 November Strauss announces he will not join a new government, thereby enabling the coalition to re-form

11 December Fifth Adenauer administration: a coalition of CDU/CSU and FDP

1963

23–26 June State visit of President Kennedy to Germany; he delivers 'Ich bin ein Berliner' speech

25 June East German Council of Ministers introduces the New Economic System

2 September British government refuses Berliner Ensemble entry to the country for the Edinburgh Festival

15 October Adenauer resigns; chancellorship passes to Ludwig ERHARD

1964

15 February Willy BRANDT elected SPD leader

2 November Border between East and West Germany is opened to allow pensioners to travel out for visits

1965

19 August End of the Auschwitz trials in Frankfurt

19 September Bundestag elections: Marginal swing to CDU/CSU; second Erhard government is formed (CDU/CSU–FDP)

1966

15 January First perfomance of *Die Plebejer proben den Aufstand* (*The Plebeians rehearse the Uprising*) by Günter Grass in West Berlin

18 April First Jewish school in post-war Germany is reopened in Frankfurt

1 October Albert SPEER and Baldur von SCHIRACH are released from Spandau prison

27 October FDP ministers leave the Erhard government over the issue of taxation levels

6 November Hessen Landtag elections: NPD wins 7.9% of the vote and is the first radical right-wing party to win seats in a German parliamentary assembly since the Nazis

30 November Erhard resigns the chancellorship

1 December Kurt Georg KIESINGER becomes chancellor at the head of the GRAND COALITION (CDU–SPD)

1967

31 January First steps towards the resumption of diplomatic relations between the Federal Republic of Germany and Romania signals the end of the HALLSTEIN DOCTRINE

20 August Lufthansa resumes flights to eastern Europe

15 October Berliner Ensemble performs for the first time in West Berlin

1968

31 January Resumption of diplomatic relations between West Germany and Yugoslavia

2 April Two Frankfurt department stores are set alight by protestors; Andreas BAADER and Gudrun Esslin are later arrested and found guilty of the arson

9 April New constitution comes into force in the GERMAN DEMOCRATIC REPUBLIC

11 April Student leader Rudi Dutschke is shot in Berlin

28 April Baden Württemberg Landtag elections: NPD wins 9.8% of votes

11 May Demonstration in Bonn against emergency legislation (*see* APO)

15 September New national gallery opened in West Berlin

4 November Violent conflicts between police and student demonstrators in West Berlin

~ Christa Wolf publishes *Nachdenken über Christa T*

1969

5 March Gustav HEINEMANN (SPD) elected president of the Federal Republic of Germany

9 May Bundestag passes reforming legislation, including the decriminalization of homosexuality and adultery

26 June Bundestag removes STATUTE OF LIMITATIONS for genocide

28 September Bundestag elections: Swing to the SPD from FDP and CDU/CSU; the extreme right NPD more than doubles its share of the vote (from 2% to 4.3%) but fails to enter parliament

21 October Willy BRANDT is elected chancellor at the head of a reforming social–liberal coalition

30 October Agreement between Federal Republic and Czechoslovakia to compensate Czechoslovak subjects of experiments in Nazi concentration camps

1970

19 March First East–West German summit meeting (between BRANDT and STOPH in Erfurt)

14 May Andreas BAADER is freed from prison

12 August Moscow treaty is signed: a non-aggression agreement between West Germany and the Soviet Union which recognizes postwar frontiers

7 December Warsaw treaty lays foundations for the normalization of relations between Poland and West Germany

22 December Franz STANGL, former commandant of TREBLINKA is sentenced in Düsseldorf to life imprisonment for his part in the holocaust

~ Comprehensive university (*Gesamthochschule*) founded at Kassel

1971

12 February 13 suspected members of the RED ARMY FACTION are arrested

3 May Walter ULBRICHT retires as first secretary of the Central Committee (ZK) of the SED

3 September FOUR-POWER AGREEMENT ON BERLIN signed by Britain, France, the Soviet Union and the USA after several months of discussions

18 November Price freeze announced in the German Democratic Republic

10 December West German chancellor Willy BRANDT receives Nobel peace prize for his OSTPOLITIK

1972

19 May Bomb attack on the SPRINGER building in Hamburg

15 June Ulrike Meinhof is arrested (*see* RED ARMY FACTION)

26 August–11 September Olympic games held in Munich and Kiel

5–6 September 11 Israelis killed during an

attack on the Israeli team in the Olympic village in Munich by the Arab guerrilla organization 'Black September'

14 September Diplomatic relations are established between Federal Republic and Poland

19 November Bundestag elections: Brandt's social–liberal coalition has a clear majority; SPD is the most popular party

10 December Heinrich BÖLL is awarded Nobel prize for literature

21 December BASIC TREATY is signed between the FEDERAL REPUBLIC OF GERMANY and the GERMAN DEMOCRATIC REPUBLIC establishing a permanent reciprocal representation in both capitals

1973

1 January Denmark, Great Britain and Ireland join the European Economic Community.

12 June Helmut KOHL is elected leader of CDU

1 August Death of Walter ULBRICHT

18 September The Federal Republic of Germany and the German Democratic Republic become members of the United Nations

19 October OPEC oil embargo: exports to West Germany are reduced to 75%

11 December Prague treaty normalizes relations between the Federal Republic and Czechoslovakia

1974

24 April GUILLAUME AFFAIR: Günter Guillaume, a member of Chancellor Brandt's staff, is arrested on suspicion of spying for East Germany

26 April PARAGRAPH 218 is reformed, removing penalties for abortion up to the twelfth week of pregnancy

2 May PERMANENT REPRESENTATIONS of diplomats from East and West Germany open in Bonn and East Berlin respectively

6 May Willy Brandt resigns as chancellor

15 May Walter SCHEEL is elected president of the Federal Republic of Germany

16 May Helmut SCHMIDT becomes chancellor of the Federal Republic of Germany

7 July West Germany wins the (football) world cup

1 October Hans-Dietrich GENSCHER is elected leader of the FDP

1975

25 February FEDERAL CONSTITUTIONAL COURT blocks government's abortion law reform

4 October Fernuniversität Hagen (similar to the Open University) opens

1976

6 May Limited reform of abortion law is agreed by the Bundestag

9 May Ulrike Meinhof is found hanged in prison

18–22 May SED party conference in East Berlin: the party is restructured and Erich HONECKER becomes party chairman and head of state

24 June Bundestag passes anti-terrorist legislation

3 October Bundestag elections: Victory for the governing SPD–FDP coalition despite large gains for CDU/CSU

30 October First demonstrations against nuclear power at Brokdorf

1 November First women's refuge (*Frauenhaus*) is opened in West Berlin

1977

1 February First issue of feminist magazine *Emma*

5 September Business leader Hanns Martin Schleyer is kidnapped by the RED ARMY FACTION

9 October Investigative journalist Günter Walraff exposes dubious journalistic practices of SPRINGER newspaper *Bild-Zeitung*

19 October Hanns Martin Schleyer's body is found in Alsace

1978

1 January Federal data protection law comes into force

1979

22 January German television begins transmission of the US series *Holocaust*

17 April First issue of *Die Tageszeitung* (taz) in Berlin

7–10 June First direct elections to the European parliament: CDU/CSU candidates win 49.2% of the vote and an absolute majority (42) of the 81 West German seats

1 July Karl Carstens becomes federal president

7 October Bremen Landtag elections: *Grüne Liste* becomes the first Green party to win more than 5% of the vote in a Landtag election

~ Volker Schlöndorff's film version of GRASS's *Die Blechtrommel* (*The Tin Drum*) is released

1980

13 January GREENS (*Die Grünen*) are founded as a national party

5 October Bundestag elections: Small swing from CDU/CSU, led by Franz-Josef STRAUSS, largely to FDP and GREENS, but the latter fail to win seats

26 October Neo-Nazi bomb at the Munich Beer Festival kills 13 people and injures over 200 others

1981

10 October 250,000 people demonstrate in Bonn against the rearmament policies on NATO and the Warsaw Pact, following the Schmidt government's commitment to the deployment of Pershing missiles

~ Wolfgang Petersen's film *Das Boot* (The Boat) is released

1982

6 March Conservative environmentalists found the Ecological Democratic Party (ÖDP)

10 June Peace demonstration by almost half a million people takes place in Bonn during NATO summit

31 July Anti-Israeli bomb at Munich airport

17 September Chancellor Helmut Schmidt cancels SPD–FDP coalition; he attempts to form a minority SPD government

1 October Helmut KOHL becomes chancellor following a CDU/CSU–FDP no-confidence vote

1983

6 March Bundestag elections: Governing coalition of CDU/CSU–FDP wins a majority; Green candidates win seats for the first time

22 April *Stern* magazine claims to have found Hitler's diaries

24 April First excerpt from the 'Hitler diaries' is published in English in the *Sunday Times*

6 May German Federal Archives declare the 'Hitler diaries' to be forgeries

26 November Pershing II missiles arrive in West Germany (at Mutlangen near Stuttgart)

2 December Bundestag lifts the parliamentary immunity of economics minister Graf LAMBSDORFF so that he can be indicted on charges connected with the FLICK AFFAIR

1984

25–30 January Chancellor Kohl visits Israel, where his visit is marked by demonstrations

23 May Richard von WEIZSÄCKER is elected federal president

14–17 June European elections: Greens replace FDP as third German party in the European parliament

1985

5 May Chancellor Kohl and US president Reagan visit Bitburg military cemetery, which contains graves of SS men, provoking a political scandal despite a visit to Belsen by the chancellor and his guest

9–10 June Federal interior minister Friedrich Zimmermann and former federal president Karl Carstens attend a rally of Sudeten Germans in Munich

14–16 June Chancellor Kohl attends a 'Silesian exiles' rally

1986

6 June Walter Wallmann becomes the first federal environment minister

~ Margareta von Trotta's film *Rosa Luxemburg* is released

1987

25 January Bundestag elections: Despite its worst electoral performance since 1949 (44.3%) the CDU/CSU remains the largest party, and the governing coalition wins a further term

17 July German Democratic Republic abolishes the death penalty except for war crimes, espionage and murder

17 August Death of Rudolf HESS in Spandau prison

7–11 September HONECKER visits the Federal Republic, the first such visit by an East German head of state

1988

4–5 March Demonstration in Dresden in support of right of East German citizens to emigrate to the Federal Republic

1 July Manfred Wörner, former federal defence minister, becomes secretary-general of NATO

1989

18 June European elections: Extreme right-wing REPUBLIKANER win 7% of the vote at the expense of CDU/CSU, which loses eight seats

19 August 900 East Germans escape over the Austro-Hungarian border

4 September First of a series of 'Monday demonstrations' in Leipzig

10 September Hungary effectively opens its border with Austria

12 September Founding of *Demokratie Jetzt* ('Democracy Now') movement in German Democratic Republic

October Thousands of East Germans leave eastern Europe by train

18 October Erich HONECKER resigns all his public offices; Egon KRENZ is elected general secretary of the SED

31 October Krenz meets Gorbachev in Moscow

4 November Half a million people demonstrate at the Alexanderplatz in Berlin

7 November Entire East German government resigns

8 November SED Politburo resigns

9 November Border between East and West Germany is opened

13 November Hans Modrow is elected East German minister-president

5 December Honecker is placed under house arrest

1990

20 January Founding of right-wing East German party German Social Union (DSU)

14 March Two-plus-Four talks (*see* TWO-PLUS-FOUR TREATY) between East and West Germany and the four wartime Allies (Britain, France, the Soviet Union and the United States)

18 March First free elections to the *VOLKS-KAMMER* (East German parliament): Conservative parties are the largest political force with 48% of the vote; SPD wins 22% and the PDS (former communists) 16%; BÜNDNIS 90, representing dissident intellectuals, wins less than 3%

12 April Lothar de Maizière is elected minister-president of the GDR

6 May First free local elections in East Germany

1 July Economic union between East and West Germany

20 September Bundestag and *Volkskammer* pass legislation for political unification of Germany

3 October Political unification of Germany

4 October First all-German parliament meets in the Reichstag building in Berlin

2 December First all-German elections: CDU/ CSU is the largest party, but is still dependent on its FDP coalition partner

1991

25 February Remaining members decide to dissolve the Warsaw pact

28 June COMECON is dissolved

September Violent attacks on GASTARBEITER, asylum seekers and other foreigners by neo-Nazi groups

29 September Bremen Landtag elections: Extreme right-wing DVU wins seats

1992

20 January Former East German border guards are tried and sentenced for manslaughter

7 February Foreign and economics ministers sign the Maastricht Treaty agreed the previous year

5 April Baden-Württemberg Landtag elections: Far right REPUBLIKANER win 10.9% of the vote

15 May Former East German leaders, including HONECKER, STOPH and MIELKE, are charged with manslaughter

17 May Foreign minister Hans-Dietrich GENSCHER resigns after 18 years

August–September Series of violent attacks on asylum-seekers' hostels in the former East Germany, initially with the support of local people and little intervention from the police

24 September Germany pays 30 million marks towards repatriation of 43,000 Romanians (over half of them ROMA AND SINTI); former STASI boss Markus Wolf is charged with treason and corruption

25 September Rhine–Main–Danube canal is opened

22–3 November Three Turks are murdered by neo-Nazis in Schleswig-Holstein

1993

3 January Vice-Chancellor Jürgen Möllemann (FDP) resigns following corruption allegations

13 January Honecker moves to Chile after charges against him are suspended

17 March East German steel workers strike for pay equal with their West German counterparts

3 May Björn Engholm resigns as SPD leader and minister-president of Schleswig-Holstein after concealing his knowledge of a CDU 'dirty' tricks campaign against him

4 May Hamburg Bürgerschaft elections of 1992 are declared invalid on account of electoral irregularities on the part of the CDU

6 May Federal transport minister Günther Krause (CDU) resigns following allegations of financial corruption

19 May Heide Simonis (SPD) becomes Germany's first woman minister-president in Schleswig-Holstein

25 May Rudolf Krause (CDU), former interior minister of Saxony, defects to REPUBLIKANER, becoming their first Bundestag member

29 May Five Turkish women and girls murdered by neo-Nazis in an an arson attack in the Ruhr

11 June Klaus Kinkel succeeds Otto Graf LAMBSDORFF as FDP leader

16 September Former East German defence minister Heinz Kessler and his deputy Hans Albrecht are jailed for their part in border shootings

26 October Erich MIELKE is sentenced to six years for the murder of two Nazis in 1931 when the statute of limitations is declared invalid on a legal technicality

28 November Saxony-Anhalt minister-president Werner Münch (CDU) and his government resign after revelations of corruption

6 December Former head of East German military intelligence Markus Wolf is jailed for treason and corruption

1994

24 March Fire bomb attack on Lübeck synagogue

12 May A large group (estimates range from 40 to 60) of neo-Nazis severely beat up five Africans in Magdeburg with the encouragement of onlookers and, according to some reports, police

23 May Roman Herzog is elected federal president

16 October Bundestag elections: Governing CDU/CSU–FDP coalition is returned with a reduced majority of 10

1995

7 May Further arson attack on Lübeck synagogue

29 June Reform of law on abortion, which remains fundamentally a crime, but not punishable if carried out in first three months

1 August Erich MIELKE is released from prison on health grounds

16 November Oskar Lafontaine becomes SPD leader

1996

18 January Ten people die in an arson attack on an asylum seekers' hostel in Lübeck

5 May Brandenburg plebiscite: voters reject union with Berlin

7 July Horst Frank becomes the first member of the GREENS to be elected mayor of a German town in Konstanz

1997

6 June Unemployment is at its highest level since the end of World War II (11.4%)

25 August Former East German leaders Egon KRENZ and Günter Schabowski are sentenced to prison terms for their responsibility for border shootings

1998

5 February Unemployment reaches 12.6%

2 March Gerhard SCHRÖDER, minister-president of Lower Saxony, becomes SPD candidate for chancellorship

26 April Saxony-Anhalt Landtag elections:

Extreme right-wing DVU wins 12.9% of the vote and 16 (of 116) seats; CDU share of the vote falls from 37% to 28%

27 September Bundestag elections: Governing centre–right coalition (CDU/CSU–FDP) loses its absolute majority, the first time a government has been defeated in the history of the Federal Republic; CDU/CSU share of the vote falls substantially, to its lowest level since 1949

27 October Chancellor Gerhard Schröder (SPD) presents his 'red–green' (SPD–GREENS/BÜNDNIS 90) coalition government

31 October SPD forms a coalition with the former Communist PDS for the first time at regional level (in Mecklenburg-Vorpommern)

7 November Wolfgang Schäuble succeeds Helmut Kohl as leader of the CDU

1999

January 1 Euro introduced for accounting purposes in Germany and ten other European Union countries

11 March Oskar Lafontaine announces the resignation of his post as finance minister, his chairmanship of the SPD and his seat in parliament

12 April Chancellor Schröder becomes SPD party leader and Hans Eichel finance minister

19 April Bundestag meets for its first regular session in Berlin

7 May Bundestag passes new citizenship law, giving children born in Germany of foreign parents dual citizenship for the first time

23 May Johannes Rau (SPD) is elected federal president

13 June European elections: Turnout falls from 60% to 45%; CDU/CSU substantially improves its share of the vote and remains the largest single German party; PDS enters the European parliament for the first time

19 September Saxony Landtag elections: Substantial gains for the PDS; with 2.1% a pro-Deutsche Mark movement wins more votes than the FDP

3 October Austrian parliamentary elections: Jörg Haider's radical right-wing FPÖ (Austrian Freedom Party) becomes – very marginally – the second largest party

30 November In the corruption scandal surrounding the financing of the CDU, former chancellor Helmut KOHL apologizes for lack of transparency

10 December Günter GRASS is awarded the Nobel prize for literature

16 December Kohl admits receiving unrecorded donations to the CDU of up to 2 million marks, but refuses to name the donors

2000

15 February Bundestag president announces CDU must pay back 41 million marks of federal subsidies following the revelations of the parties accounting irregularities

10 April Angela Merkl is elected first woman leader of the CDU as successor to Wolfgang Schäuble, following the latter's involvement in the party's finance scandal

2 October Arson attack on Düsseldorf synagogue

1 December Further financial penalties of 7.7 million marks are imposed on the CDU by the president of the Bundestag

APPENDIX II

POLITICS

2.1 **Political Leaders**

Holy Roman Emperors from Leopold I

1658–1705 Leopold I

1705–11 Joseph I

1711–40 KARL VI

1740–2 *Interregnum*

1742–5 KARL VII (Wittelsbach)

1745–65 FRANZ I (Lothringen)

1765–90 JOSEPH II

1790–2 LEOPOLD II

1792–1806 FRANZ II (from 1804, Franz I of Austria)

Emperors of Austria

1804–35 Franz I (*see* FRANZ II)

1835–48 FERDINAND I

1848–1916 FRANZ JOSEPH

1916–18 KARL I

Kings of Prussia and Emperors of Germany

1640–88 Friedrich Wilhelm, elector of Brandenburg (the Great Elector)

1688–1713 Elector Friedrich III, King FRIEDRICH I (King after 1701)

1713–40 King Friedrich Wilhelm I (the Soldier King)

1740–86 King FRIEDRICH II (Frederick the Great)

1786–97 King FRIEDRICH WILHELM II

1797–1840 King FRIEDRICH WILHELM III

1840–61 King FRIEDRICH WILHELM IV

1861–88 King/Emperor WILHELM I (regent from 1858, Kaiser from 1871)

1888 King/Emperor FRIEDRICH III

1888–1918 King/Emperor WILHELM II

2.2 **Heads of State**

Germany 1919–1945

1919–25 Friedrich EBERT (SPD)

1925–34 Paul von HINDENBURG (non-party, close to DNVP)

1934–45 Adolf HITLER (as Führer, NSDAP)

1945 Karl DÖNITZ (1–23 May, acting)

Federal Republic of Germany

1949 Karl Arnold (7–12 Sept, CDU, acting)

1949–59 Theodor HEUSS (FDP)

1959–69 Karl Heinrich Lübke (CDU)

1969–74 Gustav HEINEMANN (SPD)

1974–79 Walter SCHEEL (FDP)

1979–84 Karl Carstens (CDU)

1984–94 Richard von WEIZSÄCKER (CDU)

1994–99 Roman Herzog (CDU)

1999– Johannes Rau (SPD)

German Democratic Republic

President:

1949–60 Wilhelm PIECK (SED)

Chairman of the Council of State:

1960–73 Walter ULBRICHT (SED)

1973 Friedrich EBERT (1 Aug–3 Oct, SED, acting)

1973–6 Willi STOPH (SED)

1976–89 Erich HONECKER (SED)

1989 Egon KRENZ (24 Oct–6 Dec, SED)

1989–90 Manfred GERLACH (LDPD, acting)

President:

1990 Sabine Bergmann-Pohl (5 April–
2 Oct, CDU)

2.3 Chancellors

1871–90 Prince Otto von BISMARCK

1890–4 General Leo von CAPRIVI

1894–1900 Prince Chlodwig zu HOHEN-
LOHE-SCHILLINGSFÜRST

1900–9 Count Bernhard von BÜLOW

1909–17 Theobald von BETHMANN
HOLLWEG

1917 Georg MICHAELIS (July–Oct)

1917–18 Count Georg von HERTLING

1918 Prince Max von BADEN (Oct–Nov)

1918 Friedrich EBERT (Nov–Dec, SPD)

1918–19 Phillipp SCHEIDEMANN (SPD)

1919–20 Gustav BAUER (SPD)

1920 Herman MÜLLER (Mar–June, SPD)

1920–1 Konstantin FEHRENBACH (Centre)

1921–2 Joseph WIRTH (Centre)

1922–3 Wilhelm CUNO (non-party)

1923 Gustav STRESEMANN (Aug–Nov, DVP)

1923–5 Wilhelm MARX (Centre)

1925–6 Hans LUTHER (non-party, close
to DNVP)

1926–8 Wilhelm MARX (Centre)

1928–30 Hermann MÜLLER (SPD)

1930–2 Heinrich BRÜNING (Centre)

1932 Franz von PAPEN (June–Dec, Centre)

1932–3 Kurt von SCHLEICHER

1933–45 Adolf HITLER (NSDAP)

1945 Lutz Graf SCHWERIN VON KROSIGK
(3–23 May, acting)

1949–63 Konrad ADENAUER (CDU)

1963–6 Ludwig ERHARD (CDU)

1966–9 Kurt Georg KIESINGER (CDU)

1969–74 Willy BRANDT (SPD)

1974–82 Helmut SCHMIDT (SPD)

1982–98 Helmut KOHL (CDU)

1998– Gerhard SCHRÖDER (SPD)

2.4 German Democratic Republic: Minister-presidents (Chairmen of the Council of Ministers)

1949–64 Otto GROTEWOHL (SED)

1964–73 Willi STOPH (SED)

1973–6 Horst Sindermann (SED)

1976–89 Willi Stoph (SED)

1989–90 Hans MODROW (SED/PDS)

1990 Lothar de Maizière (CDU)

2.5 Foreign political authorities

Allied Military Governors 1945–9

British Zone:

1945–6 Sir Bernard Law Montgomery
(from Jan, Viscount Montgomery)

1946–7 Sir William Sholto Douglas

1947–9 Sir Brian Hubert Robertson

French Zone:

1945–9 Marie-Pierre Koenig

Soviet Zone:

1945–6 Georgy Zhukov

1946–9 Vasily Sokolovsky

1949 Vasily Chuikov

United States Zone:

1945 Dwight D. Eisenhower (May–Nov)

1945 George S. Patton, Jr (11–25 Nov, acting)

1945–7 Joseph T. McNarney

1947–9 Lucius D. Clay

1949 Clarence R. Huebner (May–Sept, acting)

Allied High commissioners 1949–55

British Zone:

1949–50 Sir Brian Hubert Robertson

1950–3 Sir Ivone Kirkpatrick

1953–5 Sir Frederick Hoyer-Millar

French Zone:

1949–55 André François-Poncet

Soviet Zone:

1949–53 Vasily Chuikov

1953–4 Vladimir Semyonov

1954–5 Georgy Pushkin

United States Zone:

1949–52 John J. McCloy

1952–3 Walter J. Donnelly

1953–5 James B. Conant

2.6 German governments from 1918

Council of People's Representatives

10 November–20 December 1918

Friedrich EBERT (MSPD)

Hugo HAASE (USPD)

Otto LANDSBERG (MSPD)

Philipp SCHEIDEMANN (MSPD)

Wilhelm DITTMANN (USPD)

Emil BARTH (USPD; Revolutionary Shop
Stewards)

Council of People's Representatives

20 December 1918–13 February 1919

Friedrich EBERT (MSPD)

Otto LANDSBERG (MSPD)

Philipp SCHEIDEMANN (MSPD)

Gustav NOSKE (MSPD)

Rudolf WISSELL (MSPD)

Scheidemann Administration

13 February–20 June 1919

Weimar coalition: MSPD–DDP–Centre

Chancellor Philipp SCHEIDEMANN (MSPD)

Vice chancellor Eugen SCHIFFER (DDP)

Foreign minister Ulrich, Graf von
BROCKDORFF-RANTZAU (non-party)

Interior minister Hugo PREUSS (DDP)

Finance minister Eugen Schiffer (DDP)

  Bernhard Dernburg (from 11 April, DDP)

Economics Rudolf WISSELL (MSPD)

Treasury Georg Gothein (from 21 Mar., DDP)

Justice Otto LANDSBERG (MSPD)

Defence Gustav NOSKE (MSPD)

Food Robert SCHMIDT (MSPD)

Post Johann Giesberts (Centre)

Labour Gustav BAUER (MSPD)

Without portfolio Georg Gothein (to
  21 Mar., DDP)

  Matthias ERZBERGER (Centre)

  Eduard DAVID (MSPD)

Bauer Administration

21 June 1919–27 March 1920

Weimar coalition: MSPD–Centre–DDP (from October)

Chancellor Gustav BAUER (MSPD)

Vice chancellor Matthias ERZBERGER (Centre)

  Eugen SCHIFFER (from 2 Oct. 1919, DDP)

Foreign minister Hermann MÜLLER (MSPD)

Interior minister Eduard DAVID (MSPD)

  Erich Koch-Weser (from 3 Oct. 1919,
  DDP)

Finance minister Matthias Erzberger (Centre)

  Unoccupied from 11 Mar. 1920

Economics Rudolf WISSELL (MSPD)

  Robert SCHMIDT (from 15 July 1919, MSPD)

Treasury Wilhelm Mayer (BVP)

  Unoccupied from 19 Jan. 1920

Justice Eugen Schiffer (from 2 Oct. 1919, DDP)

Defence Gustav NOSKE (MSPD)

Food Robert Schmidt (MSPD)

Post Johann Giesberts (Centre)

Labour Alexander Schlicke (MSPD)

Transport Johannes Bell (Centre)

Reconstruction Otto GESSLER (from 25 Oct.
  1919, DDP)

Without portfolio Eduard DAVID (from 5 Oct.
  1919, MSPD)

First Müller Administration

27 March–8 June 1920

Weimar coalition: MSPD–DDP–Centre

Chancellor Hermann MÜLLER (MSPD)

Vice chancellor Erich Koch-Weser (DDP)

Foreign minister Hermann Müller (MSPD)
  Adolf Köster (from 10 April, MSPD)
Interior minister Erich Koch (DDP)
Finance minister Joseph WIRTH (Centre)
Economics Robert SCHMIDT (MSPD)
Treasury Gustav BAUER (MSPD)
Justice Andreas Blunck (DDP)
Defence Otto GESSLER (DDP)
Food Andreas HERMES (Centre)
Post Johann Giesberts (Centre)
Labour Alexander Schlicke (MSPD)
Transport Johannes Bell (Centre)
  Gustav Bauer (from 1 May, MSPD)
Without portfolio Eduard DAVID (MSPD)

Fehrenbach Administration

25 June 1920–4 May 1921
Centre–right coalition: DDP–Centre–DVP

Chancellor Konstantin FEHRENBACH (Centre)
Vice chancellor Rudolf Heinze (DVP)
Foreign minister Walter SIMONS (non-party)
Interior minister Erich Koch (DDP)
Finance minister Joseph WIRTH (Centre)
Economics Ernst SCHOLZ (DVP)
Treasury Hans von Raumer (DVP)
Justice Rudolf Heinze (DVP)
Defence Otto GESSLER (DDP)
Food Andreas HERMES (Centre)
Post Johann Giesberts (Centre)
Labour Heinrich BRAUNS (Centre)
Transport Wilhelm GROENER (non-party)

First Wirth Administration

10 May–26 October 1921
Weimar coalition: MSPD–DDP–Centre

Chancellor Joseph WIRTH (Centre)
Vice chancellor Gustav BAUER (MSPD)
Foreign minister Joseph Wirth (Centre)
  Friedrich ROSEN (from 23 May, non-party)
Interior minister Georg GRADNAUER (MSPD)
Finance minister Joseph Wirth (Centre)
Economics Robert SCHMIDT (MSPD)

Treasury Gustav Bauer (MSPD)
Justice Eugen SCHIFFER (DDP)
Defence Otto GESSLER (DDP)
Food Andreas HERMES (Centre)
Post Johann Giesberts (Centre)
Labour Heinrich BRAUNS (Centre)
Transport Wilhelm GROENER (non-party)
Reconstruction Walther RATHENAU (from 29 May, DDP)

Second Wirth Administration

26 October 1921–14 November 1922
Weimar coalition: SPD–DDP–Centre

Chancellor Joseph WIRTH (Centre)
Vice chancellor Gustav BAUER (MSPD)
Foreign minister Joseph Wirth (Centre)
  Walther RATHENAU (from 1 Feb. 1922, non-party)
  Joseph Wirth (from 25 June 1922)
Interior minister Adolf Köster (MSPD)
Finance minister Andreas HERMES (from 3 Mar. 1922, Centre)
Economics Robert SCHMIDT (MSPD)
Treasury Gustav Bauer (MSPD)
Justice Gustav RADBRUCH (MSPD)
Defence Otto GESSLER (DDP)
Food Andreas HERMES (Centre)
  Anton Fehr (from 31 Mar. 1922, *Bayerischer Bauernbund**)
Post Johann Giesberts (Centre)
Labour Heinrich BRAUNS (Centre)
Transport Wilhelm GROENER (non-party)
*Bavarian Farmers' League

Cuno Administration

22 November 1922–12 August 1923
Centre–right coalition: DDP–Centre–DVP

Chancellor Wilhelm CUNO (non-party)
Foreign minister Frederic von ROSENBERG (non-party)
Interior minister Rudolf OESER (DDP)
Finance minister Andreas HERMES (Centre)
Economics Johannes Becker (DVP)

Treasury Heinrich Albert (non-party)
  Post abolished 31 Mar. 1923
Justice Rudolf Heinze (DVP)
Defence Otto GESSLER (DDP)
Food Karl Müller (Centre)
  Hans LUTHER (from 25 Nov. 1922,
  non-party)
Post Joseph Stingl (BVP)
Labour Heinrich BRAUNS (Centre)
Transport Wilhelm GROENER (non-party)
Reconstruction Gustav Müller (deputizing)
  Heinrich Albert (from 31 Mar. 1923,
  non-party)

First Stresemann Administration

13 August–6 October 1923
Grand Coalition: SPD–DDP–Centre–DVP

Chancellor Gustav STRESEMANN (DVP)
Vice chancellor Robert SCHMIDT (SPD)
Foreign minister Gustav Stresemann (DVP)
Interior minister Wilhelm SOLLMANN (SPD)
Finance minister Rudolf HILFERDING (SPD)
Economics Hans von Raumer (DVP)
Justice Gustav RADBRUCH (SPD)
Defence Otto GESSLER (DDP)
Food Hans LUTHER (non-party)
Post Anton Höfle (Centre)
Labour Heinrich BRAUNS (Centre)
Transport Rudolf OESER (DDP)
Reconstruction Robert Schmidt (SPD)
Occupied areas Johannes Fuchs (from
  24 Aug., non-party)

Second Stresemann Administration

6 October–30 November 1923
Grand Coalition: SPD (to 3 Nov)–DDP– Centre–DVP

Chancellor Gustav STRESEMANN (DVP)
Foreign minister Gustav Stresemann (DVP)
Interior minister Wilhelm SOLLMANN (SPD)
  Karl JARRES (from 11 Nov., DVP)
Finance minister Hans LUTHER (non-party)
Economics Josef Koeth (non-party)
Justice Gustav Radbruch (to 3 Nov., SPD)

Defence Otto GESSLER (DDP)
Food Gerhard, Graf von Kanitz (non-party,
  formerly DNVP)
Post Anton Höfle (Centre)
Labour Heinrich BRAUNS (Centre)
Transport Rudolf Oeser (DDP)
Reconstruction Robert SCHMIDT (to 3 Nov., SPD)
Occupied areas Johannes Fuchs (to 3 Nov.,
  non-party)

First Marx Administration

30 November 1923–3 June 1924
Centre–right coalition: DDP–Centre–BVP–DVP

Chancellor Wilhelm MARX (Centre)
Vice chancellor Karl JARRES (DVP)
Foreign minister Gustav STRESEMANN (DVP)
Interior minister Karl Jarres (DVP)
Finance minister Hans LUTHER (non-party)
Economics Eduard Hamm (DDP)
Justice Erich Hemminger (BVP)
  Curt Joël (from 15 April 1924)
Defence Otto GESSLER (DDP)
Food Gerhard, Graf von Kanitz (non-party)
Post Anton Höfle (Centre)
Labour Heinrich BRAUNS (Centre)
Transport Rudolf Oeser (DDP)
Reconstruction Gustav Müller
  Post abolished 11 May 1924
Occupied areas Anton Höfle (Centre)

Second Marx Administration

3 June 1924–15 December 1924
Centre–right coalition: DDP–Centre–DVP

Chancellor Wilhelm MARX (Centre)
Vice chancellor Karl JARRES (DVP)
Foreign minister Gustav STRESEMANN (DVP)
Interior minister Karl Jarres (DVP)
Finance minister Hans LUTHER (non-party)
Economics Eduard Hamm (DDP)
Justice Curt Joël (non-party)
Defence Otto GESSLER (DDP)
Food Gerhard, Graf von Kanitz (non-party)
Post Anton Höfle (Centre)

Labour Heinrich BRAUNS (Centre)
Transport Rudolf Oeser (DDP)
 Rudolf Krohne (from 11 Oct. 1924, DVP)
Occupied areas Anton Höfle (Centre)
 Wilhelm Marx (from 10 Jan. 1925, Centre)

First Luther Administration

15 January–5 December 1925
Centre–right coalition: Centre–DVP–DNVP–BVP

Chancellor Hans LUTHER (non-party)
Foreign minister Gustav STRESEMANN (DVP)
Interior minister Martin SCHIELE (DNVP)
 Otto GESSLER (from 26 Oct., DDP)
Finance minister Otto von Schlieben (DNVP)
 Hans Luther (from 26 Oct., non-party)
Economics Albert Neuhaus (DNVP)
 Rudolf Krohne (from 26 Oct., DVP)
Justice Josef Frenken (Centre)
 Hans Luther (from 21 Nov., non-party)
Defence Otto Gessler (DDP)
Food Gerhard, Graf von Kanitz (non-party)
Post Karl Stingl (BVP)
Labour Heinrich BRAUNS (Centre)
Transport Rudolf Krohne (DVP)
Occupied areas Joseph Frenken (Centre)
 Heinrich Brauns (from 21 Nov., Centre)

Second Luther Administration

20 January–12 May 1926
Centre–right coalition: Centre–DDP–DVP–BVP

Chancellor Hans LUTHER (non-party)
Foreign minister Gustav STRESEMANN (DVP)
Interior minister Wilhelm KÜLZ (DDP)
Finance minister Peter Reinhold (DDP)
Economics Julius CURTIUS (DVP)
Justice Wilhelm MARX (Centre)
Defence Otto GESSLER (DDP)
Food Heinrich Haslinde (Centre)
Post Karl Stingl (BVP)
Labour Heinrich BRAUNS (Centre)
Transport Rudolf Krohne (DVP)
Occupied areas Wilhelm Marx (Centre)

Third Marx Administration

16 May–17 December 1926
Centre–right coalition: DDP–Centre–DVP–BVP

Chancellor Wilhelm MARX (Centre)
Foreign minister Gustav STRESEMANN (DVP)
Interior minister Wilhelm KÜLZ (DDP)
Finance minister Peter Reinhold (DDP)
Economics Julius CURTIUS (DVP)
Justice Johannes Bell (from 16 July, Centre)
Defence Otto GESSLER (DDP)
Food Heinrich Haslinde (Centre)
Post Karl Stingl (BVP)
Labour Heinrich BRAUNS (Centre)
Transport Rudolf Krohne (DVP)
Occupied areas Johannes Bell (Centre)

Fourth Marx Administration

29 January 1927–12 June 1928
Centre–right coalition: Centre–DVP–DNVP–BVP

Chancellor Wilhelm MARX (Centre)
Vice chancellor Oskar Hergt (DNVP)
Foreign minister Gustav STRESEMANN (DVP)
Interior minister Walter von Keudell (DNVP)
Finance minister Heinrich Köhler (Centre)
Economics Julius CURTIUS (DVP)
Justice Oskar Hergt (DNVP)
Defence Otto GESSLER (non-party)
 Wilhelm Groener (from 19 Jan. 1928, non-party)
Food Martin SCHIELE (DNVP)
Post Georg Schätzel (BVP)
Labour Heinrich BRAUNS (Centre)
Transport Wilhelm Koch (DNVP)
Occupied areas Wilhelm Marx (Centre)

Second Müller Administration

28 June 1928–27 March 1930
Grand Coalition: SPD–DDP–Centre–BVP–DVP

Chancellor Hermann MÜLLER (SPD)
Foreign minister Gustav STRESEMANN
 (to 3 Oct. 1929, DVP)
 Julius CURTIUS (from 4 Oct. 1929, DVP)
Interior minister Carl SEVERING (SPD)

Finance minister Rudolf HILFERDING (SPD)
   Paul MOLDENHAUER (from 23 Dec. 1929, DVP)
Economics Julius CURTIUS (DVP)
   Paul Moldenhauer (from 11 Nov. 1929, DVP)
   Robert SCHMIDT (from 23 Dec. 1929, SPD)
Justice Erich Koch (DDP)
   Theodor von Guérard (from 13 April
   1929, Centre)
Defence Wilhelm GROENER (non-party)
Food Hermann Dietrich (DDP)
Post Georg Schätzel (BVP)
Labour Rudolf WISSELL (SPD)
Transport Theodor von Guérard (Centre)
   Georg Schätzel (from 6 Feb. 1929, BVP)
   Adam STEGERWALD (from 13 April
   1929, Centre)
Occupied areas Theodor von Guérard
   (to 6 Feb. 1929, Centre)
   Joseph WIRTH (from 13 April 1929,
   Centre)

First Brüning Administration

30 March 1930–7 October 1931
Presidential Cabinet

Chancellor Heinrich BRÜNING (Centre)
Vice chancellor Hermann Dietrich (DDP
   to 26 June 1930, then DSP*)
Foreign minister Julius CURTIUS (DVP)
Interior minister Joseph WIRTH (Centre)
Finance minister Paul Moldenhauer (DVP)
   Hermann Dietrich (from 26 June
   1930, DSP)
Economics Hermann Dietrich (to 26 June
   1930, DDP)
   Ernst TRENDELENBURG (non-party)
Justice Viktor BREDT (Business Party)
   Curt Joël (from 5 Dec. 1930, non-party)
Defence Wilhelm GROENER (non-party)
Food Martin SCHIELE (DNVP; from 22 July
   1930 CL†)
Post Georg Schätzel (BVP)
Labour Adam STEGERWALD (Centre)
Transport Theodor von Guérard (Centre)

Occupied areas Gottfried TREVIRANUS
   (to 30 Sept. 1930, KVP‡)
Without portfolio Gottfried Treviranus (from
   1 Oct. 1930, KVP)
*Deutsche Staatspartei †Christliches Landvolk
‡Konservative Volkspartei

Second Brüning Administration

9 October 1931–30 May 1932
Presidential Cabinet

Chancellor Heinrich BRÜNING (Centre)
Vice chancellor Hermann Dietrich (DSP*)
Foreign minister Heinrich Brüning (Centre)
Interior minister Wilhelm GROENER (non-
   party)
Finance minister Hermann Dietrich (DSP)
Economics Hermann Warmbold (non-party)
   Ernst TRENDELENBURG (from 6 May 1932,
   non-party)
Justice Curt Joël (non-party)
Defence Wilhelm Groener (non-party)
Food Martin SCHIELE (CL†)
Post Georg Schätzel (BVP)
Labour Adam STEGERWALD (Centre)
Transport Gottfried TREVIRANUS (KVP‡)
OSTHILFE Hans SCHLANGE-SCHÖNINGEN
   (from 5 Nov. 1931, CL)
*Deutsche Staatspartei †Christliches Landvolk
‡Konservative Volkspartei

Papen Administration

1 June–3 December 1932
'Cabinet of Barons'

Chancellor Franz von PAPEN (from 3 June,
   non-party)
Foreign minister Konstantin, Freiherr von
   NEURATH (non-party)
Interior minister Wilhelm, Freiherr von Gayl
   (DNVP)
Finance minister Lutz, Graf SCHWERIN VON
   KROSIGK (non-party)
Economics Hermann Warmbold (non-party)
Justice Franz GÜRTNER (DNVP)
Defence Kurt von SCHLEICHER (non-party)

Food Magnus, Freiherr von Braun (DNVP)

Post Paul, Freiherr Eltz von Rübenach (non-party)

Labour Hugo Schäffer (non-party)

Transport Paul, Freiherr Eltz von Rübenach (non-party)

OSTHILFE Magnus, Freiherr von Braun (DNVP)

Without portfolio Franz Bracht (non-party)
Johannes POPITZ (from 29 Oct., non-party)

Schleicher Cabinet

3 December 1932–30 January 1933
Presidential Cabinet

Chancellor Kurt von SCHLEICHER (non-party)

Foreign minister Konstantin, Freiherr von NEURATH (non-party)

Interior minister Franz Bracht (non-party)

Finance minister Lutz, Graf SCHWERIN VON KROSIGK (non-party)

Economics Hermann Warmbold (non-party)

Justice Franz GÜRTNER (DNVP)

Defence Kurt von Schleicher (non-party)

Food Magnus, Freiherr von Braun (DNVP)

Post Paul, Freiherr Eltz von Rübenach (non-party)

Labour Friedrich Syrup (non-party)

Transport Paul, Freiherr Eltz von Rübenach (non-party)

OSTHILFE Günther Gereke (CL*)

Without portfolio Johannes POPITZ (non-party)

*Christliches Landvolk

Hitler Cabinet

30 January 1933

Chancellor Adolf HITLER (NSDAP)

Vice chancellor and Reich commissioner for Prussia Franz von PAPEN

Foreign minister Konstantin, Freiherr von NEURATH (non-party)

Interior minister Wilhelm FRICK (NSDAP)

Finance minister Lutz, Graf SCHWERIN VON KROSIGK (non-party)

Economics, food and agriculture Alfred HUGENBERG (DNVP)

Justice Franz GÜRTNER (DNVP)

Defence Werner von BLOMBERG (non-party)

Post and transport Paul, Freiherr Eltz von Rübenach (non-party)

Labour Franz SELDTE (non-party)

Employment Günther Gereke (CL*)

Without portfolio Hermann GÖRING (NSDAP)

*Christliches Landvolk

FEDERAL REPUBLIC OF GERMANY
First Adenauer Administration

12 September 1949–6 October 1953
Centre–right coalition

Chancellor Konrad ADENAUER (CDU)

Vice chancellor Franz BLÜCHER (FDP)

Foreign affairs Konrad Adenauer (from 13 Mar. 1951, CDU)

Interior Gustav HEINEMANN (to 9 Oct. 1950, CDU)
Robert Lehr (from 11 Oct. 1950, CDU)

Justice Thomas DEHLER (FDP)

Finance Fritz SCHÄFFER (CSU)

Economics Ludwig ERHARD (FDP)

Food, agriculture and forestry Wilhelm Niklas (CSU)

Labour and social policy Anton Storch (CDU)

Transport Hans Christoph SEEBOHM (DP)

Post Hans Schuberth (CSU)

Housing construction Eberhard WILDERMUTH (to 9 Mar. 1952, FDP)
Fritz Neumayer (from 16 July 1952, FDP)

Refugees Hans Lukaschek (CDU)

All-German affairs Jakob KAISER (CDU)

Marshall Plan Franz Blücher (FDP)

Bundesrat Heinrich Hellwege (DP)

*Bundeskanzleramt** Walter Hallstein
Otto Lenz (28 Aug. 1950–16 Mar. 1951, CDU)

*Chancellor's office

Second Adenauer Administration

20 October 1953–October 1956

Centre–right coalition

Chancellor Konrad ADENAUER (CDU)

Vice chancellor and minister for European economic cooperation Franz BLÜCHER (FDP)

Foreign minister Konrad Adenauer (to 6 June 1955, CDU)

Heinrich von Brentano (from 7 June 1955, CDU)

Interior Gerhard Schröder (CDU)

Finance Fritz SCHÄFFER (CSU)

Economics Ludwig ERHARD (CDU)

Defence Theodor BLANK (from 7 June 1955, CDU)

Agriculture Heinrich Lübke (CDU)

Labour Anton Storch (CDU)

Transport Hans Christoph SEEBOHM (DP)

Post Siegfried Balke (from 9 Dec. 1953, non-party)

Housing Viktor-Emmanuel Preusker (FDP)

All-German affairs Jakob KAISER (CDU)

Justice Fritz Neumayer (FDP)

Refugees Theodor Oberländer (BHE*)

Bundesrat Heinrich Heliwege (to 6 June 1955, DP)

Hans-Joachim von Merkatz (from 7 June 1955, DP)

Family and youth Franz-Josef Würmeling (CDU)

Without portfolio Franz-Josef STRAUSS (CSU)

Robert Tilimans (to 12 Nov. 1955, CDU)

Waldemar Kraft (BHE)

Hermann Schafer (FDP)

Nuclear issues Franz-Josef Strauss (from 12 Oct. 1955, CSU)

*Bund der Heimatvertriebenen und Entrechteten

Third Adenauer Administration

16 October 1956–October 1957

Centre–right coalition

Chancellor Konrad ADENAUER (CDU)

Vice chancellor and minister for economic co-ordination Franz BLÜCHER (FDP)

Foreign affairs Heinrich von Brentano (CDU)

Interior Gerhard Schröder (CDU)

Finance Fritz SCHÄFFER (CSU)

Economics Ludwig ERHARD (CDU)

Defence Franz-Josef STRAUSS (CSU)

Agriculture Heinrich Lübke (CDU)

Labour Anton Storch (CDU)

Transport Hans Christoph SEEBOHM (DP)

Housing Viktor-Emmanuel Preusker (FDP)

All-German affairs Jakob KAISER (CDU)

Justice and Bundesrat Hans-Joachim von Merkatz (DP)

Refugees Theodor Oberländer (CDU)

Atomic energy Siegfried Balke (CSU)

Family Franz-Josef Würmeling (CDU)

Post Ernst Lemmer (from 14 Nov. 1956, CDU)

Fourth Adenauer Administration

24 October 1957–November 1961

CDU–CSU

Chancellor Konrad ADENAUER (CDU)

Vice chancellor Ludwig ERHARD (from 30 Oct. 1957, CDU)

Foreign affairs Heinrich von Brentano (CDU)

Interior Gerhard Schröder (CDU)

Justice Fritz SCHÄFFER (CSU)

Finance Franz Etzel (CDU)

Economics Ludwig Erhard (CDU)

Defence Franz-Josef STRAUSS (CSU)

Food and agriculture Heinrich Lübke (to Sept. 1959, CDU)

Werner Schwarz (from 8 Sept. 1959, CDU)

Labour and social affairs Theodor BLANK (CDU)

Transport Hans Christoph SEEBOHM (DP, later CDU)

Housing Paul Lücke (CDU)

All-German affairs Ernst Lemmer (CDU)

Bundesrat Hans-Joachim von Merkatz (DP, later CDU)

Refugees Theodor Oberländer (to 4 May 1960, CDU)

Hans-Joachim von Merkatz (from 26 Oct. 1960, CDU)

Atomic energy and power Siegfried Balke (CSU)

Family and youth Franz-Josef Würmeling (CDU)

Federal properties Hermann Lindrath (CDU)

Post Richard Stücklen (CSU)

Fifth Adenauer Administration
14 November 1961–October 1963
Centre–right coalition: CDU–CSU–FDP

Chancellor Konrad ADENAUER (CDU)

Vice chancellor Ludwig ERHARD (CDU)

Foreign affairs Gerhard Schröder (CDU)

Interior Hermann Höcherl (CSU)

Economics Ludwig ERHARD (CDU)

Justice Wolfgang Stammberger (to 10 Dec. 1962, FDP)

Ewald Bucher (from 11 Dec. 1962, FDP)

Finance Heinz Starke (to 10 Dec. 1962, FDP)

Rolf Dahlgrün (from 11 Dec. 1962, FDP)

Defence Franz-Josef STRAUSS (to 30 Nov. 1962, CSU)

Kai-Uwe von Hassel (from 11 Dec. 1962, CDU)

Food and agriculture Werner Schwarz (CDU)

Labour Theodor BLANK (CDU)

Transport: Hans Christoph SEEBOHM (CDU)

Housing Paul Lücke (CDU)

All-German affairs Ernst Lemmer (to 10 Dec. 1962, CDU)

Rainer Barzel (from 11 Dec. 1962, CDU)

Bundesrat and Länder Hans-Joachim von Merkatz (to 10 Dec. 1962, CDU)

Alois Niederalt (from 11 Dec. 1962, CSU)

Refugees Wolfgang Mischnick (FDP)

Atomic energy Siegfried Balke (to 10 Dec. 1962, CSU)

Family and youth Franz-Josef Würmeling (to 10 Dec. 1962, CDU)

Bruno Heck (from 11 Dec. 1962, CDU)

Treasury Hans Lenz (to 10 Dec. 1962, FDP)

Werner Dollinger (from 11 Dec. 1962, CSU)

Post Richard Stücklen (CSU)

Economic cooperation Walter SCHEEL (FDP)

Health Elisabeth SCHWARZHAUPT (CDU)

Special responsibilities Heinrich Krone (CDU)

Scientific research Hans Lenz (from 11 Dec. 1962, FDP)

First Erhard Administration
17 October 1963–October 1965
CDU–CSU–FDP

Chancellor Ludwig ERHARD (CDU)

Vice chancellor and all-German affairs Erich Mende (FDP)

Foreign affairs Gerhard Schröder (CDU)

Interior Hermann Höcherl (CSU)

Justice Ewald Bucher (to 25 Mar. 1965, FDP)

Karl Weber (from 27 Mar. 1965, CDU)

Finance Rolf Dahlgrün (FDP)

Economy Kurt Schmücker (CDU)

Defence Kai-Uwe von Hassel (CDU)

Food and agriculture Werner Schwarz (CDU)

Labour Theodor BLANK (CDU)

Transport Hans Christoph SEEBOHM (CDU)

Post Richard Stücklen (CSU)

Housing Paul Lücke (CDU)

Bundesrat and Länder Alois Niederalt (CSU)

Refugees Hans Krüger (to 31 Jan. 1964, CDU)

Ernst Lemmer (from 17 Feb. 1964, CDU)

Family Bruno Heck (CDU)

Scientific research Hanz Lenz (FDP)

Treasury Werner Dollinger (CDU)

Development aid Walter SCHEEL (FDP)

Health Elisabeth SCHWARZHAUPT (CDU)

Without portfolio Heinrich Krone (CDU)

Second Erhard Administration
26 October 1965–27 October 1966
CDU–CSU–FDP

Chancellor Ludwig ERHARD (CDU)

Vice chancellor and all-German affairs Erich Mende (FDP)

Foreign affairs Gerhard Schröder (CDU)

Interior Paul Lücke (CDU)

Justice Richard Jaeger (CSU)

Finance Rolf Dahlgrün (FDP)

Economy Kurt Schmücker (CDU)

Defence Kai-Uwe von Hassel (CDU)

Food and agriculture Hermann Höcherl (CSU)

Labour Hans Katzer (CDU)

Transport Hans Christoph SEEBOHM (CDU)

Post Richard Stücklen (CSU)

Housing Ewald Bucher (FDP)

Bundesrat and Länder Alois Niederalt (CSU)

Refugees Johann Baptist Gradl (CDU)

Family and youth Bruno Heck (CDU)

Science Hanz Lenz (FDP)

Treasury Werner Dollinger (CDU)

Development aid Walter SCHEEL (FDP)

Health Elisabeth SCHWARZHAUPT (CDU)

Chairman, Federal Defence Council Heinrich Krone (CDU)

Chancellor's office Ludger Westrick (CDU)

Kiesinger Administration

1 December 1966–October 1969
Grand Coalition: CDU–SPD

Chancellor Kurt Georg KIESINGER (CDU)

Vice chancellor Willy BRANDT (SPD)

Foreign affairs Willy Brandt (SPD)

Interior Paul Lücke (to 26 Mar. 1968, CDU)

Ernst Benda (from 2 April 1968, CDU)

Justice Gustav HEINEMANN (to 25 Mar. 1969, SPD)

Horst Ehmke (from 26 Mar. 1969, SPD)

Finance Franz-Josef STRAUSS (CSU)

Economy Karl Schiller (SPD)

Defence Gerhard Schröder (CDU)

Food and agriculture Hermann Höcherl (CSU)

Labour Hans Katzer (CDU)

Transport Georg Leber (SPD)

Post Werner Dollinger (CSU)

Housing Lauritz Lauritzen (SPD)

Bundesrat and Länder Carlo Schmid (SPD)

Refugees Kai-Uwe von Hassel (to 5 Feb. 1969, CDU)

Heinrich Windelen (from 7 Feb. 1969, CDU)

All-German affairs Herbert Wehner (SPD)

Family and youth Bruno Heck (to 1 Oct. 1968, CDU)

Aenne Brauksiepe (from 2 Oct. 1968, CDU)

Science Gerhard Stoltenberg (CDU)

Federal property Kurt Schmucker (CDU)

Development aid Hans-Jürgen WISCHNEWSKI (to 1 Oct. 1968, SPD)

Erhard Eppler (from 2 Oct. 1968, SPD)

Health Käte Strobel (SPD)

First Brandt Administration

21 October 1969–December 1972
Social–liberal coalition: SPD–FDP

Chancellor Willy BRANDT (SPD)

Vice chancellor Walter SCHEEL (FDP)

Foreign affairs Walter Scheel (FDP)

Interior Hans-Dietrich GENSCHER (FDP)

Justice Gerhard Jahn (SPD)

Finance Alex Möller (to 13 May 1971, SPD)

Karl Schiller (from 13 May 1971, SPD)

Economics Karl Schiller (to 2 July 1972, SPD)

Helmut SCHMIDT (from 7 July 1972, SPD)

Food, agriculture and forestry Josef Ertl (FDP)

Labour and social welfare Walter Arendt (SPD)

Defence Helmut Schmidt (to 6 July 1972, SPD)

Georg Leber (from 7 July 1972, SPD)

Transport and post Georg Leber (to 6 July 1972, SPD)

Lauritz Lauritzen (from 7 July 1972, SPD)

Housing and town planning Lauritz Lauritzen (SPD)

Inter-German relations Egon Franke (SPD)

Health, family and youth Käte Strobel (SPD)

Education and science Hans Leussink (to 27 Jan. 1972, non-party)

Klaus von Dohnanyi (from 15 Mar. 1972, SPD)

Economic cooperation Erhard Eppler (SPD)

Without portfolio at the chancellery Horst Ehmke (SPD)

Second Brandt Administration
15 December 1972–May 1974
Social–liberal coalition: SPD–FDP

Chancellor Willy BRANDT (SPD)
Vice chancellor Walter SCHEEL (FDP)
Foreign affairs Walter Scheel (FDP)
Interior Hans-Dietrich GENSCHER (FDP)
Justice Gerhard Jahn (SPD)
Finance Helmut SCHMIDT (SPD)
Economics Hans Friedrichs (SPD)
Food, agriculture and forestry Josef Ertl (FDP)
Labour and social welfare Walter Arendt (SPD)
Defence Georg Leber (SPD)
Transport and post Lauritz Lauritzen (SPD)
Housing and town planning Hans-Jochen Vogel (SPD)
Inter-German relations Egon Franke (SPD)
Health, family and youth Katherina Focke (SPD)
Education and science Klaus von Dohnanyi
Research and technology Horst Ehmke (SPD)
Economic cooperation Erhard Eppler (SPD)
Without portfolio Egon Bahr (SPD)
Werner Maihofer (FDP)

First Schmidt Administration
16 May 1974–February 1978
Social–liberal coalition: SPD–FDP

Chancellor Helmut SCHMIDT (SPD)
Vice chancellor Hans-Dietrich GENSCHER (FDP)
Foreign affairs Hans-Dietrich Genscher (FDP)
Interior Werner Maihofer (FDP)
Justice Hans-Jochen Vogel (SPD)
Finance Alex Möller (SPD)
Economics Hans Friedrichs (FDP)
Food, agriculture and forestry Josef Ertl (FDP)
Labour and social affairs Walter Arendt (to 15 Dec. 1976, SPD)
Herbert Ehrenberg (from 16 Dec. 1976, SPD)
Defence Georg Leber (from 7 July 1972, SPD)
Transport and post Kurt Gscheidle (SPD)
Housing and town planning Karl Ravens (SPD)

Inter-German relations Egon Franke (SPD)
Health, family and youth Katherina Focke (to 15 Dec. 1976, SPD)
Antje Huber (from 16 Dec. 1976, SPD)
Education and science Helmut Rhode (SPD)
Research and technology Hans Matthöfer (SPD)
Economic cooperation Erhard Eppler (to 4 July 1974, SPD)
Egon Bahr (8 July 1974–15 Dec. 1976, SPD)
Marie Schlei (from 16 Dec. 1976, SPD)

Second Schmidt Administration
3 February 1978–April 1982
Social–liberal coalition (SPD–FDP)

Chancellor Helmut SCHMIDT (SPD)
Vice chancellor Hans-Dietrich GENSCHER (FDP)
Foreign affairs Hans-Dietrich Genscher (FDP)
Interior Werner Maihofer (to 6 June 1978, FDP)
Gerhard Baum (from 8 June 1978, FDP)
Justice Hans-Jochen Vogel (to 26 Jan. 1981, SPD)
Jürgen Schmude (from 27 Jan. 1981, SPD)
Finance Hans Matthöfer (SPD)
Economics Otto, Graf LAMBSDORFF (FDP)
Food, agriculture and forestry Josef Ertl (FDP)
Labour and social affairs Herbert Ehrenberg (SPD)
Defence Hans Apel (SPD)
Post Kurt Gscheidle (SPD)
Transport Kurt Gscheidle (to 5 Nov. 1980, SPD)
Volker Hauff (from 5 Nov. 1980, SPD)
Housing and town planning Dieter Haack (SPD)
Inter-German relations Egon Franke (SPD)
Health, family and youth Antje Huber (SPD)
Education and science Jürgen Schmude (to 26 Jan. 1981, SPD)
Björn Engholm (from 27 Jan. 1981, SPD)
Research and technology Volker Hauff (to 4 Nov. 1980, SPD)
Andreas von Bülow (from 5 Nov. 1980, SPD)
Economic cooperation Rainer Offergeld (SPD)

451

Third Schmidt Administration

27 April–October 1982
Social–liberal coalition: SPD–FDP

Chancellor Helmut SCHMIDT (SPD)

Vice chancellor Hans-Dietrich GENSCHER (FDP)

Foreign affairs Hans-Dietrich Genscher (FDP)

Interior Gerhard Baum (FDP)

Justice Jürgen Schmude (SPD)

Finance Mannfred Lahnstein (SPD)

Economics Otto, Graf LAMBSDORFF (FDP)

Food, agriculture and forestry Josef Ertl (FDP)

Labour and social affairs Heinz Westphal (SPD)

Defence Hans Apel (SPD)

Post Hans Matthöfer (SPD)

Transport Volker Hauff (SPD)

Regional planning Dieter Haack (SPD)

Inter-German relations Egon Franke (SPD)

Health, family and youth Anke Fuchs (SPD)

Education and science Björn Engholm (SPD)

Research and technology Andreas von Bülow (SPD)

Economic cooperation Rainer Offergeld (SPD)

First Kohl Administration

4 October 1982–March 1987
Centre–right coalition: CDU–CSU–FDP

Chancellor Helmut KOHL (CDU)

Vice chancellor Hans-Dietrich GENSCHER (FDP)

Foreign affairs Hans-Dietrich Genscher (FDP)

Interior Friedrich Zimmermann (CSU)

Justice Hans Engelhard (FDP)

Finance Gerhard Stoltenberg (CDU)

Economic affairs Otto, Graf LAMBSDORFF (to 26 June 1984, FDP)

Martin Bangemann (from June 1984, FDP)

Commerce Werner Dollinger (to 29 Mar. 1983, CSU)

Food, agriculture and forestry Josef Ertl (to 29 Mar. 1983, FDP)

Ignaz Kiechle (from 30 Mar. 1983, CSU)

Labour and social affairs Norbert BLÜM (CDU)

Defence Manfred Wörner (CDU)

Post and telecommunications Christian Schwarz-Schilling (CDU)

Regional planning Oskar Schneider (CSU)

Inter-German relations Rainer Barzel (to 29 Mar. 1983, CDU)

Heinrich Windelen (from 30 Mar. 1983, CDU)

Youth, family and health Heiner Geissler (to 25 Sept. 1985, CDU)

Rita Süssmuth (from 26 Sept. 1985, CDU)

Education Dorothee Wilms (CDU)

Research and technology Heinz Riesenhuber (CDU)

Economic cooperation Jürgen Warnke (CSU)

Environment Walter Wallmann (from 6 June 1986, CDU)

Transport Werner Dollinger (from 30 Mar. 1983, CSU)

Head of federal chancellery Wolfgang Schäuble (from 15 Nov. 1984, CDU)

Second Kohl Administration

11 March 1981–12 April 1989
Centre–right coalition: CDU–CSU–FDP

Chancellor Helmut KOHL (CDU)

Vice chancellor Hans-Dietrich GENSCHER (FDP)

Foreign affairs Hans-Dietrich Genscher (FDP)

Interior Friedrich Zimmermann (CSU)

Justice Hans Engelhard (FDP)

Finance Gerhard Stoltenberg (CDU)

Economic affairs Martin Bangemann (to 28 Nov. 1988, FDP)

Helmut Haussmann (from 29 Nov. 1988, FDP)

Food, agriculture and forestry Ignaz Kiechle (CSU)

Labour and social affairs Norbert BLÜM (CDU)

Defence Manfred Wörner (to 17 May 1988, CDU)

Rupert Scholz (from 18 May 1988, CDU)

Post and telecommunications Christian Schwarz-Schilling (CDU)

Regional planning Oskar Schneider (CSU)

Inter-German relations Dorothee Wilms (CDU)

Youth, family and health Rita Süssmuth (to 25 Nov. 1988, CDU)

Ursula-Maria Lehr (from 29 Nov 1988, CDU)

Education Jürgen Möllemann (FDP)

Research and technology Heinz Riesenhuber (CDU)

Economic cooperation Hans Klein (CSU)

Environment Walter Wallmann (to 6 May 1987, CDU)

Klaus Töpfer (from 7 May 1987, CDU)

Transport Jürgen Warnke (CSU)

Head of federal chancellery Wolfgang Schäuble (CDU)

Third Kohl Administration

12 April 1989–18 May 1992

Centre–right coalition: CDU–CSU–FDP

Chancellor Helmut KOHL (CDU)

Vice chancellor Hans-Dietrich GENSCHER (FDP)

Foreign affairs Hans-Dietrich Genscher (FDP)

Interior Wolfgang Schäuble (to 25 Nov. 1991, CDU)

Rudolf Seiters (from 26 Nov. 1991, CDU)

Justice Hans Engelhard (to Jan. 1991, FDP)

Klaus Kinkel (from 17 Jan. 1991, independent, later FDP)

Finance Theo Waigel (CSU)

Economic affairs Helmut Haussmann (to 3 Dec. 1990, FDP)

Jürgen Möllemann (from 17 Jan. 1991, FDP)

Food, agriculture and forestry Ignaz Kiechle (CSU)

Labour and social affairs Norbert BLÜM (CDU)

Defence Gerhard Stoltenberg (to 31 Mar. 1992, CDU)

Volker Rühe (from 1 April 1992, CDU)

Post and telecommunications Christian Schwarz-Schilling (CDU)

Construction Gerda Hasselfeldt (to Jan. 1991, CSU)

Irmgrad Adam-Schwätzer (from 17 Jan. 1991, CSU)

Inter-German relations Dorothee Wilms (to Dec. 1990)

Youth, family and health Ursula Maria Lehr (to Jan. 1991, CDU)

Health Gerda Hasselfeldt (from 17 Jan. 1991, CSU)

Family and the elderly Hannelore Rönsch (from 17 Jan. 1991, CDU)

Women and youth Angela Merkl (from 17 Jan. 1991, CDU)

Education and science Jürgen Möllemann (to Jan. 1991, FDP)

Rainer Ortleb (from 17 Jan. 1991, FDP)

Research and technology Heinz Riesenhuber (CDU)

Economic cooperation Jürgen Warnke (to Jan. 1991, CSU)

Carl-Dieter Spranger (from 17 Jan. 1991, CSU)

Environment Klaus Töpfer (CDU)

Transport Friedrich Zimmermann (to Jan. 1991, CSU)

Günther Krause (from 17 Jan. 1991, CDU)

Minister at the chancellery Rudolf Seiters (to 25 Nov. 1991, CDU)

Friedrich Bohl (from 26 Nov. 1991, CDU)

Government spokesman Hans Klein (CSU)

Fourth Kohl Administration

19 May 1992–November 1994

Centre–right coalition: CDU–CSU–FDP

Chancellor Helmut KOHL (CDU)

Vice chancellor Jürgen Möllemann (to 3 Jan. 1993, FDP)

Foreign affairs Klaus Kinkel (FDP)

Interior Rudolf Seiters (to 4 July 1993, CDU)

Manfred Kanther (from 12 July 1993, CDU)

Justice Sabine Leutheusser-Scharrenberger (FDP)

Finance Theo Waigel (CSU)

Economic affairs Günter Rexrodt (from 22 Jan. 1993, FDP)

Food, agriculture and forestry Ignaz Kiechle (to 18 Jan. 1993, CSU)

Jochen Borchert (from 22 Jan. 1993, CDU)

Labour and social affairs Norbert BLÜM (CDU)

Defence Volker Rühe (CDU)

Post and telecommunications Christian Schwarz-Schilling (to 14 Dec. 1992, CDU)

Wolfgang Bötsch (from 22 Jan. 1993, CSU)

Construction Irmgrad Adam-Schwätzer (CSU)

Regional planning Klaus Töpfer (CDU)

Health Gerda Hasselfeldt (to 27 April 1992, CSU)

Horst Seehofer (from 6 May 1992, CSU)

Family and the elderly Hannelore Rönsch (CDU)

Women and youth Angela Merkl (CDU)

Education and science Rainer Ortleb (to 3 Feb. 1994, FDP)

Karl-Hans Laermann (from 4 Feb. 1994, FDP)

Research and technology Heinz Riesenhuber (to 18 Jan. 1993, CDU)

Matthias Wissmann (22 Jan.–6 May 1993, CDU)

Paul Krüger (from 6 May 1993, CDU)

Economic cooperation Carl-Dieter Spranger (CSU)

Environment Klaus Töpfer (CDU)

Transport Günther Krause (to 6 May 1993, CDU)

Matthias Wissmann (from 6 May 1993, CDU)

Minister at the chancellery Friedrich Bohl (CDU)

Fifth Kohl Administration
15 November 1994–27 September 1998
Centre–right coalition: CDU–CSU–FDP

Chancellor Helmut KOHL (CDU)

Foreign affairs Klaus Kinkel (FDP)

Interior Rudolf Seiters (to 4 July 1993, CDU)

Manfred Kanther (from 12 July 1993, CDU)

Justice Sabine Leutheusser-Scharrenberger (to 14 Dec. 1995, FDP)

Eduard Schmidt-Jortzig (from 15 Dec. 1995, FDP)

Finance Theo Waigel (CSU)

Economic affairs Günter Rexrodt (FDP)

Food, agriculture and forestry Jochen Borchert (CDU)

Labour and social affairs Norbert BLÜM (CDU)

Defence Volker Rühe (CDU)

Post and telecommunications Wolfgang Bötsch (to 31 Dec. 1997, CSU)

Construction Klaus Töpfer (to 31 Dec. 1997, CDU)

Eduard Oswald (from 1 Jan. 1998, CSU)

Health Horst Seehofer (CSU)

Family, women, youth and the elderly Claudia Nolte (CDU)

Education, science, research and technology Jürgen Rüttgers (CDU)

Development aid Carl-Dieter Spranger (CSU)

Environment Angela Merkl (CDU)

Transport Matthias Wissmann (CDU)

Schröder Administration
1998–
Red–green coalition: SPD–Greens/*Bündnis 90*

Chancellor Gerhard Schröder (SPD)

Vice chancellor Joseph ('Joschka') FISCHER (Greens)

Foreign affairs Joseph Fischer (Greens)

Interior Otto Schily (SPD)

Justice Herta Däubler-Gmelin (SPD)

Finance Oskar Lafontaine (to 11 Mar. 1999, SPD)

Hans Eichel (from 4 Dec. 1999, SPD)

Economics Wener Müller (non-party)

Consumer affairs, food and agriculture Karl-Heinz Funke (to 9 Jan. 2001, SPD)

Renate Künast (from 12 Jan. 2001, Greens)

Labour and social affairs Walter Riester (SPD)

Defence Rudolf Scharping (SPD)

Health Andrea Fischer (to 9 Jan. 2001, Greens)

Ulla Schmidt (from 12 Jan. 2001, SPD)

Family, the elderly, women and youth Christine Bergmann (SPD)

Transport, construction and housing Franz Münterfing (to Sept. 1999, SPD)

Reinhard Klimt (29 Sept. 1999–16 Nov. 2000, SPD)

Kurt Bodewig (from 20 Nov. 2000, SPD)

Environment Jürgen Trittin (Greens)

Education, science, research and technology Edelgard Bulmahn (SPD)

Development aid Heidemarie Wieczorek-Zeul (SPD)

2.7 Leaders of Political Parties

Federal Republic of Germany

CDU

1949–66 Konrad ADENAUER
1966–7 Ludwig ERHARD
1967–71 Kurt Georg KIESINGER
1971–3 Rainer Barzel
1973–98 Helmut KOHL
1998–2000 Wolfgang Schäuble
2000– Angela Merkel

CSU

1946–55 Hans Ehard
1955–61 Hanns Seidel
1961–88 Franz-Josef STRAUSS
1988–99 Theo Waigel
1999– Edmund Stoiber

DKP

Collective from 1990

1973–89 Herbert Mies
1990– Anna Frohnweiler
Rolf Priemer
Helga Rosenberg
Heinz Sther

FDP

1948–9 Theodor HEUSS
1949–54 Franz BLÜCHER

1954–7 Thomas DEHLER
1957–60 Reinhold Maier
1960–8 Erich Mende
1968–74 Walter SCHEEL
1974–85 Hans-Dietrich GENSCHER
1985–8 Martin Bangemann
1988–93 Otto Graf LAMBSDORFF
1993–5 Klaus Kinkel
1995–2001 Wolfgang Gerhardt
2001– Guido Westerwelle

Greens/*Bündnis 90*–Greens

Collective rotating leadership of three co-speakers 1980–91
Collective rotating leadership of two co-speakers from 1991

1980 Herbert Gruhl, August Haussleiter, Helmut Neddermeyer
1980 August Haussleiter, Petra KELLY, Norbert Mann
1980–1 Dieter Burgmann, Petra Kelly, Norbert Mann
1981–2 Dieter Burgmann, Petra Kelly, Manon Maren-Grisebach
1982–3 Wilhelm Knabe, Manon Maren-Grisebach, Rainer Trampert
1983–4 Wilhelm Knabe, Rebekka Schmidt, Rainer Trampert
1984–7 Lukas Beckmann, Jutta Ditfurth, Rainer Trampert
1987–9 Jutta Ditfurth, Regina Michalik, Christian Schmidt
1989–90 Ralf Fücks, Ruth Hammerbacher, Verena Krieger
1990–1 Renate Damus, Heide Rühle, Christian Ströbele
1991–3 Ludger Volmer, Christine Weiske
1993–4 Ludger Volmer, Marianne Birthler
1994–6 Jürgen Trittin, Krista Sager
1996–8 Jürgen Trittin, Gunda Röstel
1998–2000 Antje Radcke, Gunda Röstel
2000–1 Renate Künast, Fritz Kuhn
2001– Claudia Roth, Fritz Kuhn

KPD

1945–56 Max Reimann

NPD
1964–7 Fritz Thielen
1967–71 Adolf von Thadden
1971–91 Martin Mussgnug
1991–6 Günter Deckert
1996– Udo Voigt

PDS
1990–3 Gregor Gysi
1993–2000 Lothar Bisky
2000– Gabi Zimmer

Republikaner
1983–5 Franz Handlos
1985–94 Franz Schönhuber
1994– Rolf Schlierer

SPD
1946–52 Kurt SCHUMACHER
1952–63 Erich Ollenhauer
1964–87 Willy BRANDT
1987–91 Hans-Jochen Vogel
1991–3 Björn Engholm
1993 Johannes Rau
1993–5 Rudolf Scharping
1995–9 Oskar Lafontaine
1999– Gerhard SCHRÖDER

German Democratic Republic

CDU
1945 Andreas HERMES
1945–7 Jakob KAISER
1948–57 Otto Nuschke
1966–89 Gerald Götting
1989–90 Lothar de Maizière

KPD
1945–6 Wilhelm PIECK

SED/PDS
1946–54 Wilhelm PIECK
 Otto GROTEWOHL
1950–71 Walter ULBRICHT
1971–89 Erich HONECKER
1989 Egon KRENZ (18 Oct.–3 Dec.)
1989–90 Gregor Gysi (PDS)

2.8 Elections

Frankfurt National Assembly, October 1848: Seats

CAFÉ MILANI	37
KASINO	119
LANDSBERG	37
AUGSBURGER HOF	42
WÜRTTEMBERGER HOF	41
WESTENDHALL	41
DEUTSCHER HOF	56
DONNERSBERG	47
Independent	153
TOTAL	573

Reichstag Elections 1871–1912: share of votes (%)

PARTY	1871	1874	1877	1878	1881	1884	1887	1890	1893	1898	1903	1907	1912
DEUTSCHKONSERVATIVE PARTEI	14.1	6.9	9.7	13.0	16.3	15.2	15.2	12.4	13.5	11.1	10.0	9.4	9.2
REICHSPARTEI	8.9	7.2	7.9	13.6	7.4	6.9	9.8	6.7	5.7	4.4	3.5	4.2	3.0
NATIONAL LIBERAL PARTY	30.1	29.7	27.2	23.1	14.7	17.6	22.3	16.3	13.0	12.5	13.9	14.5	13.6
Liberals	7.2	1.0	2.5	2.7	—	—	—	—	—	—	—	—	—
Liberale Vereinigung/ FREISINNIGE VEREINIGUNG	—	—	—	—	8.4	*	*	*	3.9	2.5	2.6	3.2	†
DEUTSCHE FORTSCHRITTSPARTEI/ Deutsch-Freisinnige Partei/ FREISINNIGE VOLKSPARTEI/ FORTSCHRITTLICHE VOLKSPARTEI	8.8	8.6	7.7	6.7	12.7	17.6	12.9	16.0	8.7	7.2	5.7	6.5	12.3
DVP	0.5	0.4	0.8	1.1	2.0	1.7	1.2	2.0	2.2	1.4	1.0	1.2	†
CENTRE PARTY	18.6	27.9	24.8	23.1	23.2	22.6	20.1	18.6	19.1	18.8	19.8	19.4	16.4
WELF Party	1.6	1.8	1.6	1.7	1.7	1.7	1.5	1.6	1.3	1.4	1.0	0.7	0.7
SPD	3.2	6.8	9.1	7.6	6.1	9.7	10.1	19.8	23.3	27.2	31.7	28.9	34.8
Poles	4.5	3.8	4.0	3.6	3.8	3.6	2.8	3.4	3.0	3.1	3.7	4.0	3.6
Danes	0.5	0.4	0.3	0.3	0.3	0.3	0.2	0.2	0.2	0.2	0.2	0.1	0.1
Alsace-Lorraine	—	4.5	3.7	3.1	3.0	2.9	3.1	1.5	1.5	1.4	1.1	1.0	1.3
Anti-Semitic Parties	—	—	—	—	—	—	0.2	0.7	3.5	3.3	2.6	3.9	2.9
Others	2.0	0.9	0.5	0.3	0.3	0.2	0.6	1.0	1.7	4.5	3.5	3.0	2.0
Invalid papers	0.25	0.35	0.24	0.22	0.23	0.20	0.31	0.33	0.27	0.30	0.30	0.23	0.37
TURNOUT (%)	50.78	60.89	60.39	63.14	56.08	60.35	77.19	71.25	72.20	67.76	75.78	84.35	84.53
ELECTORATE (000s)	7656	8523	8493	9124	9090	9383	9770	10,146	10,628	11,441	12,531	13,523	14,442

* *Liberale Vereinigung* campaigning jointly with *Deutsche Fortschrittspartei*

† *Freisinnige Vereinigung and DVP* campaigning jointly with *Fortschrittliche Volkspartei*

Reichstag Elections 1919–33: Share of votes (%)

PARTY	1919*	1920	1924 (1)	1924 (2)	1928	1930	1932 (1)	1932 (2)	1933
NSDAP	–	–	6.6[†]	3.0	2.6	18.3	37.3	33.1	43.9
DNVP	10.3	14.9	19.5	20.5	14.2	7.0	5.9	8.8	8.0
DVP	4.4	13.9	9.2	10.1	8.7	4.5	1.2	1.9	1.1
CENTRE/BVP	19.7	17.9	16.6	17.3	15.1	14.8	15.9	15.0	14.1
DDP	18.6	8.3	5.7	6.3	4.9	3.8	1.0	1.0	0.9
SPD	37.9	21.6	20.5	26.0	29.8	24.5	21.6	20.4	18.2
USPD	7.6	17.9	0.8	0.3	0.1	–	–	–	–
KPD	–	2.1	12.6	9.0	10.6	13.1	14.3	16.9	12.2
TURNOUT	82.7	79.1	77.4	78.8	75.6	81.9	84.0	80.6	88.5

*1919 – Elections to the National Assembly
[†]NSDAP 1924 (1) with *Völkisch-Nationaler Block*

European elections 1979–99: Share of votes (%)

PARTY	1979	1984	1989	1994	1999
SPD	40.8	37.4	37.3	32.2	30.7
CDU/CSU	49.2	45.9	37.8	38.8	48.7
FDP	6.0	4.8	5.6	4.1	3.0
GREENS/*BÜNDNIS 90*	3.2	8.2	8.4	10.1	6.4
REPUBLIKANER	–	–	7.1	3.9	1.7
PDS	–	–	–	4.7	5.8
Others	0.8	3.7	3.8	6.3	3.7

Seats

PARTY	1979	1984	1989	1994	1999
SPD	35	33	31	40	33
CDU/CSU	42	41	33	47	53
FDP	4	–	4	–	–
GREENS/BÜNDNIS 90	–	7	8	12	7
REPUBLIKANER	–	–	6	–	–
PDS	–	–	–	–	6

Bundestag Elections 1949–98: share of votes (%)

PARTY	1949	1953	1957	1961	1965	1969	1972	1976	1980	1983	1987	1990	1994	1998
SPD	29.2	28.8	31.8	36.2	39.3	42.7	45.8	42.6	42.9	38.2	37.0	33.5	36.4	40.9
CDU/CSU	31.0	45.2	50.2	45.3	47.6	46.1	44.9	48.6	44.5	48.8	44.3	43.8	41.5	35.1
FDP	11.9	9.5	7.7	12.8	9.5	5.8	8.4	7.9	10.6	6.9	9.1	11.0	6.9	6.2
KPD/DEUTSCHE KOMMUNISTISCHE PARTEI	5.7	2.2	–	–	–	–	0.3	0.3	0.2	0.2	–	–	–	–
PDS	–	–	–	–	–	–	–	–	–	–	–	2.4	4.4	5.1
GREENS/ BÜNDNIS 90	–	–	–	–	–	–	–	–	1.5	5.6	8.3	5.0	7.3	6.7
NPD	–	–	–	–	2.0	4.3	0.6	0.3	0.2	0.2	0.6	0.3	–	–
REPUBLIKANER	–	–	–	–	–	–	–	–	–	–	–	2.1	1.9	1.8
DEUTSCHE RECHTS-PARTEI	1.8	1.1	1.0	0.8	–	–	–	–	–	–	–	–	–	–
Others	20.4	13.3	9.3	4.9	1.6	1.1	–	0.3	0.1	0.1	0.6	1.9	2.6	4.0

SUBJECT INDEX

Geography

German Democratic Republic and division of Germany

Kiaochow; Rwanda and Burundi; South-West
Africa; Tanganyika; Togoland
Communists and socialists: Bebel, August;
Bernstein, Eduard; Dietz, Johann Heinrich
Wilhelm; Heine, Wolfgang; Kautsky, Karl;
Liebknecht, Karl; Luxemburg, Rosa; Toller,
Ernst; Winnig, August; Zetkin, Clara
Conservatives and Christian conservatives:
Baden, Prince Max von; Bethmann Hollweg,
Theobald von; Bismarck(-Schönhausen),
Wilhelm von; Droste zu Fischering, Klemens,
Graf; Eulenburg, Botho, Graf zu; Heereman
von Zuydtwyck, Klemens, Freiherr; Hertling,
Georg (Friedrich), Freiherr von; Heydebrand
und der Lasa, Ernst von; Hohenlohe-Langen-
burg, Ernst, Fürst zu; Savigny, Karl Friedrich
von
**Constitution, legislation and administra-
tion:** anti-socialist laws; Bundesrat;
Burgfrieden; Gründerzeit; Kaiser; *Kulturkampf;*
Paragraph 175; Reich; Reich Chancellery;
Wilhelmstrasse
Industrialists: Benz, Carl Friedrich; Daimler,
Gottlieb; Diesel, Rudolf; Duisberg, Carl; Horn,
Hermann; Kirdorf, Emil; Siemens, (Ernst)
Werner von; Stinnes, Hugo
International relations and foreign policy:
Agadir; Algeciras Conference; Berlin, Con-
gress of; *Daily Telegraph* affair; Dual Alliance;
'hammer and anvil' speech; Moroccan crisis
of 1905; Reinsurance Treaty; Three Emperors'
League; Triple Alliance; Zabern affair
Labour, economy and infrastructure: AEG;
Berlin–Baghdad railway; Fischer Verlag; Kiel
Canal; Reichsbank; taler; *U-Bahn*
Liberals and radicals: Bennigsen, Rudolf von;
Caprivi, (Georg) Leo, Graf von; Hohenlohe-
Schillingsfürst, Chlodwig Viktor Karl, Fürst zu;
Miquel, Johannes von; Naumann, Friedrich;
Payer, Friedrich von; Schmidt, Auguste
**Nationalists, anti-Semites and radical
right:** Bülow, Bernhard, Fürst von; Drexler,
Anton; Dühring, Eugen; Lagarde, Paul Anton
de; Sonnenberg, Max Liebermann von;
Stoecker, Adolf; Vosberg, Fritz
Notables and royalty: Einem (von Rothmal-
er), Karl von; Friedrich III; Kiderlen-Wächter,

Alfred von; Ludwig II; Michaelis, Georg;
Soden, Julius, Freiherr von; Wilhelm I;
Wilhelm II; Wittelsbach
Parties, pressure groups and manifestos:
Agrarian League; Anti-Semitic People's Party;
Burschenschaften; Christian Social Party;
*Deutsche Freisinnige Partei; Deutscher Kolonial-
verein; Deutscher Nationalverband; Deutsche
Reichspartei; Deutschkonservative Partei;* Erfurt
programme; *Fortschrittliche Volkspartei;
Freikonservative Partei; Freisinnige Vereinigung;
Freisinnige Volkspartei;* Gotha programme;
Hirsch–Duncker unions; National Liberal
Party; Navy League; *Ostmarkenverein;* Pan-
German League; *Reichspartei;* SAPD; SDAP;
Socialist Unity Congress; *Soziale Reichspartei;*
SPD; Thule Society; VDA
**Public servants, diplomats and adminis-
trators:** Bernstorff, Joachim Heinrich, Graf
von; Eulenberg und Hertefeld, Philipp, Fürst
zu; Hintze, Paul von; Kühlmann, Richard
von; Lichnowsky, Karl Max, Fürst; Peters,
Karl; Richthofen, Oswald, Freiherr von;
Riezler, Kurt; Schnee, Heinrich von; Seitz,
Theodor; Strandes, Justus; Tschirsky und
Bögendorf, Heinrich von; Tucher von Sim-
melsdorf, Heinrich, Freiherr von; Wassilko,
Nikolaj, Ritter von; Wedel, Karl, Graf von

*WEIMAR REPUBLIC: NOVEMBER REVOLUTION
(1918) – appointment of Hitler (1933)*
Communists: Fischer, Ruth; Hoernle, Edwin;
Neumann, Heinz; Pieck, Wilhelm; Thal-
heimer, August; Thälmann, Ernst; Torgler,
Ernst; Wollweber, Ernst; Zaisser, Wilhelm;
Zetkin, Clara
Conservatives and Christian conservatives:
Brauns, Heinrich; Bredt, Johann Viktor;
Brüning, Heinrich; Curtius, Julius; Dertinger,
Georg; Dieckmann, Friedrich; Erzberger,
Matthias; Fehrenbach, Konstantin; Goerdeler,
Carl; Held, Heinrich; Helfferich, Karl; Hermes,
Andreas; Jarres, Karl; Joos, Joseph; Marx, Wil-
helm; Moldenhauer, Paul; Neurath, Konstan-
tin, Freiherr von; Papen, Franz von; Quaatz,
Reinhold Georg; Rheinhaben, Werner, Frei-
herr von; Schäffer, Fritz; Schiele, Martin;

APPENDIX IV

FURTHER READING

General and introductory accounts
There are now a great many general and introductory books on modern German history. Mary Fulbrook, *A Concise History of Germany* (Cambridge, 1990) is a very good short introduction to the history of Germany from the middle ages, but concentrates on the modern period. James J. Sheehan, *German History 1770–1866* (Oxford, 1989), is an excellent account of politics, society and culture in the late 18th and early 19th centuries, which avoids the widespread tendency of writing German history before 1871 in terms of the rise of Prussia. David Blackbourn, *The Fontana History of Germany: The Long Nineteenth Century* (London, 1997) is perhaps the best of recently published general accounts. Thomas Nipperdey, *Germany from Napoleon to Bismarck* (Dublin, 1996, originally published in Germany in 1983) deals with a rather shorter German 19th century (1800–66). William Carr, *A History of Germany 1815–1985* (London: Arnold, 1987) is a very readable straightforward introduction to the last two centuries. Volker Berghahn, *Modern Germany* (Cambridge, 1987) covers the 20th century from the imperial Germany of 1900 to the present, and has a useful set of statistical appendices. Mary Fulbrook, *The Fontana History of Germany 1918–1990: The Divided Nation* (London, 1991) covers the period from the end of the World War I to reunification. In addition to these general one-volume accounts, Mary Fulbrook (ed.), *German History since 1800* (London, 1997) is a useful collection of essays on important themes and has just been reissued in two volumes (London: Arnold, 2001).

Modern Germany
Few general accounts of modern German history go back much beyond the era of the French revolution. The period of '**absolutism and particularism**' identified by Michael Hughes, *Early Modern Germany 1477–1806* (Basingstoke, 1992) begins with the end of the Thirty Years War in 1648. Similarly John Gagliardo, *Germany under the Old Regime* (Longman, 1991) covers the whole of the century and half from the Peace of Westphalia to the 1790s as a single period. Peter H. Wilson's, *The Holy Roman Empire 1495–1806* (Basingstoke, 1999) and *Absolutism in Central Europe* (London, 2000) together constitute a good introduction to the empire, its institutions and the theory and practice of politics. (See also H.M. Scott (ed.), *Enlightened Absolutism* (London, 1990); M. Hughes, *Law and Politics in Eighteenth Century Germany* (Woodbridge, Suffolk, 1988).) The politics of the mid-18th century was dominated by an emergent 'dualism' in power politics within Germany: the challenge of Prussia to the hegemony of Austria and the Habsburgs. The political biographies of leading personalities can be a useful starting point, for example: G. Ritter, *Frederick*

the Great (Berkeley, 1968); T.C.W. Blanning, *Joseph II* (Harlow, 1994). Franz A.J. Szabo, *Kaunitz and Enlightened Absolutism 1753–1780* (Cambridge, 1994) deals with the role of the most distinguished Austrian minister of the time. P. Bernard, *From the Enlightenment to the Police State* (Urbana, 1991) is a biography of Pergen, Joseph's police chief. (See also J. Knudsen, *Justus Möser and the German Enlightenment* (Cambridge, 1986).) There are some very good general books dealing with Austria in the 18th century, especially Charles Ingrao, *The Habsburg Monarchy 1618–1815* (Cambridge, 1994) and Robin Okey, *The Habsburg Monarchy c.1765–1918* (London, 2001). (See also Ernst Wangermann, *The Austrian Achievement 1700–1800* (London, 1973).) K. Epstein, *The Genesis of German Conservatism* (Princeton, 1966) covers both the Enlightenment and the impact of the French revolution on German politics. The Royal Historical Association has recently published the first volume in a series of British diplomatic correspondence relating to the period: Sabine Freitag and Peter Wende (eds), *British Envoys to Germany 1816–1866, Vol. 1 1816–1829* (Cambridge, 2000).

There is no recent and easily available general account in English of the **French revolutionary period** from a German perspective. T.C.W Blanning, *The French Revolution in Germany: Occupation and Resistance in the Rhineland* (Oxford, 1983) deals with the experience of the part of Germany which was most affected, as does his earlier *Reform and Revolution in Mainz* (Cambridge, 1974). (See also J. Diefendorf, *Businessmen and Politics in the Rhineland 1789–1834* (Princeton, 1980).) Ernst Wangermann, *From Joseph II to the Jacobin Trials* (Oxford, 1959) deals with the impact of the revolution on politics in Austria. On the restoration period see R.D. Billinger, *Metternich and the German Question* (University of Delaware Press, 1991) and A. Lüdtke, *Police and State in Prussia 1815–1850* (Cambridge, 1981).

Much historical writing on Germany in the **19th century** has been dominated by the '*SONDERWEG*' debate, which concerns Germany's supposedly 'peculiar' development and 'flawed' political modernization. This peculiar path to modernity, it was suggested, was responsible for the Germany's inability to develop a liberal political culture, and thus helped explain the rise of Nazism. Hans Ulrich Wehler, *The German Empire, 1871–1918* (Leamington Spa, 1985) adopts this perspective. David Blackbourn, and Geoff Eley, *The Peculiarities of German History: Bourgeois Society and Politics in Nineteenth-Century Germany* (Oxford, 1984, first published in Germany in 1980) was the first important critique of the *Sonderweg* approach. Not least, it reflected the reluctance of a (then) younger generation of historians to see earlier periods of German history, particularly the imperial and Weimar periods, as little more than a prelude to the Third Reich. (See Geoff Eley, *From Unification to Nazism: Reinterpreting the Nazi Past* (Boston, Allen & Unwin, 1986).) This critical approach also informs the essays in a number of useful collections spanning the late 19th and early 20th centuries, including Richard J. Evans, *Rethinking German History: Nineteenth Century Germany and the Origins of the Third Reich* (London, 1987) and *Rereading German History: From Unification to Reunification 1800–1996* (London, 1997).

The political history of the early 19th century is dominated by the reforms undertaken in Prussia in the wake of defeat by Napoleon; the conservative restoration symbolized in the figure of the Austrian chancellor, Prince Klemens von Metternich; and the long-term origins of the revolutions of 1848. The focus in the mid-19th century is on the revolutions and their impact, and particularly on the question of German nationhood, relations between the German states and the origins of the unification of Germany. A good starting point is John

Breuilly, *The Formation of the First German Nation-State 1800–1871* (London, 1996). (See also T.S. Hamerow, *Restoration, Revolution and Reaction* (Princeton, 1958).) A. Sked, *The Decline and Fall of the Habsburg Empire 1815–1918* (London, 1989) questions received wisdoms both on the apparent inevitability of Austria's decline and on the nature of Metternich's regime. On Prussia see L.J. Baack, *Christian Bernstorff and Prussia: Diplomacy and Reform Conservatism 1818–1832* (New Brunswick, NJ, 1980) and J.R. Gillis, *The Prussian Bureaucracy in Crisis, 1840–1860* (Stanford,1971).

On the **German empire** there are two good recent general books in English: Volker Berghahn, *Imperial Germany* (Providence and Oxford: Berghahn Books, 1994), and Wolfgang Mommsen, *Imperial Germany 1867–1918: Politics, Culture, and Society in an Authoritarian State* (London, 1995). Roger Chickering (ed.), *Imperial Germany: A Historiographical Companion* (Westport, Connecticut and London, 1996) is a useful and stimulating collection. For an excellent concise introduction to the iron chancellor and his times see Lynn Abrams, *Bismarck and the German Empire: 1871–1918* (London: Routledge, 1995). There are many biographies of Bismarck himself; Erich Eyck, *Bismarck and the German Empire* (London: Allen and Unwin, 1968) is still among the best. (See also Lothar Gall, *Bismarck: The White Revolutionary* 2 vols (London, 1986).) On the Wilhelmine period see J.C.G. Röhl, *Germany without Bismarck: The Crisis of Government in the Second Reich* (Berkeley and Los Angeles, 1967) and James Retallack, *Germany in the Age of Kaiser Wilhelm II* (London, 1996). On Wilhelm II and the imperial court see John G. Röhl, *The Kaiser and his Court: Wilhelm II and the government of Germany* (Cambridge: Cambridge University Press, 2000). (See also Röhl and Nicolaus Sombart (eds), *Kaiser Wilhelm II: New Interpretations* (Cambridge, 1982).)

There are several very good studies of party and electoral politics, local politics and associational life for the imperial period: David Blackbourn, *Class, Religion and Local Politics in Wilhelmine Germany: The Centre Party in Württemberg before 1914* (London and New Haven, Conn., 1980); Alastair Thompson, *Left Liberals, the State and Popular Politics of Wilhelmine Germany* (Oxford, 2000); Roger Chickering, *We Men Who Feel Most German: A Cultural Study of the Pan German League 1866–1914* (London, 1985); Marilyn Chevin Coetzee, *The German Army League: Popular Nationalism in Wilhelmine Germany* (Oxford and New York, 1990); Geoff Eley, *Reshaping the German Right: Radical Nationalism and Political Change after Bismarck* (New Haven, Conn., and London, 1982); Brett Fairbairn, *Democracy in the Undemocratic State: The German Reichstag Elections of 1898 and 1903* (Toronto, 1997); Robert Gellately, *The Politics of Economic Despair* (London, 1974); Peter Pulzer, *The Rise of Political Anti-Semitism in Germany and Austria* (revised edition: London, 1988); James Retallack, *Notables of the Right: The Conservative Party and Political Mobilization in Germany 1876–1918* (London, 1988) and, by the same author, *Germany in the Age of Kaiser Wilhelm II* (Basingstoke, 1996); Stanley Suval, *Electoral Politics in Wilhelmine Germany* (Chapel Hill and London, 1985).

There is a growing literature on the **social and cultural history of imperial Germany**. Above all, see Lynn Abrams, *Workers' Culture in Imperial Germany: Leisure and Recreation in the Rhineland and Westphalia* (London, 1992); Richard J. Evans, *Death In Hamburg: Society and Politics in the Cholera Years 1830–1910* (Oxford, 1981); Matthew Jefferies, *Politics and Culture in Wilhelmine Germany: The Case of Industrial Architecture* (Oxford, 1996); Peter Fritzsche, *Reading Berlin 1900* (Cambridge, Mass.: Harvard University Press, 1996). On the culture of Berlin see Dorothy Rowe, *Representing Berlin: Sexuality and the City in Imperial and Weimar Germany* (London, 2002) and on imperial Vienna see Carl

Schorske, *Fin-de-siècle Vienna* (Cambridge, 1981) and Janet Stewart, *Fashioning Vienna: Adolf Loos's Cultural Criticism* (London, 2000).

There is an enormous literature on the origins, course and consequences of **World War I**. For an excellent short introduction to the issues around the causes of the war, see Volker Berghahn, *Germany and the Approach of War in 1914* (London, 1973). Fritz Fischer's book *Griff nach der Weltmacht* was published in English as *Germany's War Aims in the First World War* (London, 1961). (See also R.J.W. Eavans and Hartmut Pogge von Strandmann, *The Coming of the First World War* (Oxford, 1988).) There is little in English on the domestic impact in Germany of World War I, apart from Jürgen Kocka, *Facing Total War: German Society 1914–1918* (Leamington Spa, 1984). Two recent books of particular interest are John Horne and Alan Kramer, *German atrocities 1914: A History of Denial* (New Haven and London, 2001) and Vejas Gabriel Liulevicius, *War Land on the Eastern Front: Culture, National Identity and the German Occupation* (Cambridge: Cambridge University Press, 2000). Little has been published recently on the revolution of 1918. F.L. Carsten, *Revolution in Central Europe* (London, 1972) is still the best introduction to the political upheavals of the period.

There is an extensive and increasingly sophisticated literature on the **Weimar Republic**. Anton Kaes, Martin Jay and Edward Dimendberg, *The Weimar Sourcebook* (Berkeley and London, 1991), is an invaluable collection of contemporary writing. Detlev Peukert, *The Weimar Republic* (London, 1991) is the most stimulating recent general book on the republic. Among the other good general accounts, see especially Eberhard Kolb, *The Weimar Republic* (London, 1988), Helmut Heiber, *The Weimar Republic* (Oxford, 1993), both of which have been translated from German, and A.J. Nicholls, *Weimar and the Rise of Hitler* (Basingstoke, 1991). Most

aspects of the republic's history have been covered by work in English (or translated into English). The following titles comprise a necessarily small selection: Richard Bessel, *Germany after the First World War* (Oxford, 1993); F.L. Casten, *The Reichswehr and Politics* (Oxford, 1966); Gerald Feldman, *The Great Disorder: Politics, Economics and Society in the German Inflation 1914–1924* (Oxford, 1997); Theo Balderston, *The Origins and Course of the German Economic Crisis 1923–1932* (Berlin, 1993); H.A. Turner, *Stresemann and the Politics of the Weimar Republic* (Westport, Conn., 1979); Harold James, *The German Slump: Politics and Economics, 1924–1936* (Oxford, 1986); Richard Evans and Dick Geary (eds), *The German Unemployed: Experiences and Consequences of Mass Unemployment from the Weimar Republic to the Third Reich* (London, 1987); Peter D. Stachura (ed.), *Unemployment and the Great Depression in Weimar Germany* (London, 1986); Hans Mommsen, *The Rise and Fall of Weimar Democracy* (Chapel Hill, North Carolina, 1996).

Peter Gay, *Weimar Culture: The Outsider as Insider* (London, 1969) is still a useful starting point for the **cultural history of the republic**. Jeffrey Herf, *Reactionary Modernism: Technology, Culture and Politics in Weimar and the Third Reich* (Cambridge, 1986) draws attention to some of the long-term cultural continuities of the period. (See also Peter Jelavic, *Berlin Cabaret* (Harvard, 1993).) Klaus Theweleit, *Male Fantasies* (Cambridge, 1989) affords an insight into the mentalities of the radical right.

Perhaps the best-documented aspect of the history of Weimar Germany is the **rise of Nazism and the collapse of the republic**. See, in particular, W.S. Allen, *The Nazi Seizure of Power: The Experience of a Single German Town 1930–1935*; T. Childers (ed.), *The Nazi Voter* (Chapel Hill, 1983); R.F. Hamilton, *Who Voted for Hitler?* (Princeton, 1982); I. Kershaw (ed.), *Weimar: Why did German Democracy Fail* (London, 1990); A.P.

McElligott, *Contested City: Municipal Politics and the Rise of Nazism in Altona 1917–1937* (Ann Arbor, 1938); E. Rosenhaft, *Beating the Fascists? The German Communists and Political Violence 1929–1933* (Cambridge, 1983).

The standard biography of **Hitler** is Ian Kershaw's two-volume work, *Hitler 1889–1936: Hubris* (London, 1999) and *Hitler 1936–1945: Nemesis* (London, 2000). Ian Kershaw, *The Hitler Myth: Image and Reality in the Third Reich* (Oxford, 1987) deals with Hitler's 'charismatic leadership'. Alan Bullock, *Hitler: A Study in Tyranny* (London, 1952), the first biography to appear after the war, is still well worth reading. W.Carr, *Hitler: A Study in Personality and Politics* (London, 1978) is a straightforward and very readable introduction to Hitler's career. Among the better biographies of **other Nazi leaders** are R.J. Overy, *Goering: The 'Iron Man'* (London and Boston, 1984) and a collection of short biographical essays, Ronald Smelser and Rainer Zitelmann (eds), *The Nazi Elite* (Basingstoke, 1993).

Dietrich Orlow, *The History of the Nazi Party* (2 vols, Pittsburgh 1989–73) is the standard history of the NSDAP. Detlev Peukert, *Inside Nazi Germany: Conformity and Opposition in Everyday Life* (London: Penguin, 1989) is perhaps the best single-volume account in English of life in Germany under the Nazis. One of the most straightforward of the general histories of the Third Reich is Karl Dietrich Bracher, *The German Dictatorship: The Origins, Structure and Consequences of National Socialism* (Harmondsworth, 1973); another is Norbert Frei, *National Socialist Rule in Germany: the Führer State 1933–1945* (Oxford, 1993). Martin Broszat, *The Hitler State: The Foundation and Development of the Internal Structure of the Third Reich* (London, 1981), was one of the most influential 'structuralist' interpretations of the Nazi political system. Jost Dülffer, *Nazi Germany 1933–1945: Faith and Annihilation* (London, 1996) is one of the better general accounts to have been translated from

German recently. Michael Burleigh and Wolfgang Wippermann, *The Racial State 1933–1945* (Cambridge, 1991) is an important restatement of the centrality of racism and racial policy to the politics and history of Nazi Germany. Noakes and Pridham, *Nazism 1919–1945: A Documentary Reader* (4 vols, Exeter, 1983–98) is invaluable not only for its extent and the range of subject matters covered by the documents, but also for its excellent connecting commentary. Neil Gregor, *Nazism* (Oxford, 2000) is a similarly impressive collection of secondary sources.

Some of the most important historical work on **Nazi Germany** has been published as essays often in relatively inaccessible journals or books, or in German. Many of these essays are now available in one or other of the many collections of essays on Nazism. Among the best of these are Richard Bessel, *Life in the Third Reich* (Oxford, 1987); Michael Burleigh (ed.), *Confronting the Nazi Past: New Debates on Modern German History* (Cambridge, 1991); Thomas Childers and Jane Caplan (eds), *Reevaluating the Third Reich* (New York and London: Holmes, 1993); David Crew (ed.), *Nazism and German Society 1933–1945* (London, 1994); J. Noakes (ed.), *Government, Party and People in Nazi Germany* (Exeter, 1980).

Virtually every aspect of the history of Nazi Germany has been covered by historians, and important new work appears every year. The selection of titles that follows is only a small proportion of what is available. Jane Caplan, *Government without Administration: State and Civil Service in Weimar and Nazi Germany* (Oxford, 1988) is a detailed analysis of the way in which Germany was governed. There are several very readable books on the **economy under the Nazis**: William Carr, *Arms, Autarky and Aggression: A Study in German Foreign Policy 1933–1939* (London, 1972); R.J. Overy, *The Nazi Economic Recovery 1932–1938* (London, 1982) and *War and Economy in the Third Reich*

(London, 1994). Specifically on industry and industrial relations: J.R Gillingham, *Industry and Politics in the Third Reich* (London, 1985); Neil Gregor, *Daimler Benz in the Third Reich* (New Haven and London, 1998); Peter Hayes, *Industry and Ideology: IG Farben in the Nazi Era* (Cambridge, 1987) and T.W. Mason, *Social Policy in the Third Reich* (Providence and Oxford, 1993); F.L. Carsten, *The German Workers and the Nazis* (Aldershot, 1995). On the **history of women during the Third Reich** see Jill Stephenson, *Women in Nazi Society* (London, 1975) and *The Nazi Organisation of Women* (London, 1981); Alison Owings, *Frauen: German Women Recall the Third Reich* (London, 1993); and the controversial interpretation by Claudia Koonz, *Mothers in the Fatherland* (New York, 1986). (See also R. Bridenthal et al. (eds), *When Biology became Destiny* (New York, 1984).) On **propaganda** see David Welch (ed.), *Nazi Propaganda: The Power and the Limitations* (London: Croom Helm, 1983) and *The Third Reich: Politics and Propaganda* (London: Routledge, 1993). On resistance, opposition and popular opinion, see M. Geyer and J. Boyer (eds), *Resistance against the Third Reich 1933–1990* (Chicago, 1992), an excellent collection of essays, originally published as contributions to the *Journal of Modern History*; Ian Kershaw, *Popular Opinion and Political Dissent in the Third Reich: Bavaria 1933–1945* (Oxford, 1983); F.R. Nicosia and L.D. Stokes (eds), *Germans against Nazism: Nonconformity, Opposition and Resistance in the Third Reich* (New York, 1990). Robert Gellately, *Backing Hitler: Consent and Coercion in Nazi Germany* (Oxford, 2001), explores the controversial area of German support for the Nazi dictatorship. Among the most useful studies of the **Nazi police state** and its institutions are: H. Krausnick and M. Broszat, *Anatomy of the SS-State* (London, 1968); G.C. Browder, *Foundations of the Nazi Police State: The Formation of Sipo and SD* (Lexington, Kentucky, 1990); R. Gellately, *The Gestapo and German Society:*

Enforcing Racial Policy 1933–1945 (Oxford, 1990).

The number of books on **eugenics and racial policy** under the Nazis, and particularly on anti-Semitism and the holocaust, has increased rapidly in recent years. Again, the following titles constitute only a necessarily small proportion of those available: Michael Burleigh, *Death and Deliverance: Euthanasia c.1900–1945* (Cambridge, 1994); Robert N. Proctor, *Racial Hygiene: Medicine under the Nazis* (Cambridge, Mass., 1988); Berno-Müller Hill, *Murderous Science: Elimination by Scientific Selection of Jews, Gypsies and Others* (Cold Spring Harbour Laboratory Press, 1997); Paul J. Weindling, *Health, Race and German Politics between National Unification and Nazism 1870–1945* (Cambridge, 1989). The essays in Margit Szöllössi-Janze (ed.), *Science in the Third Reich* (Oxford, 2001) include contributions on eugenics and euthanasia and together constitute an original and useful collection on the impact of Nazism on the scientific and academic community in Germany. On anti-Semitism and the holocaust, see Götz Aly, *The Final Solution* (London, 1999); Omer Bartov (ed.), *The Holocaust: Origins, Implementation, Aftermath* (London, 2000); Christopher Browning, *The Path to Genocide* (Cambridge, 1994) and *Ordinary Men: Reserve Police Battalion 101 and the Final Solution in Poland* (New York, 1993); Michael Burleigh, *Ethics and Extermination* (Cambridge, 1997); David Cesarani (ed.), *The Final Solution: Origins and Implementation* (1994); Gerald Fleming, *Hitler and the Final Solution* (Oxford: Oxford University Press, 1986); Saul Friedländer, *Nazi Germany and the Jews: The Years of Persecution, 1933–1939* (London: Phoenix, 1997); H Graml, *Antisemitism in the Third Reich* (Oxford, 1992); Ulrich Herbert, *National Socialist Extermination Policies* (1999); R. Hilberg, *The Destruction of the European Jews* (New York, 1983); K.A. Schleunes, *The Twisted Road to Auschwitz: Nazi Policy towards German Jews 1933–1939* (London,

1972). On the non-Jewish victims of the holocaust see M. Berenbaum (ed.), *A Mosaic of Victims: Non-Jews Persecuted and Murdered by the Nazis* (London: Tauris, 1990). There are now several case studies of the implementation of the holocaust in various parts of Europe, although there is relatively more on eastern Europe and the Soviet Union than on the West: Michael Marrus and Robert Paxton, *Vichy France and the Jews* (New York, 1982); Zvi Gitelmann (ed.), *Bitter Legacy: Confronting the Holocaust in the USSR* (Bloomington, 1987); Martin Dean, *Collaboration in the Holocaust: Crimes of the Local Police in Belorussia and Ukraine, 1941–44* (London, 1997); Andrew Ezergailis, *The Holocaust in Latvia 1941–1944* (Riga, 1996); Randolph Braham, *The Politics of Genocide: The Destruction of Hungarian Jewry* (New York, 1982); Radu Ioanid, *The Holocaust in Romania* (Chicago, 2000).

On the **German armed forces** and the origins of World War II, see Francis Carsten, *The Reichswehr and Politics* (Oxford, 1966); M. Cooper, *The German Army 1933–1945* (London, 1978); W. Deist, *The Wehrmacht and German Rearmament* (London, 1981); Klaus-Jürgen Müller, *The Army, Politics and Society in Germany 1933–1945: Studies in the Army's Relation to Nazism* (Manchester, 1987). R.J. O'Neill, *The German Army and the Nazi Party 1933–1939* (London, 1966).

On **foreign policy**, see P.M. Bell, *The Origins of the Second World War in Europe* (London, 1986); William Carr, *From Poland to Pearl Harbour: The Making of the Second World War* (London, 1985); Klaus Hildebrand, *The Foreign Policy of the Third Reich* (London, 1973); A.B. Leach, *German Strategy against Russia 1939–1941* (London, 1973) N. Rich, *Hitler's War Aims* (2 vols, New York, 1973–4); Geoffrey Stoakes, *Hitler and the Quest for World Dominion* (Leamington Spa, 1986); G.L. Weinberg, *The Foreign Policy of Hitler's Germany* (2 vols, Chicago, 1970, 1980).

On **World War II** itself see O. Bartov, *The Eastern Front 1941–5: German Troops and the Barbarisation of Warfare* (London, 1985); Richard Overy, *Why the Allies Won* (London, 1995) and *Russia's War* (London, 1997); Gerhard L. Weinberg, *A World at Arms* (Cambridge, 1988). Four volumes are now available in English of the series *Germany and the Second World War* from the *Militärgeschichtliches Forschungsamt*, Freiburg in Bresigau/Potsdam: Wilhelm Deist, Manfred Messerschmidt, Hans-Erich Volkmann, and Wolfram Wette (eds), *Germany and the Second World War: The Build-up of German Aggression* (Oxford, 1990); Klaus A. Maier, Horst Rohde, Bernd Stegemann, and Hans Umbreit (eds), *Germany and the Second World War: Germany's Initial Conquests in Europe* (Oxford, 1991); Gerhard Schreiber, Bernd Stegemann, and Detlef Vogel (eds), *Germany and the Second World War: The Mediterranean, South-East Europe, and North Africa 1939–1941* (Oxford, 1995); Horst Boog, Jürgen Förster, Joachim Hoffman, Ernst Klink et al. (eds), *Germany and the Second World War: The Attack on the Soviet Union* (Oxford, 1998); Bernhard R. Kroener, Rolf-Dieter Muller, and Hans Umbreit (eds), *Germany and the Second World War: Organization and Mobilization of the German Sphere of Power: I: Wartime Administration, Economy, and Manpower Resources, 1939–1941* (Oxford, 2000); Horst Boog, Werner Rahn, Reinhard Stumpf, and Bernd Wegner (eds), *Germany and the Second World War: The Global War* (Oxford, 2001)

On **economy and society** in Germany during the war and the home front, see E.R. Beck, *Under the Bombs: The German Home Front 1942–1945* (Lexington, Kentucky, 1986); T. Charman, *The German Home Front 1933–1945* (New York, 1989); M. Kitchen, *Nazi Germany at War* (London, 1995); A. Milward, *The German Economy at War* (London, 1965) and *War, Economy and Society* (London, 1977); M.G. Steinert, *Hitler's War and the Germans: Public Mood and Attitude during the Second World War* (Athens, Ohio, 1977).

On **occupied Europe** see Evan Bukey, *Hitler's Austria: Popular Sentiment in the Nazi Era*, 1938–1945 (Chapel Hill and London, 2000); Philippe Burrin, *Living with Defeat: France under the German Occupation* (London, 1996); A. Dallin, *German Rule in Russia 1941–45: A Study in Occupation Politics* (London, 1981); J. Erikson and D. Dilks (eds), *Barbarossa: The Axis and the Allies* (Edinburgh, 1994); J.T. Gross, *Polish Society under German Occupation: The Generalgouvernement 1939–1944* (Princeton, 1983); Tim Kirk, *Nazism and the Austrian Working Class* (Cambridge, 1996); Tim Kirk and Anthony McElligott (eds), *Opposing Fascism: Community Authority and Resistance in Europe* (Cambridge, 1999); Mark Mazower, *Inside Hitler's Greece* (New Haven and London: Yale University Press, 1993); A. Milward, *The New Order and the French Economy* (Oxford: Oxford University Press, 1984) and *The Fascist Economy in Norway* (Oxford: Clarendon Press, 1972); T. Mulligan, *The Politics of Illusion and Empire: German Occupation Policy in the Soviet Union 1942–43* (New York, 1988).

The history of **Germany since the end of World War II** is still relatively much less well covered by works in English than the preceding decades, and few books bridge the periods before and after 1990. An added difficulty in writing about contemporary history and politics is the danger of being overtaken rather quickly by events. The collapse of the German Democratic Republic and the Soviet Union in particular prompted a general reconsideration of the history of postwar Germany (not least in light of the availability of hitherto inaccessible sources). Many of the books written before such changes in perspective nevertheless remain useful. Among the best general books on the period are Mary Fulbrook, *The Two Germanies 1945–1990* (Basingstoke: Macmillan, 1992); Peter Pulzer, *German Politics 1945–1995* (Oxford: Oxford University Press, 1995) and Lothar Kettenacker, *Germany since 1945* (Oxford: Oxford University Press,

1997). Adrian Webb, *Germany since 1945* (Harlow: Longman, 1998) is a very useful introductory guide.

On the **Allies' decision to divide Germany** after the war and the occupation, see J. Backer, *The Decision to Divide Germany* (Durham, N.C., 1978); Michael Balfour, *Four-Power Control in Germany and Austria* (Oxford: Oxford University Press, 1956); Rebecca Boehling, *A Question of Priorities: Democratic Reform and Economic Recovery in Postwar Germany* (Providence and Oxford, 1996); Norman N. Naimark, *The Russians in Germany: A History of the Soviet Zone of Occupation, 1945–1949* (Cambridge, Mass., 1995); B. Ruhm von Oppen (ed.), *Documents on Germany under Occupation* (London, 1955); G. Sandford, *From Hitler to Ulbricht: The Communist Reconstruction of East Germany* (Princeton, 1983); Tony Sharp, *The Wartime Alliance and the Zonal Division of Germany* (Oxford: Clarendon Press, 1995); F. Willis, *The French in Germany* (Stanford, 1962). On **denazification and the prosecution of war crimes**, see C. Fitzgibbon, *Denazification* (London, 1969); Nicholas Pronay and Keith Wilson (eds), *The Political Re-education of German and her Allies* (London 1985); A. and J. Tusa, *The Nuremberg Trial* (London: BBC, 1995).

On the **political history of the German Federal Republic**, see Dennis L. Bark and David Gress, *A History of West Germany* (2 vols, 1989); Tony Burkett and Stephen Padgett, *Political Parties and Elections in West Germany: The Search for a New Stability* (London: Hurst, 1986); Rob Burns and Wilfried van der Will, *Protest and Democracy in West Germany* (London, 1988); D. Childs and J. Johnson, *West Germany: Politics and Society* (London: Croom Helm, 1982); Alice Holmes Cooper, *Paradoxes of Peace: German Peace Movements since 1945* (Ann Arbor: University of Michigan Press, 1996); Marion Donhöff, *The Makers of the New Germany from Konrad Adenauer to Helmut Schmidt* (London, 1982); William Graf, *The German Left since 1945:*

Socialism and Social Democracy in the German Federal Republic (Cambridge: Oleander Press, 1977); W. Hülsberg, *The German Greens: A Social and Political Profile* (London, 1988); Eva Kolinsky, *Parties, Opposition and Society* (London, 1984); Eva Kolinsky (ed.), *The Federal Republic of Germany* (Oxford, 1991); Patrick Major, *The Death of the KPD: Communism and Anti-Communism in West Germany* (Oxford: Oxford University Press, 1998); A.J. Nicholls (ed.), *The Bonn Republic: West German Democracy 1945–1990* (Harlow, 1997); Stephen Padgett (ed.), *Adenauer to Kohl* (London, 1994); Terrence Prittie, *The Velvet Chancellors: A History of Post-War Germany* (London, 1979). On the particular difficulties of coming to terms with the past in West Germany, and the attempt by conservatives in the 1980s to find a 'usable' past, see Richard J. Evans, *In Hitler's Shadow* (London, 1989) and Charles Maier, *The Unmasterable Past: History, Holocaust and German National Identity* (Cambridge, Mass., 1988). For a more recent comparative perspective, see Jeffrey Herf, *Divided Memory in the Two Germanies* (Cambridge Mass.: Harvard University Press, 1997).

There is a growing literature on **economy, society and culture in the Federal Republic**. The following is a small selection: Volker Berghahn, *The Americanisation of West German Industry* (Leamington Spa, 1986); Volker Berghahn and Erica Carter, *How German is She? Postwar West German Reconstruction and the Consuming Woman* (Ann Arbor: University of Michigan Press, 1997); Eva Kolinsky, *Women in West Germany* (Oxford: Berg, 1989); Alan Kramer, *The West German Economy 1945–1955* (Oxford: Berg, 1990); Robert G. Moeller, *Protecting Motherhood: Women and the Family in the Politics of Post-War West Germany* (Berkeley, 1993).

On the **German Democratic Republic** see K. von Beyme and H. Zimmermann, *Policymaking in the German Democratic Republic* (Aldershot, 1984); D. Childs *The GDR: Moscow's German Ally* (London, 1983); D. Childs (ed.), *Honecker's Germany* (London, 1985); M. Dennis, *The German Democratic Republic* (London, 1988); Mary Fulbrook, *Anatomy of a Dictatorship: Inside the GDR 1949–1989* (Oxford, 1995); H. Krisch, *The German Democratic Republic* (Boulder, 1985); M. McCauley, *The GDR since 1945* (London, 1983). On the East German secret police, see David Childs and Richard Popplewell, *The Stasi* (Basingstoke, 1996).

On **East German political history** see A. Baring, *Uprising in East Germany* (New York, 1972); Peter C. Ludz, *The Changing Party Elite in East Germany* (Cambridge, Mass., 1972); M. McCauley, *Marxism-Leninism in the GDR* (London, 1979); J. Sandford, *The Sword and the Ploughshare: Autonomous Peace Initiatives in East Germany* (London, 1983); C. Bradley Scharf, *Politics and Change in East Germany* (Boulder, 1984); R. Woods, *Opposition in the GDR under Honecker* (London, 1986).

On **economy, society and culture in East Germany** see T. Bayliss, *The Technical Intelligentsia and the East German Elite* (Berkeley, 1974); G.E. Edwards, *GDR Society and Social Institutions* (London, 1985); I. Jeffries and M. Melzer, *The East German Economy* (London, 1987); Anne McElvoy, *The Saddled Cow: East Germany's Life and Legacy* (London, 1992); Robin Ostow, *Jews in Contemporary East Germany* (London, 1989); Henry Shaffer, *Women in the Two Germanies* (New York, 1981).

Although German **foreign policy** has been 'contained' within the framework of cold-war military and political alliances for over half a century, the two Germanies were right at the centre of the East–West divide, and the 'German question' and related issues produced an extensive literature, much of it ephemeral. Among the most useful perspectives in the area of foreign policy and détente are Julius W. Friend, *The Linchpin: French–German Relations 1950–1990* (New York, 1991); Philip H. Gordon, *France, Germany and the Western Alliance* (Boulder,

1995); Avril Pittmann, *From Ostpolitik to Reunification: West German–Soviet political relations since 1974* (Cambridge, 1992).

There have been many books on the origins, events and impact of 1989, none of which can really be considered histories in the proper sense: see Stephen Szabo, *The Diplomacy of German Unification* (New York, 1992).

Thematic accounts and collections which cover more than period

On the development of German national identity and nationhood, see John Breuilly (ed.), *The State of Germany* (London, 1992). On politics see also Dieter Langewiesche, *German Liberalism* (Basingstoke, 2000) and H. Grebing, *The History of the German Labour Movement* (Leamington Spa, 1985). Useful starting points for the history of German women are Ute Frevert, *Women in German History* (Providence, Rhode Island, 1990) and Lynn Abrams and Elizabeth Harvey, *Gender Relations in German History: Power, Agency and Experience from the Sixteenth to the Twentieth Century* (London, 1996). There are several wide-ranging thematic collections

in German social history, see especially, G. Iggers, *The Social History of Politics* (Leamington Spa, 1985); R.J. Evans and W.R. Lee, *The German Peasantry* (London, 1986); D. Blackbourn and R.J. Evans (eds), *The German Bourgeoisie* (London, 1991); R.J. Evans (ed.), *The German Working Class* (London, 1982); Ulrich Herbert, *A History of Foreign Labour in Nazi Germany 1880–1980: Seasonal Workers/ Forced Laborers/Guest Workers* (Ann Arbor, 1990).

There is a growing literature on the cultural history of Germany and central Europe. On the urban culture of the region from the late 18th century to the present, see Malcolm Gee et al., *The City in Central Europe* (London, 1999) and A.P. McElligott, *The German Urban Experience, 1900 to 1945: Modernity and Crisis* (London, 2001). On the culture and politics of history, memory and commemoration from the founding of the empire to the end of the 20th century, see Rudy Koshar, *From Monuments to Traces: Artifacts of German Memory, 1870–1990* (Berkeley, 2000); Ute Frevert, *Men of Honour: A Social and Cultural History of the Duel* (Göttingen, 1998).